SPORTSMAN'S PARK
in
ST. LOUIS

Home of the Browns and Cardinals at Grand and Dodier

Edited by Gregory H. Wolf

Associate Editors: James Forr, Len Levin, and Bill Nowlin

Society for American Baseball Research, Inc.
Phoenix, AZ

Sportsman's Park in St. Louis: Home of the Browns and Cardinals at Grand and Dodier
Edited by Gregory H. Wolf
Associate Editors: James Forr, Len Levin, and Bill Nowlin

Copyright © 2017 Society for American Baseball Research, Inc.
All rights reserved. Reproduction in whole or in part without permission is prohibited.

ISBN 978-1-943816-61-3
(Ebook ISBN 978-1-943816-60-6)

Cover Photo: Sportsman's Park (National Baseball Hall of Fame, Cooperstown, New York).

Book design: Gilly Rosenthol

Society for American Baseball Research
Cronkite School at ASU
555 N. Central Ave. #416
Phoenix, AZ 85004
Phone: (602) 496-1460
Web: www.sabr.org
Facebook: Society for American Baseball Research
Twitter: @SABR

CONTENTS

1 Introduction *Gregory H. Wolf*

4 Sportsman's Park *Scott Ferkovich*

12 The Milwaukee Brewers Move to St. Louis and Become the Browns in 1902 *Dennis Pajot*

20 Robert Hedges: Overlooked Visionary *Steve Steinberg*

28 Phil Ball: Cantankerous Owner; Passionate Fan *Steve Steinberg*

36 Sam Breadon: Relentless Owner *Mark Armour*

41 Bill Veeck and the St. Louis Browns *Greg Erion*

47 Three Weeks in 1953: The Fate of the Cardinals *John Bauer*

54 Anheuser-Busch Buys the St. Louis Cardinals *Russ Lake*

60 Beer and Opulence — The Day the Ballpark in St. Louis had Three Different Names *Phillip Bolda*

63 April 14, 1909. The Dawn of a New Era: The First Game at Sportsman's Park *Chip Greene*

66 April 14, 1917. A Sportsman's Park First: Pale Hose' Cicotte Hurls No-Hitter *Gregory H. Wolf*

69 May 5, 1917. On Second Thought, It's a No-Hitter for Ernie Koob *Gregory H. Wolf*

72 May 6, 1917. Bob Groom Tosses Browns' Second No-Hitter in Two Days *Gregory H. Wolf*

76 July 25, 1918. The Big Train and Sothoron Battle for 15 *Chip Greene*

79 July 1, 1920. Cardinals Fall in Their First Game in Sportsman's Park *Greg Erion*

83 July 2, 1920. Cardinals Get First Win at New Home as Doak Swashbuckles Pirates *Russ Lake*

87 August 8, 1920. Sisler First Brownie to Hit for Cycle *Richard Riis*

90 April 22, 1922. Ken Williams Clubs Three Home Runs for the Browns *Joe Wancho*

93 May 30, 1922. The Browns' 17th Hit Finally Produces the Second Run for Victory *Jeff Findley*

96 September 18, 1922. The Little World Series *Steve Steinberg*

100 August 9, 1923. A Wild Win Against the Champs *Norm King*

103 July 17, 1924. Haines Tosses Only Cardinal No-Hitter in Sportsman's Park *Gregory H. Wolf*

106 August 24, 1924. Dyer Tosses Shutout in Cards Laugher *Doug Walden*

108 July 11, 1925. George Sisler Knocks in a Career-High Seven Runs *Joe Wancho*

110 October 5, 1926. Jesse Haines Tosses Shutout and Wallops Homer in First World Series Game in the Gateway City *Gregory H. Wolf*

113 October 6, 1926. Babe Ruth First to Hit Three Homers in World Series Game *Mark S. Sternman*

117	October 7, 1926. Lazzeri's Sacrifice Fly Wins in Extra Innings *Rick Schabowski*
120	June 21, 1927. Haines Goes the Distance and Wins It on Les Bell's 13th-Inning Single *Brian P. Wood*
123	October 7, 1928. Gehrig's Two Homers Too Much for Redbirds *Richard Cuicchi*
126	October 9, 1928. The Sultan of Swat Smacks Three Homers to Sink the Cardinals *Richard Cuicchi*
129	August 21, 1930. Chick Hafey Hits for the Cycle as Cardinals Pound Phillies *Michael Huber*
132	October 4, 1930. Wild Bill Hallahan Shuts Outs Mackmen to Rekindle Redbirds Title Hopes *Gregory H. Wolf*
136	October 5, 1930. Haines Defeats Grove in Fall Classic Pitchers' Duel *J.G. Preston*
139	October 6, 1930. Double-X's Ninth-Inning Two-Run Homer Pushes the Cards to Brink *J.G. Preston*
142	July 12, 1931. Cards Set Doubles Record with Assist from Crowd *John J. Watkins*
145	October 1, 1931. Lefty Grove Subdues Redbirds in Opening Game of Fall Classic *Russ Lake*
148	October 2, 1931. The Wild Horse of the Osage Steals the Show as Wild Bill Fires Three-Hit Shutout *Gregory H. Wolf*
152	October 9, 1931. Grove Stymies Redbirds *Russ Lake*
156	October 10, 1931. Revenge Is Sweet, Even Without Pepper *Norm King*
159	June 23, 1932. The Goose Wallops Three *Gregory H. Wolf*
162	July 30, 1933. Dizzy Fans 17 for New Modern Record *Gregory H. Wolf*
165	September 16, 1933. Cardinals and Dodgers Battle Through 27 Runs, 36 Hits, and 17 Walks *Doug Feldmann*
168	September 18, 1934. Bobo Tosses No-No Through Nine, Loses in 10th *Richard Riis*
171	September 30, 1934. Dizzy Tosses Second Shutout in Three Days to Win Number 30 as Redbirds Grab Pennant on Last Day of Season *Gregory H. Wolf*
175	October 5, 1934. Paul Dean Impresses Brother Dizzy — and Comes of Age in a Hard-Fought World Series Victory *Doug Feldmann*
178	October 6, 1934. Tigers Even Series with Late-Game Offensive Explosion *C. Paul Rogers, III*
182	October 7, 1934. Bridges Outduels Dizzy for Series Lead *Ryan Parker*
185	April 29, 1936. Parmelee Bests Hubbell in Epic 17-Inning Pitchers' Duel *Gregory H. Wolf*
188	August 4, 1937. Cardiac Cards Complete Crazy Comeback While Ducky Medwick Ties Record with Four Two-Baggers *Norm King*
191	July 13, 1938. A One-Man Show: Johnny Mize Ends Slump by Blasting Three Straight Homers *Gregory H. Wolf*
194	July 20, 1938. Mize Blasts Three Home Runs for Second Time in Eight Days *Kellen Nielson*
196	May 7, 1940. Redbirds Tie NL Record with Seven Round-Trippers *Richard Riis*
199	May 24, 1940. Lights Go On In St. Louis! *Richard Riis*

202   July 9, 1940. Five National League Pitchers Combine for First All-Star-Game Shutout *Lyle Spatz*

205   July 13, 1940. Johnny Mize Triples, Scores, and Earns a Cycle as Cardinals Sweep Giants with Walk-Offs *Michael Huber*

208   August 5, 1940. Singing in the Rain: Whitehead Tosses Abbreviated No-Hitter for Last Big League Victory *Gregory H. Wolf*

211   July 19, 1941. George McQuinn Hits for Cycle *Michael Huber*

214   September 13, 1941. Cardinals lose, 1-0, in "one of the greatest games in the history of the major leagues" *Lyle Spatz*

216   September 17, 1941. Stan Musial Debuts *Joe Schuster*

220   May 30, 1942. Negro League Teams Square off on Decoration Day *Dwayne Isgrig*

222   August 25, 1942. Marion's Dash Preserves Cooper's 14-Inning Gem *Jim Wohlenhaus*

224   September 30, 1942. Ruffing Wins Opener of Series: Cardinals Do Not Go Quietly *Greg Erion*

227   October 1, 1942. Beazley Evens the Series *Greg Erion*

230   June 4, 1943. Two of a Kind: Cooper Tosses Second Straight One-Hit Shutout *Gregory H. Wolf*

233   October 10, 1943. Marius Russo's One-Man Show Leads to Yankees Win over Cardinals *Mike Huber*

236   October 11, 1943. The Yankees Bring the Championship Back to New York *James Forr*

239   July 2, 1944. Lanier Pitches Marathon Gem as Hopp Delivers Winner *Gordon Gattie*

242   October 1, 1944. Finally, The Browns! *Mike Whiteman*

245   October 4, 1944. Browns Surprise Cards in Opening Salvo of the Trolley World Series *Richard Riis*

248   October 5, 1944. Unknowns Lead Cards to Victory *Kellen Nielson*

251   October 6, 1944. The Browns' Jack Kramer Subdues the Redbirds *Michael Huber*

254   October 7, 1944. Musial's Blast Helps Cardinals Level the Trolley Car Series at Two Games Each *Ken Carrano*

257   October 8, 1944. Big Mort and Big Blasts *John Bauer*

260   October 9, 1944. St. Louis Wins! Cardinals Defeat Browns in Trolley Car Fall Classic *Gregory H. Wolf*

263   April 17, 1945. Pete Gray's Major League Debut *Chip Greene*

266   August 10, 1945. Slugfest at the Bottom of the American League *John Bauer*

269   October 1, 1946. They Needed Extra Games *Alan Cohen*

272   October 6, 1946. The Red Sox Take the Opener *Cecilia Tan and Bill Nowlin*

275   October 7, 1946. The Cat Purrs and The Kid Cracks *John Bauer*

279   October 13, 1946. Joyous Cards Hail Gameness of Brecheen and Slaughter *Phillip Bolda*

282   October 15, 1946. Country's Mad Dash and the Cat's Third Victory *Gregory H. Wolf*

286   May 21, 1947. A Dark Chapter: Jackie Robinson Debuts in the Gateway City *Chip Greene*

289　May 8, 1948. Harry Brecheen's Almost-Perfect Game *Richard A. Cuicchi*

292　July 13, 1948. Stan the Man Homers at Home in All-Star Game *C. Paul Rogers, III*

295　September 13, 1949. Munger's $50 Night *John Bauer*

298　April 30, 1950. Brecheen, Schmitz Both Go the Distance in Extra-Inning Duel *Ken Carrano*

301　August 18, 1951. Brownies Set Scoring Record at Home *J.G. Preston*

304　August 19, 1951 The Smallest Pinch-Hitter In the Game *Chip Greene*

307　August 24, 1951. Browns Fans Manage to Get It Right *Norm King*

310　September 13, 1951. Warren Spahn Earns 20th Win With One-Hitter in Rare Day-Night, Three-Team Doubleheader *Michael Huber*

313　September 30, 1951. Ned Garver Wins 20th for the 102-Loss Brownies *Gregory H. Wolf*

316　August 6, 1952. Satch Turns Back Time to Spin 12-Inning Shutout Against Tigers *Gregory H. Wolf*

319　May 6, 1953. Bobo Holloman Throws a No-Hitter in His First Major-League Start *Joe Schuster*

322　September 27, 1953. Extra-Inning Finale Ends With 100th Loss: The St. Louis Browns Depart St. Louis *Jeff Findley*

325　May 2, 1954. Musial Hits Five Home Runs, Sets ML Record In Doubleheader *Russ Lake*

330　April 16, 1955. Cardinals Outslugged by Cubs But Finally Win In 14 *Russ Lake*

333　July 9, 1957. "All my replacements did well." — Casey Stengel *Alan Cohen*

336　June 23, 1961; Stan Musial Knocks in Seven Runs *Tom Hawthorn*

339　September 14, 1961. Ken Boyer's 11 Total Bases and 11th-Inning Home Run Drive Cards to Defeat Cubs in Walk-off Fashion *Michael Huber*

342　September 2, 1962. One More Rung on the Record Book Ladder for Musial *Alan Cohen*

345　June 2, 1963. Say Hey Times Three *Alan Cohen*

348　September 29, 1963. Stan Musial's Final Game *Joe Schuster*

351　October 4, 1964. Cards Almost Mets Their Match, But Win Pennant *Norm King*

354　October 7, 1964. Schultz, Cardinals Ignore the Odds to Defeat Yankees *Frederick C. Bush*

357　October 8, 1964. Rookie Hurler Mel Stottlemyre Goes the Distance as Yankees Tie World Series *Frederick C. Bush*

360　October 14, 1964. Bouton Earns Second Victory to Extend World Series to Seventh Game *Frederick C. Bush*

363　October 15, 1964. Gibson Pitches Cardinals to Crown, Earns MVP Honors *Frederick C. Bush*

367　May 8, 1966. Cardinals' Last Game in Sportsman's Park *Greg Erion*

370　Sportsman's Park III/Busch Stadium I by the Numbers *Dan Fields*

382　Sportsman's Park: The SABR Team of Players

SPORTSMAN'S PARK IN ST. LOUIS: HOME OF THE BROWNS AND CARDINALS AT GRAND AND DODIER

BY GREGORY H. WOLF

THE INTERSECTION OF GRAND Avenue and Dodier Street on the north side of St. Louis is one of the fabled locations in baseball history. Amateurs began playing on a sandlot there as far back as the 1860s. In 1875, the first professional team in the Gateway City, the Brown Stockings of the National Association of Professional Baseball Players called Grand and Dodier its home, and played in a park with a rough wooden grandstand, the Grand Avenue Ball Grounds. That name was changed to Sportsman's Park the following year when the Brown Stockings became a charter member of the newly founded National League. In the late nineteenth century, the future of baseball at Grand and Dodier was anything but certain. The Brown Stockings went bankrupt and folded after the 1877 season, and the park sat vacant for five years, until another incarnation of the Brown Stockings occupied Sportsman's Park and dominated the American Association, a rival to the National League, winning four straight championships (1885-1888). After the AA disbanded following the 1891 season, Sportsman's Park sat vacant again, this time for a decade until the Milwaukee Brewers, a charter member of the American League relocated to St. Louis as the Browns. And that when our story for this book begins … almost.

In the winter of 1908-1909 Sportsman's Park was rebuilt and extensively remodeled and renovated. The wooden grandstand was replaced by a modern, doubled-decked steel and concrete one. It was a new dawn for ballparks in the US, as brand-new steel and concrete baseball cathedrals opened in Pittsburgh (Forbes Field) and Philadelphia (Shibe Park) in 1909, and 10 more followed in rapid succession between 1910 and 1916.

This volume focuses on the modern steel and concrete incarnation of Sportsman's Park which served as the center of professional baseball in St. Louis until the Cardinals played their last game there, on May 8, 1966. The Browns, a perennial second-division team, were the sole occupants of Sportsman's Park until 1920 when team (and ballpark) owner Phil Ball invited the Cardinals to leave their dilapidated wooden park, Robison Field, and play their games at Grand and Dodier. The rest, as some might say, is history. The Cardinals, a moribund club that had enjoyed only four winning seasons between 1900 and 1920, developed into one of the most successful teams in baseball. They captured 10 pennants and seven World Series championships between 1926 and 1964. After experiencing their longest stretch of success, in the 1920s, the Browns settled into their familiar second-division role for the remainder of their existence in St. Louis. In 1944 the Brownies won their only pennant, setting up a fairy-tale World Series with their tenants, the Cardinals. Wracked by financial problems and poor attendance, the Browns found their days in the Gateway City numbered by the time World War II was over. In 1953 Browns owner Bill Veeck sold Sportsman's Park to August Busch, who ultimately renamed it Busch Stadium, though St. Louisians and baseball fans continued to call it Sportsman's Park. At the end of the 1953 season, the Browns played their last game in "Busch Stadium," were sold in the offseason, and relocated to Baltimore. St. Louis was once again a one-team town. Like other parks of the Golden Age, Sportsman's Park showed its age by the late 1950s and early 1960s, as newer parks in Milwaukee, Los Angeles, and Minneapolis paved the way for a modern experience for fans. In May 1964, construction began on a new multipurpose sports facility in downtown St. Louis, signaling the gradual end of Sportsman's Park. On May 8, 1966, the Redbirds played their last game there and inaugurated the new Busch Stadium four days later.

This book rekindles memories of the Sportsman's Park through detailed summaries of 100 games played there from 1909 to 1966, and insightful feature essays about the history of the ballpark. The process of selecting games was agonizing, yet deliberate. Our goal was to present Sportsman's Park as a locus of baseball history—for both the National and American Leagues. About two-thirds of the games are dedicated to the Cardinals, the other third to the Browns. Some of the game summaries chronicle historic firsts, such as the Browns' (1909) and the Cardinals' (1920) first games in the steel-and-concrete structure; the Browns' first no-hitter, by little remembered Ernie Koob (1917) and the Redbirds' first no-no, by popular Jesse Haines (1924); the first time a St. Louis player belted three home runs in a game (the Browns' Ken Williams in 1922), and the first night game in the ballpark, played by the Browns in 1940. Other essays mark memorable games, such as the three All-Star Games played there (1940, 1948, and 1957) and the final games played by the Browns and Cardinals. Many essays recount great feats, like those of the Redbirds' Dizzy Dean pitching a shutout on two days' rest to win his 30th game of the season and capture the pennant for the Gas House Gang (1934), the Cardinals' Roy Parmelee and the New York Giants' Carl Hubbell battling for 17 innings (1936), and Stan "The Man" Musial belting five home runs in a doubleheader (1954). Sportsman's Park hosted 10 World Series, including the Trolley Car Series, an unlikely matchup between the Cardinals and the Browns. Included are all 33 World Series games hosted by Sportsman's Park. Many of these games have etched themselves in baseball lore, from the Babe whacking three round-trippers against the Cardinals in Game Four of the 1926 Fall Classic to the Redbirds' Game Seven victories over the Boston Red Sox in 1946 and the New Yankees in 1964, hammering the last nail in the dynasty that had ruled the AL for more than four decades.

Furthermore, the games not only just highlight the accomplishments and heroics of stars like Pete Alexander, Mort Cooper, Johnny Mize, and George Sisler, but also revive memories of forgotten or overlooked players like Bob Groom, Sig Jakucki, Jack Kramer, and Allan Sothoron of the Browns and Les Bell, Eddie Dyer, Wild Bill Hallahan, and Red Munger of the Cardinals. Also included are memorable or historic performances by the Browns' and Redbirds' opponents, such as the Chicago White Sox' Eddie Cicotte tossing the first no-hitter in Sportsman's Park (1917) and the debut of the Brooklyn Dodgers' Jackie Robinson in the Gateway City (1947).

Ten feature essays round out the volume and provide context for the stadium's history. Topics include the Milwaukee Brewers' move to St. Louis to become the Browns in 1902 and the Browns' relocation to Baltimore for the 1954 campaign, as well as beer magnate August Busch's purchase of the Cardinals in 1953, and the subsequent renaming of Sportsman's Park to Busch Stadium that same year. There are also thorough biographies of former Browns owners Robert Hedges and Phil Ball, and Sam Breadon of the Cardinals. An essay on the history of Sportsman's Park and the statistics-oriented piece "By the Numbers" round out this extraordinary volume.

This book is the result of tireless work of many members of the Society for American Baseball Research. SABR members researched and wrote all of the essays in this volume. These uncompensated volunteers are united by their shared interest in baseball history and resolute commitment to preserving its history. Without their unwavering dedication this volume would not have been possible.

I am indebted to the associate editors and extend to them my sincerest appreciation. Bill Nowlin, the second reader; fact-checker James Forr; and copy editor Len Levin each read every word of all the essays and made numerous corrections to language, style, and content. Their attention to detail has been invaluable. It has been a pleasure to once again work on a book project with such professionals, with whom I corresponded practically every day, and typically more than once.

HOME OF THE BROWNS AND CARDINALS AT GRAND AND DODIER

I thank all of the authors for their contributions, meticulous research, cooperation through the revising and editing process, and finally their patience. It was a long journey from the day the book was launched to its completion, and we've finally reached our destination. We did it! Please refer to list of contributors at the end of the book for more information.

This book would not have been possible without the generous support of the staff and Board of Directors of SABR, SABR Publications Director Cecilia Tan, and designer Gilly Rosenthol (Rosenthol Design). Special thanks to John Horne of the National Baseball Hall of Fame for supplying the overwhelming majority of photos.

We invite you to sit back, relax for a few minutes, and enjoy reading about the great games and the exciting history of Sportsman's Park.

Gregory H. Wolf
December 1, 2017

SPORTSMAN'S PARK

BY SCOTT FERKOVICH

IN BASEBALL HISTORY THERE HAVE BEEN certain street corners that through the years have become synonymous with the ballparks located at them. At the corner of Michigan and Trumbull was Detroit's Tiger Stadium. 21st and Lehigh was Shibe Park in Philadelphia. Findlay and Western was Cincinnati's Crosley Field. On the South Side of Chicago, 35th and Shields was Comiskey Park. Today, Clark and Addison carries on this tradition with Wrigley Field. To old-time baseball fans in St. Louis, there is another hallowed corner that can be added to the list: Grand and Dodier. From the days when amateur baseball clubs first laid out a rough diamond there in the mid-1860s until the Cardinals played their final game at Busch Stadium a century later, the fabled corner on the north side of St. Louis was witness to some great baseball.

In the 19th century several teams called Grand and Dodier home. The first professional circuit, the National Association of Professional Baseball Players, had a St. Louis entry in 1875, known as the Brown Stockings. They played at a park called the Grand Avenue Ball Grounds, which was really nothing fancier than a single grandstand for the paying customers. The league folded after that year.

The park's name was changed to Sportsman's Park in 1876 with the arrival of the St. Louis Brown Stockings, a charter member of the new National League. After the 1877 season, the Brown Stockings went bankrupt, and the city was without a professional baseball team for four years.

In 1882 the new American Association was formed, with yet another St. Louis Brown Stockings team. Soon the name was shortened to Browns. The team fielded some of the strongest teams of the decade, finishing first from 1885 through 1888. They were led by young player-manager Charles Comiskey. The team's owner was German-American saloonkeeper Chris von der Ahe, who renovated Sportsman's Park. By keeping ticket prices low, the Browns were annually among the league leaders in attendance, and their fans were left over with more money to spend on beer at games. Von der Ahe was a born promoter. In an effort to sell even more brew, he put up a beer garden in the right-field corner at Sportsman's Park, which, oddly enough, was in play. Eventually the rules were changed so that a ball hit into the beer garden was a home run.

The American Association folded after 1891, and the Browns rejoined the National League. Grand and Dodier, however, sat vacant for the remainder of the decade, as the Browns moved to another location in the city.

With the dawning of the new century came an upstart new "major" league, Ban Johnson's American League, which featured an entry in Milwaukee called the Brewers. After struggling their only year in the Cream City, 1901, the franchise moved to St. Louis, changed its name to the Browns, and played at the newly refurbished Sportsman's Park at Grand and Dodier.

Like most venues of the era, Sportsman's Park was a wooden structure, susceptible to fires. But in the winter of 1908-09, the Browns' ballpark underwent an extensive renovation, and by Opening Day of 1909 it featured a double-decked (and fireproof) concrete and steel grandstand. A covered single-deck grandstand extended down the left-field line. The outfield was ringed by single-decked wooden bleachers. The seating capacity was listed as 24,040. That same summer two new ballparks built of reinforced concrete and structural steel opened: Shibe Park in Philadelphia and Forbes Field in Pittsburgh. Within the next few years, many new teams would build comparable modern stadiums. The era of the Classic Ballpark had begun.

Also calling Sportsman's Park home during this time was the St. Louis University football team, under legendary coach Eddie Cochems. Football historians will quickly identify him as the originator of an offense built around the forward pass, which revolutionized the game. In 1906 the team finished with an 11-0 record, taking advantage of the forward pass to outscore its opponents, 407-11.

The National League's St. Louis Cardinals, the descendants of the Brown Stockings, had for years played at League Park, an outmoded and inadequate facility (the last wooden park, in fact, used by a major-league team). In July 1920 the Cardinals and Browns owner Phil Ball worked out an arrangement that allowed the Cardinals to move into Sportsman's Park as tenants. The Cardinals' offices were located at 3623 Dodier, the Browns' around the corner at 2911 North Grand. Both teams called Sportsman's Park home until the Browns left town for Baltimore after the 1953 season. As a result of the constant use, the field was perennially one of the worst in baseball.

The end of World War I brought an attendance boom to baseball in the early 1920s. To make room for more fans, Ball spent $500,000 to renovate the old ballpark. By the end of 1925 the park had taken on the form that it would assume for the rest of its days. The second deck now ran all the way down both foul lines. The old wooden bleachers in the outfield were replaced by concrete stands, including a covered pavilion from the right-field foul line to the center-field bleachers. The outfield distances were 351 feet to left field, 426 to dead center, and a mere 310 feet to right. The seating capacity was listed as 30,500. Sportswriter Red Smith called it "a garish, county fair sort of layout." The short distance to the right-field fence necessitated the addition in 1929 of one of the quirkiest features of the park: A 25-foot screen atop the 11½-foot wall that extended 156 feet toward center, ending at the 354-foot mark in right-center. A batted ball that hit the screen was in play. (Years later, Cardinal great Stan Musial described the effects of the screen: "[It] made it much more interesting. The ball would fly out there and the runner didn't know if it was going to hit the screen, go over it, or how it would bounce."[1]) Because of the short distance to right, outfielders tended to play shallow, and thus had a better shot of throwing out runners at third or home on singles.)

The move by the Cardinals to bigger and better digs was the catalyst that forever changed the landscape of professional baseball in St. Louis. It was perhaps the most fortuitous decision the Cardinals franchise ever made. For the first two decades of the 20th century, neither the Browns nor the Cardinals fielded particularly competitive teams. After their second-place finish in their inaugural American League season in 1902, the Browns never placed that high again until 1922. The Cardinals, meanwhile, didn't fare much better, never topping third place from 1900 to 1925. But relocating to Sportsman's Park allowed Sam Breadon, the owner of the Cardinals, to sell League Park, the club's former home. Branch Rickey, the team's manager at the time, used the money to create baseball's first farm system. By being able to develop homegrown talent on minor-league teams that they owned, the Cardinals became one of the more progressive teams in baseball. As a result, the fortunes of the two St. Louis teams went in opposite directions. From 1926, when the Cardinals went to their first World Series, until early in the 1966 season, when they abandoned the Sportsman's Park neighborhood, the club went to the fall classic ten times, winning seven times. The Browns, meanwhile, became a byword for futility, a franchise that seemingly fell off the baseball radar for decades.

The Browns came close to a pennant in 1922, but lost out to the Yankees by one game. They never seriously contended again during the decade, but featured some exciting players. Slugging left fielder Ken Williams led the league in home runs (39) and RBIs (155) in 1922, and hit .326 in his ten years as a Brown. Center fielder Baby Doll Jacobson was a consistent .300 hitter and RBI man in these years. On the mound, the Browns had one of the best baseball names ever, in Urban Shocker. The right-handed Shocker was a fine pitcher for the club from 1918 to 1924, winning 126 games, with four straight 20-win seasons. But the biggest star ever to don a Browns uniform was first baseman George Sisler. Gorgeous George played with the Browns from 1915 to 1927 (he missed 1923 with illness), hitting .344 during those years, twice topping the .400 mark. His 1922 season

SPORTSMAN'S PARK IN ST. LOUIS

was stunning: He led the league in average (.420), hits (246), runs (134), triples (18), and stolen bases (51). His OPS (on-base average plus slugging average) was 1.061. Sisler was elected to the Hall of Fame in 1939.

While the Cardinals never led the league in attendance in their years at Sportsman's Park, they did draw over a million fans in 13 different seasons. They annually outdrew their landlords by large margins. The highest single-season attendance for the Cardinals at Sportsman's Park was 1,430,676 in 1949, when they missed the pennant in a tight race with the Dodgers. The Browns, meanwhile, never topped the million mark at Grand and Dodier. Their highest single-season total was 712,918 in 1922. In a four-year stretch from 1933 to 1936, they drew fewer than 100,000 fans in a season three times, with a ridiculously low 80,922 in 1935. Even in the pennant-winning year of 1944, they attracted 508,644, fifth out of the eight American League teams.

By the middle of the 1920s, the Cardinals were beginning to come into their own as a franchise. Rogers Hornsby had emerged as perhaps the greatest right-handed hitter of all time. Certainly you cannot argue against a lifetime .358 batting average and 301 home runs. In 1926, with Hornsby as player-manager, the Cardinals reached the World Series for the first time, prevailing in seven games over the New York Yankees. In Game Four at Sportsman's Park, Babe Ruth hit three home runs, one of which cleared the pavilion roof in right field. Two years later the Babe had another three-homer game at Grand and Dodier, in Game Four of the 1928 Series, which the Yankees swept. A second Cardinals world championship fol-

Construction on Sportsman's Park was finished in 1909. It served as the home park for the Browns until 1953 and for the Cardinals from July 1, 1920, until May 8, 1966. (National Baseball Hall of Fame, Cooperstown, New York)

lowed in 1931, capping a season in which the club topped 100 victories for the first time.

Perhaps no Cardinals team is as fondly remembered as the Gas House Gang of 1934. Depression Era America fell in love with this colorful collection of hard-nosed, rough-and-tumble players who always seemed to have the dirtiest uniforms on the field.

The player-manager of the Gas House Gang was second baseman Frankie Frisch, known as the Fordham Flash for his having attended Fordham University, and his speed while starring in collegiate sports. At shortstop was scrappy Leo Durocher, a player as famous for his propensity for wearing flashy suits as for his refusal to back down from anyone who challenged him. He wasn't much of a hitter at the dish. Babe Ruth, in fact, had referred to him as the All-American Out. The batting order also boasted first baseman Ripper Collins, a Triple Crown winner in 1934 with a .333 average, 35 homers, and 128 RBIs; future Hall of Famer Joe "Ducky" Medwick also topped 100 RBIs, and added 18 home runs and a .319 average; and Pepper Martin, the hustling third baseman.

But the biggest star of the Gas House Gang was a farmboy from Lucas, Arkansas, Dizzy Dean. With a blazing fastball, the 24-year-old Dean won 30 games that year, the last National League pitcher to do so. His brother Paul won 19. Dizzy's meteoric career was cut short by injury, but it nonetheless warranted election to the Hall of Fame in 1953. He was brash, confident, and talented. But he also had a country-boy charm about him, and could tell a tale with the best of them, a quality that later helped him to forge a long career as a baseball broadcaster.

The Gas House Gang won 95 games in 1934, edging the New York Giants by two games. Their American League opponents in the World Series were the Detroit Tigers. One of baseball's most amusing fables emerged from this postseason. In Game Four, at Sportsman's Park, Dizzy was inserted as a pinch-runner at first base in the fourth inning. Trying to break up a double play, he was plunked in the forehead by the baseball on the relay throw to first base. A collective groan could be heard through Sportsman's Park as Dean lay unconscious for several moments on the field. He was carried off and taken to the hospital, before eventually being released. According to legend, a newspaper headline the next day ran, "X-Rays of Dean's Head Show Nothing." Game Seven was noteworthy for the near-riot that occurred at Navin Field in Detroit after a hard slide by Medwick into Detroit's third baseman, Marv Owen. The Gas House Gang won the last game in a blowout, 11-0, to take the world championship. The Dean brothers each won two games.

After the Depression, more and more ballparks were being outfitted with modern public-address systems. But not so at Sportsman's Park. For years announcers had to make the best of it by shouting into a megaphone while dashing around the perimeter of the field. Finally, in 1937, Sportsman's Park installed an electronic public-address system, one of the last ballparks to do so.

Starting in the 1930s, radio station KMOX began broadcasting Cardinals and Browns games. Because it was a 50,000-watt clear-channel station, games from Sportsman's Park could be heard throughout the Midwest and much of the South. This helped the Cardinals (they and the Browns were at the time the westernmost major-league teams) to develop a strong fan base throughout the nation's midsection. In 1945 broadcasting legend Harry Caray began calling games from his perch in the broadcasting booth behind home plate at Sportsman's Park. He would go on to call Cardinals games for 25 seasons before going to the White Sox and then the Cubs. One of the primary sponsors of the St. Louis broadcasts was locally brewed Griesedieck beer.

People attending games at Grand and Dodier in the 1930s would not have been able to avoid noticing the park's loudest fan. Mrs. Mary Ott, known as the Horse Lady, would tug at her ears and let out a neigh at the top of her lungs, much to the chagrin of umpires, opposing players, and the unfortunate people sitting in front of her.

In 1940 lights were installed at the ballpark. The Browns played the first night game there, on May 24, drawing a crowd of 24,827, their biggest home attendance of the season. The Cardinals played their first contest under the lights on June 4, in front of 23,500 spectators, also the most at home they would draw that year. With the sweltering hot, humid St. Louis summers, players and fans could appreciate the novelty (and the relief) of playing at night. On April 18, 1950, the Cardinals became the first team to hold their home opener at night.

From 1942 to 1946, the Cardinals experienced a stretch of excellence that saw them go to the fall classic four times, winning three of them. Their win totals in 1942, '43, and '44 were 106, 105, and 105. Stan Musial emerged as a star during this period, and the Cardinals were fortunate that he missed only one year, 1945, due to World War II. Stan the Man went on to have a long and storied career at Grand and Dodier, finishing with a .331 career batting average, 475 home runs, and what was then the most lifetime hits by a National Leaguer.

The war years were lean ones for baseball, as many stars of the game were called to serve Uncle Sam. As a result, teams were forced to fill their depleted rosters with castoffs, retreads, or unknowns who during normal times would most likely be toiling in the minor leagues. One-armed Pete Gray, who played for the Browns in 1945, came to be a symbol of wartime baseball. Despite (or because of) the roster attrition, however, the unthinkable happened in 1944. The St. Louis Browns, who had had only four winning seasons in the prior 20 years, won the American League pennant. They started strong out of the gate, winning their first nine games. They also got hot at the end, when they had to win, going 11-1 in their final 12 games, including a four-game sweep of the Yankees on the final weekend. It came down to the last game of the season at Sportsman's Park. The Browns entered the October 1 game tied with Detroit for the top spot. Before a crowd of 35,518, the largest regular-season Browns crowd ever at Grand and Dodier, they prevailed over New York, 5-2, while the Tigers lost in Detroit to the Washington Senators. The Browns were the champions of the American League, with a record of 89-65. They wound up facing the Cardinals in the only All-St. Louis World Series ever. The Browns came up short, four games to two, in what was dubbed the Streetcar Series. It was the lone World Series appearance in the long history of the Browns.

One of the most famous plays ever at Sportsman's Park occurred in Game Seven of the 1946 World Series, which featured the Cardinals against the Boston Red Sox. In the bottom of the eighth inning, with the score tied, 3-3, the Cardinals' Enos Slaughter led off with a single. The next two batters made outs, then Harry "The Hat" Walker, who got his nickname because he would constantly tug at the bill of his cap between pitches, poked a solid hit to left-center. Boston center fielder Leon Culberson ambled over, fielded it routinely, and lobbed the ball to shortstop Johnny Pesky, neither of them expecting Slaughter to continue around third and run home. Pesky perhaps hesitated just a second before gunning the ball to catcher Roy Partee. The throw was a bit up the third-base line, but it didn't matter. Slaughter slid into home safely. Many have speculated down the ages that Pesky's slight hesitation allowed Slaughter to score. In the end, it proved to be the winning run of the World Series. Before the Series started, it had been billed as a showdown between the two biggest stars on either club, Ted Williams of the Red Sox and Stan Musial of the Cardinals. Neither hit particularly well in the Series, however. Williams batted .200, while Musial was slightly better at .222.

Sportsman's Park was the last ballpark in the majors to maintain a Jim Crow section. Until the 1944 season black patrons could sit only in the right-field pavilion. But by 1947 the Browns became only the third big-league team (after the Dodgers and the Indians) to field a black player. The team had purchased two players from the Negro Leagues' Kansas City Monarchs, infielder Hank Thompson and outfielder Willard Brown. The 21-year-old Thompson didn't do much for St. Louis, playing in only 27 games with no home runs, but he did go on to have some good years with the New York Giants. Brown, who was 32, played in only 21 big-league games, hitting .179. In 2006, however, he was enshrined in

Cooperstown for his achievements in the Negro Leagues.

After their World Series appearance in 1944, the Browns finished third the next year with a record of 81-70. It was the final .500 season in their history. In July 1951, in the midst of a 102-loss season, the team was purchased by one of baseball's foremost impresarios ever, Bill Veeck. A master of promotion and theatrics, Veeck pulled off perhaps his most famous stunt on August 19, 1951, between games of a Sunday doubleheader with the Tigers. A big birthday cake was wheeled onto the field. Suddenly, a 3-foot 7-inch midget by the name of Eddie Gaedel popped out, to the delight of the crowd. Had the promotion ended there, it would have been forgotten. But it didn't, and it wasn't. When the second game got under way, Frank Saucier was scheduled to lead off the bottom of the first inning for the Browns. The fans were shocked to see Gaedel come trotting up to home plate as a pinch-hitter. When nonplussed home-plate umpire Ed Hurley asked Browns manager Zack Taylor what the big idea was, Taylor presented the man in blue with a standard player contract with Gaedel's signature on it. Veeck knew the umps wouldn't appreciate his sense of humor, so he had had the contract prepared beforehand and sent to the league office after it had closed. Hurley had to comply, and Gaedel was allowed to bat. Tigers pitcher Bob Cain threw four straight balls, and the midget took his base. Gaedel got a standing ovation from the crowd as he was removed for a pinch-runner. His uniform number, 1/8, is on display at the Baseball Hall of Fame.

Veeck and his family lived in an apartment of his own making under the stands at Sportsman's Park. He had high hopes that his promotional acumen would help to increase attendance and allow the Browns to compete with the Cardinals. Veeck himself was by no means a wealthy man, and the team operated on a shoestring budget. Among his other promotional stunts was Grandstand Managers Day, when fans in one section were given placards with words like "bunt," "steal," "swing," and "pull the pitcher." They would hold the cards up at strategic points in the game, and the players on the field had to obey the fans' decisions.

Promotions aside, the Browns didn't improve any on the field during Veeck's reign. He did sign former Negro Leagues star Satchel Paige in 1951. Paige was in his mid-40s at the time. He pitched three seasons for the Brownies, winning 18 and losing 23.

In 1953 the Anheuser-Busch brewery, maker of Budweiser beer, purchased the Cardinals, with August "Gussie" Busch, Jr. becoming team president. Veeck knew he couldn't compete with Busch's deep pockets. He tried unsuccessfully to move the Browns to greener pastures in Milwaukee. When that didn't work, he promptly sold Sportsman's Park to Busch. The tables were now turned; the Cardinals were the landlords and the Browns were the tenants.

Busch wanted to change the name of Sportsman's Park to Budweiser Stadium, but the league balked at having a ballpark named after a beer. Busch instead changed the name to Busch Stadium, after which the brewery introduced Busch Bavarian Beer in 1955. Thus, instead of naming the ballpark after a beer, they tried a different tack and named a beer after the ballpark.

By the 1953 season, it was a foregone conclusion that Veeck would be moving the Browns out of town the next season. The highlight of the year at Grand and Dodier came on May 6. Bobo Holloman, a 30-year-old career minor leaguer, pitched a no-hitter against the Philadelphia Athletics in his first major-league start, the only player ever to do so.

The final game for the Browns in St. Louis came on September 27, 1953. The club lost its 100th game of the season, in front of an intimate gathering of 3,174 fans. Jim Dyck hit a fly ball to center for the last at-bat ever by a St. Louis Brown. By Opening Day 1954, Veeck had sold the team, and the new owners had moved it to Baltimore. The Cardinals now had St. Louis all to themselves.

The old ballpark at Grand and Dodier may have had a new name, but by the 1950s Busch Stadium was in definite need of sprucing up. Years of hands-off stewardship by the Browns had left the place in a state of neglect. Gussie Busch spent over a million dollars to brighten up the ballpark. He closed the center-field bleachers and replaced them with more eye-appealing shrubbery. Every seat in the house was either repaired or replaced. Dugouts and clubhouses were renovated and expanded. Busch was also responsible for installing one of the more distinctive features of the park during its remaining years: an electronic Anheuser-Busch eagle perched atop the scoreboard in left field. After every home run, the eagle would flap its electronic wings.

Stan "The Man" Musial was the brightest star to shine at Grand and Dodier for more than two decades. From his first season, 1941, until he retired after the 1963 season Musial won no fewer than seven National League batting titles, finishing his career with the most (at the time) career hits in the NL (3,630). During his tenure, the Cardinals went to four World Series, winning three of them.

In its history Sportsman's Park played host to three All-Star Games, in 1940, 1948, and 1957. The 1957 contest involved a ballot-box stuffing controversy. Overly zealous Cincinnati fans had voted all but one of the Redlegs' position players to the game. The only non-Redleg to get voted onto the squad was Musial. Commissioner Ford Frick replaced starting Cincinnati outfielders Gus Bell and Wally Post with Hank Aaron and Willie Mays, and then decided that for future All-Star Games fans would not be casting any more ballots. Starters would now be decided by players, managers, and coaches. This policy lasted until 1970, when the vote was given back to the fans.

By the late 1950s, serious discussions began to take place about a new ballpark. Despite Gussie Busch's improvements, the stadium had begun to deteriorate. The public perception of Busch Stadium was the same as that of many other urban ballparks during this period. For one thing, the neighborhood was become increasingly dangerous. Also, the United States was becoming a car culture; people preferred to drive to baseball games, rather than take buses or trolleys as they had in previous decades. Busch Stadium, with its lack of parking, could not accommodate them. In 1964 ground was broken for what would be the future Busch Memorial Stadium, in downtown St. Louis.

That same year the Cardinals captured the pennant by one game on the last day of the season after a thrilling three-way pennant race with the Phillies and the Reds. Thanks to Philadelphia's classic late-season collapse, in which they blew the 6½-game lead they had with 12 games left to play, St. Louis went on to face the New York Yankees in the World Series. The seventh game featured Bob Gibson on the hill for the Cardinals at Busch Stadium. Gibson threw a complete game as St. Louis won by a final score of 7-5. This last championship team in Sportsman's Park's history was just on the cusp of greatness. Gibson would emerge as the most intimidating pitcher in an era filled with many of them. Lou Brock, Curt Flood, and Orlando Cepeda ignited the Redbirds' lineup in the second half of the decade. The club returned to the World Series at their new downtown stadium in 1967 and 1968.

Grand and Dodier was also the home of the St. Louis football Cardinals starting in 1960, after the franchise relocated from Chicago. The NFL's Cardinals never went to the playoffs in their six seasons at Busch Stadium. Bill and Charles Bidwill, the owners of the team, threatened to pull up stakes and move the team to Atlanta, having become disenchanted with the old ballpark and frustrated with the slow progress on the new stadium. The city eventually persuaded the Bidwill brothers to stay.

The Cardinals were scheduled to move into the new Busch Memorial Stadium for Opening Day 1966. But construction delays forced the team to continue to play at the old Busch for the first ten home games of the season. The end finally came on Sunday, May 8, an afternoon affair against San Francisco, which the Giants won 10-5. The final home run was hit by Willie Mays in the top of the ninth inning. In the bottom of the ninth, the Cardinals' Alex Johnson made the last out, hitting into a double play. Considering the occasion, a surprisingly modest crowd of 17,503 showed up. The team had had a disappointing 1965 season, and was in eighth place and playing very poorly at the beginning of 1966, which probably led to the modest crowd. There was not much "final game" fanfare for Busch Stadium; the Cardinals had scheduled a downtown parade later that day to celebrate the new stadium, and was genuinely happy to get out of the Sportsman's Park neighborhood. The ballpark area had become run-down and dangerous. A young fan was shot and killed during an armed robbery while he was hurrying to the 1964 opener. (After the May 8 game, home plate was dug up, and a few fans unbolted and carried out sections of seats, while many were content with a scoop of the outfield warning track to take home for a souvenir.)

Within six months the old ballpark at Grand and Dodier succumbed to the wrecking ball. After demolition, all that remained was the playing field. As a goodwill gesture, Gussie Busch transferred the real-estate title to the Metropolitan St. Louis Boys' Club. At this writing the grass athletic field was being used by the Boys & Girls Clubs of Greater St. Louis. A sign there noted the site of Sportsman's Park in St. Louis.

SOURCES

Benson, Michael, *Ballparks of North America: A Comprehensive Historical Reference to Baseball Grounds, Yards and Stadiums, 1845 to Present* (Jefferson, North Carolina, and London: McFarland & Company, 2009).

Feldmann, Doug, *Dizzy & The Gas House Gang: The 1934 Cardinals and Depression-Era Baseball* (Jefferson, North Carolina, and London: McFarland & Company, 2000).

Gillette, Gary, and Eric Enders, *Big League Ballparks: The Complete Illustrated History* (New York: Metro Books, 2009).

Jordan, David M., *Closing 'Em Down: Final Games at Thirteen Classic Ballparks* (Jefferson, North Carolina, and London: McFarland & Company, 2010).

Leventhal, Josh, *Take Me Out to the Ballpark.* (New York: Black Dog & Leventhal Publishers, 2011).

Smith, Ron. *The Ballpark Book: A Journey Through the Fields of Baseball Magic* (St. Louis: The Sporting News, 2000).

The Sporting News

Baseball-Reference.com

NOTES

1   Ron Smith, *The Ballpark Book: A Journey Through the Fields of Baseball Magic*, 289-90.

THE MILWAUKEE BREWERS MOVE TO ST. LOUIS AND BECOME THE BROWNS IN 1902

BY DENNIS PAJOT

IN THE FALL OF 1893, A NEW WESTERN League was formed with Milwaukee as a charter member. The first (and only) president of the Milwaukee Brewers was Matthew R. Killilea, born in the town of Poygan, Wisconsin. An 1891 graduate of the University of Wisconsin, Killilea was thereafter appointed assistant district attorney in Milwaukee County, but could not serve as he had not yet practiced law the required time. In 1894 he was an unsuccessful Democratic candidate for the Wisconsin State Assembly from Milwaukee. He was a lifelong bachelor. It was said that Killilea "is a young man of fine, natural abilities, good attainments, and has a promising future before him."[1]

Managed by Charlie Cushman in 1894, the 47-74 Brewers finished in last place, but president Killilea still claimed an $800 profit for the season.[2] That fall a new major-league was rumored in the planning stage. Slated for inclusion in this new circuit was a Milwaukee franchise to be headed by Milwaukee businessman Harry Quin, owner of Athletic Park where the Western League Brewers played. Viewing the new league talk as merely a gambit by Quin to raise their rent, the Brewers promptly relocated to new grounds on Milwaukee's far north side at 16th and Lloyd.[3]

Under a new field manager, the Brewers struggled to a 57-66 mark in 1895, but ended up approximately $10,000 ahead financially.[4] Then during the offseason, Fred Gross, owner of a local meat-packing company, who would later figure prominently in the shift of the Milwaukee club to St. Louis, was appointed club secretary.[5] A midseason change of managers did not help the sixth-place Brewers in 1896. On the financial front, officials claimed the club broke even and would have made $20,000 if it were not for a streetcar strike.[6] But this is doubtful. Ten days before the season ended it was rumored that the club was for sale, and while directors denied it, they admitted that the club would lose about $2,500. Nevertheless, offers to buy the Brewers, including a $9,000 bid by the *Milwaukee Sentinel* and a $12,000 offer by an anonymous Milwaukee businessman, were rejected. As far as president Killilea was concerned, the club was not for sale at any price (even though three losing seasons in the Western League had apparently depreciated its value).[7]

In 1897 management signed Connie Mack to manage the Brewers for $3,000, the highest salary ever given a Milwaukee manager to date.[8] Mack, recently dismissed after two-plus seasons as player-manager with the Pittsburgh Pirates, was given free rein and began to build a winner. His first Brewers club finished in fourth place with an 84-51 record and led the Western League in attendance. In the postseason estimation of the *Milwaukee Journal*, the club made a handsome profit of $22,100.[9] Mack, also a part-owner of the club, was "$2,000 richer than he would have been if he had remained in the big leagues last season."[10] The next season, Mack led the Brewers to a third-place (82-57) finish, while the club made another $20,000.[11] But when the 1899 team finished a distant sixth, club management came in for criticism, with one local writer complaining: "It looks as though the present team were run for revenue and revenue only. … The popular idea is that the Brewers are run on a very cheap basis."[12]

In 1899 there was renewed talk of a new major league, this time a revived American Association, promoted by Chris von der Ahe, recently dispossessed of his St. Louis National League franchise; St. Louis promoter George Schaefer; and Albert

Spink of the *St. Louis Dispatch*. In September an organizational meeting was held in Chicago, with 10 cities, including Milwaukee, represented by interested baseball men. The Milwaukee representatives were sporting-goods business owner Harry D. Quin and clothing store owner (and city alderman) Charles Havenor.[13] Western League President Ban Johnson took advantage of the proposed new league to seek expanded draft protection for his own league and, more importantly, to place a team in Chicago.[14] He also changed the name of his circuit to the expansive-sounding American League. It was observed that "this shrewd and unexpected move is designated to deprive the proposed new rival American Association of the benefits of a traditional title, without infringing upon the League's rights in the matter; to remove the ex-Western League from its hampering sectional basis, and to place it in the position to become nationally known."[15] Soon, backers dropped out of the American Association, and it was dead by February.[16] But once the AA threat was gone, the National League began to renege on promises made to the new AL, including refusing it permission to move a club into Chicago.[17]

Both the National League and the American League prepared for war. For the 1900 season, the formerly 12-club NL contracted to an eight-team league. This, in turn, afforded the AL the opportunity to put a team in abandoned territories like Cleveland. Soon thereafter, the National League permitted the American League to enter Chicago under the ownership of Charles Comiskey, and interleague hostilities were avoided—for the time being.[18]

Now a member of the still-minor American League, the 1900 Milwaukee Brewers played very well under Mack, finishing second, its 79-58 log bettered only by the champion (82-53) Chicago White Sox.[19] Like other AL clubs (with the possible exception of Minneapolis), the Brewers finished in the black, netting approximately $8,000 to $10,000.[20]

On November 3, 1900, the Milwaukee Baseball Club filed an amendment to its articles of incorporation, increasing the capital stock to $25,000. Principal stockholders Matthew Killilea, Fred Gross, and Connie Mack each held an equal amount of stock.[21] Later that month, Killilea stated that he would not object if Mack wished to become part-owner the AL Philadelphia franchise.[22] Mack equivocated, but by December *The Sporting News* reported, and a Philadelphia paper subsequently confirmed, that Mack had sold his stock in the Brewers and purchased an ownership interest in the Philadelphia club.[23]

On January 28, 1901, the American League reconstituted itself, admitting Washington, Baltimore, Philadelphia, and Boston to its ranks, while dropping Indianapolis, Buffalo, Kansas City, and Minneapolis. A 10-year agreement was adopted, with 51 percent of each franchise reportedly being retained by the league with a first option to purchase the club. President Johnson then declared his circuit a major league, breaking off relations with the NL. The two leagues would now go head-to-head against each other.[24]

Even before the new major got off the ground, there were rumors that the Milwaukee franchise would be transferred to St. Louis. Killilea denied it.[25] However, sources claimed that Charles Comiskey had secured old Sportsman's Park in St. Louis, and that Milwaukee would be transferred there if wartime exigencies compelled it.[26]

Intent on remaining in Milwaukee, club owners signed onetime NL batting champion Hugh Duffy to manage the team. Duffy also reportedly acquired Connie Mack's stock in the Brewers.[27] Working with management to fill out the roster, Duffy liked his club's prospects, telling a *Milwaukee Journal* reporter: "We certainly are going to have a crackerjack of a team this season. Our pitching staff is strong, and our infield can't be beat by any other team in the league. And the outfield will be there with the goods when the time comes."[28] The *Sentinel* agreed, writing that the Brewers were "exceptionally strong" and Duffy was "one of the brainiest, inside and aggressive players in the country."[29] Oddsmakers disagreed, rating Chicago a 13-to-5 favorite for the AL pennant. Milwaukee's chances were placed at 15 to 1.[30]

The Brewers' foremost problem would be their inability to sign solid National Leaguers. While most other AL clubs signed one or more big-name National Leaguers, the Brewers' best catch was outfielder John Anderson. Perhaps as a result, the $24,000 Brewers payroll was lower than those of most AL clubs, exceeding only that of Baltimore.[31]

The season itself started on a sour note. On a belated April 25 Opening Day the Brewers blew a 13-4 final-inning lead when Tigers scored 10 runs to post a 14-13 victory—still a record for ninth-inning comebacks.[32] Duffy shuffled his roster throughout the season but could not arrest the club's slide. The Brewers ended the season where they spent most of it: in last place, with a 48-89 record.[33] The Brewers' final standing was not undeserved, as the *Milwaukee Daily News* declared that the Brewers team played "the very rottenest ball ever dished up by a major league organization."[34] The team batting average of .261 was the lowest in the league, as was its run total of 641. In the field, the Brewers' 393 errors were exceeded by only two other teams, while the pitching staff gave up 828 runs, second most in the AL. The only bright spot was the play of John Anderson. In addition to batting .330, Honest John had 190 hits (second in the American League), 46 doubles (second), 99 RBIs (third), 8 home runs (fourth), and 274 total bases (third).[35]

As reflected in the columns below, the American League was competitive at the gate. As for the Brewers, an article by Ernest Lanigan in *The Sporting News* placed their biggest crowd at 10,000 for a May 26 game against the Philadelphia Athletics. But only eight Milwaukee home games drew over 5,000, and on 15 dates, attendance dropped below the 1,000 mark. Discouragingly, the last home date of the season, a doubleheader against Chicago, drew a mere 200 fans.[36]

NATIONAL LEAGUE		AMERICAN LEAGUE	
Boston	146,502	Boston	289,448
Brooklyn	198,200	Baltimore	141,952
Chicago	205,071	Chicago	354,350
Cincinnati	205,728	Cleveland	131,380
New York	297,650	Detroit	259,430
Philadelphia	234,937	Philadelphia	206,329
Pittsburgh	251,955	Washington	161,661
St. Louis	379,988	Milwaukee	139,034
	1,920,031		1,683,584[37]

Generally, the American League was pronounced a financial success. Ban Johnson claimed that only the Milwaukee club had lost money, with the *Milwaukee Sentinel* estimating the Brewers' loss at $5,000.[38] But other sources contradicted this claim. In late August,

In 1910 the Browns (47-107) finished in last place, a dubious position they held 10 times in 52 seasons. (Library of Congress)

president Killilea said that his club was set to earn from $10,000 to $15,000 for the season.[39] And on October 5, 1901, *Sporting News* correspondent B.F. Wright figured that, after the 10 percent American League fund deduction and disbursements to visiting teams, the Brewers took in about $25,850 at Milwaukee Park, and $25,075 on the road (having a road attendance of over 222,000). With revenue totaling $50,925—a little more than Cleveland, and not much less than Washington and Baltimore—Wright could not understand how Milwaukee lost money, speculating that the loss claims were intended "to reconcile the Milwaukee fans to the transfer of the club to St. Louis."[40] A contrary perspective, however, was offered by *Sporting News* correspondent Frank Patterson, who maintained that some franchise attendance reports "were at times very much exaggerated," with Milwaukee's "padded very considerable." Patterson also said Wright underestimated salaries in the American League.[41]

Whatever the truth, franchise relocation rumors resurfaced. Back on February 25, 1901, the *Milwaukee Sentinel* had stated that if the Brewers did not transfer before the 1901 season, they probably would before 1902.[42] According to a later *Sporting News* report, the American League picked Milwaukee over St. Louis for the 1901 season "for sentimental reasons." Or because Killilea had "declined to accede to the request of President Johnson, Charlie Comiskey and others prominent in the American League" to transfer his team to St. Louis "with protestations of civic pride."[43] The talk had died until June, when AL magnates meeting in Chicago said that the league would enter St. Louis and/or New York in 1902, dropping Milwaukee and/or Cleveland.[44] In late July, Killilea conferred with Comiskey and Johnson regarding a proposal to transfer the Washington franchise to New York and Cleveland to St. Louis. At that time, Killilea said he would "personally vouch for the retention of this city [Milwaukee] in the circuit." He also declared that he had just turned down a $30,000 offer for his franchise from St. Louis people, saying the franchise was not for sale at any price. He was certain that in years to come he could turn the Milwaukee club into a "money maker," and was committed to making every effort to put a strong team on the field.[45] But others, including Washington Senators owner Jim Manning, insisted Milwaukee would go to St. Louis.[46]

In August a story broke that Ban Johnson had received an option on the stock of the St. Louis National League club, and had given Killilea a chance to take up that option.[47] Privately, Johnson was committed to the transfer of the Milwaukee AL franchise to St. Louis, stating, "[T]he players at present with the Milwaukee club are popular in St. Louis and they, with a materially strengthened team, would undoubtedly be well supported there."[48] The *Sentinel* also believed the Brewers would go to St. Louis. Whatever the particulars, something was definitely brewing in St. Louis. Johnson said the American League would enter St. Louis, but declined to identify which AL city would be dropped.[49] For its part, the *Milwaukee Daily News* was sure it would not be Milwaukee because of Matt Killilea, who "has been one of the staunchest supporters of the American League, and he did as much if not more than any one person to place Ban Johnson in the comfortable berth he has today. Mr. Killilea is high in the councils of the American League and if he cares to have one of its teams here next season his wishes will be respected."[50]

In late August, Killilea again turned down an offer for his club. "An authentic source" said some National League ballplayers had formed a syndicate to purchase the Milwaukee franchise. The syndicators, unnamed but believed to be Bid McPhee, Jake Beckley, and Frank Bancroft, "are in the possession of wealth accumulated during a long term of service" and had offered Killilea $42,000 for the Brewers. Reportedly, the syndicate wanted to install the club in St. Louis, but later refocused on the Cleveland franchise when their bid for Milwaukee was turned down.[51]

By mid-September, reliable sources were again claiming that the Brewers would be transferred to St. Louis, where the roster would be composed of the best Milwaukee players and some St. Louis National League players. With Matthew Killilea ill (no doubt from the effects of the tuberculosis that would take his life), his brother Henry became head of the Brewers. Henry denied such reports, but a St. Louis dispatch alleged that Killilea had secured nine players from the National League Cardinals to play with a St. Louis club in the American League in 1902.[52] Meanwhile, Matt Killilea told Milwaukee newspapers that he wanted to retire from baseball and would not run the St. Louis club if the Brewers moved there.[53] In late September Philadelphia sources reported another transfer scenario. This one had Ban Johnson making a deal: Killilea's 40 percent stake in the Milwaukee club would be sold to a St. Louis brewer for $40,000; the franchise would relocated to St. Louis, and Matt Killilea would be president of the club.[54] In early October, Henry Killilea went to St. Louis to negotiate the disposal of the franchise, with liberal inducements being offered those opposed to the move. Upon Killilea's return to Milwaukee, St. Louis dispatches reported that the Brewers would transfer to St. Louis and that Jim McAleer would manage the club. But denials greeted these reports.[55] McAleer then went to Milwaukee to talk to Henry Killilea and Fred Gross.[56] The *Milwaukee Sentinel* wrote: "You pays your money and takes your choice" on who was telling the truth.[57] The *Evening Wisconsin* was sure the Brewers would transfer, reasoning,

It is an impossibility for Milwaukee to spend as much money in getting a team together and putting up the salaries requisite to get gilt-edged players and put a team in the field like Chicago, Philadelphia and Boston, and unless the Milwaukee fans are content to travel along as the tail-enders of the American League for another season, the best thing that can be done in the interests of the sport locally will be to quit and get into a class where Milwaukee will be able to hold its own in place of simply serving as the means to fatten the averages and standings of the other teams.[58]

However, there remained people who thought that Milwaukee could survive in the American League. The Milwaukee correspondent for *Sporting Life*, for example, wrote on September 28, 1901:

> The statement that Milwaukee cannot afford to support a team of equal caliber with Washington and Detroit is absurd. If the Milwaukee magnates engage high-salaried players, and the team makes a favorable showing—that is, winning half of their games—the patronage they will receive will surprise those who are now deriding the ability of Milwaukee for supporting first-class exhibitions of baseball. … Milwaukee will not support a tail-end team or a mediocre aggregation of ball players. It demands

the best, and when that is provided there is no limit to the extent of the patronage. … Milwaukee is a better ball town than Baltimore, Cleveland or Washington, and as good as Detroit, and if these cities can afford to secure leading talent for their respective teams for 1901, then the management of the Milwaukee Club can surely take a similar risk.[59]

Still, evidence of a franchise move kept mounting. On October 10 it was reported Hugh Duffy had resigned as manager of the Brewers, wanting to go back to Boston, but the team denied this story. The following day, Ban Johnson announced that he had signed five players from the Cardinals to play for the new AL St. Louis club. Killilea, however, still denied that any move was in the works.[60] These continuing reports and denials led *The Sporting News'* correspondent in Milwaukee to write that these were only "one of the thousand little and big things which prove how much confidence may be placed in the announcements of the base ball magnates these days. They have adopted a policy of denying and claiming everything, so that when a piece of news that is authentic is dug up, it must be supported by oaths and pledges, or it looks like the stuff that is being piped by the guess artists of the major league cities."[61] Back in St. Louis, dispatches reported that local bigwigs Gussie Busch, Zach Tinker, and George Heckel would back the club and that they wanted Matt Killilea for president.[62] Reports went so far as to name the new St. Louis players, including eight Brewers.[63] Others in the American League supported the transfer. Jim Manning and John McGraw, for example, believed that St. Louis would pay visiting clubs $5,000 more during the season than the clubs could get in Milwaukee.[64] The *Milwaukee Sentinel* attacked Johnson and his cronies.

American League magnates are exhibiting a selfish streak of well developed proportions this fall in making an attempt to deprive Milwaukee of its franchise. For years this city was the backbone of the league, supplying Johnson and his associates with the sinews of war even when the team representing Milwaukee was not considered a factor in the championship race. Now that the American League has expanded into a simon pure organization, and simply because the Brewers graced the tail end of the processions … and did not attract the people to the ball grounds as they had in preceding seasons, the other magnates now say 'T'ell with Milwaukee.'"[65]

The Milwaukee owners did not give in easily. They set a price tag of $60,000 for the franchise, believing it too high for acceptance.[66] They were right. Ban Johnson said, "There is not a club in the country that is worth $60,000 today in these troublesome times of baseball."[67] Back in St. Louis, Zach Tinker backed out, disaffected by the price tag for the Killilea stock and his inability to acquire sole control of the franchise. The Milwaukee press now believed the deal was off and that the Brewers would stay.[68] Ban Johnson decreed otherwise, calling Milwaukee a "one day town" that drew good crowds only on Sunday.[69] He stated that the Milwaukee franchise would go to St. Louis; that there would be no local money in the club; that the American League would furnish the necessary capital, and that the new St. Louis franchise would be in the league's "common possession until such time as a proper man could be found to relieve it of the holds and take personal charge."[70]

The Johnson declarations notwithstanding, the mess was not clearing up. Pitcher Bill Reidy and three other Milwaukee players said they would seek a salary increase if the club was transferred, as their contracts with the Brewers did not require them to play in St. Louis.[71] Pitcher Ned Garvin, who had been 8-20 in 1901, was dissatisfied with the situation and threatened to jump to the National League, as did infielder Billy Gilbert.[72] Shortstop Wid Conroy did more than talk, signing with Pittsburgh of the NL.[73] All the while, the AL could not find playing grounds in St. Louis at an agreeable price, until old Sportsman's Park was eventually secured.[74]

When American League magnates met in Chicago on December 2, 1901, they re-elected Ban Johnson as league president. Fred Gross was present at the meeting, but with Matthew Killilea delayed by the trains, no immediate action was taken on the

Milwaukee franchise issue.[75] Upon arrival, Killilea told newsmen, "The owners of the Milwaukee club are opposed to the transfer to St. Louis and the American League cannot make a change without the consent of the owners."[76] Word was around, however, that he wanted $48,000 for the franchise.[77] Late the following evening, the long-awaited transfer was completed. Matthew Killilea purchased the majority interest of his brother Henry, who did not want Matt in baseball because of his failing health, and transferred the Milwaukee club to St. Louis.[78] At the time, St. Louis was the fourth largest city in the country, its 1900 population of 575,238 more than twice that of Milwaukee's 285,315. Matt Killilea was recognized as president and principal owner of the new St. Louis club. Jim McAleer was named manager.[79] William Wallace Rowland of the *Milwaukee Journal*, writing under the nom de plume of Brownie, did not approve, saying, "It is a very clever trick of the American League bunch in keeping Killilea … on their staff with ground awaiting them in Milwaukee in case St. Louis should go to the bad."[80] The *Milwaukee Daily News*, bitter over the transfer, wrote that Killilea and Gross "have pink tea in their veins instead of sporting blood" for not taking a chance on Milwaukee.[81] The *Milwaukee Sentinel*, however, said of the transfer:

> The owners of the Milwaukee club removed their team to St. Louis as a business proposition. They expected to sell out, but the absence of capitalists in the Mound City to shoulder the burden made it necessary for them to carry the load themselves, and it is possible that they may make their independent fortunes as a result of the move. The Killileas and F.C. Gross stated that Milwaukee could not adequately support the expensive team they had secured; so they had to leave the city.[82]

Because of poor health, Matthew Killilea spent the winter in Texas and left George Munson, one-time secretary to Chris von der Ahe of the old St Louis Browns, to run the franchise in his absence.[83] Some, the *Milwaukee Daily News* and the *Chicago American* included, doubted if Killilea was really running the club given his health, speculating that Johnson and Comiskey were looking after the finances of the club.[84] In January 1902, Matthew Killilea sold out to a St. Louis syndicate for a reported $40,000. Then, he and brother Henry bought into the American League Boston club.[85] Six months later, Matt Killilea was dead from tuberculosis, at the age of 40.[86]

In some ways, the Brewers' transfer from Milwaukee to St. Louis was a matter of timing. In September 1901 Matthew Killilea reportedly said, "If there was no war, then Milwaukee would be sure to remain in the American League. You must fight the devil with fire, and the American League must go into the National League's territory to wage a successful war. Before peace is declared the American League will doubtless be in New York and St. Louis."[87] Time would prove Killilea correct.

Portions of this chapter were taken by permission from Dennis Pajot, *The Rise of Milwaukee Baseball: The Cream City from Midwestern Outpost to the Major Leagues, 1859-1901* (Jefferson, North Carolina: McFarland & Company 2009).

NOTES

1 Andrew J. Aikens and Lewis A. Proctor, eds., *Men of Progress, Wisconsin* (Evening Wisconsin Co., 1897), 115.

2 *1895 Spalding Baseball Guide,* 131; *Milwaukee Sentinel,* September 26, 1894.

3 *Milwaukee Journal,* October 21, 1894; *Milwaukee Sentinel,* October 21, 1894, and February 27, 1895.

4 *Milwaukee Sentinel,* September 23, 1895.

5 *Milwaukee Journal,* February 20, 1893.

6 *Milwaukee Sentinel,* October 11, 1896.

7 *Milwaukee Sentinel,* January 11 and September 13, 1896.

8 *Milwaukee Journal,* September 22, 1896.

9 *1898 Spalding Base Ball Guide,* 115; *Milwaukee Journal,* September 2, 1897.

10 *The Sporting News,* October 23, 1897.

11 *1899 Spalding Baseball Guide,* 10; *Milwaukee Sentinel,* October 15, 1898.

12 *The Sporting News,* September 30, 1899.

13 *Milwaukee Sentinel,* September 19, 1899.

14 *Milwaukee Sentinel,* September 21, 1899; *Sporting Life,* December 30, 1899.

15 *Sporting Life,* October 21, 1899.

16 *Sporting Life,* March 3, 1900.

HOME OF THE BROWNS AND CARDINALS AT GRAND AND DODIER

17 *Milwaukee Journal*, February 27, 1900.
18 *Sporting Life*, May 17, 1900; *Milwaukee Daily News*, April 12, 1900.
19 *1901 Reach Baseball Guide*, 7.
20 *Evening Wisconsin*, September 19, 1900.
21 *Milwaukee Journal*, November 5, 1900.
22 *Milwaukee Sentinel*, November 23, 1900.
23 *The Sporting News*, December 22, 1900, and February 16, 1901; *Milwaukee Sentinel*, December 25, 1900.
24 *Milwaukee Sentinel*, January 29, 1901.
25 *Milwaukee Journal*, February 20, 1901; *Milwaukee Sentinel*, February 25, 1901.
26 *Milwaukee Sentinel*, February 25, 1901.
27 *Milwaukee Sentinel*, February 3, 1901.
28 *Milwaukee Journal*, March 30, 1901.
29 *Milwaukee Sentinel*, March 31, 1901.
30 *Milwaukee Journal*, April 11, 1901.
31 *Milwaukee Sentinel*, March 21, 1901.
32 *Milwaukee Sentinel*, April 26, 1901.
33 Baseball-Reference.com.
34 *Milwaukee Daily News*, September 30, 1901.
35 Baseball-Reference.com.
36 *The Sporting News*, September 28, 1901.
37 *The Sporting News*, October 19, 1901.
38 *Milwaukee Sentinel*, September 30, 1901.
39 *Milwaukee Sentinel*, August 29 1901.
40 *The Sporting News*, October 5, 1901.
41 *The Sporting News*, October 12, 1901.
42 *Milwaukee Sentinel*, February 25, 1901.
43 *The Sporting News*, September 21, 1901.
44 *Milwaukee Sentinel*, June 5, 1901.
45 *Milwaukee Sentinel*, July 30 and August 1, 1901.
46 *Milwaukee Sentinel*, August 14, 1901.
47 *Milwaukee Sentinel*, August 9, 1901.
48 *The Sporting News*, August 24, 1901.
49 *Milwaukee Sentinel*, September 6, 1901.
50 *Milwaukee Daily News*, June 22, 1901.
51 *Milwaukee Sentinel*, August 30, 1901; *Milwaukee Daily News*, August 30, 1901.
52 *Milwaukee Sentinel*, September 15, 1901.
53 *Milwaukee Sentinel*, September 16, 1901.
54 *Milwaukee Sentinel*, September 27, 1901.
55 *Milwaukee Sentinel*, October 6 and October 10, 1901.
56 *Milwaukee Journal*, October 9, 1901.
57 *Milwaukee Sentinel*, October 11, 1901.
58 *Evening Wisconsin*, September 16, 1901.
59 *Sporting Life*, September 28, 1901.
60 *Milwaukee Sentinel*, October 11 and October 12, 1901.
61 *The Sporting News*, October 19, 1901.
62 *Milwaukee Sentinel*, October 17, 1901.
63 *Milwaukee Journal*, October 19, 1901.
64 *Milwaukee Sentinel*, October 24, 1901.
65 *Milwaukee Sentinel*, October 13, 1901.
66 *Milwaukee Sentinel*, October 20, 1901.
67 *Milwaukee Sentinel*, October 22, 1901.
68 *Milwaukee Sentinel*, October 29, 1901.
69 *Milwaukee Sentinel*, November 8, 1901.
70 *The Sporting News*, December 7, 1901.
71 *Milwaukee Sentinel*, October 31, 1901.
72 *Milwaukee Sentinel*, November 20, 1901; *Evening Wisconsin*, October 12, 1901.
73 *Milwaukee Journal*, November 21, 1901.
74 *Milwaukee Journal*, November 22 and December 7, 1901.
75 *Milwaukee Sentinel*, December 3, 1901; *Milwaukee Journal*, December 3, 1901.
76 *Milwaukee Journal*, December 3, 1901.
77 Ibid.
78 *Milwaukee Journal*, December 4, 1901; *Milwaukee Sentinel*, December 4, 1901.
79 *Milwaukee Sentinel*, December 4, 1901.
80 *Milwaukee Journal*, December 4, 1901.
81 *Milwaukee Daily News*, December 6, 1901.
82 *Milwaukee Sentinel*, December 6, 1901.
83 *Milwaukee Journal*, December 7, 1901.
84 *Milwaukee Daily News*, December 7, 1901.
85 *Milwaukee Sentinel*, January 28 and January 29, 1901.
86 *Milwaukee Sentinel*, July 28, 1902.
87 *Sporting Life*, September 28, 1901.

ROBERT HEDGES: OVERLOOKED VISIONARY

BY STEVE STEINBERG

THE FIRST OWNER OF THE ST. LOUIS Browns, from 1902 to 1915, Robert Lee Hedges was a visionary leader, years ahead of his times. He was also a shrewd businessman who maximized the value of his baseball franchise. Hedges' innovations and financial success in baseball contrasted vividly with his teams' lack of success on the diamond. He saw his club through two great baseball wars and took pride in not losing a single player to a rival league. Hedges played a critical role in settling both of those conflicts.

"Colonel Bob," as he was known, spoke out against the concentration of wealth in baseball. He was the man who hired Branch Rickey and laid out a vision of the farm system—to compete against that wealth—that Rickey later rolled out with the St. Louis Cardinals. Hedges' signing of college star George Sisler triggered a conflict that hastened the end of the three-man National Commission, baseball's governing body. When Hedges died in 1932, *The Sporting News* wrote in an editorial, "It was his pioneering and business acumen that helped to lift it (Organized Baseball) from a haphazard happy-go-lucky sort of sport into a national pastime."[1]

Robert Lee Hedges, a bold and handsome self-made man, was born in 1869 on a farm in Jackson County, near Kansas City, Missouri. His father died when he was 10, and his brothers were killed in the devastating Kansas City tornado of 1886. From the mid-1880s until 1890, he was a clerk in the office of the Recorder of Deeds in Kansas City. In the early 1890s, he started a buggy manufacturing company in Hamilton, Ohio, near Cincinnati. He sold his carriage business in the boom times of 1900, in part because he saw the threat of the emerging auto industry.

American League President Ban Johnson persuaded Hedges to buy the Milwaukee franchise of the fledging American League after the inaugural 1901 season. Former Milwaukee owner Henry Killilea remained as club president for the 1902 season. Hedges paid around $35,000 for the team and then moved it to the nation's fourth largest city, St. Louis. He called the team the Browns, a name that had been abandoned a few years before by the city's National League franchise, now known as the Cardinals. Hedges also refurbished the old Browns' Sportsman's Park, which was only a few blocks from the Cardinals' League Park.

From the start, Hedges viewed the venture as a commercial enterprise, one that would require a constant focus on the bottom line. "I went into baseball purely as a matter of business," he was quoted as saying in a July 1912 article in *McLure's* magazine entitled appropriately, "The Business of Baseball." By 1903, he moved up from secretary to president of the club.

Hedges acquired a team with modest talent. The Milwaukee Brewers had finished the 1901 season in last place. He put into play the most spectacular raid of one team by another in baseball history. Working closely with Hedges and Ban Johnson, manager Jimmy McAleer signed virtually every star from the 1901 Cardinals for the 1902 Browns.[2] The only exception was Patsy Donovan, who became the Cardinals' player-manager.

The Cardinals brought suit to stop some of the players from jumping, including star third baseman Bobby Wallace. The far-reaching case would have an enormous impact on the Browns' viability. The controversy was front-page news in St. Louis and split the city's sports fans into warring factions. Hedges prevailed that April, when the judge denied the Cardinals' injunction for a number of reasons: the abrogation of personal liberty, the violation of antitrust laws, and the lack of mutuality.[3] The reserve clause, which the owners said gave them control over players beyond the contract year, conflicted with antitrust laws, the judge declared. Wallace joined the Browns for what was then the biggest contract in baseball: $32,500 for five years, with the first year paid in advance.[4]

Hedges' raids on the Cardinals created a backlash of sympathy for the National League team. "The faithful never forgave him for wrecking the best team the town ever had," wrote the *St. Louis Times* at the start of the 1908 season. In retrospect, said Hedges, he should have followed the strategy of the New York Americans. Rather than raid the National League's Giants, they signed stars from another city, Pittsburgh.[5]

The Browns gained instant credibility, as well as viability on the ballfield. They were in first place for most of the season, only to be caught in September by the Philadelphia Athletics. The Browns re-signed all their players for 1903 except for pitcher Jack Harper, whom they didn't want back. "If any of our players are dissatisfied," said Hedges, "all they have to do is say so and we will remedy it if it lies in our power."[6]

During that giddy summer of '02, Hedges was planning for the future. "We are in

a position to pay as much as anyone for those we want."[7] And one of those he wanted was a rising star pitcher of the New York Giants, Christy Mathewson. Hedges signed him and his regular catcher, Frank Bowerman, to an "ironclad" contract (10-day clause removed), which included a cash advance. The Giants were a sorry club in disarray at the time, while the Browns were in or near first place most of that season.

The American League was looking more and more like a winner in the war with the established National League. The AL outdrew the NL by more than 30 percent in 1902. With salary inflation driving down owners' profits in both leagues, the conflict came to an end at a January 1903 peace conference.

The main sticking points were the assignment of disputed players, those who had contracts with two clubs. Superstar Ed Delahanty was awarded to his 1902 team, Washington, and not to the New York Giants, who had recently signed him. As part of the balancing act, Hedges was asked to release Mathewson back to the Giants, to placate New York owner John Brush, which he did. Almost three decades later, St. Louis sports editor Sid Keener recognized the vital yet overlooked role the owner of the Browns had played: "Hedges was the one who held the key to the famous peace treaty of 1903."[8]

Hedges was a warm and outgoing man, for which he earned the nickname "Uncle Bob." He became a fixture at Sportsman's Park, greeting his customers at the Dodier Street entrance. When Hedges died, Sid Keener recalled the Browns' owner "wearing a smile that became contagious even during his dark, dreary days as the owner of a tail-end club."[9]

The Browns didn't come close to that first year's performance during the next five years. They sank to the second division and stayed there until 1908. That year, key trades for veteran players—including pitchers Bill Dinneen and Rube Waddell, who had great comeback seasons—propelled the Browns into a spectacular pennant race. The club drew more than 600,000 fans that year, and Hedges made a profit of $165,000.[10]

Hedges took a significant portion of that profit ($75,000) and plowed it back into the ballpark.[11] He reconfigured Sportsman's Park, shifting the field 180 degrees, and remodeled and expanded the stadium, with a modern double-decked grandstand of steel and concrete. St. Louis had a long history of wooden-stadium fires, including five in the 1890s and another one in 1901. Philadelphia's Shibe Park is usually credited as the first steel and concrete sports stadium, yet Sportsman's Park, built that same year, has a claim too.[12]

The new ballpark was just one of many Hedges innovations. He took steps to clean up the image of baseball, which had been a ruffian's game with rowdy fans. He was "a reproduction of the American League policy," wrote Keener, sharing Ban Johnson's vision of baseball as a civil affair, family entertainment.[13] Hedges hired security guards and banned the sale of alcohol at Sportsman's Park, to convey a sense of safety and sobriety.

Hedges made his expectations clear that first season: "I will not stand for any rowdyism on the part of my players. I will have it suppressed if I have to set down every member of my team."[14] More than a decade later, sportswriter John Sheridan poked some fun at Hedges' Browns, who were then managed by the strait-laced Branch Rickey: "First in morals, first in sobriety, first in bed, first in the field, first in the front bench at church, and last in the American League."[15]

Hedges also popularized ladies day, letting women in free. He was one of the first owners to hire detectives to eliminate gambling in his ballpark, and recommended the double-umpire system as early as 1908. He put together a profit-sharing plan for his 1902 team and took out life insurance on his players as early as 1903.[16] Hedges was also one of the first to have announcers at games and to use an electronic scoreboard. He also "rain-proofed" his ballpark with enormous canvas tents that were rolled out when rain fell. These "baseball mackintoshes" were transported by 40-foot wagons.[17]

Most of Hedges' seasons were losing ones, yet most were also profitable ones. A shrewd asset manager, he was conservative with his money decisions. Even in 1908, when he "splurged" on veteran players (not only Dinneen and Waddell, but also Jimmy Williams, Danny Hoffman, and Hobe Ferris), his expenditure of $25,000 netted him the profit of $165,000. He also benefited from the action of the state legislature when it banned horse racing in 1905, making baseball the only big outdoor amusement.

Hedges' financial success with losing teams created resentment from other owners. They referred to "Tail-end Bob" and said he was "too canny a businessman for the good of the game" since "he wouldn't gamble for profit."[18] Yet jealousy figured in here, too, because Hedges knew how to make money at baseball like no one else. A writer for *The Sporting News* put it this way: "He always had players who cost little, to trade for players who were worth much. In this way he saved his club hundreds of thousands of dollars."[19]

Hedges was extremely active in the minor-league drafts, with the help of his scouts.[20] The Browns drafted more players than any other team in 1912 and 1913, for example. They had working relationships with a number of minor-league teams, and in December 1915 John Sheridan noted that Hedges "always had secret strings on scores of minor league players."[21] A couple of weeks earlier, a reporter for *The Sporting News* noted that Hedges got $15,000 from the Detroit Tigers in a deal that sent Big Bill James to the Motor City team.[22]

Pitcher Jack Powell, who won 117 games for the Browns, provided a window to Hedges' financial acumen. Early in 1904, Hedges traded Powell to the New York Americans for pitcher Harry Howell and $6,500. Powell would win 23 games for the 1904 New Yorkers; Howell became an anchor of the Browns' staff. Late in the 1905 season, Hedges got Powell back from New York for only $1,000. The 30-year-old Powell gave the Browns seven more solid seasons. After the 1912 season, Hedges sold Powell for $2,500, though he never appeared in another major-league game.[23]

The Browns' collapse in 1909 (a seventh-place finish) on the heels of a fine 1908 season led to a break with the only manager the team had to that point, Jimmy McAleer. Hedges then made unfortunate choices in skippers and went through three managers in less than three years.

After the club lost 107 games in 1910 and manager Jack O'Connor was let go, Hedges decided to sell his team.[24] He was worn out from losing, frustrated by the criticism from the fans, and feeling the heat from the other owners, as well as from Ban Johnson. A St. Louis syndicate paid Hedges $30,000 for an option to buy the Browns. *The Sporting News* ran an article headlined, "A Sob From Bob: The Heart of Robert Lee Will Be With Us," in which he sadly talked of the imminent sale.[25] Yet the syndicate was plagued by internal bickering and never came through with the money to close the deal.[26]

Hedges then turned to a longtime fan favorite, Bobby Wallace, to manage his team. The Browns again lost 107 games in 1911, and early in 1912 the mild-mannered Wallace readily gave up the reins. Hedges then hired fiery George Stovall as player-manager. Early in the 1913 season Stovall had a cel-

A visionary leader, Robert Lee Hedges owned the St. Louis Browns from 1902 until 1915. (Library of Congress)

ebrated run-in with an umpire, when he spat a wad of tobacco onto the face of arbiter Charlie Ferguson.

It was around this time that Hedges introduced perhaps his most far-reaching innovation. He hired as his executive assistant a lawyer and a teacher who had impressed him as a person more than as a catcher when he was on the Browns a few years earlier. His name was Branch Rickey. Hedges hired him for $7,500 a year, a very generous salary at the time.

Late in the 1913 season, Hedges promoted Rickey to vice president, secretary, and manager, replacing Stovall in the latter position. "Rickey," said the Browns owner, "combining the executive qualities in connection with the power to instruct, will be more valuable than a manager who can only play ball."[27] Perhaps thinking of his last manager, known as Firebrand Stovall, Hedges did not sound like a magnate of the early 20th century when he said, "I have had enough of the man who relies on vitriolic language to win ball games. What I want is a man of learning, a student of human nature, psychology and, incidentally, baseball."[28]

Hedges had grappled with competing with wealthier teams that could outbid him for promising players. He always had informal gentleman's agreements with minor-league clubs, under which he had "strings on" (control of) many players and later made money by selling them. Rather than simply loaning players to minor-league clubs, Hedges now wanted to buy minor-league teams and develop his own stars. He wanted Rickey to oversee this operation.[29]

In 1913, after Rickey joined the Browns, the two men tried to gain control of the Montgomery (Alabama) Southern League team, from which the sensational 1912 Browns rookie Del Pratt came. They loaned money to four Alabama businessmen to buy the club, but the deal fell apart.

In his Branch Rickey biography, Arthur Mann relates that Hedges and Rickey spent $100,000 on 30 minor-league players they drafted in September 1913. When Rickey was asked how such spending could be justified, he replied that if just two of the men became great players, it was worth it.[30] The concept that Rickey executed so brilliantly with the St. Louis Cardinals for more than two decades, starting in 1920, began with the vision Robert Hedges shared with him in 1912-1913.

Two developments prevented Hedges and Rickey from pursuing the farm system. First, the National Commission passed a law banning the ownership of minor-league teams by big-league clubs, starting in January 1914. Second, the upstart Federal League declared war on Organized Baseball and placed a team in St. Louis. Just as Robert Hedges had raided the established National League for players in 1902, the Federal League was now doing the same to the two established leagues. Player salaries again started to escalate. The farm system would have to wait.

The Federal League's announcement that George Stovall would manage (and play for) their Kansas City team was the first "shot" in this war. Hedges and Rickey realized that Stovall was secretly recruiting while he was still a member of the Browns. (After he was relieved as Browns manager, he had been kept on the team as a first baseman.) While the viability of the Federal League would unfold in the future, one thing was clear from the start: "Three clubs cannot exist in this city, and one will have to go."[31]

Early in 1914, Stovall pulled in his first "Brownie," pitcher Earl Hamilton, whom he signed for $31,000 for three years, an enormous contract at the time.[32] The promising 22-year-old pitcher had already won 29 games for the Browns. AL President Ban Johnson, who had raided the established National League more than a decade earlier, now was the defender of the status quo. "The American League will stop Hamilton if it takes every dollar of the treasury," he declared.[33] Kansas City president Charles Madison said, "Just tell Mr. Hedges that if he gives us trouble in the case of Earl Hamilton, we will strip his club of every ball player under contract. … We have the legal power and the money to back every claim we put over."[34]

The players were trying to get as much money as they could since they understood, "it's a certainty that when peace again prevails, salaries will be sliced to the core."[35] Hamilton put it succinctly: "I'm tired of playing for glory. It is a question of money."[36] Robert Hedges spoke about the early days of the American League, noting the difficulties the Federal League would present: "I worked for nothing. When my salary came around, I deposited it in the bank one day, and the next I wrote checks on my salary to pay the ball players."[37] Now, as in 1902, the Browns' owner did what he had to do to protect his interests.

He tracked Hamilton down in Kansas City, persuaded him to return to the Browns, and as some papers reported, "kidnapped" Hamilton back to St. Louis. He had become a "double-jumper." Ultimately, Hamilton never realized his potential, and Hedges suspended him a year later, for "dissolution" at an East St. Louis nightclub.[38]

Despite the fact that George Stovall met with 20 members of the Browns, not a single Brownie jumped to the new league.[39] The Federal League then increased its attention, with significant success, on the other St. Louis team, the Cardinals.[40]

Hedges' fellow American League owners refused to make deals that would have strengthened his team. Sid Keener revealed the rocky relations: "It has been common talk in American League baseball circles for years and years that other magnates would not exchange with Hedges. … The American League, failing to shoo uncle Bob out of the league, has entered into a combination to prevent him from getting his club back in the first division."[41] Keener went on to show how Cleveland owner Charles Somers had lied to Hedges about Joe Jackson's availability, saying he would not trade Jackson, shortly before he dealt him to the Chicago White Sox.

In December 1915 the Federal League war appeared about to end. All parties were wearying of the legal battles and financial losses. One of the Feds' wealthiest and most enthusiastic backers, Robert Ward of the Brooklyn team, had just died. Two of their owners, Charles Weeghman of Chicago and Phil Ball of St. Louis, were to buy established teams as part of the settlement. The Mound City was about to become a two-team city once again.

The original plan was for Ball to buy the Cardinals. Helene Britton, owner of the Cardinals since the death of her uncle in 1911, had endured five years of friction with the all-male coterie of owners. "A woman has no business in baseball" was what she kept hearing. And the Cardinals' owner known as Lady Bee pushed back. She would not be pressured into selling. She raised her price and, for all practical purposes, a sale of the Cardinals was not "in the cards."

Back on November 14, 1914, Robert Hedges said, "Maybe once again St. Louis will have to be the central figure in establishing peace in baseball." He reflected on the peace settlement of 1903, when he gave up Christy Mathewson. "I lost a pennant for St. Louis in that deal, but I brought about peace in the baseball world. ... I believe I can end this second war by selling the Browns to Mr. Ball."[42]

Though he had held his team intact and had a talented manager in Branch Rickey, Hedges' Browns finished in the second division both seasons. The Great War showed no signs of abating, and the Browns drew only 150,000 fans in 1915. The Baltimore Federal League team, which was not a party to any settlement, pursued an antitrust lawsuit against Organized Baseball. Hedges confided to Sid Keener late in 1915, after two wars, "I've lived—well, at times it seems like five years, again like fifty—in trying to keep the team together, balancing receipts and expenses."[43]

Hedges sold the Browns, including Sportsman's Park, to Phil Ball for what was reported to be between $425,000 and $525,000. Especially when the dividends he drew are considered, Hedges made an enormous return on his $35,000 initial investment. (By comparison, the Brittons sold the Cardinals two years later for $350,000.) The deal got hung up over $40,000 of outstanding liabilities that showed up on the Browns' books. It turned out that the compassionate Hedges regularly made advances to his players.

Hedges later served on the board of the Mercantile-Commerce Bank in St. Louis and as president of the National Bank of Commerce Liquidating Company. Near the end of his life, when he was battling cancer in a Santa Fe sanitarium, he spoke of buying the Cincinnati Reds for his son.[44] In late April 1932, Hedges died of lung cancer in St. Louis's Barnes Hospital.

Robert Hedges rescued the American League's weakest team in the winter of 1901-1902. He angered fellow owners for mastering a system of making money with a losing club. While other owners called him "cheap," he simply worked the system to his own benefit. Ultimately he was one of the first owners who showed that only in baseball "a man could fail and yet make 100 per cent per annum on his investment."[45]

His critics said he was too cheap, yet he was the ultimate warrior in baseball's two great wars of the twentieth century. "I am the only magnate who went though both wars without losing a man," he said.[46] And one can only wonder how and when baseball's two big wars of the twentieth century would have ended, had Robert Hedges not acted to achieve the peace.

Hedges always ran his baseball operation for "a higher class of people," not the "rowdy element." His policy was "Clean ball first, championship ball if we can. Money no object."[47] He went on two buying sprees for his Browns, in 1902 and 1908, both of which brought them just short of the pennant. Yet he did not follow up on those accomplishments, which were his only two first-division finishes. He often sold the talent he found for cash and deposited the profit in the bank, rather than putting the personnel in his lineup. "The one great mistake made by Hedges," said a writer for the *Post-Dispatch* in 1910, "was investing

$75,000 in a championship grandstand before he had a team to fit in it."

Robert Hedges deserves recognition for visualizing a farm system that would enable less wealthy teams to compete. Two years before he hired Branch Rickey, he said, "You have to develop your own players these days. None of the other club owners will sell a tried-and-not-found performer. It is simply up to the club owners to purchase the raw material, place it properly and pluck it when the proper time comes."[48]

Hedges was deeply concerned about the dangers of rich clubs dominating the national pastime, which he addressed as a parting shot in early 1916: "The chief menace of baseball … is the presence of so much big money behind certain clubs. … Until some system of shackling the millionaires and for equalizing the distribution of good playing material is devised. … (T)he moneyed fighters of the game will always be able to strengthen at the expense of the weaker. … Baseball is a big, big business, and the open sesame is 'Lots of money.'"[49]

NOTES

1. *The Sporting News*, April 28, 1932.
2. They included pitcher Jack Powell (19 wins in 1901), Willie Sudhoff (17 wins), and Jack Harper (23 wins); infielders Bobby Wallace (.324 batting average) and Dick Padden (.256); and outfielders Jesse Burkett (.376) and Emmet Heidrick (.339).
3. The latter referred to the owners' right in the standard contract to release a player on 10 days' notice. The contract didn't give the player the reciprocal right to leave on 10 days' notice. "Personal liberty consists of the right to go where one pleases," the judge wrote.
4. *The Sporting News*, December 20, 1902, and April 17, 1954.
5. *St. Louis Times*, April 23, 1908.
6. *Sporting Life*, August 2, 1902.
7. *Sporting Life*, September 6, 1902.
8. Sid Keener, *St. Louis Star-Times*, April 25, 1932.
9. Ibid.
10. The 1908 Browns drew more fans than the pennant-winning team of 1944, second only to the 1922 club.
11. *St. Louis Post-Dispatch*, December 23, 1910.
12. Since Hedges reconfigured the park, and the old grandstand became the bleachers of the new ballpark, it was not entirely new nor was it completely steel and concrete, since the bleachers were the old wooden stands.
13. Sid Keener, *St. Louis Times*, September 19, 1917.
14. *St. Louis Star*, July 6, 1902.
15. John B. Sheridan, *St. Louis Globe-Democrat*, May 4, 1915.
16. *St. Louis Post-Dispatch*, September 13, 1902.
17. *St. Louis Times*, February 13, 1912; *St. Louis Post-Dispatch*, May 7, 1908.
18. *St. Louis Post-Dispatch*, December 24, 1915; *St. Louis Times*, January 4, 1916.
19. *The Sporting News*, December 30, 1915.
20. Charley Barrett, who went on to a long career with Branch Rickey's St. Louis Cardinals, was his last scout.
21. John B. Sheridan, *The Sporting News*, December 23, 1915.
22. The Browns also got Baby Doll Jacobson in the deal.
23. John B. Sheridan, *The Sporting News*, December 30, 1915.
24. O'Connor was caught up in the middle of the Napoleon Lajoie-Ty Cobb batting race controversy, when his Browns allowed Lajoie to bunt safely seven times in a season-ending doubleheader.
25. *The Sporting News*, January 12, 1911.
26. *The Sporting News*, July 25, 1914, and July 4, 1940.
27. *St. Louis Globe-Democrat*, January 5, 1914.
28. *St. Louis Post-Dispatch*, January 4, 1915.
29. Hedges had already explored buying minor-league teams. In 1909 he had offered Frank Farrell, part-owner of the New York Americans, $45,000 for the Newark Eastern League team. (*Washington Post*, December 18, 1909.) In 1912 he wanted to buy the Kansas City team and install Rickey as its president and general manager, but Rickey wasn't available at the time.
30. Arthur Mann, *Branch Rickey: American in Action* (Boston: Houghton Mifflin, 1957), 71-72.
31. *St. Louis Post-Dispatch*, April 16, 1914.
32. *Sporting Life*, April 18, 1914.
33. *Washington Post*, April 10, 1914.
34. *St. Louis Times*, St. Louis, April 10, 1914.
35. *St. Louis Post-Dispatch*, September 30, 1914.
36. *Washington Post*, April 10, 1914.
37. *Sporting Life*, July 25, 1914.
38. *St. Louis Globe-Democrat*, May 9, 1915. The exact terms of Hamilton's new contract weren't revealed.
39. *St. Louis Star*, April 14, 1914.
40. After losing starting outfielders Steve Evans and Rebel Oakes to the new league in 1914, the Cardinals lost their third starting outfielder, Lee Magee, catcher Ivey Wingo, and pitcher Pol

Perritt in 1915. The latter two eventually stayed in the National League, but not with St. Louis, which didn't get full value in return.

41 Sid Keener, *St. Louis Times*, August 24, 1915.
42 Quoted by Sid Keener, *St. Louis Star-Times*, April 25, 1932.
43 *St. Louis Times*, December 1915 (exact date unknown).
44 *The Sporting News*, September 5, 1951.
45 *The Sporting News*, December 30, 1915.
46 *St. Louis Globe-Democrat*, January 6, 1916.
47 *St. Louis Post-Dispatch*, January 19, 1911.
48 *St. Louis Post-Dispatch*, January 14, 1911.
49 *St. Louis Post-Dispatch*, January 9, 1916.

PHIL BALL: CANTANKEROUS OWNER; PASSIONATE FAN

BY STEVE STEINBERG

PHIL BALL WAS THE OWNER OF THE St. Louis Terriers of the Federal League (1914-1915) and bought the American League's St. Louis Browns in December 1915, as part of the settlement between Organized Baseball and the upstart league.[1] In 1917 he said, "I'll pay—well, I'll go to the limit—to get a world's series for St. Louis. ... I'm just as interested in a ball game as the kids who hand their two bits over the windows for the bleacher seats."[2] He owned the Browns until his death in October 1933 but never won an AL pennant, though he came close in 1922. He was a fiery and gruff man, who, in the words of a St. Louis magazine writer, did "not affect a great softness of manner, unruffled evenness of temper or a slow and deliberate enunciation."[3] He was also the only club owner who challenged the authority of Commissioner Kenesaw Mountain Landis and did so more than once.

Philip De Catesby Ball was born in Keokuk, Iowa, on October 22, 1864, to Charles Ball, a West Point graduate who fought in the Civil War, and Caroline (Paulison) Ball. His mother wanted to name him after a great-uncle and famous commodore in the US Navy, Thomas ap Catesby Jones.[4] She did not care for "ap" and instead inserted "De" in her son's name. Charles was an engineer who started an ice business in 1878, with refrigeration equipment that produced ice.[5] The Ice and Cold Machine Company built ice plants in the South and Midwest, and Phil Ball did various jobs for his father's company, from collecting bad debts to driving an ice wagon to overseeing the construction of ice plants. The family lived in Sherman, Texas, for a number of years when Phil was a teenager. Before joining his father's company, Phil worked at many jobs, including surveying, railroad work, and hunting buffalo.[6] For this reason, Arthur Mann wrote, "Ball was a gruff and growling Iowan of 56 [b.1864] who had been everywhere and done everything."[7]

Historian Daniel Boorstin has written about the central role ice has played in "democratizing the national diet" and "homogenizing the regions and seasons."[8] Until refrigerators became common household appliances in the 1920s and 1930s, the icebox was the kitchen cold-storage unit, with blocks of ice supplied by ice plants. When Charles Ball retired to California (where he died in 1901), Phil bought his company for $20,000 and built it up.[9] In a 1932 article in *The Sporting News*, Harry Brundidge reported that Ball had 156 ice plants, including the world's largest, at Anheuser-Busch. "It has been said that I inherited my money from my father, but I never got a nickel from anybody," Ball said.[10] Although he was a civil and mechanical engineer, Ball had no technical-school training.

When Ball lived in New Orleans, he played amateur-league baseball, but his career ended when he was stabbed in a barroom brawl. Sportswriter Dan Daniel wrote, "Philip De Catesby Ball is a born scrapper. You have only to look at his determined jaw to discern that."[11]

He married Harriett Heiskell of Indiana in 1885. They had three children and then moved to St. Louis in the 1890s. His son, James, was a supervising engineer for the Ice and Cold Machine Company. His younger daughter, Phillipa (Mrs. John Nulsen), died in 1918. His older daughter, Margaret, married an accomplished ice skater, William Cady, one of the founders of the St. Louis Skating Club. In 1916 a St. Louis building from the 1904 World's Fair was converted to the St. Louis Winter Garden ice-skating rink, with the support of the Ball Ice Machine Company.[12]

The Federal League began as a Midwestern minor league in 1913, and a group of 14 St. Louis men, including Phil Ball and brewer Otto Stifel, each put up $1,000 for the city's club. When the league decided to go national and challenge Organized Baseball in 1914, only Stifel and Ball remained as owners from what was known as the "Thousand Dollar Club." Ball's fellow oil executive Harry F. Sinclair (Ball had substantial oil investments), founder of Sinclair Oil, joined them as owner of the Browns. Sinclair soon moved on to become one of the major backers of the league as a whole.[13]

When the Federal League was taking on Organized Baseball in early 1914, Ball urged his fellow owners to invest the necessary capital. "We've got the opportunity of a lifetime, but some of you fellows seemed to think too much of your bankroll. Some of you fellows seem to be showing the 'white feather' [a sign of cowardice]."[14] He told reporters later that year, "They [Organized Baseball] are going to get a financial and legal raking that they never dreamed of. … We are willing to match money and brains against anything organized ball may have to offer."[15] Ball had diversified interests beyond ice. He owned a 10,000-acre ranch and had investments in oil.

During the 1914 season the Terriers signed Cuban star Armando Marsans from the Cincinnati Reds. What *Baseball Magazine* called "the sensational Marsans case" played out in the courts.[16] The Reds secured an injunction that kept Marsans on the sidelines for more than a year. Ball tried unsuccessfully to get the injunction lifted in Judge Kenesaw Mountain Landis's court. Historian Robert Wiggins wrote that as part of the Federal League settlement, Reds owner Garry Herrmann paid Ball $2,500 in damages for keeping Marsans from playing for the Browns.[17]

Ball was pursuing one of baseball's biggest stars, pitcher Walter Johnson, for his Terriers after the 1914 season. When Johnson did not sign with the Terriers, Ball let the Federal League's Chicago Whales sign him. In return Ball got the right to pursue pitcher Eddie Plank, whom he signed for 1915.[18] When Johnson reneged on his contract with the Whales, Ball told the press, "If Johnson pitches for any team besides the Chicago Feds next season, it will be in Leavenworth, Kansas, and his identity will be hidden behind a number."[19]

In 1914 Chicago pitching great Mordecai Brown was the Terriers' manager.[20] With the team mired in seventh place in August, Ball replaced Brown with more of a disciplinarian, Fielder Jones. The manager of the 1906 world champion Chicago White Sox Hitless Wonders, Jones was lured out of retirement with an interest in the club's ownership and a hefty three-year guaranteed contract of $50,000.[21] While Jones could not turn around the Terriers at the end of the season, he achieved success the following year. The 1915 Terriers (87-67, .565) fell just short of the Chicago Whales (86-66, .566). It was the closest pennant race in major-league baseball history.[22]

Under the settlement, two Federal League team owners, Charles Weeghman of Chicago and Phil Ball, were allowed to buy existing teams of the major leagues, the Cubs and the Cardinals, respectively. Ball was anxious to acquire an established team, even though he revealed he had lost $182,000 in his two seasons with the Terriers.[23] But when Helene Britton, the owner of the Cardinals, decided not to sell (she resented the male owners trying to force out the game's only female owner), the entire settlement with the Federal League was threatened.[24]

At this point, Robert Hedges decided to sell his American League club, the St. Louis Browns, to Ball.[25] Hedges had facilitated the 1903 peace treaty between the American and National Leagues by returning Christy Mathewson to the New York Giants.[26] "Maybe once again St. Louis will have to be the central figure in establishing peace in baseball," he said.[27] Hedges sold the Browns and Sportsman's Park for what was variously reported as between $425,000 and $550,000.

The 1916 Browns (like the Cubs) had the benefit of drawing on players from two teams, the Terriers and the Browns. Ball made Jones the manager of the combined team and moved Branch Rickey, the Browns' manager, into the front office. He could not fire Rickey because Hedges had given him a contract for 1916.[28] The two men did not get along from the start. "So you're the goddamned prohibitionist!" Ball reportedly said to Rickey when they first met.[29] "Ball thought Rickey's ideas too radical, and Rickey's endless talk and large vocabulary made him uncomfortable," wrote Murray Polner in his Rickey biography. "Rickey was, in turn, uncomfortable with Ball's crudeness: he considered Ball uncouth and, in matters of baseball, virtually illiterate."[30]

The 1916 Browns finished a disappointing fifth in the AL with a 79-75 record. But 1917 was much worse, with 97 losses against only 57 wins. Rickey was gone before the start of that season; he became the president of the St. Louis Cardinals early that year, after a citizens group bought the club from Helen Britton for $375,000.[31] At first Ball supported Rickey's move. But after consulting with American League President Ban Johnson, who did not want to lose the talented Rickey to the National League, Ball changed his mind. "Just tell those bastards you can't go through with it," he told Rickey, who replied, "Mr. Ball, whether or not I ever go with the Cardinals, I'll never work another day for you."[32] The dispute headed to the courts and had an odd settlement: Rickey was enjoined from joining the Cardinals, but only for 24 hours.

In early September 1917, Ball was again in the center of a controversy—one that he created. He was so upset with a 13-6 loss to the White Sox on September 4 that he decreed he'd cut salaries $100 for every $1,000 he would lose. "If these ball players think they are getting away with something on me by 'laying down,' they are all wrong, all wrong."[33] Three of the club's players, infielders Del Pratt and Doc Lavan, and outfielder Burt Shotton, took issue with Ball and refused to suit up. Ball had not mentioned names, but these three men were having poor seasons, in no small part because of injuries.

Pratt and Lavan sued Ball for libel for $50,000 each. Ball then backtracked and said, "I have been told they [some of his men] were laying down, but that I myself am not competent to judge of that." The writer of the St. Louis magazine *Reedy's Mirror* noted that Ball "has not the polished mien one finds in some successful business men, nor the insouciance noted in others.... He is not a man whose actions bespeak craft or design. He is just a plain whole-hearted individual, with the pugnacious tenacity of a leader."[34]

Sportswriter Hugh Fullerton said that Ball should be eliminated from Organized Baseball. "The fans ought to get up a memorial to Johnny Lavan and Derrill Pratt for bringing suits against Ball," he wrote. "For a man of the Ball type to accuse men of the moral and mental standing of Lavan and Pratt is a final blow to baseball in St. Louis."[35] Both men, along with Shotton, were traded before the 1918 season. Eventually Pratt and Lavan dropped their lawsuits after receiving $2,700 each.[36]

Fielder Jones was a stern taskmaster, and his abrasive style created dissension on the Browns. Yet in early 1918, Ball told the press that Jones had been too lenient. "No more Coddling—Iron Fist to Rule Browns Hereafter" was his message.[37] Just a few months later, after a painful loss by his Browns, Jones suddenly resigned and walked away from baseball forever.[38] When Ball got the news, he erupted. "So you want to quit? You haven't an ounce of courage. Get out of my office. I wouldn't take you back if you'd work for nothing."[39]

Early in his ownership of the Browns, Ball made perhaps his best and worst baseball decisions. In 1917 he hired Bob Quinn, a decent man and sharp evaluator of baseball talent, to replace Branch Rickey as business manager. "There's really nothing to the job. All you need is bunk and bluff," Ball told him. Quinn replied, "I have never practiced bunk or bluff in my life."[40] What Quinn practiced was solid, uncanny team-building. Through trade and acquisition, he assembled a powerful club that came within one game of the 1922 AL pennant.

Fred Lieb said that Quinn once canceled a Browns home game because of damp weather; he thought Ball would make more money if the game was rescheduled. But Ball was furious. "Bob Quinn, let me tell you something. I worked myself to a frazzle at the office so I could see this game, and if you want to keep your job, don't ever do anything like this to me again."[41] Yet Quinn was no "yes man" and insisted that Ball not interfere with baseball operations. He once even walked out for a few days when Ball pushed his meddling too far.

Ball made arguably his worst baseball decision in 1920. The St. Louis Cardinals were in a desperate financial state, and their ballpark, League Park, was decrepit. Their president, Sam Breadon, who was consolidating ownership of the club, repeatedly begged Ball to allow the Cardinals to play their home games at the Browns' Sportsman's Park. In 1918, when Ball turned him down, he suggested that Breadon sell to Kansas City sportsmen.[42] Ball finally relented, even though he detested Branch Rickey, who by this point was the Cardinals manager. He felt sorry for Breadon and admired his fighting nature.

The Cardinals played their first home game in Sportsman's Park on July 1, 1920. They sold their League Park property for $275,000: $200,000 to the school board (Beaumont High School operated on the land until 2014) and $75,000 to the transit company for a streetcar turnaround. "The deal gave us money to clean up our debts, and something to work with," said Breadon. "Without it, we never could have made our early purchases of minor-league clubs."[43] Would the Cardinals have left St. Louis? It's hard to say. Instead, now Rickey's farm system would become a reality. The club had the money to start buying minor-league teams.

Ball became close friends with American League President Ban Johnson, even though they were "warring parties during 1914-1915.[44] Fred Lieb noted, "Despite Ball's truculence and quirks, he was intensely loyal."[45] When Ban lost power with the demise of the National Commission in 1920 and the rise of the commissioner system, Ball became a fierce opponent of Commissioner Landis. At one heated owners meeting in early 1920, Ball and Yankees owner Jacob Ruppert almost came to blows. When the owners voted to hire Landis later that year, Ball was the only one not to vote for the new commissioner (though he let Bob Quinn vote for the judge).

In the fall of 1924 Landis and Johnson came into open conflict, when Johnson recommended the cancellation of the World Series in the wake of the O'Connell-Dolan affair, a scandal involving attempts to throw ballgames. Landis demanded that Johnson be reprimanded; the owners responded with a resolution that humiliated Johnson. They felt they had to support Landis — or risk destroying fan confidence in the game's integrity. Eugene Murdock, Johnson's biographer, wrote, "It is unlikely that any group of subordinates had ever humiliated their superior officer so completely." Ball refused to sign the document and said, "The biggest figure in the national game has been a victim of men whose gratitude has bowed to the dollar sign."[46]

Late in his life, Johnson expressed what Ball meant to him. "I owe my life to Phil Ball. He stepped in and took charge of my case and refused to permit amputation of my leg."[47] NEA Service sportswriter William Braucher summed up their relationship: "Ball stood shoulder to shoulder with Johnson in every important battle the great old fighter had. Even the last battle that Johnson finally lost — for his life."[48]

The dramatic 1922 AL pennant race generated a large profit of around $300,000 for Ball.[49] He paid out bonuses of around $20,000 that year.[50] A decade later, Ball said, "The Browns made money for me in 1922, not before, not since. As president I get no salary, and I run the club for the pure fun of it."[51] Sportswriter Dan Daniel said that Ball set aside $250,000 each winter to run the Browns in the coming season. "I'd give anything to win with the Browns," said Ball. "Well, money is no object. Baseball is not only a hobby with me, it is a source of relaxation."[52]

In 1923 Bob Quinn left the Browns to take over the presidency of the Boston Red Sox, after Harry Frazee sold the team. Quinn had also tired of pushing back against Ball's interference. Ball felt the quiet manager of the Browns, Lee Fohl, was an ineffectual leader who had done a poor job of rallying his team after they lost two out of three games in a crucial September series against the New York Yankees.[53] With Quinn gone, Fohl now had to deal directly with his team's owner.

On July 27, 1922, controversial Browns pitcher Dave Danforth had been suspended by the league for throwing a ball whose seams were loaded with dirt or mud.[54] Quinn and Fohl sent Danforth down to the club's Tulsa farm club for the rest of the season. They did not want to bring him back in 1923, but Ball overruled them. On August 1, 1923, Danforth was again suspended, this time for throwing a doctored ball that had rough spots. When his teammates signed a petition to Ban Johnson, Fohl refused to do so. *St. Louis Times* sports editor Sid Keener wrote, "I know the character of Lee Fohl. … If Lee wouldn't sign [the petition], there must be some black smoke in the air."[55]

But Ball fired his manager a few days later and told reporters, "For the good of the game and the morale of the club, Lee Fohl is hereby relieved of his duties as manager."[56] When Fohl felt his integrity had been demeaned, Ban Johnson persuaded Ball to reword his statement: "For the good of the game as played by the Browns' team …"

Just a month later, as the Browns left for their final East Coast swing, they suspended star pitcher Urban Shocker. He had already won his 20th game of the year on August 30, his fourth consecutive 20-win season. The temperamental spitball pitcher insisted on taking his wife along on the trip, but the club's new business manager, Billy Friel, denied the request. Since Bob Quinn's departure, Phil Ball was really making all the major decisions; Friel's executive experience and reputation did not come close to that of the man he replaced.[57] Syndicated columnist Westbrook Pegler wrote that Ball's philosophy was, "Women in baseball are like gun play in a crowded street car."[58]

Ball and Friel, with Ban Johnson's full support, contended that this was the simple issue of an insubordinate employee not following team rules, as he had agreed to do in his contract. To Shocker, however, this was a violation of his personal liberty, and he took his case to Commissioner Landis, who was the ultimate arbiter. Landis was also an unpredictable "wild card" in the dispute. Even as a judge, he enjoyed defending the rights of the little guy in struggles with management. And Landis certainly did not want to uphold a position held by his nemesis, Ban Johnson.

Sportswriter Fred Lieb wrote, "There is a stick of dynamite in the Shocker case. It is fraught with danger."[59] Ball did not like to compromise when he felt he was right, and even more so in dealing with Shocker, whom he disliked. But should Landis declare Shocker a free agent, Johnson and the owners feared the reserve clause would come into challenge, opening the door to "a legal fight that might shake baseball to its foundation."[60]

Johnson decided the risk of a Landis ruling was too great, fireworks that would have made "the Last Days of Pompeii look like a wet match" by comparison.[61] He facilitated a settlement: He pulled Bob Quinn into a meeting with Shocker, in which Ball had allowed his friend Johnson to act on his behalf. Shocker signed a 1924 contract with a large salary increase, more than enough to cover the fine Ball had levied.[62] He then withdrew his hearing with Commissioner Landis. Ball wanted to trade Shocker, but he had recently hired the club's star first baseman, George Sisler, as player-manager, and Sisler wanted to keep the talented pitcher. A year later the Browns did trade Shocker, to the Yankees, after Sisler decided it was time for the unhappy pitcher to leave St. Louis.

The Browns did not come close to the pennant in the next few years. In early 1925 Phil Ball felt the brunt of St. Louis fans' ire, when outfielder Baby Doll Jacobson was locked in a salary dispute. After fans booed the club's owner in an early-season game, Ball called them "the sort of persons who throw pop bottles at umpires."[63]

After the 1925 season Ball spent hundreds of thousands of dollars to remodel and expand Sportsman's Park.[64] After the Browns finished in third place in 1925, he felt they would compete for the 1926 pennant. How wrong he was: The 1926 Browns fell to a 62-92 record and seventh place. And his tenants, the National League's Cardinals, won the World Series.[65] Ball did not renew Sisler's contract as manager and said, "The complete failure of the team this year is all the explanation that is necessary to make, I think."[66] He added a dig at the mild-mannered Sisler when he added, "The next manager of the team will be a rigid disciplinarian and a man able to command the enthusiasm of the players and their best efforts."[67]

Under new manager Dan Howley, a successful minor-league skipper, the Browns again finished seventh. Westbrook Pegler wrote about Howley's "peculiar job." "Starting with nothing, it is his duty to prevent it from becoming less."[68] Ball, acting as his own business manager, decided to rebuild his team. "Our club is loaded up with players who have had long trials and have failed to come through. We also have several malcontents who do the club no good. All the dead and dying timber will be culled."[69]

Ball was a brusque and impatient man; he always seemed to be in a hurry. Perhaps his restlessness led to his love of flying his own planes. It was not unusual for him to fly to meetings in Chicago and Detroit and return home the same day. He flew a Ryan monoplane, the same model as the one Charles Lindbergh flew across the Atlantic. Ball even bought the plant that built them.[70] In 1928 he told a reporter that he saw a future in which baseball teams would travel by airplane.[71]

In 1929 Howley tired of his owner's interference and told reporters Ball came into the clubhouse and humiliated him in front of the players. "It makes no difference where the club finishes. If we win the pennant, I'm through just the same. I'm quitting."[72] Ball replaced Howley with Browns coach (and former catcher) Bill Killefer.

In 1930 Ball had a legal showdown with Commissioner Landis. Fred Bennett was an outfielder Ball had shuttled between his minor-league farm teams for more than two years. Landis ruled that since the Browns did not bring Bennett to the major leagues, he was a free agent.[73] Ball got a temporary injunction that allowed him to keep Bennett in the minors in 1930. A judge upheld Landis, giving Bennett his freedom.[74] Ball planned to appeal, but he dropped it, he said, "at the request of the American League." Landis had been fighting a rear-guard action against the farm system, which was called "chain-store baseball." Early in 1933 the owners voted 16-0 to allow clubs to own farm teams. Ball introduced the measure.[75]

In July of 1933 Ball fired Killefer and replaced him with Rogers Hornsby. Ball earlier had told reporters, "I wish I had a fellow like Hornsby running this team. He'd make those fellows click their heels."[76] This would be Ball's last major official act as the owner of the Browns. A couple months later he took ill while vacationing at his cabin in Battle Lake, Minnesota, and died of septicemia on his 69th birthday, October 22, 1933.

Phil Ball was not amused by the saying about St. Louis, "First in shoes, first in booze, last in the American League."[77] *Brooklyn Daily Eagle* reporter Ed Hughes wrote, "Ball was willing to lose fortunes in order to feel the glow of satisfaction in owning a champion club. … He had disclosed his intention to quit the game once his Browns had 'come through.' When they failed, he kept on spending and spending and fuming at his inability to produce the winning combination." After the 1936 season, in which the Browns drew an average of only 1,260 fans a game, his executors sold the club to Don Barnes of the American Investment Company of St. Louis for $350,000.[78]

Thanks to Tom Bourke for providing genealogical and ice history information.

NOTES

1. In 1913 the Federal League operated as a minor league based in the Midwest, a year before it challenged Organized Baseball and began raiding major-league teams of players. St. Louis brewer Otto Stifel and E.E. Steininger were Ball's partners in the Terriers. At first, Stifel was the largest shareholder.
2. Sid Keener, *St. Louis Times*, September 10, 1917.
3. *Reedy's Mirror*, December 18, 1914.
4. Dick Farrington, *The Sporting News*, October 26, 1933.
5. *Ice and Refrigeration*, Chicago, September 1901, Vol XXI, No. 3. It was a modified Carré machine that cost $12,000 and made five tons of ice a day. Frenchmen Ferdinand and Edmond Carré invented ice-making machinery in the 1850s.
6. "Famous Magnates of the Federal League," *Baseball Magazine*, October 1915: 71-72.
7. Arthur Mann, *Branch Rickey, American in Action* (Boston: Houghton Mifflin, 1957), 84.
8. Daniel J. Boorstin, *The Americans: The Democratic Experience* (New York: Vintage, 1974), 327.
9. One source said that Phil paid the $20,000 for the patents. Bill Borst, *Baseball Through a Knothole* (St. Louis: Krank Press, 1980), 3.

10. Dick Farrington, *The Sporting News*, October 26, 1933. Ball said his father left what little money he had to a brother, a sister, and a third wife.
11. Dan Daniel, *The Sporting News*, February 11, 1932.
12. Susan Brownell, "Figure Skating in St. Louis—After 90 Years, 'Meet Me in St. Louis,'" St. Louis Skating Club, stlouisskatingclub.org/index.php/history-by-susan-brownell. Also, email from Susan Brownell to Tom Bourke, September 9, 2016. The rink was demolished in 1964.
13. "Famous Magnates of the Federal League," 66-74.
14. Robert Peyton Wiggins, *The Federal League of Baseball Clubs* (Jefferson, North Carolina: McFarland, 2009), 53.
15. *Washington Post*, December 4, 1914.
16. Eric Enders, "Armando Marsans," SABR BioProject, sabr.org/bioproject.
17. Wiggins, *The Federal League of Baseball Clubs*, 244.
18. *Washington Post*, December 4, 1914. The 39-year-old Plank posted a 21-11 record and a 2.08 earned-run average for the Terriers in 1915.
19. Henry W. Thomas, *Walter Johnson: Baseball's Big Train* (Washington: Phenom Press, 1995), 137-138.
20. Brown had a 12-6 record with the Terriers.
21. Grantland Rice reported this salary figure in *Collier's* magazine. David Larson, "Fielder Jones," SABR BioProject, sabr.org/bioproject.
22. The closeness of the race was the result of the teams not playing the same number of games. Ironically, Mordecai Brown was a 17-game winner for the Whales.
23. *St. Louis Post-Dispatch*, February 18, 1916.
24. *The Sporting News* of January 6, 1916, had a photo of Britton with the headline, "Never Tell Her She Must."
25. Steve Steinberg, "Robert Hedges," SABR BioProject, sabr.org/bioproject.
26. Hedges had signed Mathewson to an ironclad contract in the summer of 1902.
27. Sid Keener, *St. Louis Times*, November 14, 1914.
28. Lee Lowenfish, *Branch Rickey: Baseball's Ferocious Gentleman* (Lincoln: University of Nebraska Press, 2007), 130.
29. Peter Golenbock, *The Spirit of St. Louis: A History of the St. Louis Cardinals and Browns* (New York: Avon, 2000), 75.
30. Murray Polner, *Branch Rickey: A Biography* (New York: Atheneum, 1982), 74.
31. Frederick G. Lieb, *The St. Louis Cardinals* (New York: G.P. Putnam's Sons, 1944), 60.
32. Golenbock, 76-77.
33. *St. Louis Republic*, September 5, 1917. "Laying down" suggested throwing games by not playing well.
34. *Reedy's Mirror*, December 18, 1914.
35. Hugh Fullerton, *New York American*, September 17, 1917.
36. *Capital Times* (Madison, Wisconsin), May 8, 1918. Ball claimed he did not pay for any settlement. It is possible the American League paid the players to drop their suits. In 1919 Rickey brought Lavan and Shotton back to St. Louis, to the Cardinals.
37. This was the headline in *The Sporting News*, February 7, 1918.
38. Jones told *Baseball Magazine* (October 1915): 73, "I left the game [as player-manager of the White Sox in 1908] because I was tired of it. It is a great strain to manage a club day after day." He had a heart condition that was not known at the time. He died of heart disease at the age of 62.
39. Frederick G. Lieb, *The Baltimore Orioles* (Carbondale, Illinois: SIU, 2001), 191 (reprint of 1955 Putnam edition).
40. Rory Costello, "Bob Quinn," SABR BioProject, sabr.org/bioproject.
41. Lieb, *The Baltimore Orioles*, 190.
42. *Chicago Tribune*, November 13, 1918. The Cardinals paid the Browns an annual rent of $20,000.
43. Lieb, *The St. Louis Cardinals*, 78.
44. The two men had meetings during negotiations, and Ball was Johnson's guest at Opening Day 1915 at Chicago's Comiskey Park. Eugene Murdock, *Ban Johnson: Czar of Baseball* (Santa Barbara: Praeger, 1982), 115.
45. Lieb, *The Baltimore Orioles*, 191.
46. Murdock, *Ban Johnson: Czar of Baseball*, 211.
47. *Huron* (South Dakota) *Evening Huronite*, December 26, 1930.
48. *Altoona* (Pennsylvania) *Mirror*, April 28, 1931.
49. "Phil Ball," UPI obituary, October 22 dateline, in Baseball Hall of Fame Library Phil Ball file.
50. Dick Farrington, *The Sporting News*, October 26, 1933.
51. Harry T. Brundige, *The Sporting News*, October 20, 1932.
52. Dan Daniel, *The Sporting News*, February 11, 1932.
53. The Yankees came into St. Louis on September 16 with a one-half game lead. They took two of three games before enormous crowds and left town with a 1½-game lead. The Browns then split six games against second-division clubs and ultimately fell one game short of the pennant.
54. Steve Steinberg, "Dave Danforth: Baseball's Forrest Gump," *The National Pastime* (Cleveland: SABR, 2002).
55. Sid Keener, *St. Louis Times*, August 3, 1922.
56. *St. Louis Times*, August 6, 1923.
57. Quinn had been the business manager of the Columbus Senators of the American Association for many years.
58. Westbrook Pegler, United News, February 7, 1924.
59. Fred Lieb, *New York Evening Telegram*, December 11, 1923.

HOME OF THE BROWNS AND CARDINALS AT GRAND AND DODIER

60 *The Sporting News*, quoted in Steve Steinberg, "Urban Shocker: Free Agency in 1923," *The National Pastime* (Cleveland: SABR, 2000).

61 *St. Louis Post-Dispatch*, December 26, 1923.

62 Johnson did not want to rescind the fine because he knew that Ball's pride was involved. Quinn had maintained a good working relationship with Shocker.

63 *St. Louis Post-Dispatch*, April 19, 1925. Jacobson soon signed his 1925 contract.

64 Curt Smith, in *Storied Stadiums* (New York: Carroll & Graf, 2001), pegged the remodel cost at $500,000. The *St. Louis Post-Dispatch* said the figure was $600,000 (October 21, 1927).

65 The Browns drew only 283,986 fans and lost $75,000 in 1926; the Cardinals drew 660,428.

66 *Washington Post*, October 12, 1926.

67 Rick Huhn, *George Sisler, Baseball's Forgotten Great* (Lincoln: University of Nebraska Press, 2004), 210.

68 Westbrook Pegler, *Chicago Tribune*, March 25, 1928.

69 *Chicago Tribune*, July 27, 1927.

70 *Washington Post*, June 23, 1927; *St. Louis Globe-Democrat*, August 17, 1927; *Fairfield* (Texas) *Recorder*, June 18, 2015.

71 *Brooklyn Daily Eagle*, April 30, 1928.

72 *Altoona* (Pennsylvania) *Mirror*, July 26, 1929.

73 David Pietrusza, *Judge and Jury: The Life and Times of Judge Kenesaw Mountain Landis* (South Bend: Diamond Communication, 1998), 349-352. In the complicated case, Bennett petitioned Landis for free agency since Ball wanted to keep him in the minors for a third year. The rules of Organized Baseball limited owners' control to only two seasons.

74 Bennett hit .368 with 27 home runs for Wichita Falls of the Texas League in 1929. But he played in only 39 major-league games.

75 G. Edward White, *Creating the National Pastime: Baseball Transforms Itself, 1903-1955* (Princeton, New Jersey: Princeton University Press, 1996), 291.

76 Dick Farrington, *The Sporting News*, October 26, 1933.

77 *New York Herald Tribune*, October 23, 1933.

78 Branch Rickey played a key role in bringing Barnes and the Ball estate together, for which he was paid $25,000. Sportsman's Park was not part of the deal; Barnes negotiated the rent down from $35,000.

SAM BREADON: RELENTLESS OWNER

BY MARK ARMOUR

IN THE LONG AND SUCCESSFUL HISTORY of the St. Louis Cardinals baseball club, few people have been more important than Sam Breadon, who owned the team for 27 years and presided over nine league pennants and six World Series titles. Much of the club's success has been attributed to Branch Rickey, the team's genius general manager, who built baseball's first and largest farm system, revolutionizing the relationship between the major leagues and minor leagues and turning the Cardinals organization into a model of player development and instruction. But Breadon and Rickey worked together, and it was Breadon who funded Rickey's farm system and lobbied for its legality. Breadon sold the Cardinals in 1947, and there have been very few baseball owners who left such a legacy of success.

Samuel Breadon (pronounced BRAY-din), one of eight children, was born on July 26, 1876, to William and Jane (Wilson) Breadon. "I was born in New York and grew up in the old Ninth Ward in old Greenwich Village," recalled Sam. "Near the docks. Nothing fancy, a tough neighborhood. You had to be able to handle yourself, or you did not do so well."[1] His mother was Scottish, and his father an Irish drayman who died when Sam was a young boy. After finishing grammar school Sam dropped out to help his mother, and as a young adult he held a steady job as a bank clerk on Wall Street, earning $125 a month. In his youth he played basketball and football and boxed.

About 1902 Breadon moved to St. Louis to join two New York friends, brothers, who had gone west to open an automobile dealership and garage. It was somewhat of a risk, but young Breadon was attracted by the possibilities of the new industry. Within a year or two the brothers got wind that Breadon was looking to open his own shop, and they fired him. Some fast talking got him a concession to sell popcorn at the 1904 World's Fair, held in St. Louis. This earned him enough money to open up his own garage. A wealthy customer, impressed with his work and honesty, offered him an executive position in the Western Automobile Company, and Breadon worked his way up to the very top, buying the business himself. By 1917 Breadon and a partner owned a distributorship of Pierce-Arrow automobiles, which he held for the next 20 years.[2]

Meanwhile, Breadon had become a rabid fan of the St. Louis Cardinals, a generally struggling club in the National League. He bought into the club in the mid-1910s, and gradually increased his stake to help the struggling ownership group. In early 1919 he was on the board of directors, and that fall he was named president. As a condition of accepting this position, he worked on his partners until he was able to purchase enough stock to get 51 percent of the club. He planned to run the team, not just the board. The Cardinals had joined the National League in 1892, but had finished as high as third place just twice in their first 29 years in the league. They were also heavily in debt. At the time of Breadon's ascension, Rickey was the club's president, while serving the club as both field manager and business manager, essentially also acting as what we now call a general manager. Breadon left Rickey in the latter two positions, while also offering him a piece of the club and naming him a vice president. After the club finished sixth in 1924 and started the next year 13-25, Breadon removed Rickey as manager, leaving him to run the club off the field. "In time, Branch, you will see that I am doing you a great favor," Breadon told a disappointed Rickey. "You can now devote yourself fully to player development and scouting."[3]

The two men worked together for more than two decades, turning a struggling club into one of the more successful in the game. Their relationship grew more contentious over the years, but there can be little doubt that they needed each other. As historian Lee Lowenfish wrote, "Under their arrangement, there was no doubt that Breadon was the boss who controlled the purse strings and Rickey was the employee who engineered the baseball transactions. However, unlike many baseball owners who get so intoxicated with their power that they think they understand the mechanics of the game itself, Breadon deferred completely to Branch Rickey on the nuts and bolts of player development."[4]

Breadon's first important decision after taking control in 1920 was to sign a lease to play in Sportsman's Park, as a tenant of Phil Ball's St. Louis Browns. Cardinals Park, formerly Robison Park, had been the Cardinals' home since 1893 but was both a firetrap and in danger of collapsing. "The building inspector, who was a friend of mine, said he was afraid he couldn't let us go another season with those stands. I couldn't blame him," Breadon said.[5] He dismantled the ballpark, and sold the property and land for $275,000, which got the club out of debt and provided operating capital for the years ahead. "It was the most important move I ever made on the Cardinals," Breadon later said. "It gave us money to clean up our debts, and something more to work with. Without it, we never could have purchased the minor-league clubs, which were the beginning of our farm system."[6]

As the new Cardinals manager, Breadon named 29-year-old Rogers Hornsby, their great second baseman, who had been the best player in the National League for several years. Hornsby made Breadon look smart right away, as he rallied the club to a more respectable fourth-place showing, all the while hitting .403 and winning his second Triple Crown. The next year Hornsby led the club to a first-place showing, and a seven-game triumph over the Yankees in the World Series. It was the first championship for the Cardinals since their days in the American Association in the 1880s.

Late in the 1926 season, Breadon and Hornsby got into an argument about a series of in-season exhibition games Breadon had arranged, which Hornsby thought was more than his tired players needed. During a heated disagreement, Hornsby apparently used choice words to insult his boss. Not forgetting the slight, after the season Breadon traded his pennant-winning hero-manager to the New York Giants for star second baseman Frankie Frisch and pitcher Jimmy Ring. Though Cardinals fans were livid, they soon learned that Breadon and Rickey were generally willing to trade the team's most popular players if they thought they were nearing the end of their peak years. After Hornsby, the Cardinals later dealt Dizzy Dean, Joe Medwick, Jim Bottomley, Chick Hafey, Johnny Mize, Mort Cooper, Walker Cooper, and many others. Rickey was able to find young replacements with their careers ahead of them, and the pennants piled up.

Though Breadon gave Rickey a fair amount of authority, he followed the team closely on a daily basis, and often left to himself the decision to hire and fire the Cardinals manager. In fact, he had a quick trigger in this area. Besides Hornsby, he replaced Bill McKechnie just a half season after he had won a pennant, and then Gabby Street a year and a half after Street's team had won two more pennants. Not counting interim managers, Breadon presided over nine managerial changes in 27 years despite tremendous on-field success.

It was Rickey who first conceived of the idea of operating a farm system, but it was Breadon who paid for it. Rickey convinced his boss that the club could save money by signing and developing its own players on its own minor-league clubs rather than paying the high prices demanded from independent minor-league teams. And it was Breadon who had to fight for the right to operate the farm system in the major-league boardrooms, a fight that occasionally grew contentious since Commissioner Kenesaw Mountain Landis was adamantly opposed to the idea.

By 1940 the Cardinals owned or had working agreements with 32 minor-league teams, controlling more than 600 players. One of the brilliant side effects of this extensive system was that Rickey could both sell the developed players the Cardinals did not need, and also sell Cardinals stars once they hit their early 30s, knowing he had other players ready to step in. Breadon and Rickey traded the 28-year-old Dean to the Cubs in 1938 for $185,000 and three players—Dean had hurt his arm the previous year after altering his pitching motion due to the foot injury he had suffered during the 1937 All-Star Game, and Rickey thought he might not return to his old self. Most importantly, Rickey had convinced Breadon that the system could produce new players. It always had, and it would again. During their long run of success from 1926 to 1949, when they finished first or second 18 times, the Cardinals never purchased a player from another organization.[7]

Rickey generally got all the credit for the moves that worked out well, but he also developed a reputation from his players and the press for being cheap or heartless. But Breadon, who gave little indication that he desired more attention for himself, deserves to share both the credit and the reputation — he set the salary budgets and approved the ballplayer sales Rickey was praised or derided for. "There was never a decision made in which I didn't have the final say," Breadon later said. "Many of Rickey's moves I approved, others I rejected."[8]

By the late 1930s, Breadon had sold his auto business, making the Cardinals his sole business interest. Coincidentally, after winning five pennants in nine years, in 1935 the Cardinals began a seven-year pennant drought. During this period Breadon began to meddle a bit more in the affairs of the team, including the firing of a few Rickey protégés in the farm system, causing a gradual deterioration of their relationship. In 1938 Commissioner Landis freed more than 70 Cardinals farmhands, claiming that the Cardinals controlled players on more than one team in some minor leagues, allowing the Cardinals to affect their pennant races. Breadon was apparently embarrassed by this decision, while Rickey was upset that Breadon did not fight it. In 1939 Breadon, who prided himself on maintaining great health and physical appearance, suffered a severe spinal injury when he was thrown from a horse. His recovery was difficult and slow, and Lowenfish opined that Breadon never completely recovered physically or emotionally from the accident.[9]

In February 1941, Breadon informed the board of directors, which included Rickey, that he would not be renewing Rickey's contract after the 1942 season. His stated reason was that the current economic climate, including America's possible entrance into a world war, made Rickey's large salary ($50,000, plus large bonuses for his share of player sales) an unwanted burden. This was likely part of Breadon's reasoning, but the two men's deteriorating relationship and the club's failure to win pennants for the previous six years were surely factors as well. The Cardinals lost a tough pennant race to the Dodgers in 1941, and then won the World Series in 1942, with Rickey still running the team. Rickey moved to Brooklyn to run the Dodgers, with more historic accomplishments ahead of him. n their remaining years as rival executives, the two men always spoke kindly of each other, at least publicly.

While the Cardinals were having another great year in 1943, Breadon fended off any attempts to mitigate Rickey's previous contributions. "I don't want to be placed in a position of 'crowing' about the way things are going in the wake of Rickey's departure," Breadon said. "After all, we had a good foundation built. But I've seen all angles of the game for the last quarter of a century and if I didn't know something about running a ballclub now, I'd be pretty damned dumb."[10]

Breadon's reputation as a tight-fisted owner only grew once he became more the public face of the team. Brothers Mort (pitcher) and Walker (catcher) Cooper held out in 1945 before capitulating just before Opening Day. Walker was soon in the armed forces, but Breadon traded Mort to the Boston Braves in late May. When Jorge Pasquel of the Mexican League plucked several major-league players in 1946, in defiance of the long-held reserve clause, it was the disgruntled Cardinals who suffered the biggest losses — star pitcher Max Lanier, pitcher Fred Martin, and infielder Lou Klein.

The Cardinals finished the 1946 regular season tied with the Dodgers, forcing a three-game pennant playoff. At a banquet held after the final regular season game, Breadon was chided from the lectern by writer Roy Stockton. "It looks, Sam," said Stockton, "as if you sliced the baloney too thin this time."[11] Breadon shrugged it off, and the Cardinals went on to beat the Dodgers and then the Red Sox in the World Series. It was Breadon's sixth championship.

In November 1947 Breadon sold his majority share (75 percent) of the Cardinals to a group headed by his longtime friend Robert F. Hannegan and Fred Saigh, Jr., a prominent St. Louis attorney. The price for Breadon's shares was reported to be $3 million, the highest such figure in baseball history, and a pretty fair return on his initial $2,000 investment. "This is not a pleasant day for me," Breadon said, "but every year I am less sufficient and at my age it is time to quit."[12] He later told Dan Daniel, "I am seventy years of age [actually 71]. I am in fine condition. As far as I know I might live to be ninety. But I felt that, in justice to my family, I should put my estate in order. This meant selling my stock in the Cardinals."[13]

Despite his reputation as a tight-fisted owner, Breadon could be very generous. One of the stars of his first World Series team was the great pitcher Pete Alexander, whom the Cardinals got off waivers in June 1926 only to see him return to stardom for a few more years. Alexander had a difficult life after his career was over, and at the time of his death in 1950 it was revealed that the Cardinals (under Breadon) had for many years paid him $50 per month, which Alex thought was a pension, to allow him to live a little better.[14] In 1948 Mort Cooper, having washed out of baseball soon after Breadon discarded him, was arrested for passing three bad checks. Breadon, who was retired, paid his bond, and later talked the Cubs' Phil Wrigley into signing Cooper and giving him one last shot.[15]

Breadon's marriage to Josephine in 1905 yielded a daughter, Frances. He married Rachel (Ray) Wilson in 1912, and the couple adopted their own daughter, Janet. Breadon was said to be the life of many parties in his younger days, and he earned the nickname "Singing Sam" because he often sang in barbershop quartets. Before his accident on his horse in 1939, he was an avid swimmer and horseman, and worked out by taking groundballs during the Cardinals' spring-training season. By the time he reached middle age he was more interested in golf and retiring early so he could read in bed.[16]

Breadon succumbed to cancer on May 8, 1949, at age 72. He had been a patient at St. Joseph's Hospital in St. Louis for several weeks. He was survived by his wife and daughters. At his request, there was no funeral service, and his ashes were dropped from a plane over the Mississippi River. Branch Rickey, who worked for Breadon for two decades, said he was "deeply grieved over the passing of one of the game's finest sportsmen and outstanding businessmen. We always got along splendidly, even after I returned to Brooklyn."[17]

In the ensuing decades, Breadon's role as the head of one of baseball's best organizations has been often overlooked. The most recent attempt to rectify this came in 2012 when Breadon was on the ballot considered by the Hall of Fame's Veteran's Committee, though he was not elected. The Cardinals have had much success in their history, and their 11 World Series victories are topped only by the New York Yankees. But it is worth remembering that their success began when Sam Breadon bought the club, and that six of the 11 titles came during his reign.

NOTES

1. Daniel M. Daniel, "Sam Breadon Left Indelible Imprint on Baseball Operation," *Baseball*, July 1949, 261.
2. Lee Lowenfish, *Branch Rickey—Baseball's Ferocious Gentleman* (Lincoln: University of Nebraska Press, 2009), 120.
3. Lowenfish, *Branch Rickey*, 150.
4. Lowenfish, *Branch Rickey*, 122.
5. John Kieran, "How to Buy a Ball Club," *New York Times*, undated clipping in Breadon's file at the National Baseball Library.
6. Mark Tomasik, "Top 5 reasons why Sam Breadon should be in Hall," retrosimba.com, November 15, 2012.
7. Warren Corbett, "Eddie Dyer," SABR's Baseball Biography Project, sabr.org/bioproject.
8. Fred Lieb, "Flashbacks—Sam Breadon," *The Sporting News*, November 18, 1943.
9. Lowenfish, *Branch Rickey*, 298.
10. Dick Farrington, "Breadon Nixes 'Mr. Brain' Idea as Birds Soar Without Rickey," *The Sporting News*, June 24, 1943.
11. Bob Broeg, *Memories of a Hall of Fame Sportswriter* (Champaign, Illinois: Sports Publishing LLC, 1995), 157.

12 Associated Press, "Not Pleasant, But It Is Time to Quit," *New York World Telegram*, November 24, 1947.

13 Daniel M. Daniel, "Sam Breadon Left Indelible Imprint On Baseball Operation," *Baseball*, July 1949, 261.

14 Jan Finkel, "Pete Alexander," SABR's Baseball Biography Project, sabr.org/bioproject.

15 Gregory H. Wolf, "Mort Cooper," SABR's Baseball Biography Project, sabr.org/bioproject.

16 J. Roy Stockton, "Singing Sam, the Cut-Rate Man," *The Saturday Evening Post*, February 22, 1947, 140.

17 "Baseball Mourns Breadon," *New York World Telegram*, May 11, 1949, page unknown.

BILL VEECK AND THE ST. LOUIS BROWNS

BY GREG ERION

BY 1951 THE BROWNS WERE DECIDedly moribund. They had been last in the American League in attendance every year since 1946 and the usual question one asked before the start of the season was whether they might finish in seventh or eighth place. Underfinanced, Charles and William DeWitt wanted out of what they saw as a no-win situation. The only way they had been able to continue running their team was through the sales of their more promising players, but by 1951 even this option was thinning out. They began to quietly let word get out that they were looking to sell the team.

Their plan to put the Browns up for sale soon came to the attention of Bill Veeck. One of the most colorful characters in baseball history, Veeck grew up with the sport—his father, William Veeck Sr., had been president of the Chicago Cubs in the 1930s. Young Veeck followed in his father's footsteps, first as treasurer of the Cubs and then as part-owner of the Milwaukee Brewers in the Double-A American Association. Taking on the financially strapped Brewers in midseason 1941, Veeck and co-owner Charlie Grimm soon turned things around. Offering a precursor of things to come, Veeck staged numerous promotional events ranging from offering free lunches to giveaways of pigeons and blocks of ice. He introduced night games at the Brewers' Borchert Field and offered morning games for night-shift defense workers during World War II.[1] Attendance nearly tripled over the previous season. During five years of ownership Grimm and Veeck won three pennants.

Veeck first attempted to get into the majorleague market in late 1942, by trying to purchase the Philadelphia Phillies. Once gaining ownership, his plan was to fill the roster with players from the Negro Leagues—four years in advance of Jackie Robinson breaking the color barrier. Quite probably because of this, the league owners awarded the Phillies to another prospective buyer.[2]

In 1946 Veeck was able to purchase the Cleveland Indians. He immediately began to work his promotional skills on the team. Efforts ranged in all directions from introducing Ladies' Day, refurbishing Municipal Stadium, and offering radio broadcasts of the games—all the while talking with fans and getting their take on how to improve the team's draw and popularity. While these efforts were radical departures from the staid habits of Veeck's predecessors, in 1947 he initiated an even greater change, signing Larry Doby, the first African American to play in the American League.

In 1948 Veeck added legendary Negro League pitcher Satchel Paige to the roster. The presence of Doby and Paige proved vital in helping the Indians win the pennant and the 1948 World Series. Performance on the field generated success at the box office. A major-league record 2,620,627 fans attended Cleveland's regular-season games. In 1945, the year before Veeck purchased the team, just 558,182 fans had come through the Indians' turnstiles. One year after winning the Series, Veeck sold the team. He was getting a divorce and settlement terms demanded that he jettison the Indians.

A little over a year and a half later, with his divorce settled and newly remarried, Veeck jumped at the chance to get back in the game as an owner. Negotiations commenced in early May. By June Veeck secured an option on the DeWitts' shares in the Browns.[3] His ability to purchase the team depended on his obtaining 75 percent ownership of the club. According to *The Sporting News*, Veeck and his partners needed to meet that percentage threshold under Missouri law to "liquidate the present Browns set-up, pay off minority stockholders and form a new corporation entirely owned by Veeck and his associates."[4] The DeWitts held 58 percent of the shares; Veeck was given 12 days to purchase 114,000 shares and gain the remaining 17 percent he needed. The day before the deadline, Veeck was 8,500 shares short of his goal but a last-minute purchase of 8,572 shares from a Browns board member on July 3 put him over the top.[5]

Including Veeck, 16 members of the syndicate ended up owning 222,000 of the Browns 275,000 shares — giving them slightly over 80 percent control of the club.[6] Most versions of the deal pegged Veeck and his syndicate as having purchased the team for $1,750,000. The DeWitts had bought the club for approximately $1,000,000 in 1949.[7]

A day after meeting the deadline Veeck went to the ballpark. "I moved all over the park and talked to every fan I could reach. ... These are people we are going to serve. I want to know what they want, what they like, what they think of the ball club."[8] What fans thought of the club was probably not positive, as the Browns were swept in a doubleheader by, ironically, the Cleveland Indians. The double loss entrenched their hold on last place; they were the worst team in major-league baseball. Of Veeck's decision to purchase the Browns, John Lardner wrote, "Many critics were surprised to know that the Browns could be bought because they didn't know the Browns were owned."[9]

Veeck immediately went to work on several fronts to upgrade the ballpark, increase interest in the Browns and improve the team. Responding to women's complaints that Sportsman's Park needed a thorough cleaning, Veeck arranged for the St. Louis Fire Department to hose down the upper deck.[10] Within days during a doubleheader on July 6, he announced that soft drinks and beer were on the house; he personally handed out several buckets of cold beer while visiting the bleachers.[11] As if these activities were not enough, Veeck reached out to a then highly regarded Browns minor leaguer named Frank Saucier, who had decided to leave the game rather than play for the salary he was offered. Veeck tracked down Saucier, who was working for an oil company, and signed him to a contract. Never mind that Saucier would fail with the Browns. That Veeck would go all out to improve his team impressed the fans. Over the next several months, Veeck crisscrossed the region drumming up support for the team.

These were minor efforts compared with subsequent endeavors Veeck put forth that season. On August 19 the Browns hosted the Detroit Tigers for a doubleheader. Between games a celebration marking the 50th anniversary of the founding of the American League was scheduled to take place. The event included a procession of 1901 vintage automobiles and comic performances by baseball clown Max Patkin. As a finale a giant cake rolled out on the field commemorating the event. A midget dressed in a Browns uniform popped out of the cake. All this was considered below Veeck's promotional standards.

Then the second game began and the midget, one Eddie Gaedel, was announced as a pinch-hitter for the Browns.[12] After verifying that Gaedel had signed a viable contract, the umpires allowed him to bat. Tigers pitcher Bob Cain walked Gaedel on four pitches, whereupon he was removed for a pinch-runner. Veeck's action proved controversial, especially to fellow baseball owners, whose approach to the game was decidedly more conservative than that of the Browns' lively owner. Brash as Veeck was, he brought excitement to the game with this and numerous other events, promotions, and efforts to lure fans into the ballpark. Less than a week later, on August 24, Veeck arranged to let fans manage a game. Manager Zack Taylor sat in a rocking chair near the dugout and watched as fans picked a lineup and made strategic decisions during the contest.[13] The Browns finished last but attendance rose from approximately 4,000 per game to over 5,000 after Veeck took over.

Veeck's long-term goal was to outhustle the Cardinals promotionally. He had a daunting task ahead of him. The Cardinals were a much better team, they had a legacy of winning, and their players, like Stan Musial and Red Schoendienst, were huge draws. However, Redbirds owner and financial expert Fred Saigh was a novice in baseball circles. Veeck felt that through consistent promotions, endless publicity, and gradually building the Browns into a contending team he would succeed drawing away Cardinal fans over time.

During the 1952 season Veeck followed this strategy and to some extent succeeded. Attendance increased from 293,270 to 518,796—a substantial jump. Of equal importance, Cardinals attendance dropped from 1,013,429 to 913,113—still a decided edge over the Browns but moving in the right direction from Veeck's perspective. On the field, the Browns marginally improved, winning a dozen more games to finish seventh.

Veeck's biggest challenge going into 1953 was to increase the team's revenue. It was estimated that the Browns would have to draw approximately 850,000 fans to break even.[14] Promotions to draw fans to the park were improving attendance, but slowly. Seeking an additional source of income, Veeck overreached. After the 1952 season ended, appreciating the possibilities of televised games, he proposed to fellow American League club owners that they share radio and television revenue with visiting teams. Veeck's proposal, admittedly self-serving given the Browns' dearth of popularity, was shot down 7 votes to 1, each team deciding to negotiate separate deals. At that point Veeck retaliated, saying that a "no pay, no television" policy would be implemented. Teams would not broadcast their games from St. Louis unless the Browns got part of the earnings when playing games on the road. Other teams, including the Yankees, Red Sox, and Indians, countered Veeck by refusing to schedule profitable night games. Veeck had taken on owners he would soon learn he could ill afford to antagonize.

As Veeck was involved in these maneuverings, a rapidly developing situation took place in the National League that would have a profound overall effect on baseball history and on the St. Louis Browns specifically.

The Browns' departure from St. Louis was ironically set in motion by misfortune that befell the Cardinals when Fred Saigh, owner of the team, was indicted for income-tax evasion. Pleading no contest to the charges, Saigh expected to pay a fine for his actions. Instead, on January 28, 1953, he was not only fined $15,000 but also sentenced to 15 months in jail. On hearing this, Saigh realized his ownership of the team was finished. "This means, of course, that I will have to dispose of the Cardinals. There is no way I can stay in baseball."[15] Within days Saigh met with National League President Ford Frick to establish plans for divesting himself of the franchise. He was given until February 22 to make a deal to sell the Cardinals. After that date, they would come under the control of a board of trustees.[16] Once it became known that Saigh had to sell, offers came in from numerous groups, including one that could have involved shifting the Cardinals to Houston, Texas.[17]

Several weeks later, two days before the February 22 deadline, Saigh sold the team to the Anheuser-Busch brewing company. His intent in selling to Anheuser-Busch was to keep the team in St. Louis. In describing the transaction, Saigh said, "During the past weeks I have had serious offers for the Cardinals but all of them involved moving the club away from St. Louis." One of the most serious later offers involved a consortium of Milwaukee businessmen intent on shifting the team to their city; one of the attractions: the recently completed County Stadium, which had a capacity of over 34,000.[18] Milwaukee baseball fans did not have to wallow in disappointment at losing the Cardinals for long. The sale of the Cardinals to the cash-rich brewery set off a series of repercussions within the baseball world that would bring Milwaukee its own team and force the Browns out of St. Louis.

When Veeck heard that Anheuser-Busch had purchased the Cardinals, he realized that his efforts to promote his team had no chance to succeed against the financial juggernaut. When August "Gussie" Busch, president of the brewery, came to Sportsman's Park for the first time as owner of the Redbirds, Veeck welcomed him: "Glad to see you. But I'm afraid you're going to offer us a little difficult competition." Busch's smiling, "You're right" confirmed that the Browns could succeed only if they moved elsewhere.[19]

There were two viable options for Veeck to pursue. Both Baltimore and Milwaukee had built ballparks of sufficient capacity to support major-league baseball. Veeck's inclination was to move to Milwaukee, the site of his earlier accomplishments with the American Association Brewers. But there was a significant snag to that option. Lou Perini, owner of the Boston Braves, held territorial rights to baseball in the Milwaukee region.

Perini wanted out of Boston; in 1952 his Braves drew just 281,278 fans — the worst in the major leagues, losing nearly $600,000 for the year.[20] Realizing he could not compete with the Red Sox, Perini considered his options. Eager to move the Browns to Milwaukee, Veeck offered Perini $750,000 for the rights to the market. Perini stalled him off.[21] Early in March, just weeks after Saigh sold out to Anheuser-Busch, Perini announced that the Braves were moving to Milwaukee.

Thwarted by Perini's action, Veeck turned his attention to seeing if he could shift the Browns to Baltimore, now his only viable option.

Baltimore had hosted a major-league team during the first two years of the American League's existence only to lose the franchise to New York in 1903. Over the ensuing years, even while hosting the International League's Baltimore Orioles, the city of Baltimore yearned to regain major-league status. Baltimore's existing Memorial Stadium gave it an advantage over other cities seeking a major-league franchise. Recently rebuilt, the 31,000-capacity ballpark was ready for big-league competition.[22]

While Veeck maintained that the major turning point for his deciding to move was Anheuser-Busch's decision to purchase the Cardinals in the spring of 1953, he had sent out feelers to Jack Dunn III, who owned the minor-league Orioles, in the fall of 1952.[23] Dunn was receptive to giving Veeck territorial rights for the move if he could have an ownership stake in the franchise.[24]

Even earlier, in the summer of 1952, Veeck initiated discussions with Baltimore city officials concerning Memorial Stadium. Baltimore's Mayor Thomas J. D'Alesandro Jr. and local attorney Clarence Miles, who were spearheading efforts to gain a major-league franchise, worked to develop an agreement that would establish temporary seating for 13,500 fans to accommodate the fast-approaching 1953 season.[25] A viable lease agreement was created and long-range plans were established to increase permanent seating accommodations for 50,000. Veeck, needing working capital, agreed to sell 20 percent of the ballclub's stock to local businessmen.[26]

Believing financial plans and operational requirements had been worked out for the Browns to shift to Baltimore, Veeck sought approval of the American League. While Veeck was an outstanding entrepreneur, in many ways a visionary for the game, in the realm of intraleague politics, he was quite naïve.

His constant publicity-seeking efforts, whether by having a midget bat in a game or having fans "manage" a game, struck more staid owners as distinctly garish and therefore offensive. More seriously, his wrangling over radio and television rights and scheduling of night games created enemies. Additionally, owners were concerned that the Browns shifting to Baltimore, would hurt attendance for the Philadelphia and Washington clubs — concerns that in the end proved credible. Another argument was that if the shift were allowed, the International League's continued viability was at risk, particularly on the eve of a new season. The proposed action was too sudden.

These and other roadblocks, including possible exposure to legal proceedings, all coalesced into the American League owners denying Veeck's request to transfer the Browns to Baltimore by a 6-to-2 vote, with Veeck and the Chicago White Sox being the sole supporters of his request. The owners wanted Veeck out of the game.

Their feelings were soon echoed by Browns fans in St. Louis once Veeck's plans became known. He had worked himself into a corner. The Browns were forced to stay in St. Louis for the 1953 season. Local interest in the team Veeck had built up over the previous two seasons plummeted. The Browns dropped into last place, losing 100 games. Attendance fell under 300,000. Veeck had become a pariah in the city.

By the end of 1953, several developments had taken place. Veeck sold Sportsman's Park to Anheuser-

Busch for $1.1 million. Additionally, he sold off marketable players to stave off bankruptcy. And of great collective interest to American League owners, movement of the Braves from Boston to Milwaukee proved a resounding success, with attendance soaring from less than 290,000 in Boston to over 1.8 million in Milwaukee. This was incentive to grant Veeck's renewed interest in moving to Baltimore. Even so, his effort failed again in a 4-to-4 vote. It became clear to Veeck that the right to move to Baltimore could be approved—as long as Veeck was not part of the ownership.

Immediately after the vote denying Veeck's efforts to move to Baltimore on September 27, 1953, Baltimore's representatives sought to retool the proposal through several avenues. One was to hint at potential legal actions, including an assault on baseball's sacred player reserve clause. The other was to restructure the financial package by buying out Veeck. An offer was formulated to pay Veeck's asking price of $2.4 million. Financing was also arranged to buy the International League Orioles for $350,000 and to pay a $48,749 indemnity to the International League for its loss of Baltimore territorial rights. The American League approved the deal on October 1, enabling Bill Veeck to realize a $1 million gain on his investment and allowing the discharge of various debts as well as realize some profit for him and his fellow investors.[27]

With this action, the 51-year run of the St. Louis Browns ended. The team would play in Baltimore in 1954 and end up with the exact record it had in 1953: 54 wins and 100 losses. Fortunately for the Orioles, the hapless Philadelphia A's won three games fewer, to finish in last place. Despite not improving on their 1953 performance on the field, the Orioles did something the Browns had never come close to achieving. Baltimore's return to the majors attracted 1,060,910 fans through the turnstiles.

The shift from St. Louis to Baltimore proved to have a ripple effect on the American League. Fears that placing a team in Baltimore would oversaturate the region were proved correct: Both the Philadelphia A's and Washington Senators saw declining attendance. After the 1954 season, the A's moved to Kansas City. After the 1960 season the Senators franchise moved to Minneapolis-St. Paul.

NOTES

1 Paul Dickson, *Bill Veeck, Baseball's Greatest Maverick* (New York: Walker & Company, 2012), 63-69; Nick Acocella, *Baseball's Showman*, espn.com/classic/veeckbill000816.html.

2 Dickson, *Bill Veeck*, 67-80, and 357-366. Dickson goes into depth on Veeck's efforts as well as analyzing the validity of subsequent documentation concerning this aspect of Veeck's career.

3 That option was obtained from Mark Steinberg, a St. Louis investment broker who had purchased the note from the DeWitts. Rumors were about that the DeWitts might sell the club to Frederick C. Miller, a Milwaukee brewer whose intentions were to shift the franchise to Milwaukee. Steinberg's action forestalled that possibility. The note represented approximately 56 percent of the Browns stock. Bob Broeg, "Veeck's Friend Buys Browns $700,000 Note," *The Sporting News*, May 23, 1951: 4, and Frederick G. Lieb, *The Baltimore Orioles: The History of a Colorful Team in Baltimore and St. Louis* (Carbondale, Illinois: Southern Illinois University Press, 1955), 214.

4 Ray Gillespie, "Veeck Party Forms New Corporation," *The Sporting News*, July 4, 1951: 2.

5 Dickson, *Bill Veeck*, 185-186.

6 A breakout of how shares were distributed was not publicized. "Reorganized Browns Boast Only Sixteen Shareholders," *The Sporting News*, July 11, 1951: 16.

7 Ray Gillespie, "Veeck Deal Shows Rocketing Value of Major Franchises," *The Sporting News*, October 7, 1953: 5, and James Quirk and Rodney D. Fort, *Pay Dirt: The Business of Professional Team Sports* (Princeton, New Jersey: Princeton University Press, 1992), 400.

8 Bob Burnes, "Bill's Magic Touch Spurs Lagging Gate," *The Sporting News*, July 18, 1951: 2.

9 Bill Veeck with Ed Linn, *Veeck—as in Wreck: The Chaotic Career of Baseball's Incorrigible Maverick"* (New York: G.P. Putnam's Sons, 1962), 213.

10 Bob Burnes, "Sports Shirt Veeck Collars Browns Fans," *The Sporting News*, July 18, 1951: 4.

11 Veeck and Linn, *Veeck*, 215.

12 Gaedel pinch-hit for the aforementioned Saucier, who would have only 14 at-bats in his abbreviated career.

13 The fans who "managed" were winners of an essay contest. The Browns won, 5-3. Dickson, *Bill Veeck*, 191-196.

14 Gerald Eskenazi, *Bill Veeck: A Baseball Legend* (New York: McGraw-Hill Book Company, 1988), 105.

15 Ray Gillespie, "Owner Given 15 Months, $15,000 Fine," *The Sporting News*, February 4, 1953: 11.

16 Dan Daniels, "3 Trustees to Be Named to Run Club," *The Sporting News*, February 11, 1953: 4.

17 Peter Golenbock, *The Spirit of St. Louis: A History of the St. Louis Cardinals and Browns* (New York: Avon Books, Inc., 2000), 56, 397.

18 Ray Gillespie, "Head of Beer Firm Is New Prexy of Club," *The Sporting News*, February 25, 1953: 3.

19 Dickson, *Bill Veeck*, 208.

20 Harold Kaese, *The Boston Braves: 1871-1953* (Boston: Northeastern University Press, 2004), 283.

21 Veeck and Linn, *Veeck*, 281-282.

22 Originally built as a football stadium, it was eventually reconfigured in 1950 to host the minor-league Orioles. Philip J. Lowry, *Green Cathedrals: The Ultimate Celebration of Major League and Negro League Ballparks* (New York: Walker & Company, 2006), 18.

23 James Edward Miller, *The Baseball Business: Pursuing Pennants and Profits in Baltimore* (Chapel Hill: University of North Carolina Press, 1990), 29.

24 Jack Dunn III, with whom Veeck was dealing, is not to be confused with his grandfather, who owned the International League Baltimore Orioles in the 1920s. baseball-reference.com/bullpen/Jack_Dunn_III.

25 D'Alesandro's daughter, Nancy Pelosi, became speaker of the US House of Representatives in 2007.

26 Veeck's attempt to transfer and then sell the Browns is detailed in Miller, *The Baseball Business*, 29-35.

27 Miller, *The Baseball Business*, 35.

THREE WEEKS IN 1953: THE FATE OF THE CARDINALS

BY JOHN BAUER

FRED SAIGH HAD NOT EXPECTED THE outcome. The St. Louis Cardinals owner walked into Judge Roy Harper's federal courtroom on January 28, 1953, prepared to plead no contest to two counts of tax evasion in exchange for withdrawal of three other counts. The government's investigation concluded that Saigh's tax returns from 1944 to 1950 showed unreported income of $413,179, for which Saigh owed almost $400,000 in unpaid taxes and penalties.[1] Also, the Cardinals' tax returns for 1948 and 1949 showed unreported income of $330,978, resulting in a tax deficiency and penalties totaling $159,542.[2] Saigh's acquisition of the Cardinals—with partner and former US Postmaster General Robert Hannegan—occurred through what Saigh described as a tax gimmick involving no personal funds; now, it may have seemed that Saigh had been caught playing fast and loose with the tax code.

Fred Saigh did not expect that he would have to sell his club. Saigh, owner of all but seven shares of Cardinals stock after buying out the ailing Hannegan in 1949, anticipated big things for the team. The Cardinals had yet to win a pennant during his tenure, but a third-place finish in 1952 with an 88-66 record generated optimism for 1953. Citing the Cardinals' strong second half to the 1952 season, Saigh used the occasion of the club's Christmas party to forecast a pennant.[3] He also hoped that talk of building a proposed riverfront arch would be replaced with talk of a new riverfront stadium,[4] thereby allowing the Cardinals to escape tenancy at Sportsman's Park, controlled by the Browns and their president, Bill Veeck. In early January, Saigh spent 10 days in the Middle East checking on his other business interests. He even packed some baseballs for the trip. For the Cardinals owner, it seemed like business as usual.

It would not be business as usual. Saigh believed he would plead the matter and pay a fine. That is how these cases were disposed of, he understood.[5] Judge Harper, however, sentenced Saigh to 15 months in prison and fined him a total of $15,000. Harper gave Saigh until May 4 to handle his affairs before reporting to prison. The assistant US attorney, Ted Bollinger Jr., may have had some insight into the apparent severity of the sentence. Bollinger said afterward that the court viewed Saigh as uncooperative with the federal investigation. He disclosed that Saigh offered a job to a government agent investigating his tax records, but Saigh claimed later that he meant nothing improper in doing so. After Harper passed sentence, Saigh became visibly shaken and angry at the court, and had trouble controlling his voice in the courtroom.[6] Saigh's lawyer, Robert H. McRoberts Sr., argued that sparing Saigh's wife and mother the stress and rigors of a trial was his client's principal concern in pleading no contest. Further, because Saigh "is key to the entire Cardinal organization,"[7] a trial would have been detrimental both to the Cardinals and to baseball. The consequences of the sentence sinking in, Saigh said, "This means I must dispose of the Cardinals. I cannot stay in baseball."[8]

With the National League due to meet on January 30, two days after his sentencing, Saigh did not have much time to figure out a plan. He said, "I will confer with National League President Warren Giles and Baseball Commissioner Ford Frick in New York. As there are developments concerning the Cardinals, announcements will be made."[9] Developments were underway, in fact, though Giles felt compelled to disclose that he had not received an application related to the transfer of ownership of the Cardinals.

After an hour-long meeting on January 29 with Frick and Giles in New York, Saigh announced that he would select "three civic-minded St. Louisans"[10] to act as a trustees committee to operate the club until he could dispose of his stock. Saigh promised to name the trustees committee, which would have to be acceptable to Frick and the NL, by February 22. Saigh intended to handle club affairs until completion of the sale, but removed himself from active participation in National League business and appointed longtime Cardinals vice president William Walsingham Jr. to represent the club at league meetings. Frick expressed his regret about the circumstances. "I certainly hated to see this happen. This plan was Saigh's. He's a battler, a game little guy who never has been a bigger man than he was today. He certainly was entitled to bow out of baseball with all the grace possible under these unfortunate circumstances."[11] Saigh reiterated his commitment to sell: "I've said I don't want to embarrass baseball and that I'd sell. I don't want anyone running the club for me, either, and I won't sell at a loss. But I'm interested only in selling to people who plan to operate the Cardinals where they belong — in St. Louis."[12]

It was anticipated that Walsingham, the nephew of former Cardinals owner Sam Breadon, would be appointed by the trustees to operate the club until completion of the sale. With Saigh's intent to keep the team in St. Louis and Walsingham's experience with the team, Walsingham positioned himself as the one to watch as the sale progressed. Walsingham acknowledged his status as a player in negotiations, claiming he had been approached by financial interests willing to back him in taking over the Cardinals.[13] Walsingham added that he had met with five or six "substantial" groups interested in the Cardinals while in New York, but urged his potential backers to let him first discuss matters with Saigh.[14] For his part, Saigh offered that he preferred for Walsingham to gain control of the club.[15]

It was becoming quickly apparent, however, that Walsingham would have competition if he hoped to emerge with control of the Cardinals. Although Saigh had said the club would stay put, syndicates based in Milwaukee, Houston, and Washington expressed almost immediate interest.[16] Milwaukee and Houston groups had previously explored purchasing the Cardinals with the clear intent of relocating the team. Because of their status as tenants of the Browns, the Cardinals could be perceived as vulnerable to leaving St. Louis regardless of their greater popularity. (The Cardinals outdrew the Browns by approximately 400,000 fans in 1952.) Veeck believed St. Louis would become eventually a one-team city, and he intended for the Browns to be that team, but first he hoped the Cardinals would leave town.

Because the Cardinals were implicated in Saigh's personal tax issues, a quick sale seemed unlikely. Further, there were concerns that Saigh might establish a high price that could delay sale of the club. During the National League meeting just after Saigh was sentenced, a question was raised about what action to take if he delayed the sale of his stock or reneged on his commitment to sell. Collectively, the NL agreed that the door "already was irrevocably closed"[17] by Frick to any further participation in baseball by Saigh. While Frick could clearly act under his power to deal with conduct detrimental to baseball, he did not seem inclined to force the issue with Saigh. After all, because Saigh led the push to oust Frick's predecessor, Happy Chandler, it might have been said that Frick owed his job, at least in part, to the Cardinals owner. Frick confirmed his plan for patience toward Saigh: "I don't intend to see a deadline put on the length of the trusteeship to force Saigh to sell at a sacrifice. He has taken these steps voluntarily to avoid embarrassing baseball and we're not unappreciative."[18] Giles also announced that the league had accepted the procedure outlined by Saigh, and "[a]fter [the February 22 deadline for naming the trustees committee,] Saigh will dispose of his stock as quickly as he can. Naturally, we won't rush him into accepting an unnecessary loss."[19]

With regard to the price of the club, the starting point appeared to be the $4,060,000 for which Saigh and Hannegan acquired the Cardinals in 1947. This figure had its critics. One source within baseball, likely thinking of the Cardinals' lack of title to a stadium, thought this price might be high by $2,000,000.[20] To enhance the attractiveness of the Cardinals for possible buyers, Saigh reportedly looked into purchasing Sportsman's Park from the Browns.[21] It is difficult to imagine that he would have gotten anywhere with Veeck on that matter. Another baseball executive opined that the Cardinals' presence in Saigh's tax case brought the value down to around $3,500,000.[22] When Saigh fielded calls, he instructed prospective buyers not to bother if their offers were not in the $4,250,000 to $4,500,000 range.[23] Saigh's valuation was based largely on the Cardinals' physical assets, which he claimed were worth $3,000,000 alone. Saigh tied his estimates to the value of the Cardinals' minor-league properties, and most of that $3,000,000 was directly related to farm teams in Houston ($1,400,000); Rochester, New York ($800,000); and Columbus, Ohio ($600,000). Saigh added to that figure the excellent financial condition of the Cardinals as well as the intangible value of the team drawing fans into St. Louis from a region encompassing 11 or 12 states.[24]

By February 1 Saigh claimed to have received 30 to 40 bids[25] with most of the interest coming from outside St. Louis. Similar to other growing cities without major-league baseball, Houston wanted it. George Strake, a Houston oilman and philanthropist, seemed like the man to provide it. In fact, Strake's interest in the Cardinals preceded Saigh's ownership. In a wire-service story the day after Saigh's sentencing, Strake was quoted as saying, "I was definitely interested in the purchase of the Cardinals prior to their sale by Sam Breadon to Bob Hannegan and Fred Saigh. I have had no reason to keep up with the financial side of the Cardinals since then. Nor do I know what their present assets or liabilities are."[26] He added that he could become interested again in buying Cardinals "if it is a good business deal."[27] During the NL meeting on January 30, there were reports about a Houston group inquiring about the Cardinals, but the group was not identified. Indeed, other Houston residents who previously figured into attempts to acquire a major-league team "emphasize they knew of no recent attempts to reopen negotiations."[28] The extent of any momentum to move the Cardinals to Houston was thus unclear. The *Paris (Texas) News* appended to the wire-service story an excerpt from a *Houston Post* column mentioning that the minor-league (and Cardinals-owned) Houston Buffs were expected to operate as usual regardless of what happened to ownership of the Cardinals.[29] The *Lubbock Evening Journal* added to its story that the *Houston Post* sports editor believed Frick would assume control of the Cardinals and negotiate a sale to Walsingham.[30] If Houston wanted the Cardinals, it was not clear who would be leading the effort.

Houston was not the only source for stories related to the Cardinals. Milwaukee also figured prominently in sales news and rumors. With a new 34,000-seat stadium but no major-league team, Milwaukee desperately wanted to upgrade from the current American Association Brewers. An actual Milwaukee brewer, Frederick Miller, confirmed his prior interest in the Cardinals. Miller had previously inquired about the Boston Braves and the Browns, in addition to the Cardinals, in order to secure major-league baseball for Milwaukee. Miller claimed to have spoken to Saigh about purchasing the Cardinals in 1952 but said, "I dropped the thing right there" when Saigh quoted Miller a $4,000,000 price tag.[31] With Saigh putting the team on the market, rumors surfaced that Miller might be getting involved again through intermediaries.

Additional groups figured into news reports about the sale. Washington radio executives Howard Stanley and Nat Allbright formed a six-man syndicate to buy the Cardinals; there was no indication that their interest was tied to relocation. Although Detroit already had the Tigers, two groups with ties to the Motor City expressed interest. Sportscaster Harry Wismer headed a syndicate that wanted to move the team to Detroit. Wismer, who would become the original owner of the team that became the New York Jets, sought Frick's assistance in dealing with Tigers owner Spike Briggs, who was reluctant to share his ballpark with another club.[32] Another Detroit group, possibly including members of the Ford family, was said to be willing to operate the club in St. Louis if it could not be moved to Detroit.[33] Charles Margiotti, a former Pennsylvania attorney general, and Harold Klein, a New York lawyer representing trucking interests, also spoke with Saigh although their plans were unknown. John Jachym, a former Cardinals scout who previously headed a seven-man syndicate that bought and later sold a minority interest in the Washington Senators, expressed interest on behalf of a Pacific Coast syndicate "if the price is right."[34] Los Angeles was known to want big-league baseball. Pittsburgh real-estate man Charles Morris reported that Saigh offered his stock to him for $4,250,000.[35] A three-man Arkansas syndicate was revealed to have made an offer, but there was no indication whether their interest was tied only to enhancing their financial portfolio or if they also planned to move the team.[36]

Meanwhile, as Saigh fielded inquiries and offers for the club, he and his lawyers began negotiating with the Internal Revenue Service on February 11 to keep the Cardinals free from government liens. There were concerns that any liens could interfere with salary payments to players, trades with other clubs, and contracts with concessionaires and radio and television stations. At the center of the tax issue concerning the Cardinals was that just as Saigh and his lawyers claimed his personal tax liability was much less than the government claimed, they also contended that the Cardinals' tax liability was closer to $15,000 than the $160,000 claimed by the IRS.[37] The reason the Cardinals factored into Saigh's tax liability is that personal loans obtained by Saigh and Hannegan when they purchased the club were alleged to have been repaid by the club. The government intended to declare in anticipated civil litigation that Saigh should have reported that repayment as personal income or a constructive dividend.[38] Because the repayment of those loans reduced the corporate tax paid by the Cardinals, the club also had added tax liability. Government lawyers, however, seemed reluctant to place restraints on Cardinals operations, and Saigh's lawyers told them that any back taxes and penalties related to the Cardinals would be agreed on in any contract for the sale of club. Saigh's lawyers planned to offer to post a bond or sum of money equal to the highest figure claimed by the IRS in order to keep the Cardinals free of liens through the sale. Remaining mindful of his personal May 4 deadline for reporting to prison, Saigh hoped a successful resolution of the Cardinals' tax issues would hasten completion of the sale.

As IRS negotiations continued, Saigh spoke dismissively in public about those who had reached out to him by that point, grumbling about a lack of progress in negotiations and complaining that only publicity seekers had contacted him.[39] Saigh also had yet to name his proposed trustees committee. Saigh's apparent insistence on sticking to a $4,250,000 price tag for the Cardinals may also have contributed to the delay. Saigh was expected to announce his trustees committee on February 20, still ahead of his original deadline. Giles confirmed that Saigh had yet to submit names for league approval but added, "We are assuming he will carry forth on the program he volunteered to us."[40]

Saigh would not have to follow through on his commitment to appoint a trustees committee. On the day he was expected to announce his appointments, another announcement revealed Anheuser-Busch's plans to purchase the Cardinals. Brewery president August Busch Jr. would become president of the ballclub and retain Walsingham as vice president and operating head of the baseball organization. Saigh would receive significantly less than the $4,250,000 upon which he was reputedly insisting. The purchase price was $3,750,000; of that, $2,500,000 would be paid to Saigh and $1,250,000 represented assumption of debt. Saigh claimed to be satisfied, and Giles announced that the NL had already approved the deal. Busch was slated to take over on March 11 after the expected approval by Anheuser-Busch shareholders.

During the Anheuser-Busch press conference, Saigh confirmed that he had received offers that might have resulted in the Cardinals leaving St. Louis.[41] He characterized local interest as "purely speculative."[42] Local bankers David Calhoun and James Hickok entered the scene on Busch's behalf, with apparent instructions to watch the situation and take any necessary steps to keep the Cardinals in town.[43] Calhoun and Hickok offered that Saigh "said he would even be willing to make a sacrifice if it were possible to have the Cardinals remain in St. Louis."[44] Saigh said that "[w]hen it became apparent that an out-of-town group was ready to purchase the Cardinals at a price which I felt was a fair value for the club, I informed Mr. Busch and his associates of the impending sale. They expressed their serious interest in having the club remain here."[45]

After the press conference, additional details emerged about the groups that had sought to purchase the Cardinals and move them. A Milwaukee syndicate was understood to have had the inside track on winning the bidding for the team. The possibility of a deal being reached must have been serious enough, because Cardinals front office employees were told two weeks before the Anheuser-Busch announcement that their expenses would be paid if they wished to move to Milwaukee.[46] During the Anheuser-Busch stockholder meeting on March 11 to approve the purchase, brewery vice president John Wilson revealed that a Milwaukee group had offered $4,100,000 for the Cardinals. Indeed, Saigh had made arrangements to travel to New York on February 13 to obtain approval to sell the club to a Milwaukee group.[47] To be sure, the decision to sell the Cardinals and move them to Milwaukee was not a choice only for Saigh and the Milwaukee syndicate. Two NL clubs were believed to have opposed the move.[48] Moreover, the Milwaukee bid was conditioned upon NL approval to move the team as well as American Association approval to shift the minor-league Brewers to another city.[49] Considering that Boston Braves owner Lou Perini owned the Brewers—and, as events would prove, was considering his own options—Saigh would have had work to do to accommodate potential Milwaukee buyers. When the Anheuser-Busch transaction went through, this group turned its attention to the Browns, who would undergo their own relocation drama over the following year.

Houston interests were also negotiating with Saigh. One syndicate was headed by George Kirksey, a public relations executive in Houston and a former sportswriter. Saigh disclosed later that two Texas groups had made creditable bids for the Cardinals,[50] one of which was Kirksey's. Kirksey visited St. Louis in early February with a proposal for Anheuser-Busch to sponsor Cardinals broadcasts if Houston acquired the team.[51] His group was believed to have made an eleventh-hour attempt to outbid Anheuser-Busch, and subsequently requested consideration if that deal fell through. Just as National League approval to move the Cardinals to Milwaukee was not a given, relocation to Houston would have posed a different set of issues. Giles pointed out his own doubts that enough clubs would favor moving to any city outside the immediate area of the current circuit. While Milwaukee fit within the existing footprint of major-league baseball in the early 1950s, Houston did not. Giles suggested that "[c]ities aspiring for major league membership must reach for their goal through the organization of a third big league, rather than by incorporating in the present circuits."[52] Later in the decade, a number of cities pursued the possibility of the third major league, and Giles appeared to offer an open invitation to a new circuit.

The Cardinals' sale to Anheuser-Busch contributed to a chain of events that would remake the baseball map. To Veeck, it was clear that because he could not run Anheuser-Busch out of St. Louis, he would not run the Cardinals out of town either. Within a month of the announcement of the sale, the American League rebuffed Veeck's request to move the Browns to Baltimore. The Browns would play a lame-duck season at Sportsman's Park as an Anheuser-Busch tenant after Veeck sold the stadium. Milwaukee would have major-league baseball in 1953, when Perini secured NL approval to move the Braves from Boston. The Braves' first game at Milwaukee County Stadium was played against the Cardinals. There would be no Houston Cardinals, and the booming oil city would have to wait until 1962 for big-league baseball. As for Fred Saigh, he kept his appointment with federal prison. Seeing what baseball would do for Anheuser-Busch, Saigh bought a large block of brewery stock shortly after his release. That transaction would make him a millionaire many times over through ownership of stock in the company that owned the team he never wanted to sell.

SOURCES

In addition to the sources in the Notes, the author also consulted:

Veeck, Bill (with Ed Linn). *Veeck as in Wreck: The Autobiography of Bill Veeck* (Chicago: University of Chicago Press, 2001).

NOTES

1. "Saigh Pleads No Contest to 2 Tax Evasion Counts, U.S. Would Drop 3 Others," *St. Louis Post-Dispatch*, January 28, 1953: 1A.
2. Ibid.
3. Harold Tuthill, "Saigh Predicts Cards Pennant in '53, Praises Rookie Crop," *St. Louis Post-Dispatch*, December 24, 1953: 8A.
4. Ibid.
5. Peter Golenbock, *The Spirit of St. Louis: A History of the St. Louis Cardinals and Browns* (New York: Dey Street Books, 2001), 397.
6. "Saigh Gets Jail Term; Cardinals' Fate Moot," *New York Times*, January 29, 1953: 1.
7. "Saigh Gets 15-Month Term, Fined $15,000; Walsingham May Take Over Cardinals," *St. Louis Post-Dispatch*, January 29, 1953: 3A.
8. Ibid.
9. Ibid.
10. "Saigh to Set Up Citizens' Group to Run Cardinals Until He Sells," *St. Louis Post-Dispatch*, January 30, 1953: 1A.
11. Ibid.
12. Ibid.
13. Ibid.
14. "Saigh Offers Harper Apology for Remarks on Television Show," *St. Louis Post-Dispatch*, January 31, 1953: 7A; "Saigh Back in City, Meets Heavy List of Prospective Cardinal Buyers," *St. Louis Post-Dispatch*, February 2, 1953: 3A.
15. "Saigh Offers Harper Apology."
16. "Saigh to Set Up Citizens' Group": 4A.
17. "Saigh Drops Out of Organized Baseball After Meeting With Frick and Giles," *New York Times*, January 31, 1953: 19.
18. "Saigh Offers Harper Apology."
19. Dan Daniel, "3 Trustees to Be Named to Run Club," *The Sporting News*, February 11, 1953: 5.
20. Bob Broeg, "Birds 'Sound Organization,' Declares V-P," *The Sporting News*, February 4, 1953: 12.
21. Oscar K. Ruhl, "Settlement of $558,901 Tax Claims on Saigh Discussed," *The Sporting News*, February 18, 1953: 14.
22. "Saigh Back in City."
23. "Saigh Offers Harper Apology."
24. "$4,250,000 'Fair' Asking Price for Cardinals, Saigh Contends," *St. Louis Post-Dispatch*, February 5, 1953: 5A.
25. "Ford Family, Harry Wismer Listed Among Prospective Cardinal Buyers," *The Sporting News*, February 11, 1953: 5.
26. "Strake Is Still Interested in Buying Cardinals," *Bryan (Texas) Daily Eagle*, January 29, 1953: 8.
27. Ibid.
28. Ibid.
29. "Texan May Bring Cardinals to Houston, If Price Okay," *Paris (Texas) News*, January 29, 1953: 16.
30. "Sale of Cardinals Expected After Owner Is Sentenced," *Lubbock (Texas) Evening Journal*, January 29, 1953: 8.
31. "Miller Kept on Trying for Big Time Ball," *The Sporting News*, April 1, 1953: 7.
32. "Wismer to Seek Frick's Aid," *New York Times*, February 4, 1953: 35.
33. "Ford Family, Harry Wismer Listed."
34. "Saigh Begins Preliminary Talks With Possible Buyers of Cardinals," *St. Louis Post-Dispatch*, February 3, 1953: 3A.
35. "Ford Family, Harry Wismer Listed."
36. "Arkansas Financiers in Bid for Cardinal Club," *Bryan (Texas) Daily Eagle*, February 20, 1953: 11.
37. "Saigh Thinks U.S. Tax Claim of $558,901 Is Much Too High," *St. Louis Post-Dispatch*, February 9, 1953: 3A.
38. "Talks Under Way on Settlement of $558.901 U.S. Tax Claim on Saigh," *St. Louis Post-Dispatch*, February 11, 1953: 1A.
39. Ruhl.
40. "Saigh Believed Ready to Name Trustee Board," *St. Louis Post-Dispatch*, February 19, 1953: 3A.
41. "Cards Kept in St. Louis by Sale to Busch," *The Sporting News*, February 25, 1953: 3.
42. Ibid.
43. Ibid. Saigh later credited the two bankers with convincing Busch to buy the Cardinals for the benefit of the brewery, disputing accounts that Busch was the driving force behind buying the Cardinals to keep them in St. Louis. See Golenbock, 397.
44. "Cards Kept in St. Louis."
45. Ibid.
46. "Cardinals Ball Club Sold to Anheuser-Busch Inc. by Fred Saigh for $3,750,000," *St. Louis Post-Dispatch*, February 20, 1953: 4C.
47. Ibid.
48. John Wray, "Wray's Column," *St. Louis Post-Dispatch*, February 22, 1953: 2F.

49 Ray Gillespie, "Busch Ready to Be 'Active' Boss of Redbirds," *The Sporting News*, March 4, 1953: 8.

50 Golenbock, 397.

51 "Texas Group Wanted Busch to Buy Cards' Radio Rights," *The Sporting News*, March 4, 1953: 10.

52 "No Chance for N.L. Club to Shift Now, Says Giles," *The Sporting News*, March 4, 1953: 2.

ANHEUSER-BUSCH BUYS THE ST. LOUIS CARDINALS

BY RUSS LAKE

THE PLAYERS ON THE TRAIN CARRYing the St. Louis Cardinals back to Union Station should have been vibrant and fun-loving as it rolled through the Land of Lincoln on October 2, 1949. The Redbirds had thumped the Chicago Cubs, 13-5, at Wrigley Field in the season finale that afternoon. Thanks to a thrilling pennant race, the 1949 Cardinals set a home attendance mark of 1,430,676 at Sportsman's Park, but they came up short again and suffered their third straight second-place finish in the National League. They lost by a single game to the Brooklyn Dodgers after dropping six of their last nine games. Most of the players sat in the private parlor car with their eyes closed thinking about lost chances over the prior 10 days. Manager Eddie Dyer talked softly with his wife in a closed compartment, and wondered how long it might be before his team would get this close again.[1] Farther down the tracks, their landlord, the St. Louis Browns, wrapped up a dismal season of their own by losing 101 games while drawing fewer than 271,000 spectators. Although the two franchises paired to win five pennants and three world championships in the 1940s, those seasons of glory seemed far behind in the rearview mirror when the calendar turned to a new decade.

The 1950 Cardinals finished fifth and fell into the second division for the first time since 1938, while the Browns maintained their losing ways in both games and attendance. The Browns seemed to graciously shrug at the "laughing stock" slogan attached to them — "First in shoes, first in booze, and last in the American League."[2] As different managers came and went for both Mound City squads during the next couple of seasons, a war of nerves between the two team presidents also broke out and festered. In the most noteworthy squabbles, new Browns owner Bill Veeck demanded that the Cardinals' Fred Saigh sign a new ballpark lease, and Veeck snatched up Cardinals pitcher Harry "The Cat" Brecheen for double the salary Saigh was paying him. Saigh later claimed that the Browns had tampered with Brecheen before the Cardinals released the veteran southpaw at the end of the 1952 season.[3]

In actuality, the maverick mannerisms of Veeck, along with his multiple Barnum & Bailey promotion tactics seeking to woo area fans to the Brownies, were the least of Saigh's worries. Saigh had been indicted by a grand jury earlier in the year for federal income-tax evasion, and despite proclaiming his innocence of the charges in an article in the *St. Louis Post-Dispatch*, had to consider selling the Cardinals. "The Cardinals are a great ballclub and I would not want them to be hurt in any way even though I believe that I will be completely vindicated," Saigh said. "I don't have this coming to me. I'm completely shocked because I understood that a settlement was being made. I'd better say no more until I see my lawyer."[4]

The citizens of St. Louis and its metropolitan area had embraced a pair of major-league baseball teams for 50 years, but they were now perplexed as they read about the possibility that one or both might be sold and leave town. Rumors periodically circulated either about baseball teams relocating or about a third league forming to satisfy the growing number of cities wanting professional baseball. Lou Perini, the beleaguered owner of the Boston Braves, certainly made baseball fans think about other deserving locales when he voiced his concerns and projections to *The Sporting News:* "The country is ripe for (a third major league). Eventually it is going to happen. Such cities as Houston, Toronto, Montreal, Milwaukee, and the areas surrounding San Francisco and Los Angeles can support one."[5] During a late-summer automobile trip to the Southwest, Saigh listened to a solid financial proposal from Houston investors for the sale and transfer of the Cardinals to Texas. Saigh declined their overture and stated, "The Cardinals have been nurtured through the years by a tremendously loyal audience in the Midwest area. So long as it's within my power, I'll never desert St. Louis for the money involved in any proposed transfer. No, money would not be the deciding factor. There would have to be other considerations more important, considerations I don't care to go into."[6]

As January 28 1953, the time to defend himself in court, approached, Saigh remained committed to St. Louis. After consultation with his lawyer, Saigh, not wanting a lengthy jury trial, decided to switch his plea from not guilty to nolo contendere in hopes of a lighter sentence. His decision backfired in the worst way when the judge, in a surprise judgment, sentenced him to 15 months in federal prison and fined him $15,000. Saigh staggered toward the bench and pleaded that his aged mother would be alone, but Judge Roy Harper snapped at him and reminded him what his no contest meant.[7] Harper, who had once been employed as the business manager of a lower-level Cardinals farm club,[8] showed no favors and gave Saigh four months to get his personal and business affairs in order before his sentence began.[9]

Saigh met with Commissioner Ford Frick in New York during the winter meetings, and later announced that he would divest himself of his treasured ballclub for the good of baseball. The commissioner agreed with Saigh's plan to appoint a three-member committee of civic-minded people from St. Louis to run the club until the sale. Frick acknowledged his admiration for the embattled Saigh. "He is doing this to spare baseball any repercussions and we salute him for it," the commissioner said. "He certainly was entitled to bow out of baseball with all the grace possible under these unfortunate circumstances."[10]

Veteran Cardinals All-Star Stan Musial said he understood that "business was business," but added that he felt sorry for Saigh and wondered what was down the road for the team.[11] The beleaguered Saigh analyzed several local bids for the Cardinals, but determined that none of them would work out. Just before spring training in 1953, a Milwaukee syndicate swiftly worked themselves in as the front-runners to buy the club. A sale approved by National League owners would result in the franchise being transferred to the "beer and cheese capital" in Wisconsin. It was early February and Saigh knew he had little time left to get a purchase arrangement that he felt was acceptable, so he told his St. Louis office employees that they would be paid for moving expenses and compensated for losses selling their homes since it appeared Milwaukee would be acquiring the team.[12]

As Saigh prepared to return to the Big Apple to meet with Frick and get the sale to the Milwaukee group approved, he was suddenly asked to postpone his trip because a new St. Louis entity was prepared to negotiate with him. Saigh agreed to halt his business plans after he learned that David H. Calhoun, president of St. Louis Union Trust Company, and James P. Hickok, executive vice president of First National Bank, were representing Anheuser-Busch to discuss a sale of the Cardinals to the brewery. The two well-known area businessmen, who had both been considered for the commissioner's approved three-person civic committee, convinced Saigh that Anheuser-Busch had a serious interest in acquiring the ballclub to keep it in St. Louis. Saigh laid out his request to Calhoun and Hickok and stated that he would take less money than the Milwaukee group had offered. (It was later announced to be about $4 million.[13])

A deal was readily consummated and a 6:00 A.M. press conference to announce the sale agreement was scheduled for February 20 at First National Bank downtown. The early hour was to allow the *St. Louis Post-Dispatch* to fully report the proceedings in its evening edition.[14] The elaborate session was staged in the bank's sixth-floor directors room. In addition to local newspaper and wire services, area radio and television stations were there. As the "changing of the guard" commenced, Saigh stood and opened with a timeline to describe how the Anheuser-Busch offer to purchase the team and keep it in St. Louis had been conveyed to him.[15]

Fifty-three-year-old August A. Busch Jr., president of the brewery, would assume the same role with the Cardinals on March 11 after a vote by the Anheuser-Busch stockholders. Busch began his formal statement with these words: "During its 100 years of existence, Anheuser-Busch has shared in all St. Louis civic activity. The Cardinals, like ourselves, are a St. Louis institution. We hope to make the Cardinals one of the greatest baseball teams of all times, and we propose to further develop our farm clubs." William Walsingham Jr., the nephew of the late Cardinals owner Sam Breadon, would retain his position as vice president and operating head of the baseball organization. Several directors of Anheuser-Busch and legal counsel of the brewery were in attendance. This was the first time that the Cardinals would be owned by a corporation rather than a single owner or a small group of investors. Busch said the Cardinals would not sell stock to the public.[16]

National League President Warren Giles journeyed from Cincinnati to be present at the proceedings and had already approved the transaction between Saigh and the brewery. Giles said: "The sale of the Cardinals was appropriate and beneficial to St. Louis, the Cardinals and the National League. It was appropriate that an institution like Anheuser-Busch would identify itself with the Cardinals. I am glad to welcome Busch and his associates to the National League and to baseball." Giles was quizzed about any obstacles from other team owners and responded that he saw no problem with approval of the sale. He said that had the Cardinals been sold to someone who wanted to relocate the club, it would have been necessary to receive unanimous consent from all National League clubs to move forward.[17] Although Busch was known as a sportsman within the high-society circles, it was with show horses and hunting clubs, so the personal welcome to the sport of baseball from Giles was beneficial.[18] Longtime comrades and acquaintances referred to Busch as "Colonel" or "Gus," which is what he preferred over "Augie" or "Gussie."[19]

Saigh appeared very subdued after his initial narrative of the transaction, but he did answer several questions pertaining to monetary details of the sale. The total financial outlay from Anheuser-Busch was headlined as $3.75 million with Saigh receiving $2.5 million, which was what he had requested. Busch confirmed that the brewery would assume $1.25 million in debt, and Saigh acknowledged that he had deposited $1 million in escrow to guard the new ownership against additional liabilities. Busch seemed well informed as he replied to myriad queries with short but ardent responses. He said the Anheuser-Busch purchase of the Cardinals was done completely from a sports angle and was not a product sales weapon, and that he would honor the rival Griesedieck Brothers beer-sponsorship contract of Cardinals radio broadcasts. Sportsman's Park was not part of the transaction since it was owned by the Browns, with whom the Cardinals had a secure stadium lease guaranteed through 1960. Busch wished the Browns luck in the coming season and said he hoped they remained in St. Louis. Busch indicated that he would be active in the management of the Cardinals, and he endorsed incumbent manager Eddie Stanky. He said he would be heading to St. Petersburg, Florida, soon to watch the team participate in spring training.[20]

KSD Radio, owned by the *Post-Dispatch*, taped the press conference and scheduled a playback of the event for 7:00 P.M.[21] KSD-TV, also owned by the newspaper, filmed an interview to be broadcast later in the morning introducing Busch. KSD special-events director and newscaster Frank Eschen was flanked on his right by Saigh, with Saigh's attorney just behind him. Busch and Warren Giles stood on Eschen's left as the interview commenced. Eschen first received a concise statement from Saigh that he had indeed sold the Cardinals. As Eschen shifted to move the microphone and speak to Busch, Saigh forlornly placed his hands on his hips, bowed his head, and slipped off-camera to his right, but apparently had his escape pathway blocked. Saigh looked back to see that his lawyer had turned left and was squeezing awkwardly behind the three men who were in front of a large backdrop curtain. With no option to move out of the way, an obviously distraught Saigh drooped his shoulders and followed his attorney for an unplanned "out with old, in with new" scene as the camera rolled and Eschen's dialog continued.[22]

Eschen commented, "Now, congratulations are in order for you, Colonel Busch, for the fine thing that you have done in buying the St. Louis Cardinals." Busch replied, "Well, thank you very much. We are delighted to be the owners of the Cardinals, and we are going to start to give the fans everywhere the finest baseball that is known in the United States." Eschen concluded, "Well, I'm sure that you will fully live up to the old Cardinal tradition."[23] Busch had little time to process what Eschen might have meant by "the old Cardinal tradition" because a brewery associate had leaned in to inform him that he and his entourage were late for a tour of the administrative offices at Sportsman's Park and to meet several employees of the ballclub.

Busch excused himself and returned to the room where the papers had been signed to retrieve a fountain pen. Unknowingly, he walked in on Fred Saigh sitting alone at the table, with his hands over his face, sobbing. Busch never told anyone about witnessing this until years later.[24] As Busch entered the car for his ride to the ballpark, he thought back to how he eventually sold the idea of purchasing the St. Louis Cardinals to the brewery's board of directors the week before. He had convinced them with an entirely different vision than what he had stated at the morning's press conference. When Busch concluded the closed-door presentation to the brewery leaders, he emphatically predicted, "Development of the Cardinals will have untold value for our company. This is one of the finest moves in the history of Anheuser-Busch."[25]

Meanwhile, team officials had contacted Cardinals manager Eddie Stanky at St. Petersburg during morning spring-training drills. Stanky, starting his second season as the Redbirds' skipper, was asked to be in his office at Al Lang Field for a phone call in the early afternoon. With no knowledge of what had taken place in St. Louis, he assumed a player deal was in the making. When Stanky answered the telephone, it was Fred Saigh on the line explaining that he had sold the club to Anheuser-Busch. Stanky asked Saigh if he was satisfied with the deal, and Saigh replied in the affirmative. Stanky, who was under contract through 1954, responded to Saigh, "Then it's all right with me. I'm very sorry, as you know, that you had to do this." Stanky was grateful to Saigh for giving him his first opportunity to manage a major-league club, saying later, "Our relations were extremely pleasant. There was never one iota of interference with the operation of the club on the field. If my relations with the new owners are half as good as they were with Mr. Saigh, it will be 100 percent satisfactory." Stanky also spoke briefly to Busch and John Wilson, an officer of the brewery, and said he was happy for them before inviting both to the club's training camp.[26] Busch had affirmed earlier that he felt Stanky was one of the best managers in the game.[27]

Player reaction to the sale ranged from reflective to tongue-in-cheek. Veteran second baseman Red Schoendienst recalled, "Before Busch bought the Cardinals, he had Stan and I and [traveling secretary] Leo Ward out to his hunting lodge for lunch. We were talking about the ballclub, and what was going happen to the franchise, and both Stan and I suggested that Busch buy the team. His response was that he didn't know much about baseball, but I wonder if he already had been thinking about it and just wanted to see what our reaction would be."[28] A pair of unidentified St. Louis players were a bit loose with their retorts. "I guess if we go into a tailspin, they'll call us the 'Busch' team of the league," said one. Another jokingly said, "I always liked that Budweiser. Hey, do you think they'll take the Redbirds off our uniforms and put beer bottles there?"[29]

Busch got to Sportsman's Park for his planned visit to the team headquarters nearly an hour late. Bill Veeck had been waiting in his Browns office for a courtesy visit from Busch, but now, pressed for time, he took it upon himself to walk over to the Cardinals outer offices to meet his new intracity rival. Busch was summoned and the two owners warmly shook hands. Veeck said, "It's nice to have you. We're glad to see you. But I'm afraid you're going to offer us some difficult competition." Busch replied with a grin, "You're right." Glancing around the workplace surroundings with piqued interest, Veeck offered, "You know this is the first time I've ever been in this office." Busch replied, "Well, it's my first time too."

Noting that he had an apartment in the ballpark, Veeck said, "You know I live right next door, you must come and see me." Busch responded, "You bet your sweet life I will. You've got to come see me and we must visit each other often." With that, the two men shook hands again, and Veeck departed for a downtown appointment.[30]

As he moved rapidly through the two floors of the Cardinals offices, Busch's main interest in the building was whether it was fireproof. He looked closely at the names on the large blackboards and listened intently as Cardinals scout Joe Monahan and minor-league director Joe Mathes explained the rosters and the method by which players were transferred from one team to another. Busch posed for several pictures with team employees. Fred Saigh, who was present for the orientation, declined to be in any of the photographs.[31]

In his last act as owner of the Cardinals, Saigh went to St. Petersburg on March 8 to talk with Stanky, watch a game against the New York Yankees, and speak briefly with the players about the sale.[32] Busch had ventured to Hot Springs, Arkansas, for 10 days' rest before traveling to Florida to see his squad in action. Busch donned a Cardinals cap and uniform shirt, grabbed a bat, and took some practice swings against relief pitcher Eddie Yuhas. When he did not connect with the soft tosses delivered by Yuhas from about 30 feet away, Stanky cracked that Yuhas might find himself on another club if Busch didn't hit the next one.[33] Busch delivered a clubhouse talk to the team, attended games, and visited the Cardinals' minor-league camps in Daytona Beach, Florida, and Albany, Georgia.[34] Since a slight rift had developed in St. Petersburg regarding the Cardinals' lease, Busch met with Mayor Sam Johnson and local baseball ambassador Al Lang to get a new agreement in the works to continue at the longtime spring training facility.[35]

Busch returned to St. Louis to make an early April inspection of Sportsman's Park before the season began, and demonstrated that he had not paid much attention to his surroundings in the few times he had attended a major-league baseball game in St. Louis. After scrutinizing the grim conditions of the concession areas and the restrooms, he rasped, "I'd rather have my ballclub play in Forest Park."[36] Busch was appalled at how small and decrepit the ballpark seemed, and lectured associates about how ashamed he would be to bring his friends out to the ballpark. An angry Busch made a list of demands to his landlord to fix the place up, but Veeck said that he had no money to do anything.[37] The warmth the men had shown several weeks earlier had just turned frigid, and the future of "Baseball in St. Loo" would quickly shift to an unforeseen, but predictable pathway.

SOURCES

In addition to the sources cited in the Notes, the author accessed Retrosheet.org, Baseball-Reference.com, SABR.org/bioproj, and *The Sporting News* archive via Paper of Record. Additional websites accessed were newspapers.com and stltoday.com.

NOTES

1. Stan Musial, as told to Bob Broeg, *The Man Stan: Musial, Then and Now* (St. Louis: Bethany Press, 1977), 139.
2. Evault Boswell, "The Bad News Browns," *Missouri Life*, May 2016. missourilife.com/life/the-bad-news-browns/, accessed September 15, 2016.
3. Ray Gillespie, "Bill Veeck Is 'Trying to Laugh Brecheen Case Out of Court,' Says Fred Saigh, Filing Charges," *The Sporting News*, November 12, 1952: 9.
4. "Saigh to Put His Baseball Future Up to Frick, Giles; Indicted on Tax Charge," *St. Louis Post-Dispatch*, April 24, 1952: 1.
5. Clif Keane, "Perini Gives Hub Two Years to Back Braves," *The Sporting News*, October 1, 1952: 1, 6.
6. Bob Broeg, "Houston Bid for Major Club Five Years Too Early — Saigh," *The Sporting News*, November 5, 1952: 7.
7. Bob Broeg, *Memories of a Hall of Fame Sportswriter* (Champaign, Illinois: Sagamore Publishing, 1995), 218.
8. Ray Gillespie, "Judge Who Sentenced Saigh Was Card Farm Executive," *The Sporting News*, February 4, 1953: 12.
9. Ray Gillespie, "Owner Given 15 Months, $15,000 Fine," *The Sporting News*, February 4, 1953: 11.
10. Dan Daniel, "Saigh Studies Flock of Bids for Cards," *The Sporting News*, February 11, 1953: 5.
11. Musial as told to Broeg, 148.
12. Rob Rains, *The St. Louis Cardinals, the 100th Anniversary History* (New York: St. Martin's Press, 1992), 128.

13. "Cardinals Ball Club Sold to Anheuser-Busch," *St. Louis Post-Dispatch*, February 20, 1953: 4.
14. Broeg, *Memories of a Hall of Fame Sportswriter*, 219.
15. "Cardinals Ball Club Sold."
16. Ibid.
17. "Cardinals Ball Club Sold to Anheuser-Busch Inc. by Fred Saigh for $3,750,000," *St. Louis Post-Dispatch*, February 20, 1953: 1.
18. "New Cardinals President Busch Long Active in Field Sports," *St. Louis Post-Dispatch*, February 20, 1953: 4.
19. Broeg, *Memories of a Hall of Fame Sportswriter*, 221.
20. *St. Louis Post-Dispatch*, February 20, 1953: 1.
21. "Cardinals Ball Club Sold."
22. Video Production, *St. Louis Cardinals, A Century Of Success, 100 Years of Cardinals Glory* (St. Louis Cardinals and Major League Baseball Properties, Inc., 1992).
23. Ibid.
24. Peter Hernon and Terry Ganey, *Under the Influence, the Unauthorized Story of the Anheuser-Busch Dynasty* (New York: Simon & Schuster, 1991), 212.
25. Hernon and Ganey, 213.
26. J. Roy Stockton, "Cardinals Look Forward to New Owner's Visit to Florida Training Camp," *St. Louis Post-Dispatch*, February 21, 1953: 6.
27. *St. Louis Post-Dispatch*, February 20, 1953: 1.
28. Red Schoendienst with Rob Rains, *Red: A Baseball Life* (Champaign, Illinois: Sports Publishing, 1998), 71.
29. J. Roy Stockton, *St. Louis Post-Dispatch*, February 21, 1953: 6.
30. "August Busch Jr. Visits Cardinals' Offices, Takes Over March 11," *St. Louis Post-Dispatch*, February 21, 1953: 1.
31. *St. Louis Post-Dispatch*, February 21, 1953: 4.
32. Dan Daniel, "Saigh, in Farewell to Game, Foresees End of Two-Club Ball in Three Cities," *The Sporting News*, March 18, 1953: 9.
33. Red Byrd, "'We're Behind You on Every Play,' Busch Assures Cards," *The Sporting News*, March 25, 1953: 11.
34. Red Byrd, "Busch Inspects Cardinals' Farm Camp at Albany, Ga.," *The Sporting News*, March 18, 1953: 9.
35. Frederick G. Lieb, "'Busch Heals St. Pete Rift With Redbirds," *The Sporting News*, March 25, 1953: 11.
36. Broeg, *Memories of a Hall of Fame Sportswriter*, 221.
37. Peter Golenbock, *The Spirit of St. Louis, A History of the St. Louis Cardinals and Browns* (New York: Avon Books, Inc., 2000), 405.

BEER AND OPULENCE – THE DAY THE BALLPARK IN ST. LOUIS HAD THREE DIFFERENT NAMES

BY PHILLIP BOLDA

ON FRIDAY, APRIL 10, 1953, AUGUST Anheuser "Gussie" Busch Jr., head of the firm that purchased the St. Louis Cardinals from Fred Saigh less than two months earlier, announced that the Anheuser-Busch brewery had also purchased Sportsman's Park for $1.1 million from Bill Veeck, the owner of St. Louis Browns.

He said the park would be known as Budweiser Stadium, in honor of the brewery's chief product. But before the day ended, he revised his announcement—the ballpark would actually be known as Busch Stadium "in memory of the founder and past presidents of Anheuser-Busch Inc. Realizing that Budweiser is a brand name of our product, we decided the name would not be appropriate."[1]

What happened that day has long been an object of speculation, and for some, "Budweiser Stadium" has come to represent the moment the "deep pockets" of corporate world would change baseball. Budweiser Stadium is still cited as the tipping point, and comes up in discussions of the public's distaste for the corporate naming of public stadiums. Gussie Busch was seen as a lout who had never sat through an entire nine-inning game—but through modern practices of corporate marketing and public relations he was later portrayed as a conservator preserving the very best traditions of the game.

Al Fleishman, co-founder of Fleishman-Hillard, a St. Louis public-relations firm, remembered doing a considerable amount of damage control as a participant in the purchase of the Cardinals and Sportsman's Park. Gussie, Fleishman noted later, had actually signed the papers to purchase the Cardinals without informing the Anheuser-Busch board, or many members of the Busch family.[2]

Among civic leaders in St. Louis it was said, "Gussie Busch didn't say good morning unless Al Fleishman told him to. Fleishman became become an important St. Louis civic leader while successfully managing the images of Gussie Busch, the Busch family, and the Cardinals.[3]

Reaction to Gussie Busch's initial announcement didn't stop when he backed away from the new name. It was a flashpoint for those who opposed corporate ownership, the rapid commercialization of the game, and the fusing of baseball and beer. They cynically noted that Gussie soon introduced Busch Bavarian Beer to once again bring the ballpark and his product together.

And for those who knew the business side of baseball in 1953, it must have been seen as a nearly unforgivable self-inflicted wound. Gussie Busch's coming to baseball had meant swallowing the idea that, for the first time, a franchise would operate as a subsidiary of large corporation. Gussie Busch was president of the team, not the sole owner. Behind him stood a marketing behemoth that cared only how baseball could better sell beer.

Founded by Gussie's grandfather Adolphus, Anheuser-Busch was second to Schlitz in 1954 and was not even the dominant beer in Sportsman's Park. St. Louis-based Falstaff beer sponsored the Browns radio broadcasts and was prominent among scoreboard advertisers; another brewery in the Gateway City, Griesedieck, sponsored the Cardinals. But under Gussie Busch—and with a successful presence in baseball—Anheuser-Busch became the largest brewer in the United States and remained so for the next 50 years.

As the weekend began, the *St. Louis Post Dispatch* printed a critical editorial complaining about "making a sandwich board of Sportsman's Park."[4] The Metropolitan Church Federation of St. Louis, already uneasy about brewery ownership of the Cardinals, expressed outrage at naming a ballpark for a brand of beer.[5] Those targeting baseball's antitrust issues included political leaders from cities clamoring for major-league franchises of their own. And much of the public perceived the beer industry as somehow dishonest, crass, or even immoral.

Baseball Commissioner Ford Frick reportedly knew of Gussie Busch's original announcement half an hour before it was made.[6] He made no public comment on that day and it is not known if he ever spoke directly to Busch on the matter, although the press generally gave him the credit for Busch's quick reversal.

Events in St. Louis baseball had required Frick's intervention for weeks. He spent considerable time persuading Busch to set up a new corporate entity to govern the franchise that—although owned by the brewery—would act as a buffer from the appearance of direct corporate control.

It had been Frick's edict that forced Fred Saigh, who faced a prison sentence from federal court for tax evasion, to sell the Cardinals to Busch at a fire-sale price in February 1953. Busch's deep pockets quieted rumors of a move of the Cardinals to another city, but also pushed the Browns out, making the first franchise shifts in major-league baseball in 50 years inevitable.

A few weeks before selling Sportsman's Park, Bill Veeck attempted to move the St. Louis Browns to Milwaukee. Frick, pressured by Boston Braves owner Lou Perini, blocked the move. On March 13, 1953, Perini moved his Braves to Milwaukee. Veeck was stranded in Busch Stadium for the 1953 season before selling the Browns to local Baltimore owners, who moved the team and renamed them the Orioles in 1954.

Federal antitrust laws prevented breweries from being their own distributors or owning their own taverns or beer gardens. The end of Prohibition left a flurry of state and local laws regulating the sale and consumption of alcohol. Baseball's own antitrust issues also loomed large. In the 1940s a number of players had bolted major-league baseball and signed with the Mexican League, including Cardinals pitchers Max Lanier and Fred Martin and infielder Lou Klein. Frick's predecessor, Happy Chandler, suspended the players when they attempted to return to major-league baseball. Legal actions by those players resulted in head-on challenges to baseball's reserve clause. Chandler had withdrawn the player suspensions in 1949 when faced with defeat in federal court. But baseball's legal structure had been shown to be vulnerable.

Busch's combination of beer and baseball precipitated even more federal attention when the US Senate examined legislation to make the antitrust laws applicable to teams affiliated with the alcoholic beverage industry—namely, the St. Louis Cardinals. The purchase of the Cardinals had particularly raised the ire of Colorado Senator Edwin Johnson. Citing the team's stadium—now rechristened Busch Stadium—and the Clydesdale-drawn wagon on the playing field, Johnson charged that the franchise was a subsidiary of the brewer, and exclaimed, "Mr. Busch's lavish and vulgar display of beer wealth and beer opulence in the operation of the Cardinal Ball Club should disturb baseball greatly."[7]

Johnson proposed legislation to block the sale of the team to Anheuser-Busch and threatened Gussie Busch with a subpoena from the Senate Judiciary Committee.[8] (Senator Johnson convened his subcommittee in April 1954 for hearing on a revised version of the bill, stripping the antitrust exemption from any baseball franchise owned by a corporation. The hearing featured testimony from Cardinals catcher Joe Garagiola regarding player contracts. The bill did not move forward to the Senate.)[9]

Not coincidentally, Senator Johnson was the president of the Denver Bears of the Western League, and the league's treasurer. He had been concerned that the rapid expansion of national television broadcasts of major-league games and radio broadcasts through the ad hoc networks set up by the Cardinals would "encroach" upon the minors.[10] Johnson had been a speaker at the New York baseball writers' dinner in February, where he threatened to expose major-league baseball as a "cruel and heartless monopoly."[11]

The Sporting News had responded by calling Johnson an "articulate spokesman" for the interests of baseball fans.[12]

Fleischman suggested that the threats were dropped as the senator's economic self-interests were clearly known. In a twist of fate, Busch later hired Bob Howsam, Johnson's son-in-law, as the Cardinals' general manager.

In the months immediately after gaining control of the Cardinals, Busch seemed to be everywhere in *The Sporting News* and the baseball press. He sought to calm other owners' fears of his deep pockets, and dismissed charges that he would simply buy the best players. He attended games, standing in ticket lines to inspect their efficiency. He reintroduced promotions such as Ladies Day. He held a ballyhooed family party at his mansion for Cardinals players, staff, and the writers who covered the team, with special gifts for the many wives and children in attendance.

Gussie used his ornate, custom-built railroad car to travel to the minor-league franchises he owned, including local Anheuser-Busch distributors in the festivities. He hosted New York sportswriters at a well-attended luncheon at Toots Shor's in New York. Fleishman recalled later that Busch had been horrified by condition of the "decrepit" Sportsman's Park, saying that would rather the Cardinals played in Forest Park—the site of the 1904 St. Louis World's Fair.[13] Gussie invested an additional $1.5 million of company money in Sportsman's Park, redesigning it, replacing or repairing every seat, removing the advertising from outfield walls, planting shrubbery in the center-field bleachers, installing new loges, erecting a new scoreboard, and remodeling the dugouts and clubhouses.[14]

St. Louis fans persisted in calling the facility Sportsman's Park, a title that had endured at Grand and Dodier since 1881, and with Busch's attention to the fan experience it would come to be hailed as one of the truly classic ballparks.[15]

Gussie's charm and seeming benevolence, along with careful public expenditures of his private wealth and corporate resources, soon had baseball writers referring to him to as "beer's super-salesman, sportsman and latter-day baseball buff."[16] Veeck would come to represent those who sought to operate major-league franchises without personal wealth or corporate resources, enhancing his image as a hustler, con man, and promoter extraordinaire.[17]

SOURCES

In addition to the sources cited in the Notes, the following were consulted:

Lisle, Benjamin Dylan. "'You've Got to Have Tangibles to Sell Intangibles': Ideologies of the Modern American Stadium, 1948-1982," Dissertation, University of Texas-Austin, May 2010.

McGuire, John M. "Brown Out: Brewery's Purchase of the Cards Doomed Veeck's Browns," *St. Louis Post Dispatch*, February 21, 1993.

NOTES

1 United Press International, "Sadder but Wiser: Name Park Busch Stadium/Frick Rules Out Budweiser," *New York Herald Tribune*, April 11, 1953.

2 John M. McGuire, "Versions Differ on the Purchase of the Cards by Anheuser-Busch," *St. Louis Post Dispatch*, February 21, 1993.

3 "100 People Who Shaped St. Louis," *St. Louis Magazine*, December 27, 2007.

4 "Sadder but Wiser."

5 McGuire.

6 "Sadder but Wiser."

7 Christian H. Brill and Howard W. Brill, "Take Me Out to The Hearing: Major League Baseball Players Before Congress," *Albany Government Law Review*, Volume 5, Issue 1, 2012.

8 McGuire.

9 Red Smith, "Capitol Capers," *Sarasota Journal*, April 12, 1954.

10 McGuire.

11 "Senator Johnson's Warning on Majors' Video Policy," *The Sporting News*, February 11, 1953.

12 Ibid.

13 McGuire.

14 Al Hirshberg, "Mistakes Helped Lose Braves for Hub, Says Scribe," *The Sporting News*, March 23, 1953.

15 Roger Angell, "The Series, Two Strikes on the Image," *New Yorker*, October 24, 1964.

16 Gerald Holland, "Gussie Busch's Kind of Day," *Sports Illustrated*, May 20, 1957;

"Capitol Capers."

17 Bill Veeck and Ed Linn, *The Hustler's Handbook* (New York: Simon & Schuster, 1989).

THE DAWN OF A NEW ERA: THE FIRST GAME AT SPORTSMAN'S PARK

April 14, 1909: Cleveland Indians 4, St. Louis Browns 2, at Sportsman's Park

BY CHIP GREENE

THE CITIZENS OF ST. LOUIS HAD SEEN a lot of baseball played in the ballpark that stood at the intersection of Dodier Street and Grand Avenue. They had never seen it like this, though.

After a single season in the upstart American League, the Milwaukee Brewers franchise was relocated to the "Gateway to the West" in the fall of 1901. The team borrowed a name from the past, the Brown Stockings, and moved into the city's vacant Sportsman's Park, the one along Dodier and Grand. The ballpark hadn't housed a team in 10 years, not since the original Browns, of the National League, left Sportsman's Park and moved to a ballpark several blocks northwest. For a time, they also called that one Sportsman's Park, and the club ultimately changed its name to the Cardinals.

For a while, Grand Avenue's Sportsman's Park kept its character. In 1875, when August Solari opened his quaint 8,000-seat Grand Avenue Grounds for the original Brown Stockings, he situated home plate in the ballpark's northeast corner, the one bounded by Dodier and Grand. As the new Browns took up residence for the 1902 season, however, home plate was moved to the ballpark's northwest corner, bordered by Sullivan Avenue and Spring Street. There it remained for the next seven years, backed by a wooden grandstand.

Much advancement took place in ballpark architecture over those seven years. By the end of the 1908 season, as one mediocre Browns team after another toiled in their wooden home, new ballparks made of concrete and steel had been built in Philadelphia and Pittsburgh. It was time, then, to modernize Sportsman's Park, to furbish it, too, with concrete and steel, and to enlarge the grand old park to accommodate the unprecedented growth that baseball was enjoying. In 1909, Browns fans would cheer for their team in, if not a brand-new ballpark, in one that looked nothing like they had ever seen.

The first and perhaps most symbolic change in Sportsman's alignment was a complete reversal of the field's layout: home plate was moved from the northwest corner to the southwest, where it was now bordered by Dodier Street and Spring Avenue. Most impressively, a two-tiered concrete and steel grandstand that spanned from first base to third base was erected behind the new home-plate location, and the old wooden grandstand that had stood behind the old home plate was transformed into a spacious new left-field pavilion made of concrete. When construction was completed, Sportsman's Park had been transformed into a gleaming new 25,000-seat jewel that represented the Browns' future.

Naturally, the public was eager to get a look at the rebuilt Sportsman's Park. Under the conditions, though, the crowd perhaps failed to live up to all that the event may have promised. When Opening Day arrived on April 14, 1909, it brought an unseasonably cold day, one in which "even the peanut boys sat about hugging themselves to keep warm."[1] Some intrepid fans arrived early and in great numbers to stake out choice viewing locations in the outfield. Indeed, reported the press the following day, "The crowd was out on the field behind the ropes a long time before the game started."[2] They weren't necessarily in a placid mood, either. In a throng that stood rows deep, with many spectators perched on "benches, [or] boards set on anything that the crowd could lay its hands on to gain a point of vantage," the enthusiastic patrons waged a "never-ending battle with the policemen on guard at the ropes."[3] Continuously, "the bluecoats shoved the crowd back," as "those in the third, fourth and fifth rows crowded forward."[4] Battling mightily to keep things under control, "the officers would almost be carried off their feet."[5]

What must have most astonished the crowd behind the ropes, of course, looking up from ground level, was the sheer size of the new ballpark, particularly the new two-level grandstand behind home plate. In describing the grandstand, a sportswriter noted, "One look at the comparatively small structure that was the grandstand last year and a comparison with the big stand was enough to convince everyone that they might as well try to hunt for the haystack needle as to find anybody in the new park."[6]

If the crowd on the field, though, was undaunted by the cold, the chill higher up in the atmosphere seemed to have kept some folks away from the ballpark's gaudy new grandstand. For while the first level was "crowded almost to its limit," the second level, "with the exception of the boxes, which were almost all filled," was not. That small crowd likely had to do with the chill wind that "swept through the stand with a whistle that went through almost any amount of wraps."[7]

Out in left field, meantime, the site of the old wooden grandstands that for the previous seven years stood behind the old home plate, the new concrete pavilion was "filled, but not overcrowded."[8]

All in all, wrote the press, "Whether it was the chilly wind or the fact that the park is so much larger than last year, the crowd could not seem to show the enthusiasm they displayed last year. … The cheering seemed light. There seemed to be a lack of concerted noisemaking."[9] Perhaps it was the play on the field, though, which had for so long been less than stellar, that generated such tempered applause.

With the exception of their first year in St. Louis, when they finished in second place, the Browns had never been very good. True, in 1908 they'd won 83 games and finished above .500 for the third time in their seven-year history; yet they'd finished only in fourth place, so contending for a championship re-

Workhorse Jack Powell started the first game for the Browns in their new home, Sportsman's Park. He won 245 games and lost 254 in his 16-year career (1897-1912). (Library of Congress)

mained elusive. Perhaps, though, this year they would build on that moderate success and finally make a run.

In 1909, however, that success was not to be. On this day, the Cleveland Naps, led by superstar player-manager Napoleon Lajoie, visited Sportsman's Park for the season's opening three-game series. After a thrilling American League pennant chase the previous year, during which Lajoie's Naps played and lost one more game than the champion Detroit Tigers and finished an agonizing second, just a half-game behind, the Naps looked to repeat their high level of play. On the mound for Cleveland in St. Louis was the brilliant Addie Joss, winner of 92 games over the past four seasons. Opposing Joss was 34-year-old right-hander Jack Powell.

The flame-throwing Joss eventually became one of baseball's immortals. John Joseph "Red" Powell is less acclaimed in baseball lore, but he was entering his

13th big-league season with 209 wins and was one of his era's toughest pitchers. He would prove as much on this day. Displaying "perfect control" and "speed that increased as the game progressed," Powell "allowed just five hits to the heavy-slugging Naps" and "outpitched" Joss, who had "neither the speed nor control to match Powell."[10] Still, Powell's toughness wasn't enough, for, as it was reported the next day, although the "Browns beat [the Naps] down for eight innings … in one frame, the fourth, Lajoie and his tribe won the game."[11]

Key to the Naps' win were two critical Browns errors and a lack of speed on the basepaths. During that Naps fourth inning, Browns shortstop Bobby Wallace and third baseman Hobe Ferris, both normally surehanded fielders, committed miscues. Those mistakes, together with three Naps hits, accounted for four runs in the frame. Although St. Louis touched Joss for eight hits, including three doubles, two Browns runners were cut down at second, one on a perfect throw from the outfield, and the other on a steal attempt. Were it not for those chances, plus the defensive blunders, the press opined, "Powell should have been the victor by a score of 2-1," rather than the 4-2 loser.[12]

Despite the Browns loss, the next day it was reported that the team "played a game of ball that was a delight to the estimated 25,000 fans who swarmed [the] new park. … Not one of them left the place discouraged."[13] When the game was ended, the "rush for the streetcars was fierce. … [C]ars ran one after another" and "hundreds and hundreds had to wait for an available seat."[14]

It was a scene that in one way or another would be repeated many times over the next 57 years as

St. Louis's baseball fans headed home after yet another game at their beloved Ballpark at Dodier and Grand.

SOURCES

In addition to the sources cited in the Notes, the author also accessed Retrosheet.org, Baseball-Reference.com, and www.SABR.org

NOTES

1   *St. Louis Post-Dispatch*, April 15, 1909: 17.
2   Ibid.
3   Ibid.
4   Ibid.
5   Ibid.
6   Ibid.
7   Ibid.
8   Ibid.
9   Ibid.
10 James Crusinberry, "Lack of Speed Still Injures Browns' Play," *St. Louis Post-Dispatch*, April 15, 1909: 10.
11 Ibid.
12 Ibid.
13 Ibid.
14 *St. Louis Post-Dispatch*, April 15, 1909: 17.

A SPORTSMAN'S PARK FIRST: PALE HOSE'S CICOTTE HURLS NO-HITTER

April 14, 1917: Chicago White Sox 11, St. Louis Browns 0, at Sportsman's Park

BY GREGORY H. WOLF

CHICAGO TRIBUNE SPORTSWRITER I.E. Sanborn confidently predicted that barring injuries to key players, the White Sox would capture the 1917 AL pennant.[1] One of the team's strengths, he opined, was its "great" and "well-balanced" pitching staff, led by Red Faber; however, Sanborn conceded that it lacked a star like Walter Johnson or Eddie Walsh. The White Sox' 32-year-old right-hander Eddie Cicotte proved Sanborn wrong.

A durable, yet often inconsistent hurler, Cicotte had flashed signs of brilliance since his first full season in 1908, with the Boston Red Sox, and his subsequent acquisition by the White Sox in July 1912. He finished second in the AL in ERA in 1913 (1.58) and again in 1916 (1.78) when he concluded the season on a tear, yielding just four earned runs in 48⅔ innings in September and winning all five of his decisions. With a 119-100 record in parts of 10 seasons, Cicotte's success rested on a mesmerizing knuckleball and a series of trick pitches, especially the shine ball. Cicotte made only 19 starts among his 44 appearances in 1916, but Pale Hose skipper Pants Rowland looked to 5-feet-9 "Knuckles" to play a bigger role in 1917 — if there was a season.

The estimated 10,000 fans at Sportsman's Park in the Gateway City on Saturday afternoon, April 14, 1917, for the final contest of the three-game season-opening series between the St. Louis Browns and the Chicago White Sox might have been confused when they saw players marching in unison with bats on their shoulders, led by a drill sergeant. Weeks earlier, AL President Ban Johnson had ordered all teams to practice military drills during spring training, as pressure mounted on the United States to enter World War I, which had ravaged Europe since 1914. On April 6, just days before the regular season began, the United States declared war on Germany. Former league MVP Eddie Collins of the White Sox praised the exercise regimen for preparing players physically for the season and instilling the discipline needed to succeed as a team.[2] Baseball would go on despite calls that the season be suspended.

With temperatures hovering in the 40s and dark, ominous skies overhead, the White Sox came out swinging against 25-year-old Browns southpaw Earl Hamilton, who had also started the season opener just three days earlier, yielding only five hits and three runs (none earned) in 7⅓ innings in the Browns' eventual 7-2 loss. After Collins drew a two-out walk and moved to third on Shoeless Joe Jackson's double, he scored on Happy Felsch's single. Cuban-born center fielder Armando Marsans made a running catch on Chick Gandil's deep fly to save two more runs and end the inning.

In what proved to be the Browns' only scoring chance of the game, Cicotte walked leadoff hitter Burt Shotton, who stole second when shortstop Swede Risberg dropped the catcher's throw, but was stranded on third.[3]

The White Sox offense exploded in the second inning. Hamilton faced only two batters (hitting Buck Weaver and surrendering a double to Ray Schalk) before yielding to reliever Jim Park. "One would think that [Park] had desecrated the American flag," wrote W.J. O'Connor in the *St. Louis Post-Dispatch*. "He got along with the enemy like percussion caps and dynamite. The explosion was terrific."[4] All four batters Park faced hit safely. Cicotte's single knocked in two runs; Risberg followed Nemo Leibold's single with a double to plate Cicotte; and Collins's single increased Chicago's lead to 5-0. With two men on, right-hander Tom Rogers made his big-league debut against Shoeless Joe. According to Sanborn, Rogers's "first attempt was a wild throw," permitting Risberg to score.[5] Jackson ultimately walked; and he and Collins moved up a station on Felsch's sacrifice bunt, the first out of the frame. After Gandil's fly ball drove home Collins, and Weaver reached on first baseman George Sisler's error (the first of five Brownie miscues), the Browns suffered the ultimate indignity when the White Sox executed a daring double steal.[6] Jackson scored from third to make it 8-0, while Weaver rounded second and was thrown out going to third to end the inning.

The first two innings, noted the *Tribune* in utter amazement, lasted 40 minutes.[7] The *Post-Dispatch* opined solemnly that "after the first six or eight runs nobody kept cases on the Chicago score."[8]

Among the best control pitchers of the era, Cicotte "wobbled some" in the third, according to the *Tribune*, yielding consecutive two-out walks to Shotton and Ward Miller.[9] But Risberg snared Sisler's scorching liner to end the frame.

Rogers settled down enough after his baptism of fire to last seven innings, yielding just two hits but also walking four. The White Sox made it 9-0 in the fourth when Collins drew a free pass, moved to third on a hard-hit grounder by Jackson (which Sanborn noted was "scored as error to [shortstop Doc] Lavan by St. Louis's blind official scorer"[10]), and subsequently raced home on Felsch's out. After loading the bases with no outs in the sixth on a walk to Leibold, a single by Risberg, and a bunt single by Collins, Jackson and Felsch each drove in runs on outs for an 11-0 lead.

Staked to a seemingly insurmountable early-inning lead, Cicotte cruised through the Browns lineup. In the fifth he hit Lavan who was quickly erased in a 6-4-3 double play. The Browns' most exciting play, and the game's most controversial one, occurred with two outs in the seventh. Jimmy Austin hit what the *Post-Dispatch* called a "sizzling drive" straight to first sacker Chick Gandil. "Jimmy's drive had whiskers like a German who was trapped for ten days on Vimy Ridge," wrote O'Connor, making reference to the brutal battle between primarily Canadian and German troops on the Western Front that had concluded two days earlier with well over 10,000 casualties in four days of fighting. While the *Tribune's* Sanborn suggested the ball "flitted through Gandil's mitt," O'Connor opined that "ordinarily this would have been scored a hit." Casting doubt on the official scorer's intention in the midst of Cicotte's no-hitter, O'Connor added, "[T]here was ominous unanimity in the belief that … (the scoring decision) was an egregious error."[11]

Despite the humiliating score, skipper Fielder Jones's Brownies did not roll over, making up for their offensive woes with some excellent defensive stops. In the eighth, Collins and Jackson belted deep drives to

Eddie Cicotte led the AL in wins (28), ERA (1.53), and innings pitched (346) in 1917 for the world champion Chicago White Sox. (Library of Congress)

center field. "The Cuban tore back and captured both of them brilliantly," wrote Sanborn in a compliment to Marsans.[12] O'Connor was even more effusive in his praise. "Marsans has only one peer as a defensive man," he opined, naming the Cleveland Indians' Tris Speaker as the standard-bearer at that position.[13] In the ninth, right-hander Kewpie Pennington relieved Rogers, retiring three of the four batters he faced in his only big-league appearance. Third baseman Austin helped out his hurler by making what the *Tribune* called a "spectacular catch" of Weaver's foul when "he slid under it to protect himself from hitting the grandstand."[14]

Cicotte was at his "best at the finish," gushed Sanborn.[15] The Michigan native made quick work of the Browns in the ninth, retiring Miller, Sisler, and Del Pratt on infield popups to complete the no-hitter in 2 hours and 2 minutes to win with "apparent ease."[16] Cicotte fanned five and walked three in recording the sixth White Sox no-hitter in franchise history, and the first since teammate Joe Benz beat the Cleveland Naps, 6-1, on May 31, 1914. Future Hall of Famer Ray Schalk had also donned the tools of ignorance for that no-hitter, and would be behind the plate for the White Sox' next one, too, on April 30, 1922, when Charlie Robertson tossed the first perfect game in team history (and fifth in big-league history) to beat the Detroit Tigers, 2-0.

The Browns exacted revenge of sorts against Cicotte on May 5 at Sportsman's Park when Ernie Koob tossed the second no-hitter in Browns history, albeit a controversial one, defeating the Pale Hose, 1-0. The *Tribune* initially reported that Koob had tossed a one-hitter;[17] but hours after the game, the official scorer, John B. Sheridan, a St. Louis sportswriter, changed Buck Weaver's first-inning hit to an error on second baseman Ernie Johnson. The following day, the Browns' Bob Groom tossed a no-hitter against Chicago in the second game of a doubleheader. It was the first time in big-league history that a team had thrown no-hitters on consecutive days.

Sanborn's prediction that the White Sox would win the pennant was correct. They won 100 games, owing in large part to the emergence of Cicotte as the AL's best pitcher. He led the league in wins (28), ERA (1.53), and innings (346⅔), while completing 29 of his 35 starts among 49 appearances. Cicotte defeated the New York Giants in Game One of the World Series. He made three appearances in Chicago's Series victory, yielding just four earned runs in 23 innings in three appearances.

SOURCES

In addition to the sources cited in the Notes, the author also accessed Retrosheet.org, Baseball-Reference.com, the SABR Minor Leagues Database, accessed online at Baseball-Reference.com, SABR.org, and *The Sporting News* archive via Paper of Record.

NOTES

1. I.E. Sanborn, "Sox Should Win Flag Unless Stars Are Hurt," *Chicago Tribune*, April 8, 1917: A1.
2. Edward T. Collins, "Eddie Collins Tells Benefits of Army Drills," *Chicago Tribune*, April 15, 1917: A1.
3. According to "Notes," *Chicago Tribune*, April 15, 1917: A1, Shotton was credited with a stolen base; however, the box scores in Baseball-Reference.com and Retrosheet.org do not credit him with a stolen base.
4. W.J. O'Connor, "Browns Hitless Before Cicotte, Sox Go Over, 11-0," *St. Louis Post-Dispatch*, April 15, 1917: 35.
5. According to I.E. Sanborn, "Cicotte Pitches No-Hit Game for Sox," *Chicago Tribune*, April 15, 1917: A1, Rogers made a wild pitch; however, the box scores in Baseball-Reference.com and Retrosheet.org do not credit Rogers with a wild pitch.
6. Contemporary newspaper reports mentioned the stolen bases; however, the box scores in Baseball-Reference.com and Retrosheet.org do not credit Jackson or Weaver with one.
7. I.E. Sanborn "Cicotte Pitches No-Hit Game for Sox," *Chicago Tribune*, April 15, 1917: A1.
8. O'Connor.
9. Sanborn, "Cicotte Pitches No-Hit Game for Sox."
10. Ibid.
11. Ibid.
12. Ibid.
13. O'Connor.
14. "Notes," *Chicago Tribune*.
15. Sanborn, "Cicotte Pitches No-Hit Game for Sox."
16. Ibid.
17. I.E. Sanborn, "Koob Tames Sox in One Hit Game, 1-0," *Chicago Tribune*, May 6, 1917: 1.

ON SECOND THOUGHT, IT'S A NO-HITTER FOR ERNIE KOOB

May 5, 1917: St. Louis Browns 1, Chicago White Sox 0, at Sportsman's Park

BY GREGORY H. WOLF

AN INCORRECT HEADLINE IS A PUBlisher's nightmare. The most famous such blunder occurred the day after the presidential election in 1948 when the *Chicago Tribune* proclaimed "Dewey Defeats Truman" in the first edition of the morning paper on November 3.[1] Thomas E. Dewey had been leading in the polls and the *Tribune*'s managing editor, J. Loy "Pat" Maloney, went with his gut instinct, even though results on the West Coast had not been completely tallied. Thirty-one years earlier, as the 1917 baseball season was still in its infancy, Ernie Koob of the St. Louis Browns "tantalized and teased" the Chicago White Sox, holding them hitless in Sportsman's Park in the Gateway City on May 5.[2] The next day the *Tribune*'s headline read, "Koob Tames Sox in One Hit Game, 1-0."[3] How did the *Tribune*, and other papers across the country using wire services for their sports reports get it wrong? Koob's no-hitter, opined sportswriter W.J. O'Connor in the *St. Louis Post-Dispatch*, was "hardly immaculate," and added, "[I]t was slightly tainted, stained with doubt in its very incipiency."[4]

Skipper Fielder Jones's Browns were itching to get back on the diamond on Saturday, May 5, to play the first game of a six-game series against the White Sox. The "dark, dank, dismal days of sunless Spring," as O'Connor put it, had forced the postponement of the Browns' games with the Detroit Tigers the previous two days.[5] Coming off their first winning season in eight years and just their fourth in franchise history as a charter member of the AL, the Browns had split their first 16 games, and were in fourth place, three games behind the front-running Boston Red Sox. The Pale Hose (11-7), piloted by Pants Rowland, had pennant aspirations, having finished runners-up to the Red Sox the previous year. However, the club had lost five of its last seven games to fall out of first place.

The inclement weather and poor field conditions suggested an advantage for the hurlers. Chicago sent its ace, 33-year-old right-handed knuckleballer Eddie Cicotte, to the mound. On April 14 the 11-year veteran, with a career record of 121-101 (2-1 thus far in '17), had opened the season by hurling the first no-hitter in the history of Sportsman's Park, defeating the Browns, 11-0. The Brownies countered with Koob, a 24-year-old southpaw and part-time starter who had entered the season with a 15-13 career record. In his last outing, on April 29, he was scorched for four hits and four runs in just 1⅔ innings of relief against the Cleveland Indians, but notched the victory to improve his record to 2-1.

After Koob fanned leadoff hitter Shano Collins to start the game, Buck Weaver hit a sharp grounder to second baseman Ernie Johnson, in what proved to be the most important and controversial play of the afternoon. A journeyman infielder making his first career start at the keystone sack, Johnson replaced the injured Del Pratt, generally acknowledged as one of the best second basemen of the era. Johnson "gave it a valorous battle," opined O'Connor, while sportswriter I.E. Sanborn of the *Tribune* noted that Johnson "tore in and tried to pull a brilliant stop."[6] O'Connor poetically described Johnson's struggles in the *Post-Dispatch*: He "fielded [the ball] with his chest, and knocked it silly at his feet. He then laid a prehensile paw on the pill and came up with ample time" to throw to first baseman George Sisler. "But he suddenly lost his prehensileness and threw the ball over his shoulder like a superstitious person throwing salt to avoid a fight."[7] Weaver easily reached first as Johnson searched for the ball behind him. Johnson's fumbling act, noted O'Connor, instantly evoked a debate in the press box about whether Weaver deserved a hit or Johnson an error. The official scorer, John B. Sheridan, a St. Louis sportswriter, ruled immediately and emphatically that it was a hit. Johnson redeemed himself just moments later. Koob scooped up Eddie Collins's grounder back to the mound and tossed to Johnson to initiate an inning-ending twin killing. "Johnson has a great arm for a middle man in double-murders," gushed O'Connor.[8]

The Browns threatened to tally the game's first run in the bottom of the third when light-hitting Doc Lavan (batting just .135 entering the game) popped a one-out single over first baseman Chick Gandil's head. After Koob walked, Burt Shotton loaded the bases when second baseman Eddie Collins misplayed his grounder.[9] Cicotte, one of the game's most notorious shine-ballers, escaped the jam when Jimmy Austin grounded to shortstop Swede Risberg and Sisler struck out on what the *Post-Dispatch* considered "three bad balls."[10]

The fifth proved to be Koob's "severest test," according to O'Connor, when the White Sox advanced as far as second base for the first and only time of the game.[11] Gandil led off with a grounder and raced 180 feet following shortstop Lavan's two-base throwing error. After Risberg and Ray Schalk were retired on "anemic flies" to right fielder Baby Doll Jacobson, Cicotte walked. Lavan then atoned for his miscue by fielding Shano Collins's grounder and beating Cicotte to the bag to squelch the rally.[12]

The outcome of the game rested on Austin's routine pop-up behind second base in the sixth. According to the *Post-Dispatch*, Risberg, calling off second sacker Eddie Collins and center fielder Happy Felsch, "tangoed back and hesitated," but fumbled the ball for an error, enabling the speedy Austin to reach second.[13] Up stepped Sisler, emerging as one of the league's best hitters, who entered the game batting .381, third highest in the AL. Sisler lined a single to right field to drive in Austin for the game's only run.

In parts of four seasons, Ernie Koob produced a 23-31 career record including 6-14 in 1917. (Library of Congress)

O'Connor described the game as "featureless ... as pitched battles always are."[14] Save for Johnson's muff in the first, Koob set down the White Sox, the big leagues' highest-scoring team in 1917, without the help of any exceptional defensive gem; nonetheless, he profited from heads-up, fundamentally sound ball. As tension mounted in the pitchers' duel, Risberg drew a one-out walk in the seventh, Koob's fifth free pass (all with two outs) of the game. Third baseman Austin fielded Schalk's lazy grounder to initiate the Browns' second double play, in exciting 5-4-3, around-the-horn fashion.

As the game wore on, "grave doubt," wrote the *Post-Dispatch*, arose in the press box about the hit awarded to Weaver in the first.[15] Koob had thrown two shutouts in his career, a five-hitter against the Washington Senators and a marathon 17-inning, 14-hitter against Boston that ended in a tie, but had never seriously flirted with a no-no.

The Browns tried to add on when Armando Marsans, the third Cuban-born big-league player and the first to start regularly, led off the seventh with a double and moved to third on Johnson's sacrifice bunt. He broke for home when Lavan grounded up the middle. Eddie Collins fielded the ball cleanly and rifled a strike to his fellow future Hall of Famer, Ray Schalk, who tagged Marsans at the plate. Koob fouled out to end the frame.

Koob "moved merrily along," gushed O'Connor, "mowing 'em down with great éclat."[16] He retired all six batters he faced in the eighth and ninth to finish the game in 1 hour and 34 minutes. Without celebrations, the contestants retired to their clubhouses; the Brownies delighted with Koob's one-hit shutout. Koob "throttled Comiskey's de lux twenty-four cylinder machine," praised the *Tribune*.[17] Cicotte, a tough-luck loser, surrendered just five safeties.

While the ballpark emptied and the players dressed, Sheridan harbored doubts about his first-inning ruling. He "sought sounder counsel," wrote the *Post-Dispatch*, and conferred with umps, players, and coaches.[18] According to the paper, "to a man" all parties agreed that Johnson deserved an error and Koob a no-hit game. The *Post-Dispatch* admitted there was a "suspicion of gang ethics" and attempts by the Browns to influence Sheridan's decision but O'Connor tried to defuse those accusations. "The able and honorable official scorer yielded reluctantly under the preponderance of evidence and erased the hit, substituting an error."[19] Koob was credited with the first no-hitter by a St. Louis Browns pitcher in Sportsman's Park, and just the second in franchise history.[20]

"I made a rank error," Ernie Johnson told the *St. Louis Star and Times* the next day.[21] "The ball was hit straight at me and although I got in front of it, it hopped out of my hands. But as it fell 'dead' at my feet, I still had a second chance to get the batter. … [A] throw to Sisler would have had him but the ball slipped out of my hand and flew over my shoulder."

Sheridan's flip-flop caused a scandal. The Base Ball Writers Association of America lodged a formal protest with the both league offices on May 6. It also polled its members on a resolution asking both league presidents to instruct official scorers that their rulings cannot be reversed except in cases on "misinterpretation of the rules."[22] There was also an unsuccessful attempt to change Sheridan's decision back to a hit.

SOURCES

In addition to the sources cited in the Notes, the author also accessed Retrosheet.org, Baseball-Reference.com, the SABR Minor Leagues Database, accessed online at Baseball-Reference.com, SABR.org, and *The Sporting News* archive via Paper of Record.

NOTES

1. Tim Jones, "Dewey defeats Truman," *Chicago Tribune*. chicagotribune.com/news/nationworld/politics/chi-chicago-days-deweydefeats-story-story.html.
2. W.J. O'Connor, "No-Hit Game Nets Koob and Browns One-Run Victory," *St. Louis Post-Dispatch*, May 6, 1917: 1S.
3. I.E. Sanborn, "Koob Tames Sox in One Hit Game, 1-0," *Chicago Tribune*, May 6, 1917: 1.
4. O'Connor.
5. Ibid.
6. O'Connor; Sanborn.
7. O'Connor.
8. "Sisler, Who Leads Cobb in Batting, Strikes Out With Bases Filled," *St. Louis Post-Dispatch*, May 6, 1917: 1S
9. There is some discrepancy on this play. The *Post-Dispatch* and the *Chicago Tribune* charged Collins with an error; the game account on Baseball Reference.com does not.
10. "Sisler, Who Leads Cobb in Batting, Strikes Out With Bases Filled."
11. O'Connor.
12. O'Connor.
13. "Sisler, Who Leads Cobb in Batting, Strikes Out With Bases Filled."
14. O'Connor.
15. Ibid.
16. Ibid.
17. Sanborn.
18. O'Connor.
19. Ibid.
20. The first no-hitter in Browns history belongs to Earl Hamilton who beat the Detroit Tigers, 5-1, at Navin Field on August 30, 1912.
21. "Koob Is Entitled to a No-Hit Game, E. Johnson Claims," *St. Louis Star and Times*, May 7, 1917: 11.
22. "Baseball Writers to Protest Koob's No-Hit Contest," *Pittsburgh Daily Post*, May 7, 1917: 7.

BOB GROOM TOSSES BROWNS' SECOND NO-HITTER IN TWO DAYS

May 6, 1917: St. Louis Browns 3, Chicago White Sox 0, at Sportsman's Park

BY GREGORY H. WOLF

IT WAS ALMOST AS IF SPORTSWRITERS had a sense of relief following Bob Groom's no-hitter against the Chicago White Sox in the Gateway City. Nothing "remotely resembled a hit," declared beat writer W.J. O'Connor in the *St. Louis Post-Dispatch*;[1] Groom's gem was "free from stain or taint," offered the *Chicago Tribune's* I.E. Sanborn.[2] A day earlier, Groom's St. Louis Browns teammate Ernie Koob had subdued the South Siders on what newspapers reported was a one-hit shutout. Hours after that game, the official scorer, St. Louis sportswriter John B. Sheridan, changed a controversial first-inning hit by Buck Weaver to an error on second baseman Ernie Johnson. Koob was credited with the Browns' first no-hitter, but the incident unleashed a protest by sportswriters, and an attempt to have Sheridan's decision overruled. (It wasn't.) There was no such concern in what O'Connor described as Groom's "Homeric effort" which began with the hurler tossing two hitless frames of relief in the first game of the Browns doubleheader sweep.[3]

The Browns and White Sox were headed in opposite directions. Koob's tainted no-hitter pushed skipper Fielder Jones's squad one game above .500 (9-8), tied with the New York Yankees for third place, 2½ games behind the Boston Red Sox. After a strong start to the season, manager Pants Rowland's White Sox were reeling. The team had lost six of its last eight games, and was in second place (11-8).

An estimated 20,000 spectators braved a cool, raw day with temperatures hovering in low 50s to take in a Sunday afternoon twin bill. The "outpouring at Sportsman's Park gives pause to those who have figured that major league baseball was slipping," suggested sportswriter John Wray in the *Post-Dispatch*.[4] The overflow crowd included fans lined up several deep in the outfield, cordoned off by a rope.

In the first game, the Browns exploded for five runs in the fourth inning but held a precarious 5-4 lead to begin the eighth inning. Into the game stepped Bob Groom, a 32-year-old right-hander who began his ninth season with a 109-129 record since debuting for the Washington Senators in 1909. A former 20-game winner, Groom was a sturdy workhorse, averaging 258 innings and 14 wins per campaign in his career; he had also led his league in losses twice (26 as a rookie in 1909; and 20 with the St. Louis Terriers of the Federal League in 1914). Making his fifth relief appearance among his seven outings thus far in '17, Groom held the White Sox hitless in two innings, though he looked wobbly at times, issuing three walks in the Browns' eventual 8-4 victory, their fifth win in sixth games.

Minutes later Groom was back on the mound as the Browns starter in the second game, but did not look anything like a pitcher who could toss a no-hitter. He issued a walk to leadoff hitter Nemo Leibold, then benefited when his batterymate, Hank Severeid, picked up Weaver's poorly-placed sacrifice bunt in front of the plate and fired a strike to shortstop Doc Lavan to initiate a 2-6-3 twin killing.

The Browns came out swinging against 31-year-old right-hander Joe "Butcher Boy" Benz, making his first start of the season. Benz (62-64 in parts of six seasons) had authored a no-hitter on May 31, 1914, defeating the Cleveland Naps, 6-1, at Comiskey Park. After George Sisler reached on a two-out single, Baby Doll Jacobson whacked a "tremendous double" which, according to the *Post-Dispatch*, "almost killed

HOME OF THE BROWNS AND CARDINALS AT GRAND AND DODIER

Bob Groom pitched a no-hitter in the same year he tied for the AL lead in losses (19). In his 10-year career he posted a 119-150 record. (Library of Congress)

Umpire [Billy] Evans, who was doing duty on the speedways."[5] Sisler rounded third and scored easily. The *Chicago Tribune* blamed the tally on a "boner" by the White Sox' right fielder. "[I]f Leibold had let the ball roll into the crowd," opined Sanborn, "Sisler would have been held at third" and Jacobson credited with a ground-rule double.[6]

Groom worked around another leadoff walk in the second — his fifth free pass in 14 batters in the two games — to Shoeless Joe Jackson, who was subsequently caught stealing.

The Browns picked up another run in the second when Johnson doubled to right and moved to third on Severeid's out. He scored on Lavan's grounder to first baseman Chick Gandil, whose throw to catcher Ray Schalk was not in time to nab the speedy, sliding Johnson.

Groom and Benz traded zeroes over the next five frames. Groom hit Weaver with one out in the fourth, but then picked him off first for the final out of the inning. The South Siders had their best scoring chance in the sixth when Swede Risberg drew Groom's third and final free pass to lead off the inning, and then advanced a station on Schalk's sacrifice, and another on Benz's roller to first baseman Sisler. Then, in what was described as a "great play" by sportswriter Clarence Lloyd of the *St. Louis Star and Times*, Severeid "speared [Leibold's pop foul] a foot from the concrete stand" to end the frame with Risberg stranded on the hot corner.[7]

Benz yielded only eight hits in his route-going outing, but they came at inopportune times. The Indiana native of German stock quashed a Browns rally in the sixth after Sisler and Jacobson led off with consecutive singles, but was not so lucky two innings later in an action-packed eighth. Jimmy Austin led off with a single and moved to third on Sisler's third single of the game. After Sisler stole second on Jacobson's strikeout, Cuban-born Armando Marsans hit a tapper to third baseman Weaver, whose strike to Schalk easily erased Austin at the plate while Sisler reached third and Marsans first. Reports differed about how the Browns tallied their final run, with Johnson at the plate. According to the *Post-Dispatch*, the Browns attempted a daring double steal; Schalk's throw to second caught Marsans in a rundown while Sisler scored.[8] The *Tribune* reported that Benz caught Marsans off first, and in the ensuing rundown Sisler sneaked home. "Gandil and Risberg took so much time retiring [Marsans] a run scored," wrote Sanborn.[9]

The Browns faithful were on their feet when Groom took the mound in the ninth. "I will admit that I got terribly nervous in that ninth inning," said Groom, noting that a teammate alerted him to his no-hitter. "I had gone along for eight innings without knowing that the Sox hadn't made a hit off me."[10] The scoreboard at Sportsman's Park did not show hits and errors, only the run totals. Perhaps Groom was thinking about the only other time he had flirted with a no-no. A year earlier, on April 21, 1916, Groom held the Cleveland Indians hitless for 8⅓ innings at Sportsman's Park when Elmer Smith doubled home Tris Speaker in the Browns' 11-1 victory.[11]

After Schalk popped up to short for the first out, it was no laughing matter when pinch-hitter Eddie Murphy hit a tricky grounder that drew Sisler far off first base. Racing to cover the bag, Groom took Sisler's throw to retire Murphy for the second out. Groom had retired 11 straight batters and was just one out from a no-hitter. When Leibold took Groom's first two pitches, Severeid walked the ball back to Groom, reported the *Star and Times*. "[P]ut everything you have on that ball now and don't lose this fellow," Severeid supposedly told his hurler.[12] Groom retired Leibold on a weak grounder to Sisler, who scooped up the ball and raced a few steps to first to secure Groom's no-hitter; it had taken a mere 81 minutes.

Fans poured onto the field to celebrate Groom's accomplishment, the second Browns no-hitter in as many days, and the third no-hitter at Sportsman's Park between the Browns and White Sox in three weeks. The South Siders' Eddie Cicotte authored the first no-hitter in the history of Sportsman's Park on April 14. Groom was "hoisted on the shoulders of a half dozen men who carried him to the coop," reported the *Star and Times* excitedly.[13] Groom fanned four and faced just 28 batters, one over the minimum. There was "no flaw in Groom's no-hit game," added Sanborn, praising the pitcher's complete dominance.[14] Home plate umpire Dick Nallin called both Groom's and Koob's no-hitters; as of 2017 Nallin is the only umpire to be behind the plate for no-hitters on consecutive days.

Described as "intensive entertainment" by the *Post-Dispatch*, the Browns doubleheader sweep of the eventual World Series champion White Sox pushed them into second place, 1½ games behind Boston.[15] It proved to be the Brownies' high-water mark of the season. The club lost 15 of its next 19 games en route to its 13th losing season since entering the AL as a charter member in 1901. (The club was founded as the Milwaukee Brewers, and relocated to St. Louis in 1902.)

Groom, who had hurled a no-hitter as a member of the Portland Beavers of the Class-A Pacific Coast League in 1906, lost his next start, three days later to the White Sox to conclude the team's six-game series, yielding 11 hits and four earned runs in seven innings. In what proved to be his final full season in the big leagues Groom finished with nine victories and tied teammate Allan Sothoron for the AL lead in losses (19). Waived by the Browns in the offseason, Groom pitched ineffectively for Cleveland in 1918, finishing with a 119-150 record in parts of 10 seasons.

SOURCES

In addition to the sources cited in the Notes, the author also accessed Retrosheet.org, Baseball-Reference.com, the SABR Minor Leagues Database, accessed online at Baseball-Reference.com, SABR.org, and *The Sporting News* archive via Paper of Record.

NOTES

1. W.J. O'Connor, "Bob Groom Pitches 11 No-Hit Innings, As Browns Beat Sox Twice, Gaining Second Place," *St. Louis Post-Dispatch*, May 7, 1917: 14.

2. I.E. Sanborn, "Sox Defeated Twice; Held Without a Hit by Groom of Browns," *Chicago Tribune*, May 7, 1917: 20.

3. O'Connor.

4. John Wray, "Wray's Column," *St. Louis Post-Dispatch*, May 7, 1917: 14.

5. "Team That Jinxed Browns in 1916 Beaten Three Times in Two Days," *St. Louis Post-Dispatch*, May 7, 1917: 17.

6. Sanborn.

7. Clarence Lloyd, "Brownies, Aided by Groom's Great Game, Reach Second Place," *St. Louis Star and Times*, May 7, 1917: 11.

8. "Team That Jinxed Browns in 1916 Beaten Three Times In Two Days."

9. Sanborn.

10. "I Didn't Know I Had No Hit Game on Way Until Eighth—Groom," *St. Louis Star and Times*, May 7, 1917: 11.

11. "Jones Is Repaid for His Faith in Pitcher Groom," *St. Louis Star and Times*, April 22, 1916: 11.

12. "I Didn't Know I Had No Hit Game on Way Until Eighth—Groom."

13. "Fans Carry Groom on Shoulders From Park," *St. Louis Star and Times*, May 7, 1917: 11.

14. Sanborn.

15. "Team That Jinxed Browns in 1916 Beaten Three Times In Two Days."

THE BIG TRAIN AND SOTHORON BATTLE FOR 15

July 25, 1918: Washington Senators 1, St. Louis Browns 0 (15 Innings), at Sportsman's Park

BY CHIP GREENE

PERHAPS NO BASEBALL SEASON HAS ever begun with more uncertainty than the 1918 pennant chase. As the season began, the United States had been at war for a year, during which time major-league players had been largely unaffected by the world's events. On July 1, 1918, however, the sport's privileged existence was shattered when Secretary of War Newton Baker ruled that baseball was "non-essential" to the war effort, and mandated that ballplayers either seek war-related jobs or face military draft eligibility. This "work or fight" decree severely threatened the National Pastime's equilibrium.

Of course, baseball's owners immediately protested Baker's decision. In turn, Baker, who admitted to little knowledge of baseball's business or how best to enact the order, agreed to postpone his decree until September 1; he also committed to meet on July 24 with baseball's representatives to discuss how the work-or-fight order might be implemented. Unsure how the ruling would affect the season, the American League announced that unless it was given some assurances as to what to expect from the War Department, it to cease operations.

Under this cloud, the regular season progressed. One might think that given the vagueness of Baker's order the players naturally would have become preoccupied with their immediate futures, causing their performances to suffer. Not so for everyone. Case in point: Walter Johnson, one of the sport's preeminent stars. In the midst of baseball's maelstrom, the Big Train produced one of the most dominant exhibitions of his legendary career.

On July 25 Johnson's Washington Senators opened a four-game series against the St. Louis Browns at Sportsman's Park in the Gateway City. Fresh from a four-game sweep of the Chicago White Sox, the Senators came into the game in third place in the American League, with a 47-41 record. With Senators manager Clark Griffith home in D.C. awaiting the outcome of Secretary Baker's meeting, George McBride directed the team. Scarcely could McBride imagine how little his managerial instincts would be required on this day.

Across the field, the Browns, too, were skippered by a new manager, although one who'd already been on the job for a month. The Browns' 88th game of the season was the first home game for Jimmy Burke, the team's third manager of the season.[1] After a seven-year playing career and a 90-game managerial stint in 1905 with the crosstown Cardinals, Burke had spent four seasons the Detroit Tigers coaching staff (1914-1917) before taking the Browns' helm on June 28, 1918, in the team's 63rd game. From that date, amazingly, the Browns spent the next 25 games on the road, so this was the first time the home crowd saw the new manager of their sixth-place squad. As it turned out, Burke and the fans were both in for an agonizing afternoon.

If Walter Johnson was assuredly going to be tough for the Browns to beat, his opponent promised to be no less a challenge for the Senators' offense. Twenty-five-year-old right-hander Allan Sothoron was that most enigmatic of Deadball Era pitchers, a spitballer. In fact, already this season Sothoron, who came into the game on a personal five-game winning streak, had gotten the best of the Big Train just 18 days earlier, when they squared off in Washington. Sothoron won, 3-0, allowing just three singles. Sothoron had notched wins in both of his previous starts against

Coming off an AL-high 19 losses in 1917 (tied with teammate Bob Groom), Allan Sothoron went 12-12 in 1918 with a 1.94 ERA. (Library of Congress)

Washington (with one loss in relief), while Johnson had gone winless in his two starts against the Browns (with one save in relief). With a 10-8 record and 1.97 ERA, Sothoron was the Browns' ace; so, too, was Johnson (16-10, 1.33) for the Senators. This game, then, had the makings of a classic pitchers' duel.

The confrontation more than lived up to its potential. For Sothoron, the story of this afternoon was not that he allowed 12 Senators hits, but that in spite of those hits, his "exhibition, while not quite so impressive as Johnson's, still was really deserving of more credit, for the Senators had numerous scoring opportunities, all of which, until the final stanza, Sothoron succeeded in erasing."[2] For Johnson, the game was marked not simply by a paucity of Browns runners on the basepaths, but by the degree to which he proved "positively invincible"[3] in the few instances when the batters did reach base. That each man offered his best was vital to their respective teams, for, as the press related the next day, "It became apparent early in the game that one run by either club would win the contest."[4]

One look at the line score suggests how the game's suspense grew. Over the first three innings, neither team scored; nor were any runs plated in the fourth, fifth, or sixth innings. While over this period Sothoron may have had to quell some of the Senators' aforementioned "numerous scoring opportunities,"[5] Johnson, with just a few exceptions, totally handcuffed the Browns. After the first six St. Louis batters had been retired in order, Earl Smith coaxed a leadoff walk in the third inning, finally giving the Browns a baserunner. Yet, after Smith advanced to second on a sacrifice by the next batter, Les Nunamaker, the inning ended with Smith standing on second base.

The fourth inning presented the Browns with what was their best scoring chance of the game. When it failed, however, Johnson became virtually unhittable. Batting second for the Browns and leading off the bottom of the inning was Jimmy Austin, whom Johnson retired for the first out. Next up was the brilliant George Sisler. As Johnson fired, Sisler swung and lined one down the left-field line; the speedy Sisler stopped at third with a triple. To the plate strode the cleanup hitter, lefty-swinging Ray Demmitt. In this, his sixth major-league season, Demmitt would post a career-best 61 RBIs, and here he "strove mightily to tally Sisler,"[6] driving a fly ball to right field. But as Sisler broke for home, Frank "Wildfire" Schulte, 35 years old and in his final season, fired a "beauty bright peg"[7] to catcher Eddie Ainsmith, who tagged Sisler for the out. Sisler's hit had been the Browns' first of the game. It would be a while before they got another.

For the next seven innings the Browns had no answers for Johnson's offerings; in each inning, he retired the side in order. Yet Sothoron, too, "clung firmly to the pace set by his illustrious adversary,"[8] so the scoreless game moved to the 12th. That inning, St. Louis finally got its second hit, when Nunamaker singled to left field. After Nunamaker advanced to second on Sothoron's sacrifice, the Browns seemed poised to score, but again Johnson stranded the runner. Both starters moved on to the 13th.

That inning, the Browns mounted their final scoring threat, but again came up empty. With one out, Demmitt blasted a double off the right-field wall. As Demmitt took a long lead off second, however, Ainsmith rifled a throw to shortstop John "Doc" Lavan,[9] who tagged him out. The next batter, Jack Tobin, pushed a "fluke"[10] bunt safely past Johnson but when he subsequently tried to steal second, he too was retired Ainsmith-to-Lavan. It was the Browns' last gasp.

Though Sothoron had allowed 10 hits through 14 innings, the Senators had not scored. Their drought ended with two outs in the top of the 15th inning. Following an Eddie Foster single up the middle, Joe Judge came to the plate. As Foster ran with Sothoron's pitch, Judge hit a long, high fly to right-center field, where it fell for a double. Foster scored standing up, and the Senators led 1-0. Johnson ended the game in the bottom of the inning.

It had been a sensational outing for the Big Train. In 10 of 15 innings he had retired the Browns in order, and from the fifth inning to the 12th not one St. Louis batter had reached first. Remarkably, too, with just four hits and two walks, the Browns had left just two men on base. Known for strikeouts, Johnson fanned only three. With those accomplishments, it was hard to argue with the writer who contended that "when a club gets but four hits in 15 innings and scores not one run during that time, there isn't much chance for victory."[11]

Indeed, there wasn't.

SOURCES

In addition to the sources cited in the Notes, the author also consulted:

thisgreatgame.com/1918-baseball-history.html.

facs.org/about%20acs/archives/pasthighlights/crowderhighlight.

Retrosheet.org.

Baseball-Reference.com.

NOTES

1 The first two managers had been Fielder Jones (with a 22-24 record) and Jimmy Austin (7-9).

2 "Johnson Winner Over Sothoron in 15-Inning Combat," *St. Louis Post-Dispatch*, July 26, 1918: 16.

3 Ibid.

4 Ibid.

5 For this game summary the author could rely only on game descriptions, none of which provided specifics as to the Senators' scoring chances in any inning other than the last.

6 *St. Louis Post-Dispatch*, July 26, 1918: 16.

7 Clarence F. Lloyd, "Sothoron Is Beaten in 15-Round Duel by Famed Fireball King," *St. Louis Star and Times*, July 26, 1918: 11.

8 *St. Louis Post-Dispatch*, July 26, 1918: 16.

9 Lavan had been acquired by the Senators from the Browns on December 15, 1917, but the 1918 season was his only one in Washington. In early September of 1918, Lavan, a naval surgeon, reported to the Great Lakes Naval Training Station, where in addition to his medical duties he also managed the baseball team. Upon his death in 1952, Lavan was buried at Arlington National Cemetery.

10 *St. Louis Post-Dispatch*, July 26, 1918: 16.

11 Ibid.

CARDINALS FALL IN THEIR FIRST GAME IN SPORTSMAN'S PARK

July 1, 1920: Pittsburgh Pirates 6, St. Louis Cardinals 2, at Sportsman's Park

BY GREG ERION

AT THE END OF JUNE 1920 THE National League pennant contenders were tightly bunched behind the defending champion Cincinnati Reds. The Brooklyn Dodgers, Chicago Cubs, and St. Louis Cardinals were in a virtual tie for second, three games out. The greatest surprise among these contenders was the Cardinals — the year before, they had finished seventh, 40½ games out.[1]

Thus, as the Cardinals hosted a three-game series against the Pirates beginning July 1, an estimated 20,000 fans came to see their club in action.[2] Attendance was no doubt swelled by an annual benefit for the St. Louis Tuberculosis League, which included an assortment of races, field events, and musical entertainment. Local society women walked through the stands selling programs that held the promise of various prizes. An exhibition game involving Army and Navy personnel preceded the Cardinals-Pirates contest at what was described as "the Browns Park," a descriptive that popular usage would change to "the Cards Park" within a few years.[3]

The *St. Louis Post-Dispatch* faithfully covered these events; not until the fourth paragraph of the article did it touch on the day's most significant development, and then only in passing. The Cardinals were playing their first "Championship contest" (as the *Post-Dispatch* expressed it), in Sportsman's Park. It was an occurrence that would have profound implications for the Browns and Cardinals over the ensuing years. This was unrealized in the next day's coverage of the game. A mundane recounting of the contest carried the day.[4]

The matchup featured Ferdie Schupp, 8-4 for far, against the Pirates' Hal Carlson, who began the contest with a 5-6 record. Pittsburgh, in sixth place, just five games behind the Reds (and two behind St. Louis) drew first blood in the third on Carson Bigbee's triple and Max Carey's single. Another Pirates tally came the next inning off the bat of Walter Barbare, whose double followed Howdy Caton's double to make it 2-0.

Carlson held St. Louis scoreless until the bottom of the eighth, when Cliff Heathcote slammed his second home run of the year. St. Louis then tied the game in the bottom of the ninth on Doc Lavan's double and pinch-hitter Austin McHenry's one-out single.

Henry had batted for Schupp, whose 10 hits and three walks surrendered remarkably yielded just two runs for Pittsburgh. He was replaced in the 10th by Bill Sherdel, the Cardinals' main relief pitcher that year. Sherdel had done yeoman work for the club, and would do so for years to come, but this would not be one of his better efforts. He gave up four hits and a walk, aided by first baseman Jack Fournier's wild throw, as the Pirates scored four times. St. Louis went quietly in the bottom of the inning to give Pittsburgh a 6-2 victory.

The results of the game had no bearing on a pennant race eventually won by Brooklyn. Pittsburgh ended the season in fourth; St. Louis, plagued by ineffective pitching, faded into a tie for fifth, encouraged, however, that at 75-79 they almost reached .500, substantially better than they had done in 1919. Rogers Hornsby, at .370, won the first of six consecutive batting titles, starting a run that included three seasons over .400.

Quite often the importance of a major-league game is measured by the outcome of the contest,

SPORTSMAN'S PARK IN ST. LOUIS

Ferdie Schupp, who posted a 61-39 record in his 10-year career (1913-1922), was the Cardinals' starter in their first game in Sportsman's Park. (Library of Congress)

often by what might have been accomplished either individually or by either club. In this game Hornsby had two singles in four at-bats. But what he or anyone else accomplished on the field this day was not the significant story. This was the Cardinals' first home game at Sportsman's Park, a field they would use for the next 46 years. That the Cardinals could use Sportsman's Park for their home games would prove of significant importance not only to their franchise but also to their rival St. Louis Browns.

A review of major-league baseball in St. Louis over the years rightfully focuses on the Cardinals. There was a time, however, when the favored team in St. Louis was the American League Browns—not the Cardinals. Until 1926, when the Cardinals won their first pennant and world championship, the Browns regularly outdrew their National League counterparts to the tune of over 50,000 fans per year on average.

The Browns were the better team in the early 1920s, and came breathtakingly close to a pennant in 1922, finishing just one game behind the Yankees.

While the Cardinals, in retrospect, might be seen as a greater draw in those years because of Hornsby, the Browns had just as big a pull in first baseman George Sisler. The same year, 1920, that saw Hornsby lead the league with his .370 average, Sisler batted .407 with a then major-league-record 257 hits.

How allegiance gradually shifted from the Browns to the Cardinals was based on several factors. One involved the Cardinals' promotion of what was called the Knothole Gang, an effort that arranged for free tickets to mostly underprivileged youth. This program gained scores of loyal Cardinals fans for decades. Another development involved Branch Rickey's move from the Browns to the Cardinals. The Browns' wealthy, irascible, and unpredictable owner, Phil Ball, did not appreciate Rickey's talents and Rickey, seeking better opportunities, was lured to the Cardinals. Although he was mediocre as a field manager, his visionary efforts as a general manager in developing an expansive minor-league farm system were peerless. By the time Rickey left the Cardinals in 1942 he had earned the club six pennants and four World Series championships.

Despite these factors, what really cemented the Cardinals' future in St. Louis—and the Browns' eventual departure to Baltimore—was how they gained access to Sportsman's Park, and how it saved the franchise.

By 1920, Robison Field, the Cardinals' home ballpark for decades, was in a state of serious disrepair. Built in 1893, the wooden structure had outlived its usefulness. Cardinals president Sam Breadon lacked the wherewithal to refurbish it—he estimated it would cost over half a million dollars to do so.[5] As the 1920 season approached, the structure had become a firetrap, ready to collapse. Breadon was warned that the ballpark would not pass a fire inspection.[6]

Desperate, and without the cash to fix the ballpark or build a new one, Breadon approached Ball to see if he could rent Sportsman's Park for Cardinals home games. Sportsman's Park had been used by the Browns since 1902 and had received a major overhaul in 1909 with construction of steel and concrete grandstands.

Ball rebuffed Breadon in large part because he was offended at Rickey having left the Browns for the Cardinals years before. "Are you crazy, Sam? I wouldn't let Branch Rickey put one foot inside my ballpark. Now get out yourself."[7] Facing financial calamity, Breadon was persistent; after several attempts, he finally asked Ball to listen to his plea. Ball relented.

As historian Fred Lieb told it later, Ball told Breadon, "I was a poor boy—a very poor boy—in New York. I came here to St. Louis, nearly starved at first, but eventually made some money in the automobile business. I got into the Cardinals with that fan group—soon got in over my head—and much of my money is in the club. We're heavily in debt, and our only chance to salvage what we put into it is to sell the Cardinals' real estate (Robison Field) for $200,000, get out of debt, and move to Sportsman's Park. You're a rich man, Mr. Ball; money doesn't mean anything to you, but I'm about to go broke, and only you can save me."

Ball respected determination, and behind his blustery façade rested the temperament of a caring man. Breadon's entreaty hit its mark. "Sam, I didn't know you were hooked so bad. I admire your frankness, and what's more I admire a fighter, a man that doesn't quit easily. Get your lawyer to draw up a contract, insert a rental figure you think is fair and I'll sign it. Even if it included having that Rickey around the place."[8]

With Ball agreeing to take on the Cardinals as tenants, Breadon was able to sell Robison Field for $275,000, clear outstanding debts and provide working capital for the future. One of the main initiatives Breadon and Rickey could now pursue was establishment of the productive minor-league system that would eventually create a competitive team for decades to come.[9] This, and a growing allegiance created out of the Knothole Gang, would bury the Browns.

By itself the game of July 1, 1920, between the Cardinals and Pirates was of no great importance in the scheme of things. Where it was played would prove to have a lasting impact on two major-league franchises.

SOURCES

In addition to the sources cited in the Notes, the author also accessed Retrosheet.org and Baseball-Reference.com.

NOTES

1. "Cards' Biggest Local Attendance This Year, Welcomes Team Home," *St. Louis Post-Dispatch*, July 1, 1920: 37.
2. "National League," *The Sporting News*, July 8, 1920: 6.
3. "Cards Biggest Local Attendance."
4. Edward P. Balinger, "Sherdel Hammered for Four Hits in Vicious Exhibition," *St. Louis Post-Dispatch*, July 2, 1920: 10.
5. Joan M. Thomas, Robison Field, SABR BioProject, sabr.org/bioproj/park/88929e79.
6. Mark Armour, "Sam Breadon," in *The 1934 St. Louis Cardinals, The World Champion Gas House Gang* (Phoenix: Society for American Baseball Research, 2014): 239.

7   Golenbock, Peter, *The Spirit of St. Louis: A History of the St. Louis Cardinals and Browns*, (New York: Avon Books, Inc., 2000), 267.

8   Frederick G. Lieb, *The Baltimore Orioles: The History of a Colorful Team in Baltimore and St. Louis*, (Carbondale, Ilinois: Southern Illinois University Press, 1955),191-192.

9   Armour. 239

CARDINALS GET FIRST WIN AT NEW HOME AS DOAK SWASHBUCKLES PIRATES

July 2, 1920: St. Louis Cardinals 3, Pittsburgh Pirates 0, at Sportsman's Park

BY RUSS LAKE

THE ST. LOUIS CARDINALS' OWNER, Sam Breadon, generally shunned publicity. Nevertheless, Breadon knew that the way to attract more fans to the games was to have a winning team and also to get more information about the games to the fans.[1] The June 24, 1920, issue of *The Sporting News* steadfastly questioned how the newbie Breadon and his associates would be able to take care of the bugs and allow their improving ballclub to be showcased at the dilapidated Cardinals plant (Robison Field), located at the end of Vandeventer Avenue.[2]

Breadon had been wheeling and dealing, but was not yet tipping his "Cards." He soon let the media in on the monetary details of an agreement with Browns owner Phil Ball to lease Sportsman's Park.[3] Subsequently, the July 1 publication of "The Base Ball Paper of the World" reversed its previous week's concern and touted Breadon as a genius for his coup in the venue switch.[4] This edition came out on the same date that the Redbirds hosted the Pittsburgh Pirates in their first game at Sportsman's Park, which was viewed by an overflow gathering in the annual benefit game for the St. Louis Tuberculosis Society.[5] All seemed perfect, except for the final score of Pirates 6, Cardinals 2, in 10 innings.

At least one individual at the Cardinals' inaugural loss was decidedly more upset about leaving an important article inside the ballpark after the conclusion of the extra-frame affair. An appeal in the *St. Louis Post-Dispatch* spelled out the situation: *GOLD MESHBAG — Lost, at Sportsman's Park Thursday: containing small amount of money and owner's cards. Call Forest 4370: reward.*[6]

While the Cardinals players could not do anything about the missing handbag, they were determined to "right the ship" and earn a triumph during the midafternoon tilt on Friday, July 2. The fourth-place Cardinals had lost four straight and stood at 34-32. Pittsburgh had also been struggling lately and possessed a 30-30 record, good for fifth. The Pirates' first-year manager, George Gibson, settled on 28-year-old southpaw Earl Hamilton, fittingly born in Gibson, Illinois.[7] Hamilton's father happened to be in St. Louis on business and was able to watch his son pitch.[8]

Cardinals skipper Branch Rickey tabbed 6-foot right-hander Bill Doak, who was coming off a bout with ptomaine poisoning.[9] "Spittin' Bill" was 8-7, with a 3.57 ERA, as he neared the halfway mark of his ninth major-league season. Rickey had to order his regular first baseman, Jack Fournier, to the bench due to a lingering hand injury.[10] Utilityman Hal Janvrin played first and batted leadoff for St. Louis. Janvrin had not played a full game at first in over four years.

Unlike the day before, plenty of seats were available. Five price levels were offered with the ducats ranging from 50 cents to $1.50,[11] and could be purchased in advance on North Broadway at Dengler & Hatz Cigar Store inside the Boatmen's Bank Building.[12] A paid crowd of 2,500 passed through the gate along with an additional 1,500 members of the Knot Hole Gang to watch the Cardinals in steamy 93-degree heat.[13]

SPORTSMAN'S PARK IN ST. LOUIS

Bill Doak tossed a six-hit shutout to record the Cardinals' first victory in Sportsman's Park. He posted a 169-157 record in his 16-year career (1912-1924; 1927-1929). (Library of Congress)

Born in Pittsburgh, the 29-year-old Doak strolled to the hill with a 15-11 career record versus the Pirates. He was a deliberate worker who used a large red handkerchief to wipe his brow during the game. He relied on good control, an effective curve, and a signature spitball.[14] In the top of the first, Max Carey singled and advanced to second when right fielder Joe Schultz fumbled the ball, but Doak pitched out of the trouble.[15] Hamilton, despite giving up two hard-hit balls and benefiting from a shoe top grab of a little popup by first baseman Charlie Grimm, retired the first six St. Louis batters.[16]

Hamilton, who was 2-3 with a 3.11 ERA, saw his luck go south in the third when Doc Lavan singled to right. With the hit-and-run on,[17] Pickles Dillhoefer came through with a double to right and Lavan scored. Doak's bunt moved his batterymate to third, and Dillhoefer came home when Janvrin's hard grounder caromed off second baseman Walter Barbare for an infield hit to make it 2-0. Cliff Heathcote forced Janvrin, and then the young center fielder was caught napping and picked off first by Hamilton.[18]

In the fifth, Barbare knocked a one-out infield hit that went off Doak's glove. With the Pirates attempting the hit-and-run, Schmidt drove a liner to right-center that the left-handed Heathcote dashed over for to make a backhanded catch, forcing Barbare to race back to first. Pittsburgh turned in three defensive gems of its own during the bottom half when third baseman Possum Whitted stabbed a tricky hopper by Schultz, spun and fired low to Grimm, who scooped up the peg. Lavan sent a deep drive down the line that left fielder Carson Bigbee raced for and caught in front of the fence. Dillhoefer's bid for another hit was foiled when his smash glanced off Hamilton's mitt and was scooped up by shortstop Howdy Caton, who fired to first for the putout.[19]

The Pirates were looking for a way to get to Doak in the sixth, but failed to deliver even after two free passes from the Cardinals hurler. Bigbee was out on a close play after second baseman Rogers Hornsby knocked down his grounder and threw quickly to Janvrin. Carey walked, but Dillhoefer, the catcher, made an alert snap throw and picked the speedster off first. Billy Southworth also walked, but was left on when Whitted flied out to Schultz in deep right.[20]

St. Louis started strong in the bottom half when Doak and Janvrin opened with singles. After Heathcote forced Janvrin at second, Milt Stock grounded slowly to Caton, who fired home to Schmidt. Doak was tagged out after a rundown, but Heathcote maneuvered to third and Stock slipped in to second. Hornsby worked the count to 3-and-1 and Hamilton fired outside for ball four, but Heathcote, trying to steal home on the pitch, was tagged on the heel by Schmidt and called out by plate umpire Cy Rigler for the third out.[21] Heathcote indignantly whirled, grabbed a nearby glove, and accidentally shoved it into Schmidt's face when he actually meant the physical abuse for the arbiter.[22]

Another argument over a close play took place in the seventh. With one away for the Pirates, Janvrin ranged to his right to field Grimm's groundball. Doak covered first base and caught Janvrin's toss just as Grimm hit the dirt with a head-first dive for the bag. Umpire Charlie Moran signaled out and Grimm was not pleased as he lay flat across the base protesting the decision. The Cardinals' Austin McHenry launched his third consecutive long drive to the outfield in the home half, but Southworth put this one away, just as center fielder Carey had run down his first two clouts.[23]

The bottom of the eighth featured plenty of action on the basepaths for St. Louis. Rookie right-handed reliever Johnny Meador had taken over on the mound for Hamilton. Two walks, a sacrifice, and a force put Cardinals runners on the corners with two outs. Stock came through with a line-drive single to right, plating Dillhoefer for a 3-0 lead and sending Heathcote to third base. The Cardinals again tried some trickery as Rickey signaled for a double steal; however, Caton, after taking Schmidt's late throw to second, whipped the ball over to third and nipped Heathcote trying to return to the base.[24]

With a three-run lead, Doak went after the complete-game conquest. A one-out double to right-center by Caton, followed by Grimm's infield hit brought the tying run to the plate. But Doak prevailed for his ninth win by getting a force out and a routine fly ball to center field,[25] securing his shutout and giving the St. Louis Cardinals their first regular-season victory at the intersection of Grand and Dodier.

The time of game was 1 hour and 40 minutes. Overall, the base-on-balls total (six) skunked the strikeout figure (0), with six hits in the line score for each team, and St. Louis committing the only error. Many of the fans exiting the ballpark headed for the busy streetcar transit stops and stations that could return them home via the 485-mile track network within and near the city.[26]

The game's hero, Bill Doak, eventually made history off the field as well as on it. After baseball outlawed the spitball, Doak was a prominent voice in the successful effort to allow 17 pitchers, including himself, who used the pitch to continue throwing it for the remainder of their careers. Also, Doak approached the St. Louis-based Rawlings Sporting Goods Company with a proposal for a new model of baseball glove with webbing that made it easier for fielders to catch the ball. Doak's design marked a significant evolution in the role of the glove, transforming it from primarily a means of protection, and Rawlings sold the Bill Doak model for years to come.[27]

SOURCES

In addition to the sources cited in the Notes, the author also accessed Retrosheet.org, Baseball-Reference.com, SABR.org/bioproj, and *The Sporting News* archive via Paper of Record. Additional websites accessed were newspapers.com and stltoday.com.

NOTES

1. Rob Rains, *The St. Louis Cardinals, the 100th Anniversary History* (New York: St. Martin's Press, 1992), 30.
2. "Babe Draws Crowd but Ping Does Work," *The Sporting News*, June 24, 1920: 1.
3. Rains, 26.
4. "Cards Sure Move to a Place in the Sun," *The Sporting News*, July 1, 1920: 1.
5. Robert L. Tiemann, Cardinal Classics, *Outstanding Games From Each of the St. Louis Baseball Club's 100 Seasons*, 1882-1981 (St. Louis: Baseball Histories, Inc., 1982), 100.
6. *St. Louis Post-Dispatch*, July 2, 1920: 32.
7. Edward Callary, *Place Names of Illinois* (Urbana: University of Illinois Press, 135). Gibson was later renamed Gibson City by the US Post Office Department.
8. "Notes of the Game," *Pittsburgh Daily Post*, July 3, 1920: 10.
9. Edward F. Balinger, "Doak Has Pirates at Mercy and Cardinals Score Whitewash, 3-0," *Pittsburgh Daily Post*, July 3, 1920: 10.
10. "Notes of the Game," *Pittsburgh Daily Post*, July 3, 1920: 10.
11. *The Sporting News*, July 1, 1920: 8.
12. *St. Louis Post-Dispatch*, July 2, 1920: 22.
13. "Janvrin Is Sent to Initial Sack by Boss Rickey," *St. Louis Post-Dispatch*, July 2, 1920: 24.
14. Steve Steinberg, "Bill Doak," SABR Baseball Biography Project, sabr.org/bioproj/person/1359e4e2.
15. "Play-by-Play," *Pittsburgh Daily Post*, July 3, 1920: 10.
16. "Notes of the Game," *Pittsburgh Daily Post*, July 3, 1920: 10.
17. Charles J. Doyle, "Failure to Hit Bill Doak Cost Buccos Hard Battle, 3 to 0," *Pittsburgh Post-Gazette*, July 3, 1920: 9.
18. "Play-by-Play," *Pittsburgh Daily Post*, July 3, 1920: 10.
19. "Play-by-Play," *Pittsburgh Post-Gazette*, July 3, 1920: 9.
20. Ibid.
21. "Play-by-Play," *Pittsburgh Post-Gazette*, July 3, 1920: 9.
22. "Notes of the Game," *Pittsburgh Daily Post*, July 3, 1920: 10.
23. Ibid.
24. "Play-by-Play," *Pittsburgh Post-Gazette*, July 3, 1920: 9; James M. Gould, "Cardinals 3, Pittsburg 0," St. Louis Star, July 2, 1920: 20.
25. Ibid.
26. Tim O'Neill, "A Look Back—Hodiamont Line Street Car Closed Out After 107 Years of Service," *St. Louis Post-Dispatch*, May 23, 2010, stltoday.com.
27. Steinberg.

SISLER FIRST BROWNIE TO HIT FOR CYCLE

August 8, 1920: St. Louis Browns 11, Washington Senators 4 (Game Two of Doubleheader), at Sportsman's Park

BY RICHARD RIIS

"They've called Ty Cobb the Georgia Peach for the last 15 years," wrote Dean Snyder, nationally syndicated columnist and sporting editor of the Newspaper Enterprise Association, "but at this point in the drama enters Peachy George. It now remains for the world to start calling the Brown star the Great George Sisler."[1]

With Cobb temporarily relegated to the background due to a protracted slump that saw him hitting under .300 as late as June 2, and then by being sidelined for a month after colliding with teammate Ira Flagstead in pursuit of a fly ball, the St. Louis Browns first baseman had emerged from Cobb's shadow as arguably baseball's premier hitter.

The 27-year-old Sisler, now in his sixth campaign with the Browns, had hit better than .300 all but his rookie season, and above .340 for the past three years, but was finally capturing national attention by seizing a place at or near the front of the batting race since Opening Day.

On June 14 Sisler passed the .400 mark and kept on going, reaching as high as .434 on June 28. Although his average dipped into the .390s in late July, on the morning of August 5 Sisler, having hit safely in 10 straight games, was in second place among the AL leaders at .403, just ahead of Chicago's Shoeless Joe Jackson at .397, and Yankees slugger Babe Ruth at .392. Topping them all was Tris Speaker, the veteran leader of the Cleveland Indians, whose torrid hitting in June and July had pushed his average to a phenomenal .421.

With the Browns stuck in a distant fifth place at 47-51, far behind the contending Indians, Yankees, and White Sox, the attention of St. Louis fans was focused primarily on Sisler and his progress at the plate as the Washington Nationals, a half-game up on the Browns at 46-49, arrived in town on August 5 for a four-game series.

The Browns won the first two games, 2-1 and 14-7, with Sisler collecting three hits in nine at-bats, extending his hitting streak to 12 games. After a scheduled day off, the clubs met again for a Sunday doubleheader.

The Browns took the opener, 3-2, in the ninth on a double by Earl Smith, a wild throw by center fielder Sam Rice that allowed Smith to take third, and a single by Jack Tobin. Sisler smacked two hits, a single and a double, in four at-bats.

A pair of right-handers, Elam Vangilder (2-5) for the Browns and Eric Erickson (10-9) for the Nationals, started on the mound for the second game. Washington was the first to score, tallying a pair of runs in the third inning. After Patsy Gharrity walked and Erickson bunted him to second, Joe Judge singled to center, scoring Gharrity. Judge was subsequently called out stealing second on a contested call that loomed larger when the following hitter, Clyde Milan, hit only the 15th home run of his of his 14-year career into the right-field stands for a 2-0 lead.

St. Louis took its revenge in the bottom of the third when Joe Gedeon walked and Sisler, who tallied a single in the first inning, doubled to right center, advancing Gedeon to third. Baby Doll Jacobson drove Gedeon and Sisler home with a game-tying double. Erickson bobbled Ken Williams's smash back to the mound and then threw the ball away, allowing Jacobson to score and Williams to take second. Smith flied to center, but Tobin singled to right, scoring Williams to put the Browns up 4-2.

George Sisler led the majors in batting with a .407 average in 1920 and a .420 mark two years later. He hit at a .340 clip in his 15-year career. (Library of Congress)

Bucky Harris's double to left, an infield single by Howard Shanks, and a sacrifice fly by Jim O'Neill gave the Nationals a third run in the fourth inning but a great defensive play possibly prevented further damage. Shanks stole second and Gharrity reached base on an error by Smith at third. Erickson hit a grounder past Vangilder, but second baseman Gedeon grabbed the ball in back of second, tumbled, and threw the pitcher out at first from a sitting position.

Sisler belted his 14th home run of the season with Gedeon on base in the bottom of the fourth, giving the Browns a 6-3 lead.

St. Louis skipper Jimmy Burke, who had pulled Vangilder for a pinch-hitter in the fourth inning, brought in right-hander Bill Burwell to pitch. Although Burwell allowed a single to Milan and hit Braggo Roth with a pitch, the Nats failed to score in the fifth.

Gharrity came close to a homer in the sixth when his long drive to left caromed off the wall inches short of going over. Williams snared the ball on the rebound to hold Gharrity to a double. Ericksen left Gharrity stranded when he tapped back to the mound for the third out.

A single by Wally Gerber and a walk to Gedeon put two runners on as Sisler came to the plate in the bottom of the sixth. Sisler, who had singled in the first, doubled in the third, and homered in the fourth, hit a low liner to center which bounced off Rice's shins and rolled to the wall. Both Gerber and Gedeon scampered home and Sisler pulled into third with a triple, giving him a cycle for the game. Sisler attempted to score when Williams was thrown out at first on a grounder to Harris at second, but was tagged out at the plate on the relay from Judge to catcher Gharrity.

Judge hit a solo homer in the seventh to cut the St. Louis lead to 8-4, but the Browns retaliated in the bottom of the frame with a triple by Josh Billings and a single by Burwell. Two batters later, Sisler, hitting for the fifth time in the game, came to the plate with the bases full but went down swinging.

St. Louis added two more in the eighth. Jacobson and Williams singled. After Jacobson was picked off second by Gharrity, Smith poked a base hit to center, with Williams scoring on an errant throw to the infield, his second of the afternoon, by Rice. Tobin's sacrifice fly brought Smith home to make the score 11-4.

Burwell set the Nationals down in the ninth, giving the Browns a sweep of the doubleheader and the four-game series, and evening their record for the season at 51-51.

Under the scoring rules of the day, Vangilder was awarded the win despite pitching only four innings. Although he'd been hammered for 16 hits and 11 runs, 10 of them earned, Eric Erickson pitched a complete game for the losers. Washington manager Clark Griffith had his reasons. "With a double bill in Chicago tomorrow staring him in the face, the National boss was obliged to leave Erickson in throughout the entire second game, although it was apparent early in the game that the big Swede was not at his best."[2]

George Sisler's 6-for-9 day at the plate raised his batting average to .407, the same average with which he would win the batting title at season's end. His hitting streak, standing now at 14 games, would extend to 25 games before it was stopped by Philadelphia's Scott Perry on August 24. Sisler, the first Browns player to hit for the cycle, would duplicate the feat almost a year to the day later, on August 13, 1921, against the Detroit Tigers, in the Motor City.

SOURCES

In addition to the sources listed in the notes, the author also consulted the *New York Times*, *St. Louis Post-Dispatch*, *St. Louis Star-Times*, *The Sporting News*, and *Washington Post*.

NOTES

1. Dean Snyder, "Sisler Heralded as the New Ty Cobb," *Fitchburg* (Massachusetts) *Sentinel*, August 9, 1920: 6.
2. Jack Nye, "Double Defeat Handed Griffmen Gives Browns Clean Sweep of Series," *Washington Herald*, August 9, 1920: 8.

KEN WILLIAMS CLUBS THREE HOME RUNS FOR THE BROWNS

April 22, 1922: St. Louis Browns 10, Chicago White Sox 7, at Sportsman's Park

BY JOE WANCHO

THE DOORMATS OF THE AMERICAN League, also known as the St. Louis Browns, were making their way northward in the AL standings. In 1918 and 1919 they finished in fifth place. In 1920 they inched up to fourth. And when the curtain came down on the 1921 season the Browns were looking up at only New York and Cleveland in the junior circuit. Though they finished 17½ games off the pace, and just 1½ games ahead of the fourth-place Senators, it would be hard not to notice that the Browns were putting together quite a ballclub.

A capsule look at the Browns in 1921 shows that George Sisler led the team in batting with an astounding .371 average. Gentleman George led the league in stolen bases (35) and tied with teammate Jack Tobin for the league-best in triples (18). The hard-hitting outfield was Tobin in right field and "Baby Doll" Jacobson in center, who both hit .352, and left fielder Ken Williams, who batted .347 and led the Browns in home runs (24) and RBIs (117). Catcher Hank Severeid (.324) and third baseman Frank Ellerbe (.288) contributed to the offensive firepower. The team's .303 batting average was third in the league. On the mound, Urban Shocker led the league with 27 wins.

But would the Browns, and the rest of the American League for that matter, have enough heft to knock off New York in 1922? Indeed, the Browns and their AL brethren caught a big break as the season got under way. After the 1921 World Series, won by the New York Giants over the Yankees, Bob Meusel and Babe Ruth took part in a barnstorming tour. This was a common practice among players of the day to earn extra money during the offseason. However, members of the teams that played in the World Series were forbidden to barnstorm. Commissioner Kenesaw M. Landis fined Meusel and Ruth $3,362 apiece, which equaled the players' shares from the World Series. In addition, each player was suspended for the first six weeks of the 1922 season. The Yankees would have to make do without their star players until May 20. The Yankees would still be a formidable foe to their opponents. But perhaps they were just a little less intimidating.

On April 22, 1922, the Browns hosted the Chicago White Sox at Sportsman's Park. On the mound for the hometown heroes was Dixie Davis. The right-handed hurler won 18 games in 1920 and 16 in 1921. He also led the league in walks both years as well. It would not be going out on a limb to say that Davis's lack of control was his Achilles' heel. On the hill for the White Sox was José Acosta. The Havana native spent much of his career as a relief pitcher and spot starter. After posting identical 5-4 records for Washington in 1920 and 1921, Acosta was sent to the Philadelphia Athletics with Bing Miller in exchange for Joe Dugan. Then Philadelphia sold Acosta to Chicago. The starting assignment would be the only one of the season for the diminutive Acosta (5-feet-6, 134 pounds).

Tobin led off the home half of the first inning with a walk. Browns manager Lee Fohl put the sacrifice on and Ellerbe bunted back to the mound. Tobin checked into second base. Sisler followed with a single that plated Tobin. Then Williams came to the plate and launched a home run that cleared the bleacher seats and landed on Grand Avenue. The two-run blast was the left fielder's first round-tripper of the season, and after one inning, the Browns had jumped out to a 3-0 advantage.

That lead held until the sixth inning. True to form, Davis had yielded four walks in the first five innings, but so far had surrendered only one base hit. He was the beneficiary of two double plays that nullified Chicago threats. Acosta righted himself after the first frame, keeping the three-run deficit a manageable one.

But in the top of the sixth inning, the White Sox put two on base, on an error by Browns shortstop Wally Gerber and a walk to Eddie Collins. Harry Hooper, the former Red Sox star and future member of the Hall of Fame, deposited a Davis pitch into the right-field seats to tie the game at three.

But the Browns answered immediately when Sisler led off the bottom of the frame with a single to center field and Williams followed with his second homer. This time, the home run was of the line-drive variety. But the Browns were not done, as a single by Severeid was followed by back-to-back doubles by Gerber and Marty McManus. The Browns were in front 7-3 and Acosta's afternoon was over.

With two outs in the bottom of the seventh, Sisler again reached base with a single to left off reliever Lum Davenport. Sisler stole second base, and went to third on a throwing error by Chicago catcher Ray Schalk. Williams followed with a mighty clout into the right-field stands to set a new American League record with three home runs in a game.

St. Louis scored an unearned run in the bottom of the eighth inning, and with a 10-3 lead in hand, the Browns looked to be on Easy Street. Not so fast, as the top of the ninth inning proved to be quite adventurous. Davis fell into his old bugaboo of the free pass, and walked the first three batters he faced. With one out, Ernie Johnson singled to right field, and the score became 10-5. After Hervey McClellan popped out to third base, Collins walked to again load the bases. With a 2-and-0 count on Hooper, Fohl finally had seen enough. He removed the starter and summoned Shocker from the bullpen. The old spitballer Shocker was used mostly as a starter and was the ace of Fohl's staff, but he lost Hooper to make the score 10-6. The walk was charged to Davis, who surrendered a career-high 11 bases on balls in the game. Johnny Mostil followed in the Chicago lineup and Shocker issued him yet another free pass. St. Louis was leading 10-7 and the go-ahead run was coming to the plate, but Bibb Falk ended the suspense, grounding to Gerber, who threw to third base to force Hooper. The Browns won to raise their season record to 5-4.

Attendance at the game was reported at just over 3,000. No doubt they left the park that day following the 1:42 affair happy, and maybe a bit relieved.

But Ken Williams was just getting started. Between April 22 and 29 he smashed nine home runs in seven games. His power surge prompted L.C. Davis of the *St. Louis Post-Dispatch* to write this tribute to the slugger:

> *Whose name is on every tongue? Ken Williams*
> *Whose praises are now daily sung?*
> *Ken Williams*
> *Who is the rooter's joy and pride?*
> *Who gives the pesky pill a ride?*
> *And separates it from its hide? Ken Williams*
>
> *Who is our most admired youth? Ken Williams*
> *Who makes the fan forget Babe Ruth?*
> *Ken Williams*
> *Who is the guy so calm and cool?*
> *Who swings his trusty batting tool?*
> *And knocks the pellet for a gool? Ken Williams.*[1]

Comparisons between Williams and Babe Ruth began to pour from writers' pens in national magazines. But Williams refused to buy into the debate. "I have never made any claim that I could equal Babe Ruth as a home-run hitter," he said. "On the other hand, I know I am not his equal. No player in the game could hope to match Ruth over a full season's course. I have done my best. But I have never had in mind trying to beat Babe for I know it can't be done."[2]

Ken Williams indeed lived in anonymity when compared to Babe Ruth, or even with some of his teammates on the Browns. The baseball correspondent who covered the St. Louis clubs for *The Sporting News* illustrated the point with the following anecdote: "A photographer was told to go out and get a picture of Ken Williams swinging at the plate — and the well meaning camera artist proceeded to shoot Bill Jacobson. ... Imagine the text and illustration that would have been incident to Babe Ruth hitting three home runs in one ball game! Sporting editors would have wired every syndicate in operation to rush story and photographs. But Ken hits three of them and a photographer on the ground doesn't even know which is Ken or Bill Jacobson. ..."[3]

NOTES

[1] Roger A. Godin, *The 1922 St. Louis Browns: Best of the American League's Worst* (Jefferson, North Carolina: McFarland, 1991): 50.

[2] John J. Ward, "A Rival for Babe Ruth?" *Baseball Magazine*, July, 1922: 359-360.

[3] Godin, 47.

In 1922 slugger Ken Williams led the AL in home runs (39) and the majors in RBIs (155). (Library of Congress)

THE BROWNS' 17TH HIT FINALLY PRODUCES THE SECOND RUN FOR VICTORY

May 30, 1922: St. Louis Browns 2, Detroit Tigers 1 (16 Innings; Game Two of Doubleheader), at Sportsman's Park

BY JEFF FINDLEY

THE AMERICAN LEAGUE REGULAR season consisted of 618 games in 1922, none of which exceeded the 16-inning matchup between the St. Louis Browns and Detroit Tigers on May 30. Hosting the Tigers and already in the thick of a pennant race, the Browns had suffered a narrow 6-5 loss in the morning game of the Memorial Day doubleheader, and needed the split to keep pace with the New York Yankees.

Reports that day are conflicting, but a St. Louis newspaper reported that 22,000 attended the afternoon matchup.[1] The Tigers were operating without the services of player-manager Ty Cobb, who was dealt an indefinite suspension that morning by American League President Ban Johnson for reportedly "trying to pulverize [umpire Frank] Wilson's feet"[2] the day before as Cobb kept stepping on Wilson's toes as he argued umpire decisions multiple times. Outfielder Harry Heilmann suffered the same fate for his role in the contentious debate, so neither was eligible for the Memorial Day contests.

The Browns sent Urban Shocker to the mound. The Browns ace was making his eighth start in the month of May; just three days earlier he had hurled 9⅓ innings in a 2-1 loss at the Chicago White Sox. Shocker, a spitball artist who won 187 games in his major-league career, already had nine wins under his belt in the first two months of the season.

Cobb's Tigers countered with John "Red" Oldham, a Maryland-born southpaw starting his seventh game of the 1922 campaign. Oldham had saved the morning game for Detroit, inducing a game-ending groundout by future Hall of Famer and 1922 American League Most Valuable Player George Sisler to salvage a 6-5 win.

Sisler posted his first of four hits in game two when he drove a high fly over the head of Tigers left fielder Bobby Veach in the bottom of the first, but he had to settle for a long single when he missed the bag on the turn at first base. It was the most excitement recorded in the early innings, as Shocker and Oldham scattered a total of three hits in the opening three innings.

Frank Ellerbe, in his second season with the Browns after arriving in exchange for Earl Smith of the Washington Senators a year before, put St. Louis on the scoreboard in the bottom half of the fourth when he doubled to left-center to drive in Ken Williams. It was the second hit of the inning and only the fourth off Oldham, but it staked the always-tough Shocker to a lead.

With Cobb sidelined, coach Dan Howley took the reins of the Tigers, although his role was mostly that of messenger, with Cobb watching the game and calling the shots from a box just in the rear of the Tigers' bench.[3] (Howley, along with Browns trainer William Bierhalter, would exercise more influence in a game less than two months later when the two were pressed into action as umpires in a Browns-Tigers matchup in Detroit after the scheduled arbiters missed a train connection from Buffalo and did not arrive for the game.[4])

Shocker marched on unscathed through the middle innings. A great stop by second baseman Marty McManus in back of second left two Tigers runners on base in the top of the seventh, and after

93

eight innings Shocker had relinquished only five hits while striking out five.

The last inning of regulation told a different story. With the Tigers still trailing 1-0, Bob Jones started a Detroit rally with one out by beating out a roller to third. Ira Flagstead followed, but with a 1-and-1 count on him, Larry Woodall came on to pinch-hit and popped out to Sisler. Down to their last out, the Tigers finally put something together. Topper Rigney's single sent Jones to third and then Johnny Bassler singled to right, driving in Jones with the equalizer. The game moved to extra frames when Shocker set down Oldham on three pitches.

With the first major-league night game still 13 years away,[5] natural sunlight provided the only illumination of the day. With a 3:00 P.M. first pitch the game ambled toward dusk as no serious scoring threat occurred in the 10th or 11th inning, and Oldham was stranded at third in the top of the 12th. The next two innings showed no change in the score, and both starters had completed 14 innings.

With one out in the top of the 15th, Detroit leadoff hitter Fred Haney singled to left. Several Browns players surrounded umpire Brick Owens, voicing their displeasure over his rulings on balls and strikes to Haney, and it culminated with the ejection of Shocker and right fielder Jack Tobin. Harry Bullion of the *Detroit Free Press* described it this way: "Shocker became so enraged over what he thought was a strike on Haney in the fifteenth that he threw a bat Haney left at the plate after hitting safely with a crash against the grandstand, and was invited to stay out of the festivities. Tobin supported Shocker so vociferously that he, too, got the gate."[6]

The next morning Ban Johnson informed manager Lee Fohl that Tobin was suspended indefinitely. He would sit for five games before returning to the lineup on June 6. Johnson's telegram made no mention of Shocker.[7]

With Shocker done for the day, Fohl substituted former University of Missouri left-hander Hubert "Hub" Pruett, making only the seventh appearance of his major-league career. Pruett struck out George

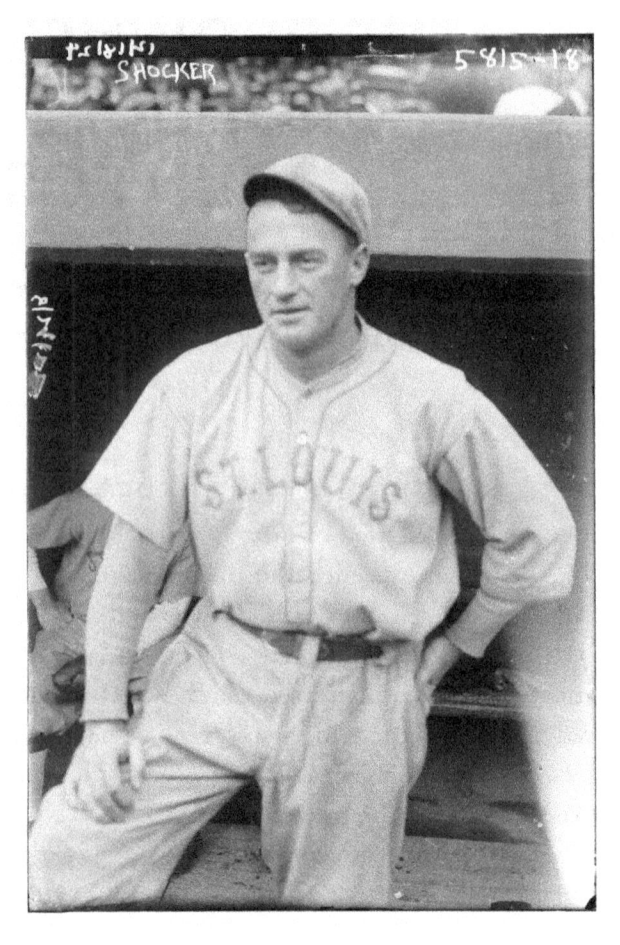

Urban Shocker won 20 or more games for four straight seasons (1920-1923) for the Browns, and finished with a 187-117 career record. (Library of Congress)

Cutshaw and Danny Clark, the Tigers' second- and third-place hitters, and the threat was averted.

With one out in the bottom of the 15th, Ken Williams of the Browns started a rally with a double down the right-field line. Oldham, who had allowed just one run in 14⅓ innings, was replaced by Ole Olsen, a rookie whose major-league career would last just two seasons. Of the pitching change, the *Free Press* said: "Instructions were given to Howley by Manager Cobb, who was hidden from view near the rear entrance to the dugout, to insert Olson *[sic]*, a right hander, against Ellerbe, who bats the same way."[8] Olsen was successful in closing out the inning, striking out Ellerbe and, after intentionally walking McManus, retiring the opposing pitcher, Pruett, on a liner to end the frame.

The fateful 16th started with Pruett, who fanned two in relief of Shocker the inning before, continuing his dominance by striking out Veach and Jones before Bert Cole, now playing center field in Flagstead's original spot in the batting order, grounded to third baseman Ellerbe for the third out. The top of the Browns' lineup awaited Olsen.

When Tobin was granted his departure in the 15th inning, Cedric Durst quietly replaced him in right field. A left-handed hitter, Durst was making his major-league debut. His leadoff infield single was one of only 12 at-bats during the season.

Wally Gerber sacrificed Durst to second. After intentionally walking Sisler, Olson got Baby Doll Jacobsen, 0-for-8 in the game, to fly out deep to center field. Next came Tharon Patrick "Pat" Collins. The seldom-used backstop had only seven previous plate appearances in 1922, but three of them resulted in safeties. He continued to make the most of his opportunities, driving an Olsen offering to center field and scoring Durst with the game-winner.

The victory left the Browns just 2½ games behind the Yankees in a pennant chase that wasn't decided until just two days remained in the season, with the Browns ultimately finishing one game off the pace.

Shocker and Oldham both toiled for 14⅓ innings, neither of them posting a decision. Oldham allowed one run and 15 hits and struck out four. Shocker was a touch better, allowing one run and 11 hits while striking out eight.

George Sisler posted four hits in six official at-bats, and walked twice to boost his average to .426, on his way to a staggering final mark of .420.

And for Cedric Durst, his major-league debut featured the most efficient stat line of all.

One at-bat. One hit. One run scored.

The game-winner.

SOURCES

In addition to the sources cited in the Notes, the author also accessed Retrosheet.org and Baseball-Reference.com.

NOTES

1   *St. Louis Star and Times*, May 30, 1922.

2   Harry Bullion, "Intentional Walk Is Costly to Cole," *Detroit Free Press*, May 30, 1922.

3   "Tales of the Tigers," *Detroit Free Press*, May 31, 1922.

4   Harry Bullion, "Bengals Twice Get Five in One Inning," *Detroit Free Press*, July 24, 1922.

5   "MLB Holds First Night Game," history.com/this-day-in-history/mlb-holds-first-night-game.

6   Harry Bullion, "Bengals Grab First but Fail in Second," *Detroit Free Press*, May 31, 1922.

7   "Johnny Tobin Draws Indefinite Suspension; Shorten Replaces Him," *St. Louis Post-Dispatch*, May 31, 1922.

8   Harry Bullion, "Bengals Grab First but Fail in Second."

THE LITTLE WORLD SERIES

September 18, 1922: New York Yankees 3, St. Louis Browns 2, at Sportsman's Park

BY STEVE STEINBERG

IN 1922, THE DEFENDING AMERICAN League champion New York Yankees and the St. Louis Browns battled for first place all season long. The pennant was at stake when the Yankees came to Sportsman's Park on a mid-September weekend for a three-game "Little World Series" with only a half-game lead over the Browns. After the teams split the first two contests, the final game slipped away from the Browns in the ninth inning. "It was one of the most nerve-racking finishes ever flaunted before a St. Louis public," John Sheridan wrote in the *Globe-Democrat*. "That one inning will remain indelible in the memory of the fans who witnessed it—to the grave. It was a nightmare."[1]

Browns owner Phil Ball had additional field boxes constructed; they would serve him well when his team reached the World Series. Sportsman's Park had crowds of close to 30,000 for each of the games, including almost 10,000 behind ropes in the outfield, "making a farce of what should be the greatest series of the season to date."[2] The contracted playing field figured to make the games high-scoring affairs, with many ground-rule doubles.

The Yankees won the first game of the series, 2-1, when they beat their old nemesis, Urban Shocker, on Saturday. He had already lost to them six times in 10 decisions this year, though he came into the game with an overall record of 23-15. In the bottom of the ninth, Yankee center fielder Whitey Witt was hit by a soda bottle thrown from the bleachers and knocked unconscious. For a few seconds, as fans spilled out of the stands and the Yankees came charging out of their dugout, many with bats in hand, the game seemed in danger of slipping out of control.

The Yankees won the game "amid scenes of riot and disorder never before seen on an American ball field," wrote Monitor in the *New York World*."[3] Home-plate umpire Billy Evans recalled the time a St. Louis bottle had knocked him unconscious and fractured his skull in this ballpark, on September 15, 1907. The Browns' team doctor, Robert Hyland, said that Witt was fortunate the injury was not more severe than a laceration and slight concussion. Both Browns owner Phil Ball and American League President Ban Johnson put up rewards to apprehend the bottle-thrower. Ball announced that bottled refreshments would not be sold in the bleachers for the rest of the series.

The Browns won the second game, on Sunday, a 5-1 five-hitter tossed by screwball pitcher Hub Pruett, who "held the slugging Yanks in the hollow of his hand," in the words of the *New York Times* reporter.[4] The rookie pitcher (who would finish the season with a 7-7 record and a 2.33 earned-run average) had handcuffed the great Babe Ruth all season long, repeatedly striking him out on that fadeaway pitch.

With the pennant hanging in the balance, the third game, on Monday, September 18, would climax with a series of moves and countermoves befitting a World Series Game Seven. The Yankees started Joe Bush, going for his 25th win. Browns manager Lee Fohl tabbed Dixie Davis, a journeyman who had won 34 games for them in 1920-1921.[5] With so much at stake, Davis responded with the game of his life.

The Monday game drew 30,000, the biggest home crowd of the season. Long before the age of blogs and the internet, the center-field fans had communicated with each other and showed up wearing white shirts. Throughout the game, when the Yankees were at bat, they swayed back and forth, which gave the New Yorkers a difficult hitting backdrop.

HOME OF THE BROWNS AND CARDINALS AT GRAND AND DODIER

Journeyman pitcher Dixie Davis won 34 games for the Browns in 1920-1921. (Library of Congress)

For seven innings Davis held the Yankees to just two hits, both of them infield hits by Witt. At this point, the Yankees had scored but one run in 22 innings. Bush was almost as effective. "On an open field," New York sportswriter Frank O'Neill wrote, "Bush would have had a shutout. Joe was never better in his long and interesting life."[6] However, St. Louis held a 2-0 lead, by virtue of routine fly balls that went into the crowd for what Monitor called "St. Louis two-baggers."[7]

The eighth inning started well for the Browns; Davis retired Witt for the first time that day. Then Joe Dugan doubled for the first legitimate hit of the game for New York. Davis then struck Ruth out on three pitches.[8] Now came the first of a series of breaks—lucky breaks for the Yankees, bad breaks for the Browns. Wally Pipp singled off Davis's glove. The ball dribbled to second baseman Marty McManus, who had no chance of throwing Pipp out but compounded the matter by throwing to first, rather than holding onto the ball. He threw the ball away, and Dugan came in to score. Davis then rebounded by striking out Bob Meusel with a called strike three. The Browns were now just three outs away from taking back first place, but their lead had been cut to one run, 2-1.

After Bush retired the Browns in the bottom of the eighth, right-hander Davis returned to the mound. Incredibly, Yankees catcher Wally Schang got another infield hit off Davis's glove. Manager Miller Huggins went to his bench and sent lefty Elmer Smith to the plate to pinch-hit for Aaron Ward.[9] Smith was an excellent pinch-hitter; he would finish his career 39-for-123 in that role, for a .317 batting average.[10] The very first pitch to him got away from catcher Hank Severeid. On the passed ball, Schang moved to second.

Lee Fohl then made a move that would be discussed for years. He decided to pull Davis. "Davis was to be pitied," wrote the reporter of the *World*. "He pitched a remarkable game, one entirely unexpected for him, but Fohl apparently had no confidence in him when things began to break badly."[11] Yet Fohl later explained that he had something very different on his mind. He went for the lefty-lefty matchup, a strategy not commonly used in 1922.[12] "I took [Davis] out because I thought we could win with the shift."[13]

Fohl then brought in the previous day's pitcher, the southpaw Pruett. Roy Stockton of the *St. Louis Post-Dispatch* noted that this was where many of the second-guessers were focusing: not so much on whether Davis should have been pulled, but on whether Pruett was the one to have been brought in. Sid Keener, the sports editor of the *St. Louis Times*, understood. "Fohl's plan was to get Smith out of the game by calling for a southpaw."[14] In that he succeeded. With the lefty now pitching, Huggins pulled Smith in favor of right-handed-hitting utilityman Mike McNally.

McNally laid down a bunt. Catcher Severeid threw low and wide to the foul side of third, and Schang slid in safely. It was an aggressive move, going for the lead runner. A perfect throw would have nipped Schang. There were now runners at the corners and no one out. Pruett then walked Everett Scott on four pitches; the game accounts indicate it was not intentional.[15]

Fohl now pulled Pruett for Urban Shocker, who had saved a number of games for the Browns in the past three seasons.[16] Huggins decided to let Joe Bush, a good hitter, bat for himself.[17] He grounded to McManus, who threw home. The throw was in the dirt, but Severeid got it on the first bounce to force Schang. But then Whitey Witt, with bandages still wrapped around his forehead from his injury, stroked a clean single up the middle, scoring McNally and Scott. The fans were stunned; the Yankees had taken the lead, 3-2. "Here was divine retribution, or poetic justice of the first order," wrote Harry Schumacher.[18] Shocker then retired Joe Dugan on an inning-ending double play.

The heart of the Browns' lineup went quietly in the bottom of the ninth. George Sisler's record-setting hitting streak ended at 41 games.[19] He would finish the season with a .420 batting average, but a recent shoulder injury had taken its toll. In this critical series, he managed but two hits in 11 at-bats.

One New York paper captured the dramatic finish this way. "Already St. Louis had raised the brimming bowl to its lips to drink deep of the nectar. … Almost before they knew it, the Browns were beaten and the sounds of reverie died. The silence was sepulchral."[20] John Sheridan summed up the heartache of Browns fans. "Just like the old-time story books in which we used to read about fairies vanishing, so did a one-run lead the Brownies held going into the final inning waft into oblivion."[21]

The Yankees held on to win the pennant by one game.

Postscript:

In a sidebar to Dixie Davis's obituary in the *Sporting News* of February 10, 1944, it was noted that this game of September 18, 1922, "has been the subject of more telephone inquiries than any other sports event of Mound City history," including Grover Alexander's 1926 World Series heroics.

NOTES

1. John B. Sheridan, *St. Louis Globe-Democrat*, September 19, 1922.
2. While it was not uncommon for teams of this era to allow fans on the field, neither the Giants nor the Yankees allowed them onto their home field, the Polo Grounds, despite the potential revenue they would have generated.
3. *New York World*, September 17, 1922. "Monitor" was the pseudonym of sportswriter George Daley. The Browns would later apprehend the bottle-thrower, a youngster. Supposedly, the bottle did not hit Witt directly, but rather flew up to his forehead when Whitey stepped on it.
4. *New York Times*, September 18, 1922.
5. Davis had made three trips to the majors without a win in the 1910s: the 1912 Reds, 1915 White Sox, and 1918 Phillies.
6. *New York Sun*, September 19, 1922. In the fourth inning, the crowd let Browns outfielder Baby Doll Jacobson catch Wally Pipp's fly ball. Yankee manager Miller Huggins protested that Pipp should be awarded a double. But the umpires ruled that Jacobson fell against the outfield ropes (behind which the fans stood) and did not go behind them. Twice during the game, Ruth tried to penetrate the wall of fans, unsuccessfully, as Jacobson and Williams both earned doubles and later scored.
7. *New York World*, September 19, 1922. The *New York American* said one of the doubles was almost a home run. Often there were such conflicting accounts of plays in different papers. Since this was long before the advent of video, there is no way to resolve these differences.
8. Ruth went 0-for-4 in this game and was not a factor.
9. Smith was best known as a Cleveland Indians hero in the 1920 World Series, when he hit the first grand slam in post-season play.
10. Smith was an excellent pinch-hitter; he would finish his career 41-for-132 in that role, for a .311 batting average; see retrosheet.org. As a pinch-hitter, Smith was 4-for-14 (.286 batting average) in 1922 and would go 10-for-21 (.476) in 1923.
11. *New York World*, September 19, 1922.
12. Smith had played for Tris Speaker's Indians, where he was regularly platooned in the outfield with Smoky Joe Wood. Speaker had popularized the concept, which was then called a "double-batting shift" or "reversible" hitters. The word "platooning" did not even exist in baseball at the time.
13. *St. Louis Times*, September 19, 1922.
14. Sid Keener, *St. Louis Times*, September 20, 1922.
15. The *Globe-Democrat*, for example, said that Pruett seemed rattled after McNally's bunt, suggesting the walk was not intentional.
16. From 1920 to 1922, Shocker appeared in relief 29 times and earned 12 (retroactive) saves.
17. A career .253 hitter with 7 home runs and 59 doubles, Bush hit .325 in 1921 and .326 in 1922.
18. *New York Globe and Commercial Advertiser*, September 19, 1922.
19. Sisler had broken Ty Cobb's consecutive-game hitting streak of 40 the day before. None of the newspapers mentioned the nineteenth-century marks of Willie Keeler (44 in 1897) or Bill Dahlen (42 games in 1894).
20. *New York Evening Telegram*, September 19, 1922.
21. John B. Sheridan, *St. Louis Globe-Democrat*, September 19, 1922.

A WILD WIN AGAINST THE CHAMPS

August 9, 1923: St. Louis Cardinals 13, New York Giants 12, at Sportsman's Park

BY NORM KING

2, 15, 25, 33, 37.

Don't worry. This isn't a brainteaser where you have to guess the next number in the sequence. These figures are statistics from a wild and wacky major-league game played on August 9, 1923, between the reigning world champion New York Giants and the hometown St. Louis Cardinals. It included 12 errors (eight by the Giants and four by the Cardinals), 15 innings, 25 runs (St. Louis won 13-12), 33 hits, and 37 players used (including six pitchers by each team).[1]

"The game dragged through three hours and thirty-eight minutes and was a very weird affair, made up of some good baseball, but a great deal more that was decidedly bad," said the *New York Times*.[2]

The Giants, led by the Little Napoleon, John McGraw, were headed toward their third straight National League pennant, and entered the game with a 69-36 record, seven games up on second-place Pittsburgh.[3] Branch Rickey, another legendary baseball figure managed the Cardinals, who were 16½ games behind the Giants at 53-53. Since this was an era where one would find wild cards only in a game of canasta, the Redbirds were effectively out of the race. That didn't mean they didn't want to win, as they had halted the Giants' six-game winning streak the day before with a 4-3 victory.

Bill Doak, one of the few pitchers still allowed to use the spitball after it was outlawed in 1920, started for the Cardinals. Although he had a moderately successful career (169-157 with ERA titles in 1914 and 1921), Doak had an impact on baseball that changed the game forever. In the game's early days, gloves were little more than padding for the hand. Doak developed the idea of adding webbing to the glove between the thumb and forefinger to make catching the ball easier, and worked with the Rawlings Sporting Goods Company to bring his idea to fruition. The revolutionary Rawlings "Bill Doak" model baseball glove was introduced in 1920, and was sold until 1953.

Neither Doak's glove nor his saliva helped him on this day. He had a 5-10 record entering the game, but with a respectable 3.26 ERA. He exited the game with a less-respectable 3.54 ERA, as he faced only four batters, all of whom scored. After Ross Youngs and Freddie Maguire singled, Frankie Frisch, who went into the game batting .355, deposited a ball into the right-field bleachers to give the Giants a quick 3-0 lead. When Irish Meusel doubled, Rickey replaced Doak with Johnny Stuart. Stuart induced Casey Stengel (the Ol' Perfessor was in McGraw's grad school at the time) to ground out to first, allowing Meusel to reach third.[4] George "High Pockets" Kelly brought Meusel home with a sacrifice fly to complete the scoring. Youngs' single kept alive a hitting streak that eventually reached 12 games, and raised his batting average to .350.

Giants starter Art Nehf entered the game with a 9-8 record and a reputation for delivering when it was needed most. He had pitched complete-game victories for McGraw to clinch each of the previous two World Series, including a 1-0 victory in Game Eight of the 1921 fall classic.[5] His 5.28 ERA was enough to encourage the Cardinals to think they had a good chance to eat into New York's lead, and they did, with two runs in the bottom of the first. Max Flack led off with a lucky-bounce single past second, moved to second on Ray Blades' groundout, then scored on Rogers Hornsby's single. The Rajah moved up on Sunny Jim Bottomley's groundout, then scored on Milt Stock's single. The Giants led 4-2 after one.

HOME OF THE BROWNS AND CARDINALS AT GRAND AND DODIER

In the second, the Cardinals gave a good indication of what kind of game it would be when they scored two runs on one walk, one hit, and errors by Maguire and Hank Gowdy. Virgil Barnes relieved Nehf with two out in the inning, even though both Cardinal runs were unearned. The game was tied 4-4 after two, and the fun was just beginning.

"Spectators saw the Giants, heroes of 38 errorless games this season, kick the ball about in the early innings like the rankest Municipal League team," wrote Herman Wecke in the *St. Louis Post-Dispatch*.[6]

The teams exchanged runs in the third. Irish Meusel doubled to extend a hitting streak that would reach 15 games, and came home on Kelly's single. Eddie Ainsmith got that one back for the Cards when he was safe on a fielder's choice, stole second, and scored on Stuart's single.

St. Louis took its first lead of the game in the fourth, thanks to more bad Giants defense. After Blades singled, Youngs dropped Hornsby's fly ball, putting two on. After Jim Bottomley popped to first and Stock forced Hornsby at second, Heinie Mueller tripled to score two. Maguire then bobbled Ainsmith's grounder, which brought Mueller home, and then threw the ball past Kelly at first, for his second error on the same play and third of the game. It was now 8-5 Cardinals. Scorecards were starting to look pretty messy by this point.

New York got one back in its half of the fifth, using the typical McGraw-style small-ball game. After Frisch doubled, Meusel walked, and then was forced at second on a Stengel groundball. Frisch, now on third, showed why he was nicknamed the Fordham Flash as he stole home as part of a double steal, making the score 8-6.

Ah, but the baseball gods can be cruel, as Frisch went from hero to goat in the bottom of the inning. Claude Jonnard was pitching for New York and

A career .289 hitter, Milt Stock twice had at least 200 hits in a season. (Library of Congress)

got himself in a bases-loaded jam with two out. He seemed on his way to getting out of the inning unscathed when Stock hit a grounder back to the box. The ball, however, hit Jonnard's glove and bounced toward third, where Frisch picked it up and threw it down the right-field line, bringing home two more runs and increasing the Cardinals' lead to four.

Then a strange thing happened; nobody scored in the sixth or the seventh. In the eighth, Gowdy decided that now was a good time to hit his only home run of the season, which sliced the lead to 10-7. Many teams would find it daunting to face a three-run deficit going into the ninth, but the Cardinals committed the second-highest number of errors in the National League in 1923 (232). Factor in the overall goofiness of the game, and the Giants had reason for optimism. That optimism proved warranted when they scored three unearned runs to tie the game on three hits and two errors. It was now on to extra innings, where the game went from crazy to bizarre.

After a scoreless 10th, New York caught Rickey and the Cardinals napping in the 11th. Pitcher number six for the Giants, Jack Scott, had been inserted into the eighth spot in the batting order, and was the first due up in the inning. Ninth-place hitter Frank Snyder led off instead and singled. Scott then came up and he singled as well. Both runners ended up scoring, thanks in part to a Hornsby error. According to the rules, Snyder would have been called out for batting out of order if the Cardinals had appealed, but they didn't.[7]

"And yet, when Frank Snyder and John [sic] Scott batted out of turn in the eleventh inning and singled, Rickey was as unobservant as a seventh son of a seventh Heine Mueller," wrote the *St. Louis Post-Dispatch*."[8]

We'll never know what the writer meant by the seventh son of a seventh Heine Mueller, but Hornsby atoned for his error (this seemed to be a day of atonement for a lot of players) when he smacked a two-run homer in the bottom of the inning to tie it 12-12 and keep the game going. Finally, in the bottom of the 15th, Ainsmith scored from second on a single by winning pitcher Lou North (3-3), who went four hitless innings for the win. Scott (9-7), who pitched 6⅔ innings of relief, was the loser.

Besides the wild action, lead changes, and unusual goings on, the game was interesting because a number of players, lesser-known and Hall of Famers alike, had spectacular days. Frisch whacked a home run and two doubles, raising his average to .357; he also scored three runs. Hornsby went 2-for-5 with three RBIs to keep his average at .401 (He "slumped" to .384 by the end of the season, but still won his fourth of six straight batting titles.) Stock brought his average over the .300 mark by going 4-for-8. Stuart, who came on in relief of Doak, pitched 7⅓ innings, more than any other hurler that day, and even got into the hitting act, going 2-for-4, with one run scored and one RBI.

Wecke summed up the game nicely: "It is doubtful if St. Louis fans will ever be treated to another game of baseball just like the one put on exhibition yesterday by the Cardinals and the world's champion Giants yesterday."[9]

SOURCES

In addition to the sources listed in the Notes, the author also used: Bill Doak biography by Steve Steinberg, sabr.org

NOTES

1. The Giants used 20 players in all, the Cardinals 13.
2. "Cards Beat Giants in 15 Innings," *New York Times*, August 10, 1923: 8.
3. "The Little Napoleon" was McGraw's nickname.
4. In his SABR biography of Stengel, Bill Bishop wrote that Stengel and McGraw would often spend hours talking about strategy and tactics.
5. The World Series was a best-of-nine affair from 1919 to 1921.
6. Herman Wecke, "It Appears that Frank Snyder Was the Boy Who Caused the Disorder in the Giants' Batting Order," *St. Louis Post-Dispatch*, August 10, 1923: 16.
7. Scott and Alex Gaston, who replaced Snyder behind the plate, batted out of turn twice, but the Cardinals said nothing.
8. "Rickey Keeping Score When Snyder and Scott Bat Out of Turn in 11th," *St. Louis Post-Dispatch*, August 10, 1923: 16.
9. Wecke.

HAINES TOSSES ONLY CARDINAL NO-HITTER IN SPORTSMAN'S PARK

July 17, 1924: St. Louis Cardinals 5, Boston Braves 0, at Sportsman's Park

BY GREGORY H. WOLF

WHEN CARDINALS RIGHT-HANDer and future Hall of Famer Jesse Haines retired in 1937 after 18 seasons with the club, he held the franchise record for wins (210), innings pitched (3,203⅔), starts (387), and complete games (209), and had helped guide the Redbirds to five NL pennants and three titles. Haines's pitching records have all since been surpassed, but there is one that can never be broken. On July 17, 1924, Haines tossed the only National League no-hitter in the history of Sportsman's Park, the steel and concrete stadium built in 1909. "I started as I always do," said Haines of his fateful performance against the Boston Braves, "trying the corners with my curve on the outside to right-handed hitters and keeping the fast one close to the handle of the bat."[1] "[N]ot even a questionable hit," opined the *St. Louis Post-Dispatch*,[2] while the *Boston Globe* gushed, "nothing doubtful whatsoever about Haines' brilliant accomplishment."[3]

Best remembered as a knuckleball pitcher, the 30-year-old Haines was primarily a fastball/curveball pitcher at the time of his no-hitter. He began experimenting with the knuckler in 1923, and credited Philadelphia Athletics pitcher Eddie Rommel, the first big leaguer to use the knuckleball extensively, for teaching him the pitch. Unlike Rommel, who gripped the pitch with the tips of his index and middle fingers, Haines gripped the ball with the first knuckles on those fingers with the ball resting against the inside of his ring finger. The result was a hard knuckler that came straight down and did not flutter like Rommel's. "[My knuckler] acted like a spitball," said Haines. He had a breakout season in 1923, winning 20 games, and seemed primed for stardom, but his knuckler suddenly vanished. "Thought I had [the knuckler] in 1923," said Haines, "but it eluded me the next years."[4] Haines struggled in 1924. "[He] has not been a wonderful pitcher this season," offered the *Post-Dispatch* bluntly.[5] Entering the game against Boston, Haines (4-12) had lost eight of his last nine decisions, and had a 66-66 career record.

Branch Rickey, the Cardinals' 42-year-old skipper in his sixth season guiding the club, needed big Jess to kick it up a notch. Despite winning the first two games of a six-game series with Boston, St. Louis had the worst record in the majors (32-49), a whopping 22½ games behind the New York Giants. The Braves, en route to their third consecutive season with at least 100 losses, were an early-season surprise under Dave Bancroft, who assumed the role of player-manager for the first time in his Hall of Fame career. However, despite a 16-16 start, the Tribe (33-48) was in sixth place.

A Thursday-afternoon game between two bad teams would not normally be a hot ticket, but it was the annual Tuberculosis Day in the Gateway City. The *Post-Dispatch* estimated that 15,000 people showed up at Sportsman's Park, yet derided the crowd as "apathetic." "The many ladies in attendance," suggested the paper, "gave passing attention to the ball game" and seemed more interested in the music, festivities, and the "variegated color in the stands."[6]

Following Haines's 1-2-3 first, the Cardinals took their swings at Boston's 25-year-old right-hander Tim McNamara (6-4), who sported a lackluster 12-21 career record in parts of three seasons. Seeming a "bit unsteady," according to the *Boston Herald*, McNamara yielded a one-out single to Wattie Holm, who extended his hitting streak to 17 games.[7] The hot-hitting rookie, who entered the game batting .362, moved to second on a wild pitch, and then scored on Rogers Hornsby's single.

After fanning four of the first eight batters he faced, Haines walked his mound opponent, but second baseman Hornsby redeemed the cardinal sin by making an impressive grab of Gus Felix's "low line drive" to end the frame.[8] It was the Rajah's second stellar defensive play of the game, following his scoop of Cotton Tierney's hard grounder an inning earlier.

Haines's single in the third led to the Redbirds' second run. He moved up a station on a sacrifice bunt, and scored when Felix misplayed Jim Bottomley's fly to center field.

Leading the majors with a .405 batting average entering the game, Hornsby belted his second of three singles in the fifth with one out. Bottomley, who finished runner-up to Hornsby in the race for the batting title the previous season (.384 to .371), also singled. After Ray Blades flied to center and Specs Toporcer, widely considered the first position player to don eyeglasses, was hit by a pitch to load the bases, Cuban-born Miguel Gonzalez (to whom the *Post-Dispatch* referred with his given name instead of the more common anglicized nickname Mike), hit a routine grounder to second baseman Ernie Padgett. The rookie's throw to first sailed over Stuffy McInnis's head, enabling Hornsby to scamper home. Jimmy Cooney followed with a single to drive in Bottomley and Toporcer, for a 5-0 lead.

The rest of the game revolved around Haines, who profited from good defense, including his own, to record the final 12 outs. After Haines walked both McNamara and Bill Cunningham in the sixth, Casey Stengel smashed a bullet back to the mound "with such force that it almost took off the pitcher's glove," according to St. Louis sportswriter Dent McSkimming.[9] The *Boston Globe* reported that the 6-foot Haines knocked down the ball, which rolled toward third. "For several moments it was a question whether the big pitcher would recover in time," but Haines retrieved the orb and rifled it to Bottomley to end the inning.[10]

In his 18 years with the Cardinals (1920-1937), Jesse Haines pitched for five pennant winners and three World Series champions. (National Baseball Hall of Fame, Cooperstown, New York)

Two additional defensive gems helped keep the no-hitter intact. In what was described as the "most remarkable fielding play of the day," Hornsby corralled another sharp grounder by Tierney in the seventh. The crowd gasped the next inning when Mickey O'Neil hit a blooper to short center, but Holm was playing shallow and made a difficult catch seem routine, according to the *Globe*.[11]

Haines needed only six pitches to retire the side in the ninth. Felix flied to right field on the first pitch and Cunningham popped up to short on a 1-and-2 count. Up stepped Stengel, whose heroics in the 1923 World Series had made him a household name. The Braves acquired the journeyman flychaser from the Giants in the offseason, after he went 5-for-12 in the World Series, including game-winning home runs in Games One and Three, as the Giants almost knocked off the New York Yankees. Praised by the *Post-Dispatch* as the "biggest batter of the whole Boston team and one of the most dangerous pinch-hitters in either major league," Stengel hit an 0-and-1 grounder to Hornsby, whose throw to Bottomley ended the game in one hour and 43 minutes. "[T]hat fellow had great stuff on the ball," said the rough-and-tumble Stengel, still decades removed from the "Old Perfessor" moniker. "Wonderful speed and pretty good control."[12] Haines's batterymate was equally impressed. "Haines had greater speed than I have ever found him using before," said Gonzales.[13]

The loss went to McNamara who yielded 12 hits and five runs, but just one earned, in seven innings. Johnny Cooney, whose brother Jimmy started at short for the Cardinals, set down the side in order in the eighth.

The no-hitter was poetic justice for Haines, who finished with five strikeouts and three walks while facing 30 batters. As a rookie in 1920, he was in a grueling pitchers' duel with the Chicago Cubs' Pete Alexander in his last start of the season on October 1. Haines hurled 9⅔ hitless frames, from two outs in the sixth until one out in the 16th, in a game he eventually lost in the 17th inning, 3-2.

Notwithstanding his no-hitter, Haines continued to struggle in 1924, finishing with an abominable 8-19 record. After another poor campaign (13-14) in 1925, Haines miraculously rediscovered his knuckler. "Not until mid-summer 1926 did the mystery of it come back to me," he explained. "And then I started to throw a slow ball. That helped me as much as the knuckler."[14] Haines emerged as one of the Redbirds' most consistent hurlers, going 95-43 over the next six seasons (1926-1931), twice notching 20 wins.

Haines's no-hitter is widely considered the first in Cardinals history; however, two hurlers for earlier teams based in St. Louis also tossed no-hitters at home. On July 15, 1876, the Brown Stockings' George Washington Bradley beat the Hartford Dark Blues in the first no-hitter in the history of the National League. The game took place at the wooden-framed Grand Avenue Ball Grounds, on the site of the future Sportsman's Park. In his first professional start, Ted Breitenstein of the American Association Browns held the Louisville Colonels hitless on October 4, 1891, also at the Grand Avenue Ball Grounds, which by that time had been renovated and was affectionately called Sportsman's Park. The American Association disbanded after the 1891 season, and the Browns joined the NL in 1892. The teams played as the Browns, Perfectos, and, since 1900, as the Cardinals.

SOURCES

In addition to the sources cited in the Notes, the author also accessed Retrosheet.org, Baseball-Reference.com, the SABR Minor Leagues Database, accessed online at Baseball-Reference.com, SABR.org, and *The Sporting News* archive via Paper of Record.

NOTES

1. Billy Evans, "Hitless Hero Says Good Control Gave Him Record Game," *Olean* (New York) *Times*, September 17, 1924: 7.
2. Dent McSkimming, "Jess Haines No-Hit, No-Run Game Against Boston," *St. Louis Post-Dispatch*, July 18, 1924: 19.
3. "Jess Haines of St. Louis Enters Pitching Hall of Fame," *Boston Globe*, July 18, 1924: 10.
4. Neil Russo, "Batters Knuckled Under to Haines and Schultz," [publication unknown], September 6, 1964. Jesse Haines player file at the National Baseball Hall of Fame.
5. "Haines Has Won 5 Games and Lost 12; So Far This Year," *St. Louis Post-Dispatch*, July 18, 1924: 6.
6. McSkimming.
7. "Jess Haines of St. Louis Shuts Out Braves Without a Hit—Only Three Reach First," *Boston Herald*, July 18, 1924: 7.
8. "Jess Haines Pitches No-hit Game for Cards," *Evening News* (Harrisburg, Pennsylvania), July 18, 1924: 17.
9. McSkimming.
10. "Jess Haines of St. Louis Enters Pitching Hall of Fame."
11. Ibid.
12. McSkimming.
13. Ibid.
14. Eugene F. Karst, director of information, St. Louis Cardinals Press release, 1928. Jesse Haines player file at the National Baseball Hall of Fame.

DYER TOSSES SHUTOUT IN CARDS LAUGHER

August 24, 1924: St. Louis Cardinals 17, Brooklyn Robins 0 (Game Two of Doubleheader), at Sportsman's Park

BY DOUG WALDEN

THE CARDINALS ENTERED THE 2 P.M. doubleheader with the Brooklyn Robins far off the pace in the National League race. Winners of only 50 of their 118 games to this point in the season, the disappointing club was sixth in the National League, ahead of only the Philadelphia Phillies and Boston Braves. The third-place Robins, on the other hand, were hoping to stay in the thick of the pennant race. They were 67-52, seven games behind the first-place New York Giants with just over one month to go.

The Cardinals' offense was led by their hitting sensation, second baseman Rogers Hornsby. Entering the doubleheader, Hornsby was leading the National League in hitting at .423, was second in runs scored with 92 and third in home runs with 19. The Cardinals' other hitting star, first baseman Jim Bottomley, led the team in RBIs with 78. After taking the first game from the Robins in dramatic fashion, 7-6, on a home run by Hornsby in the bottom of the ninth, St. Louis sent 24-year-old Eddie Dyer to the mound in the second contest. Dyer entered the game with a record of 5-10 and an ERA of 5.28, having pitching very poorly in his five previous games (32 hits and 20 earned runs over 18⅔ innings). He was opposed by Robins rookie starter Jim Roberts, 0-2 with an ERA of 7.08. It figured to be a high-scoring affair — and it was, at least on one side of the line score.

In a quick 1-hour and 43-minute effort, Dyer had his best stuff as he walked two and scattered seven singles to pick up his sixth win and his only shutout of the season as the Cardinals smoked the Robins, 17-0. Still officially a rookie after only short stints with the Cardinals in 1922 and 1923, Dyer was in command throughout the game and was aided by four Cardinals double plays.

Roberts did not fare nearly as well. The Cardinals sent 49 batters to the plate, getting 25 hits and two walks off Roberts and reliever Tiny Osborne. Hornsby started the scoring with a first-inning triple and came home on Bottomley's single.[1] After picking up single tallies in each of the first two innings, the Cardinals rocked Brooklyn for seven more in the fourth, aided by a critical error by shortstop Johnny Mitchell. The outburst chased Roberts, who would not win a game in his short major-league career. Against Osborne the Cardinals added a single run in the fifth, two in the seventh, and five in the bottom of the eighth to close the scoring. Osborne took one for the team, getting tagged with 8 runs and 15 hits in 4⅓ innings of work.

Reserve catcher Verne Clemons, giving a breather to first-stringer Mike Gonzalez, who was behind the plate in the opener, led the Cardinals offense with a double and four singles in five plate appearances. Bottomley and reserve shortstop Specs Toporcer each had four hits. Hornsby, the hero of the first game, and left fielder Ray Blades each contributed three hits. Dyer, not a bad hitter himself, chipped in at the plate with a double, a walk, a sacrifice, and three RBIs in his five plate appearances, raising his batting average for the season to .254. The whitewash ranked as the third most lopsided shutout in National League history and the fourth most lopsided in major-league history to that point.[2]

The Cardinals were playing with a patchwork crew in this second game of the doubleheader. In the first game starting pitcher Leo Dickerman was hit by a pitch and suffered a broken arm, and starting shortstop Jimmy Cooney dislocated his thumb on a play at third base. The injuries continued in the nightcap as Wattie Holm, an outfielder who was filling in at third base, broke a bone in his right foot while fielding a groundball.[3]

The 17-0 shutout ranked among Dyer's most memorable mound performances. While pitching for Rice Institute (later Rice University) in 1921, Dyer threw a no-hitter, besting future White Sox Hall of Famer Ted Lyons of Baylor.[4] In his first major-league start with the Cardinals, Dyer shut out the Chicago Cubs 3-0 on September 9, 1923, scattering eight hits.[5] The lopsided victory over Brooklyn was Dyer's only other major-league shutout.

In 1928 Dyer began a new career as a manager in the Cardinals' budding farm system. In 1946 he succeeded Billy Southworth as manager of the Cardinals and the team won the World Series against the Boston Red Sox that year. He managed the team through the 1950 season.

Unfazed after their humiliating defeat, the Robins immediately went on a 15-game winning streak, which placed them virtually even with the first-place Giants on September 6 as they approached the final three weeks of the regular season. However, the Giants closed the season with wins in 11 of their last 17 games to capture the NL pennant by 1½ games. The Cardinals, meanwhile, finished their season with 25 of 32 games on the road and limped in with a disappointing record of 65-89 (.422), 28½ games behind the first-place Giants.

SOURCES

In addition to the sources cited in the Notes, the author also accessed Retrosheet.org, Baseball-Reference.com, and SABR.org.

NOTES

1 *New York Times*, August 25, 1924.

2 Ronald C. Liebman, "The Most Lopsided Shutouts," SABR Research Journal Archives, research.sabr.org/journals/lopsided-shutouts.

3 *St. Louis Post-Dispatch*, August 25, 1924; "Rickeyites Have Four Performers on Hospital List," *St. Louis Star and Times*, August 25, 1924.

4 Warren Corbett, "Eddie Dyer," SABR BioProject. sabr.org/bioproj/person/b3e94581.

5 "Cubs Blanked by Recruit," *New York Times*, September 10, 1923.

GEORGE SISLER KNOCKS IN A CAREER-HIGH SEVEN RUNS

July 11, 1925: St. Louis Browns 10, Washington Senators 5, at Sportsman's Park

BY JOE WANCHO

THE WASHINGTON SENATORS WERE feeling plenty good about themselves. The reigning world champions had won 10 of their last 13 games as they rolled into St. Louis on July 11, 1925. The Senators were in the midst of their Western swing having split a four-game set with the White Sox in Chicago. As the Senators geared up for the four-game series against the Browns, they were 3½ games ahead of second-place Philadelphia. The Browns, despite winning six of their last seven games, were in fifth place, 13½ games off the pace.

The Senators had a strong outfit, starting with the pitching staff, led by Walter Johnson and Stan Coveleski. On this day, Dutch Ruether toed the slab for the visitors. Ruether, who sported a 9-3 record, was matched up with the Browns' Joe Giard. The rookie southpaw, from Ware, Massachusetts, entered the game with a 1-2 record. His Achilles' heel was the free pass. By the end of the season, despite a record of 10-5, his total walks (87) doubled his strikeouts (43).

Both teams could fill the box score with explosive offensive statistics. The Nats fielded one of the greatest infields of their era with Joe Judge at first base, Bucky Harris at second, Roger Peckinpaugh at short, and Ossie Bluege at the hot corner. Earl McNeely was the center fielder, and he was flanked by Goose Goslin in left field and Sam Rice in right. Muddy Ruel was the backstop. McNeely would end the season with the lowest batting average of the regulars, .286. As a team, Washington hit .304.

St. Louis countered with George Sisler at first base. Second baseman Marty McManus combined with Bobby LaMotte at short (Wally Gerber was nursing a sore leg) to form the keystone combo. Gene Robertson manned third base. Ken Williams, Baby Doll Jacobson, and Harry Rice made up the Browns' outfield, left to right. Leo Dixon and Pinky Hargrave shared catching duties. Although Dixon was an outlier with an average of only .224, the Browns hit .298 as a team.

The Senators and Browns were both led by player-managers, not an uncommon occurrence then. Harris led the Senators, while Sisler was the Browns' skipper. Both were in their second season leading their squads.

Right-handed-hitting Joe Harris, who started at first base against the lefty Giard, slashed a pitch to left field with one out in the top of the second inning. Williams misjudged the ball and Harris landed at third with a triple. He scored on a single by Bluege, and the visitors took the early 1-0 lead.

Ruether escaped unharmed in the bottom of the third inning. He surrendered two walks and made a throwing error to load the bases, but Jacobson struck out to end the threat.

Goslin added to the margin in the fourth with a solo shot to right field, his 11th home run of the season. In the bottom of the frame, Hargrave led off with a double. Two walks later the bases were loaded as Sisler came to the plate. There would be no goose eggs on the scoreboard this time as Sisler sent a triple to right-center. Three runs crossed the plate and the Browns led 3-2 after four innings.

The Senators unraveled in the fifth inning, as two errors and three walks contributed to a six-run inning for St. Louis. Ruether, whose throwing error allowed Jacobson to advance to third base, was ejected by home-plate umpire Harry Geisel. The other error was committed by shortstop Everett Scott, who replaced

Peckinpaugh in the first inning after Peck was injured on a hot smash by LaMotte. The big blow in the inning was a grand slam by Sisler off reliever Allen Russell. The Browns blew the game open with a 9-2 advantage. All six runs were unearned.

"It's the timing of the swing," said Sisler. "Perfect timing is what enables a little man, even, to get long hits."[1] The seven RBIs were a career high for Sisler.

McManus ended the scoring for the Browns in the sixth inning when he hit a solo shot off reliever Spencer Pumpelly. It was Pumpelly's only big-league game; he worked one inning. The Senators scored three runs in the eighth inning, but for the most part they were meaningless as the Browns cruised to a 10-5 victory.

Giard went the distance to even his record at 2-2. Ruether was tagged with the loss and dipped to 9-4. The Senators made four errors. Ruether issued seven free passes which, combined with two errors of his own doing, led to his downfall.

Washington went 7-7 on its Western jaunt. After sweeping three at Cleveland to end the trip, the Senators were in a virtual tie for first place with the Athletics, who had the edge in winning percentage. But the Senators ultimately prevailed and captured their second straight pennant, only to lose to Pittsburgh in the World Series.

The Browns made a gallant effort, posting a 50-33 record from July to October, but ended up in third place, 15 games back of Washington. As for Sisler, he ended the season batting .345 with 12 home runs and 105 RBIs. It was the ninth straight year that Gentleman George batted above .300, including two seasons in which he batted over .400 (.407 in 1920 and .420 in 1922).

In 1920 Sisler was within 12 hits of breaking Ty Cobb's single-season record of 248, set in 1911. There were 11 games remaining in the season. Sportswriter F.C. Lane of the *St. Louis Post-Dispatch* wrote the following poem in the September 22, 1920, edition of the paper:

Who is the present king of swat?
George Sisler
Who pounds the pill around the lot?
George Sisler
Who is it when he's on the job,
Evokes the plaudits of the mob,
As in the palmy days of Cobb?
George Sisler
Who is the greatest guy on earth?
George Sisler
Who gives the fans their money's worth?
George Sisler
Who is the bird who doesn't pose,
As hero in the movie shows,
But busts the pellet on the nose?
George Sisler[2]

Sisler accomplished that and more. He totaled 21 hits in the final 11 games to set a new record with 257. Indeed, George was doing a lot of pellet busting.

NOTES

1 Rick Huhn, *The Sizzler: George Sisler, Baseball's Forgotten Great* (Columbia: University of Missouri Press, Columbia, 2004), 201-202.

2 Huhn, 93-94.

JESSE HAINES TOSSES SHUTOUT AND WALLOPS HOMER IN FIRST WORLD SERIES GAME IN THE GATEWAY CITY

October 5, 1926: St. Louis 4, New York Yankees 0, at Sportsman's Park

Game Three of the World Series

BY GREGORY H. WOLF

"SCREAMS, SHRIEKS, WHOOPS, BAWLS, howls, hollers, roars swept through the ballyard with the weird noise raised by cow bells, auto horns, whistles, rattles, and musical instruments," wrote Damon Runyon about the wild scene at Sportsman's Park for first World Series game ever played in St. Louis.[1] A member of the National League since 1892, the Cardinals had spent most of their existence mired in the second division until they captured an unexpected pennant in 1926. As the Cardinals and the New York Yankees prepared for Game Three in the Gateway City, the national media appeared awestruck by the enthusiasm of long-suffering baseball fans. "Baseball in this western citadel is not a recreation or an amusement," wrote Grantland Rice, "it's more a fever, a frenzy, a furor and a flaring flame."[2]

The pandemonium in St. Louis actually started the day before, on October 4, when the Redbirds arrived at the Washington Avenue train station at 3:50 P.M. to be greeted by thousands of fans. After losing the opening game of the fall classic, 2-1, to the favored Yankees, the Cardinals had taken Game Two, 6-2, behind an overpowering four-hit, 10-strikeout masterpiece by 39-year-old graybeard Pete Alexander. The Redbird faithful paid tribute by closing businesses and shops and accompanying the club on a parade for dozens of blocks through the city. "The town thought, slept, dreamed and ate baseball," raved sportswriter James R. Harrison in the *New York Times*.[3]

The party didn't stop after the parade. According to the *St. Louis Post-Dispatch*, thousands of fans had lined up by midnight for grandstand seats, creating a festive and raucous environment outside of the park, located at the intersection on Grand Avenue and Dodier Street on St. Louis's north side.[4] The gates opened at 8:30 on Tuesday morning to a throng of already hoarse and overly anxious fans. Sportswriter William F. Allen of the *Post-Dispatch* remarked that the commotion was unprecedented with the city practically closed and traffic jams bringing to a halt even the vast network of trolley cars.[5]

The celebratory atmosphere was tempered only by gloomy and ominous skies with unseasonably cool temperatures hovering in the low 60s. Nonetheless, a record crowd in excess of 38,500 had packed Sportsman's Park.[6] "It would have taken a cyclone, and earthquake, and a tidal wave to have kept St. Louis away from the ball park," chimed in Harrison in the *Times*.[7] By noon the dark clouds gave way to brilliant sunshine, enabling both teams to conduct batting practice before a sea of red-clad fans.

Soon after St. Louis Mayor Victor Miller threw out the ceremonial first pitch, home-plate umpire George Hildebrand yelled "Play ball" at approximately 1:30. Taking the mound for the Cardinals was Jesse Haines, a 33-year-old right-hander with a career record of 96-91 in seven years with the club. Since winning 20 games in 1923, he had struggled with his knuckleball and his fastball had seemingly lost its zip, leading many to wonder if he was washed up.[8]

An ankle injury limited Haines primarily to relief appearances for the first nine weeks of the '26 season, but he returned with a vengeance, finishing with a 13-4 record. Nonetheless, few sportswriters gave "Old Jess" a chance against the Bronx Bombers.

The Yankee "invaders were treated with disdain," wrote Harrison about the chorus of boos that greeted each batter.[9] Encouraged by the cajoling spectators, Haines retired the first six batters he faced. "The fans are nutty," Graham McNamee announced flatly as he called the game on WEAF radio in New York, the first World Series broadcast on radio.[10]

Erstwhile Cardinals skipper Miller Huggins, who guided the Yankees to their fourth pennant since becoming manager in 1918, surprised many by sending 33-year-old southpaw Dutch Ruether to the rubber. Acquired in a trade with the Washington Senators on August 27, Ruether went 2-3 in his five starts with the Yankees to conclude his 10th big-league campaign with a 124-89 slate. After yielding an innocuous one-out single to Billy Southworth in the first, Ruether encountered some trouble in the next frame when Chick Hafey stroked a one-out double down the left-field line, but was left stranded on third.

Joe Dugan led off the Yankees' third with a single, a promising sign given that the Bombers had managed just 10 hits and four runs in their previous 19 innings. After backstop Bob O'Farrell made what *Times* sportswriter Richards Vidmer described as a "great lunging catch [with Ruether at bat] as the ball swerved toward the stands and then twisted back toward the diamond," Haines issued a two-out walk to Earle Combs, giving the Yankees two baserunners for the first time since the sixth inning of Game One, but the team failed to score.[11]

The Cardinals threatened in the third when Haines hit a sharp yet routine grounder to first, pulling Lou Gehrig off the line. According to Harrison, Ruether was late in covering, enabling Haines to reach base.[12] Taylor Douthit walked and both runners moved up a station on Southworth's sacrifice bunt. But Ruether retired Rogers Hornsby and cleanup hitter Jim Bottomley to escape the jam.

Under rapidly darkening skies spitting rain, Babe Ruth led off the fourth with a single and moved to second on Bob Meusel's grounder. Just when it appeared that Haines might be in trouble, the umpires ordered the players off the field. Approximately 30 minutes later, Haines was back on the rubber warming up. Seemingly rejuvenated by the rest, Old Jess quickly dispatched Gehrig and Tony Lazzeri.

Unlike Haines, Ruether seemed out of sorts after the delay, yielding a leadoff single to Les Bell and walking O'Farrell with one out. The tenor of the game, and perhaps the entire Series, changed on the next at-bat. Light-hitting Tommy Thevenow hit a tailor-made double-play grounder to second baseman Lazzeri, whose throw to shortstop Mark Koenig forced O'Farrell. According to Harrison, Koenig was slow to cover second and thus "threw from a needlessly awkward position," and watched as the ball bounded past Gehrig's ankle.[13] Bell rounded third and scored the game's first run. After the game the press lambasted Koenig, a 22-year-old in his first full big-league season. He "tossed away the third game of the current world series with a double play and salvation in sight," scowled the *Times's* Vidmer, who described Ruether as "very much vexed and somewhat sulky" after Koenig's error.[14] Seemingly indifferent facing Haines, Ruether "grooved one for his pitching rival," continued Vidmer. Haines, a lifetime .187 batter thus far in his career with one round-tripper, deposited the first pitch over the right-field wall for a two-run blast and a 3-0 Cardinals lead. The "clamor was so great that the eardrums quivered," wrote Harrison of the crowd's reaction. "There has never been a noise like it on a ball field."[15]

Buoyed by his offensive heroics, Haines retired the side in the fifth on three deep fly balls, after which the Redbirds took their whacks at Ruether. Billy Southworth lined a leadoff single and advanced to third on Hornsby's single to center. Bottomley's grounder drove in Southworth for the Cardinals' fourth and final run, sending Ruether to the showers.

While relievers Bob Shawkey and Myles Thomas hurled 3⅔ innings of one-hit ball to keep the Yankees in the game, Haines refused to break under pressure.

He worked around a leadoff single in the sixth by Combs and one by Gehrig in the seventh. Looking fatigued to begin the eighth, Haines issued a walk to pinch-hitter Ben Paschal and had a 2-and-0 count on Combs when Hornsby ordered Flint Rhem and Art Reinhart to begin warming up in the bullpen. Mustering some youthful energy as black clouds returned, Haines fanned Combs on a 3-and-2 pitch and then retired Koenig and Ruth on weak infield grounders. "Haines' fastball came hopping out of the gloom," opined Harrison with an air of incredulity.[16]

According to the *Times*, Yankee batters had "tightened up" and were swinging at bad balls.[17] Gehrig's one-out single in the ninth, the team's fifth hit, barely had a chance to quiet the crowd before shortstop Thevenow scooped up Lazzeri's lazy grounder to initiate a 6-4-3 twin killing and conclude the game in 1 hour and 41 minutes.

Sportswriters were quick to heap praise on Haines, widely hailed as one of the good guys of baseball in an era defined by hard living (and hard drinking). "[N]ot many pitchers of the present even have thrown a fastball faster than Haines threw today," gushed Harrison about the hurler, who recorded just 46 strikeouts in 183 innings in '26. "There is no telling what would have happened if Haines had not had that fast ball, his courage and a wise head," he continued.[18] Haines tossed 111 pitches, fanned three and walked three. The Yankees' leadoff hitter reached base five times, but Haines was best in the pinches. Not known for compliments, Hornsby added, "I think he's the fastest man in the National League, second only to Dazzy Vance."[19]

The "Yankees had their chances, but they flittered them away," wrote Vidmer dejectedly. Their "murderous attack ... vanished, evaporated, dissolved, disappeared."[20] In a succinct summation of the game, the *New York Times* announced: "The Yanks played dully in a dull game."[21] A story of David defeating Goliath suddenly seemed like a distinct possibility.

SOURCES

In addition to the sources cited in the Notes, the author also accessed Retrosheet.org, Baseball-Reference.com, the SABR Minor Leagues Database, accessed online at Baseball-Reference.com, SABR.org, and *The Sporting News* archive via Paper of Record.

NOTES

1. Damon Runyon, reprinted in "Seeing Ourselves as Others See Us," *St. Louis Post-Dispatch*, October 6, 1926: 2.
2. Grantland Rice, reprinted in "Seeing Ourselves As Others See Us," *St. Louis Post-Dispatch*, October 6, 1926: 2.
3. James R. Harrison, "Cards Lead Series; St. Louis in Ecstasy as Yanks Lose, 4-0," *New York Times*, October 6, 1926: 1.
4. "Noisy Fans Tell World St. Louis Is Proud of Cardinals," *St. Louis Post-Dispatch*, October 5, 1926: 2.
5. William F. Allen, "New Record Set With 38,500 Fans Packing the Park," *St. Louis Post-Dispatch*, October 5, 1926: 1.
6. The *St. Louis Post-Dispatch* estimated the crowd to be approximately 38,500. Baseball-Reference gives the paid attendance as 37,708 as did the *New York Times*.
7. Harrison.
8. Gregory H. Wolf, "Jesse Haines," BioProject. Society for American Baseball Research (SABR), sabr.org/bioproj/person/afeb716c.
9. Harrison.
10. Graham McNamee, reprinted in "Seeing Ourselves as Others See Us," *St. Louis Post-Dispatch*, October 6, 1926: 2.
11. Richards Vidmer, "Koenig's Error Starts Yankees to Downfall," *New York Times*, October 6, 1926: 16.
12. Harrison.
13. Ibid.
14. Vidmer.
15. Harrison.
16. Ibid.
17. Ibid.
18. Ibid.
19. "Cards Hail Haines as a Double Star," *New York Times*, October 6, 1926: 17.
20. Vidmer.
21. Harrison.

BABE RUTH FIRST TO HIT THREE HOMERS IN WORLD SERIES GAME

October 6, 1926: New York Yankees 10, St. Louis Cardinals 5, at Sportsman's Park

Gave Four of the World Series

BY MARK S. STERNMAN

THE AMERICAN LEAGUE HOME-RUN leader with 47 in 1926, Babe Ruth had hit only four in his first 25 World Series games. Then he gave "the greatest exhibition of batting a World's Series ever saw"[1] and become the first player to hit a trio of homers in a postseason game as the Yankees evened the 1926 World Series at two games apiece with a 10-5 triumph over the Cardinals.

New York had scored only four times in the first 26 innings of the Series. "We hope to get going today," said Yankees manager Miller Huggins. "Our bats can't be tied indefinitely. The boys are bound to get some hits out of their system."[2]

In the first three games St. Louis received excellent starts from Bill Sherdel, Pete Alexander, and Jesse Haines. Game Four starter Flint Rhem, who had a career record of 10-15 entering the season only to lead the National League with 20 wins in 1926, began strongly by fanning Earle Combs and Mark Koenig. But Ruth put New York on top, 1-0, with a blast "a mile high [that] seemed a mile long. It went away out over the pavilion and came down among the mass of fans in Grand Avenue, who couldn't get into the park and stood out there listening to the cheering."[3]

Following Ruth, cleanup hitter Bob Meusel walked, but when he tried to score from first base on a single to right by Lou Gehrig, a throw from Billy Southworth to Rogers Hornsby to Bob O'Farrell cut him down at home.

New York starter Waite Hoyt went 16-12 in the regular season. He was facing the Cardinals for the first time since tossing a scoreless inning against them in his big-league debut as a member of the Giants in 1918. Hoyt's reacquaintance with the Cardinals quickly turned sour as St. Louis tied the game thanks to a trio of singles by Taylor Douthit, Southworth, and player-manager Hornsby. With men at second and third, Hoyt avoided further damage when he fanned Chick Hafey to end the frame.

Tony Lazzeri doubled off Rhem to start the second but, in more adventures in bad New York baserunning, fell victim to a Douthit-to-Tommy-Thevenow-to-Les-Bell relay while trying to stretch his hit into a triple. On a nice play, Bell "made a desperate drive to lay the ball on the sliding Yankee."[4] The last three New York batters had homered, walked, singled, and doubled, but the Yankees had just one run to show for all of these productive plate appearances.

Hoyt set down the Cardinals in order in the bottom of the second, and Rhem again retired Combs and Koenig in the top of the third to face Ruth with two outs and nobody on base. "Rhem threw Ruth a slow ball … as big as a derby hat, but the motion was deceptive and the Babe had started a quick swing when he saw that he was shooting too soon. Then, so quickly that you could barely perceive the motion, he pulled back again and took a long, slow swipe. … He banged the baseball … over the roof of the right field pavilion close to the middle of the park."[5] New York led 2-1, a score that would hold until the top of the fourth inning.

With one out in that frame, Rhem walked Lazzeri. Next Joe Dugan lifted one to shallow left-center. As sportswriter Grantland Rice described the

SPORTSMAN'S PARK IN ST. LOUIS

Babe Ruth walloped 15 round-trippers in only 129 at-bats in the World Series. (Library of Congress)

scene, "Both Douthit and Hafey started for the ball. They were traveling at top speed after the manner of two taxicabs attempting to cross the street from opposite directions when the collision took place. One had just reached the ball when the other struck him with the force of a tornado."[6] Dugan got credit for a double, and Lazzeri raced home with the third Yankee run. Hank Severeid singled, but Douthit got his second outfield assist in three innings by throwing out Dugan at home.

Down 3-1, St. Louis rallied in the bottom of the fourth. With one out, Hafey singled and O'Farrell reached on a Koenig error. In his postgame analysis, Huggins said, "Koenig … tried to do too much: He was trying to scoop the ball and throw it with the one motion, overeager to make the kill."[7]

Thevenow doubled to score Hafey and cut the Yankees' lead to 3-2. Specs Toporcer batted for Rhem and hit a sacrifice fly to tie the game, and then Douthit doubled in Thevenow to give the Cardinals a lead for the first time, 4-3. All three St. Louis runs in the inning were unearned. Southworth followed with a single to left, and Douthit tried to score. According to the radio broadcaster, "Ruth relayed it home with a perfect throw, a gorgeous throw and gets Douthit trying to come in from second base. Babe Ruth nor no other man ever made a better throw than that. … Babe shot it like an arrow and Severeid did not have to move for it."[8]

Art Reinhart relieved Rhem but failed to retire a batter. Combs walked and Koenig doubled him in to knot the game, 4-4. Reinhart walked Ruth and Meusel to load the bases, and threw two balls to Gehrig. "Here was the point where Hornsby should have acted," wrote the *New York Times's* James Harrison. "He had Herman Bell warmed up, and it was no secret that Reinhart was now in the clouds. The left-hander steadied a little, but [after] the count was two and two, he walked Gehrig, forcing Koenig in and sending New York ahead" with a 5-4 lead.[9] Hi Bell came in with the bases loaded and none out. A Lazzeri sacrifice fly and a Dugan squib to the catcher gave the Yankees two more runs to make the score 7-4.

New York expanded on its lead in the top of the sixth. Bell gave up a single to Combs and fanned Koenig before yielding Ruth's third homer of the game, this time to deep center field, to extend the Yankee lead to 9-4. The 39-year-old Alexander, in his 16th season in the majors, wrote, "It was one of the longest, if not the longest drive I have seen since I have been in baseball."[10]

After the game, in response to an assertion that the blast had gone almost 600 feet, the slugger admired his own prodigious feat. "Boy, that was a darling," Ruth proudly exclaimed.[11]

Meusel followed with a single, but Southworth earned his second assist of the game, matching Douthit, by throwing out Meusel trying to stretch the hit into a double. That saved a run as Gehrig followed with a double before Lazzeri popped to short.

O'Farrell and Thevenow gave the Cardinals a good start with singles to start the bottom of the sixth, but Hoyt escaped unscathed.

New York tallied its final run in the top of the seventh thanks to a Severeid single, Hoyt's sacrifice, and a double by Combs.

Wild Bill Hallahan, a back-of-the-bullpen reliever who walked more than five batters per nine innings in 1926 but who would become a frontline starter for St. Louis in the 1930s and the NL starter in the first All-Star game, in 1933, lived up to his nickname by walking the bases loaded in the top of the eighth, an inning that also featured the lone sacrifice bunt of Gehrig's 34-game World Series career. Severeid fouled to Les Bell at third, however, to strand a trio of Yankees.

St. Louis still trailed 10-4 going into the bottom of the ninth. Hornsby reached on a one-out single, advanced to second on Jim Bottomley's grounder, and scored on a two-out single by Les Bell. But Hoyt secured the 10-5 win by getting Hafey to pop to Severeid. According to Brooklyn manager Wilbert Robinson, Hoyt's "good control of a high fast one and a low curve made half of them of no value to the Cardinals."[12]

The Yankees had relied on heavy hitting to compensate for losing four runners on the bases. New

York would ultimately fall to the Cardinals in Game Seven on another aggressive baserunning adventure that failed—when Ruth was caught stealing to end the game.

NOTES

1 "Ruth's Great Exhibition," *The Sporting News*, October 14, 1926.

2 William F. Allen, "Crowd at Game Today Likely to Set New Record," *St. Louis Post-Dispatch*, October 6, 1926 (evening edition).

3 James Crusinberry, "Ruth Gets 3 Homers; Yanks Win, 10-5," *Chicago Tribune*, October 7, 1926.

4 J. Roy Stockton, "Yankees 3, Cardinals 1 (3½ Innings); Ruth Hits Two Home Runs," *St. Louis Post-Dispatch*, October 6, 1926 (evening edition).

5 Westbrook Pegler, "Finders Is Keepers When the Babe Swings the Bat," *Chicago Tribune*, October 7, 1926.

6 Grantland Rice, "Cardinals Crushed as Babe Ruth Smashes Three Mighty Home Runs," *Boston Globe*, October 7, 1926: 12; "Douthit played out the game, but the next day was stiff and sore, and Hornsby advised him to stay on the side lines" for the rest of the Series. "Alexander Joins Immortals in Cardinals' Series Triumph," *The Sporting News*, October 14, 1926.

7 "'I Told You So!' Huggins Chortles," *New York Times*, October 7, 1926.

8 "Radio Description of Fourth Game," *New York Times*, October 7, 1926.

9 James R. Harrison, "Ruth Hits 3 Homers and Yanks Win 10-5; Series Even Again," *New York Times*, October 7, 1926.

10 Grover C. Alexander, "Alexander Takes Hat off to Babe," *Boston Globe*, October 7, 1926: 12.

11 Associated Press, "Spirit of Cards Broken by Yank Attack: Huggins," *Chicago Tribune*, October 7, 1926.

12 Wilbert Robinson, "Ruth Really Great, Robinson Declares," *New York Times*, October 7, 1926.

LAZZERI'S SACRIFICE FLY WINS IN EXTRA INNINGS

October 7, 1926: New York Yankees 3, St. Louis 2 (10 Innings), at Sportsman's Park

Game Five of the World Series

BY RICK SCHABOWSKI

A CROWD OF 39,552, THE LARGEST of the three games at Sportsman's Park in the 1926 World Series, saw the road team win for the third time in the Series as the New York Yankees defeated St. Louis, 3-2, in 10 innings to move to within one win of a world championship.

The pitching matchup was a rematch of Game One, the Yankees' Herb Pennock versus the Cardinals' Bill Sherdel. This game was as well pitched as the opener, which New York won 2-1. The Yankees went down in order in the top of the first. After Babe Ruth made the last out of the inning, grounding out to first, he had a surprise waiting for him when he returned to the dugout. Pere Marquette Council 271, Knights of Columbus, of Boston, which counted Ruth as a member, presented him with a basket of flowers.

With one out in the bottom of the first, the Cardinals' Billy Southworth reached base on an error by shortstop Mark Koenig. Southworth stole second but didn't score as Rogers Hornsby grounded out to the pitcher and Jim Bottomley grounded out to second base.

After Bob Meusel grounded out to third to start the second inning, the Yankees got back-to-back singles by Lou Gehrig and Tony Lazzeri, putting runners on the corners. The threat ended when Joe Dugan ground into a second-to-first double play. Bob O'Farrell singled with two out in the bottom of the inning, but Tommy Thevenow made the third out, flying out to center. The third inning was three up, three down for both teams.

The Yankees' Ruth was stranded at first base after a one-out walk in the top of the fourth. In the home half, the Cardinals took the lead. With one out Bottomley hit a shot to left that a charging Ruth misplayed for a double. Bottomley scored when Les Bell singled to right. Chick Hafey fouled out to Ruth, who made a spectacular catch, leaning into the left-field box seats. The St. Louis fans who had jeered Ruth when he took the field in the bottom of the inning acknowledged his effort with applause. The inning ended when Bell was thrown out attempting to steal second base.

Speaking after the game about Ruth's difficult play, Yankees manager Miller Huggins said, "That catch by Ruth in the fourth on Hafey's foul fly was a great catch and showed that the Babe is a leader in his fighting spirit when he is ready to risk his neck for an almost impossible catch."[1]

The pitchers' duel continued in the fifth inning. The Yankees went down in order. O'Farrell singled leading off the Cardinals' half of the inning, but he was stranded after Thevenow grounded out, Sherdel struck out, and Wattie Holm made the third out on a grounder to short.

The Yankees tied the game in a bizarre top of the sixth. Pitcher Pennock led off the inning with a double that left fielder Hafey lost in the sun. The Cardinals had Pennock picked off second on a perfect throw by O'Farrell, but Thevenow dropped the ball for an error as he tried to make the tag. Earle Combs walked, then Koenig singled to left, scoring Pennock with the tying run and advancing Combs to second.

After Ruth struck out for the first out of the inning, a bizarre play occurred after Sherdel's first pitch to Meusel. Sherdel caught the return throw from O'Farrell awkwardly and hurt his left index finger. He had to leave the field for treatment as Jesse Haines warmed up hastily in the bullpen. But Sherdel returned to the mound. He retired Meusel on a fly to right, Combs moving to third. After Gehrig walked, loading the bases, Lazzeri drove a fly ball to deep right. On most days Lazzeri would have had a grand slam, but a strong wind blew the ball back into play, and Southworth made the catch.

Ruth had ruined the Cardinals in Game Four, blasting three home runs. Player-manager Hornsby tried something different in Game Five. "We gave Ruth nothing but slow balls on the inside to hit during the game," he told sportswriters after the game. "That's what I have instructed my pitchers to use every time the Yankee slugger comes to the plate. Sherdel worked the trick effectively."[2] (In that era, sportswriters were wont to "clean up" players' quotes and rephrase them in the King's English.)

Pennock retired the Cardinals in order in the bottom of the sixth, and Sherdel did likewise to the Yankees in the top of the seventh. After the seventh-inning stretch, the Cardinals regained the lead. Bell stroked a leadoff double to left and after Hafey flied out to left, Bob O'Farrell got his third hit, a single to left, scoring Bell and making it 2-1.

The Yankees had the top of the order due in the eighth. Leadoff batter Combs singled but the Yankees were unable to advance him. Koenig flied out to left field, Ruth grounded to Sherdel, who threw to short to force Combs, and Meusel grounded to third base for the third out.

The Cardinals leadoff batter, Wattie Holm, was up first in the eighth and he walked. He was forced out at second on Southworth's grounder to shortstop. Hornsby ended the inning by grounding into a double play, second to short to first.

New York tied the game in the top of the ninth. Gehrig reached second on a blooper to left and moved to third as Lazzeri beat out a bunt. As Joe Dugan walked to the plate, manager Huggins pulled him for pinch-hitter Ben Paschal. Dugan reacted childishly, throwing his bat in the air and storming back to the clubhouse. Unfazed, Paschal hit a bloop single to shallow center field to score Gehrig with the tying run and advance Lazzeri to second. A bunt had worked earlier in the inning, so why not try it again? Hank Severeid laid down a weak bunt, which Cardinals catcher O'Farrell played perfectly, throwing to third to force Lazzeri. Sherdel avoided further damage when Thevenow made a brilliant stop of Pennock's grounder and flipped to Hornsby to force Severeid, and then Combs grounded out to second. The Cardinals went down in order in the bottom of the ninth. Bottomley popped out to second, Bell grounded out to third, and Hafey popped out to short. Game Five was headed to extra innings.

Koenig led off the top of the 10th with a single to left and advanced to second on Sherdel's wild pitch. Ruth walked and Meusel moved the runners into scoring position with a bunt to the pitcher. Gehrig was walked intentionally, loading the bases. Lazzeri then lofted a fly to left, scoring Koenig with the go-ahead run. The Yankees loaded the bases when Mike Gazella, who replaced Dugan at third in the bottom of the ninth, was hit by a pitch. But Severeid's pop fly to second ended the inning with the Yankees leading 3-2.

The Cardinals went quietly in the bottom of the 10th. O'Farrell lifted a foul pop to third, Thevenow singled to right. Jake Flowers pinch-hit for Sherdel and popped out to Gehrig, and the game ended on Holm's grounder to third.

Huggins was very pleased with his team's play. "The fighting spirit won for us in a tough pitchers' battle," he said. "That was the thing that most impressed me out there on the field today. It was fight, fight, fight with my men from the time the first ball was thrown, and their demonstration of the true fighting spirit was crowned with success. You can't beat a fighting spirit like that. It is not to be denied. The boys were never licked, despite great pitching by Sherdel. We had great pitching on our side. We had the day's best pitching. Pennock was at his best. He pitched in masterly fashion. But the fighting spirit was the big thing."[3]

Hornsby tried to be optimistic, even though his club was now on the brink of elimination. "Had it not been for a whole carload of bad breaks we would have won," he said. "… The breaks can't go that way all the time, and we'll fight and make our own breaks tomorrow and Sunday."[4]

Pennock was happy to pick up the win. "[Sherdel] pitched a better game than I did, but all the breaks were against him," the future Hall of Famer said. "You will have to go a long way to see a better pitched ball game."[5] One can't disagree; both pitchers went the distance, pitching 10 innings.

SOURCES

In addition to the sources cited in the Notes, the author consulted BaseballReference.com, retrosheet.org, and SABR.org.

NOTES

1. "Yankees' Courage Won, Says Huggins," *New York Times*, October 8, 1926: 17.
2. "World Series Sidelights," *St. Louis Post Dispatch*, October 8, 1926: 44.
3. *New York Times*, October 8, 1926.
4. J. Roy Stockton, "Two Pop Flies That Escaped Cardinals Fielders Caused Sherdel's Defeat," *St. Louis Post Dispatch*, October 8, 1926: 44.
5. Ibid.

HAINES GOES THE DISTANCE AND WINS IT ON LES BELL'S 13TH-INNING SINGLE

June 21, 1927: St. Louis Cardinals 6, Chicago Cubs 5, (13 Innings, Game One of Doubleheader) at Sportsman Park

BY BRIAN P. WOOD

ON TUESDAY, JUNE 21, 1927, AT Sportsman's Park, the reigning World Series champion St. Louis Cardinals hosted the Chicago Cubs in a doubleheader. The Cardinals trailed the Cubs by two games for second place and were four behind the first-place Pittsburgh Pirates. Chicago, recently off a recent 12-game winning streak, had lost three of its last four.

A crowd of 10,000 plus "3,000 members of the Knothole gang"[1] looked forward to a duel between Jesse Haines and "Sheriff" Blake of the Cubs. Haines, unlike most knuckleballers, gripped the ball with his knuckles instead of his fingertips to increase the velocity of his pitches.[2] Blake, on the other hand, relied on keeping his fastball and a fast-breaking curveball low. He was known for being a quick worker and for his extensive use of the rosin bag.[3]

In the top of the first, Cubs rookie Earl Webb, in the middle of a .300 season, stroked the first hit of the game, a one-out single past shortstop Tommy Thevenow that advanced Eddie Pick (on via an error) to second. Haines retired the next two hitters to keep the Cubs scoreless.

In the Cardinals' first, Taylor Douthit bunted for a single. First baseman Charlie Grimm made a nice stop of a grounder by Frankie Frisch, forcing Douthit. After Frisch stole second, one of his league-leading 48 for the season, Jim Bottomley flied to Riggs Stephenson in left. Frisch made an ill-advised decision to take third. Riggs Stephenson had a weak throwing arm but got enough on the throw to cut down Frisch and end the threat. But in the third, Frisch, who entered the game with a .364 batting average, atoned for that mistake with a solo home run, his fifth of the season—for a 1-0 Cardinals lead.

In the Cardinals' fourth, center fielder Hack Wilson lost a two-out fly ball by Thevenow in the sun. Ruled a double, it put runners on second and third, but Haines contained the Cubs for no runs.

Douthit singled to center to lead off the bottom of the fifth. A groundout and a fly out by Bottomley (a sacrifice fly under the scoring rules of the time) moved him to third, and Wattie Holm plated the Cardinals' center fielder with a looping single to left, increasing the St. Louis lead to 2-0.[4]

Stephenson singled past third in the Cubs' sixth and Mike Gonzalez singled past second, putting runners on first and second. Clyde Beck's triple drove both runners home,[5] tying the game, 2-2. Blake hit a fly into left-field foul territory, but it was not deep enough for Beck to score. Haines then struck out 5-foot-5 Sparky Adams looking to end the inning.

In the sixth another fly ball by Thevenow gave Wilson problems, and this time he dropped it for a two-base error. But Haines escaped again without any damage. Wilson's adventure foreshadowed a similar set of sun-assisted plays two years later, when he lost two balls in the sun in the seventh inning of Game Four of the 1929 World Series, resulting in a single and a three-run inside-the-park home run. The Philadelphia Athletics scored 10 runs that inning against Wilson's Cubs to overcome an 8-0 deficit. Chicago lost the game (the losing pitcher, coincidentally, was Blake) and eventually the Series. This game's sun-related miscues, however, did not directly contribute to any runs.

Wilson fared no better at the plate. He became irate and had to be separated from home-plate umpire Cy Pfirman after being called out on strikes to end the seventh. Wilson shoved Pfirman and almost knocked down the Cubs' captain, Grimm, who was trying to calm the situation.[6]

As the ninth inning began, the teams were tied, 2-2. For the Cubs, Beck doubled to left-center. Blake tried to lay down a sacrifice bunt but Haines threw out Beck at third. Adams singled to right and Blake sailed into third. Next, Pick grounded to first baseman Bottomley, whose wild throw to the plate allowed Blake to score the go-ahead run.[7] The Cubs led for the first time, 3-2.

Frisch began the bottom of the ninth with a single to center. Holm's one-out single put runners at first and third, and a single to center by Billy Southworth scored Frisch, tying the game, 3-3. An intentional walk loaded the bases with two outs. Cardinals skipper Bob O'Farrell called on George "Specs" Toporcer, considered to be the first position player to wear eyeglasses,[8] to pinch-hit for Thevenow, who was batting below .200 for the season, but was 3-for-4 this day. With the winning run on third, Blake stopped Toporcer's scorcher up the middle and forced Holm at home, sending the game into extra innings.

New Cubs pitcher Charlie Root allowed a two-out hit by Frisch in the 10th but Frisch was thrown out attempting to take an extra base for the second time when Wilson's throw to Beck erased him as he tried to stretch his single into a double.

In the next two innings, Haines gained strength, surrendering only a single to Root, the pitcher's 12th hit of a career high 27 in 1927. But Frisch made a spectacular play ranging to his right and grabbed Pick's grounder to force Root and end the 11th.

The Cubs' Webb led off the 12th by powering his 12th home run of the season over the roof of the right-field pavilion, giving Chicago a 4-3 lead. But St. Louis quickly tied the game when Johnny Schulte homered over the right-field pavilion roof in the bottom of the 12th.

Once again, the Cubs struck in the 13th. Gonzalez, a light-hitting catcher who would tally only 13 homers in a 17-year major-league career, banged out his only home run of the season into the busy right-field pavilion (four home runs were hit there in the game) to make it 5-4. Finding their backs against the wall once more, the Cardinals answered. Douthit knocked a triple to the left-field wall. Pick snatched Frisch's grounder at third and froze Douthit before getting the out at first. However, Bottomley singled to center, tying the game, 5-5 (one of his 124 RBIs in 1927). A groundout and intentional walk put runners on first and second with two outs. Up to the plate stepped Les Bell, who singled to left field. Bottomley scored from second, giving St. Louis a 6-5 victory in 13 innings. Four lead changes and five ties punctuated the back-and-forth contest. Chicago could not hold three one-run advantages in the last five innings.

Neither team took advantage of its opportunities. Although the two teams combined for 32 hits, (19 for St. Louis, 13 for Chicago), they left 27 runners on base (16 for St. Louis and 11 for Chicago). The starting pitchers held firm in the clutch giving up just three hits in 22 at-bats with runners in scoring position.

Root, the losing pitcher, went on to lead the National League in games pitched (48), innings pitched (309), walks (117), and victories (26), all career highs. He placed fourth in the NL MVP voting. Frisch placed second, batting .337 with only 10 strikeouts. One spot behind him was the man the Cards traded for him prior to the 1927 season, Rogers Hornsby of the New York Giants.

Haines also produced career numbers in 1927, topping the league in complete games (25) and shutouts (6), plus a career-best 24 wins and a 2.72 ERA, finishing eighth in the MVP voting. This was one of three extra-inning complete games the knuckleballer pitched in 1927, including another game of 13 innings and one of 11.

The Cardinals swept the doubleheader beating the Cubs, 12-3, in the nightcap and tying Chicago for second, 2½ games behind first-place Pittsburgh. Bottomley socked two triples in the second game[9] but Thevenow broke his ankle sliding into second base and was on the shelf for nearly three months.[10]

Hack Wilson's struggles with the arbiters continued into the second game. In his first at-bat, Ernie Quigley called him out on strikes, and Wilson, after again expressing his displeasure, found himself ejected from the game for the first time in his career.

Skipper Joe McCarthy joined in and received his first career walking papers, too.

The Cardinals ended the season in second place behind Pittsburgh. Streaky Chicago gained first place on July 7 during a nine-game winning streak, only to later lose 9 of 12 and fall out of first. The Cubs rebounded and on August 19 sported a five-game lead over the Pirates. However, losing 16 of 20 dropped them out of contention, and they finished in fourth place.

SOURCES

In addition to the sources listed in the Notes, the author also consulted baseball-reference.com and retrosheet.org.

NOTES

1 J. Roy Stockton, "Cards 6, Cubs 5 (First Game); Four Homers in Game," *St. Louis Post-Dispatch,* June 21, 1927: 13. Irving Vaughn of the *Chicago Tribune* reported the attendance as 15,000. Retrosheet and Stockton said it was 10,000. Stockton also reported the 3,000 Knothole gang members.

2 "Cards All-Time Top 40 — Jesse Haines #16," The Cardinal Nation, scout.com/mlb/cardinals/story/617326-cards-all-time-top-40-jesse-haines-16?s=321 February 8, 2007.

3 Gregory H. Wolf, "Sheriff Blake," SABR BioProject, sabr.org/bioproj/person/d30272b3.

4 From 1926 to 1930, a fly ball caught in the outfield that resulted in a runner advancing to any base was scored as a sacrifice and the batter was not charged with an at-bat. Under today's rules it is a sacrifice fly only if a runner scores on the play. John Schwartz, "The Sacrifice Fly," Society for American Baseball Research, research.sabr.org/journals/sacrifice-fly.

5 The *St. Louis Post-Dispatch*'s said the ball was hit to left-center field and the *Chicago Tribune* said it was hit to right-center field.

6 The *Chicago Tribune*'s Irving Vaughan, showing his partisan colors, described Pfirman as "one of the league's unique umpires who is guided by his sense of smell and not sight." Irving Vaughan, "Cardinals Take 2 From Cubs, 6-5, 12-3," *Chicago Tribune,* June 22, 1927: 19.

7 Associated Press, "Cardinals Nest in Second Place by Double Victory Over Cubs," *Omaha World,* June 22, 1927: 7.

8 A nineteenth-century pitcher, Will White, who played from 1877 to 1886, was the first player to wear glasses. Toporcer's use of spectacles paved the way for position players to do so. Bill Koenig, " Spectacular Players Can Wear Spectacles," *USA Today, Baseball Weekly,* June 6, 1996. By 1951, Toporcer lost his eyesight because of detached retinas. Fred Lieb, "Specs Toporcer: Still Tops," *St. Petersburg Times,* January 13, 1971: 4C.

9 Several references state that Bottomley hit three triples in the second game, but Retrosheet shows only two.

10 Associated Press, "Thevenow Suffers Fracture of Ankle," *Omaha World,* June 22, 1927: 7.

GEHRIG'S TWO HOMERS TOO MUCH FOR REDBIRDS

October 7, 1928: New York Yankees 7, St. Louis Cardinals 3, at Sportsman's Park

Game Three of the World Series

BY RICHARD CUICCHI

BEFORE THE START OF THE 1928 World Series, former major-league pitcher Walter Johnson predicted, "To me, the St, Louis Cardinals should make short work of the New York Yankees. The Yankees don't look good. They haven't looked good for a while."[1] The Big Train couldn't have been more wrong.

Going into Game Three at St. Louis's Sportsman's Park, the Yankees were riding high with resounding wins in the first two games. Babe Ruth, Lou Gehrig, and Bob Meusel had provided most of the firepower in those games, prompting Ruth to say, "We served notice that from here on out, there'll be a lot of dynamite in those Yankee bats."[2] His proclamation would turn out to be true.

In fact, not only had the Yankees' bats inflicted damage on Cardinals pitching, but also New York pitchers Waite Hoyt and George Pipgras shut down the Cardinals' potent offense, yielding just seven hits in the first two games.

The paid admissions for Game Three were 39,602, but *The Sporting News* estimated that 42,000 were in attendance, a Sportsman's Park record. This suggested that Cardinals fans were still enthusiastic about their chances despite what happened in Games One and Two.[3] The Cardinals had planned to sport new uniforms for this game, but manager Bill McKechnie had to abandon that idea for his regulars when uniforms for several of the players were too small. A few of the reserves did wear the new uniforms.[4] However, sartorial splendor would turn out to be the least of McKechnie's problems.

With Herb Pennock unavailable to pitch in the Series because of a sore arm, Yankees manager Miller Huggins turned to 32-year-old journeyman Tom Zachary to face the Cardinals in Game Three.[5] The Yankees had acquired Zachary from the Washington Senators in a waiver deal on August 23 to shore up a pitching staff beset by injuries. He wound up winning three games in six starts during the regular season.

Jesse Haines, a 20-game winner during the regular season, drew the starting assignment for McKechnie. The 35-year-old's World Series experience included two wins over the Yankees in the 1926 World Series, won by the Cardinals.

St. Louis jumped out on top with two runs in the bottom of the first inning. It was one of only three times in the entire Series that the Cardinals held a lead. Jim Bottomley, who led the Cardinals in home runs (31) and RBIs (136) during the season, tripled to score Andy High and Frankie Frisch, who had reached on infield singles. Bottomley's hit was misjudged by Yankees center fielder Cedric Durst, who charged in only to find that he was headed in the wrong direction.[6]

The Yankees responded in the top of the second inning on Gehrig's solo home run into the right-field pavilion, his second of the Series. Zachary pitched out of a jam caused by errors by third baseman Gene Robertson and second baseman Tony Lazzeri in the bottom half of the inning.

After Ruth singled in the top of the fourth inning, Gehrig laced a screaming line drive into center field, where Taylor Douthit tried to make a diving catch, but the ball skipped past him and rolled to the flagpole. The other two Cardinals outfielders were unable to back up Douthit because the ball had been hit so hard.[7] Gehrig raced around the bases for an inside-the-park home run, with Ruth scoring ahead of him to give New York a 3-2 lead. Combined with the two earlier Cardinals losses, Gehrig's freak round-tripper seemed to take the wind out of the Cardinals' sails.

Zachary yielded the Cardinals' third run in the bottom of the fifth on Andy High's double, which scored Douthit, who had been hit by a pitch. This tied the score, 3-3.

But the Yankees rose to the occasion again in the sixth. With Haines still pitching, the Yankees scratched out three unearned runs thanks to a bizarre, Keystone Cops type of play. Ruth reached first base when his grounder to second forced Mark Koenig, who had singled. After Gehrig drew a walk, Meusel hit a groundball to third baseman High, who attempted to start a double play. High's throw to second forced Gehrig, but Frisch's relay got past Bottomley and the ball rolled to the fence behind first base. As Bottomley ran to retrieve the ball, Ruth rounded third base and started for home. Bottomley's throw to catcher Jimmie Wilson beat Ruth at the plate. Umpire Bill McGowan initially called Ruth out, but Ruth's aggressive slide jarred the ball loose. McGowan changed his call and the Yankees were back on top.[8] Wilson recovered in time to fire the ball to second in an effort to nab Meusel, who was advancing on the throw home, but no one was covering the bag—Frisch was still sprawled on the ground, where Gehrig had knocked him head-over-heels on a takeout slide. The ball sailed into center field and Meusel ended up at third. Tony Lazzeri then walked. With Gene Robertson batting, Meusel and Lazzeri executed a double steal, on which Meusel scored. Lazzeri then scored on Robertson's single, making the score 6-3.

The Yankees scored another unearned run in the seventh inning, while Zachary held the Cardinals scoreless after the fifth, for a final score of 7-3. The Yankees optimized their seven hits, turning them into seven runs, while the Cardinals could manage only three runs on their nine hits. Zachary's complete-game win included one walk and seven strikeouts. It was his third victory in World Series competition. Haines, who was relieved in the top of the seventh inning, took the loss for the Cardinals.

A joyous Zachary commented about his mixed performance, "I guess there isn't much that I can say. I might have done better and I guess I might have done worse. The big thing, though, is that we won. I felt fine all through the game, except in the last few innings, when I started to get tired in the legs."[9]

After the game Wilson explained the play at home. "If (Ruth) hit me any other way than he did, why, then, he's out. But he kicked the side of my head first, then struck my chest protector and I went over. You are bound to spread when a 225-pound guy falls on top of you."[10]

Yankees manager Huggins, worried that his team might be over-confident in Game Four the next day, addressed his players with cautionary words about letting this victory go to their heads. He told them there would be no celebrating that night, since was still another game to be won.[11]

However, Ruth, who provided a guest article for a St. Louis newspaper, declared after the game, "It's all over but the shouting." He asserted that Lou Gehrig was the hero of the Series based on his eight runs batted in the three games. "You know when a fellow is hitting like that, his mere presence up there at the plate is a threat the other fellows can't overlook," the Bambino wrote.[12]

Cardinals manager Bill McKechnie recapped his team's loss: "We were bad. We started hitting today, but what did that get us? The breaks went against us when they could do the other side the most good. The Yanks shouldn't have scored a run in that sixth inning. That Ruth play at the plate, when he knocked the ball out of Wilson's hand and scored, and that crash of Gehrig against Frisch at second were tough on us, but we're not kicking. That's part of the game." Optimistically, McKechnie added, "It they can win three games, so can we. Nothing is impossible. And this thing isn't over until the fourth game is won."[13]

Gehrig and Ruth, the foundational members of the renowned Murderer's Row, were responsible for most of the offensive punch by the Yankees through the first three Series games. Gehrig had five hits, eight RBIs, three home runs, and four runs scored, while Ruth accounted for seven hits, driving in one run and scoring six. Including their performances in the clinching Game Four, the slugging duo would go on to set several World Series records.[14]

The Game Three loss further demoralized the Cardinals, who had been favored to win the Series thanks in part to injuries to several Yankees — Pennock blew out his arm in August and Earle Combs was available for only pinch-hitting duties due to a broken finger, while Ruth, Koenig, and Lazzeri soldiered on at less than 100 percent. It was New York's seventh straight victory in a World Series game, which set a new record. (They swept the Pirates in four straight in the 1927 Series.)

The Yankees' Game Four win two days later allowed them to gain revenge for their loss to the Cardinals in the 1926 World Series. The championship also evened their overall World Series record at that point at 3-3.

SOURCES

In addition to the sources mentioned in the Notes, the author also consulted:

Baseball-Reference.com.

Cantor, George. *Inside Sports World Series Factbook* (Detroit: Visible Ink Press, 1996).

Creamer, Robert W. *Babe: The Legend Comes to Life* (New York: Simon and Schuster, 1974).

Gallagher, Mark. *The Yankee Encyclopedia 6th Edition* (Champaign, Illinois: Sports Publishing, LLC, 2003).

Krueger, Joseph J. *Baseball's Greatest Drama* (Milwaukee: Joseph J. Krueger, 1945).

NOTES

1 Leigh Montville, *The Big Bam* (New York: Doubleday, 2006), 275.

2 Mike Eisenbath, *The Cardinals Encyclopedia* (Philadelphia: Temple University Press, 1999), 452.

3 "Three Straight for Yanks Upsets All Predictions," *The Sporting News*, October 11, 1928: 3.

4 "Gossip of the Game," *The Sporting News*, October 11, 1928: 5.

5 Eisenbath.

6 "Gossip of the Game."

7 William McKechnie, "We Presented Yanks with 6 of 7 Runs, Says M'Kechnie," *St. Louis Post-Dispatch*, October 8, 1928: 13.

8 Eisenbath, 453.

9 "Yanks Make Merry; Cards Are Silent," *New York Times*, October 8, 1928: 17.

10 Charles Dunkley, "Ruth Kicked the Ball Out of My Hand, Says Jim Wilson," *St. Louis Post-Dispatch*, October 8, 1928: 13.

11 *New York Times*, October 8, 1928: 17.

12 Babe Ruth, "Ruth Believes Cards' Morale is Broken," *St. Louis Post-Dispatch*, October 8, 1928: 14.

13 *New York Times*, October 8, 1928: 17.

14 At the end of the 1928 World Series, Ruth held single-season World Series records for batting average (.625) and runs scored (9) and was tied for the lead in total bases (22), while holding second place in OPS, or on-base plus slugging percentage (2.022). Gehrig led all players in on-base percentage (.706), slugging percentage (1.727), OPS, (2.433), and home runs (4), and was tied for first in RBIs (9). As of 2017 Ruth was still tied for first in total bases and in third place in batting average and runs scored. Gehrig still held the record for slugging percentage and OPS.

THE SULTAN OF SWAT SMACKS THREE HOMERS TO SINK THE CARDINALS

October 9, 1928: New York Yankees 7, St. Louis Cardinals 3, at Sportsman's Park

Game Four of the World Series

BY RICHARD CUICCHI

Not even the all-powerful Kenesaw Mountain Landis could predict the future. At 11:00 A.M. on October 8, with a steady rain falling, the commissioner decided to postpone Game Four of the 1928 World Series. When the skies had cleared by 1:00 P.M., Landis looked a bit foolish and many fans were understandably upset.[1] In reality, the Cardinals could have used the extra day of rest to regroup, as the gloomy weather matched their demoralized disposition after they suffered their third consecutive loss to the New York Yankees the day before.

On the other hand, Yankees manager Miller Huggins had to warn his players against "making whoopee" because of their commanding lead over the Cardinals.[2] Any overconfidence would have been well-founded, because the Yankees had overmatched the favored Cardinals in the first three games. Yankees pitchers stifled the Cardinals' offense, while Lou Gehrig was terrorizing St. Louis pitching. But Babe Ruth would steal the limelight in the final game.

The Cardinals sported their new game uniforms for Game Four before a home crowd of 37,331. The Redbirds had been prevented from wearing them in Game Three because many of them didn't fit.[3] However, the new uniforms and an extra day of rest didn't help the Cardinals alter their fortunes, as the Yankees swept them in the Series for their second consecutive championship.[4]

Huggins tapped Waite Hoyt for his second starting assignment of the Series. The 29-year-old right-hander had limited the Cardinals to one run on three hits in Game One. He was opposed by lefty Bill "Wee Willie" Sherdel, a 21-game winner who had taken the loss in Game One, giving him three consecutive World Series losses to the Yankees since 1926.

In the first inning Ruth grounded into a double play, which would be his only significant blemish that day. The Cardinals didn't score in the bottom of the first even though they got two runners on base via a double and a walk.

The Cardinals were able to draw first blood in the bottom of the third inning. Ernie Orsatti, who started in center field in place of the struggling Taylor Douthit, doubled to center field. Andy High advanced Orsatti to third when he beat out a bunt, and Frankie Frisch followed with a sacrifice fly to center field that scored Orsatti.

The Yankees responded in the top of the fourth inning with a solo home run by Ruth over the right-field pavilion roof. Gehrig followed with a walk and Tony Lazzeri singled, but Sherdel got out of the inning without further damage.

Hoyt gave up another run in the bottom of the fourth inning on two costly errors by the Yankees. Earl Smith led off with a single to right field. Rabbit Maranville hit a potential double-play ball to second base. Lazzeri flipped to shortstop Mark Koenig to force Smith but Koenig's relay was off-target and Maranville advanced to second base. With Orsatti batting, Hoyt threw wildly on a pickoff attempt at second, which allowed Maranville to score and the Cardinals to regain the lead, 2-1.

The Yankees threatened again in the fifth and sixth innings, but were unable to score, leaving a total of five runners on base.

With one out in the top of the seventh inning, Sherdel got two strikes on Ruth. When Ruth turned to argue the second strike call, Cardinals catcher Earl Smith promptly whipped the ball back to Sherdel, who then abruptly threw an apparent third-strike pitch to Ruth. However, umpire Cy Pfirman quickly declared a "no pitch." Cardinals manager Bill McKechnie and his players argued the umpire's decision, but to no avail. After Ruth and Sherdel exchanged heated words, Ruth got his revenge, belting his second home run of the game to tie it.[5] Gehrig immediately followed with another homer, his fourth of the Series, to give New York a 3-2 lead.

Up to that point, Sherdel had kept the Yankees in check. After the game, baseball pundits argued that perhaps he had become unnerved by the umpire's call. Official scorers commented that Sherdel had actually made a legal pitch—his feet were on the rubber when he retrieved the ball from the catcher and took a windup, while Ruth was still standing in the batter's box. However, before the Series a conference between the umpires and the teams decided that use of the "quick return" (also known as quick pitch) would not be allowed, even though the National League had permitted it during the regular season.[6]

After the back-to-back home runs, Bob Meusel singled, chasing Sherdel. Pete Alexander came on in relief but couldn't quell the rally. The Yankees scored two more runs—one more charged to Sherdel and one to Alexander. The Yankees had forged a 5-2 lead they would never relinquish.

In the top of the eighth inning, the Yankees scored two meaningless runs, since the Cardinals were already a deflated team. However, the manner in which the Yankees scored put an exclamation point on the way they had dominated the Cardinals in the Series. Cedric Durst, who replaced Ben Paschal in center field at the top of the inning, hit a leadoff home run off Alexander. Then, in his fifth at-bat, Ruth put another layer of icing on the cake for the Yankees when he hit his third home run of the game. Ruth had previously performed this feat against the Cardinals in Game Four of the 1926 World Series.

The Cardinals scored once more in the bottom of the ninth inning before Ruth caught the final out of the game in dramatic fashion: a running catch of Frankie Frisch's foul fly to left field. Forgetting a gimpy knee that had plagued him during the Series, Ruth chased the ball down near the edge of the extra box seats that lined the playing field and speared it among fans whose papers and scorecards went flying. He ran to the dugout with the ball raised high in the air, while fans screamed for him to toss them a souvenir. The exuberant Ruth kept the ball, taking it to the clubhouse, where he exclaimed as he brandished it, "There's the ball that says it's all over!"[7]

The final score was 7-3. Hoyt pitched a complete game, yielding 11 hits and three walks while striking out eight. He put runners on base in six of his nine innings. Suffering his second loss of the Series, the hard-luck Sherdel also gave up 11 hits and three walks, while yielding four earned runs in 6⅓ innings.

The Yankees' sweep of the Cardinals was a surprise in some quarters. The Cardinals had been favored because numerous Yankees were banged up, including Herb Pennock (arm), Earle Combs (wrist), Lazzeri (shoulder), Gehrig (beaned in the final game of the season), and Ruth (knee). Furthermore, the Cardinals' confidence going into the Series was high, since they had defeated the Yankees in the 1926 World Series.[8]

McKechnie allowed his pitchers to throw to Ruth during the Series, contrary to the strategy Cardinals manager Rogers Hornsby employed in 1926 when St. Louis walked Ruth 11 times. Ruth walked only once in 1928, and he capitalized on the pitches in the strike zone with a then-World Series record .625 batting average.[9]

The Cardinals' skipper offered no excuses for his team's collapse. He remarked in his guest column in the *St. Louis Post-Dispatch* on October 11, "What other explanation of the rout can there be? Here was a team of healthy athletes opposed to a club supposed to be crippled from Ruth to the clubhouse boy. The crippled team comes on the field and makes the healthy club look like a collection of misfits."[10]

Understandably, Ruth received most of the national attention in the World Series for his three round-trippers in Game Four. James Harrison proclaimed in the *New York Times*, "If there is any lingering doubt, if anywhere in this broad land there were misguided souls who believe that Babe Ruth was not the greatest living ballplayer, they should have seen him today."[11]

Yet Gehrig arguably had a better overall Series. His four home runs and .545 batting average were momentous, too. His slugging percentage of 1.727 and OPS of 2.433 remain World Series records. Even Ruth himself declared Gehrig the hero of the Series. "(Gehrig) getting on base safely in nine consecutive times at bat deserves all the honors. … We think he's the greatest coming player in the business. Watch him and see."[12]

There were no good numbers on the Cardinals' side. They batted .206 as a team while their pitchers racked up an ERA of 6.09. (Alexander's ERA, over five innings, was 19.80.)

The defeat of the Cardinals was the third World Series victory for the Yankees and they were on their way to becoming one of the most storied major-league franchises.[13]

SOURCES

In addition to the sources mentioned in the Notes, the author also consulted:

Baseball-Reference.com.

Cantor, George. *Inside Sports World Series Factbook* (Detroit: Visible Ink Press, 1996).

Creamer, Robert W. *Babe: The Legend Comes to Life* (New York: Simon and Schuster, 1974).

Gallagher, Mark. *The Yankee Encyclopedia 6th Edition* (Champaign, Illinois: Sports Publishing LLC, 2003).

Krueger, Joseph J. *Baseball's Greatest Drama* (Milwaukee: Joseph J. Krueger, 1945).

NOTES

1. "Cardinal Plumage Droops in Listless Trio of Lost Games," *The Sporting News*, October 11, 1928:1.
2. Leigh Montville, *The Big Bam* (New York: Doubleday, 2006), 276.
3. "Gossip of the Game," *The Sporting News*, October 11, 1928: 5.
4. The Yankees had defeated the Pittsburgh Pirates in four straight games in the 1927 World Series.
5. Montville, 277.
6. J. Roy Stockton, "Ruth's Three Home Runs Enable Yanks to Sweep Series," *St. Louis Post-Dispatch*, October 10, 1928: 22.
7. Montville, 277.
8. Montville, 275.
9. John Devaney and Burt Goldblatt, *The World Series: A Complete Pictorial History* (Chicago: Rand McNally & Company, 1981), 121.
10. William McKechnie, "It Had to Be, All McKechnie Can Say of Rout," *St. Louis Post-Dispatch*, October 11, 1928: 28.
11. Montville, 276.
12. Babe Ruth, "We Say It With Base Hits; That's All—Babe Ruth," *St. Louis Post-Dispatch*, October 10, 1928: 22.
13. As of 2016 the Yankees had won a record 27 World Series championships.

CHICK HAFEY HITS FOR THE CYCLE AS CARDINALS POUND PHILLIES

August 21, 1930: St. Louis Cardinals 16, Philadelphia Phillies 6, at Sportsman's Park

BY MICHAEL HUBER

ON THIS STEAMY AUGUST AFTERnoon, the bespectacled outfielder Chick Hafey etched his name into the St. Louis record books and helped launch his team on a historic run to the National League pennant. As the Cardinals pounded out 19 hits in beating the Philadelphia Phillies, 16-6, in the first game of a five-game series, Hafey became the first Cardinals player to hit for the cycle in Sportsman's Park. It wasn't much of a contest; the Phillies' six runs didn't come until they had fallen behind by 13.

Entering the contest, the Cardinals were in fourth place with a record of 62-56, while the visiting Phillies were in the cellar with a mark of 40-78, already 31 games behind the National League-leading Chicago Cubs. J. Roy Stockton of the *St. Louis Post-Dispatch* wrote, "Despite the general belief that the fans are especially fond of slugging only about 2000 persons attended."[1] Although the hard-hitting Phillies resided in the National League cellar, five of their starters in this game were batting better than .300, with Lefty O'Doul and Chuck Klein near .400. On the other hand, their pitching staff allowed almost seven earned runs per game. That proved to be evident in this game. For the Cardinals, every starting position player had a batting average over .300. More importantly, the St. Louis pitching staff was allowing two fewer runs per game than the Phillies.

Cardinals starting pitcher Burleigh Grimes tossed a complete game despite allowing 11 hits and six runs (five earned).[2] Phillies starter Claude Willoughby lasted only one-third of an inning, facing five batters, and allowing all five to reach. Taylor Douthit started the bottom of the first inning with a single to right but was thrown out trying to stretch the hit into a double. Sparky Adams and Frankie Frisch drew back-to-back walks, and Jim Bottomley singled past second baseman Fresco Thompson, driving in Adams with the Cardinals' first run. With Hafey batting, Frisch and Bottomley pulled off a double steal. Hafey then sent a Willoughby offering into the left-center-field seats for a three-run homer, and the score was suddenly 4-0. That's when Philadelphia manager Burt Shotton[3] pulled Willoughby for reliever Harry Smythe. Smythe and fellow reliever Buz Phillips did not fare any better, as the trio of Philadelphia hurlers gave up 19 hits and three walks in the game. St. Louis posted multiple runs in each of the first four innings.

With one out in the second, Grimes and Douthit singled. Adams's single knocked in Grimes. Frisch followed with a two-run double. After Bottomley grounded out, Hafey sent a short pop fly to left field. Phillies shortstop Tommy Thevenow raced back to make the catch, but collided with left fielder O'Doul and dropped the ball. The official scorer credited Hafey with a triple and another run batted in to make it 8-0.[4] O'Doul injured his leg in the collision and although he finished the inning in the field, he was replaced by Bernie Friberg in the top of the third inning.

Grimes helped his own cause with a two-run double in the bottom of the third.[5] In the St. Louis fourth, singles by Bottomley, Hafey, and Gus Mancuso brought the Cardinals' run total to 11 and sent Smythe to the showers. Charley Gelbert greeted Phillips with a double to left-center field, and Hafey and Mancuso scampered across the plate. St. Louis led by 13-0 by the time the Phillies came to bat in the top of the fifth inning. Hafey, already with a home run, triple, and single in four innings, batted again in the fifth inning and flied out to Klein in right field.

Philadelphia's bats awakened in the top of the seventh. Friberg singled, Klein doubled, and Don Hurst reached on an error by first baseman Bottomley as Friberg scored. Pinky Whitney singled to bring Klein around. An out later, with Whitney at first base and Hurst at third, Spud Davis hit a sacrifice fly to Douthit in center, driving in Hurst. Whitney, thinking there were already two outs, was running with the crack of the bat and was doubled off first. The Phillies were limited to three runs on three hits.

In the bottom of the seventh, the Cardinals scored three unearned runs. After Adams reached on an error by third baseman Whitney, Bottomley came up with two outs and stroked a single to right field, putting runners at the corners. Hafey then drove a Phillips pitch into left field for a double, driving in Adams and completing the cycle. He and Bottomley scored when George Watkins singled to right.

The Phillies added three more runs in the ninth inning on three singles, a hit batsman, and a walk. However, it was too little, too late, and the game ended with the score St. Louis 16, Philadelphia 6.

As a team, St. Louis batters had six doubles, a triple and a home run. Hafey's home run was his 23rd of the season; the triple was his 11th. Hafey almost accomplished a "reverse natural" cycle, but his order was home run, triple, single, double.[6] His line score for the game was 4-for-5 with three runs scored and five runs batted in. The Cardinals batted an amazing 10-for-19 with runners in scoring position. Frisch and Bottomley helped Hafey lead the charge, with Hafey and Bottomley collecting four hits and Frisch scoring two runs and driving in two.[7] Every starting player for St. Louis got at least one hit.

Chick Hafey was a star with the Cardinals and one of the best right-handed batters in the game. Despite being one of the first major-league position players to wear eyeglasses,[8] from 1928 through 1930, the future Hall of Famer batted .337, averaging 27 home runs and 114 runs batted in. He led the National League in batting in 1931 with a mark of .349 and led the Cardinals in Wins Above Replacement in 1929 (4.3)

Over a four-year stretch (1928-1931), Chick Hafey averaged 24 home runs and 110 RBIs, and batted .340. (National Baseball Hall of Fame, Cooperstown, New York)

and 1931 (4.2). WAR didn't exist as a statistic then, and was compiled retrospectively. As a member of the Cincinnati Reds, Hafey batted cleanup in the inaugural All-Star Game in 1933.

Hafey became the seventh batter in franchise history (and the third since they became the Cardinals in 1900) to hit for the cycle and the first to hit for the cycle at Sportsman's Park. The two Cardinals who hit for the cycle before him, Bottomley (July 15, 1927) and Cliff Heathcote (June 13, 1918), also attained their cycles against the Phillies, but those two rare accomplishments took place in Philadelphia.[9]

Defensively, the Cardinals turned five double plays. (They led the National League in 1930 with 176 double plays turned.) In pitching a complete game, Grimes struck out four and walked four, facing 39 Philadelphia hitters.

The Cardinals went on to take four more from the Phillies and sweep the five-game series, outscoring Philadelphia 50-28. It was part of what would be a nine-game winning streak.[10] Grimes won the series opener; he also earned the victory in the series finale. Willoughby took two losses for Philadelphia (this game and the fourth game of the series). From August 20 to the end of the 1930 season, the Redbirds were red-hot, finishing the campaign by winning 31 of their final 37 games and nosing out the Chicago Cubs by two games for the NL pennant. The Phillies finished dead last, 40 games behind the Cardinals, who fell to another Philadelphia team, the Athletics, in the World Series.[11]

NOTES

1. J. Roy Stockton, "Hafey Hits 23rd Homer; Two Men on Base at Time," *St. Louis Post-Dispatch*, August 21, 1930: 13.

2. Grimes began 1930 with the Pittsburgh Pirates but was traded to the Boston Braves during the final days of spring training on April 9. On June 16 he was traded to St. Louis. His record with the '30 Cardinals was 13-6 with a 3.01 earned-run average.

3. Burt "Barney" Shotton managed the Phillies for six seasons (1928-1933), had a won-lost record of 370-549, and never finished better than fourth. The fourth-place finish came in 1932, the only season the Phillies finished above .500 from 1918 to 1948. He did much better at the helm of the Brooklyn Dodgers (1947-1950), winning 326 games and losing 215 while claiming two NL pennants. St. Louis manager Gabby "Old Sarge" Street, was in his first season as Cardinals skipper in 1930. He finished the season with a 92-62 record and the pennant, and then he won 101 games and the World Series title in 1931. In five seasons with St. Louis, Street's record was 312-242.

4. This might be one of the very few times in history that the play-by-play (in both Retrosheet and Baseball-Reference) lists a "triple to shortstop."

5. Grimes was a good hitter, batting .263 with the Cardinals in 1930. In 19 seasons and 1,535 at-bats, he posted a .248 batting average and drove in 168 runs.

6. A "reverse natural" cycle occurs when a batter hits the home run first, then the triple, then the double, and finally the single.

7. In addition to Hafey, Frankie Frisch and Jim Bottomley are Hall of Famers. Frisch had been NL Most Valuable Player in 1931 and Bottomley had earned that honor in 1928.

8. Greg Erion, "Chick Hafey," posted online at sabr.org/bioproj/person/96ae4951.

9. *mlb.mlb.com/mlb/history/rare_feats/index.jsp?feature=hit_for_cycle*. Three St. Louis batters hit for the cycle in the nineteenth century, one of them twice: Fred Dunlap (St. Louis Maroons, May 24, 1886), Tip O'Neill (St. Louis Browns, April 30, 1887, and May 7, 1887), and Tommy Dowd (St. Louis Browns, August 16, 1895).

10. This nine-game stretch of victories equaled the Cardinals' longest win streak of the season, from May 7 to 16. From May 7 to 26, the Cardinals won 17 of 18 games, landing them in first place in the National League. But they then lost 14 of the next 16 games, plunging them to fourth place, where they remained until late August.

11. The Cardinals lost to the Athletics in six games in the 1930 World Series, giving Philadelphia back-to-back championships. In 1931 St. Louis and Philadelphia met again in the fall classic, and this time the Cardinals won, in seven games.

WILD BILL HALLAHAN SHUTS OUTS MACKMEN TO REKINDLE REDBIRDS TITLE HOPES

October 4, 1930: St. Louis Cardinals 5, Philadelphia Athletics 0, at Sportsman's Park

Game Three of the World Series

BY GREGORY H. WOLF

The mood was gloomy and subdued at Sportsman's Park in the Gateway City on October 4, 1930, as the Cardinals prepared to face the seemingly invincible Philadelphia Athletics in the third game of the World Series, having lost the first two contests in the City of Brotherly Love. There was "none of the concerted cheering, none of the sustained enthusiasm," reported the *St. Louis Post-Dispatch*, comparing the atmosphere to that of previous fall classics in the city when the Redbirds upset the powerful New York Yankees in 1926 and then lost four straight to the Bronx Bombers in 1928.[1]

Bill Hallahan, the Cardinals' southpaw, "retouched that somber world series picture," gushed sportswriter J. Roy Stockton. He shut out the mighty Mackmen on seven hits to rekindle the Cardinals' hope of joining the 1921 New York Giants as the only team in World Series history to capture a title after losing the first two games.[2]

Praise for Hallahan's performance was effusive. "A red-breasted but thoroughly lion-hearted Cardinal brought down a White Elephant," pronounced John Drebinger of the *New York Times*.[3] "[Hallahan] hurl[ed] horsehide-covered thunderbolts from this mound," wrote Roy Alexander of the *Post-Dispatch*, while Stockton lauded Hallahan for "pour[ing] his darting curves and his flashing fast balls through the strike zone."[4]

Outscored 11-3 in the first two games of the World Series, the 92-62 Cardinals seemed overmatched by the Athletics (102-52), who appeared to be en route to their second consecutive championship. St. Louis sportswriter Sid Keener blamed the losses on "powder-puff punching and erratic pitching."[5] Hallahan, a 28-year-old who had entered the 1930 season with just six victories in parts of three campaigns, entered the game having established himself as the Redbirds' ace, posting a 15-9 record and establishing a reputation as one of the hardest throwers in baseball as he led the NL in strikeouts (177). But true to his nickname, Wild Bill, he also walked a league-high 126 in 237⅓ innings. Connie Mack, the A's owner-manager and master of subterfuge, gave no inkling who he'd send to the mound in Game Three. Fifteen minutes before the game, Lefty Grove (28-5) and swingman Eddie Rommel were warming up.

On a sunny, warm 80-degree Saturday afternoon, Sportsman's Park was packed with an estimated 40,000 spectators, hundreds of whom had waited since 11:00 A.M. the previous day hoping to purchase a bleacher ticket and then sell it for a few dollars' profit as the Great Depression tightened its grip on the Mound City.

The Cardinals "looked entirely too clean," opined Stockton, as they took the field in brand-new white uniforms instead of their sweat- and dirt-stained ones.[6] A rough-and-tumble squad, the Cardinals had led the NL in scoring (1,004 runs) while all eight starters batted at least .300. Backstop Jimmie Wilson, who had missed the first two games of the Series with a sore ankle, donned the tools of ignorance to help

Bill Hallahan posted a 102-94 record with a 4.03 ERA in his 12-year career, but saved his best for the World Series, going 3-1 with a sparkling 1.36 ERA in 39 innings. (National Baseball Hall of Fame, Cooperstown, New York)

steady the potentially erratic Hallahan in what proved to be an anxious first frame. After Max Bishop led off with a single, Hallahan fanned Jimmy Dykes on a curve that "looked like a jug handle," wrote Stockton.[7] After a walk to Mickey Cochrane, Hallahan punched out Al Simmons, whose .381 season average led the AL, on three pitches. Shortstop Charley Gelbert knocked down Jimmie Foxx's grounder through the box, but his throw to second was not in time to erase Cochrane. With the bases loaded, Hallahan made Bing Miller look silly on a curve in the dirt to fan the side and end the threat. It was a good omen for the Redbirds: every A's hit in the first two games had figured in runs.

The A's "had the air of conquerors as they came on to the field," wrote Alexander. "They're big, thick-necked, brawny fellows beside whom the Cardinals looked very youthful and just a bit spindle-shanked."[8] On the slab was a surprise starter—34-year-old left-hander Rube Walberg, who had an 88-79 record in parts of nine seasons, including 13-12 in an inconsistent campaign in 1930. Walberg looked sharp, though, setting down the first nine Redbirds he faced.

Meanwhile Hallahan still struggled with his control. In the third he issued consecutive one-out walks to Dykes and Cochrane, then escaped the jam when Simmons hit into a 6-4-3 inning-ending twin killing. The Cardinals faithful breathed another sigh of relief.

After Hallahan's 1-2-3 fourth, Taylor Douthit, hitless in nine at-bats in the Series thus far, walloped a home run to left field. The smash was like "an explosion that must have reverberated around the world like the shot at Lexington," wrote Drebinger excitedly.[9] Unshaken, Walberg retired the next three batters.

The Cardinals struck again in the fifth when Ray Blades, fresh off a fielding gem the previous inning when he grabbed Bishop's smash off the right-field screen and held him to a single, drove a one-out single of his own to center. Wilson, described by Stockton as a "smart hit-and-run batter," moved Blades to third on a single.[10] Gelbert followed with a single to left, driving in Blades. When Simmons fumbled the ball, the slow-footed Wilson tried for third but was gunned down on a perfect strike from Bucketfoot Al. Walberg's afternoon ended when he walked Hallahan. Right-hander Bill Shores, who had posted a 12-4 record as a swingman, retired Douthit to end the threat.

Hallahan faced the heart of the A's order in the sixth, retiring Cochrane on easy grounder to second sacker Frankie Frisch. Simmons followed with a hefty smash off the pavilion wall in right field. George Watkins, who had replaced Blades in right to start the frame, fielded the ball cleanly to hold Simmons to a double. Foxx, who had finished third in the AL with 156 RBIs to go along with 37 round-trippers and a .335 batting average, hit a foul ball to the first-base side, seemingly out of play. In the defensive gem of the game, first baseman Jim Bottomley ran 40 feet from the bag, and according to St. Louis sportswriter

Herman Wecke, "gripped the rail of the box seats with his bare hand, reached far over the heads of the spectators," and made the catch.[11] Miller then flied out to end the threat.

Entering the seventh nursing a precarious two-run lead, Hallahan recorded two quick outs. Then he walked Shores and surrendered a single to Bishop, leading many to "wonder if Bill was weakening," according to Stockton.[12] On a day when everything seemed to go right for Wild Bill, though, Dykes chopped at curve in the dirt and grounded harmlessly to Bottomley.

Bespectacled Chick Hafey led off the seventh with what Stockton called a "whistling drive" that "crashed against the bleachers wall a yard from the foul line" for a single.[13] Watkins followed with a single that center fielder Mule Haas "foolishly" threw to third in a bid to erase Hafey.[14] The throw was late, enabling Watkins to advance to second. Mack, dressed in his usual suit, sat on the temporary bench in front of the box seats that had been erected on the dugouts. The Tall Tactician, who had flapped his scorecard all game long, moving his players into position, recognized a turning point. He waved for shortstop Joe Boley to move in toward the plate with Wilson at bat, but the move backfired. The right-handed hitting Wilson, who had batted .325 and .318 in 1929 and 1930, respectively, hit a sharp grounder through the left side of the infield to drive in Hafey and Watkins for a 4-0 lead, sending Shores to the showers. "Had [Boley] stayed back," wrote Stockton, "he would have stopped Wilson's grounder."[15] In relief came ageless wonder 46-year-old Jack Quinn, who yielded a two-out single to Douthit, but ended the frame with runners on the corners to keep the A's within striking distance.

With Cochrane, Simmons, and Foxx due up in the eighth, Mack sent Grove to the bullpen to warm up in case the A's mounted a comeback. After Cochrane was retired on a grounder to short, Simmons lined a single to right. Foxx hit a tailor-made double-play ball to Frisch, who bobbled the ball to wipe out any chance of a twin killing; his hurried throw to first beat Foxx by a split-second. Miller's grounder to short ended the frame.

In the eighth the slumping Bottomley doubled down the right-field line with one out for his first hit in 12 at-bats in the series. Hafey's double into the right-center-field gap drove in Sunny Jim for the Redbirds' fifth tally.

Jimmy Moore, pinch-hitting for Haas, singled to lead off the ninth, but the Redbirds bullpen remained silent. Home-plate umpire Harry Geisel momentarily interrupted the game when a spectator tried to distract Boley with a mirror. Hallahan needed no smoke and mirrors to win this game. He retired the next two batters before yielding his fifth and final walk of the game, to Bishop. Playing it safe, Street sent Jim Lindsey and Syl Johnson to warm up, but they barely had a chance to stretch their arms. Hallahan notched his sixth punchout, fooling Dykes on an outside curve, to end the game in 1 hour and 55 minutes. The Cardinals' 5-0 victory was just the second win for an NL team in the last 16 World Series games.[16] More importantly for the Redbirds, their title hopes were revived.

SOURCES

In addition to the sources cited in the Notes, the author also accessed Retrosheet.org, Baseball-Reference.com, SABR.org, and *The Sporting News* archive via Paper of Record.

NOTES

1   Roy Alexander, Fans Stand All Night and Enter Park Without Rush; Little Selling of 'Places,'" *St. Louis Post-Dispatch*, October 4, 1930: 1.

2   J. Roy Stockton, "Hallahan Blanks Athletics; 5-0, to Give Cardinals First Series Victory; Douthit's Homer Starts the Scoring," *St. Louis Post-Dispatch*, October 5, 1930: 17.

3   John Drebinger, "Hallahan Shuts Out Athletics by 5 to 0 as Cards Come Back," *New York Times*, October 5, 1930: S1.

4   J. Roy Stockton, "Hallahan Blanks Athletics; 5-0, to Give Cardinals First Series Victory; Douthit's Homer Starts the Scoring."

5   Sid Keener, "Hallahan Will Pitch Today's Game With A's," *St. Louis Star and Times*, October 4, 1930: 1.

6   J. Roy Stockton, "Cards Defeat Athletics, 5-0; First Victory. Hallahan Yields Only Seven Hits and Strikes Out Six; Douthit Poles a Home Run," *St. Louis Post-Dispatch*, October 4, 1930: 11.

7   Ibid.

8   Roy Alexander, "Roar of Crowd Spurs Cardinals to First Victory of World Series," *St. Louis Post-Dispatch*, October 5, 1930: 1.
9   Drebinger.
10 Stockton, "Cards Defeat Athletics, 5-0."
11 Herman Wecke, "Cardinals Say Victory Turned Tide of Series," *St. Louis Post-Dispatch,* October 5, 1930: 1C.
12 Stockton, "Cards Defeat Athletics, 5-0."
13 Ibid.
14 Ibid.
15 Ibid.
16 Since the Cardinals beat the Yankees in Game Seven of the 1926 World Series, the AL had beaten the NL in 14 of 15 games. The Yankees swept the Pittsburgh Pirates in 1927 and the Cardinals in 1928. The A's defeated the Chicago Cubs in five games in 1929 and had taken the first two games in 1930.

HAINES DEFEATS GROVE IN FALL CLASSIC PITCHERS' DUEL

October 5, 1930: St. Louis Cardinals 3, Philadelphia Athletics 1, at Sportsman's Park

Game Four of the World Series

BY J.G. PRESTON

WITH THE CARDINALS TRAILING the Philadelphia A's two games to one in the 1930 World Series, most St. Louis fans expected Cardinals manager Gabby Street to send Burleigh Grimes to the mound in Game Four at Sportsman's Park, especially with ace Lefty Grove scheduled to pitch for the visitors. Grimes had 240 career wins to that point and been the Cardinals' best pitcher since coming to the team in a trade with the Boston Braves in June; he had also thrown a complete-game five-hitter, albeit in a losing effort, in Game One of the Series against Grove four days earlier.

But Grimes, known as "Ol' Stubblebeard" because he never shaved on days when he pitched, was freshly shaved when he arrived at the ballpark that day.[1] Instead, in a game the Cardinals could ill afford to lose, Street gave the ball to 37-year-old Jesse Haines, who had yet to pitch in the Series. "If I am going to win this Series, Haines has got to win a game for me," Street said, "and I might as well find out right now if he can come through."[2]

Street may have had some second thoughts about his choice in the early going. Max Bishop led off the game for the A's with a smash single down the first-base line that might have gone for extra bases had first baseman Jim Bottomley not gotten a glove on it. Bishop went to second base on Jimmy Dykes' sacrifice, took third on a wild pitch, and scored on a two-out single by Al Simmons. Jimmie Foxx then reached on an infield hit when Cardinals second baseman Frankie Frisch couldn't handle his twisting groundball, and Bing Miller followed with a slow bouncer that shortstop Charlie Gelbert charged to field behind the mound. "On any other shortstop Bing probably would have reached first and the bases would have been loaded," James C. Isaminger wrote in the next day's *Philadelphia Inquirer*, "but Gelbert is one of the most powerful throwers in baseball and he simply burned the ball to Bottomley and beat Miller there by a step" to end the inning.[3]

Haines got in trouble again after retiring the first two batters in the second inning. Grove reached base when Frisch fumbled his groundball for an error, and then Bishop walked after fouling off two full-count pitches. That led Street to call on Jim Lindsey to start warming up in the Cardinals bullpen. But Dykes grounded out to end the threat … and after that the A's batters were baffled. Haines allowed only one hit over the final seven innings and no Philadelphia runner got as far as third base.

Meanwhile Haines helped his own cause in the bottom of the third. With one out, Gelbert slashed a hit down the first-base line that, according to Isaminger, struck a temporary stand in right field and took a violent bounce past right fielder Miller. By the time Miller got the ball back to the infield, Gelbert had reached third with a triple. That brought Haines to the plate. Grove's first pitch was called a strike and Haines fouled off the second, but then Haines hit a ball up the middle through Grove's legs for a single to tie the game, 1-1. (Haines wasn't a bad hitter, with a .246 average during the 1930 season. And exactly four years prior to this game he had hit a home run while pitching a shutout against the Yankees in Game Three of the 1926 World Series.)

The key moment of the game came in the bottom of the fourth. After Grove retired the first two Cardinals, Chick Hafey hit a ball to right field that struck the wall on the fly and then dropped between the wall and a wire screen that had been built in front of it to protect outfielders. Hafey circled the bases while Miller tugged at the wire to try to get the ball. The umpires called it a ground-rule double.[4]

The next batter, Ray Blades, hit a routine groundball to Dykes near the third-base bag. Hafey was running on contact with two outs and had practically reached third by the time the ball was fielded. (Newspaper accounts had Blades anywhere from one to six feet away from Dykes once the ball was gloved.) "Hafey came to a dead stop within a step of Dykes," according to *St. Louis Star* sports editor Sid Keener.[5] Dykes "had only to turn around and tag Hafey to retire the side," Isaminger wrote.[6]

But Dykes threw to first base to try to retire Blades. His throw was wide and first baseman Foxx "extended as far as he could and finally left the bag and knocked the ball down in front of him," wrote Isaminger. "Hafey, quickly sizing up the situation, took a chance and charged full tilt for the plate." Foxx didn't realize right away that Hafey was trying to score; when he did, he made a throw home that "was both half-hearted and slow," according to Isaminger, allowing Hafey to score what would turn out to be the winning run.

"The uproar which followed beggars description by the most trenchant pen," wrote the *Inquirer*'s Stan Baumgartner. "The huge concrete stadium was turned into an inferno of noise. Wave after wave of hysterical yells piled up against each other until the park rocked."[7] (The crowd of 39,946 was the largest ever to see a baseball game in St. Louis to that point.)

Dykes was charged with an error, but Foxx "was equally culpable with Dykes for the loss of the game," in Isaminger's view.[8] Dykes disagreed. "I can't alibi on that one and I won't try," he said after the game. "I thought maybe I was too far up to get back in time to tag [Hafey]. I thought the moment I grabbed the ball that I would go back and touch him, but I changed my mind, as there were two out. So I threw to first. It was a rotten throw and that's all there is to it. Nobody but myself is to blame."[9]

The error left Blades on first base. He went to third on a hit-and-run single by Jimmie Wilson. Gelbert then hit a ball that bounced off Grove (one report said off his shin, another said off his bare hand) for a single, scoring Blades to make it 3-1 in favor of St. Louis.

And that held up as the final score, as the A's managed only three baserunners against Haines after that, all on walks. Grove went the distance for the A's, allowing just five hits, all in the third and fourth innings when the Cardinals scored their runs. "Grove pitched good enough ball to win," wrote Walter S. Cahall in the *Inquirer*, "but his playmates played just bad enough to lose."[10]

"Grove was good, but Haines was better," Foxx (or his ghost writer) wrote in his syndicated newspaper column the next day. "That sums up why we lost."[11]

The A's had a .294 team batting average in 1930 but mustered only four singles off Haines.[12] "I had to pitch mighty carefully against this great ball club," Haines said while sitting in a rocking chair on the front porch of his hotel after the game. "I pitched a great many balls during the game [123, according to the *Philadelphia Inquirer*].[13] This was because I was afraid to give such fine hitters as Simmons, [Mickey] Cochrane and Foxx a chance to get hold of a good one. All the time I was trying to make the A's hit at bad balls. I used three styles of pitching, a fast ball, a curve and a half-speed knuckle ball which acted as a change of pace."[14]

The Cardinals' win tied the Series, 2-2, with Game Five to follow the next day at Sportsman's Park. "I can't see how we can lose the Series now," Bottomley said. "We have the A's on the run."[15]

SOURCES

Game stories in the *St. Louis Post-Dispatch*, *St. Louis Star*, and *Philadelphia Inquirer* were accessed via Newspapers.com. Stories in *The Sporting News* were accessed via PaperofRecord.com.

NOTES

1 Stan Baumgartner, "Tasty Tidbits Served for the Fans, Red Hot Off the Series' Griddle," *Philadelphia Inquirer*, October 6,

1930: 16. The derivation of Grimes's nickname is included on his page at the Baseball Hall of Fame's website, baseballhall.org/hof/grimes-burleigh.

2 "Haines Hero of Fourth Game, When He Allows Four Hits," *The Sporting News*, October 9, 1930: 7.

3 James C. Isaminger, "Haines Bests Grove in Twirlers' Clash to Deadlock Classic," *Philadelphia Inquirer*, October 6, 1930: 14.

4 Baumgartner, "Tasty Tidbits."

5 Sid Keener, "Sid Keener's Column," *St. Louis Star*, October 6, 1930: 14.

6 James C. Isaminger, "A's Give Due Credit to Callahan, Haines," *The Sporting News*, October 9, 1930: 1.

7 Baumgartner, "Jimmy Dykes' Error Costly to Mackmen," *Philadelphia Inquirer*, October 6, 1930: 15.

8 James C. Isaminger, "Haines Bests Grove in Twirlers' Clash to Deadlock Classic."

9 James L. Kilgallen (International News Service), "Haines Explains How He Elected to Pitch to Stop Athletics," *St. Louis Star*, October 6, 1930: 14.

10 Walter S. Cahall, "Footnotes of A's-Cards Battle," *Philadelphia Inquirer*, October 6, 1930: 14.

11 Jimmie Foxx, "Foxx Still Thinks Macks Should Be Favorites to Win," *St. Louis Star*, October 6, 1930: 14.

12 The A's had four or fewer hits in a game only seven times during the 1930 regular season.

13 "Pitched Balls" chart, *Philadelphia Inquirer*, October 6, 1930: 14.

14 Kilgallen.

15 Jim Bottomley, "Haines' Fine Game Tribute to Street, Bottomley States," *St. Louis Star*, October 6, 1930: 14.

DOUBLE-X'S NINTH-INNING TWO-RUN HOMER PUSHES THE CARDS TO BRINK

October 6, 1930: Philadelphia Athletics 2, St. Louis Cardinals 0, at Sportsman's Park

Game Five of the World Series

BY J.G. PRESTON

OF ALL SEASONS, THE LEAST likely in which to expect a pitchers' duel in the World Series would have been 1930. That year major-league teams scored an average of more than 5½ runs per game, the most for any season since 1896, and nearly 10 percent more than the height of the "steroid era" of the late 1990s and early 2000s. And the offenses of the World Series participants were even more robust: The Philadelphia Athletics averaged nearly 6.2 runs per contest, while the St. Louis Cardinals led the National League with an average of more than 6.5 runs per game and posted a .314 team batting average — pitchers included!

But neither team performed to that standard in the spotlight of the fall classic. The Cardinals scored a total of three runs in losing the first two games of the Series in Philadelphia, and the A's scored just one run while losing the next two games at Sportsman's Park.

"It's the strain of the big show that stops us," said Cardinals center fielder Taylor Douthit, who hit .303 during the 1930 regular season and .083 in the World Series. "A batter goes up to the plate gripped, trying to bear down, with the result he is not free. A ballgame is different during the season. If we miss we feel we'll get even the next day. In a World Series we try to get a safe one each time we go to the plate, and we are too tight."[1]

Game Five saw both teams struggle at the plate. The Cardinals' Burleigh Grimes and Philly's George Earnshaw hooked up in a classic, each allowing just two hits through the first seven scoreless innings.

The Cards had the first scoring opportunity of the day in the third inning. Charlie Gelbert led off with a walk and advanced to second on Grimes's sacrifice bunt. Douthit hit a groundball to A's third baseman Jimmy Dykes, whose error the previous day had cost his team the game. Gelbert was halfway to third base and stopped when Dykes fielded the ball. "Dykes chased Gelbert back to second and a throw to [second baseman Max] Bishop would have retired him," James C. Isaminger wrote in the *Philadelphia Inquirer*, "but Jimmy, for some reason, never threw at all and charged after Gelbert to tag him. As [Dykes] reached to put the ball on him, Gelbert dived into the keystone and was safe as Dykes sheepishly realized his error of judgment."[2]

Douthit reached first on the fielder's choice, giving the Cardinals two baserunners, but Earnshaw got out of the jam. Sparky Adams popped out and Frankie Frisch was retired when A's first baseman Jimmie Foxx made a nice play on his sharply hit groundball close to the foul line.

Neither team advanced a runner past first base again until the bottom of the seventh when, with two out, the Cardinals' Jimmie Wilson got a base hit to center field and stretched it to a double when Mule Haas held onto the ball too long after fielding it and was slow throwing to second. Earnshaw intentionally walked Gelbert to pitch to Grimes, who was not an automatic out; Burleigh batted .263 with the Cardinals in 1930, stroked two hits off Lefty Grove in the first game of the Series and posted a .248 average in his 19-year major-league career. But Grimes was retired on a hard-hit ball to right-center field that

Haas tracked down, and the game remained scoreless going into the eighth inning.

That's when the A's threatened to finally put a run on the scoreboard. With one out, Haas put down a bunt toward third base and reached on a single when Grimes mishandled it and threw late to first. With Joe Boley at bat, Haas took off for second; Wilson's throw was in time to retire him and umpire Harry Geisel called him out, but Frisch dropped the ball and Geisel reversed the call, putting a Philadelphia runner on second base for the first time in the game. Frisch threw the ball to the ground and argued that he had held onto the throw long enough, but to no avail. Boley then hit a chopper over Grimes that the pitcher fielded. Haas slid into third ahead of Grimes's throw, Boley was credited with a single, and the visitors had runners on the corners with one out.

A's manager Connie Mack then surprised many of those in attendance by removing Earnshaw—who was working on a two-hit shutout and had thrown only 83 pitches—for pinch-hitter Jimmy Moore, who walked on five pitches to load the bases. With the infield in, Bishop hit a groundball to first baseman Jim Bottomley, who threw home to retire Haas on a force out. Dykes followed with a grounder to Gelbert at short for the final out, leaving the game scoreless.

Mack's choice to pitch the bottom of the eighth was his ace, Lefty Grove—who had thrown 107 pitches *the day before* in winning Game Four.[3] Frisch reached base with a two-out single, but cleanup hitter Bottomley followed with a strikeout, his third of the game. A .304 hitter during the regular season (and .310 lifetime) who was the National League's Most Valuable Player in 1928, Bottomley managed just one hit in 22 at-bats during the Series.

Grimes's first pitch to Mickey Cochrane leading off the top of the ninth was a ball, but then a called strike and a foul put Grimes ahead in the count 1-and-2 before Cochrane worked out a walk. That brought the dangerous Al Simmons to the plate. Simmons had led the American League with a .381 batting average during the regular season, with 36 home runs and 165 runs batted in. Grimes decided to taunt the slugger.

"When [Simmons] went through a lot of fussy motions, adjusting his cap and sticking his uniform shirt down into his uniform trousers ... Grimes gave him the horse laugh," J. Roy Stockton wrote in the *St. Louis Post-Dispatch*. "He gave him more than that. ... Grimes openly made fun of Simmons."[4] (An Associated Press account said Grimes had "engaged in a running exchange of insults" with the A's throughout the game.[5])

If Grimes was trying to get into Simmons's head, it seems to have worked. Simmons swung hard at the first pitch and missed, and then hit a popup into shallow left field that shortstop Gelbert caught. That brought another fearsome hitter to the plate: the 22-year-old Foxx, who had hit 37 home runs and driven in 156 runs during the regular season. When he retired after the 1945 season, Foxx had 534 home runs, second only to Babe Ruth.

Grimes said his first pitch to Foxx was a curve; Foxx said he didn't see any curve to it. He swung and connected. "The ball soared toward left center," Stan Baumgartner wrote in the *Inquirer*. "From the moment it started on its way there was no question as to where it was going to land. [Left fielder] Chick Hafey and Taylor Douthit gave it a half-hearted chase for a few steps, praying that some miracle, some air pocket would halt its flight and bring it down. But they were futile hopes. The speeding apple landed far up in the left center bleachers."[6]

Having finally scored against Grimes, the A's turned the pitcher's taunts back on him. "As he rounded third, scoring ahead of Foxx, Cochrane put his hands to his ears and waved them derisively at Grimes," E. Roy Alexander wrote in the *Post-Dispatch*. "Earnshaw, sitting near Connie Mack on the bench, waved his hand at the Cardinal pitcher in a gesture of contempt. Joe Boley and Bing Miller ran out from the bench and danced a few steps, concluding their performance by giving Grimes a Bronx cheer."[7]

Back in Philadelphia, A's fan George McQuilkin heard Foxx's home run on the radio broadcast of the game just as his wife, Adelaide, was delivering an 8-pound boy. In honor of the occasion, the McQuilkins named their son James Foxx McQuilkin.[8]

Given a two-run lead, Grove didn't squander it. Pinch-hitter Ray Blades walked with one out in the bottom of the ninth, but Grove retired Wilson on a groundball and struck out Gelbert to give the A's a three-games-to-two lead in the series. The Cardinals never got a runner as far as third base in the game.

The A's won their second straight championship two days later back in Philadelphia, when Earnshaw—pitching on one day's rest—beat the Cards, 7-1. (Earnshaw had also started consecutive games in the 1929 World Series. No one has done that since.) One year later Grimes and Earnshaw would meet again at Sportsman's Park, this time in Game Seven of the World Series—and with a different result.

SOURCES

Game stories in the *St. Louis Post-Dispatch*, *St. Louis Star*, and *Philadelphia Inquirer* were accessed via Newspapers.com. Stories in *The Sporting News* were accessed via PaperofRecord.com.

NOTES

1. Sid Keener, "Sid Keener's Column," *St. Louis Star*, October 7, 1930: 16.
2. James C. Isaminger, "Foxx' Homer in Ninth Beats Cardinals 2 to 0 and Gives Macks Series Lead," *Philadelphia Inquirer*, October 7, 1930: 22.
3. Pitch counts for Game Four are in the *Philadelphia Inquirer*, October 6, 1930: 14. Pitch counts for Game Five are in the *Philadelphia Inquirer*, October 7, 1930: 23.
4. J. Roy Stockton, "Grimes Has His Fun With Simmons; Foxx Breaks It Up With Home Run," *St. Louis Post-Dispatch*, October 7, 1930: 14.
5. Associated Press, "Grimes Dusts Al Three Times in 4th," *Philadelphia Inquirer*, October 7, 1930: 22.
6. Stan Baumgartner, "Foxx Goat One Day and Hero the Next as A's Forge Ahead," *Philadelphia Inquirer*, October 7, 1930: 22.
7. E. Roy Alexander, "Crowd on Edge Watching Duel of Pitchers," *St. Louis Post-Dispatch*, October 7, 1930: 14.
8. Dora Lurie, "Parents to Name New Heir After A's Slugger," *Philadelphia Inquirer*, October 7, 1930: 24. James Foxx McQuilkin died in 2003. His death date and his mother's first name were found on Ancestry.com.

CARDS SET DOUBLES RECORD WITH ASSIST FROM CROWD

July 12, 1931: St. Louis Cardinals 17, Chicago Cubs 13, at Sportsman's Park

BY JOHN J. WATKINS

FANS BEGAN ARRIVING AT DODIER Street and Grand Boulevard shortly after daybreak on Sunday, July 12, lining up for general-admission tickets to the afternoon's doubleheader.[1] All reserved seats had been sold in advance, and a record turnout was anticipated.[2] The first-place Cardinals held a six-game lead over the visiting Chicago Cubs, with New York and Brooklyn sandwiched in between, but Chicago had won three of four against St. Louis at Wrigley Field earlier in the week.[3]

Sportsman's Park seated about 34,400, but paid attendance was a record 45,715.[4] The overflow crowd ringed the outfield, shrinking the playing area and turning routine fly balls into ground-rule doubles. Under what *The Sporting News* called "unspeakable" playing conditions,[5] the teams combined for 23 doubles in the second game to set a major-league record after collecting nine in the opener.[6] The Cardinals' 13 doubles in the nightcap were the most by a team in the modern era,[7] and one of them possibly played a role in deciding the National League batting title.

The ballpark gates were opened at 9:00 A.M. and "long before noon every unreserved seat in the park was occupied and spectators were standing two and three deep in the aisles in the back of the stands."[8] After ropes were stretched from foul line to foul line in front of the outfield wall, fans were allowed onto the field. But with no police or ushers to keep them behind the ropes, the spectators "spread like water breaking through a dam, out and all over the field."[9]

The Cubs were then taking infield practice, but that quickly ground to a halt. When grounders were hit to the infielders, fans "dashed in front of the Cub players in a wild scramble for each baseball."[10] The spectators then circled the dugouts to get a close look at the players. "It was like a mob of children, suddenly given a chance to inspect wild animals in their dens."[11]

With the threat of rain in the air, Cardinals owner Sam Breadon led policemen, ushers, umpires, and players in clearing the field so that the first game could begin. Eventually, the spectators took up posts around the outfield about 70 feet beyond first base, 150 feet past second, and 100 feet from third. But they rushed toward baseballs hit in their direction, fighting among themselves and even pushing aside players to get souvenirs. Under the threat of forfeit, the fans later moved back toward the fences, but even so, "a solid outfield fly was sure to fall among the customers for a double."[12] The Cubs rallied for five runs in the seventh inning of the opener to defeat the Cardinals, 7-5.

Playing conditions deteriorated for the second game, with the worst situation in left field. The spectators began the game "50 or 75 feet beyond third base and ... edg[ed] closer and closer toward the infield, until the late innings a ball that dropped over the third baseman's head was gobbled up by the insatiable mob."[13] Spectators even lined the wall behind home plate, hoping to grab a foul ball.[14] Miraculously, there were only two reported injuries, both in the stands. One spectator sprained an ankle on the crowded steps, and another was taken to a hospital with a possible fractured spine after he was pushed onto the field from his seat in the first row of the bleachers.[15]

The scoring started early.[16] Chicago got two runs in the first inning against veteran right-hander Flint Rhem, who had lost to the Cubs in his previous start, on July 7. Footsie Blair led off with a pop fly to shallow center field that went for a double when Pepper

Martin slipped and fell. Woody English reached on an error, and Kiki Cuyler drew a walk. After Hack Wilson struck out, Blair and English scored when shortstop Sparky Adams, the Cardinals' regular third baseman who was substituting for the injured Charley Gelbert,[17] fumbled Rogers Hornsby's groundball and then threw high to first. Cuyler, who had moved to third, attempted to score when Danny Taylor flied to center, but Martin threw him out to end the inning.

St. Louis immediately answered with three runs against Pat Malone, a hard-throwing right-hander who had beaten the Cardinals twice in the past week—a 10-inning complete game on July 5 and a two-inning relief stint two days later. Ripper Collins doubled into the overflow crowd to drive in George Watkins with the first Redbird run. Chick Hafey brought home Collins with another double into the crowd, and Martin singled in Hafey.

The Cardinals held that 3-2 edge until the top of the fourth, when the Cubs scored four runs. After Charlie Grimm and Gabby Hartnett reached on consecutive singles, Rhem cleanly fielded Malone's bunt but threw wildly to first. Grimm scored, Hartnett went to third, and Malone wound up at second. Blair cleared the bases with a three-run homer onto the pavilion roof in right field.

Chicago's lead did not last long, however, as St. Louis erupted for seven runs in the bottom of the inning. Gus Mancuso and Ernie Orsatti, batting for Rhem, both doubled into the crowd to start the rally. Adams then singled to center, with Orsatti scoring on Taylor's error. Malone struck out Watkins, but Frankie Frisch doubled, advancing Adams to third and prompting Hornsby to bring in Guy Bush. The wiry right-hander walked Hafey to load the bases, and Martin followed with a single to drive in two runs. Andy High's double scored Hafey, and Mancuso drove in Martin and High with his second double of the inning, a short fly ball that fell untouched after shortstop English and left fielder Wilson got their signals crossed.

But the Cubs tied the game in the top of the fifth with four runs against reliever Allyn Stout, a rookie right-hander who faced four batters without recording an out. After Taylor walked and Grimm reached on Adams' third error of the game, consecutive doubles by Harnett and pinch-hitter Les Bell, batting for Bush, produced three runs. The fourth came after manager Gabby Street replaced Stout with another rookie right-hander, Paul Derringer. After Blair struck out, English doubled to drive in Bell, the run charged to Stout. At the halfway point the score was knotted, 10-10.

From that point the Redbirds took control. They added three runs in the fifth on doubles by Frisch and Collins off Charlie Root following Ed Baecht's walks to Adams and Watkins; two in the sixth against Sheriff Blake on a walk to Adams, a wild pitch, a double by Watkins, and singles by Frisch and Collins; and two off Blake in the eighth on a walk to Frisch and doubles by Collins and Hafey. The Cubs managed a run in the sixth on Derringer's wild pitch and scored twice in the ninth on doubles by Blair and English when fans in the outfield grabbed the ball.

Derringer picked up the win, allowing three runs on seven hits in five innings. Baecht, who pitched to only two batters in the fifth inning and walked both, took the loss. Derringer and Malone each surrendered five doubles, Blake allowed four, and Rhem gave up three. Four hitters had three doubles each (Collins, English, Hartnett, and Mancuso), while three had two apiece (Blair, Frisch, and Hafey). Ironically, Sparky Adams, who led the league with 46 doubles that season, managed only a single in four at-bats after going 0-for-1 as a pinch-hitter in the first game.

Most of the 23 doubles were of the ground-rule variety, landing in the overflow crowd.[18] And most of those were routine fly balls that would have been caught under normal playing conditions. Both games of the twin bill produced 32 two-base hits; *The Sporting News* estimated that only six of those would have been legitimate doubles.[19] More than 100 baseballs were lost to spectators during the doubleheader—46 in the first game, 59 in the second.[20]

The outcome of the doubleheader had no impact on the pennant race; St. Louis finished with a 101-53 record, 13 games in front of the runner-up New York

Giants and 17 ahead of the third-place Cubs. But the second game may well have affected the batting title, which Hafey won by a fraction over teammate Jim Bottomley and Giants first baseman Bill Terry. Hafey started the first game and was 0-for-1 before being replaced by Orsatti. He had two doubles in the second game, however, and at least one of them — his two-bagger in the first inning — went into the overflow crowd. Bottomley played only in the first game and had one hit, a single.

Assuming that the ball Hafey hit into outfield crowd would have been caught, he would not have won the batting crown. Hafey finished the season with 157 hits in 450 at-bats for a .348889 average. Terry was second at .348609 and Bottomley third at .348168.[21] Take away that ground-rule double, and Hafey would have finished with 156 hits, dropping his average to .346667.

NOTES

1. J. Roy Stockton, "45,715 Pay to See Cardinals and Cubs Burlesque Double Bill," *St. Louis Post-Dispatch*, July 13, 1931: 1B.
2. "Rhem and Hallahan to Pitch Today," *St. Louis Post-Dispatch*, July 12, 1931: 1E; "Cards' Box Office Will Remain Open Nights This Week," *St. Louis Star*, July 10, 1931: sec. 2, 1.
3. Irving Vaughan, "Cubs Rout Cardinals Twice Before 45,000," *Chicago Tribune*, July 8, 1931: 25.
4. "Crowd Statistics," *St. Louis Post-Dispatch*, July 13, 1931: 1B. In response to a query eight years later, the Cardinals reported the paid attendance as 45,770. See J. Roy Stockton, "Extra Innings," *St. Louis Post-Dispatch*, August 11, 1939: 2B. The previous record was 39,600 during the 1930 World Series. For a regular-season game, 38,296 had paid to watch the Cardinals play the Giants on May 20, 1928. See "St. Louis Fans Surge on Field to Set Record," *The Sporting News*, July 16, 1931: 2.
5. "St. Louis Fans Surge on Field to Set Record."
6. Baseball Almanac, baseball-almanac.com/rb_2b2.shtml. See also "Record for Doubles," *Chicago Tribune*, July 13, 1931: 22; "Cards, Cubs Divide; Crowd Sets Record," *New York Times*, July 13, 1931: 20; "23 Doubles in One Game Breaks Mark Made in '83," *The Sporting News*, July 16, 1931: 5. The 32 doubles in the doubleheader were also a record. Baseball Almanac, baseball-almanac.com/rb_2b2.shtml.
7. The Chicago White Stockings had 14 doubles against the Buffalo Bisons on July 3, 1883. Baseball Almanac, baseball-almanac.com/rb_2b2.shtml.
8. Stockton, "45,715 Pay to See Cardinals and Cubs Burlesque Double Bill."
9. Ibid.
10. Ibid.
11. Ibid.
12. Irving Vaughan, "Cubs Lose to Cards, 17-13, after Winning, 7-5," *Chicago Tribune*, July 13, 1931: 21.
13. Stockton, "45,715 Pay to See Cardinals and Cubs Burlesque Double Bill."
14. Ibid.
15. "Fans Pay $46,629 to See Cards and Cubs in Twin Bill," *St. Louis Star*, July 13, 1931: Sec. 2, 2.
16. The play-by-play in this account is based on Retrosheet.org and Vaughan, "Cubs Lose to Cards, 17-13, after Winning, 7-5." However, neither source is complete regarding the ground-rule doubles into the crowd.
17. Gelbert had a bruised heel, while Adams was in the lineup despite a pulled leg muscle. Utility infielder Jake Flowers, who had been badly spiked at Wrigley Field earlier in the week, managed to play the first game at shortstop but was forced to sit out the second because his wound had opened. "Cards Carry on With Patched Lineup; Play to Record Crowd," *The Sporting News*, July 16, 1931: 1.
18. The *St. Louis Star*'s report of the doubleheader states that there were 23 ground-rule doubles in the second game. Gillespie, "Record Crowd of 45,715 Turns Card-Cub Contests into Slugfests." As noted in the text, however, Blair's pop fly to center field leading off the game went for a double because Martin slipped and fell, and Mancuso wound up at second on a popup to left in the fourth because of a misunderstanding between English and Wilson. The account of these plays is taken from Vaughan, "Cubs Lose to Cards, 17-13, after Winning, 7-5."
19. "Cards Carry on With Patched Lineup; Play to Record Crowd." J. Roy Stockton of the *St. Louis Post-Dispatch* concurred, writing that "not more than five or six of the two-baggers would have been anything but easy outfield flies under normal conditions." Stockton, "45,715 Pay to See Cardinals and Cubs Burlesque Double Bill."
20. "Fans Pay $46,629 to See Cards and Cubs in Twin Bill."
21. David L. Fleitz, *Silver Bats and Automobiles: The Hotly Competitive, Sometimes Ignoble Pursuit of the Major League Batting Championship* (Jefferson, North Carolina: McFarland & Co., 2011), 94.

LEFTY GROVE SUBDUES REDBIRDS IN OPENING GAME OF FALL CLASSIC

October 1, 1931: Philadelphia Athletics 6, St. Louis Cardinals 2, at Sportsman's Park

Game One of the World Series

BY RUSS LAKE

ANTICIPATION OF THE 1931 WORLD Series steadily peaked all summer in the St. Louis area as the Cardinals clinched their fourth National League pennant in mid-September. The Redbirds eventually finished 13 games better than the runner-up New York Giants, but their previous league flags, in 1926, 1928, and 1930, were all secured by meager two-game margins as those campaigns came down to nail-biting conclusions. A rematch against the powerful Philadelphia Athletics, who defeated the Cardinals in the 1930 World Series, along with the promise of hosting the opening game at Sportsman's Park for the first time helped heighten fans' eagerness for the calendar to turn to October.

The Athletics arrived via train in the late afternoon of September 30, and were welcomed by St. Louis Mayor Victor Miller and a crowd of several hundred at Union Station.[1] The A's Connie Mack had earlier praised his 107-win squad after they wrapped up their third consecutive American League crown, boasting, "I have confidence in its ability to set a new record by capturing its third straight world championship."[2]

Gabby Street of the Cardinals piloted his St. Louis players to a franchise record 101 victories, but seemed annoyed when asked who would win the Series. "I have always felt that a ballclub should do its playing on the field, and for that reason I am not going to begin shouting that we will win the World's Series," said Street.[3]

Many of the major-league managers had their predictions published in *The Sporting News*. Most of them voted the "party line" and tabbed their respective league representative as the eventual world champion. Bill Killefer of the St. Louis Browns offered some praise for the Cardinals, but declared, "I look for a short Series with the A's a decisive winner."[4] Giants skipper John McGraw predicted a close Series and concluded his analysis: "The most significant feature of the advance preparation for the Series was the absolute confidence of the Cardinals."[5]

Street knew his players were confident and ready to take on the two-time defending world champions. In the middle of each team's lineup was its league's batting champion—Al Simmons for Philadelphia and Chick Hafey for St. Louis. The slugging left fielders would feature prominently in the middle of the batting order. Simmons hit .390 for the season, and had catcher Mickey Cochrane (.349) hitting in front of him with first baseman Jimmie Foxx (30 home runs and 120 RBIs) behind him. Hafey squeaked in as tops in the NL at .349, which gave him a very narrow margin over New York's Bill Terry. Hafey would be complemented by veteran first baseman Jim Bottomley (.348 in 108 games), and relative newcomer Johnny "Pepper" Martin (.300), who would patrol center field. Street had a couple of late-season injuries to deal with: the losses of stalwart pitcher Jesse Haines (right shoulder)[6] and possibly starting third baseman Sparky Adams (ankle sprain). Reserve infielder Andy High was tabbed to start at the hot corner for Game One.[7]

While Mack felt good about his hitters, he knew that the key to capturing a best-of-seven series would be his pitching staff. Just before Game One, Mack offered that he did not know yet who would start in the opening game.[8] Most notable was Bob "Lefty" Grove, who led the majors by posting a 31-4 mark, with the possibility that George Earnshaw (21-7) or Waite Hoyt (10-5) might get the nod. Grove won two games with a 1.42 ERA in 19 innings in the 1930 World Series, but was actually overshadowed by Earnshaw, who also posted a pair of victories and compiled a 0.72 ERA in 25 innings. Hoyt had been claimed off waivers from Detroit in early July, and came on board with 10 World Series starts on his résumé. Mack ultimately decided on the southpaw Grove to start the first game.

October 1 finally arrived and the ex-catcher Street, who celebrated his 49th birthday the day before, announced that rookie Paul Derringer, 18-8, with a 3.36 ERA, would start Game One. The 6-foot-3 right-hander, just shy of 25 years old, had led the Cardinals' staff with four shutouts. Street's lineup for Game One included only two left-handed batters, High and Bottomley.[9] Mack put his batting order together and gave it to coach Eddie Collins, who later met at home plate with Redbirds' second baseman Frankie Frisch to present the lineup cards to arbiter Bill Klem just before the 1:30 P.M. start.[10]

Ideal weather greeted the crowd of 38,529, with the high temperature expected to reach 80 degrees. The Sportsman's Park fans were relatively quiet before they let out a mighty cheer as the Cardinals took the field in their new white uniforms. Underneath the new attire, as tokens of good luck, were the same stained sweatshirts that had not been washed since the season began.[11] After the band played the last note of "The Star Spangled Banner," umpire Klem called "Play Ball" as Philadelphia's Max Bishop walked to the batter's box.[12] The 1931 World Series was about to begin.

Derringer's opening pitch was low and outside, but the youngster came back to strike out Bishop, and then he fanned Mule Haas. After a wide pitch to start Cochrane, Derringer got the A's catcher to ground out to shortstop for the third out. With just nine deliveries, Derringer walked to his dugout after completing a perfect first inning. Grove overmatched High and struck him out on three pitches to start the bottom half, but Wally Roettger singled to center. Frisch singled to right and Roettger raced to third. Bottomley, 1-for-22 with nine strikeouts in the 1930 Series, lined an RBI single over second to put St. Louis up, 1-0. Grove fanned Hafey, but Martin knocked a double off the right-field pavilion screen to score Frisch and send Bottomley to third. After allowing four safeties and a pair of tallies, Grove induced a groundball out from Jimmie Wilson to end a shaky first.[13]

The second inning was impressive for Derringer as he notched two more strikeouts with the A's again going down in order. Charley Gelbert almost solved Grove to begin the bottom half, but Bing Miller hauled in his drive to deep right. High singled with two outs, but was left stranded. The Athletics managed their first baserunner in the third when Jimmy Dykes opened with an infield single off High's glove. Dykes motored to third on Dib Williams's single past first before Grove was called out on strikes. Bottomley fielded Bishop's hard grounder and fired to the plate to put Dykes out in a rundown going catcher to third to catcher. But just as Derringer appeared ready to escape the jam, Haas followed with a clutch RBI double to put Philadelphia on the board. Derringer seemingly became unnerved as he lost his control and walked Cochrane and Simmons to force in the tying run. Foxx then smacked a two-run single back through the box to put the A's up 4-2 before the side was finally retired. Grove settled down and recorded his first three-up and three-down frame in the Cardinals' third.[14]

Both hurlers were able to pitch out of trouble from the fourth through the sixth, benefiting from good defense, avoiding the extra-base hit, and inducing timely twin killings. The Athletics padded their lead in the seventh when Simmons followed Cochrane's single by drilling an offspeed pitch into the left-field bleachers to give Philadelphia a 6-2 margin. "I am afraid that Al's home run has convinced the Cardinals that a slow ball is not Al's batting weakness," said Mack after the game.[15]

Jake Flowers hit for Derringer to open the bottom of the inning and was the victim of a fine defensive play from Dykes at third base for the first out before Grove finished another scoreless half, despite allowing two more hits.[16] Syl Johnson took the mound for the Cardinals to start the eighth and worked two perfect innings. Grove retired six of the last seven St. Louis hitters he faced to gain his third career post-season win and give the Athletics an early edge in the World Series. There were no errors, and the contest took one hour and 55 minutes to complete.

Simmons and Foxx led the Mackmen as five of Philadelphia's runs were funneled through their plate appearances. The Cardinals, with Martin going 3-for-4 with a stolen base, tagged Grove for 12 hits, the most safeties the left-hander had ever allowed in World Series action, but St. Louis left nine men on base and finished 2-for-10 with runners in scoring position. Derringer took the loss, and pitched admirably for five of his seven frames. He struck out nine, compared to seven for Grove, but allowed three walks, and six earned runs on 11 hits.

Mack heaped postgame praise on Derringer, saying, "I think Derringer will develop into one of the greatest pitchers in baseball. His mistake today was pitching too hard at the start. He forgot that there were eight other men working on his side. His strenuous efforts in those first two innings prevented him from being as effective as he should have been later on."[17] Nonetheless, as the discouraged rookie hurler left the ballpark, Derringer waved off the many autograph hounds seeking his signature.[18]

SOURCES

In addition to the sources noted in this game account, the author also accessed Retrosheet.org, Baseball-Reference.com, SABR.org/bioproj, newspapers.com, and *The Sporting News* archive via Paper of Record.

NOTES

1. "Athletics Arrive for First World Series Game Tomorrow," *St. Louis Post-Dispatch*, September 30, 1931: 1B.
2. "Major Managers Stick With Their Own Leagues in Series Selections," *The Sporting News*, October 1, 1931: 5.
3. Ibid.
4. Ibid.
5. Ibid.
6. Gregory H. Wolf, "Jesse Haines," SABR BioProject, sabr.org/bioproj/person/afeb716c.
7. J. Roy Stockton, "Cardinals in Final Workout Still Hopeful Adams Can Play," *St. Louis Post-Dispatch*, September 30, 1931: 1B, 3B.
8. "Major Managers."
9. Herman Wecke, "World Series Highlights," *St. Louis Post-Dispatch*, October 1, 1931: 1B.
10. E. Roy Alexander, "Cards First on Field; Many in Line at Gates Wait All Night," *St. Louis Post-Dispatch*, October 1, 1931: 1B.
11. Ibid.
12. Ibid.
13. "The Game, Play-by-Play," *St. Louis Post-Dispatch*, October 1, 1931: 1B.
14. Ibid.
15. William E. Brandt, "Mack Is Cheered by Men's Batting," *New York Times*, October 2, 1931: 20.
16. Ibid.
17. Brandt, "Mack Is Cheered."
18. Wecke, "World Series Highlights."

THE WILD HORSE OF THE OSAGE STEALS THE SHOW AS WILD BILL FIRES THREE-HIT SHUTOUT

October 2, 1931: St. Louis Cardinals 2, Philadelphia Athletics 0, at Sportsman's Park

Game Two of the World Series

BY GREGORY H. WOLF

BILL HALLAHAN "CAST A SPELL OF IMpotence over the bats of the slugging Athletics," gushed St. Louis scribe J. Roy Stockton after the Cardinals southpaw's overpowering three-hit shutout of heavily favored Philadelphia.[1] Hallahan "pitched magnificently," in the eyes of sportswriter S.O. Grauley of the *Philadelphia Inquirer*. "His curve ball was just wild enough to keep the Athletics in a continued puzzle."[2] But as impressive as Hallahan was, Pepper Martin, the "Wild Horse of the Osage," stole the headlines with his daring baserunning and by scoring both Redbirds runs in a tightly played Game Two of the 1931 World Series.

The Hallahan-and-Pepper show came at a precipitous time. Following the Athletics' 6-2 victory in the opening contest of the fall classic, the mood at Sportsman's Park on Friday afternoon for Game Two was subdued. The crowd "showed discouragement [and] lacked the cheering and pep of game one," lamented E. Roy Alexander in the *St. Louis Post-Dispatch*, noting that the attendance of 35,947 was more than 2,500 fewer than on the previous day.[3] The invincible-looking A's, winners of 107 games and shooting for their third straight title, hushed the Midwestern throng in batting practice as sluggers Al Simmons, Jimmie Foxx, and company pounded balls over the fence. To make matters worse for the rough-and-tumble Cardinals, A's owner-skipper Connie Mack sent right-hander George Earnshaw to the mound. "Big Gawge," as Philadelphia sportswriters liked to call him, was coming off his third consecutive season with at least 20 victories; however, more ominous was his commanding performance against the Cardinals in the 1930 World Series when he permitted just two earned runs in 25 innings and won two games as the A's emerged victorious in six games.

Cardinals skipper Gabby Street's ace in the hole was Hallahan. One of baseball's hardest throwers, Hallahan had emerged as a legitimate ace the previous season, his first as a full-time starter, posting a 15-9 record. He also shut out the A's on a seven-hitter in Game Three of that year's World Series. Hallahan's 19 victories tied for the NL lead in 1931, but true to his "Wild Bill" moniker, the hurler with a "sphinx face and pug nose" (according to Redbirds beat writer Sid C. Keener) paced the circuit in walks as well as punchouts for the second year on a row.[4]

After Hallahan set down the A's in order in the first, including swinging strikeouts of Mule Haas and Mickey Cochrane, the Cardinals threatened when George Watkins lofted a one-out single to short center. Haas was caught napping as Watkins raced to second, just beating Haas's throw. Watkins was left stranded, but his heads-up play epitomized the club's "small ball" mentality.

The Cardinals' speed was on full display in the second when the red-hot Martin, greeted by a loud ovation for his 3-for-4 performance in Game One, belted a one-out liner to left. When Simmons slightly fumbled the ball, Martin rounded first and slid into second in a cloud of dust.[5] Martin, who swiped 16 of the Cardinals' big-league best 114 stolen bases, took advantage of Earnshaw's slow delivery and bolted for third, sliding in head-first and easily evading Cochrane's late throw. Martin tallied the game's first run on Jimmie Wilson's sacrifice fly to center.

Appearing unhittable, Wild Bill retired the first 11 batters he faced until Cochrane drew a two-out walk in the fourth. He encountered his first trouble of the game in the fifth, yielding a leadoff free pass to Foxx and then surrendering his first hit, a single by Bing Miller. After Jimmy Dykes moved up both runners on a sacrifice bunt, Hallahan played the percentages by walking Dib Williams to face Earnshaw.[6] Although he was no slouch at the plate (30-for-114 and 13 RBIs in '31), Earnshaw hit into a 6-4-3 inning-ending twin killing.

It looked as though the A's might score their first run in the sixth when Cochrane smashed what Stockton considered a "dangerous looking" one-out liner to right field with Haas on first via a single.[7] But Watkins made a "sensational catch" as he crashed into the pavilion wall to save a run.[8]

Earnshaw rolled through the Cardinals lineup, setting down nine straight batters before Frankie Frisch, the 1931 NL MVP, doubled with one out in the sixth; however, Big Gawge needed some runs.[9] The A's threatened again, in the seventh, when Foxx led off with a single. After a two-out walk to Williams, Hallahan unleashed a wild pitch facing Earnshaw, permitting Miller (whose grounder had forced Foxx at second) to reach third. Hallahan fanned Earnshaw to end the rally, though, as the St. Louis faithful exhaled.

In the seventh Pepper Martin "put on a real display of dazzling baseball," wrote James C. Isaminger of the *Philadelphia Inquirer*, and had the crowd "spellbound."[10] Martin led off with a single, swiped second, and moved to third on Wilson's grounder. With manager Street calling for a squeeze play, Charlie Gelbert bunted back to the mound. According to the *Post-Dispatch*, Cochrane "had the plate well blocked" and it looked as if Martin would be out.[11] However, Earnshaw's poor throw pulled Cochrane off the plate.[12] In what proved to be one of the defining moments of the Series, Martin executed a perfect hook slide to elude Cochrane's reach and made it 2-0. Martin "stole the game away from the clutching hands of the mightiest catcher in baseball," exclaimed sportswriter Stan Baumgartner in the *Inquirer*, comparing his daredevil tactics to those of Ty Cobb.[13]

A scoreless eighth during which both hurlers issued two-out walks gave way to what Baumgartner described as a "pulsating and nerve-racking ninth" when the "A's had the chance they seldom muff."[14] Hallahan, whose "wildness made the contest a thriller," according to Stockton, began the frame by issuing his sixth walk, to Foxx.[15] After Miller flied out, Dykes drew a walk as tension mounted, but Hallahan had ice in his veins. He fanned Williams looking, then met with his batterymate Wilson to discuss how to approach Jimmy Moore, pinch-hitting for Earnshaw.

The final sequence of events led Isaminger to pronounce that "Never in a World's Series did a game have a more theatrical ending."[16] In a succession of weird plays, Moore swung at a third strike on a sharp-breaking curve in the dirt. (Some reports claimed that Wilson had dropped the ball.) According to sportswriter Herman Wecke, Moore headed to the dugout apparently thinking that the game was over, while Cardinals fans swarmed the field.[17] But the game was anything but over as "entire playing field resembled a corner-lot ball game," opined Keener.[18] Inexplicably, Wilson "almost pull[ed] a Merkle," wrote Stockton.[19] After a short hesitation, Wilson fired the ball to third baseman Jake Flowers as both Foxx and Dykes had taken off with two strikes in what looked like a double steal. Almost simultaneously, A's coach Eddie Collins yelled to Moore and told him to run back to first and not to the dugout; then Collins charged toward home-plate umpire Dick Nallin to argue that Moore should be safe on first because Wilson did not tag him or throw him out following the third strike in the dirt. Nallin agreed. Wilson was charged with an error, the game's first, and the bases were loaded.

Philadelphia had caught a break. Now it was up to Max Bishop to capitalize on it while Hallahan had to keep his wits. Needing a single to tie the game, Bishop lofted a 0-and-1 pitch toward foul territory.

First baseman Jim Bottomley raced toward the temporary field box seats, tracking the orb. Sunny Jim lunged for the ball with his glove stretching over the railing to make what the sports pages across the country universally hailed as a "spectacular catch" as he tumbled into spectators to end the game in a nail-biting 1 hour and 49 minutes.[20]

The game will be "buzzed over during the entire winter around the stove league," predicted the *Inquirer's* Grauley.[21] The Cardinals' 2-0 victory was hailed as an immediate World Series classic. The Redbirds rode Hallahan, described by Baumgartner as a "half-pint southpaw with the kick of a keg in his sturdy left arm."[22] In a scintillating performance against the reigning three-time pennant-winning A's, Wild Bill made 132 pitches (53 balls), including 28 in the final inning, and struck out eight.[23] "[H]is fast ball zipped past batters," said batterymate Wilson. "He had a curve that stood them on their heads."[24] Martin, a 5-foot-8 ball of energy, served as the team's inspiration, collecting two of the club's six hits, swiping two bases, scoring both runs, and making his case as one of the most disruptive and exciting players in baseball.

While sportswriters from the Gateway City and the City of Brotherly Love surrounded the two stars of the game, Wilson seemed dejected in a euphoric clubhouse. Eventually he had the chance to explain what many called his bonehead move, one that could have cost the Cardinals a victory. "Moore's swing was not a complete follow-through," he said, adding that he couldn't hear Nallin's call and thought it might have been a ball. He admitted he had hesitated and then threw to third because Foxx was running. In the end, Bottomley's catch made sure that Wilson was no Merkle.

SOURCES

In addition to the sources cited in the Notes, the author also accessed Retrosheet.org, Baseball-Reference.com, SABR.org, and *The Sporting News* archive via Paper of Record.

NOTES

1. J. Roy Stockton, "Martin Hits Safely Twice, Steals Two Bases, Scores Both Runs; Hallahan in Form," *St. Louis Post-Dispatch*, October 2, 1931: 1C.
2. S.O. Grauley, "Tables Turned for Cards by Hallahan Just as Last Year," *Philadelphia Inquirer*, October 3, 1931: 17.
3. E. Roy Alexander, "35,947 See Second Game, Smaller Than Opening Day Crowd," *St. Louis Post-Dispatch*, October 2, 1931: 1C.
4. Sid C. Keener, "Wilson's Explanation of Play That Nearly Made Him a 'Merkle,'" *St. Louis Star and Times*, October 3, 1931: 3.
5. Stockton.
6. Although BaseballReference.com and Retrosheet.org describe the play as an intentional walk, contemporary play-by-play reports do not; rather, they describe it as four consecutive bad pitches (inside and outside). See S.O. Grauley, "Pursue That Elusive World's Series Pellet Here Tracing the Contest to Marvel at Hallahan's Brilliance and to Condole with the Macks," *Philadelphia Inquirer*, October 3, 1931: 19.
7. Stockton.
8. "The Game, Play-by-Play," *St. Louis Post-Dispatch*, October 2, 1931: 1C.
9. Frisch's smash down the left-field line was officially ruled a ground-rule double because of fan interference.
10. James C. Isaminger, "A's Defeated, 2-0; Hallahan and Martin Put Cards in Race," *Philadelphia Inquirer*, October 3, 1931: 1.
11. Stockton.
12. Isaminger.
13. Stan Baumgartner, "Pepper Martin Hero as Hallahan Hurls Three-Hit Triumph," *Philadelphia Inquirer*, October 3, 1931: 19.
14. Ibid.
15. Stockton.
16. Isaminger.
17. Herman Wecke, "Stupid Play by Wilson Gives Home Fans Scare in the Ninth," *St. Louis Post-Dispatch*, October 2, 1931: 1C.
18. Keener.
19. Stockton. Merkle refers to the New York Giants rookie Fred Merkle, whose baserunning blunder against the Chicago Cubs on September 23, 1908, led to his being forced at second base for the game's final out instead of a game-winning hit. [Merkle never made it to second as he headed for the dugout as fans poured onto the field after Moose McCormick, who was on third, scored what appeared to be the game-winning run.] Given the ensuing chaos, play did not resume and the game was declared a tie. The Cubs won the makeup game, and eventually the pennant—by one game over the Giants—and went on to capture the World Series.

20   Stockton.

21   Grauley, "Tables Turned for Cards by Hallahan Just as Last Year."

22   Baumgartner.

23   Pitch counts are from Grauley, "Tables Turned for Cards by Hallahan Just as Last Year."

24   Keener.

GROVE STYMIES REDBIRDS

October 9, 1931: Philadelphia Athletics 8,
St. Louis Cardinals 1, at Sportsman's Park

Game Six of the World Series

BY RUSS LAKE

THE DAY BEFORE GAME SIX OF THE 1931 World Series, more than 500 baseball fans crowded into the Union Station Midway to wait for the St. Louis Cardinals' special train to arrive.[1] The gathering was celebratory in manner as their team returned home sporting a three-games-to-two advantage over the favored Philadelphia Athletics.

An arrival message board at the station publicized a statement related to the captivating Mound City center fielder by displaying "Pepper Martin and Red Birds, 12:45 P.M." on the marquee.[2] Pepper Martin, who had transitioned from untested rookie to national phenomenon in less than a week, hurried with his wife from the team's rear car to the front end to try to exit without notice. But the crowd was there and surged forward with a roar. Martin grinned, blushed, and obliged a local photographer's request for some camera shots.[3]

"Everybody in St. Louis wonders what you really look like, 'Pep.' Come over here and pose for a good picture," said the cameraman. "All right," said Pep. "I'll pose. Let 'er go."[4] Martin, dressed in a brown suit and a tan sombrero cocked on the back of his head in approved Oklahoma style, finally made it out of a 20th Street side door to secure a taxi for the ride to their hotel.[5] Police struggled almost frantically to get the Martins and outfielder Chick Hafey into the taxicab and then keep boys and even men from climbing all over the cab.[6]

Later that evening, Martin returned to the hotel lobby carrying two huge bundles and was asked by teammate Jimmie Wilson what he had under his arms. "Two gallons of ice cream," replied Martin. "What's the idea?" asked another player. "Oh, ever since I was a kid I dreamed of being a big league star—making lots of money and buying as much ice cream as I could eat—and now I have done it," concluded Martin.[7]

Martin's .667 batting average and his running the basepaths with abandon had produced four steals with five runs scored, while his overall hustle afforded him the unique moniker of "The Wild Horse of the Osage." Upon learning that there was a new home plate installed at Sportsman's Park due to the previous "dish" being dug up by a souvenir hunter after Game Two, a scribe jokingly remarked that Martin would have been accused of stealing it had that happened in Philadelphia.[8]

With all of the positive ink applied to Martin, some consternation from Cardinals team officials percolated when a wire story appeared about first baseman Jim Bottomley. E. T. Bales, sports editor of the *Chattanooga News*, repeated in his column an unfounded report "from two authoritative sources" that Bottomley had been sold to the Chicago Cubs for the 1932 season.[9] Branch Rickey of the Cardinals and William Veeck of the Cubs denied the report.[10] Bales responded, "Of course they can't let it get out now while Bottomley is playing in the World Series for the Cardinals."[11]

Gabby Street altered his lineup before Game Five by shifting Martin to cleanup with the struggling Bottomley batting sixth, and his decision produced positive results as the two men combined for five hits. Street conveyed confidence, "If we'd had any luck in the first game, the series would be over right now. But what's the difference, it's taking just a little longer."[12]

HOME OF THE BROWNS AND CARDINALS AT GRAND AND DODIER

Connie Mack was concerned about his Philadelphia team on both sides of the baseball. He was worried about the inability of his players to hit consistently against the Cardinals' hurlers, and the inability of his pitchers to stop the hitting of Martin.[13] After five games, the A's were batting just .217 to the .257 mark posted by the Redbirds.

For Game Six, it would be the same mound matchup as Game One with Bob "Lefty" Grove for the Athletics going against the Cardinals' Paul Derringer. Grove was 1-1 and had been tagged for 23 hits, but just four of those safeties had gone for extra bases. In 17 innings, he had given up six runs, struck out nine and walked just one. Derringer was 0-1 in two appearances covering eight frames, and had allowed six runs on 11 hits, fanned 10, and permitted three walks. Jake Flowers would be at third base for St. Louis as the ankle problem affecting Sparky Adams would keep him out for the remainder of the series.[14]

A crowd of 39,401 jammed into Sportsman's Park anticipating that the Redbirds would clinch the championship in six games as the A's had done versus St. Louis in 1930. John Heydler, president of the National League, was all smiles as he stated, "This certainly looks like our year. The Cardinals have played great baseball against a great club."[15] Pepper Martin was so busy signing scorecards that he missed most of fielding practice, but he received a great ovation as he ran to his outfield position. Once he got there two men dashed from the stands and across the field to present the Cardinals ace with a rifle.

Pepper Martin – the Wild Horse of the Osage – was one of the most disruptive players of his generation, terrorizing opponents on the basepaths and hitting .298 for his career. (National Baseball Hall of Fame, Cooperstown, New York)

Teammate Wally Roettger trotted over, not to help Martin, but to inspect the gift.[16]

Exceptional baseball weather was present as Derringer warmed up to begin the contest. Max Bishop took a called third strike on a 2-2 count to begin the game and protested mildly to veteran plate arbiter Dick Nallin, who was umpiring in his fourth World Series.[17] Derringer took the possible clincher to heart as he put up four scoreless innings, giving up just one hit, and striking out three. Meanwhile, Grove matched zeroes with Derringer while allowing two singles and fanning a pair. Martin, who was 5-for-8 (.625) versus Grove, was retired on a pop foul to first and a line drive to center. This had to hearten those pulling for the A's because Martin's fame was growing so fast that the daily sports question had changed from "Who won the game?" to "What did Martin do?"[18]

It all fell apart for Derringer in a flash. On a Jimmie Foxx grounder to open the fifth, Flowers' throw pulled Bottomley off first for an error. A bunt sent Foxx to second base before Jimmy Dykes drew a walk. Foxx broke in the "new" home plate when he scored on a single to center by Dib Williams. After Grove fanned, Derringer became too careful with the top of the A's order and then lost his composure. Bishop walked, and another free pass on a disputed full-count pitch to Mule Haas forced Dykes home. Mickey Cochrane's hard grounder went off the glove of second baseman Frankie Frisch for another tally. Derringer's stint ended after he walked Al Simmons to plate the fourth run. Syl Johnson relieved a seething Derringer, and retired the 10th batter of the inning, Foxx, on a pop fly to shortstop.[19] All of the runs were unearned, but it was little solace with the score now reading Philadelphia 4, St. Louis 0.

Grove permitted a single to Hafey to open the Redbirds' fifth, but then retired the next three batters. The Cardinals finally tallied in the sixth when Flowers, who had doubled, scored after Frisch lined a two-out single past Foxx into right field.[20] Martin, looking to extend the inning, popped out to second baseman Bishop in short right. In the seventh, Street went with right-hander Jim Lindsey, who had been effective in Game Four. But on this afternoon Lindsey gave up four runs (two earned) on three singles, a hit batsman, another bases-loaded walk, and a dropped fly ball by Hafey, which concluded the carnage, let in two runs and yielded an 8-1 Philadelphia advantage.

The Cardinals' faithful saw little that mattered during the final three innings. Cochrane was charged with the first Philadelphia error of the series when he mishandled a third strike and allowed a batter to reach first to start the ninth. One out later, Martin walked. But Grove worked out of the jam and earned his second complete-game win in the series with a sparkling five-hit, seven-strikeout performance that took one hour and 57 minutes. The pair of fielding miscues by Flowers and Hafey factored in six of the Athletics' eight runs.

Derringer was still steaming afterwards about the perceived mid-game missed strike that plated the Athletics' second run. "The ball I pitched to Haas with a 3-2 call in the fifth inning was a perfect strike, but Umpire Nallin called it a ball."[21] Derringer thundered. "I don't mind being beaten, but I hate to be robbed — and by an American League umpire."[22] While Street affirmed his hurler's scrutiny of Nallin's judgement, Martin, who was held hitless for the first time in this Fall Classic, noted, "The umpires are human, like everybody else, and make mistakes, but they're trying to do their best."[23] Martin also praised Derringer, "He's a great pitcher. I played with him last year at Rochester, and I ought to know. The breaks just went against him, that's all."[24]

Martin predicted that the Cardinals would win Game Seven.[25]

Connie Mack stopped long enough to offer his assessment, "I said when we came back we would keep the championship in the American League and today's game certainly did not change my thought on the matter."[26]

SOURCES

In addition to the sources noted in this game account, the author also accessed Retrosheet.org, Baseball-Reference.com, SABR.org/bioproj, newspapers.com, and *The Sporting News* archive via Paper of Record.

HOME OF THE BROWNS AND CARDINALS AT GRAND AND DODIER

NOTES

1. "Street Names Paul Derringer To Pitch Tomorrow," *St. Louis Post-Dispatch*, October 8, 1931: 1B.
2. Walter W. Smith, "Pepper's' Big Show Arrives Here," *St. Louis Star-Times*, October 8, 1931: 19.
3. Ibid.
4. 'Photo Caption', *St. Louis Star-Times*, October 8, 1931: 19.
5. Smith, "Pepper's' Big Show Arrives Here."
6. "Street Names Paul Derringer To Pitch Tomorrow": 3B.
7. Stan Baumgartner, "Through The Series Sieve As Connie Cut The Cards," *Philadelphia Inquirer*, October 10, 1931: 16.
8. "Gossip of Sixth Game," *The Sporting News*, October 15, 1931: 6.
9. Author's Note-The report by E. T. Bales proved untrue as Bottomley remained with the Cardinals for the 1932 season. He was subsequently traded to the Cincinnati Reds on December 17, 1932.
10. "Reported Sale of Bottomley Denied by Branch Rickey," *St. Louis Star-Times*, October 8, 1931: 19.
11. 'United Press', "Bottomley Sold, Report," *Pittsburgh Press*, October 8, 1931: 29.
12. "Worried," *The Pittsburgh Press*, October 8, 1931: 29.
13. "Happy," *The Pittsburgh Press*, October 8, 1931: 29.
14. Herman Wecke, "Earnshaw Likely to be Mack's Pitcher; High to Play Third," *St. Louis Post-Dispatch*, October 8, 1931: 1B.
15. Ibid.
16. Wecke, "Grimes and Earnshaw to Pitch Tomorrow; Mound Duel Likely," *St. Louis Post-Dispatch*, October 9, 1931: 1C-2C.
17. "Grimes and Earnshaw."
18. "Introducing The World Series Hero," *Pittsburgh Press*, October 8, 1931: 29.
19. J. Roy Stockton, "Cards Lose 8-1; Deciding Game Tomorrow," *St. Louis Post-Dispatch*, October 9, 1931: 1C.
20. Ibid.
21. "Grimes and Earnshaw."
22. Baumgartner, "Derringer Bitter At Umpire Nallin," *Philadelphia Inquirer*, October 10, 1931: 16.
23. Pepper Martin, "'Think I'll Do It,' Martin Confides As He Visions Victory," *Philadelphia Inquirer*, October 10, 1931: 1.
24. Ibid.
25. Ibid.
26. "Derringer Bitter."

REVENGE IS SWEET, EVEN WITHOUT PEPPER

October 10, 1931: St. Louis Cardinals 4, Philadelphia Athletics 2, at Sportsman's Park

Game Seven of the World Series

BY NORM KING

GABBY STREET WANTED REvenge, so he went to the firm of Hallahan and Grimes.

Street, in his second year as Cardinals manager, wanted to avenge his team's loss to the A's in the 1930 World Series, which Philadelphia won in six games. He had his chance as the day dawned on Game Seven of the 1931 Series, thanks to Wild Bill Hallahan, who won Games Two and Five, and Game Three winner Burleigh Grimes. It was only fitting that both pitchers were involved in the game that won it all.

This series pitted two teams that boasted great staffs. Philadelphia led the American League with a 3.47 ERA, while the Cardinals ranked second in the National League with a mark of 3.45. The clubs had vastly different offensive styles. The Athletics had three sluggers who would reach the Hall of Fame. Jimmie Foxx's 30 home runs represented half the total of the entire Cardinal team. Al Simmons had 22 and Mickey Cochrane launched 17. Cochrane's total would have led the Cardinals. Future Hall of Famer Chick Hafey had 16 to lead St. Louis, while the only other Redbird to reach double figures was George Watkins, with 13. Conversely, St. Louis ran rings around the A's. Their 114 stolen bases led the National League, while Philadelphia was last in the American League with 25.

Street had legitimate cause for concern going into the for-all-the-marbles matchup, as the A's had pounded his Cards, 8-1, in Game Six, and the Philadelphia starter for Game Seven, George Earnshaw (21-7, 3.67 ERA during the season), had pitched very well. He gave up only two earned runs on six hits in a 2-0 loss in Game Two; then threw a two-hit shutout in Game Four, which the A's won, 3-0.

"After taking the play away from their White Elephant rivals in the forepart of the competition, and coming home for the concluding games, the Cards slumped so miserably yesterday that hope for their victory today seemed given up by all the red-shirted players." wrote United Press sports reporter L.S. Cameron.[1]

Street put his team's fate in Grimes's damp hand. Grimes, one of baseball's last (legal) spitballers, was 17-9 with a 3.65 ERA in one of the last seasons of his Hall of Fame career.[2] He pitched brilliantly in his only other Series start, going into the eighth inning of Game Three with a no-hitter and winning 5-2.

Grimes's mastery over the A's continued at the beginning of Game Seven, as he retired the first three Philadelphia hitters in order in the first. Third baseman Andy High led off for St. Louis in the bottom of the inning, and how he got to that spot is an interesting story. Sparky Adams was the Cardinals' third baseman and leadoff hitter during the regular season, but on September 20 he sprained his ankle rounding first base during, of all things, a pregame skills competition between his team and the Brooklyn Dodgers. After High played Game One and Jake Flowers Game Two, Street inserted Adams into the lineup for Game Three, but his gimpy ankle forced him to leave after the fifth. Prior to Game Four, Flowers was injured during the pregame warm-up when a groundball jumped up and hit him in the face. He started the game — no one had heard of concussion protocols in 1931 — but left after the first due to dizzy spells. Adams started Game Five but departed after limping to first with a leadoff single off Waite Hoyt. High took over in both games. Flowers played Game Six, but his fifth-inning throwing error on a Jimmie Foxx grounder led to four unearned runs.

Hence, High started Game Seven. He got to play on a beautiful, sunny day, too, with the temperature in the mid-70s. Oddly enough, Sportsman's Park was only half full. After more than 39,000 watched the Cardinals lose Game Six, only 20,805 showed up for the clincher. They got their money's worth.

Ignoring the low turnout, the Cardinals wasted no time showing Earnshaw that Game Seven was not going to be like Game Four. Both High and number-two hitter George Watkins singled to start the Cardinals' first, and moved up on a sacrifice by Frankie Frisch. Earnshaw uncorked a wild pitch, allowing High to score the game's first run, while Watkins moved to third.

The next batter was Street's not-so-secret weapon, one Johnny Leonard Roosevelt "Pepper" Martin, who was in his first full season in the majors. Martin had already tied what was then the World Series record with 12 hits in the first five games, with one home run, five RBIs, and four stolen bases.[3] He walked and promptly stole his fifth base of the Series.

Ernie Orsatti was the next hitter, and he struck out, but Cochrane dropped the third strike and when he threw to first to get Orsatti, an alert Watkins darted for home. Foxx's return throw to the plate was off the mark, and the Cardinals had a quick 2-0 lead. Jim Bottomley struck out to end the inning.

Grimes breezed along with his two-run lead. He gave up two hits in the second but came out of the inning unscathed, and made up for walking Max Bishop in the third by picking him off first base. His teammates rewarded Grimes for that move in the bottom of the inning. High smacked his second straight single to lead off, and then Watkins launched his only round-tripper of the Series over the right-field pavilion. St. Louis led 4-0 going into the fourth.

An early four-run lead didn't mean much against a team with sluggers like Foxx and Simmons, and Earnshaw did his part by settling down and not allowing a baserunner through the next four innings. However, Grimes also continued pitching well. He had some trouble in the fifth when he gave up two hits, but a double play ended that threat. He was perfect in the sixth and struck out the side in the seventh, including Foxx and Simmons.

Things got interesting in the eighth as Grimes, who was pitching despite being in great pain from appendicitis, began to tire. After Dib Williams struck out, Grimes walked Phil Todt, who was pinch-hitting for Earnshaw. Todt moved to second when Bishop grounded to third. Mule Haas got the second walk of the inning — only Grimes's third of the game — but Cochrane lined out to Grimes for the third out.

Many managers, no doubt, have cursed the person who thought that games shouldn't end after the eighth inning. The Redbirds' skipper was probably one of them, using blue language as Grimes started the ninth by walking Simmons. Pitching 101 says it's never a good idea to walk the leadoff hitter, especially when the guy behind him, Foxx, had driven in 120 runs during the season. But Foxx didn't come through this time, fouling out to catcher Jimmie Wilson. One away. The next batter, Bing Miller, had the Cardinals sniffing the $4,480-per-man World Series money when he grounded into a force play at second base. Two down.

That's when Grimes really got into trouble; he walked Jimmy Dykes and then Williams singled to load the bases. Up came Doc Cramer, living every kid's dream — Game Seven, ninth inning, two out, bases loaded, with the chance to be a hero. Okay, so a two-run single isn't how these fantasies usually play out, but Cramer's hit did make the game closer and brought Grimes's day to an end. Street brought Hallahan in to face Bishop, who flied out to, appropriately, Martin, and the celebration began.

"People and automobiles began to appear on the streets that a moment before had been virtually deserted," wrote the *St. Louis Post-Dispatch*.

"Downtown, the streets looked like Sunday afternoon, until Pepper Martin caught that last fly."[4]

SOURCES

In addition to the sources cited below, the author also used:

Baseballhall.org.

Faber, Charles. "Burleigh Grimes," in *The 1934 St. Louis Cardinals: The World Champion Gas House Gang* (Phoenix: Society for American Baseball Research, 2014).

NOTES

1. L.S. Cameron, "Cards Defeat Macks to Win World Series," *Pittsburgh Press*, October 11, 1931: 1.

2. According to BaseballAlmanac.com, 17 pitchers were allowed to continue using the spitball after it was outlawed in 1920. Three other pitchers still threw the wet one in 1931: Red Faber, Clarence Mitchell, and Jack Quinn. Grimes was the last of the group, retiring after the 1934 season.

3. Three other players had 12 hits in a World Series before Martin: Buck Herzog for the New York Giants in 1912, Shoeless Joe Jackson for the Chicago White Sox in 1919, and Sam Rice for the Washington Senators in 1925.

4. "Noisy Celebration on Streets When Cards Win Series," *St. Louis Post-Dispatch*, October 10, 1931: 1.

THE GOOSE WALLOPS THREE

June 23, 1932: St. Louis Browns 14, New York Yankees 10, at Sportsman's Park

BY GREGORY H. WOLF

GOOSE GOSLIN WAS A DANGERous hitter, suggested St. Louis sportswriter Charles Regan, especially for pedestrians walking along Grand Boulevard in front of Sportsman's Park, located on the north side of the Gateway City. Regan wondered whether the future Hall of Famer "would hurt many people" with his next moon shot in a slugfest with the New York Yankees.[1]

"The Bronx Bombers versus the Brownie Bashers" would have been an appropriate epithet to describe the teams' four-game series, which concluded on Thursday, June 23. On paper, skipper Bill Killefer's sixth-place Browns, coming off consecutive seasons with at least 90 losses, were an unlikely match for the league-leading Yankees, who had ridden roughshod over the competition since the beginning of the season en route to a 43-18 record. After losing the first two games (3-1 and 11-8) courtesy of late-inning Yankees rallies, the Browns exploded for 10 runs in the sixth inning of the third game and cruised to a 17-10 victory to improve their record to 31-31.

As the Great Depression tightened its stranglehold on St. Louis, catapulting the city's employment to an estimated 25 percent, Sportsman's Park was filled with only about 2,000 patrons to see the Browns conclude their 17-game homestand.[2] That figure was actually about 500 more than the team's season average, the seventh of 18 consecutive seasons that the Browns finished last in AL attendance. Hopefully none of spectators expected a pitchers' duel on a warm, sunny afternoon with temperatures in the mid-80s. Toeing the rubber for the Browns was hard-throwing right-hander Bump Hadley, acquired on April 27 along with outfielder Bruce Campbell from the Chicago White Sox in exchange for budding star shortstop Red Kress. In parts of seven seasons, Hadley had compiled a 63-61 record, including 5-5 thus far in '32. His biggest bugaboo was control, and in the first inning he lacked it completely, walking four batters, including bases-loaded free passes to Lou Gehrig and Bill Dickey, giving the Yankees a 2-0 lead.

The Browns teed off against Yankees right-hander George Pipgras, whose 82-57 career slate, including 7-4 in '32, was enviable to any Brownie hurler. After Jack Burns and Campbell whacked consecutive doubles to cut the Yankees' lead in half, Goslin spanked one "high in the air," wrote Regan, "falling into Grand Boulevard without much fanfare" for a 3-2 Browns lead.[3]

Goslin's blast was music to Killefer's ears. Acquired from the Washington Senators in a blockbuster trade for future Hall of Fame flychaser Heinie Manush and pitcher General Crowder in June 1930, Goslin had averaged 20 round-trippers, 113 RBIs, and a .333 batting average in the previous eight campaigns (1924-1931). However, the New Jersey native had been a disappointment entering the Yankees series with just five homers and a .298 average. Two days earlier, he finally had gotten on track, belting a grand slam and tying his career-high single-game mark with six RBIs. To be competitive, the Browns needed their cleanup hitter to regain his form.

Hadley walked the bases full in the second but escaped the jam. Pipgras, who tied Lefty Grove for the AL lead with 24 victories in 1928, was having his own case of the "Hadleys." He walked Fred Schulte, who eventually scored on Campbell's single. Up stepped Goslin, who smashed a "whistling liner into the pavilion far down near the centerfield bleachers," as the

St. Louis Star and Times put it, to increase the Browns' lead to 6-2 and send Pipgras to the showers.[4]

The Browns gave rookie right-hander Johnny Allen, coming off his third shutout in his last seven starts, a rude welcome to the Midwest. In the third, Schulte's single and Burns's second double led to two more runs in what had quickly transformed into a laugher. On the other hand, one could never count out the Yankees, the highest-scoring team in the majors.

The visitors from Gotham City staged their comeback in the fourth when Earle Combs led off with a single and scored on Gehrig's 18th round-tripper of the season, a towering shot over the right-field pavilion.[5] The 29-year-old Gehrig was playing in his 1,103rd consecutive game, which tied teammate Joe Sewell for the second longest such streak in big-league history, though still far behind Everett Scott's 1,307. Hadley issued two more walks in the fifth. One of the men granted a free pass, Tony Lazzeri, scored on Combs's single to make the game interesting, 8-5.

Had the Rookie of the Year Award existed in 1932, Johnny Allen would have been the likely recipient with a sparkling 17-4 record, but on this day the country boy from North Carolina struggled. Jim Levey led off the fifth with a single and scored on Schulte's single. After a walk to Burns, Goslin did his best impression of the Sultan of Swat by belting a bullet, which, according to Regan, "scooted across [the field] on a terrific line that just skimmed the roof of the pavilion" before landing on Grand Boulevard to put the Browns up by seven runs, 12-5.[6]

Goslin's stature among AL sluggers of the 1920s and 1930s is often overlooked due to the prodigious exploits of Babe Ruth and Gehrig, as well as Philadelphia A's teammates Jimmie Foxx and Al Simmons. From 1924 to 1931, Goslin finished in the top seven in home runs every season, despite playing in Washington's Griffith Stadium, one of the largest in baseball. Goslin became just the third hitter in AL history to hit at least three home runs in a game three times, joining Ruth and Gehrig, whose record-setting four-home-run outburst against the A's three weeks earlier put him in exclusive company with four such games. Goslin was only the second St. Louis hitter, Cardinal or Brown, to whack three homers in a contest at Sportsman's Park, following Ken Williams's feat on April 22, 1922, against the White Sox.

Given Hadley's wildness (he'd go on to lead the majors with 171 walks) and the general ineptitude of the Browns staff (with its collective 5.01 ERA), the game was far from over despite the Browns' 12-5 lead. Hadley increased his walk total to 11 with free passes to Gehrig and Ruth to lead off the sixth and was yanked in favor of George Blaeholder. Victimized by six runs (five earned) in a two-inning start just two days earlier, Blaeholder fared no better in this game, retiring only two batters while yielding a two-

Goose Goslin walloped 248 round-trippers, knocked in 1,612 runs, and batted .316 in his 18-year Hall of Fame career. (National Baseball Hall of Fame, Cooperstown, New York)

run single to Lazzeri and an RBI double to pinch-hitter Sam Byrd. Combs's run-scoring single off the Browns third pitcher, Wally Hebert, made it 12-9.

McCarthy probably rued his decision to call on southpaw reliever Ed "Satchelfoot" Wells to start the sixth. On the positive side, the nine-year veteran retired three batters; however, he also surrendered three doubles, the latter two by Levey and Schulte, producing two more runs to push the Browns' lead to 14-9.

The game's scoring ended with Ruth's clout over the right-field pavilion, his 22nd of the season, to lead off the seventh. Goslin's attempt to join Gehrig as the second modern-day member of the four-home-run club failed in the seventh when he fanned.

The Yankees, concluding their 16-game Western swing and their 26th road game in their last 29 contests, were probably looking forward to the Pullman coaches on an overnight train back to New York. The Browns were probably sorry to see the Yankees leave town, a sentiment the club rarely harbored. Following the pitching duel between Lefty Gomez and Hebert in the first game, which featured just seven safeties (three by the Browns), the Browns offense exploded for 46 hits and 39 runs in the next three contests; true to their moniker, the Bombers pounded out 38 hits and scored 31 times.

Hadley's pitching line was a nightmare: a career-high 11 walks and seven runs (six earned) in just five innings, but he picked up the victory. Pipgras, charged with six runs in 1⅔ innings, took the loss.

Goslin finished the best four-game series of his career with 14 RBIs and four homers; he scored eight times. His seven RBIs in this game set a career high. He went on to hit 17 homers and drive in 104 runs, marking the eighth of 11 times he surpassed the century mark.

SOURCES

In addition to the sources cited in the Notes, the author also accessed Retrosheet.org, Baseball-Reference.com, SABR.org, and *The Sporting News* archive via Paper of Record.

NOTES

1   Charles "Kid" Regan, "Goslin's Homers Feature Browns Winning Stride," *St. Louis Star and Times*, June 24, 1932: 22.

2   Attendance estimate from William E. Brandt, "Goslin's 3 Homers Put Yankees to Rout," *New York Times*, June 24, 1932: 26.

3   Regan.

4   Ibid.

5   Play-by-play courtesy of James M. Gould, "Goslin Hits Three Home Runs; Two Are Made off Pipgras," *St. Louis Post-Dispatch*, June 23, 1932: 15.

6   Regan.

DIZZY FANS 17 FOR NEW MODERN RECORD

July 30, 1933: St. Louis Cardinals 8, Chicago Cubs 2, at Sportsman's Park

BY GREGORY H. WOLF

"[HE] PITCHED WITH DEVASTATING speed, his curves breaking fast and baffling the best of the Cubs hitters," gushed the Associated Press after Dizzy Dean's record breaking performance.[1] The 23-year-old Cardinals hurler fanned 17 to set a post-1900 record for most strikeouts in a game. St. Louis sportswriter L.C. Davis exulted that "the Great Dean proceeded to turn out a masterpiece that dwarfed all his former efforts."[2] J. Roy Stockton of the *St. Louis Post-Dispatch* praised Dean as the "brilliant young Cardinals pitcher, whose skill, showmanship and color make him the Babe Ruth of the National League."[3]

The Cardinals were in dire need of Dean's heroics as they prepared for a Sunday-afternoon doubleheader against the Chicago Cubs to conclude a season-long 23-game homestand. The Redbirds had overcome a sluggish start and were tied for first place as late as June 17. Then they lost 24 of their next 37 games. Club owner Sam Breadon, notoriously quick to replace his skippers, fired Gabby Street, who had led the underdog Cardinals to a World Series victory over the Philadelphia Athletics in 1931, and replaced him with the NL MVP of that squad, second baseman Frankie Frisch. St. Louis had won its first four games for the Fordham Flash, and was in now in fourth place (50-45), eight games behind the New York Giants. Player-manager Charlie Grimm's reigning pennant-winning Cubs (53-44) had been the hottest team in baseball, having won 15 of 17 games before a three-game sweep in Pittsburgh cooled them off. Their losing streak reached four when Pepper Martin belted a three-run walk-off home run in the first game of a three-game set with the Cardinals the day before.

The pitching match-up featured two of the league's best right-handers. The Cubs' Guy Bush, the "Mississippi Mudcat," was a slick-dressing, good-looking 31-year-old who had fashioned a 125-87 record in parts of 11 campaigns, including an 11-8 mark thus far in '33. Dizzy Dean needed no introduction to even the casual baseball fan of the time. In just his second full season in the majors, Dean had captured the country's attention in the height of the Great Depression with his down-home, eccentric stories about growing up in Arkansas. He had won 25 and 26 games respectively in his first two seasons of Organized Baseball. As a rookie with St. Louis in 1932 he went 18-15 and led the majors in strikeouts (191). He entered the game with a 13-11 record, but had recently struggled, yielding 16 runs (15 earned) and 25 hits in his last 22⅔ innings. Dean probably had been overworked; he had relieved in 12 games in addition to his 20 starts. Given some extra rest by his new skipper, Dean was making his first start in a week.

According to the *St. Louis Post-Dispatch*, the Sunday-afternoon twin bill drew a crowd of 29,500 to Sportsman's Park, located at the intersection of Grand Avenue and Dodier Street on the city's near north side.[4] Dean, the NL's biggest drawing card, looked rusty. Cubs leadoff hitter Mark Koenig stroked a double to center, and scored on Billy Herman's single to center. Kiki Cuyler hit a popup to Dean, who attempted some shenanigans. He "grounded" the pop fly, letting it fall, hoping for a double play. Dean's antics confused first baseman Pat Crawford, who was "balled up in the trick technique" as Edward Burns put it in the *Chicago Tribune*.[5] The umpires didn't fall for it, though, and Cuyler was called out on an infield-fly ruling. Dean then whiffed Babe Herman and Frank Demaree to end the inning. He settled down in the second and third innings, striking out three batters.

No slouch at the plate, Dean got the Cardinals on the board in the third, belting a double down the third-base line. He moved to third when Pepper "The Wild Horse of the Osage" Martin hit a screamer back to the mound that caromed off Bush's glove for an infield hit, and subsequently scored on Frisch's sacrifice fly to tie the score, 1-1.[6]

The Cubs took the lead in the fourth. Martin committed the Cardinals' only error of the game when he fumbled a sharp grounder to third by leadoff hitter Demaree, who scored on Gilly Campbell's double to left. (The run was unearned.) Dean retired the next three hitters, but for the only inning of the game did not register a strikeout. He made up for it in the fifth, striking out the side, and increased his total to 10 with two more punchouts in the sixth.

The Cardinals, led by the league's highest-scoring offense, broke through in the sixth. Crawford drew a one-out walk and Joe "Ducky" Medwick singled to left field, where Cuyler fumbled the ball, allowing both to advance a station. Ernie Orsatti smashed a double that ricocheted off first baseman Harvey Hendrick's glove, enabling Crawford and Medwick to score, giving the Cardinals a 3-2 lead. After Jimmie Wilson's single drove in Orsatti, Leo Durocher's double off the wall plated Wilson and ended Bush's rough afternoon (10 hits and 6 runs, all earned, in 5⅓ innings). Burleigh Grimes, a 39-year-old spitballer, took the mound. Facing Dean, his first toss was a wild pitch, sending Durocher to third. Dean followed with a run-scoring single to make it 6-2.

St. Louis tacked on two more runs in the eighth. Medwick led off with his fourth single of the game and moved to second on Orsatti's sacrifice. With Wilson on first via a walk, Durocher hit what Ed Burns considered an easy double-play ball to shortstop Billy Jurges, whose throw to second baseman Billy Herman nabbed Orsatti. But Herman misfired on the relay toss to Hendrick, permitting Medwick to scamper home. Dean smacked a double off the center-field wall, his third hit of the game, to drive in Durocher for the Redbirds' eighth and final run.

After Billy Herman led off the eighth with a single, Dean overpowered the Cubs, fanning six of the next seven batters he faced. His only blemish was a leadoff double by Babe Herman in the ninth. Dizzy struck out pinch-hitter Jim Mosolf to complete the Cardinals' 8-2 victory in one hour and 42 minutes.

Dizzy's 17 strikeouts, 12 of them swinging, set a new modern single-game record.[7] Since 1900 four pitchers had whiffed 16: Cincinnati's Frank "Noodles" Hahn (1901), Christy Mathewson of the New York Giants (1904), Rube Waddell of the St. Louis Browns (1908), and Brooklyn's Nap Rucker in 1909. In 1884, when the pitching mound was located 50 feet from home plate, Charlie Sweeney of the NL Providence Grays struck out 19.

Dean was his typical exuberant self after the game. "[Frisch] gave me a chance to rest a week, and I believe I pitched my best game as a result," said Dizzy, who walked just one. "I was at my best when the game ended."[8] J. Roy Stockton went so far as to suggest that Dean might have had more "had he paid attention to the fanning business earlier."[9] Dean's batterymate Jimmie Wilson also set a big-league record for most putouts by a catcher (18), including one foul popup he caught.

The Cardinals took the second game of the doubleheader, 6-5, highlighted by Ducky Medwick's three-run homer and Pepper Martin's three runs scored, to stay undefeated for player-manager Frisch. The *Post-Dispatch* opined that the Sportsman's Park faithful were "convinced that the Cardinals could not be counted out of the pennant race."[10] Dean stoked their belief. "No kidding, I actually do believe the Cardinals will win the flag this year," he said after facing his younger brother Paul "Daffy" Dean, pitcher for the Columbus Red Birds, in an exhibition in Ohio on July 31.[11]

The Cubs released "Old Stubblebeard" Grimes after the game. The following day the future Hall of Famer signed with the Cardinals.

So moved by Dean's record-breaking performance, St. Louis sportswriter L.C. Davis wrote a poem in his honor.

> 17 — Count 'Em — 17
> Nine hearty cheers for "Dizzy" Dean,
> The new-crowned strike-out king;
> At his new mark of seventeen,
> The pitchers now can fling
> While carving for himself a niche,
> With but a single walk,
> He showed the world he can pitch,
> As well as he can talk.
> The batters were completely cowed
> And eating from his hand;
> Like wheat before the scythe they bowed,
> As one by one they fanned.
> And graybeards to their sons someday
> Will speak of "Dizzy" Dean,
> And tell them all about the day
> He struck out seventeen.[12]

Dean finished the season with a 20-18 record and once again led the majors in strikeouts (199) for the Cardinals, who finished in fifth place. In his injury-shortened career, Dizzy struck out 10 or more batters in a game on eight occasions.

SOURCES

In addition to the sources cited in the Notes, the author also accessed Retrosheet.org, Baseball-Reference.com, the SABR Minor Leagues Database, accessed online at Baseball-Reference.com, SABR.org, and *The Sporting News* archive via Paper of Record.

NOTES

1. Associated Press, "Marks Set in Cards' Double Win," *Cincinnati Enquirer*, July 31, 1933: 10.
2. L.C. Davis, "A Sport Salad," *St. Louis Post-Dispatch*, August 1, 1933: 2B.
3. J. Roy Stockton, "Cards Idle for Day After Dean's Record 17-Strikeout Show," *St. Louis Post-Dispatch*, July 31, 1933: 1B
4. Stockton.
5. Edward Burns, "Cubs Lose to Cards, 8-2, 6-5; Deans Fans 17 For New Record," *Chicago Tribune*, July 31, 1933: 17.
6. Both the *Chicago Tribune* and *St. Louis Post-Dispatch* report that the Cardinals scored their first run in the third inning. The incomplete game accounts on Baseball-Reference.com and Retrosheet.org show that the Cardinals scored their first run in the first inning.
7. Stockton.
8. "Dean Praises Frisch and Predicts 1933 Pennant," *St. Louis Post-Dispatch*, August 1, 1933: 3B.
9. Stockton.
10. Ibid.
11. "Dean Praises Frisch and Predicts 1933 Pennant."
12. Davis.

CARDINALS AND DODGERS BATTLE THROUGH 27 RUNS, 36 HITS, AND 17 WALKS

September 16, 1933: St. Louis Cardinals 14, Brooklyn Dodgers 13 (10 Innings), at Sportsman's Park

BY DOUG FELDMANN

BY THE TIME THE 1933 NATIONAL League season was winding down on September 16, the St. Louis Cardinals had joined the Brooklyn Dodgers—their guests that day in Sportsman's Park—in battling for little more than pride. The Cardinals had been mathematically eliminated from the pennant race the previous afternoon and stood 10½ games out of first place through 144 games.

Since the dismissal of Gabby Street as manager on July 23, the Cardinals' on-field leadership had been assumed by second baseman Frankie Frisch. To date, Frisch had steadied the club into fourth place with a record of 77-66 while his former team, the New York Giants, had built a commanding 7½-game lead on the Chicago Cubs and the Pittsburgh Pirates entering play that day. The Dodgers were mired further down in sixth place with a record of 57-80, sitting nearly a full 30 games from the top.

Yet, despite the lack of impact, the afternoon's affair would have on the pennant race, Cardinals owner Sam Breadon was hopeful for a large Saturday crowd with a doubleheader in store.

He would be disappointed. So would the people who stayed home.

Relatively few souls jumped off the "70 Grand" streetcar line that ran by the ballpark. A total of 6,200 women were admitted free of charge for a ladies day promotion, and they were joined by only 2,800 paying customers. The fans who made the effort to be present, however, were entertained. "Those baseball boys had a rip-snorting time at the corner of Grand Boulevard and Dodier Street," concluded J. Roy Stockton, the Cardinals beat writer for the *St. Louis Post-Dispatch*.[1]

Greeted with clear late-summer skies and steamy 92-degree temperatures, the Cardinals took the field. On the mound was Tex Carleton, who brought a 15-10 record and a 3.24 earned-run average into the contest and who, along with fellow second-year pitcher Dizzy Dean, had become a mainstay in Frisch's rotation. After Buzz Boyle led off the game with a single, Carleton quieted the Dodgers bats over the rest of the first inning before the Cardinals came to the plate for the first time.

Carleton was opposed by Walter Beck, a native of nearby Decatur, Illinois. When the season's final statistics were totaled, Beck led the National League in runs allowed; and in subsequent years with the Phillies, he would earn the nickname "Boom-Boom"—the sound that would echo through the park when his pitches ended up against the metallic outfield wall at the Baker Bowl in Philadelphia. But for now, Beck—after posting earned-run averages of 5.56 and 4.41 in limited duty in his first two major-league seasons with the St. Louis Browns—had found a groove. As he took the mound in Sportsman's Park he carried a respectable 3.62 ERA, solidifying a spot in Max Carey's rotation as he made his 32nd start of the season.

The Cardinals pushed across a run in the first inning in their classic small-ball fashion, with Pepper Martin drawing a walk, stealing second, advancing to third on a fly ball by Frisch, and scoring when Brooklyn right fielder Johnny Frederick misplayed a drive off the bat of rookie sensation Joe Medwick.

They increased their lead to 2-0 in the second when Leo Durocher singled home Gene Moore, who had doubled in his first start in a Cardinals uniform.

A bunt single by Lonny Frey started a six-run rally for Brooklyn in the third inning. Frey was well known locally, having attended a Cardinals tryout two years earlier after losing his job at a St. Louis meat-packing plant due to the Great Depression. Playing sandlot ball on the evenings and weekends, Frey went unsigned by his hometown Cardinals after the tryout but inked a deal with the Dodgers organization a year later.

Five more Dodger hits followed Frey's—including a double by Beck—propelling Brooklyn to a 6-2 lead. But the Cardinals answered with six of their own in the bottom half, five of which came off Beck before he was relieved by Rosy Ryan. Five of the runs were unearned, due to three errors by first baseman Sam Leslie.

A three-run homer by Medwick in the sixth upped the Cardinals' advantage to 11-6. After Brooklyn cut the lead to 11-8, the Cardinals added to the lead again on a triple steal in the seventh, with George Watkins swiping home, Frisch third, and Medwick second. St. Louis relievers Bill Hallahan, and Syl Johnson faltered, however, and permitted three Brooklyn runs to send the game into extra innings with a 12-12 score.

A triple by Frey gave the Dodgers the lead in the top of the 10th, but the Cardinals responded once again. Durocher reached base with the 17th walk issued by the afternoon's erratic pitchers and he scored on a double by Martin (as he swung, the bat slipped out of Pepper's sweat-soaked hands—yet he still drove the ball into the gap in right-center). Watkins then followed with the winner, a blue-darter down the right-field line that rolled to the wall and plated the cheering Pat Crawford.

The 14-13 final score had taken an "interminable" 3 hours 28 minutes to play, a length quite common by modern standards but a veritable marathon in the 1930s. Johnson picked up the win while Ray Benge—normally a starter who was thrust into a relief role on the long afternoon—was tagged with his 17th loss for permitting the 10th-inning Cardinal tallies. The 14 runs by the Cardinals and 13 by the Dodgers were the third most and second most scored respectively by each club during the season.

Frey led the Dodgers at the plate with four hits and three RBIs. Beck drove in three himself, while Tony Cuccinello added three hits to the attack. For the Cardinals, the first five hitters in the lineup—Martin, Watkins, Frisch, Medwick, and Rip Collins—posted two hits apiece, while the young Medwick continued to establish himself as one of the great new run-producers in the game with five RBIs. Patrolling center field for the Cardinals all day long was the newcomer Moore, a promising young player who only a day earlier had arrived from the team's farm club at Houston in the Texas League. In addition to his second-inning double, Moore walked, scored twice, and had an RBI in the first game, and then knocked a triple in the second game before it was halted by darkness after four innings.

"When they finally got around to squaring off for the second encounter, the shades of night were falling fast and darkening many a kitchen, where lonely husbands were looking longingly for the can opener," Stockton wrote of the tired teams—and of the ladies day attendees still there watching them.[2]

The next afternoon was "Dizzy Dean Day" at Sportsman's Park, as the city lauded its star pitcher. "His gifts included a new Buick, a crate of baby chicks, and five pigs."[3] While Frisch spent the remainder of 1933 positioning the Cardinals for their title run in '34, the end was near for the two-year stint of Carey at the helm of the Dodgers, as his coach Casey Stengel would get the next shot at the manager's job in Brooklyn.

SOURCES

In addition to the sources listed below, the author also consulted Baseball-Reference.com, Retrosheet.org, and SABR.org

NOTES

1 J. Roy Stockton, "Cardinals Outscore Brooklyn, 14-13; Second a Fadeout," *St. Louis Post-Dispatch*, September 17, 1933: 1F.

2 Ibid.

3   Robert Gregory, *Diz: The story of Dizzy Dean and Baseball During the Great Depression* (New York: Penguin Books, 1992), 117.

BOBO TOSSES NO-NO THROUGH NINE, LOSES IN 10TH

September 18, 1934: Boston Red Sox 2, St. Louis Browns 1 (10 Innings), at Sportsman's Park

BY RICHARD RIIS

"Buck Newsom pitched a no-hit game
But gets no credit for the same,
 As in the tenth he lost it.
For in that inning Lady Luck
Hauled off and took a poke at Puck,
 And off the records crossed it."[1]

LOUIS NEWSOM, NICKNAMED "BUCK" when he arrived in the majors before adopting "Bobo" during his post-Browns tenure with the Washington Senators,[2] received brief looks from the Brooklyn Robins in 1929 and 1930 and the Chicago Cubs in 1932 before his breakout season in 1933 (30 victories for the Los Angeles Angels of the Pacific Coast League) convinced the Browns to take him in the Rule 5 draft.

After starting the 1934 season in the bullpen, Newsom was promoted to the rotation by the end of April. Despite compiling a losing record for the second-division Browns, he soon established himself as one of the better pitchers in the AL, and his colorful "country boy" personality and eccentric ways made him a favorite of fans and sportswriters.

Winners of only four of their last 15 games, the Browns, holding onto fifth place but 28½ games behind the league-leading Tigers, lost yet again, 3-0, in the opener of a four-game series with the fourth-place Boston Red Sox at Sportsman's Park on September 17.

Newsom got the pitching assignment from Browns manager Rogers Hornsby for the second game of the series. Although the big right-hander's 17 losses were one behind the White Sox' Milt Gaston for most in the AL, his 15 wins and 4.04 ERA placed him among the league's top 10 in each category.

Control issues, as evidenced by 133 walks in 236⅓ innings, were Newsom's signature vulnerability. In three previous starts against Boston, Newsom had gone 1-2, but had issued 15 bases on balls in 22 innings; in three relief outings against the Sox he'd pitched seven innings and walked nine, but earned a victory on June 17 when the Browns came from behind to win.

Newsom's opponent this day was Wes Ferrell. Ferrell, 13-5, had started three games against the Browns and won all three, each a complete game and one a shutout, with a combined ERA of 1.33.

Neither team managed a hit in the first inning, but the Red Sox were able to put together a run without the benefit of a base hit in the second. Roy Johnson and Skinny Graham walked, and an error by Browns second baseman Ski Melillo on an attempted pickoff allowed the runners to advance to second and third. After an infield out by Rick Ferrell, Wes's brother and batterymate, Newsom walked Ed Morgan, loading the bases. Lyn Lary's groundball to short was scooped up by Alan "Inky" Strange, who tossed to Rollie Hemsley at the plate, but Johnson beat the throw to score the game's first run.

With the bases loaded and an opportunity to break the game wide open, Wes Ferrell, as adept at the plate as he was on the mound and batting .297 with four home runs, fell behind 0-and-2 in the count. Then he took a pitch he believed was outside but which umpire Lou Kolls called a third strike. Ferrell, known for a hair-trigger temper, exploded, unleashing a tirade of epithets at Kolls.

It was unclear to witnesses if Ferrell simply verbally assaulted Kolls or actually shoved him, as the arbiter reported to the league office, but after a few seconds Kolls called to Red Sox manager Bucky Harris, "Get another pitcher ready; this one is through."[3] At that, brother Rick sprang from the dugout with a few choice words of his own, and was also tossed.

Newsom, aware of Hornsby's rule that a pitcher ahead 0-and-2 in the count was subject to a $20 fine if the next pitch was over the plate, had also run in from the mound to agree with both Ferrells that the pitch had been a ball. Kolls chased Newsom back to the mound.

Newsom escaped the inning without further damage, except for a $20 fine from Hornsby for the location of the pitch and the temerity of arguing in the opposition's favor. After a review the following day by AL President Will Harridge, the Ferrell brothers were suspended and fined for "conduct detrimental to the best interests of baseball."[4] Wes was suspended for five games and fined $100; Rick drew a three-game suspension and also was fined $100.

Rube Walberg, a former 20-game winner with the 1929-1931 pennant-winning Philadelphia Athletics but now doing mostly bullpen duty in Boston, replaced Wes Ferrell on the mound for the Red Sox and Gordie Hinkle took Rick's place behind the plate.

The Browns mustered a hit here and there off Walberg, with nothing to show for it until the bottom of the sixth. A base hit by Hemsley followed by an errant throw by center fielder Mel Almada and a single by Strange broke the Browns' scoreless streak at 26 consecutive innings and tied the score, 1-1.

Newsom, meanwhile, continued to baffle the Boston lineup. Despite the gift of five walks and errors by Strange and Melillo, the Red Sox failed to reach him for another run or anything approaching a base hit through eight innings.

In the Red Sox' ninth, Morgan drove a liner that center fielder Ray Pepper misplayed for an error. With Morgan on third and one out, Lary tried to execute a squeeze play but missed the pitch, and Morgan was run down between third and home. Newsom had not allowed a hit through nine. The Browns in their half failed to capitalize on a double by Debs Garms and the game went into extra innings knotted at 1-1.

In the top of the 10th inning, Walberg grounded out to Melillo but then Newsom grew wild, walking Max Bishop and Billy Werber. Almada flied out to Garms in left field, but Roy Johnson, worked the count to 3-and-2, then slapped the next pitch on the ground between shortstop and second base. Strange lunged for the ball but it skipped off the tip of his glove and rolled into center field as Bishop raced home from second with the go-ahead run. Newsome retired Graham to end the inning, but the no-hitter was gone, and the Browns were down 2-1.

With one out in the Browns' final turn, Ollie Bejma, batting for Bruce Campbell, doubled, but Walberg struck out Melillo and got Hemsley to foul to Morgan in back of first to close out the game.

The usually punchless Browns had managed eight singles and two doubles but had been able to push across only one run. Buck Newsom had pitched nine innings of no-hit ball, but owing to a penchant for walking batters was forced to carry on into a 10th inning, where again his inability to find the plate and the solitary hit he allowed cost him both the no-hitter and the game. He ended up walking seven batters while striking out nine.

At the time, Newsom's feat was recognized as a no-hitter, with the notation that he'd surrendered a hit in the 10th inning. Newsom never counted it as anything less. No official gate count was recorded for the game, but those in the press box that day put the crowd at under 1,000. When challenged in later years about his recall, Newsom would always reply, "Were you there? If you were, I woulda seen you."[5]

In 1991 a rule change by Major League Baseball redefined a no-hitter as follows: "An official no-hit game occurs when a pitcher (or pitchers) allows no hits during the entire course of a game, which consists of at least nine innings."[6] Previously recognized no-hitters of fewer than nine innings or those like Newsom's in which the first hit had been allowed in extra innings were stricken from the official record books.

Buck Newsom had lost again.

"He failed to make the Hall of Fame,
But pitched a great ten-inning game
While yielding just one bingle.
When Johnson hit to Alan Strange,
The pellet bounced just out of range,
And turned into a single."[7]

SOURCES

In addition to the sources listed in the notes, the author also consulted the *Boston Herald*,

Los Angeles Times, *New York Times*, *Poughkeepsie Eagle-News*, *St. Louis Star-Times*, and *The Sporting News*.

NOTES

1. L.C. Davis, "The Passing Show," *St. Louis Post-Dispatch*, September 20, 1934: 16.
2. Jim McConnell, *Bobo Newsom: Baseball's Traveling Man* (Jefferson, North Carolina: McFarland, 2015), 71.
3. James M. Gould, "Newsom Pitches Nine Hitless Innings, but Loses in Tenth, 2-1," *St. Louis Post-Dispatch*, September 19, 1934: 16.
4. "Ferrell Brothers Suspended for Row," *Decatur* (Illinois) *Herald*, September 20, 1934: 12.
5. McConnell, 63.
6. Lyle Spatz, *Historical Dictionary of Baseball* (Lanham, Maryland: Scarecrow Press, 2013), 249.
7. Davis.

DIZZY TOSSES SECOND SHUTOUT IN THREE DAYS TO WIN NUMBER 30 AS REDBIRDS GRAB PENNANT ON LAST DAY OF SEASON

September 30, 1934: St. Louis Cardinals 9, Cincinnati Red 0, at Sportsman's Park

BY GREGORY H. WOLF

"IF A SHOWMAN HAD ARRANGED IT," opined the AP's Paul Mickelson, "he couldn't have staged a more dramatic finish than that of today."[1] The pennant hopes of the St. Louis Cardinals hinged on the last day of the season. A victory over the lowly Cincinnati Reds guaranteed the Redbirds the pennant; their loss and a victory by the New York Giants against Brooklyn would result in a tie and force an unprecedented playoff. Cardinals player-manager Frankie Frisch called on the hurler who had led his team to an unlikely September surge and to the cusp of its fifth pennant in nine years, Dizzy Dean, whom sportswriter Hugh Fuller hailed as "greatest single figure of the 1934 major league season."[2]

After consecutive second-division finishes, the Cardinals were not among the pennant favorites as the 1934 season began. However, they surprisingly battled the Giants and Chicago Cubs for first place for much of the summer, led by a strong mound corps that included the Dean brothers, 24-year-old Dizzy and 21-year-old rookie Paul, often called Daffy, and a high-scoring, rollicking offense. Trailing the Giants by seven games on September 6, the Cardinals got hot and commenced what St. Louis sportswriter J. Roy Stockton described as "the most spectacular story-book stretch drive in the history of the major leagues."[3] The "Gas House Gang," so known for its rough-and-tumble personalities and style of play, won 18 of 23 games to take a one-game lead over skipper Bill Terry's Giants on the eve of the last day of the regular season.

"There is no question in my mind," said Frisch when asked who the 1934 National League MVP should be. "Dizzy Dean."[4] The eccentric right-hander from Arkansas might have been the game's biggest attraction after Babe Ruth. He had led the NL in innings pitched and strikeouts as a rookie in 1932 and won 20 games in 1933, but his 1934 campaign was one for the ages. He won 14 games by the All-Star break, including a career-best 17-inning outing against Cincinnati on July 1. He was at his best when the Cardinals needed him most. He entered the season finale with victories in his last six starts of the month (and also relieved four times). With the Cardinals trailing the Giants by a half-game with three games left in the season, Dean tossed a seven-hit shutout against the Reds for his 29th victory in the first game of the three-game series to pull the Redbirds into a tie. "I never saw [a ballclub] with more courage or more confidence" said Frisch, who called on his Dizzy to perform his magic again on two days' rest.[5]

Sportsman's Park, the 25-year-old stadium that the Cardinals had called home since 1920, was jam-packed with 37,402 fans.[6] It was the biggest crowd since a doubleheader against the Cubs drew in excess of 45,000 on July 12, 1931. "The aisles were crowded and it was tough for spectators to move around," wrote the *Post-Dispatch*.[7] Just as the game began, the Cardinals faithful let out a collective groan as the

SPORTSMAN'S PARK IN ST. LOUIS

The most famous pitcher of his generation, Dizzy Dean won 30 games in 1934, the last NL pitcher to accomplish the feat. (National Baseball Hall of Fame, Cooperstown, New York)

scoreboard posted four runs for the Giants in the first inning against Brooklyn in the Polo Grounds.

The score of the Giants-Dodgers game put additional pressure on Dean facing the last-place Reds (52-98), a whopping 41 games behind the Cardinals, and the lowest-scoring team in the big leagues. Dean retired the side in order, the final out coming on the first of several exceptional defensive plays by the Cardinals when left fielder Ernie Orsatti made a "spectacular diving catch" of Mark Koenig's low fly, somersaulting afterward.[8] Cincinnati skipper Chuck Dressen protested the ruling, to no avail. "The gods of opportunities were with the Cardinals," mused Paul Mickelson, noting the Reds' "lost opportunities" and "freakish bounces" throughout the game.[9]

The Redbirds wasted no time taking their hacks at 27-year-old right-hander Si Johnson, who entered the game with seven wins and a league-high 21 losses. Jack Rothrock hit a "vicious" one-out single over second base, and moved to second on Frisch's single.[10] After Ripper Collins drew a two-out walk to load the bases, rookie Bill DeLancey belted a single against the right-field pavilion screen to drive in Rothrock and Frisch for the game's first runs. Left fielder Harlin Pool made a nifty running catch on Orsatti's hard fly to end the frame.

Staked to an early two-run lead, Dean blew through the next three innings, yielding two hits. While he subdued the Reds on what the *Post-Dispatch* lauded as "brilliant pitching," Lady Luck continued to smile on the Cardinals fielders.[11] With two outs in the third, Sparky Adams lined a bullet off Dean's leg but the ball caromed into Ripper Collins's glove. The 5-foot-9 first baseman from Altoona, Pennsylvania, sauntered to the bag for an inning-ending out. In an even more peculiar play, Gordon Slade led off the fourth by ducking from Dean's wild pitch, but in doing so he inadvertently hit the ball back to the mound where Dean stabbed it and tossed to Collins for another easy out.[12] The fourth inning ended when shortstop Frisch fielded Pool's liner and slid into second to force Koenig, who had singled.

Johnson "lost control" in the fourth, wrote the *Post-Dispatch*, loading the bases by hitting Collins and walking DeLancey and Orsatti with no outs.[13] Leo Durocher greeted right-handed reliever Benny Frey with a single to drive in Collins. The Cardinals tacked on two more when the "Wild Horse of the Osage," Pepper Martin, lined a one-out single to left to give the Cardinals a 5-0 lead.

After Dean worked around a one-out double down the right-field line by Adam Comorosky in the fifth, the Cardinals added another run on DeLancey's 13th home run, a towering shot over the right field pavilion.

Despite the Cardinals' commanding six-run lead to start the seventh inning, Frisch was not taking any chances with the pennant on the line and the outcome of the Giants-Dodgers game still up in the air. After Pool led off with a infield single, Frisch motioned for starters Wild Bill Hallahan and Tex Carleton to start warming up in the bullpen. Moments after Dean retired Wes Schulmerich on a pop foul to DeLancey, Sportsman's Park erupted in collective cheer when the scoreboard announced that the Dodgers had tied the Giants, 5-5 in the eighth. Dean issued a walk to Comorosky then retired Clyde Manion and pinch-hitter Frank McCormick to escape a jam and keep his shutout intact.

Buoyed by a vivacious crowd, Joe "Ducky" Medwick, who had been named earlier to his first of seven consecutive NL All-Star teams, walked to lead off the seventh against reliever Allyn Stout. Collins followed with his 200th hit and 35th home run of the season, a shot over the right-field pavilion to give him 128 RBIs. After Durocher's two-out single, Dean got into the hit parade with a single. (Adept with the bludgeon, Dean batted .246 [29-for-118] in '34). Martin fouled out to end the frame. The Redbirds tallied their ninth and final run in the eighth on DeLancey's third hit of the game, a two-out single driving in Frisch, to tie his career high with four RBIs.

While the Giants-Dodgers game moved into extra innings, Dean took the mound in the ninth, and in the words of the *Post-Dispatch,* "closed the game with a grand flourish of power," but not without a few minutes of tension.[14] Pool led off with a single and moved to third on Schulmerich's double. It was the first time Dean had yielded more than one hit in any inning, and the first time a runner had advanced to third. Comorosky drew Dean's third walk of the game to load the bases. With the bullpen quiet, Dean fanned Manion and pinch-hitter Ted Petoskey for his sixth and seventh punchouts of the game. Around this time, the ballpark burst into its third collective cheer. The scoreboard had just announced that Brooklyn had defeated New York in 10 innings. The Cardinals had won the pennant. The *Post-Dispatch* reported that the crowd went wild and confetti fell from the upper deck of the stadium.[15] Keeping his composure in the mounting melee, Dean retired Adams on a popup to DeLancey to end the game in 2 hours and 1 minute.

There was a "mad rush" of fans onto the field, reported the *Post-Dispatch*, as soon as DeLancey corralled the ball.[16] Dean was led by a "flying squadron of coppers" to the clubhouse, where the Redbirds celebrated the pennant.[17] "[It was a] triumph of a ball club with every man on the squad doing his share," exclaimed Frisch ecstatically.[18]

In fashioning his second shutout in three days and his league-high seventh of the season, the hurler, whose given name was Jay Hanna, picked up his 30th victory of the season, the first to reach that mark since Pete Alexander in 1917. Dean finished one of the most memorable campaigns in big-league history with a 30-7 record and 2.66 ERA in 311⅔ innings and led the league in strikeouts (195) for the third straight season.

SOURCES

In addition to the sources cited in the Notes, the author also accessed Retrosheet.org, Baseball-Reference.com, the SABR Minor Leagues Database, accessed online at Baseball-Reference.com, SABR.org, and *The Sporting News* archive via Paper of Record.

NOTES

1. Paul Mickelson, Associated Press, "Dizzy Pitches 30th Victory," *Detroit Free Press*, October 1, 1934: 13.
2. Hugh Fullerton, AP, "Dizzy Dean Star of Climb of St. Louis to Pennant," *The Bee* (Danville, Virginia), October 1, 1934: 8.
3. J. Roy Stockton, "Dizzy, Worn Out by His Efforts in Final Dash, May Require Long Rest," *St. Louis Post-Dispatch*, October 1, 1934: section 2, 1.
4. Frankie Frisch, "Frisch Says He Never Played On Club With More Courage or Confidence Than the Cardinals," *St. Louis Post-Dispatch*, October 1, 1934: section 2, 1.
5. Ibid.
6. The *St. Louis Post-Dispatch* gave the attendance as 37,402; the Associated Press gave the figure 35,274. BaseballReference.com uses the AP figure.
7. "Final Game Drew Largest Crowd Since Cubs' Double Header of 1931," *St. Louis Post-Dispatch*, October 1, 1934: Section 2, 3.
8. "How Cardinals Won," *San Bernardino* (California) *County Sun*, October 1, 1934: 9.
9. Mickelson.
10. "How Cardinals Won."
11. "Dizzy Dean's 30th Victory Is Seventh Straight and Seventh Shutout of Year," *St. Louis Post-Dispatch*, October 1, 1934: section 2, 1.
12. "How Cardinals Won."
13. "Dizzy Dean's 30th Victory Is Seventh Straight and Seventh Shutout of Year."
14. Ibid.
15. Ibid.
16. Ibid.
17. Ibid.
18. Frisch.

PAUL DEAN IMPRESSES BROTHER DIZZY — AND COMES OF AGE IN A HARD-FOUGHT WORLD SERIES VICTORY

October 5, 1934: St. Louis Cardinals 4, Detroit Tigers 1, at Sportsman's Park

Game Three of the World Series

BY DOUG FELDMANN

After the Detroit Tigers and St. Louis Cardinals split two contests in the Motor City, the 1934 World Series moved down into the dry, dust-beaten heartland for Game Three. It was the first postseason game in St. Louis in three years, and an opportunity for those in the Midwest — far removed from the cluster of big-league teams found on the Eastern Seaboard — to witness baseball's ultimate battle.

"When the World Series comes to town," Westbrook Pegler observed in covering the scene for the *Chicago Daily News*, "there is a stirring and churning through the cotton belt and the southwest, and up they come … the knowing, critical gaze of the most expert class of customers in the country … the nuts from the true baseball country where the ball players are raised for the big city trade."[1]

Many had lined up outside the ballpark for hours, hoping to buy any remaining tickets. They had arrived from the distant hinterlands in any manner they could — as hitchhikers, as stowaways jumping onto open train boxcars, or by packing into the back of a flatbed jalopy.

"There were wide hats in the audience," noticed Pegler during the day, "and the high and whiny voice of the Texas and Oklahoma trade was heard in the uproar. … Arkansas too, and rural Missouri and little towns in Tennessee and Mississippi, where nothing much happens and a World Series within driving distance is not to be missed. … There is a long spell between planting and picking when there isn't much to do but play ball or go to minor league games. You can't hurry cotton."[2]

It was indeed a pilgrimage for these fans, as they had also come to watch one of their own ply his trade.

With the remainder of the Series yet to unfold, the game would perhaps be the capstone moment in the magnificent rookie season of 22-year-old pitcher Paul Dean, himself a sharecropper in the Arkansas cotton fields before entering professional baseball three years earlier.

Before he had even taken his first jog in spring training for the Cardinals in Bradenton back in February, Dean was already being promoted for a salary increase by his famous older brother Jay, who was better known as Dizzy. For the sake of alliteration, sportswriters had planted the nickname of Daffy on Paul; but in reality he was inward and quiet, and let his sibling do the talking.

After a rough start to the season, Paul found a groove and crafted a 2.70 ERA in the month of August, followed by a 1.93 mark in September. By season's end he had posted a record of 19-11 and notched 5.79 strikeouts per nine innings, the best ratio in baseball. Paul had been nearly as dominant as Dizzy in the second half of the schedule — his high point a no-hitter against the Dodgers in Brooklyn on September 21, which immediately followed a three-hit shutout Diz had authored in the opener of a doubleheader that day. Paul had also logged an impressive six wins in seven decisions against the defending World Series champions, the New York

Giants — including three victories over legendary hurler Carl Hubbell.

None of Paul's regular-season laurels now mattered, however, as his ultimate test stood before him. In being handed the ball by manager Frankie Frisch in the pivotal third game, Paul would go up against curveball artist Tommy Bridges of the Tigers. Bridges had won five of his last six starts in September, and had won 22 games during the season for Detroit — second only to Schoolboy Rowe (24) on the team — while pacing the Tigers with 275 innings pitched and 151 strikeouts.

Even though his club had beaten Cardinals pitchers Bill Hallahan and Bill Walker in an extra-inning affair in Game Two, Detroit player-manager Mickey Cochrane was scratching his head in mapping out a solution for the Series with the brothers lurking. "For always there are the Deans to taunt them," *St. Louis Post-Dispatch* beat writer J. Roy Stockton noted colorfully, "two lanky, steel-armed pitching devils, sinister figures in American League eyes, ubiquitous and stalking, ready and certain to enter the fray when the need arises."[3]

The thermometer recorded an unseasonably warm temperature of 77 degrees at Dean's first pitch at 3:00 P.M., as 34,073 had crammed into the edifice at Grand and Dodier. It was the first time Paul had taken the mound in six days, while Bridges had last pitched five days earlier when he threw four no-hit innings against the St. Louis Browns in Detroit before Cochrane pulled him to rest his arm.

Charlie Gehringer singled after Paul retired the first two batters, but Hank Greenberg, one of baseball's top run producers, popped to catcher Bill DeLancey to end the inning. It was the first of many Tigers assaults Dean would need to sidestep.

The Cards scored in each of the first two innings on a pair of sacrifice flies — the first by Jack Rothrock after leadoff batter Pepper Martin had tripled, and the second by Dean himself to drive in Rip Collins. St. Louis extended its lead to 4-0 in the fifth inning, as Martin again started things with "a double against the chicken wire in right field" before Rothrock tripled him home.[4] Frisch followed with a single to score Rothrock, a blow that sent Bridges out of the game.

"[Elon] Hogsett walked slowly into the box," Pegler recounted the situation as the relief pitcher entered with nobody out, "surveyed a gloomy situation calmly, and flexed his left arm with a few practice shots at Cochrane's mitt."[5] Hogsett immediately induced Joe Medwick to hit into the first Detroit double play of the series. He next got a hand from Cochrane, who threw out Collins trying to steal after normally surehanded shortstop Billy Rogell committed his first of two errors in the game. Collins was one of three Gas House Gang members Cochrane would nab on the bases during the afternoon to help keep the Tigers close.

All the while, Paul bent but did not break, permitting baserunners in every Detroit frame until he finally enjoyed a one-two-three inning in the seventh — and again in the eighth. And though Paul frequently got into trouble, Frisch never lost faith as "Dizzy was down in the bullpen warming up just for exercise in the eighth and ninth innings."[6]

The Tigers threatened again in the ninth, breaking up the shutout bid when Greenberg drove a long triple to center field with two out, sending home speedster Jo-Jo White from first. But Paul refocused, getting Goose Goslin on a popup to Frisch at second to end the game and put the Cardinals ahead in the Series two games to one. Martin, Frisch, and Collins each stroked two hits to lead the Cardinals attack while DeLancey contributed a double. The frustrated Tigers stranded 13 runners and left the bases loaded twice.

"As the game ended, Brother Dizzy slung his sweater over his shoulder and walked up fast, shouldering ball players, customers, and policemen aside to intercept Daffy at the lip of the Cardinals' dugout," Pegler wrote. "He placed his left hand on Daffy's shoulder, looked him dead in the eye, and solemnly acknowledged that next to his older brother, Daffy was the best pitcher in the world."[7] And while still alive in the series, the Tigers appeared to be a beaten team. "They have the look of losers," Pegler asserted, "whereas the Deans are overbearing even when mediocre."[8]

In the home clubhouse, Paul's teammates surrounded him in appreciation once again. "Dean sat in front of his locker, declaring he was never so tired in his life," reported Charles Dunkley of the *St. Louis Globe-Democrat*. "He was dripping with perspiration and puffing like a racehorse."[9] When asked to speak, Paul uttered a simple respect for the Tigers' bats. "They didn't give me much trouble. I was faster the last two innings than at any time during the game. I don't hold no ballclub cheap, and that's the reason I beared down."[10]

After Paul's win in Game Three, a car with New York license plates approached Dizzy outside the ballpark. The occupants offered him a ride home — which he accepted. Although Diz arrived safely, the incident prompted Cardinals owner Sam Breadon to provide the Deans with armed guards for the remainder of the World Series, in fear of their being kidnapped or extorted by gamblers.

"Shucks, nobody's going to kidnap me. Not in this town," Dizzy scoffed. "Even if they did, that wouldn't do Detroit no good, 'less'n they took Paul too, and I guess two Deans would be more than they could handle."[11]

So it would be for the Tigers.

SOURCES

In addition to the sources listed below, the author also consulted Baseball-Reference.com, Retrosheet.org, and SABR.org

NOTES

1. Westbrook Pegler, "Cards Take Game Three," *Chicago Daily News*, October 6, 1934: 3C.
2. Ibid.
3. J. Roy Stockton, "Carleton Pitches for Cards Today, Auker for Tigers," *St. Louis Post-Dispatch*, October 6, 1934: 1.
4. Westbrook Pegler, "Cards Take Game Three," *Chicago Daily News*, October 6, 1934: 3C.
5. Ibid.
6. Ibid.
7. Ibid.
8. Ibid.
9. Charles Dunkley, "Dean Stands Tall," *St. Louis Globe-Democrat*, October 6, 1934: 5.
10. Ibid.
11. J. Roy Stockton, "Dizzy Too Friendly, Is Put Under Guard," *St. Louis Post-Dispatch*, October 6, 1934: 1.

TIGERS EVEN SERIES WITH LATE-GAME OFFENSIVE EXPLOSION

October 6, 1934: Detroit Tigers 10,
St. Louis Cardinals 4, at Sportsman's Park

Game Four of the World Series

BY C. PAUL ROGERS, III

DOWN TWO GAMES TO ONE IN THE 1934 World Series, the Detroit Tigers evened the count in Game Four with a resounding 10-4 win in a lengthy 2 hours and 43 minutes before 37,492 disappointed Sportsman's Park fans. It was a game full of misadventures, dominated by Dizzy Dean's attempt to run the bases. After slow-footed Spud Davis singled in the fourth inning, Dean, who fancied himself an excellent baserunner, ran onto the field to pinch-run before Cardinals manager Frankie Frisch could send anyone else out.[1] Pepper Martin then hit a double-play groundball to second baseman Charlie Gehringer, who scooped it up and tossed to shortstop Bill Rogell to force Dean at second. Dean, however, came into the base standing up and Rogell's relay throw nailed him squarely in the head, sending him straight to the ground.

According to the *New York Times*, Dean was "out cold as a mackerel."[2] His brother Paul and others eventually carried him fireman's style from the field to the great concern of Cardinals fans, since he was slated to toe the rubber for the pivotal Game Five the next day.[3] Dean recovered quickly, however, and after X-rays that evening was pronounced fit to start the next day. Although apocryphal, the story is often told that a St. Louis newspaper reported the next morning that "Doctors x-rayed Dizzy's head and found nothing."[4]

The starting pitchers were Tex Carleton for the Cardinals, who had a 16-11 regular-season record, versus submariner Elden Auker of the Tigers, who had been 15-7. Both were former college football players,[5] prompting Grantland Rice to write, "Here were two ex-collegians trying to steal the show from the brush and the sage—from the boys of the open road and the school of the harder way."[6]

Before the game began, the Cardinals' band played "Take Me Out to the Ballgame."[7] Then, after a scoreless inning and a half, the Cardinals struck in the bottom of the second beginning with a sharp single to center by Joe Medwick and Rip Collins's ringing double off the pavilion screen in right that sent Medwick to third. Ernie Orsatti then hit a long sacrifice fly to Goose Goslin in left to drive in Medwick before Auker was able to retire the side without further damage.

The Tigers quickly responded after two outs in the top of the third against the side-winding Carleton on a double past first by Mickey Cochrane, two walks and Rogell's single to center, which plated two runs and sent the Tigers to a 2-1 lead. Detroit would not trail again although plenty of entertaining, if not particularly pristine, baseball remained.

After Rogell's hit, Frisch gave Carleton a quick hook and brought in 43-year-old Dazzy Vance in relief. Hank Greenberg greeted Vance with a single off shortstop Leo Durocher's glove to drive in the third run of the inning. Down 3-1, the Cardinals bounced back in the bottom half when, with two outs, Rogell lost Frisch's high bounder in the sun.[8] Medwick walked on a 3-and-2 count and Collins followed with a whistling shot to center on the first pitch to drive in Frisch and make it a one-run margin, 3-2.

In the fourth the Tigers extended the lead back to two runs without a hit thanks to shoddy fielding by the Cardinals. With one out Jo-Jo White worked a walk from Vance, stole second, and went to third on the play when catcher Bill DeLancey's throw got past Frisch covering and Martin muffed centerfielder Orsatti's return throw to third. Vance promptly uncorked a wild pitch to enable White to scoot home to extend the score to 4-2.

The Cardinals managed to tie the score in the bottom half of the inning in spite of Dean's misadventure on the basepaths. Orsatti led off with a single to center, and then barreled into second on Durocher's groundball to Marv Owen at third, causing Gehringer to bobble the throw while covering the bag.[9] With runners on first and second, Davis, batting for Vance, singled to deep right field to drive in Orsatti and send Durocher to third. Durocher actually scored the Cardinals' fourth run to tie the score when Dean intercepted Rogell's relay throw with his noggin on what should have been Martin's double-play groundball.[10] According to Grantland Rice, the impact of the ball on Dean's head sounded like the backfire of an automobile as the ball bounced 30 feet in the air and ended up 100 feet away in Greenberg's glove in short right field.[11]

After Bill Walker replaced Vance on the mound for St. Louis, the teams traded goose eggs for the next two innings. The Cardinals, however, wasted a scoring chance in the bottom of the fifth when with runners on first and second and one out, Greenberg snagged Orsatti's liner to first and threw behind Medwick, who had misread the ball and strayed too far off the bag at second, to double him up and end the threat.

The Tigers wasted Pete Fox's first-pitch double off the wall in the top of the sixth. In the bottom half, Durocher led off with a single past Owen but didn't advance as Auker bore down to retire the next three batters.

Thus, even with the Cardinals' sloppy play, the game remained tied heading into the top of the seventh. The Tigers, who faced a three-games-to-one deficit if they lost, rallied for a go-ahead run thanks to more bungling by the Cards. Gehringer led off with a single to center and was sacrificed to second by Goslin. Rogell then grounded to Durocher at short who threw to Martin at third to try to nail Gehringer but Martin dropped the throw for his third error of the game, leaving runners on first and third with one out.[12] Greenberg then lofted a long fly to center that Orsatti got a late jump on because of the sun. The ball slipped out of his glove for a double that scored Gehringer and sent Goslin to third. But with runners now on second and third with one out, Walker managed to avoid further damage, retiring Owen on a liner to Jack Rothrock in right, and, after an intentional walk to Fox to load the bases, getting Auker on a groundout to Frisch.

As the bottom of the seventh got underway, the public-address announcer informed fans that Dean was okay, prompting relieved applause from the crowd.[13] It would be the last opportunity for the hometown fans to cheer. The Cardinals went out in order, highlighted by Greenberg's great stop of Medwick's hard grounder to first.

St. Louis totally unraveled in the top of the eighth. White started the Tigers' rally with a walk and was safe at second when Walker, still on the mound for the Cardinals, threw Cochrane's sacrifice past Durocher covering at second. Gehringer sacrificed the runners to second and third, and then an intentional walk to Goslin loaded the bases with one out. With a count of two strikes and a ball, Rogell singled just past Durocher's glove to drive in two runs and send Goslin to third. Greenberg then laced the first pitch far off a fan's outstretched hands in front of the right-center-field wall for a double to drive in Goslin with the third run of the inning.[14]

That was it for Walker, who was relieved by 41-year old Jesse Haines. Marv Owen slashed Haines's first pitch for a line single to right to score Rogell and send Greenberg to third. Fox then struck out swinging on a 3-and-2 pitch as Owen took off for second. When DeLancey, the Cardinals catcher, threw to second, Greenberg took off from third and beat Frisch's hurried throw to the plate by kicking the ball from DeLancey's grasp as the Tigers successfully executed a double steal for another tally.[15] The carnage came to five runs on three hits and two more Cardinals errors as Detroit extended its lead to 10-4.

The Cardinals managed a hit in each of their last two innings, but were unable to score as Auker finished his complete game, scattering 10 hits and allowing four walks while striking out only one to close out the 10-4 victory. After the game, Frisch said, "We played like a lot of sandlotters. There was no one especially to blame. We all had a finger in the pie."[16]

True to his word, Dizzy Dean did start for the Cardinals the following day, but lost 3-1 to Tommy Bridges as the Tigers took a 3-2 Series lead before the teams returned to Detroit for Games 6 and 7. Once there, Paul Dean outdueled Schoolboy Rowe 4-3 to even the Series at three games apiece. The climatic Game Seven was anything but as Dizzy Dean, pitching with one day's rest, shut out the Tigers 11-0 to win the world championship.[17]

SOURCES

Besides the sources listed in the Notes, the author consulted the following:

Alexander, Charles C. *Breaking the Slump—Baseball in the Depression Era* (New York: Columbia University Press, 2002).

Barthel, Thomas. *The Fierce Fun of Ducky Medwick* (Lanham, Maryland: The Scarecrow Press, 2003).

Barthel, Thomas. *Pepper Martin—A Baseball Biography* (Jefferson, North Carolina: McFarland & Company, 2003).

Berkow, Ira, ed. *Hank Greenberg—The Story of My Life* (New York: Time Books, 1989).

Bevis, Charles. *Mickey Cochrane—The Life of a Baseball Hall of Fame Catcher* (Jefferson, North Carolina: McFarland & Company, 1998).

Durocher, Leo, with Ed Linn. *Nice Guys Finish Last* (New York: Simon and Schuster, 1975).

Golenbock, Peter. *The Spirit of St. Louis—A History of the St. Louis Cardinals and Browns* (New York: Avon Books, 2000).

Kurlansky, Mark. *Hank Greenberg—The Hero Who Didn't Want to Be One* (New Haven: Yale University Press, 2011).

Lieb, Frederick G. *The St. Louis Cardinals* (New York: G.P. Putnam's Sons, 1945, reprinted by Southern Illinois University Press, 2001).

Lieb, Frederick G. *The Detroit Tigers* (New York: G.P. Putnam's Sons, 1946, reprinted by Kent State University Press, 2008).

Shapiro, Milton J. *The Dizzy Dean Story* (New York: Julian Messner, 1963).

Skipper, John C. *Charlie Gehringer—A Biography of the Hall of Fame Second Baseman* (Jefferson, North Carolina: McFarland & Company, 2008).

Smith, Curt. *America's Dizzy Dean* (St. Louis: The Bethany Press, 1978).

NOTES

1   According to one quote of Frisch, "The hard-playing S.O.B. was down there running himself for Davis." Bob Broeg, *The Pilot and the Gas House Gang* (St. Louis: The Bethany Press, 1980). See also Robert E. Hood, *The Gashouse Gang*, (New York: William Morrow and Company, 1976), 132; Vince Staten, *Ol Diz—A Biography of Dizzy Dean* (New York: Harper Collins, 1992),144-45; Richard Bak, *Cobb Would Have Caught It—The Golden Age of Baseball in Detroit* (Detroit: Wayne State University Press, 1991), 269. In his autobiography, Frisch wrote that "Diz was red hot to run for [Davis]. Why not? He was a fine base runner." Frank Frisch as told to J. Roy Stockton, *Frank Frisch: The Fordham Flash* (Garden City, New York: Doubleday, 1962), 173-74. After the game Frisch was quoted as saying, "Dean kept pulling my sleeve and begging me to use him." Wray's Column, "Did Frankie Boot One?" *St. Louis Post-Dispatch*, October 7, 1934: 19.

2   John Drebringer, "Tigers Rout Cards, 10-4, Pounding Five Pitchers to Square Series at 2-2," *New York Times*, October, 7, 1934: S3.

3   Paul Dean later said he knew his brother was all right when he came to because he was talking. Asked what Dizzy was saying, Paul said, "Nuthin'. He was just talking." Broeg, 140-41.

4   Elden Auker with Tom Keegan, *Sleeper Cars and Flannel Uniforms* (Chicago: Triumph Books, 2001), 53; Robert Gregory, *Diz* (New York: Viking, 1992), 225.

5   Carleton had played at TCU while Auker had played at Kansas State.

6   Grantland Rice, "The Storm Breaks—Fortunate Recovery of Dean Is Only Bright Spot for Those Tiger-Chewed Cards," *Detroit Free Press*, October 7, 1934: 3.

7   "Martin Discovers That Fans Forget," *New York Times*, October 7, 1934: S3.

8   Alan Gould, "Cards Bow to Tigers," *Los Angeles Times*, October 7, 1934: Part VI a, 2; Charles P. Ward, "Tigers Unleash Bats, Trounce Cards, 10-4, and Even Series," *Detroit Free Press*, October 7, 1934: 17.

9   Grantland Rice described Orsatti as "pulling a Marty Brill blocking act by jolting the ball from Gehringer's grip." Rice, *Detroit Free Press*: 3.

10 Dean was running on the inside of the basepath instead of out toward the outfield grass. Rogell thought Dean had no business trying to pinch-run (Bak, 269), but he felt bad that he had nailed Dean, saying, "[T]he play was too fast for me to see Dizzy blaring into second standing up." William M. Anderson,

HOME OF THE BROWNS AND CARDINALS AT GRAND AND DODIER

The Glory Years of the Detroit Tigers—1920-1950 (Detroit: Wayne State University Press, 2012), 252.

11　Rice, *Detroit Free Press:* 3. Not surprisingly, Frisch received a lot of criticism for allowing Dean to pinch-run. Sportswriter Paul Gallico noted that "Frankie Frisch took a million dollar asset and used him on a ten-cent job." Doug Feldman, *Dizzy and the Gashouse Gang* (Jefferson, North Carolina: McFarland & Company, 2000), 156.

12　By the end of the game, the Cardinals had committed five errors, making a total of 11 in just four games. For their part, the Tigers had committed eight errors by the game's end. Herman Wecke, "This Series One of Most Loosely Fielded in History," *St. Louis Post-Dispatch*, October 7, 1934: 18.

13　James P. Dawson, "Game at St. Louis Told Play by Play," *New York Times*, October 7, 1934: S3.

14　Greenberg raced to third on the hit and Rogell also scored from first, but after Frisch protested, the umpires ruled the hit a double and sent Greenberg back to second and Rogell to third. Dawson, *New York Times*: S3.

15　Rice, *Detroit Free Press,* 3. Owen moved to third when DeLancey let Frisch's throw get away for the second Cardinals error of the inning.

16　Feldman, 156.

17　Game Seven is remembered mostly for Joe Medwick's kicking of Marv Owen at third after a triple in the sixth inning which brought the score to 9-0. Medwick claimed that Owen came close to spiking him, prompting his kicking action. Frustrated Detroit fans pelted Medwick with fruit, vegetables, and bottles when he took his position in left field the next inning, prompting Commissioner Kenesaw M. Landis to remove him from the game. J. Roy Stockton, *The Gashouse Gang and a Couple of Other Guys* (New York: A.S. Barnes & Company, 1945), 129-130; V. Owen, *The Adventures of a Quiet Soul—A Scrapbook of Memories* (San Jose: The Rosicrucian Press, 1996), 70-75.

BRIDGES OUTDUELS DIZZY FOR SERIES LEAD

October 7, 1934: Detroit Tigers 3, St. Louis Cardinals 1, at Sportsman's Park

Game Five of the World Series

BY RYAN PARKER

THE ST. LOUIS CARDINALS HAD BEEN favored to win the 1934 World Series. But after dropping Game Four to the Detroit Tigers in a humbling beat-down, 10-4, the Series was tied at two games apiece and the status of the Cardinals' de-facto leader, Dizzy Dean, was uncertain. Had momentum swung in favor of the Tigers?

In Game Four, the day before, Dean, the Cardinals' star pitcher, pinch-ran for pinch-hitter Spud Davis in the fourth inning of Game Four, the day before a scheduled start. It was an interesting choice; Dean was not known for his speed. Player-manager Frankie Frisch later said he made the move because of Dean's ability to motivate the team with his play. When Pepper Martin grounded to second, Tigers shortstop Billy Rogell's throw nailed Dean in the head and the pitcher had to be carried off the field by eight of his teammates.[1] Though the beaning prevented a double play and allowed the Cardinals to score and tie the game, it was not enough as the Tigers eventually rallied.

As the sun rose on October 7, the day of Game Five, many shadows still seemed to be lurking in the Cardinals clubhouse. The team physician, Dr. Robert F. Hyland, put Dean through a series of tests at what the *Post-Dispatch* called a laboratory. After reviewing two X-rays of Dean's head, the doctor determined that there was no skull fracture. He even stated that the right side of the head, the side struck with the ball, was working even better than the left side![2] The only noticeable difference in Dean before the game was his reluctance to sign the balls and programs of fans, something he normally did.[3] As expected, Dean, who won the Series opener, took the mound for the Cardinals. He faced off against Detroit's Tommy Bridges, who had been hammered by the Cards two days earlier in Game Three.[4]

The Tigers struck first. With one away in the second inning, Hank Greenberg worked a walk and Pete Fox hit a double that sent Greenberg home from first.[5] That lead held up until the sixth inning, which proved to be the downfall for the Cardinals. Dean gave up a leadoff home run to Charlie Gehringer, whose blast bounced off the façade of the right-field pavilion. After Goose Goslin popped out, Rogell stroked a single to center. The ball rolled through Chick Fullis's legs and he compounded his error by not hustling after the ball. By the time Joe Medwick came out of position in left field to retrieve the ball and throw it in, Rogell was on third.[6] Rogell tagged up and scored the Tigers' third and final run when Greenberg flied out to right field. With the exception of a double by Martin, the Cardinals did nothing in the sixth to help their cause and entered the seventh inning behind 3-0.[7] In the seventh, the Cardinals finally managed to get on the board thanks to Bill DeLancey's home run, which landed on the roof of the right-field pavilion for their only run of the day.[8]

The Cards didn't die easily, though. With a man on first and one out in the eighth, Pepper Martin slashed a deep drive to left-center that looked like trouble. But fleet-footed center fielder Jo-Jo White raced into the gap, "looking like a man with all the demons in creation at his heels," and made the grab in front of the wall.[9] In the ninth, St. Louis had a man on with one out. Ripper Collins smoked one to right that hit high off the pavilion screen, just missing a home run. Fox played it perfectly, holding Collins to a single. The Tigers had two men up in the bullpen but they stuck with Bridges, and with runners on the corners the left-hander stiffened again, striking out DeLancey on three straight curveballs.[10] Pinch-hitter Ernie Orsatti hit a sharp grounder but Rogell made a nice play and flipped the ball to Gehringer for the force on Collins to end the game.

The Detroit papers dramatically described Dean's loss to the Tigers as his Waterloo and compared it to the Brooklyn Bridge collapsing.[11] In reality it was a very tight game with only a few mishaps on the Cardinals' part that determined the game. Both pitchers hurled superbly. Dean went eight innings and yielded only six hits and fanned six; Bridges gave up seven hits and struck out seven. The difference came from Dean's three walks, one that led to a run, and Fullis's key misplay in the sixth inning.

The Cardinals, obviously upset about falling behind in the Series to the Tigers, focused much of their angst on home-plate umpire Brick Owens. The first grievance was an incident that occurred in the third inning. Pepper Martin attempted to steal second base, with two outs and Jack Rothrock at the plate. Tigers catcher Mickey Cochrane's throw struck Rothrock's bat and fell onto the infield, not allowing the play to be made at second. Owens immediately called Rothrock out at the plate for interference to end the inning. The Cardinals captain, Leo Durocher, insisted that Rothrock's bat was still resting on his shoulder when Cochrane made the throw and that there was no way possible for Rothrock to have stuck out his bat in a manner to interfere with the throw as Rothrock had to step away from the plate to avoid a tight, inside pitch.[12]

Owens' other major offense, according to the Cardinals, was his pitch-calling. Frisch, who claimed to never have griped about balls and strikes in his life, said the called strikes against DeLancey in the ninth inning were so low and outside that he never could have reached them.[13] In a way it was true that DeLancey and the other Cardinals were finding Bridges' pitches unreachable, but it is more likely that Bridges was throwing great stuff that day, particularly his curveball. Babe Ruth who was in attendance for Game Five, even commented on Bridges' good play and remarked that he was better in the Series than he had been during the season.

Cochrane praised his pitcher as having one of the best pitching performances he had seen that season with a curveball that was breaking three to four feet away.[14] Chicago sportswriter Irving Vaughn agreed with the Detroit catcher, declaring that the Cardinals met what was known as one of the best curveballs in the American League.[15] Vaughn made the point that the Cardinals striking out seven times did not tell the whole story of how Bridges' stuff frustrated them even when they did make contact. The Cardinals just could not make solid contact with the ball; the result was repeated "easy bounders and easy pop ups."[16] Bridges threw three balls to a batter only twice, and each time he was able to come back with a strikeout.[17]

As the teams boarded trains to head back to Detroit for the final games of the Series, there was a great contrast in moods. The once underdog Tigers now had a 3-games-to-2 advantage and were very eager to finish the Series at home. The favored Cardinals were now in a do-or-die situation. They were not yet beaten but resembled their star pitcher, Dean; as the *St. Louis Star* reported him to look, the "swagger had gone out of his shoulders," and the same could be said for the rest of the team.[18] The question now was whether they could get their swagger back and keep from losing to the Series to the Tigers in Detroit.

SOURCES

In addition to the sources cited in the Notes, the author also consulted Baseball-Reference.com and Retrosheet.org.

NOTES

1. "Dizzy Dean Hurt as Cards Lose," *St. Louis Post-Dispatch*, October 7, 1934: 19.
2. " 'Dizzy' Not Even Dizzy, After Being Hit in the Head, Tests Show," *St. Louis Post-Dispatch* October 8, 1934: 16.
3. Ibid.

SPORTSMAN'S PARK IN ST. LOUIS

4 W.J. McGoogan, "Bridges to Pitch for Tiges Today and Rowe in Next Game." *St. Louis Post-Dispatch*, October 7, 1934: 17.

5 "Tommy Bridges Pitches Tigers Into Series Lead in Fifth Tilt," *The Sporting News*, October 11, 1934: 7.

6 "Gossip of Fifth Game," *The Sporting News*, October 11, 1934: 7.

7 "Umpire Brick Owens, Not Tigers, Beat Us, Says Durocher: Game, Play-by-Play," *St. Louis Post-Dispatch* October 8, 1934: 14.

8 "Tommy Bridges Pitches Tigers Into Series Lead."

9 John Drebinger, "Bridges Outpitches Dizzy Dean and Tigers Win to Gain 3-2 Lead in Series," *New York Times*, October 8 1934: 20.

10 James Dawson, "Play-by-Play Summary of St. Louis Game," *New York Times*, October 8, 1934: 20

11 Grantland Rice, "Dizzy's Waterloo: Bridges Pitches Rings Around the Great Big Bogey Man Dean and Humbles Holdenville," *Detroit Free Press*, October 8, 1934: 11-12.

12 Leo Durocher, "Cards' Captain Says Decision on Rothrock Indefensible," *St. Louis Post-Dispatch*, October 8, 1934: 14.

13 "Jubilant Tigers Sure Rowe Will Win Title Today: Cardinals Still Raging at Umpire Owens," *Chicago Tribune*, October 8, 1934: 19.

14 Ibid.

15 Irving Vaughan, "Tommy Makes Rivals Pop up, Roll Out, Fan: Batters Can't Work Him for Walk," *Chicago Trbune*, October 8, 1934: 19.

16 Ibid.

17 Ibid.

18 "Cardinals Lost Again to Tigers Because No Storybook Hero Arose to Save Them," *Chicago Trbune*, October 8, 1934: 19.

PARMELEE BESTS HUBBELL IN EPIC 17-INNING PITCHERS' DUEL

April 29, 1936: St. Louis Cardinals 2, New York Giants 1 (17 Innings), at Sportsman's Park

BY GREGORY H. WOLF

"There is a new heroic figure in the Cardinals picture," gushed St. Louis sportswriter J. Roy Stockton after Roy "Tarzan" Parmelee emerged victorious in an epic 17-inning pitchers' duel with Carl Hubbell to defeat the New York Giants, 2-1.[1] Parmelee, who finished with a six-hitter, "gave a masterful demonstration of his skill," opined John Drebinger of the *New York Times*.[2]

The Giants and Cardinals began the 1936 campaign as likely challengers to dethrone the reigning pennant-winning Chicago Cubs. The runner-up Redbirds, led by feisty player-manager Frankie Frisch, who had guided the Gas House Gang to their last title two years earlier, had won 96 games in 1935, but started slowly in '36. They were in sixth place (4-5), three games behind the Giants (8-3). Since taking over for the legendary John "Little Napoleon" McGraw during the 1932 season, player-manager Bill Terry had skippered the Giants to at least 90 wins in his first three full seasons and to a World Series title in 1933.

The first game of the three-game series, scheduled for Tuesday, April 28, was billed as a match-up between right-handers Parmelee, whom the Cardinals had acquired from the Giants in the offseason in exchange for infielder Burgess Whitehead; and Hal Schumacher, winner of 61 games in the last three seasons.[3] When the game was postponed by rain, Terry gave the start to Hubbell, the league's best hurler. Known for his screwball, the 32-year-old southpaw had amassed a record of 146-88, including wins in his two starts thus far in '36. He had won 23, 21, and 23 games respectively in the last three seasons, and was named NL MVP in 1933. That year he tossed an 18-inning complete game to defeat the Cardinals, 1-0, in the Polo Grounds. As fate would have it, his former teammate would exact revenge on behalf of the Cardinals. Parmelee, with a career record of 41-31 in parts of eight seasons, relied on a more standard repertoire of heaters and curves. "His powerful arm can throw a ball with a swiftness that would do credit to the greatest speed pitcher of the game," opined F.C. Lane in *Baseball Magazine*.[4]

A modest crowd of about 3,500 was at Sportsman's Park on a Wednesday afternoon to witness what the *Post-Dispatch* subsequently described as "the most brilliantly played game in years."[5] The Great Depression had hit hard in the Gateway City, where unemployment had hovered around 30 percent since 1930. Attendance at the ballpark sank to an average of 3,327 in 1933, rising to 5,819 three years later.

After Parmelee yielded a two-out hit to Mel Ott in the first, a seemingly unimportant event in the bottom half of the frame foreshadowed the final play of the game. Future Hall of Famer Travis "Stonewall" Jackson fumbled Pepper Martin's two-out grounder to third for an error. The 32-year-old Jackson, a career shortstop, had been moved to third base the previous year after the team acquired Dick Bartell. Martin moved to second on Medwick's single before Johnny Mize grounded back to Hubbell. St. Louis waited 11 innings for another good scoring opportunity.

Parmelee and Hubbell mowed down the opposition for 11 scoreless innings. The crowd was "on edge as one thrill followed another," according to Stockton.[6] In the tense environment, the Cardinals' bench jockeys, led by Martin, Frisch, and Leo "The Lip" Durocher, harassed their counterparts mercilessly. The Gas House Gang "used to be nervy, noisy and noisesome," wrote Harold Parrott of the *Brooklyn Eagle*, "but now they're twice as bad. Jibes, some laughable, some mean, some of fighting pitch, spewed out of the mouth of the Cardinal dugout."[7]

The Giants caught a break in the 12th. After Whitehead drew a walk, Terry played small ball for a run. On his manager's orders, Ott, who eventually led the NL in round-trippers in 1936 for the third of six times, sacrificed Whitehead to second. Cleanup hitter Hank Leiber, coming off an impressive campaign (.331-22-107), belted a single to drive in Whitehead for the first run of the game. "The Cardinals bristled with resentment," exclaimed the *Post-Dispatch*.[8] In what seems like an apocryphal story, Durocher, the Redbirds' combative shortstop, came to the mound to console Parmelee. "It's just one run," yelled the Lip. "Bear down on the next two hitters and we'll get that one back."[9] Parmelee retired Sam Leslie and Travis Jackson to end the frame.

Ducky Medwick, who entered the game leading the majors with a .452 batting average, started the Cardinals' rally in the 12th with a one-out single to center. Mize followed with a tricky fly to short right field. Seemingly intent on making a shoestring catch, Ott charged the ball, but "decided to play it safe," and let it hit the ground.[10] The ball took a peculiar bounce, hitting him in the chest and rolling away, enabling Medwick to reach third and Mize second. Hubbell met with his infielders, then gave Spud Davis a free pass to fill the bases. Speedy rookie Stu Martin replaced Mize as a pinch-runner representing the winning run. Charley Gelbert lined a single to right, driving in Medwick, but Ott made a perfect throw home to nail Martin, who "was out by such a wide margin he didn't even bother to slide," wrote Stockton, adding that some veteran members of the Gas House Gang were irritated by Martin's failure to take out the catcher, Gus Mancuso.[11]

Described as a "broad-shouldered, stout-hearted but mild-mannered and modest right-hander,"[12] Parmelee worked around a leadoff single to Jo-Jo Moore in the 14th, the only hit he surrendered in the last five innings of the game, and a walk to Mancuso to lead off the 16th. The next batter in both cases missed a bunt on a fastball, resulting in Moore getting picked off first and Mancuso being thrown out easily at second.[13] "Parmelee's speed was too much for the Giants," wrote the *Post-Dispatch*.[14]

Weakening in the 16th, Hubbell yielded consecutive two-out singles to Frisch and Martin, and then loaded the bases with an intentional pass to Medwick. Ripper Collins, who had replaced Mize at first base, was next. He was a dangerous hitter but was batting a paltry .182 entering the game. His weak grounder forced Medwick at second and ended the inning.

With "shadows stretching from the grandstand to the bleachers," the umpires met after the 16th inning to determine if they should call the game, effectively ending it as a tie, a normal though rare occurrence in the days before stadium lights.[15] (Lights were installed at Sportsman's Park in 1940.) The umpires informed the managers that the 17th would be the final frame regardless of the outcome.[16]

After Parmelee put yet another zero on the scoreboard, the Cardinals had one last shot. Slow-footed catcher Spud Davis lined a leadoff double down the right-field line, and was replaced by pinch-runner Lynn King. Hubbell met with his infielders again to discuss strategy. Possessing the era's best control, "King Carl" issued yet another free pass, to Gelbert, to play for a twin killing. After Durocher lined out to center field, Parmelee followed with what sportswriters universally considered a routine double-play ball, but sure-handed All-Star shortstop Bartell fumbled it, filling the bases. Terry Moore, who had been on fire, batting .421 entering the game, hit a chopper to Jackson at third. On what appeared to be another routine play, Jackson threw wildly toward home, drawing Mancuso off the plate, as King slid across with the winning run after 3 hours and 41 minutes.

"Apparently beaten at one stage of the 17-inning diamond struggle," chimed the *Post-Dispatch*, Parmelee "deserved the victory."[17] In the game of his life, Parmelee hurled the longest complete-game victory in Cardinals history, and tied Dizzy Dean for the most innings pitched in a game (records Parmelee still held as of 2017). Parmelee struck out nine, walked four, and yielded only six hits, never more than one in an inning. In a heartbreaking loss, Hubbell surrendered 11 safeties and fanned six. Only twice since Parmelee's and Hubbell's grueling gems have two pitchers come close to hurling complete games as long in the same contest. Jack Harshman beat Al Aber on August 13, 1954, and Juan Marichal defeated Warren Spahn on July 2, 1963, each game by a score of 1-0 in 16 innings.[18]

As exciting as the Cardinals' victory was, it was pushed from the front page of the *St. Louis Post-Dispatch* by the death of Harry Hoffmann, a local bartending legend, longtime fan, and friend of team owner Sam Breadon. Hoffmann suffered a heart attack at the game and died minutes before the Cardinals won.[19]

Inspired by Parmelee's performance, St. Louis sportswriter L.C. Davis composed the following verse:

"One to Parmelee"
There was a young man named Leroy
Who was once in the Giants employ;
Though he postponed the winning
Till the seventeenth inning
To the Cardinal fans he brought joy.[20]

SOURCES

In addition to the sources cited in the Notes, the author also accessed Retrosheet.org, Baseball-Reference.com, the SABR Minor Leagues Database, accessed online at Baseball-Reference.com, SABR.org, and *The Sporting News* archive via Paper of Record.

NOTES

1. J. Roy Stockton, "Parmelee Emerges as Pitching Hero in 17-Inning Victory," *St. Louis Post-Dispatch*, April 30, 1936: 2B.
2. John Drebinger, "Cardinals Defeat Giants in 17th, 2-1," *New York Times*, April 30, 1936: 23.
3. J. Roy Stockton, "Cardinals' Game Rained Out; Athletics 4, Browns 2," *St. Louis Post-Dispatch*, April 28, 1936: 1B.
4. F.C. Lane in *Baseball Magazine*, June 1934, quoted in Bill James and Rob Neyer, *The Neyer/James Guide to Pitchers* (New York: Fireside, 2004), 335.
5. The *St. Louis Post-Dispatch* estimated the attendance at 3,500; the *New York Times* gave a figure of 4,500.
6. "Parmelee Emerges as Pitching Hero in 17-Inning Victory."
7. Harold Parrott, "Giants in Misery While in Missouri," *Brooklyn Daily Eagle*, April 30, 1936: 20.
8. "Parmelee Emerges as Pitching Hero in 17-Inning Victory."
9. Ibid.
10. Ibid.
11. Ibid.
12. Ibid.
13. "Red Bird Notes," *St. Louis Post-Dispatch*, April 30, 1936: 2B.
14. Ibid.
15. In the days before stadium lights, ties were rare, yet expected. From 1931 to 1936, the Cardinals had five tied games; the Giants had eight, including four in 1933 and three in 1935.
16. "Parmelee Emerges as Pitching Hero in 17-Inning Victory."
17. Ibid.
18. Jack Harshman of the Chicago White Sox hurled a nine-hit shutout to beat the Detroit Tigers and Al Aber on August 13, 1954, at Comiskey Park. Minnie Miñoso's one-out triple won the game. In a storied contest, San Francisco's Juan Marichal limited the Milwaukee Braves to eight hits over 16 innings on July 2, 1963. Warren Spahn, then 42 years old, surrendered a one-out home run to Willie Mays for the only run of the game.
19. "Harry Hoffmann, 'The Count,' Dies at Ball Game," *St. Louis Post-Dispatch*, April 30, 1936: 1A.
20. L.C. Davis, "Spot Salad," *St. Louis Post-Dispatch*, May 1, 1936: 2C.

CARDIAC CARDS COMPLETE CRAZY COMEBACK WHILE DUCKY MEDWICK TIES RECORD WITH FOUR TWO-BAGGERS

August 4, 1937: St. Louis Cardinals 7, Boston Bees 6, at Sportsman's Park

BY NORM KING

You know you've been to a great ballgame when you leave the stadium with a raspy voice after your team wins. It's easy, then, to imagine that 2,303 St. Louis Cardinals fans were just this side of laryngitis when they left Sportsman's Park on August 4, 1937, after watching their team roar back from a four-run deficit with two out in the bottom of the ninth to defeat the Boston Bees, 7-6.

It was a steamy 90-degree day as the two teams took the field with little to play for; the 45-49 Bees were in fifth place, 16 games behind the league-leading Chicago Cubs, while the fourth-place Cardinals, 49-43, were 11 games back.[1]

"It sure don't seem right to see a team in Cardinal uniform 10 [sic] games behind the leaders at no time, 'spcially [sic] in August," said Grover Cleveland Alexander, one of several former Cardinal greats in attendance.[2]

The pitching matchup pitted 30-year-old rookie sensation Lou Fette against journeyman veteran Bob Weiland, who was having one of his better seasons. Fette (pronounced Fetty), was a feel-good story. After toiling for nine years in the minors, he finally got his shot in "The Show" in 1937 and blew away the opposition. He went into this game with an astounding 13-3 record on his way to a 20-10 season (He was not the only age 30-plus Braves rookie to win 20 games that year. Jim Turner, 33, went 20-11). "Fette was a country boy from Missouri, a quiet, hard-working mature pitcher who had paid his dues in coming up through the low minors year after year, and he was ready," wrote Sol Gittleman.[3]

Weiland had ping-ponged between the majors and minors for years. Except for his rookie season in 1928, in which he won his only decision—a 1-0 victory over some Philadelphia Athletics benchwarmers on the last day of the season—he had lost more games than he won every year. He was 7-9 at game time, but would go on to finish above .500 for the first time in his career, at 15-14.

Fette faced a very strong Cardinals batting order, led by Joe "Ducky" Medwick, who was batting .397 and would go on to win the Triple Crown with a .374 batting average, 31 home runs, and 154 RBIs. Medwick had a season for the ages, as the only batting categories he didn't lead the league in were triples (he finished sixth) and on-base percentage (fourth). Johnny Mize (.364, 25, 113) could easily have been MVP were it not for Medwick's amazing season. These sluggers helped the Cardinals finish second in runs scored in the National League with 789.[4]

One of those runs came in the third inning, when Mize hit his 14th home run of the season, part of a 4-for-5 day that extended his hitting streak to 12 games. That 1-0 lead didn't last long, as Boston came back with three in the fourth without the benefit of an extra-base hit. Vince DiMaggio, Tony Cuccinello, and Gene Moore started the inning off with singles, with Joe's younger brother scoring on Moore's hit. With Cuccinello on third, Weiland committed a balk, which made the score 2-1. Weiland walked Gil

English with first base open, but that strategy backfired when Elbie Fletcher singled to bring Moore home with the third run.

Boston extended its lead with a run in the fifth. Weiland walked Bobby Reis, who moved up on an infield out, and then scored on a single by DiMaggio. St. Louis got that one back in the bottom of the inning when Terry Moore and Stu Martin hit back-to-back singles. Mize hit into a fielder's choice, forcing Martin and sending Moore to third. Moore then scored on Medwick's double. Boston led 4-2 after five, and Weiland was done for the day.

At this point, the game turned into one of those affairs where the fans think the manager is a genius or a complete idiot, depending on how his moves work out. Cardinals manager Frankie Frisch looked as though he earned his degree from Fordham when he brought in Ray Harrell, who pitched a perfect sixth inning, and Sheriff Blake, who moseyed to the mound for a scoreless seventh.

But then came the eighth, which left fans wondering why Frisch took Harrell out after his perfect inning, this being the era when relievers sometimes worked three or four innings at a time. It was high noon for Blake, as he gave up two runs. The rally started again with the firm of DiMaggio, Cuccinello, and Moore hitting consecutive singles to load the bases. After Blake struck out English, he walked Fletcher to force in DiMaggio, after which Frisch replaced Blake with Mike Ryba. Ryba got Ray Mueller on an infield out, but Cuccinello scored and made the score 6-2, Boston.

That was how the score stood in the bottom of the ninth, when the Bees blew it, giving up five runs with two out. The fans' voices were still in good shape, as they hadn't had much to cheer about to this point. A number had probably already headed to the exits. Yogi Berra had yet to say it ain't over 'til it's over, but for all we know this may have been the game that inspired the maxim from the St. Louis-born ballplayer-philosopher.

The rally started with Moore on second thanks to a one-out walk and a groundout by Martin. Mize was the next batter and he singled to drive home Moore. Medwick then came up with a chance not only to drive Mize home, but also to tie the major-league record of four doubles in one game last accomplished by Frankie Hayes of the Philadelphia Athletics on July 25, 1936. With the kind of season Medwick was having, of course he came through, giving him a 4-for-5 day and a .403 average for the season. Mize's run made the score 6-4; Bees skipper Bill McKechnie had seen enough, and brought in Guy Bush.

For McKechnie, who was later elected to the Hall of Fame as a manager, this was not one of his better decisions. The first man Bush faced, Don Padgett, singled to bring in Medwick. The tying run was now on base and the lead was down to 6-5.

The next batter, Don Gutteridge, faced two prospects no player wants—an 0-for-5 afternoon and of being the last out of the game. But he came through with a crucial single; the Bees tried to throw Padgett

In 1937 Joe "Ducky" Medwick had one of the best seasons in history, winning the Triple Crown (31-154-.374); leading the NL in runs, hits, doubles, and slugging; and winning the MVP award. (National Baseball Hall of Fame, Cooperstown, New York)

out at third on the hit, and not only was Padgett safe, but Gutteridge also moved to second on the play. With the winning run in scoring position, Frisch sent Pepper Martin in to pinch-hit for Leo Durocher; Boston made the standard move of walking Martin intentionally to load the bases.

What was Frisch to do next? He adopted the if-you-want-something-done-you-have-to do-it-yourself approach and strode to the plate to pinch-hit for Mickey Owen. The old vet decided to make the last hit of his major-league career a memorable one, smacking Bush's first pitch down the right-field line for a double, driving home Padgett and Gutteridge to complete the comeback and set off a state of pandemonium. Medwick led a charge of Cardinals who rushed to Frisch from the dugout and tried to put him on their shoulders.

"Old Frank thought they ought to know better and blushed, but he liked it just the same," wrote J. Roy Stockton in the *St. Louis Post-Dispatch*. "It's great to have your men for you like that."[5]

SOURCES

In addition to the sources listed in the Notes, the author also used:

(Fort Lauderdale, Florida) *Evening Independent*.

New York Times.

onthisdayincardinalnation.com.

SABR biography of Bill McKechnie by Warren Corbett.

SABR biography of Frankie Frisch by Fred Stein.

Weathersource.com.

NOTES

1 Starting on August 4, the New York Giants went 41-17 to take the pennant by three games over Chicago. The Giants lost the World Series to the New York Yankees in five games.

2 J. Roy Stockton, "Sh! It's the Ghosts of Cardinal Teams That Rallied — Rising Up to Overcome Bees in the Ninth," *St. Louis Post-Dispatch*," August 5, 1937: 2B.

3 Sol Gittleman, *Reynolds, Raschi and Lopat: New York's Big Three and the Yankee Dynasty of 1949-53* (Jefferson, North Carolina: McFarland & Company, 2007): 13.

4 The Cubs led with 811.

5 Stockton.

A ONE-MAN SHOW: JOHNNY MIZE ENDS SLUMP BY BLASTING THREE STRAIGHT HOMERS

July 13, 1938: Boston Bees 10, St. Louis Cardinals 5, at Sportsman's Park

BY GREGORY H. WOLF

"For weeks on end, the once fell bludgeonings of Johnny Mize were but a ghastly whisper," opined the *St. Louis Post Dispatch* about the slugger's prolonged slump in 1938.[1] After bursting on the scene as a rookie in 1936, batting .329 and knocking in 93 runs, the stout 6-foot-2 Georgian laid a legitimate claim as the best left-handed hitter in the National League the following season with a .364 batting average, 25 homers and 113 RBIs. Mize also formed with his teammate, 1937 MVP and Triple Crown winner Joe "Ducky" Medwick (.374 BA, 31 HR, 154 RBIs), the most potent one-two punch in Redbird history. But at almost the halfway point of the '38 campaign, the 25-year-old Mize was batting a measly .269 with only five homers, and just one in his last 76 at-bats. "[His] failure at the plate has been one of the [Cardinals'] major disappointments," declared the Associated Press.[2]

Cardinals skipper Frankie Frisch was on the hot seat. The *Post-Dispatch* pronounced his team a "complete washout."[3] Coming off a fourth-place finish, the team was expected to challenge the New York Giants for the pennant in '38, but was mired in one of its worst slumps in recent memory. St. Louis had lost its last six games and 10 of 11, and were in seventh place (29-41), 16 games behind the Giants, as it prepared to play the ninth game of a season-long 21-game homestand. Many were speculating when club owner Sam Breadon, notoriously fickle with his managers, would fire Frisch, who had led the club to its last championship, as a player-manager in 1934. "I haven't quit on this club as yet," said Breadon. "I know they must be better than they've looked."[4] Hardly a ringing endorsement.

After posting just their third winning season in the last 16 years, the Boston Bees had started off well under first-year pilot Casey Stengel in 1938, but had recently skidded, having lost 10 of their last 15 games, and were in fifth place (32-34).

A crowd of 7,846 showed up on a Wednesday afternoon at Sportsman's Park to take in an afternoon of baseball on Tuberculosis Day after the Cardinals had drawn less than half that total (3,583) in the two previous games combined against Cincinnati. The Cardinals, like the other 15 big-league teams, acutely felt the effects of the Great Depression. The pregame festivities for the annual fundraising event included 17 bands performing together on the field and 1,000 Boy Scouts doing stunts.[5]

Fundamentally sound defense had been a hallmark of previous Cardinals teams, but this year's club struggled, finishing with 199 errors, just two fewer than Philadelphia's league high. Hoping to light a fire under the players, Frisch rearranged his fielders against Boston, which had changed its name from the Braves to the Bees after a horrendous campaign in 1935 (38-115). Rookie Lynn Myers debuted at shortstop, pushing starter Don Gutteridge to third base, giving 35-year-old Joe Stripp a rest. Utilityman Don Padgett replaced rookie Enos Slaughter in right field, and Herb Bremer donned the tools of ignorance to spell the durable 22-year-old Mickey Owen behind the plate. Frisch's move turned out to be a disaster. "[They] played in the field like the awkward squad

Hall of Famer Johnny "The Big Cat" Mize belted three home runs in a game on six occasions and paced the NL in round-trippers four times. (National Baseball Hall of Fame, Cooperstown, New York)

of a school for ungainly boys," criticized the *Post-Dispatch* sharply.[6]

Gene Moore led off for the Braves by stroking a double off Fiddler Bill McGee. In his first full season, the 28-year-old right-hander had an unsightly 2-8 record despite a sturdy 2.83 ERA. The next three hitters, suggested the *Post-Dispatch*, "should have been retired in order."[7] Myers fumbled Johnny Cooney's tricky grounder and threw late to Mize at first; no error was charged. Gil English hit what appeared to be a routine double-play ball, but after Cooney was erased at second, Mize dropped the relay throw, as Moore crossed the plate. Once again, no error was charged. Tony Cuccinello grounded to Meyers, who again fumbled, drawing an error. In what was beginning to look like an episode from *The Three Stooges*, Padgett misplayed Max West's liner to right field, plating English. As the ball rolled to the wall, Cuccinello scored and West reached second.

One can only wonder what the demonstrative Frisch was yelling at this point. But the comedy of errors continued. When Bremer dropped a pitch by McGee, West broke for third and slid in safely for a stolen base while Gutteridge dropped the ball. After Mize made what Gerry Moore of the *Boston Globe* considered a sensational catch of Elbie Fletcher's bullet, Ray Mueller walked, and Rabbit Warstler singled to right to drive in West for the Bees' fourth run.[8]

Boston tacked on three more in the third, courtesy of more sloppy play by the Cardinals. With two outs, Cuccinello on first, and Mueller on third, the Bees pulled off a double steal, reminiscent of Stengel's years playing for his mentor John McGraw and his Deadball Era tactics with the Giants. Cuccinello slid in safely for the game's fifth run as Bremer dropped a relay throw. Warstler lined a triple to deep center to drive in West and then scored himself when center fielder Frenchy Bordagaray's throw went wild for the Redbirds' third and final charged error of the game. McGee's log of the day was forgettable: six hits, seven runs (three earned), and two walks in three innings.

Trailing 7-0 in the bottom of the fourth, the Cardinals took their whacks against Bees starter Milkman Jim Turner. The 34-year-old right-hander had debuted the previous season. He won 20 games and paced the National League in ERA (2.38), complete games (24), and shutouts (5) for manager/pitching guru Bill McKechnie, now the Cincinnati skipper. With Medwick on first, Mize walloped a homer onto the right-field pavilion roof to get the Redbirds on the board.

Held scoreless in the fourth and fifth innings by Cardinals swingman Roy Henshaw, the Bees tallied a run off the 5-foot-8 southpaw in the sixth on Moore's RBI single, driving in Warstler.

Mize accounted for the next three Cardinals runs. In the sixth he drove a pitch from Turner over the 33-foot-high screen that stretched across most of right field to prevent cheap homers, over the pavilion roof, and onto Grand Boulevard. In the eighth he repeated the blast onto the street, with Medwick on first with his third single of the game, to make it 8-5, and give the Cardinals a glimmer of hope. It was the first time a Cardinals player had belted three homers in a game at Sportsman's Park, home of the American League's St. Louis Browns since its opening in 1909, and the Cardinals since July 1, 1920.

Right-hander Ray "Cowboy" Harrell's troubles in the ninth inning, in his second inning of mop-up work, were indicative of the Cardinals' frustrating day. With two outs, rookie West, batting just .210 entering the game, parked a pitch on the right-field roof for a 9-5 Bees lead. Fletcher followed with a single, stole the club's fourth base of the contest, and then scored on Mueller's single, the Bees' 13th safety of the game.

Turner, who had been rocked for 12 hits, ceded to Dick Errickson in the ninth. The rookie right-hander set down the side in order to preserve Turner's victory and ended the game in 2 hours and 14 minutes.

Mize's record-tying three consecutive home runs and five RBIs put a definitive end to the good-natured Southerner's slump. "Perhaps Mize will hit from now on and perhaps a few more things will happen," said Breadon.[9] The impatient owner probably did not expect the kind of fireworks Mize would subsequently provide. A week later he became the first major leaguer to hit three home runs in a game twice in one season when he turned the trick in a 7-1 victory over the Giants. He also knocked in five runs in the second game of a doubleheader on July 20 at Sportsman's Park. For the remainder of the season, Mize was the most destructive force in the league, batting .391 and slugging .744.

The Cardinals finished in sixth place with their worst record (71-80) since 1924, leading to Frisch's dismissal with 16 games remaining. Mize made a run at the Triple Crown, finishing second in batting (.337), third in home runs (27), and fifth in RBIs (102), while leading the NL in slugging (.614) and total bases (326) for the first of three consecutive seasons, and also triples (16).

Mize cranked three or more home runs in a game six times in his career, compiling 359 homers in parts of 15 seasons.

SOURCES

In addition to the sources cited in the Notes, the author also accessed Retrosheet.org, Baseball-Reference.com, the SABR Minor Leagues Database, accessed online at Baseball-Reference.com, SABR.org, and *The Sporting News* archive via Paper of Record.

NOTES

1. "The Sinking Cardinals," *St. Louis Post-Dispatch*, July 16, 1938: 4A.
2. Associated Press, "Cards Lose to Bees, 10-5," *Decatur* (Illinois) *Herald*, July 14, 1938: 9.
3. "Wray's Column," *St. Louis Post-Dispatch*, July 15, 1938: 1B.
4. J. Roy Stockton, "Breadon Says He Has Not Quit on the Cardinals Yet," *St. Louis Post-Dispatch*, July 15, 1938: 2B.
5. Gerry Moore, "Mize Gets Three Homers, But Bees Win by 10-5," *Boston Globe*, July 15, 1938: 9.
6. "Mize Hits Three Straight Homers but Cards Lose," *St. Louis Post-Dispatch*, July 14, 1938: 1B.
7. Ibid.
8. Moore.
9. Stockton.

MIZE BLASTS THREE HOME RUNS FOR SECOND TIME IN EIGHT DAYS

July 20, 1938: St. Louis Cardinals 7, New York Giants 1, at Sportsman's Park

BY KELLEN NIELSON

JOHNNY MIZE, A COUNTRY BOY FROM Demorest, Georgia, had been given the nickname of Big Cat because of his defensive prowess, but it was Mize's offense that made him a star early in his career. Mize had a fine pedigree, being a distant cousin of Ty Cobb and a relation to Babe Ruth through marriage. But in 1938, his third year, Mize had been struggling. Just eight days earlier Mize showed a spark of his power returning when he blasted three home runs in a loss to the Boston Bees at Sportsman's Park in St. Louis, becoming the first Cardinal to accomplish the feat since George Watkins did it in 1931.

The three-homer game was about all Mize had to celebrate in the first half of the 1938 season. The young Cardinals slugger had been mired in somewhat of a slump, especially considering his extraordinary first two seasons in the majors. In his rookie year, 1936, Mize had clubbed 19 home runs and driven in 93 runs with a .329 batting average. The next campaign was even better as the left-handed hitter avoided the sophomore jinx, hitting .364 with 25 home runs and 113 RBIs. The Cardinals expected more of the same from Mize in '38, but after 81 games Mize was batting .278 with eight home runs (three in that one game) and 38 runs driven in. Mize's power outage had continued in the six games since he belted three home runs. He hit .280 in that stretch with just two extra-base hits—a double and a triple—and two RBIs. On this day, Mize was to regain his form.

A crowd of 8,404 came out for the Wednesday doubleheader in St. Louis. Manager Frankie Frisch's Redbirds beat Bill Terry's Giants, 7-2, in the opener behind lefty Clyde Shoun's complete game. Mize went 0-for-4 with two RBIs on a groundout and an error.

Frisch was having his worst season as manager. His team came into the game with a 33-45 record. He had never had a team finish below .500 in his previous five years heading the Cardinals. This was also Frisch's first year as a nonplaying manager, after he had spent the previous five years as a player-manager. Frisch had enjoyed some success early in his managerial tenure. He had won more than 90 games in each of his first two full seasons, including a World Series title in 1934; but the Cardinals had had little success since then, with their win total decreasing every year since that championship. The team's declining fortunes led somewhat of a rift between the Cardinals' owner, Sam Breadon, and their general manager, Branch Rickey. Rickey had wanted to replace Frisch, but Breadon won out and Frisch stayed on.

The embattled manager had been facing calls from the media for his removal. Frisch said of the tough '38 campaign, "This is the toughest season I ever had in baseball. Sure I have worried. One can't take the failure of the Cardinals with a happy-go-lucky smile. But I believe our team will cause a lot of trouble before the season is over."[1]

The Giants were the two-time defending National League champs and had gotten off to a hot start. They had won 12 of their first 13 games, including 11 in a row. But they had been struggling lately. In first place for most of the year, they had lost the lead to the Pittsburgh Pirates on July 14. After a few days of lead changes, the Giants came into the second game of the doubleheader with a 50-32 record, 1½ games behind the Pirates. The *St. Louis Post-Dispatch* reported that according to the New York Betting Commission the

Giants were no longer the odds-on favorite to win the National League pennant.[2]

For the second game the Cardinals started another lefty, Bob Weiland. Weiland had arguably been the club's best pitcher. Coming into the game he was 8-7 with a 3.54 ERA. He had not fared well versus the Giants, however. In four previous games against New York Weiland had gone 1-3 with a 4.45 ERA. Clydell "Slick" Castleman got the start for the Giants. The young right-hander was 4-3 so far with a 4.30 ERA and had beaten the Cardinals twice, both in complete games.

The Cardinals continued where they left off in the first game. Mize came up in the first inning with two men on and delivered a three-run bomb to give the Cardinals a lead. He followed with a solo in the fourth off Castleman and another in eighth off Bill Lohrman. The Cardinals tacked on another two runs with RBIs from Jimmy Brown and Herb Bremer. Weiland scattered nine hits in the complete-game, 7-1 victory, with the lone New York run coming on Mel Ott's 21st home run of the year. Castleman surrendered only four home runs in 1938, half of them to Mize in this one game.

With the two victories and the offensive outburst newspapers, across the country heralded the return of the Gas House Gang. The *Brooklyn Daily Eagle* lamented, "The Giants appeared to be coming apart at the seams," and added that this was "the cruelest blow the club has had to take all season."[3]

The two defeats were disastrous for the Giants. *New York Times* writer John Drebinger aptly described the effects of the twin bill: "The Giants' desperate dash in the wake of the pace-setting Pirates suffered something of a compound fracture today as Onkel Franz Frisch's deflated Gas House Gang, apparently steaming along on borrowed gas, rode right over Colonel Bill Terry's band wagon in both ends of a double header."[4] The Giants never recovered and never came closer to retaining the National League title. They finished in third place, five games behind the Chicago Cubs.

The Gas House Gang days did not last and Frisch was fired with 16 games remaining in the season. Third-base coach Mike Gonzalez was named the interim manager. Gonzalez, a native of Cuba, became the first Latino to manage in the majors.

Mize's game was overshadowed by the news that the third-place Chicago Cubs had fired their manager, Charlie Grimm, and replaced him with Gabby Hartnett.[5] Mize, however, was the real story of the day, becoming the first man to have two three-home run games in a season. Mize would set a torrid pace for the remainder of the year. In his final 74 games, Mize hit .390 with a .486 on-base percentage and a .708 slugging percentage. He blasted another 16 home runs while driving in 59 runs. Before his career was over, Mize had a record six three-home-run games. This one was the only one of the six his team won; it lost four and tied one.

Mize's slump in the early part of 1938 proved to be an aberration; he hit 27 home runs in 1938. In 1939, his 28 homers led the National League and in 1940 his 43 homers led both leagues. In both 1947 (51) and 1948 (40), Mize also led the majors in home runs. He finished his career with 359 home runs. He was voted into the Baseball Hall of Fame by the Veterans Committee in 1981.

SOURCES

In addition to the sources cited in the Notes, the author also consulted

Baseball-Reference.com, Retrosheet.org, and SABR.org.

NOTES

1. Dick Farrington, "Frisch Says Players Forget Camp Stuff," *Sporting News* July 28, 1938: 3.

2. "Giants No Longer Odds-on Favorite to Win the Pennant," *St. Louis Post Dispatch*, July 21, 1938.

3. Ed Hughes, "Terry Machine Coming Apart at All Points," *Brooklyn Daily Eagle*, July 21, 1938: 14

4. John Drebinger, "Double Loss to Cards Drops Giants Game and a Half Below Leading Pirates," *New York Times*, July 21, 1938.

5. Hartnett would lead the Cubs to the National League pennant. They lost to the New York Yankees in the World Series.

REDBIRDS TIE NL RECORD WITH SEVEN ROUND-TRIPPERS

May 7, 1940: St. Louis Cardinals 18, Brooklyn Dodgers 2, at Sportsman's Park

BY RICHARD RIIS

AS THE 1940 SEASON BEGAN, THE Cardinals were sputtering in the early going. Losers of their first three games and eight of their first 13, the runners-up to the Cincinnati Reds for the 1939 pennant were limping along a game and a half ahead of the miserable Boston Braves at the bottom of the standings.

In contrast, the Brooklyn Dodgers broke fast from the gate, winning their first nine games before finally losing 9-2 to the Reds. The Dodgers thus headed for St. Louis for a three-game series with the Cardinals with a record of 9-1 and sitting atop the National League standings.

Arriving in the Gateway City by airplane, only the fourth major-league team after the Reds, Cardinals, and Red Sox to fly, the Dodgers showed the stuff of a first-place ballclub by rallying for four runs in the ninth to take the series opener. 9-6, and followed with a 6-2 victory to raise their record to 11-1, while the Cardinals dropped into last place.

"Quite as shocking as the Dodgers' electrifying start," wrote one syndicated scribe, "is the utter collapse of the St. Louis Cardinals, the team experts picked to dethrone the Cincinnati Reds."[1]

It certainly didn't help that the Cards' slick-fielding rookie shortstop, Marty Marion, injured a knee in the first game of the series and would be on crutches for the rest of the month, or that All-Star center fielder Terry Moore had sprained his shoulder making a diving catch in the same game and would miss the next seven games.

Despite the Cardinals' 5-10 record, there were some signs of life on the team. Catcher Don Padgett was hitting .349 and had driven in a team-high nine runs. Right fielder Enos Slaughter was hitting .377, second highest among NL batsmen, and left fielder Joe "Ducky" Medwick was not far behind at .353. A lack of other baserunners, though, had limited the pair to only three RBIs each.

Dodgers player-manager Leo Durocher wasn't counting the Cardinals out just yet.

"The Cards have plenty of power and they'll get going. They're a better ballclub than they've shown. They gotta be. Mize, Medwick, Padgett, Slaughter—say, that's a murderer's row for you."[2]

Nobody could have anticipated, however, the explosion of offense from the St. Louis lineup in the third and final game of the series.

Only 2,298 faithful fans were on hand at Sportsman's Park on a mild Tuesday afternoon to witness the fireworks. St. Louis skipper Ray Blades sent veteran Lon Warneke (0-2) to the mound, while Durocher tabbed Hugh Casey (2-1) to start for Brooklyn.

With Marion out of commission, the Cardinals had an infield problem. Blades put second baseman Stu Martin at third base—a position he had never played before in Organized Baseball—moved third sacker Jimmy Brown to shortstop, inserted untested rookie utilityman Eddie Lake at second base, and hoped this would do.

It was Padgett who started the Cards' long-ball frenzy by homering off Casey in the second inning. Brown followed with a triple, but was caught in a rundown and tagged out when the next batter, Johnny Hopp, bounced one to Dodgers third baseman Cookie Lavagetto.

Lake poled his first career homer to lead off the third inning for St. Louis. Martin then singled. Slaughter tripled, scoring Martin, and Medwick singled, scoring Slaughter. Johnny Mize then deposited his fourth home run of the season in the right-field seats to make it 6-0 in favor of the Cardinals.

The Dodgers continued to do little of anything at the plate, and Hugh Casey returned to the mound for the fourth inning. "Let me keep pitching," Casey implored Durocher, "I need the work."[3] Durocher did make one change, sitting himself down and sending 21-year-old rookie Pee Wee Reese in to take his place at shortstop. In the inning, Stu Martin took Casey deep for another Cardinals home run and a 7-0 lead.

Warneke, coasting on a two-hit shutout, retired the Dodgers in order in the fifth and sixth innings, and the Cardinals struck again in the bottom of each frame with an RBI double by Hopp and a two-run double by Lake in the fifth, and a two-run homer by Medwick and a run-scoring fly ball by Brown in the sixth that put St. Louis up 13-0.

The Dodgers finally showed some life in the eighth when Reese led off with a single and Dixie Walker, hitting for the battered Casey, singled Reese to third. After Charlie Gilbert popped out to third, Pete Coscarart grounded to Brown at short, who flipped to Lake at second for the force out, as Reese scored the first Brooklyn run. Jimmy Ripple and Johnny Hudson, spelling Lavagetto at third base, each singled, allowing Coscarart to score, before Babe Phelps flied out to center to end the inning.

Left-hander Max Macon, who had come up with the Cardinals in 1938, took the mound for Brooklyn in the bottom of the eighth. Hugh Casey had pitched seven innings and been pounded for 15 hits, including five home runs, and 13 runs, an ignominious pitching line that would remain unmatched by another major-league starter for more than 70 years.

He asked to stay in there," said Durocher. "He hadn't had much work, and as long as the game was gone, I let him continue."[4]

The removal of Casey did nothing to cool the Cardinals' hot bats. With one out, Mize slugged his second homer of the game. After another out, Joe Orengo, hitting for Brown, singled and stole second. Hopp singled, scoring Orengo for the Cardinals' 15th run. Warneke got in on the action, stroking a double to score Hopp. Lake then clubbed his second homer of the game, a two-run shot that made it 18-2. Macon finally induced Martin to hit a grounder to Dolph Camilli at first, who stepped on the bag to retire the side.

It wasn't the Cardinals' feats at the plate that drew the loudest ovation of the afternoon, however. A great cheer arose from the stands when Bill DeLancey strode from the home dugout in the top of the ninth inning to replace Don Padgett as catcher. The Cardinals' receiver from the world champion "Gas House Gang" of 1934 had been forced to retire after the 1935 season after contracting tuberculosis.

The Cardinals established a Class-D farm team in Albuquerque, New Mexico, in 1937 and hired the convalescing DeLancey as its manager. He led the Albuquerque Cardinals to two Arizona-Texas League championships and regained enough strength to return to the field for brief periods as a player—nine games in 1938 and 19 games in 1939. By 1940, his health had improved to the point that he was able to return to the big league Cardinals as the team's third-string catcher. As DeLancey took the field, it marked his first time on a major-league diamond in nearly five years. DeLancey would only play 15 games in 1940 before retiring a second time, eventually succumbing to his illness on November 28, 1946, his 35th birthday.

With Warneke still on the mound, Camilli hit a foul in back of third that Martin caught for the first out. Roy Cullenbine singled, but Reese flied out to left. Max Macon, left in to bat for himself, poked a single, advancing Cullenbine to second. Warneke then fanned Gilbert for the final out.

In the 18-2 pounding of the Dodgers, the Cardinals shattered two batting records and tied another. The team's 49 total bases topped the NL mark of 47 established by the Giants in 1931. Their seven total homers tied a NL record shared by five others and fell one short of the major-league record of eight set on June 28, 1939, by the New York Yankees in a game against the Philadelphia Athletics. The Cardinals' 13 extra-base hits tied the modern major-league record held by the Tigers and matched twice before by the Cardinals.

Not to be overlooked was the fine pitching performance of Lon Warneke, who pitched shutout ball for seven innings, weakening only in the eighth when he was reached for four of the nine hits he allowed in the game and the Dodgers' only two runs.

As for Hugh Casey, as a Brooklyn sportswriter put it, "There is no pitcher on the club who hates losing worse than [Casey] and he can get downright mean about it. He gave the Redbird sluggers something to remember him by. One by one they hit the dirt and he actually did hit three of them—Padgett, Mize, and Slaughter. Padgett and Mize had previously hit homers off Casey but Slaughter's worst offense was a triple."[5]

SOURCES:

In addition to the sources listed in the Notes, the author also consulted:

Decatur (Illinois) *Herald.*

New York Times.

St. Louis Star-Times.

The Sporting News.

Baseball Reference.com.

Retrosheet.org.

NOTES

1 George Kirksey, "Collapse of Cards Stuns Baseball World," *Daily Times* (New Philadelphia, Ohio), May 3, 1940: 7.

2 "Lippy Leo Respects Bill Terry's Pitcher," *St. Louis Post-Dispatch*, May 7, 1940: 12.

3 Tommy Holmes, "Dodgers Relax After Pinning Back of Ears," *Brooklyn Daily Eagle*, May 8, 1940: 17.

4 "Casey Wanted to Stay In," *The Sporting News*, May 16, 1940: 1.

5 Holmes.

LIGHTS GO ON IN ST. LOUIS!

May 24, 1940: Cleveland Indians 3, St. Louis Browns 2, at Sportsman's Park

BY RICHARD RIIS

FOR NEARLY 15 MINUTES 25,562 excitedly impatient fans had been shouting and clapping their hands in unison. The claps turned to applause when St. Louis Mayor Bernard Dickmann finally emerged from the dugout, strode to a microphone behind home plate, and formally welcomed the crowd to the night's special event.

Hosting chores were then turned over to St. Louis Browns' President Don Barnes, who introduced a handful of dignitaries, including AL President Will Harridge. Finally, Kenesaw M. Landis, commissioner of baseball, was invited to press a button wired into the ballpark's electrical system, and, to an audible gasp from the crowd, 764 1,500-watt bulbs on eight steel towers and 250 additional lights installed in the pavilion, bleachers, and other public areas burst into brilliance, illuminating every corner of Sportsman's Park.

Less than one year earlier, Browns vice president and general manager Bill DeWitt had made clear the club's opposition to introducing night baseball in St. Louis.

"Our main object right now," said DeWitt, "is to get a winning ballclub. It's next to impossible to sell a tailender to the public, nights or afternoons. I'm positive on that point. We're tailenders now and I doubt that we'd increase our patronage at night in sufficient numbers to meet the cost of installing lights."[1]

But the numbers from elsewhere in the major leagues were hard to ignore. While the Browns drew an average of 2,480 to 11 home games against the White Sox in 1939, the White Sox drew 30,000 in their one night game against the Browns in Chicago.[2] In 11 games with the Indians in St. Louis, the average crowd numbered 1,050; the Browns played before 16,467 in one night game in Cleveland.[3] Even the seventh-place Athletics could boast of hosting 120,000 fans for their seven night games in Philadelphia, nearly equaling the Browns' total home attendance of 109,000 for the entire 1939 season.[4]

The basic plans required to install lights at Sportsman's Park were already in hand. Blueprints had been drawn up in 1937, but a dispute over how the cost was to be split between the Browns and the Cardinals and which team would get to play the first game under the lights caused the project to be put aside.

Faced with the box-office numbers from around the league, resistance to night baseball within the financially strapped Browns organization crumbled, and on January 18, 1940, the club's board of directors unanimously approved the installation of lights at Sportsman's Park at a cost of $174,000,[5] contingent on half of the tab being paid by the tenant St. Louis Cardinals. Cardinals owner Sam Breadon gave the project his approval the following day.

Estimates were that the construction of light towers and installation of lights would take less than four months. By agreement between the two clubs, the Browns would host the first night game, against the Indians on May 24, while the Cardinals would make their nighttime debut against the Brooklyn Dodgers on June 4. With only one minor setback—a wind and rain storm on May 14 that tore a light reflector from one of the towers, sending it crashing into the seats as spectators for a Browns-Yankees game, just postponed, were leaving the grandstand—the project was completed on schedule.

Devoted fans and the curious began to file into Sportsman's Park on the evening of the 24th as early as 5:00 P.M. The lights were turned on at 7:45 to allow the Browns and the Indians to take fielding practice, after which the lights were extinguished in preparation for the scheduled ceremonies.

By game time, 24,827 cash customers and 735 pass-gate attendants filled the stands, the largest turnout for the Browns since a June 1928 game that brought Babe Ruth and the New York Yankees to town.

"It was carnival time in North St. Louis," one observer said in describing the scene in and around the ballpark. "The neighborhood was lighted up like downtown, but the lights were brighter. Night baseball became a debutante in a bright, gleaming dress.

"Sportsman's Park's neighbors entered into the spirit of the occasion. They sat on their porches and watched the lights go on, and thrilled to the roar of the crowd that cheered the Browns and the Indians."[6]

Starting that night for Browns was Elden Auker, winner of three of his first five decisions for the 11-15 club. Auker, a submarine hurler who had won 15 and 18 games for the 1934-1935 pennant-winning Detroit Tigers, had been acquired by St. Louis after an unhappy 9-10 season in Boston in which he had feuded on and off with Red Sox manager Joe Cronin.

Tapped for 18-10 Cleveland was 21-year-old fireballing sensation Bob Feller. Feller had galvanized the baseball world by tossing a 1-0 no-hitter against the White Sox on Opening Day, and owned a 5-2 record, a stingy 2.56 ERA, and 51 strikeouts in 59⅔ innings coming into the game.

Auker got off to a good start, retiring the Indians in order in the first inning. Feller, on the other hand, found himself in trouble right away, walking leadoff hitter Alan "Inky" Strange and allowing Walt Judnich to drive a pitch off the screen in right field for a double. After George McQuinn went down swinging, Rip Radcliff, hitting .391 overall and .477 over his last 10 games on his way to a .342 season, was given an intentional pass. With the bases now loaded, Feller fanned Chet Laabs on three straight pitches. But third baseman Ken Keltner booted a hard-hit grounder off the bat of Harlond Clift, and Strange sprinted home with the first run of the game.

Auker continued to make short work of the Indians, retiring three straight in the second and the first two hitters in the third before Feller, catching an outside curveball, drove the ball into the lower deck of the right-field pavilion, tying the game with his first major-league home run.

Cleveland snapped the tie in the fourth inning when Jeff Heath knocked a double off the wall in left-center and scored on a single to left by Rollie Hemsley. Rookie Ray Mack, who had been made the Tribe's regular second baseman after brief stints with the club in 1938 and 1939, and who was pacing the club in the early going with a .340 average, looped a double to right, scoring Hemsley with an insurance run to make it 3-1.

The Browns managed only three more hits off Feller between the second and seventh innings, but broke through again in the eighth. McQuinn opened with a single to left before taking off on Radcliff's third hit of the night, a double to left-center. Taking a wide turn around third, McQuinn collided with an Associated Press photographer but managed to untangle himself from the unlucky lensman and scattered camera parts to score without a play being made.

With Radcliff representing the tying run on second and one out, Laabs bunted up the third-base line. Feller pounced on the ball and tossed it to Keltner, who scrambled back to third to make the tag on a sliding Radcliff. Clift then flied to center, and Laabs was thrown out on an attempted steal of second, Hemsley to shortstop Lou Boudreau.

Auker disposed of the Indians in order in the ninth and Feller finished off the Browns in the same manner to end the game.

Feller struck out nine in going the distance, scattering seven hits and walking only two, for his sixth victory of what would be a career-high 27 for the season. Feller won the "triple crown" of pitching in 1940, leading the AL in wins, strikeouts, and ERA, as well as in games pitched, starts, complete games, shutouts, and innings pitched.

Auker took a hard-luck loss, hurling nine innings and surrendering nine hits and three runs while striking out six.

The outcome of the game may have been a disappointment to 25,000-plus Browns fans, but the reviews of the game under the lights were nonetheless excellent.

"After the Browns' last batter had been retired," the sports editor of the *St. Louis Star-Times* wrote the following day, "the huge crowd moved toward the exit gates, everyone voicing the sentiment of Mr. Baseball Fan of 1940 — that night baseball in the majors is here to stay."[7]

SOURCES

In addition to the sources listed in the notes, the author also consulted:

Akron Beacon-Journal.

Cincinnati Enquirer.

Cleveland Plain Dealer.

Freeport (Illinois) *Journal-Standard.*

New York Times.

Sandusky (Ohio) *Star-Journal.*

The Sporting News.

NOTES

1. Sid Keener, "Sid Keener's Column," *St. Louis Star-Times*, June 8, 1939: 30.
2. Sid Keener, "Sid Keener's Column," *St Louis Star-Times*, January 23, 1940: 16.
3. Ibid.
4. E.G. Brands, "St. Louis Greets Nocturnal Ball With Third Largest Attendance in the Browns' History," *The Sporting News*, May 30, 1940: 5.
5. Robert Morrison, "Sportsman's Park to Have 'Best Lighting in World,'" *St. Louis Post-Dispatch*, May 22, 1940: 14.
6. James Toomey, "North St. Louis Finds It Likes Night Baseball — Even Outside Park," *St. Louis Star-Times*, May 25, 1940: 6.
7. Sid Keener, "Sid Keener's Column," *St Louis Star-Times*, May 25, 1940: 6.

FIVE NATIONAL LEAGUE PITCHERS COMBINE FOR FIRST ALL-STAR-GAME SHUTOUT

July 9, 1940: National League 4, American League 0, at Sportsman's Park

1940 All-Star Game

BY LYLE SPATZ

UNDER A BROILING MIDSUMMER sun, five National League pitchers combined to throw the first shutout in All-Star Game history. With their 4–0 victory in the 1940 contest, the Nationals had now won three of the last five games, after having lost the first three.

Although the American League Browns and National League Cardinals shared Sportsman's Park, the NL was the home team for this game. The Cardinals' successes over the past 15 years had made them by far St. Louis's more popular team, as shown by the mostly National League adherents in the crowd of 32,373. Among the spectators were Commissioner Kenesaw Landis, AL President Will Harridge, and NL President Ford Frick.

The boos that greeted Dodgers' outfielder Joe Medwick were an early indication that it was a predominantly Cardinals crowd. Medwick, a former Cardinals favorite, was making his first appearance at Sportsman's Park since his recent trade to Brooklyn. Meanwhile, Browns fans had little to cheer about. They had only one player on the AL squad, first baseman George McQuinn, who was in uniform but recovering from a thigh injury and never got into the game.

The heavily favored American Leaguers managed just three hits and two walks against Cincinnati's Paul Derringer and Bucky Walters, Brooklyn's Whit Wyatt, Chicago's Larry French, and New York's Carl Hubbell. Luke Appling of the Chicago White Sox, who doubled in the second inning, was the only American Leaguer to get as far as third base.

Boston Bees outfielder Max West's first-inning three-run homer off the Yankees' Red Ruffing provided all the offense the Nationals would need, although they added a final run against Bob Feller in the eighth. Ruffing and Derringer had also started the 1939 game in New York, making this the first time that two pitchers had started against each other in consecutive All-Star games. (They'd also been the opposing pitchers in Game One of the 1939 World Series.)

Pittsburgh's Arky Vaughan led off the home first with a bad-hop single over second baseman Joe Gordon's head. Billy Herman of the Cubs, who had three of the Nationals' seven hits, followed with a hit-and-run single that put runners at first and third. Next up was West, a third-year man playing in his first (and what would be his only) All-Star Game. National League manager Bill McKechnie of Cincinnati had made an overnight decision to start West in right field. His original choice was to use the Giants' Mel Ott, a member of each NL squad since 1934.

West, a native Missourian, smashed an 0-and-1 pitch into the covered pavilion in right-center field. His home run was the first by a Boston National Leaguer in an All-Star Game and the first ever by a batter in his first All-Star at-bat.

Later, West confessed that he wasn't sure what he had hit; however, Ruffing said: "It was a low fastball, but it seemed to be faster after he swung."[1]

That one pitch was enough to make the Yankees' right-hander the losing pitcher on what was overall a very poor day for the four-time defending champions. Despite their fourth-place position, four other Yankees joined Ruffing in the starting lineup. Another, Red Rolfe, was selected but missed the game with an injury. Washington's Cecil Travis replaced him. Yankees manager Joe McCarthy, who had managed the American League in the previous four games, had asked to be excused for this one, and Joe Cronin of the Red Sox was handling the team.

None of the Yankees did well this afternoon. Center fielder Joe DiMaggio (0-for-4), second baseman Gordon (0-2, two strikeouts), right fielder Charlie Keller (0-for-2, one strikeout), catcher Bill Dickey (0-for-1), and Ruffing (0-for-1) were a combined zero for 10 against National League pitching. But then no one else on the AL squad did much better. Appling had an eighth-inning single to go along with his double, and Detroit Tigers pitcher Bobo Newsom had a sixth-inning single. Those were the AL's only hits. In addition to West furnishing the highlight of the game for the NL, West also furnished the lowlight. He injured his left hip when he crashed into the right-field wall attempting to catch Appling's second-inning double. The National League team trainer, Dr. Richard Rohde, administered first aid as West lay on the ground, and after a few minutes he was able to walk off on his own power. Bill Nicholson of the Cubs replaced West in right field.

Derringer pitched the first two innings, walking Boston Red Sox left fielder Ted Williams (playing in his first All-Star Game) in the first inning and allowing Appling's double in the second. Each came with only one out, but both times the next two batters, Yankees in both cases, couldn't take advantage. Derringer got Keller and DiMaggio after the walk to Williams and Dickey and Gordon after Appling's double.

Derringer's Cincinnati teammate, Bucky Walters, retired the American Leaguers in order in the third and fourth innings and then turned it over to Wyatt. The Dodgers right-hander set down the Americans in order again in the fifth, before yielding Newsom's single leading off the sixth.

McKechnie had replaced his entire infield to start the inning, so when Travis followed Newsom's hit by bouncing into a double play, it went from Brooklyn second baseman Pete Coscarart to Boston shortstop Eddie Miller to Cincinnati first baseman Frank McCormick.

In all, McKechnie used 22 of his roster of 25 players, leaving out only Philadelphia pitchers Kirby Higbe and Hugh Mulcahy and Dodgers shortstop (and rival manager) Leo Durocher. Cronin used 18 players. Only three men played the entire game: DiMaggio, American League home-run leader Jimmie Foxx, and Cardinals center fielder Terry Moore. Foxx's selection made him the only player in either league who had been picked for each of the eight All-Star Games.

McKechnie brought in Cubs left-hander French to pitch the seventh. Like Wyatt, he too set the side down one-two-three in his first inning and gave up a leadoff single in his second. That was to Appling, but French retired the next three batters without Appling ever advancing. The last two, pinch-hitter Ray Mack and his Cleveland teammate Feller, batting for himself, went down on strikes. Mack was one of four Indians and nine American Leaguers chosen for their first All-Star Game.

Facing Feller in the eighth, Mel Ott led off with a walk, moved to second on a sacrifice bunt by McCormick, and scored on Harry Danning's single to right.

The Giants' Danning was the National League's leading hitter (.343) and RBI man (58), but McKechnie had chosen to start Ernie Lombardi, Derringer's regular-season batterymate, behind the plate. In the middle three innings he used Brooklyn's Babe Phelps, which enabled Wyatt to pitch to his regular-season batterymate.

First-half statistics appeared to count for little to both managers. Of the top five in each league, only White Sox shortstop Appling was in the starting lineup. Five didn't even make the team: the Browns' Rip Radcliff, the White Sox' Taft Wright, and the Tigers' Barney McCosky—the numbers two, four, and five hitters in the AL—and the Dodgers' Dixie Walker and the Cubs' Jimmy Gleeson—the numbers two and four hitters in the NL.

Red Sox outfielder Lou Finney was the AL's leading hitter at .359, but he did not appear until the sixth inning. Same for Detroit's Hank Greenberg, the major leagues' RBI leader with 71. Greenberg, the starter at first base in 1939, replaced Williams in left.

Hubbell, Danning's Giants batterymate, came on in the ninth and after striking out Cleveland's Ken Keltner issued a walk to Finney. Hubbell then ended the game by getting Greenberg on a foul out to Danning and DiMaggio on a fly to Giants left fielder Jo-Jo Moore.

The scarcity of baserunners led to the shortest game (by time) in All-Star history—one hour and 53 minutes. Yet despite its brevity and the oppressive heat of a typically torrid St. Louis afternoon, the fans had a wonderful afternoon.

NOTES

1 Roscoe McGowen, "Jubilant Victors Reconstruct game," *New York Times*, July 10, 1940.

This account is adapted from Vincent, David, Lyle Spatz, and David W. Smith, *The Midsummer Classic: The Complete History of Baseball's All-Star Game* (Lincoln: University of Nebraska Press, 2001).

JOHNNY MIZE TRIPLES, SCORES, AND EARNS A CYCLE AS CARDINALS SWEEP GIANTS WITH WALK-OFFS

July 13, 1940: St. Louis Cardinals 7, New York Giants 6 (Game One of Doubleheader), at Sportsman's Park

BY MICHAEL HUBER

THE *NEW YORK TIMES* DESCRIBED THE outcome of a 1940 midseason New York Giants-St. Louis Cardinals doubleheader: "The Giants' efforts to better their position in the National League flag race suffered two jolts today when they went down before the Cardinals in both ends of a double-header both times in the last inning."[1] The two teams were heading in different directions. On this day, the sixth-place Cardinals swept the third-place Giants, and both victories were in walk-off fashion.

Billy Southworth was the third manager of the season for St. Louis, having taken over from interim manager Mike Gonzalez (who succeeded the fired Ray Blades) on June 14, with the Cardinals mired in last place with a 15-29 record. St. Louis won its first six games with Southworth at the helm, but coming into this doubleheader the Cardinals had lost six straight. In the end, Southworth piloted the team to a 69-40 record, for a third-place finish at 84-69.[2] In the other dugout, Bill Terry's Giants were skidding. Although they came into the doubleheader with a record of 41-28, they found themselves at 62-62 by early September and an 11-game losing streak in the final month of the season propelled New York downward to a final record of 72-80.

A Saturday-afternoon Ladies' Day crowd of 7,325 was on hand at Sportsman's Park for the contests.[3] This was only the second game played after the All-Star Game, which also had been played at Sportsman's Park.[4] In the opening game of the doubleheader, Carl Hubbell took the mound for the Giants and Lon Warneke started for the Cardinals.

The *St. Louis Post-Dispatch* reported that, prior to this season, Hubbell and Warneke[5] were "veterans of the pitching wars and rivals in many a mound duel, but both had taken early showers before the thing was over."[6]

Hubbell, a future Hall of Famer, was the ace of the Giants' pitching staff. A perennial All-Star, he had copped two National League Most Valuable Player Awards, in 1933 and 1936. *The Sporting News* named him the Major League Player of the Year in 1936.[7] In three World Series, he had a 4-2 record, accompanied by a 1.79 earned-run average. At 37 years old, he struggled in 1940, allowing 220 hits in 214⅓ innings. Although he started the season well, compiling five straight complete-game victories in May and June, his season ERA of 3.65 was the highest it had been in 10 years. (He came into this game with a 3.38 mark and a record of 5-4.) At season's end his 11 wins for the year were just behind Hal Schumacher (13) and Harry Gumbert (12) for the team lead.

Warneke had been a star in his earlier years, winning at least 20 games three times from 1932 to 1935 while pitching for the Chicago Cubs. He was traded to the Cardinals in 1937 and won 18 games. Although he was 31 years old and a little past his prime by 1940, he remained a reliable starter.[8] His 5-7 record entering the game belied an impressive 2.83 ERA.

The Giants scored first. In the top of the second, singles by Babe Young, Tony Cuccinello, and Billy Jurges plated a run. Hubbell squandered this early lead by offering up back-to-back doubles to the Cardinals' Marty Marion and Mickey Owen in the bottom of the second. Later in the inning, Warneke helped his own cause with an RBI single to center, and St. Louis led, 2-1. In the third inning, with two outs, Johnny Mize cracked his 22nd home run of the season. He added a double and a single off Hubbell later in the game.

In the fourth inning, the Giants "finished Lon with a withering five-hit blast which sent four runs across."[9] Young singled past second base, Harry Danning doubled to left, and Mel Ott looped a single into center field, driving in both Young and Danning. Cuccinello and Jurges followed with singles, with Ott scoring. At this point Southworth lifted Warneke in favor of Jack Russell. Russell got Hubbell to ground into a double play, but Cuccinello scored the fourth run of the inning on the play. All four runs were charged to Warneke. In the sixth, New York pushed across a solo run to make it 6-3.

St. Louis sent up two pinch-hitters (Don Padgett for Owen and Don Gutteridge for Russell) in the seventh against a trio of pitchers (Hubbell, Jumbo Brown, and Red Lynn), and the Cardinals came away with three more runs to knot the score at 6-6.

In the bottom of the ninth inning, with Lynn trying to preserve the tie, Mize strode to the plate having already hit a single, double, and homer. He launched a drive to deep center, over the head of Giants center fielder Frank Demaree. The ball hit the wall and rebounded from the concrete, 412 feet from home plate.[10] Left fielder Jo-Jo Moore retrieved the ball and threw it to the infield. Shortstop Jurges bobbled the relay before he fired home to the catcher, Danning. Mize, who never stopped running hard, was waved toward the plate. According to the *St. Louis Post-Dispatch*, "Mize looked like a gone goose, but Danning took his eye off the ball to see whether he'd have Mize by ten feet or 20 and that was his undoing. He fumbled the bounding ball and Mize scored the winning run, providing the Cardinals with the walk-off 7-6 victory."[11] The official scorer ruled it a triple and an error on Danning. Mize's three-base smash "sent the opener crashing down on the ears of the Giants."[12] The scoring decision actually enabled Mize to hit for the cycle.

Mize had a 4-for-5 game, driving in two runs. The Cardinals collected 13 hits to the Giants' 11. Young's three singles and two runs scored paced the New York offense.

In Game Two of the doubleheader, the Cardinals once again worked late-inning magic to secure the victory. They loaded the bases with one out, but the Giants were close to surviving the jam when Jimmy Brown hit into a force play at home plate for the second out. Pitching to Terry Moore, Giants hurler Hy Vandenberg appeared to stop in the middle of his windup. This would have constituted a balk, thus ending the contest, but home-plate umpire George Magerkurth did not make the call. Instead, Moore delivered a single to left center while the crowd "yelled happily."[13] Two games, two ninth-inning walk-off wins for the homestanding Cardinals.

Mize, inducted into the Hall of Fame in 1981 by the Veterans Committee, was a 10-time All-Star with the Cardinals, the Giants, and the New York Yankees. In 1940 he led the National League in home runs (43) and led both leagues in RBIs (137), slugging (.636), and OPS (1.039). He started the season with 43 bats, causing him to remark in 1953, "To this day I wonder what would have happened if I had started the season with sixty-one bats."[14] He placed second in the voting for the NL Most Valuable Player Award in 1939 and 1940.

In 1940 six major-league players hit for the cycle.[15] Mize was the third batter of the season to do so. His cycle followed that of the Giants' Danning by exactly four weeks. Complementing his 5-for-9 performance at the plate for the two games in this doubleheader, Mize flashed his leather. He had 23 putouts in the two games at first base, including robbing Demaree of sure extra bases by snaring his line drive in the first game.

NOTES

1 John Drebinger, "Giants Drop Pair to Cards, 7-6, 4-3," *New York Times*, July 14, 1940: 61.

2 Southworth's Cardinals finished the 1940 season in third place. He helmed the St. Louis squad for the next five seasons, garnering two second-place finishes and three pennants (including World Series championships in 1942 and 1944). His 577 victo-

3   J. Roy Stockton, "Mize Bats in One Victory and Terry Moore the Other," *St. Louis Post-Dispatch*, July 14, 1940: 36. The box score in the *New York Times* lists an attendance figure of 3,056. However, according to the *Post-Dispatch*, the "doubleheader attracted a Ladies' day crowd of 7,325, including 3,056 paid, 2,615 women, 1,240 boys, and 414 girls."

4   In 1940 the National League prevailed over the American League in the All-Star Game, 4-0. The Cardinals' Mize and Moore started the game. The Giants had five players on the squad, all reserves: Harry Danning, Carl Hubbell, Billy Jurges, Jo-Jo Moore, and Mel Ott. Of the seven players, only Danning had a hit (and an RBI, driving in Ott, who had walked in the bottom of the eighth inning). Hubbell has been retroactively credited with a save. (In 1940 the save was not an official statistic.)

5   Exactly two months earlier in the season, Warneke had the unique distinction of umpiring in a game between his Cardinals and the Cincinnati Reds. Four years after he retired from pitching, he became a major-league umpire.

6   Stockton.

7   In 1936 Hubbell led the National League in victories (26), winning percentage (.813), earned-run average (2.31), and WHIP (1.059). By 1940 his innings pitched and effectiveness had steadily declined.

8   This game saw Warneke allow his most earned runs in the season (5). He allowed five earned runs four more times in 1940; still, he finished the season with a 16-10 record and 3.14 ERA.

9   Drebinger.

10 Ibid.

11 Stockton.

12 Drebinger.

13 Ibid.

14 Jerry Grillo, "Johnny Mize," posted online at sabr.org/bioproj/person/a7ac6649.

15 Players who hit for the cycle in 1940 were Harry Craft (Cincinnati Reds, June 8), Harry Danning (Giants, June 15), Mize (Cardinals, July 13), Buddy Rosar (New York Yankees, July 19), Joe Cronin (Boston Red Sox, August 2), and Joe Gordon (Yankees, September 8).

(Note: The first paragraph begins: "ries in five-plus seasons gave him a .648 winning percentage. In 1946 he took over managerial duties for the Boston Braves and guided them to the 1948 World Series.")

SINGING IN THE RAIN: WHITEHEAD TOSSES ABBREVIATED NO-HITTER FOR LAST BIG-LEAGUE VICTORY

August 5, 1940: St. Louis Browns 4, Detroit Tigers 0 (Six Innings, Game Two of Doubleheader), at Sportsman's Park

BY GREGORY H. WOLF

"For some time now Large John has been in danger of being booted clear back to his Texas domicile," declared sportswriter W. Vernon Tietjen in the *St. Louis Star and Times* about the Browns' embattled pitcher John Whitehead.[1] The AP noted that the robust right-handed hurler almost "ate his way out of the majors."[2] The result was a two-month midseason banishment to the Double-A Toledo Mud Hens in the American Association to shed some weight and, suggested Tietjen, "make him more fit for the mound than the easy chair."[3] With his big-league career in jeopardy, "Silent John" surprised his detractors by tossing a rain-shortened six-inning no-hitter against the Detroit Tigers in his second start after the demotion. Far from inaugurating a fairy-tale chapter, though, the victory proved to be Whitehead's last in his career. But for 78 minutes, Whitehead was atop the baseball world, and in "superb form as he handcuffed the Tigers," gushed beat writer W.J. McGoogan in the *St. Louis Post-Dispatch*.[4]

In the midst of a season-long 24-game homestand, skipper Fred Haney's Brownies (42-59) were in seventh place, 18½ games behind the league-leading Tigers, whom they hosted for a four-game series beginning with a doubleheader on Monday, August 5, at Sportsman's Park. In front of a paltry crowd of 2,158, the Tigers emerged triumphant in the first contest, 9-2, led by Schoolboy Rowe's six-hitter. The victory proved costly, however, as six-time All-Star second baseman Charlie Gehringer injured his right leg while scoring in the ninth inning on a damp field caused by light rain. ("The Mechanical Man" ultimately missed the next nine games.)

On paper, the second game seemed like a laugher for pilot Del Baker's squad from the Motor City. Longtime stalwart and three-time 20-game winner Tommy Bridges, who owned a 157-107 record in parts of 11 seasons, including 7-5 thus far in 1940, faced off against Whitehead. Sportswriter George Kirksey opined that Whitehead once "looked like one of the most promising pitchers in baseball," after beginning his career with eight consecutive victories as a member of the Chicago White Sox in 1935.[5] However, the "high and fast life in the big time was too attractive" for the hurler, thought Kirksey, as Whitehead struggled with weight issues, and was traded to Browns in early June of 1939. Following a one-win season, Whitehead was slotted for mop-up duty in 1940, but struggled both before and after his demotion. He had lost all three of his decisions thus far, bringing his career record to 48-54, and sported an atrocious 8.44 ERA in 21⅓ frames.

Under dark, ominous skies, Whitehead came out firing strikes. He set down the first seven Bengal batters before issuing a one-out walk in the third to rookie Scat Metha, who had replaced Gehringer, but was left stranded when Bridges fanned and Dick Bartell fouled out.[6]

If Bridges had a bugaboo, it was his control. For six consecutive seasons (1931-1936) he had issued at least 100 walks, and free passes proved to be his demise in this game. He walked Joe Grace to lead off the third. After George McQuinn's grounder forced Grace at second, rookie Wally Judnich sent Bridges' offering "over top of the right field pavilion," wrote Charles P. Ward in the *Detroit Free Press*, for his 20th round-tripper of the campaign, giving the Browns a 2-0 lead.[7]

Detroit's second and final baserunner of the game was Hank Greenberg, en route to his second AL MVP award. Shortstop Johnny Berardino fielded the slugger's chopper but threw wildly to first sacker McQuinn, the Browns' only miscue of the game. Slugger Rudy York lined sharply to Judnich in center field to end the frame.

"[L]oose defensive work," wrote Tietjen, "hardly the kind you would expect from a club that proposes to succeed the Yankees to the American League throne," characterized the Tigers' fourth.[8] Fielding was a thorn in the Tigers' tail all season long; their 194 errors were second to the Philadelphia A's 238. Harlond "Darkie" Clift beat out a bunt to the mound, then scampered all the way to third when Bridges committed one of the club's two errors in the game by tossing errantly over York's head at first. Light-hitting Don Heffner followed by chopping a single off the plate to drive in Clift for the Browns' third run.

St. Louis tacked in another run in the fifth when Bridges loaded the bases on walks to Rip Radcliff, Clift, and Heffner. The final of those was intentional in order to set up an inning-ending double-play opportunity facing slow-footed catcher Bob Swift. The rookie foiled that plan with an infield groundout that plated Radcliff, who had entered the doubleheader with the highest batting average in baseball (.361).

While Whitehead "showed fine control and had the Tigers hitting the ball into the dirt," in the words of Ward in the *Free Press*, he also benefited from some excellent defensive support.[9] According to McGoogan, right fielder Joe Grace made two one-handed catches of liners that "seemed ticketed for the fence," saving potential extra-base hits.[10] Whitehead, an adept fielder despite his girth (he led AL pitchers with 60 assists in 1936), fielded what McGoogan considered one of the "most difficult chances" by snaring Barney McCosky's "lazy bounder over his head" and sending a bullet to McQuinn.[11]

With the Browns leading 4-0 after 5½ innings, home-plate umpire Harry Geisel halted the game at approximately 6:30 as the intermittent light rain had morphed into a heavy shower an inning earlier and the field deteriorated rapidly. An hour later, he called the game because of the field conditions. The game officially lasted 1 hour and 18 minutes. The Browns' 43rd victory matched their total from the entire 1939 season. The Tigers' loss dropped them into a tie with the Cleveland Indians atop the AL standings, but they went on to capture the pennant by one game over the Tribe.

Whitehead's name graced headlines in sports pages across the country the next day. He punched out two and walked one in hurling the 52nd complete game and ninth shutout of his career. It was the Browns' first no-hitter since another quirky game when Bobo Newsom held the Boston Red Sox hitless through nine innings on September 18, 1934, only to yield a hit and lose the game, 2-1, in the 10th. The Browns' previous regulation no-hitters were by Ernie Koob and Bob Groom, who turned the trick against the Chicago White Sox on consecutive days, May 5 and May 6, 1917. (As of 2016 it marks the only time in major-league history that teammates tossed no-hitters on successive days.)

In September 1991, baseball's Committee for Statistical Accuracy changed the definition of a no-hitter. Led by Commissioner Fay Vincent, the committee declared that only a game lasting at least nine innings and ending with zero hits is considered a no-hitter. Fifty no-hitters were erased from the record books, most notably the 12-inning perfect game by Harvey Haddix of the Pittsburgh Pirates against the Milwaukee Braves on May 26, 1959, which he lost on Joe Adcock's walk-off double in the 13th. Struck, too, from the list of no-hitters were Newsom's and Whitehead's, the former because of a hit in the 10th, the latter because it was not nine innings.

SOURCES

In addition to the sources cited in the Notes, the author also accessed Retrosheet.org, Baseball-Reference.com, SABR.org, and *The Sporting News* archive via Paper of Record.

NOTES

1. W. Vernon Tietjen, "Whitehead Pitches Six-Inning No-Hit Game and Wins, 4-0," *St. Louis Star and Times*, August 6, 1940: 15.

2. Associated Press, "Schoolboy Wins, Bridges Beaten," *Battle Creek* (Michigan) *Enquirer*, August 6, 1940: 11.

3. Tietjen.

4. W.J. McGoogan, "Browns to Bat Against Newsom in Night Game," *St. Louis Post-Dispatch*, August 6, 1940: 1B.

5. George Kirksey, United Press, "Tigers Held Without Hits by Whitehead," *Belvidere* (Illinois) *Daily Republican*, August 6, 1940: 6.

6. Neither Baseball-Reference.com nor Retrosheet.org has a box score for this game. Information about plays is garnered from newspapers.

7. Charles P. Ward, "Rowe Wins Opener, 9-2. Rain Shortens Nightcap," *Detroit Free Press*, August 6, 1940: 11.

8. Tietjen.

9. Ward.

10. McGoogan.

11. McGoogan.

GEORGE MCQUINN HITS FOR CYCLE

July 19, 1941: St. Louis Browns 9, Boston Red Sox 3 (Game One of Doubleheader), at Sportsman's Park

BY MICHAEL HUBER

GEORGE MCQUINN LED THE OFfense as the Browns swept the Boston Red Sox, 9-3 and 4-3, in a doubleheader at Sportsman's Park on July 19, 1941. McQuinn's 4-for-5 performance in the first game included the only batter's cycle of the 1941 season.

McQuinn, considered the best defensive first baseman in the American League at the time, was member of the American League All-Star Team in 1939 and 1940, and would be an All-Star three more times after that.[1] As a fielder he was compared with Joe Kuhel, Hal Chase, and Hall of Famer George Sisler.[2]

This pleasant Saturday afternoon was Ladies Day as Sportsman's Park. Women were admitted "without even having to pay tax and service charge and everybody receiving a cloisonné lapel pin, or a radio or a diamond wrist watch," a St. Louis sportswriter noted with a chuckle.[3] Nonetheless, the announced attendance was a mere 2,620. (Two weeks earlier, the Browns had combined Ladies Day, Stockholders Day, Children's Day, and Soldiers Day to entice fans to the ballpark. J. Roy Stockton, the baseball beat writer for the *St. Louis Post-Dispatch*, commented, "You can see what's wrong with the Browns. They just don't give away enough things. One day they gave away tickets, five to each of the stockholders, and they won two games. Then they gave away admission and radios and lapel pins and watches and they win two more."[4])

Johnny Allen (1-5) and Elden Auker (6-11) were the starting pitchers for the Browns, facing Broadway Charlie Wagner (4-5) and Mickey Harris (3-8) of the third-place Red Sox.

Future Hall of Famer Dizzy Dean was nine days into his new job as the play-by-play broadcaster for Browns and Cardinals home game on St. Louis radio station KWK. in St. Louis. A Boston scribe wrote, "Opinion here is divided on Dizzy's descriptive ability, his supporters claiming that the erstwhile great one's homespun philosophy will overcome the frequent errors of identity he makes."[5]

After Wagner retired the first two batters in the bottom of the first innings, McQuinn "inaugurated the bombardment ... by whacking his 11th round-tripper over the whole right-field works." The ball sailed over the right-field pavilion roof. An inning later Joe Grace homered, sending the ball bouncing off the pavilion roof. In the third, McQuinn tripled with two outs and scored on Wally Judnich's single to right, making the score 3-0. After Wagner walked Roy Cullenbine, he was lifted for Jack Wilson, who retired Grace on a grounder to second to end the inning.

St. Louis was facing a lineup with five All-Stars,[6] yet the 37-year-old Allen, a former 20-game winner who appeared to be on his last legs, cruised. His only major hiccup came in the top of the fourth inning, when Boston's Lou Finney led off with a single, raced to third on Stan Spence's double down the third-base line, and scored (and Spence advanced to third) on a passed ball by catcher Rick Ferrell which a Boston sportswriter opined could have been ruled a wild pitch.[7] Red Sox player-manager Joe Cronin stroked a double, his 100th hit of the season, driving in Spence. Jimmie Foxx followed with a walk, and he and Cronin advanced on a wild pitch. Allen retired the next two batters, but Browns shortstop Johnny Berardino misplayed Johnny Peacock's grounder and Cronin scored the third run for Boston to tie the game.

The Browns immediately roared back, sending 10 batters to the plate against Wilson and Nels Potter in the bottom of the fourth and scoring four runs, all after two men were out. They used four singles (one by McQuinn), a walk, and a hit batsman to plate the runners, leaving the bases loaded.

The Browns put runners on base in every inning except the eighth. McQuinn doubled off Potter with one out in the sixth to complete the cycle. In the bottom of the seventh, with the score 7-3, Grace led off with a walk, then back-to-back doubles by Berardino and Rick Ferrell gave St. Louis two more runs. There was no more scoring. The Browns pounded out 12 hits and drew six walks.

After the Boston fourth, Allen allowed just four singles and two walks the rest of the game. His wild pitch was his eighth of the season. By limiting the Red Sox to two earned runs, Allen lowered his ERA to 6.24. He made one more start for the Browns, on July 24, before being placed on waivers.[8]

McQuinn completed his cycle in four successive at-bats. The first baseman scored three runs and drove in two in the first-game victory. He then had a 1-for-4 performance in the nightcap, which the Browns won, 4-3. McQuinn scored one of those runs. (Fans would have to wait two years, until July 3, 1943, before the next cycle in the major leagues, by Red Sox rookie outfielder Leon Culberson.)

Like McQuinn, Roy Cullenbine drove in two runs in the July 19 twin bill. Cullenbine batted .378 in May and .352 in June, and at the end of the day he was hitting .358. He faded to a season-ending average of .317. For Boston, Ted Williams was batting .393 at the end of the day on his way to a .406 batting average, the last major-league player to bat over .400.

The next day, July 20, featured another doubleheader between the Red Sox and the Browns. Again the Browns swept, 6-3 and 10-0. All three Red Sox runs in the first game came on a pinch-hit home run by Ted Williams in the ninth inning, "all that saved the relapsing Red Sox from a double dose of whitewash."[9] McQuinn hit three home runs in the twin bill, two in the first game and one in the second. For the twin bill, he was 5-for-8, with four RBIs and five runs scored. His batting average at the end of the day

George McQuinn was a six-time All-Star first baseman in his 12-year career. After years of suffering on many poor Browns teams, he won a World Series with the New York Yankees on 1947. (National Baseball Hall of Fame, Cooperstown, New York)

was .322, but he tailed off considerably and finished the season at .297.

In sweeping the Red Sox in two doubleheaders, the Browns had won seven of their last eight games and "looked like a team that might make a loud noise the remainder of the season,"[10] though after the two sweeps they were still deep in seventh place with a 34-51 record, 24½ games behind the league-leading New York Yankees. The Browns had been in seventh or eighth place in the American League since May 1. After the July 19 sweep, the Browns won 38 and lost 33, sneaking into sixth place. On June 5 Luke Sewell had taken over as St. Louis manager, succeeding Fred Haney. His record for the remainder of the season was 55-55. Sewell stayed at the helm through 1946, taking the Browns to the World Series in 1944. For the Red Sox, Joe Cronin was in his seventh of 13 seasons as manager. In 1941 the team won 84 games and lost 70 (.545), and finished in second place, 17 games behind the Yankees. In 15 seasons as manager for Washington and Boston, Cronin's winning percentage was .540, so this was a "typical" season. He did win the American league pennant in 1933 with the Senators and in 1946 with the Red Sox. (Cronin relinquished the managerial reins to become the Red Sox general manager in 1948, and later served from 1959 until 1973 as president of the American League.)

Coincidentally, the previous time a player hit for the cycle at Sportsman's Park, it was before a Ladies Day crowd. The Cardinals' Johnny Mize did it against the New York Giants on July 13, 1940. The Cardinals swept a doubleheader that day, too.[11]

Postscript

The author thanks Lisa Tuite of the *Boston Globe* for her assistance with obtaining sources.

NOTES

1. McQuinn was an American League All-Star in 1939, 1940, 1942 (all with the Browns) and in 1947 and 1948 (with the Yankees). He did not play in the 1939, '40, or '42 games, but was the starting first baseman in 1947 and 1948.
2. C. Paul Rogers, "George McQuinn," sabr.org/bioproj/person/394ab9a8.
3. J. Roy Stockton, "Allen and Auker Beat Red Sox, 9-3, 4-3," *St. Louis Post-Dispatch*, July 20, 1941: 35.
4. Ibid.
5. Gerry Moore, "Browns Twice Top Faltering Red Sox," *Boston Sunday Globe*, July 20, 1941: 21. Dean had started broadcasting on July 10. See Joseph Wancho's biography of Dizzy Dean at sabr.org/bioproj/person/40bc224d.
6. The 1941 Red Sox had Bobby Doerr, Ted Williams, Joe Cronin, Jimmie Foxx, and Dom DiMaggio elected to the All-Star Game. Only Roy Cullenbine represented the Browns.
7. Moore.
8. On July 30, 1941, Johnny Allen was selected off waivers by the Brooklyn Dodgers, and spent parts of the next three seasons with Brooklyn.
9. Gerry Moore, "Sox Again Lose Two to Browns," *Boston Globe*, July 21, 1941: 2.
10. Associated Press, "Browns Turn Back Red Sox, 9-3 and 4-3," *New York Times*, July 20, 1941: S3.
11. See "Johnny Mize Triples, Scores and Earns a Cycle as Cardinals Sweep Giants with Walk-Offs" from July 13, 1940.

CARDINALS LOSE, 1-0, IN "ONE OF THE GREATEST GAMES IN THE HISTORY OF THE MAJOR LEAGUES"

September 13, 1941: Brooklyn Dodgers 1, St. Louis Cardinals 0, at Sportsman's Park

BY LYLE SPATZ

HISTORIAN BILL JAMES HAS CALLED the 1941 Brooklyn Dodgers "that close to being a perfect team," citing their lineup that had future Hall of Famers Joe Medwick in left field, Pee Wee Reese at shortstop, and Billy Herman at second base and included such other luminaries as Pete Reiser, Dixie Walker, and Dolph Camilli. "In the history of baseball, that is probably as close as any team has ever come to putting out a lineup of eight legitimate stars," James wrote.[1]

On September 11, 1941, those Dodgers arrived in St. Louis for their final three games against the St. Louis Cardinals, with whom they had waged a season-long battle for the National League pennant. Brooklyn's lead was one game, with just over two weeks left in the season.

The local press was calling it the "Little World Series," the same designation sportswriters had used for the crucial late-season series played at Sportsman's Park between the St. Louis Browns and the New York Yankees in 1922. Baby Doll Jacobson, the star center fielder of that Browns team, visited the Cardinals dressing room to wish them luck.[2]

The Dodgers won the first game, 6-4, on Dixie Walker's two-run single in the 11th inning. It was a sloppily played game, with each team committing four errors. Brooklyn's lead grew to two games. The crowds were as rabid at Sportsman's Park as they had been at Ebbets Field two weeks earlier, and tension on the field was as great as it was in the stands.

The bench jockeys from both teams had taunted one another all afternoon, and several players had lodged complaints with umpire Al Barlick. The Dodgers' aggressively belligerent manager, Leo Durocher, was at the forefront of all the complaints and arguments, as he always was. Before the September 12 game, NL President Ford Frick met with Durocher, Cardinals manager Billy Southworth, and the umpires and ordered them to tone down the badgering and arguing.

St. Louis, behind the pitching of Howie Pollet and Max Lanier, won the middle game of the series, 4-3, setting up the rubber game on Saturday. Brooklyn's lead was again down to one game, and unless the two teams ended the season deadlocked, this would be their final meeting.

The third game, on Saturday, September 13, drew a crowd of 32,691, Sportsman's Park's largest non-Sunday crowd since 1927. Cardinals fans were as devoted to their team as Dodgers fans were to theirs. Durocher started Whit Wyatt (19-10), while Southworth chose Mort Cooper (13-6).

Because of the stakes involved, this game between the Dodgers and Cardinals was among the most dramatic ever in the history of these longtime rivals. Through seven innings, neither team could score. Wyatt, normally a fast worker, was pitching at a much more deliberate pace than usual and had been in trouble in the fifth and sixth innings.

In the fifth the Cardinals had runners at first and third with no outs, but Wyatt struck out Gus Mancuso and Cooper, and Jimmy Brown grounded out. After retiring the first two batters in the sixth, he gave up a single to Johnny Mize and hit Estel Crabtree with a pitch. A passed ball by catcher Herman Franks allowed the runners to move up a base. Durocher chose to intentionally walk Frank Crespi and pitch to Marty Marion. Loading the bases in that situation was a daring move, but Wyatt justified it by getting Marion on a pop fly to his opposing shortstop, Pee Wee Reese.

Meanwhile, Brooklyn had managed five walks against Cooper, but the Cardinals right-hander had allowed no hits. Dixie Walker ended the potential no-hitter in the eighth inning with a one-out double to right-center. Next up was Billy Herman, who also ripped a double to right-center, driving in what would be the game's only run. "Walker, running as if a horde of red demons were on his heels, galloped across with the all-important run," wrote Roscoe McGowen in the *New York Times*.[3]

Walker said after the game that he stole catcher Mancuso's sign and signaled Herman that the next pitch would be a curveball. "Billy's eyes bugged out so far that I was sure the Cardinals would catch on and switch," he said.[4]

Wyatt retired the last six St. Louis batters, including a strikeout of pinch-hitter Enos Slaughter to end the game and give him his 20th win. Slaughter, along with Terry Moore, had been out for the past month. He had taken batting practice, but his shoulder was still too sore for him to play the field. The pinch-hitting appearance was his first game action since the injury.

Speaking of this game years later, Wyatt said, "I think that was the best game I ever pitched in my life." When Slaughter came up to pinch-hit in the ninth, Durocher came out and said, "You know this fellow can hurt you, don't you?"[5] Wyatt did know, but he struck out the rusty Slaughter on three fastballs.

Despite losing Moore and Slaughter, Cardinals president Branch Rickey waited until four days after this game to bring up the team's best prospect, outfielder Stan Musial, from the International League's Rochester Red Wings. "Why didn't he bring Musial up earlier? That's what all the players wanted to know," remembered Johnny Mize. "We might have gone ahead and won the pennant."[6]

That winter Walker discussed the three games in St. Louis with *The Sporting News*'s editor, J.G. Taylor Spink. "I have been in baseball for some years, but that series of three games with the Cardinals was the most thrilling of my life," Dixie told Spink. "We won that series because we rode the younger St. Louis players into the jitters." Walker called Wyatt's win over Cooper "one of the greatest games in the history of the major leagues."[7]

NOTES

1. Bill James, *The New Bill James Historical Baseball Abstract* (New York: Free Press, 2001), 207.

2. Bill Borst, "Showdown in St. Louis," *The National Pastime* (1991): 63-64.

3. Roscoe McGowen, *New York Times*, September 14, 1941.

4. *Brooklyn Daily Eagle*, December 11, 1952.

5. Thomas Liley, "Whit Wyatt—The Dodgers' 1941 Ace," in David L. Porter, ed., *Biographical Dictionary of American Sports: Q-Z* (Westport, Connecticut: Greenwood Press), 47.

6. Donald Honig, *Baseball When the Grass Was Real* (New York: Coward, McCann & Geoghegan, 1975), 92.

7. J.G. Taylor Spink, "Always Something Doing With Dixie," *The Sporting News*, December 25, 1941.

STAN MUSIAL DEBUTS

September 17, 1941: St. Louis Cardinals 3, Boston Braves 2, at Sportsman's Park

BY JOE SCHUSTER

IN SPRING TRAINING BEFORE THE 1941 season, the St. Louis Cardinals listed Stan Musial on the roster as a pitcher.[1] His numbers from the previous year would suggest this was sensible. Although he also played the outfield on days he was not on the mound and had finished among the top 10 hitters in the Florida State League with his .311 average, he also ranked among the best hurlers in the circuit, leading the league in won-loss percentage with an 18-5 record and ranking in the top 10 in victories and ERA (2.62) among pitchers with at least 100 innings on the mound.[2]

Hidden in those statistics, however, was an arm injury Musial suffered diving for a fly ball in August that kept him out of 20 games.[3] Early in the 1941 preseason, the injury's effect was evident in several abysmal outings that made Musial a candidate for release.[4]

However, Ollie Vanek, manager of the Cardinals' Class-C Western Association team in Springfield, Missouri, had once managed a Redbirds farm team near Musial's hometown of Donora, Pennsylvania, and had seen him work out for scouts before the Cardinals signed him. Mindful of his performance at the plate in 1940, Vanek asked the organization if it would allow him to add Musial to his roster.[5]

Given that second chance, Musial caught fire immediately. For the first two months of the season his batting average hovered around .400.[6] By late July he was running away from the rest of the league in nearly every offensive category, hitting .379 with 26 home runs, 94 RBIs, and a .739 slugging average. The Cardinals promoted him to Double-A Rochester in the International League, where he batted .326 over the last six weeks of their season, helping the team run off a streak of 16 wins in its final 20 games that put the team in the International League playoffs.

Once the playoffs ended, St. Louis called Musial up to the big leagues. The news received relatively modest attention in the press. The *St. Louis Post-Dispatch*, for example, reported that the team had added Musial to the roster, summarizing his season's statistics, but giving considerably more attention in the article to first baseman Ray Sanders, who had finished second in the American Association in RBIs and among the leaders in batting average and home runs.[7] St. Louis's other major daily paper, the *Globe-Democrat*, gave Musial even less ink, merely listing his name along with four other players the team had brought up.[8]

As it turned out, Sanders did not play for the Cardinals until the next season, while a week after the press reported his recall, Musial found himself in the starting lineup for a team fighting for the pennant.

When Musial joined the club, it was in second place, 1½ games behind Brooklyn, and struggling through an offensive dry spell: Over the previous 15 games, the team had hit a combined .218 and had managed to go 8-6-1 over that stretch largely on the strength of its pitching.[9]

It was because of this slump and Billy Southworth's desire for outfield reinforcement through the last two weeks of the pennant chase that the Cardinals decided to bring Musial up in September rather than wait until the next spring.[10]

reported to Sportsman's Park on Tuesday, September 16. His arrival was marked by a photo session, for which he and fellow call-up Erv Dusak

A converted pitcher, 20-year-old Stan Musial hit .426 (20-for-47) as a September call-up in 1941 and the rest is history. (National Baseball Hall of Fame, Cooperstown, New York)

posed for an AP photographer admiring each other's new Cardinals white home uniforms.[11] Musial already wore what would become one of the most iconic numbers in baseball history, 6, which clubhouse attendant Butch Yatkeman had given him simply because the number was available and the jersey fit.[12]

He made his major-league debut the next day, in the second game of a doubleheader against the lowly Boston Braves, who were in seventh place among eight teams, 32 games out of first. The Cardinals had taken the opener, 6-1, thanks to five unearned runs in the eighth, to keep pace with Brooklyn, which had won its game against the Pittsburgh Pirates to hold onto a 1½-game lead over St. Louis.

For the nightcap, Southworth shuffled his outfield. He rested center fielder Terry Moore, who had returned to the team only three days earlier from a month's layoff after being hit in the head by a pitch; moved Johnny Hopp from left field to center, shifted Estel Crabtree from right field to left, and started Musial in right and batted him third.[13] He sent southpaw Max Lanier, 8-8, against the Braves' Jim Tobin, a right-handed knuckleballer who had the misfortune of being a good pitcher on a bad team: he ended the year among the top 10 in several key statistical categories and, despite finishing 12-12, earned a handful of votes for MVP.

It was a pleasant afternoon, in the high 80 degrees and the sky clear as a ladies-day special drew 7,713 fans to the park. After Lanier set down the Braves in order in the top of the first, the Cards put their leadoff hitter on base when Jimmy Brown singled, but he was doubled off when Braves center fielder Gene Moore made a spectacular catch on a Hopp line drive to the wall and Brown couldn't get back to first before the throw.[14] That brought Musial to the plate for his first major-league at-bat.

In his 1964 autobiography, *Stan Musial: The Man's Own Story*, which he wrote with sportswriter Bob Broeg the year after he retired as a player, Musial described his debut: "[The] first knuckleball I'd ever seen. It fluttered up the plate, big as a grapefruit but dancing like a dust devil. Off-stride, fooled, I popped up weakly to Sibby Sisti, playing third base for Boston."[15]

Although he'd been flummoxed in the first, by the time Musial came to the plate again, in the bottom of the third of a still-scoreless game, with two outs and runners on first and second thanks to an infield single by Lanier and a walk to Hopp, he'd figured out how to hit the pitch. As he said in his autobiography: "I learned to delay my stride, cut down on my swing and just stroke the ball."[16]

Fittingly for the player who, when he retired 22 years later, held the National League record for doubles, Musial laced the ball to the wall in right-center for a two-base hit, driving in the first two of what would eventually be 1,951 career RBIs and giving the Cardinals a 2-0 lead.[17]

Tobin settled in after that and held the Cards to only one hit — a single by Musial — between the fourth inning and the eighth. Lanier, meanwhile, was limiting the Braves to two hits through the first six.

In the top of the seventh, however, two defensive lapses by St. Louis allowed Boston to tie the score. With one out, Creepy Crespi misplayed a groundball and Eddie Miller followed it with a drive to right that Musial, "who appeared nervous … didn't play too well," allowing the Braves to get on the board.[18] Boston added its second run on a single by Moore.

In the ninth Boston threatened. Carvel Rowell led off with a double and first baseman John Dudra bunted along the first-base line but rather than advance, Rowell stayed put. The *Globe-Democrat* account of the game said Rowell's decision likely cost his team a run because shortstop Marty Marion had to range far to his left to snag a groundball by Frank Demaree that would have plated Rowe had he advanced.[19] Marion's play effectively ended the threat as Lanier retired the side on a groundout by Johnny Cooney.

That set up a sudden and dramatic finish in the bottom of the inning. Leading off, Crabtree watched the first pitch go by for a ball and then drove the second, a low knuckler, to the pavilion roof "with the ease of Ben Hogan lofting a No. 9 iron."[20] The win moved the Cards to within a game of Brooklyn.

In the aftermath, the headlines went, rightly so, to Crabtree, a 37-year-old reclamation project for St. Louis that year; the team had plucked him out of the minors, where he had played the last seven-plus seasons after spending three years in the major leagues. Not only had he hit the walk-off winner in the second game of the afternoon, he had also homered in the opener.

But Musial, too, earned ink. Southworth told reporters he was "impressed" by his performance.[21] The *Post-Dispatch* noted that, without his play, Lanier would have been saddled with a disappointing loss.[22]

In the end, the Cardinals fell short of the pennant, finishing 2½ games behind Brooklyn, but Musial made plain through his play that he would be a force in the game. That September he appeared in a dozen games, hitting .426 and driving in seven runs. It was impressive enough that, despite his limited résumé that season, he earned votes for the Rookie of the Year award.[23]

SOURCES

In addition to the sources cited in the Notes, the author also accessed Retrosheet.org, Baseball-Reference.com, and SABR.org.

NOTES

1 "East Coast Breezes," *The Sporting News*, March 13, 1941: 8.

2   Unless otherwise noted, all statistics are from Baseball Reference: baseball-reference.com/players/m/musiast01.shtml.

3   Jan Finkel, "Stan Musial," Society for American Baseball Research Biography Project. sabr.org/bioproj/person/2142e2e5. Accessed September 19, 2016.

4   James Giglio, *Musial from Stash to Stan the Man* (Columbia: University of Missouri Press, 2001), 39.

5   George Vecsey, *Stan Musial: An American Life* (New York: Ballantine Books, 2011), 77

6   "Latest Batting and Pitching Averages," *The Sporting News*, July 3, 1941: 12.

7   "Cardinals Buy Sanders from Columbus Farm," *St. Louis Post-Dispatch*, September 10, 1941: 15.

8   "Pollet and Lanier Face Braves Today," *St. Louis Globe-Democrat*, September 17, 1941: 4B.

9   "Good Pitching Helps Birds Win Twin Bill from Braves," *St. Louis Post-Dispatch*, September 18, 1941: 15.

10 "Cards Send Hurry Call for Musial and George Kurowski," *Dunkirk* (New York) *Evening Observer*, September 16, 1941: 12.

11 "They're Redbirds Now," *St. Louis Post-Dispatch*, September 17, 1941: 11.

12 Vecsey, 84.

13 "Lanier and Tobin Hurl Nightcap," *St. Louis Post-Dispatch*, September 17, 1941: 11.

14 Martin J. Haley, "Birds One Game Behind After 6-1, 3-2 Triumphs," *St. Louis Globe-Democrat*, September 18, 1941: 3B.

15 Stan Musial and Bob Broeg, *Stan Musial: "The Man's" Own Story, as Told to Bob Broeg* (Garden City, New York: Doubleday & Company, 1964), 49.

16 Ibid.

17 James P. Dawson, "Cardinals Subdue Braves, 6-1, 3-2; Crabtree's Homer Takes Nightcap," *New York Times*, September 18, 1941: 32.

18 W. Vernon Tietjen, "Cards, Game Behind, to Start Cooper Today," *St. Louis Star-Times*, September 18, 1941: 22.

19 Haley.

20 Ibid.

21 Ibid.

22 "Good Pitching."

23 "Pete Gets Big Pat from 'Chi' Writers," *The Sporting News*, December 25, 1941: 5.

NEGRO LEAGUE TEAMS SQUARE OFF ON DECORATION DAY

May 30, 1942: New York Black Yankees 8, Birmingham Black Barons 4, at Sportsman's Park

BY DWAYNE ISGRIG

ON A WARM SATURDAY AFTERnoon in May, with the nation's list of war dead growing as the country battled in two theaters of war, the baseball fans of St Louis were given a rare treat. Big-league black baseball came to town and put on a show at Sportsman's Park. The New York Black Yankees defeated the Birmingham Black Barons, 8-4. Such was the scene, with more than 11,000 spectators present, on the first Decoration Day of World War II.

The game was won and lost in the course of the fifth inning when the Black Yankees' bats feasted on Birmingham pitching, stringing together six runs on seven hits.[1]

St Louis had hosted big-league black baseball until 1931, when the economic turmoil of the Great Depression forced the Negro National League out of business. During the 1910s and up to the formation of Rube Foster's Negro National League (NNL) in 1920, the city was home to the St Louis Giants. The Giants hit a financial snag in 1921 that led to a change in ownership and a new name—the Stars—for 1922. The Stars continued in the NNL and were a powerful team, winning pennants in 1928, 1930, and 1931 behind stars like Cool Papa Bell, Willie Wells, and Mule Suttles.[2] The Stars played their home games at Stars Park, located near the intersection of Compton and Laclede Avenues, close to the campus of St. Louis University, about two miles south of Sportsman's Park. After the NNL folded and the Stars' reign ended, it became rare for the Mound City to host big-league black baseball games.

While some big-league stadiums, like Forbes Field in Pittsburgh, Griffith Stadium in Washington, and Comiskey Park in Chicago, hosted black baseball regularly, Negro League teams rarely played at Sportsman's Park. The ballpark, at the corner of Grand and Dodier, was the home to the Browns and the Cardinals and the seating was segregated. Black patrons were allowed to sit only in the section known as the right-field pavilion, a practice that would not end until 1944.[3]

But with the winds of war came change. Even in 1941, prior to the United States entering World War II, some things were beginning to change. In cities throughout the country, there was a push for greater inclusion for black workers in war jobs. A. Philip Randolph and the March on Washington Movement made strides in gaining greater inclusion in factories. President Franklin D. Roosevelt issued Executive Order 8802, which established the Fair Employment Practices Committee to try to ensure nondiscriminatory hiring practices in factories that supplied war materials under federal government contracts. Satchel Paige twice brought teams to St. Louis in 1941 to play at Sportsman's Park, once on the Fourth of July, a game that saw Paige and the game's organizers push for and achieve more inclusive seating practices for black patrons at the ballpark, and again in October versus Bob Feller and his major league all-stars.[4]

One of the interesting highlights of the game on Decoration Day between the Black Yankees and Black Barons was the pitching of Gene Smith for the New York team. In the words of one scholar, Smith was a "power pitcher, he had a good fastball and slider," who had three no-hitters during his career.[5] On this day at Sportsman's Park, though he was erratic, with two wild pitches, a hit batsman and 11 walks. Nonetheless, Smith pitched a complete game and surrendered only five hits. In a few tight spots over the course of the game, Smith was able to buckle down and make the pitches he needed to strand Black Barons on the bases.

The Black Yankees began the scoring in the second inning with two runs. The Black Barons countered with three in the third to take the lead.

Things would stay that way until the fifth inning, when the Black Yankees opened the floodgates with six runs crossing the plate.

Dan Bankhead, who would later play with the Brooklyn Dodgers, appeared in relief in the game for the Black Barons. Bankhead, one of a family of five brothers who played in the Negro Leagues, was a hard-throwing right-handed pitcher. He was known for a "blazing fastball and a tantalizing screwball."[6] When Bankhead debuted with the Dodgers on August 26, 1947, joining teammate Jackie Robinson, he became the first black pitcher in the National League. Bankhead hit a home run in his pitching debut though his time on the mound was not so successful, as he appeared in 52 games over parts of three seasons with an ERA of 6.52. Bankhead and Robinson finished the year with the Dodgers losing to the Yankees in the World Series.[7]

Local fans had a special treat in the game thanks to the fact that the Black Yankees fielded three players from St. Louis: Smith, Leslie "Chin" Green, and Dan Wilson. The Black Barons had only one player from St. Louis on their roster, of Bill Bradford. One local writer noted that the Black Barons were "shopping around for more after seeing what three could do."[8]

Before the marquee game, fans were treated to a beauty pageant with the title of Miss Midwest on the line. There was also a patriotic display with a boys and girls drum and bugle corps demonstration. As Normal "Tweed" Webb of the *St. Louis Argus* noted, "even in the midst of the baseball spectacle, the war was not forgotten."[9]

There was also a preliminary contest featuring two local teams. The Cosmopolitan Insurance Company (Cosmo) and the East St. Louis Colts squared off for local bragging rights. Doc Brackens toed the slab for the Colts while Lefty Whitlock pitched for the Cosmo club. Whitlock and the Cosmo team won the game, 7-1.[10]

NOTES

1   *Chicago Defender*, June 6, 1942; *St. Louis Argus*, June 5, 1942; *St. Louis Post-Dispatch*, May 31, 1942.

2   Dick Clark and Larry Lester, eds., *The Negro Leagues Book* (Cleveland: Society for American Baseball Research, 1994); John Holway, *The Complete Book of Baseball's Negro Leagues: The Other Half of Baseball History* (Fern Park, Florida: Hastings House Publishers, 2001).

3   *Chicago Defender*, May 13, 1944; *St. Louis Argus*, May 19, 1944.

4   *Chicago Defender*, July 12, 1941; Andrew Kersten, *A. Philip Randolph: A Life in the Vanguard* (Lanham, Maryland: Rowman and Littlefield Publishers, 2007); *St. Louis Argus*, July 11, 1941; *St. Louis Globe-Democrat*, July 4, 1941, October 6, 1941; *St. Louis Post-Dispatch*, July 4, 1941.

5   James A. Riley, *The Biographical Encyclopedia of the Negro Baseball Leagues* (New York: Carroll and Graf/Richard Gallen, 1994).

6   Riley.

7   Lyle Spatz, ed., *The Team That Forever Changed Baseball and America: The 1947 Brooklyn Dodgers* (Lincoln, Nebraska: University of Nebraska and Society for American Baseball Research, 2012); Jules Tygiel, *Baseball's Great Experiment: Jackie Robinson and His Legacy* (New York: Vintage Books, 1984);

8   *St. Louis Argus*, June 5, 1942; *St. Louis Globe-Democrat*, May 30, 1942.

9   *Pittsburgh Courier*, May 30, 1942; *St. Louis Argus*, June 5, 1942; *St. Louis Star-Times*, May 27, 1942.

10   *St. Louis Argus*, June 5, 1942.

MARION'S DASH PRESERVES COOPER'S 14-INNING GEM

August 25, 1942: St. Louis Cardinals 2, Brooklyn Dodgers 1 (14 Innings), at Sportsman's Park

BY JIM WOHLENHAUS

Described as "the largest throng to see a night game in the Mound City," a capacity crowd of 33,527, including 267 servicemen, packed Sportsman's Park to see the invading Brooklyn Dodgers face the hometown St. Louis Cardinals on August 25, 1942.[1] The Sporting News praised the game as "one of the tensest, most dramatic games ever played in Sportsman's Park," with the Cardinals emerging victorious, 2-1, in 14 thrilling innings.[2] "It also was the toughest contest of the season in St. Louis," continued the publication, "and the longest night game in the league since Larry MacPhail started the nocturnal shows in Cincinnati in 1935."[3]

What made this game so interesting to the fans of St. Louis was that they had trailed Brooklyn in the standings all season to this point and were poised to make a charge.

The 1942 Dodgers were tied for the third-best record through 81 games since 1901 with a record of 58-23. The Cardinals were 50-31, eight games behind.[4] The trend for Brooklyn continued as St. Louis was 10 back on August 5, their worst deficit of the year. Then the Cardinals started to turn it around and went 44-9 while Brooklyn went 31-20 for the remainder of the 1942 season. The Cardinals won the pennant by two games in one of the most impressive stretch drives in major-league history, and this late-August series was when things started to get serious.

The two teams had played each other 17 times previously in 1942 and the Cardinals had won nine. After this night's game the teams would meet four more times. Since the low point of the Cardinals' season (measured by games behind) on August 5 until the 25th, the Cardinals had scored 122 runs, an average of 5.8 per game. Brooklyn had scored 68, an average of 4.2, and not surprisingly the Dodgers' lead had narrowed from 10 games to 6½.

This game was the second of a four-game series and started off as a pitchers' duel. The two starters, Whitlow Wyatt for Brooklyn and Mort Cooper for St. Louis, were facing off for the fourth time in the season. Wyatt was 1-2 with a 5.40 ERA in those matchups while Cooper was 2-1 with a 2.11 ERA. Overall, Cooper had 15 wins and 7 losses with a 2.04 ERA, while Wyatt had 15 wins and 4 losses, and a 2.71 ERA.

Through the first eight innings, manager Leo Durocher's Dodgers had been on base seven times with five hits, an error, and a walk. The walk and error were each erased by the next batter via double-play balls. Only twice was more than one runner on base: In the fifth Billy Herman doubled and Mickey Owen walked, but then Wyatt grounded into a 6-4-3 double play. In the seventh, Joe Medwick and Herman singled back-to-back with two outs, but Owen grounded out to first baseman Johnny Hopp to end that threat.

Brooklyn was its own worst enemy in the ninth. After Pete Reiser fouled to third baseman Whitey Kurowski, Dolph Camilli doubled to right and tried to get the game closer to closure by stretching it to a triple. A fine throw from right fielder Enos Slaughter to Kurowski led to a rundown with Marty Marion receiving the throw from Kurowski and Marion then throwing it back to Kurowski, who tagged Camilli for the second out of the inning. Dixie Walker, the next batter, singled, but Medwick forced Walker at second.

Billy Southworth's Cardinals had only four hits through nine innings, although they did augment them with four walks and benefited from a throwing error by Owen, the Brooklyn catcher. There were two mild threats. Walker Cooper led off the fifth with a single but was forced out by Hopp. Owen tried to double Hopp off first after catching Kurowski's foul pop but his throw was wild and Hopp advanced to second. However, after an intentional walk to Marion, Mort Cooper flied out to end the inning.

In the sixth, after one out, Terry Moore and Slaughter walked consecutively, but Musial popped to short and Walker Cooper flied out to end that threat.

Scoreless after nine, the game went into extra innings.

In the next three innings, with the game still scoreless, probably the most exciting moments came in the 12th, when Durocher started questioning a ball call on Walker, who eventually flied out to Moore in center. After Medwick singled, Durocher came out of the dugout and confronted the home-plate umpire, George Barr. Durocher was immediately ejected. Barr later tossed Brooklyn coach Charlie Dressen in the bottom of the inning for continuing to argue balls and strikes after Marion had walked.

The game went into the 13th inning before either team scored. The Dodgers got on the scoreboard first. Owen led off with a single and Wyatt sacrificed him to second. Two batters later, Lew Riggs hit a single to score Owen with the game's first run.

In the Cardinals' half of the 13th, Slaughter walked with one out and Musial moved him to second with a single. Walker Cooper came through with another single and Slaughter scored the tying run. Larry French relieved Wyatt and induced pinch-hitter Coaker Triplett, batting for Hopp, to ground into an inning-ending 4-3 double play.

In the top of the 14th the Dodgers went out on three harmless infield outs by Camilli, Walker, and Medwick. Kurowski led off the Cardinals' half of the inning with a single. After Les Webber relieved French, Marion laid down a sacrifice bunt. First baseman Camilli tried to get the lead runner, Kurowski, at second but the throw was too late. Runners on first and second and nobody out.

Mort Cooper hit a tapper to the mound. Webber threw to Riggs to get Kurowski at third. There were still runners on first and second, but now one out. Jimmy Brown walked, loading the bases for Moore. With the infield drawn in, he hit a smash to third baseman Riggs, who fell attempting to field the ball. He scrambled to his feet and fired home but it was too late to get Marion, who came across with the winning run. After 3 hours and 30 minutes of hard-fought baseball, the Cardinals had prevailed, 2-1.[5] The victory went to Mort Cooper, who pitched all 14 innings, surrendering 10 hits and just one walk.

St. Louis won the next day's game in walk-off fashion as well, before losing the series finale. But the Cardinals had reduced Brooklyn's once seemingly insurmountable lead to 5½ games on their way to an eventual pennant and World Series championship.

SOURCES

In addition to the sources in the Notes, the author also accessed his own game scoresheet, BaseballReference.com, and Retrosheet.org.

NOTES

1. *The Sporting News*, September 3, 1942: 11.
2. Ibid.
3. Ibid.
4. David Nemec, *The Great Book of Baseball Knowledge* (Lincolnwood, Illinois: Masters Press, 1999), 417.
5. As it turned out, the final numbers for the August 25 game were like those of the May 20 game, a 1-0 St. Louis victory. In that game both pitchers threw complete games. Wyatt gave up four Cardinals hits and Cooper gave up two Dodgers hits.

RUFFING WINS OPENER OF SERIES: CARDINALS DO NOT GO QUIETLY

September 30, 1942: New York Yankees 7, St. Louis Cardinals 4, at Sportsman's Park

Game One of the World Series

BY GREG ERION

USUALLY THE OPENING GAME OF A World Series generates a great deal of excitement. Hometown fans are thrilled that their club has reached the ultimate series to determine who will reign as the world champion. While that occurred in 1942, it played out against a different, more somber backdrop.

World War II was well under way. All attention was focused on the horrific conflict between German and Russian forces to determine who would gain mastery over Stalingrad. Nearer to home, hearts were with sons, brothers, fathers, and other loved ones in the Pacific, where at that moment the US struggle to hold Guadalcanal against repeated Japanese efforts captured daily newspaper headlines. The war demanded concern. The Series offered momentary distraction from that concern.

Specifically, that distraction would take place at Sportsman's Park in St. Louis, where the hometown Cardinals were appearing in the World Series for the first time since 1934. Their rivals were the New York Yankees, favored to win, favored at 4-to-1 odds.[1] Those odds were born of considerable logic. The Yankees had appeared in 12 Series, including five of the last six, during which they won 20 of 24 games, including sweeps in 1938 and 1939. Their roster included the likes of Joe DiMaggio, Bill Dickey, Charlie Keller, Phil Rizzuto, and Joe Gordon, who would be named the American League Most Valuable Player for 1942. DiMaggio, Gordon, and Keller each drove in over 100 runs for a team that led the league in runs scored. The pitching staff, equally adept, contained such talents as Tiny Bonham (21-5), Spud Chandler (16-5), and Red Ruffing (14-7). At 2.91, their team ERA was the American League's best. Their 13th pennant was a foregone conclusion by the end of August. They finished nine games ahead of the Boston Red Sox.

Not only did the Yankees have a strong team, they also were familiar with Sportsman's Park, having regularly played the American League Browns there during the regular season. Thus any hometown advantage the Cardinals might have enjoyed, their familiarity with the poorly maintained infield that plagued visiting players, or the idiosyncrasies of play in the outfield, was largely negated.[2]

The Cardinals, by contrast, had to generate a stunning 21-4 run in September, part of a 44-9 effort, to pull ahead of the Brooklyn Dodgers, clinching the pennant on the last day of the season. They too led their league in hitting and runs scored. Their ERA of 2.55 was easily the best in the majors. As opposed to the mostly veteran Yankees, the Cardinals lineup was made up of relative youngsters like 21-year-old Stan Musial, 24-year-old Whitey Kurowski, and 25-year-old Marty Marion. Twenty-four-year-old rookie Johnny Beazley (21-6) and Mort Cooper (22-7) led the pitching staff. Overall, the team was nearly two years younger than its American League counterparts. Unlike the Yankees, the Cardinals' experience in the World Series was virtually nil.[3]

Overshadowing all was a constant reminder that World War II was its height. These reminders manifested themselves in various ways. Military personnel around the world were able to hear the Series via shortwave radio, and the Army Emergency Relief Fund received part of the gate receipts.[4] The war effort had priority on rail transportation. Giants manager Mel Ott, bumped off his train en route to the Series by military personnel, never made it. He returned to New York. Johnny Sturm, the Yankees' first baseman in the 1941 World Series, was on hand to watch the game—as a corporal in the Army. Lieutenant Hank Greenberg, the 1940 Most Valuable Player, attended as well.[5] But for the war, both players would have been on major-league rosters. Dozens of other players serving in various branches of the military could have made the same claim.

Managerial talent for the Series pitted experience vs. newness. Yankees skipper Joe McCarthy was looking for his seventh championship. His counterpart, Billy Southworth, was looking for his first. Southworth had managed St. Louis in 1929 for part of the season. The team got off to a mediocre start and Southworth lost his job, demoted to manage the Cardinals' minor-league team in Rochester. After several years, he left baseball. Eventually he rejoined the Cardinals organization and in 1940 received the call to take over the Redbirds. Now he was facing the most successful manager in World Series history. Southworth choose Mort Cooper to start. His 22-7 record, compiled on the strength of a league-leading 1.78 ERA, made Cooper's selection an easy one.

McCarthy named Red Ruffing to open the Series. The 37-year-old Ruffing had solid credentials in postseason play. He held the record for most World Series victories (six); he had started eight Series games. This was his seventh World Series. There were 34,769 fans at Sportsman's Park to see the apparent David vs. Goliath contest. New York drew first blood in the fourth on DiMaggio's single, a walk to Dickey, and Buddy Hassett's RBI double. The Yankees scored again in the fifth on Red Rolfe's single, Roy Cullenbine's double, and a run-scoring infield grounder, making it 2-0.

In the eighth New York struck again with three runs on three hits and a dropped fly ball by Enos Slaughter in left. The 5-0 lead appeared to be more than enough for Ruffing, who had kept the Cardinals from scoring. And hitting. The Redbirds were hitless through seven. In the bottom of the eighth Ruffing struck out Harry Walker and got Jimmy Brown to pop up to Rizzuto. With Brown's popup Ruffing set a record—no other pitcher had gone so deep into a Series game without allowing a hit. Former teammate Monte Pearson had no-hit the Reds in 1939's World Series before giving up a single to Ernie Lombardi with one out in the eighth. Another former teammate, Herb Pennock, had also pitched 7⅓ innings of hitless ball in 1927 against the Pirates. Both times the Yankees had gone on to sweep the Series.

Pennock was four outs away from pitching the first no-hitter in World Series history. Then, with two outs in the eighth, Terry Moore, the Redbirds' center fielder, broke Ruffing's hold by singling to right. Any solace the Cardinals might have gained from breaking up Ruffing's hitless effort vanished in the top of the ninth when New York scored two more runs thanks to two errors on throws by relief pitcher Max Lanier. Going into the bottom of the ninth, St. Louis was down 7-0.

Musial popped out to Dickey to open the ninth. Walker Cooper, Mort's brother and batterymate, reached on an infield hit—just the second hit off Ruffing. When Johnny Hopp flied out to left it looked as if Ruffing was going to pick up his eighth complete game in World Series play, but it was not to be. Three hits (including Marion's two-run triple and Ken O'Dea's RBI single) and a walk later, McCarthy was forced to relieve Ruffing with Spud Chandler. Moore and Slaughter greeted Chandler with singles. The bases were loaded, the score stood at 7-4. The Cardinals had batted around and Musial came to bat once again. Musial had made the first out of the inning; he would make the last out, grounding to Hassett at first, who flipped the ball to Chandler for the final putout.

New York had firmly handled the Redbirds until the ninth. They had almost let the game get away from them. Ruffing received credit for his seventh and final World Series win. His record stood until Whitey Ford broke it 19 years later, in 1961, when Ford achieved the eighth of what would become a record 10 World Series victories.

The Yankees had won the ninth opening game of the last 10 World Series in which they had appeared. This victory served to reinforce the feeling that they would make quick work of the less-experienced Cardinals. The 4-to-1 odds laid out before the Series looked more and more like a sure thing.

St. Louis had played sloppily, with four errors leading to four unearned runs. Their ace, Mort Cooper, had not impressed the home crowd. He had given up five runs in 7⅔ innings. Ruffing had stymied the offense until the ninth. It was a daunting experience. St. Louis needed to win the next game — no team had ever emerged victorious in a best-of-seven World Series after losing the first two games.[6]

While they looked bad, the Cardinals had confidence in themselves. As Musial later recalled, "In '42 we played the New York Yankees during spring training and beat them three out of five games. We played against them all the time in the spring and that was a plus. We knew they were a tough club, a good club, but the Yankees didn't faze us."[7]

Did Musial's perspective have merit? Was the Redbirds' rally in the ninth an omen of things to come or a last-gasp effort? The Cardinals would soon find out.

SOURCES

In addition to the sources cited in the Notes, the author also accessed Retrosheet.org, Baseball-Reference.com, and SABR.org.

NOTES

1. Jack Cavanaugh, *Season of '42: Joe D., Teddy Ballgame, and Baseball's Fight to Survive a Turbulent First Year of War* (New York: Skyhorse Publishing, 2012), 234-235.
2. Peter Golenbock, *The Spirit of St. Louis: A History of the St. Louis Cardinals and Browns* (New York: Avon Books, 2000), 232.
3. Cardinals with previous World Series exposure were limited to reserve catcher Ken O'Dea, closer Harry Gumbert, and reliever Whitey Moore, each of whose experience was limited.
4. Bill Gilbert, *They Also Served, Baseball and the Home Front, 1941-1945* (New York: Crown Publishers Inc., 1992), 70.
5. "Notes of Yank Victory in Curtain-Raiser," *The Sporting News*, October 8, 1942: 13.
6. The Giants came back to win after being down 2-0 in 1921, but that was a best-of-nine series.
7. Golenbock, 244.

BEAZLEY EVENS THE SERIES

October 1, 1942: St. Louis Cardinals 4, New York Yankees 3, at Sportsman's Park

Game Two of the World Series

BY GREG ERION

DESPITE ST. LOUIS'S LAST-INNING HEroics the previous day, the fact remained that New York had taken Game One of the 1942 World Series. Going into Game Two on October 1, the Cardinals faced a must-win situation—no team had ever come back to win a best-of-seven Series after dropping the first two contests.[1] And even if they won the Cardinals faced the daunting challenge of traveling to Yankee Stadium for the next three contests, an experience many found intimidating when playing for the first time on the field of Ruth and Gehrig.

John Drebinger, longtime sportswriter for the *New York Times*, saw the Cardinals' late rally as a minor aberration in the Yankees' march toward another world championship. "And so as the years roll on, apparently do (Red) Ruffing and the Yanks even though occasionally the rolling gets a bit bumpy."[2]

Yankees manager Joe McCarthy sought to take the second contest with Ernie Bonham. The 29-year-old Bonham, ironically nicknamed Tiny for his 6-foot-2, 215-pound frame, was 21-5 during the season with a league-leading 22 complete games and an impressive 2.27 ERA. He had built his record on pinpoint control, a solid fastball, and a tricky forkball. Bonham's experience in postseason play was impressive; he had beaten the Brooklyn Dodgers, 3-1, in the 1941 World Series, in a complete-game, four-hit effort to clinch the title

Cardinals skipper Billy Southworth countered with 24-year-old rookie Johnny Beazley, whose 21-6 record and 2.13 ERA were as impressive as Bonham's. Beazley, who made the team in spring training, was being rooted on by three of his former high-school teammates. He had signed a note while in school in Tennessee promising they would be his guests if he ever played in a World Series. He made good on his commitment by arranging for them to come to Sportsman's Park to watch the contest.[3]

Despite the Cardinals' precarious position, they did not show any sign of being overwhelmed. They were loose; possibly surviving a grueling pennant race with the Dodgers minimized the pressure they should have felt. Perhaps it was a sense of youthful naiveté—theirs was the youngest team in the majors.[4] Or maybe it was because of their jovial trainer, Harrison "Doc" Weaver, who had entertained the club down the stretch drive with his mandolin and endless playing of Spike Jones's hillbilly song "Pass the Biscuits, Mirandy," which contributed to a relaxed clubhouse. Weaver went beyond being the jolly court jester. He had a secret weapon—a "double whammy" hex often unleashed with devastating results—or so the Cardinals believed.[5]

For the 34,255 spectators at Sportsman's Park the main question revolved around which Cardinals team would show up, the one that made four errors and just one hit over eight innings or the one that banged out six hits and four runs in their last at-bat? They would not have long to find out.

Beazley opened the game by walking Phil Rizzuto, then retired the next three hitters. In the bottom of the inning, Jimmy Brown worked a leadoff walk against Bonham. It was Bonham's only walk of the game but it proved timely. Terry Moore attempted a sacrifice bunt, and Bonham, thinking he could force Brown out at second, threw to the bag but he failed to account for Brown's speed. Umpire Cal Hubbard called Brown safe. Enos Slaughter and Stan Musial both made outs and it looked as if Bonham would escape damage. As Bonham began to pitch to Walker Cooper, second baseman Joe Gordon darted toward second, attempting to hold Brown closer to the bag. Cooper lined the ball right to the spot Gordon had just vacated. The ball rolled all the way to the wall, the double scoring both Brown and Moore for a 2-0 St. Louis lead.

Had Bonham thrown to first on Moore's bunt or Gordon stayed in position, things would have been different. On such plays do games turn. Johnny Hopp flied out to end the inning. Counting the previous day's game, St. Louis had scored six runs in the last two innings against the Yankees.

Over the next five innings New York garnered five hits and a walk but could not score. In the bottom of the seventh Hopp singled to right with one out, his second hit of the game. The only other hit was Cooper's run-scoring single in the first, as Bonham had proved almost as effective as Beazley. Now, with Hopp on first, Whitey Kurowski sliced a drive down the left-field line with Charlie Keller in futile pursuit. Umpire George Magerkurth ruled that the ball had landed fair, just inside the line. Kurowski ended up at third with a triple as Hopp scored to make it 3-0. New York disputed Magerkurth's call to no avail.

The top of the eighth began with Rizzuto striking out and Rolfe grounding to second. Roy Cullenbine scratched out an infield single. It was the Yankees' sixth hit; up to this point Beazley had done well in scattering New York's offensive efforts. But with the Yankees desperate to get something going, Cullenbine, after getting a long lead off Beazley, stole second with Joe DiMaggio at bat. The Yankees' cleanup hitter then singled, driving Cullenbine home with New York's first run of the game. As St. Louis fans were absorbing this turn of events, Keller drove a pitch onto the roof of the right-field pavilion, making it a brand new ballgame, 3-3.

St. Louis started the bottom of the eighth as New York had at the top of the frame. Brown and Moore went down quietly before Slaughter doubled, aggressively taking third when Rizzuto failed to come up

In his first full season in the majors, Johnny Beazley won 21 games and tossed two complete-game victories in the World Series for the world champion Cardinals in 1942. (National Baseball Hall of Fame, Cooperstown, New York)

cleanly with Cullenbine's throw from right. With the go-ahead run on third, Bonham now faced Stan Musial.

Musial hadn't gotten the ball out of the infield his first three at-bats. Having made the first and third outs in the previous day's ninth inning rally, he was still looking for his first safety in the Series—of all the regulars he was the only one who had failed to hit safely. Although he hit .315 during the regular season, third in the National League, he had not yet established himself as one of baseball's icons. With a 0-for-7 skein, Musial was working toward being St. Louis's offensive goat.

That prospect was quickly eliminated when Musial slapped a groundball single over second to drive in Slaughter with the Cardinals' fourth run. Cooper flied out to end the inning and St. Louis went into the top of the ninth with a one-run lead.

Beazley found himself in immediate trouble when Bill Dickey opened the inning with an infield single. McCarthy lifted the 35-year-old Dickey for pinch-runner Tuck Stainback, whom the Yankees had used sparingly during the year. He appeared in just 15 games, mostly as a pinch-runner, often for Dickey.

Buddy Hassett singled to right and one of the most crucial plays of the Series unfolded. Stainback, off with the hit, headed toward third but Slaughter grabbed the ball and threw on a line to Kurowski, nailing Stainback at third by yards. Instead of runners on first and third with no outs, the Yankees had Hassett at first with one out. Red Ruffing, pinch-hitting for Bonham, flied to left. Although it might seem odd to have one pitcher hit for another pitcher, Ruffing was one of the best hitting pitchers in the game, and arguably as capable as Frank Crosetti or Jerry Priddy on an otherwise threadbare Yankee bench. Rizzuto grounded out and the Series was tied at one game apiece.

The Cardinals were jubilant. Beazley, congratulated by Southworth and team owner Sam Breadon, was ecstatic, "Hey you guys! Now we know them fellers can be beat. Let's go and get them." Outfielder Harry Walker chimed in, "Hot Daddy! We're after 'em now. Get them in New York too." [6]

The Yankees clubhouse was quiet and tense. When a reporter asked coach Earle Combs a question about the game, he "flared up in an outburst few had thought was possible from the coach." There was a pervasive feeling that bad calls by the umpiring crew had cost them the game.[7]

The momentum was shifting. St. Louis might have received breaks on various calls, including Brown beating Bonham's throw to second in the first inning and Kurowski's barely fair triple in the seventh. But St. Louis had shown something; its speed (Brown) and defense (Slaughter) were forces to be reckoned with. Most important, the Cardinals realized that the Yankees were not invincible—and more to the point, so did New York.

Besides talent, there could have been something else at play. Although Weaver might have been applying hexes, he wasn't the only Cardinal dabbling with the supernatural. After the game Beazley told reporters he had been given a rabbit's foot by a fan. Whether things mystical would accompany St. Louis to Yankee Stadium remained to be seen.

SOURCES

In addition to the sources cited in the Notes, the author also accessed Retrosheet.org and Baseball-Reference.com.

NOTES

1. Nor would one until 1955 when the Dodgers took the World Series from the Yankees after dropping the first two contests in the seven-game Series. The Giants dropped their first two games against the Yankees in 1921, but that was a best-of-nine Series.

2. John Drebinger, "Yankees Set Back Cardinals By 7-4 In Series Opener," *New York Times*, October 1, 1942: 1.

3. "Beazley Makes Good on a Promise," *The Sporting News*, October 8, 1942: 13.

4. baseball-reference.com/leagues/MLB/1942.shtml.

5. Bob Broeg, "Cards Mourn Dr. Weaver, Trainer, Morale-Builder," *The Sporting News*, June 1, 1955: 36.

6. "Cardinals Confident After Win," *Hartford Courant*, October 2, 1942: 17.

7. See James P. Dawson, "Victory Proves Cards Are Unawed By Yankee Might…" *New York Times*, October 2: 1942, 18, and "Blow That Beat Bonham Foul—McCarthy," *The Sporting News*, October 8, 1942: 14.

TWO OF A KIND: COOPER TOSSES SECOND STRAIGHT ONE-HIT SHUTOUT

June 4, 1943: St. Louis Cardinals 5, Philadelphia 0, at Sportsman's Park

BY GREGORY H. WOLF

ST. LOUIS HELD ITS COLLECTIVE breath when reports emerged at the beginning of 1943 season that pitcher Mort Cooper's right elbow was aching. To call Cooper an integral part of the Redbirds was an understatement. In what was then arguably the best season ever by a Cardinals pitcher, Cooper won the NL MVP award in 1942, leading the circuit in wins (22), ERA (1.78), and shutouts (10). He beat the rival Dodgers five times as the Cardinals edged Brooklyn by two games to capture the pennant and subsequently beat the Yankees in the World Series.

Skipper Billy Southworth's Cardinals were widely expected to take pennant once again in 1943. Unlike Brooklyn, which had lost starters Pee Wee Reese and Pete Reiser to Uncle Sam and the war effort, the St. Louis club was intact from the previous campaign. The Redbirds overcame a sluggish start and were in second place (24-14), a half-game behind Brooklyn, as they prepared for the second game of a four-game set against the Philadelphia Phillies as part of a season-longest 27-game homestand. The Phillies were baseball's biggest surprise thus far in 1943. After averaging almost 107 losses in the previous five seasons, the club was in fifth place (18-20) under veteran manager Bucky Harris, hired in the offseason to turn the moribund franchise around.

Cooper was pitching on borrowed time. In late June 1941 he underwent what was then potentially career-ending surgery to remove bone spurs in his right elbow. Defying expectations, he returned six weeks later and made 13 starts in August and September. Pain-free for most of 1942, Cooper supposedly chewed aspirin by the dozen to numb the pain in 1943.[1] The 30-year-old hurler with a career record of 65-38, including 5-3 thus far in the season, showed no signs of discomfort on the mound. In his previous start, four days earlier at Sportsman's Park, he tossed his first career one-hitter, defeating Brooklyn, 7-0, in the first game of a doubleheader on May 31. The only hit was Billy Herman's double to lead off the fifth inning. Cooper's gem got scant coverage in the sports pages, which focused on Brooklyn's 41-year-old emergency starter, Fat Freddie Fitzsimmons, who tossed seven scoreless innings of four-hit ball to beat the Cardinals, 1-0, in the second game.

The Friday evening contest between the Cardinals and Phillies under the lights at Sportsman's Park drew a modest crowd of 6,008, in addition to 669 service men and women, and 197 blood donors.[2] A Missouri native, Cooper loved pitching in the heat and humidity of St. Louis, but he was concerned that the unseasonably cool temperature (mid-60s) after a day of rain might bother his elbow. He needn't have worried.

While Big Mort breezed through the first three frames, setting down all nine batters, 5-foot-8 Philadelphia right-hander Charlie Fuchs faced the potent Cardinals offense, which led the league in hitting and finished second in scoring in '43. The 29-year-old wartime hurler dispatched the first six batters he faced before shortstop Glen Stewart fumbled Jimmy Brown's hot grounder. Marty Marion walloped a deep shot but center fielder Buster Adams made what W.J. McGoogan of the *St. Louis Post-Dispatch* described as a "great running catch in right center" to save a run.[3] Brown moved to third on Cooper's single, and then scored on Harry Walker's two-out single. En route to his first of two All-Star berths, Walker entered the game on fire, batting .488 (21-for-43) in his

Mort Cooper compiled a 65-22 record with 23 shutouts over a three-year stretch (1942-1944) as the Cardinals captured three straight pennants and two World Series titles. (National Baseball Hall of Fame, Cooperstown, New York)

last 12 games. Stan Musial drove home Cooper with a single to increase his hitting streak to 21 games, during which he batted .392 (31-for-79) while scoring and driving in 18 runs.

"Cooper had his fast ball snapping over the plate and the Phillies could do nothing with it," wrote the *Post-Dispatch*.[4] With pinpoint control, Cooper mesmerized the Phillies with a repertoire of pitches. In addition to his heater, described as "blurred lightning, with a hop at the end," Cooper often fed right-handers a forkball.[5] According to sportswriter Jack Cuddy, that pitch "approaches the plate in drunken fashion," fluttering like a knuckler; though the pitcher himself compared it to a spitball.[6] Left-handers tried their luck against screwballs that Cooper threw down and away so they could not be pulled.

Through seven innings Cooper had not yielded a hit or walk, and he had thrown 12 consecutive hitless innings extending from his previous start. The only Phillies baserunner was Pinky May, whose tapper to the mound in the sixth Cooper fumbled. May was immediately erased when Mickey Livingston hit a grounder to second baseman Lou Klein, who started a 4-6-3 double play.

Cooper's hitless streak ended when Jimmy Wasdell singled to left field to lead off the eighth. "I couldn't put it in a better spot for him if I'd hung it upon a string," said Cooper to St. Louis sportswriter J. Roy Stockton about the location of his fastball.[7] Unlike Billy Herman's blooper, which fell near the right-field foul line out of Musial's reach, Wasdell's single was a clean, hard-hit line drive.[8]

Philadelphia's one and only hit must have awakened the Cardinals hitters, dormant since the third inning. Walker lined a one-out single, and then scored on cleanup hitter Ray Sanders' double to right-center field to make it 3-0. Ken O'Dea, given the start instead of All-Star catcher Walker Cooper, the pitcher's younger brother, followed with his first round-tripper of the season, a two-run shot which, according to the *Post-Dispatch*, went "deep into the pavilion in right center," for a 5-0 lead.[9]

Cooper breezed through a 1-2-3 ninth, retiring Danny Murtaugh to complete the game in one hour and 42 minutes. He finished with five strikeouts and walked none while facing 28 batters. Fuchs pitched well, too, yielding just eight hits and walking one; two of the five runs were unearned.

"It was disappointing," said Cooper in response to coming oh-so-close to a no-hitter for a second straight game. "Every pitcher wants to do that some day."[10] The stout, 6-foot-3, 210-pound hurler was in an otherwise good mood, especially pleased with his location and stuff. "My forkball was working pretty good. I throw it side-armed or straight overhand depending on the batter."[11] Sportswriters seemed sympathetic to the jovial Cooper, who never tossed another one-hitter, or came close to a no-hitter, in his career. "Lady Luck certainly is tantalizing big Mort Cooper," wrote Cuddy.[12]

Southworth continued leaning heavily on Cooper for the rest of the season. The staff ace, Cooper tied for the NL lead in wins (21) with Pittsburgh's Rip

Sewell and Cincinnati's Elmer Riddle, and finished second in ERA (2.30, behind teammate Max Lanier's 1.90), complete games (24), and shutouts (6).

While Cincinnati's Johnny Vander Meer set the standard by tossing consecutive no-hitters in 1938, contemporary accounts of Cooper's gem completely overlooked that he became just the second pitcher to toss consecutive one-hit shutouts in the modern era (defined as since 1893, when the pitcher's rubber was moved back to 60 feet 6 inches from home plate). The New York Giants' Rube Marquard (1911) was the only other. The Chicago Cubs' Lon Warneke tossed consecutive one-hitters in 1934, but gave up two runs in the second game. Howard Ehmke of the Boston Red Sox (1923) and the Washington Nationals Max Scherzer (2015) are the only pitchers to a no-hitter followed by a one-hitter (or vice-versa). A trio of nineteenth-century hurlers tossed consecutive one-hitters, including Hugh Daily (1884 in the Union Association), Toad Ramsey of the American Association Louisville Colonels in 1886, and Charlie Buffinton for the NL Philadelphia Quakers in 1887. Like Ehmke, Ed Cushman of the Milwaukee Brewers in the Union Association, yielded just one hit over two complete games.[13]

NOTES

1. Gregory H. Wolf, "Mort Cooper," SABR BioProject. sabr.org/bioproj/person/9c707ace.
2. W.J. McGoogan, "Mort Cooper Hurls Second Straight One-Hit Game," *St. Louis Post-Dispatch*, June 5, 1943: 6A.
3. Ibid.
4. Ibid.
5. Jack Cuddy, United Press, "Mort Copper Hurls Second One-Hitter," *Pittsburgh Press*, June 5, 1943: 7.
6. Ibid.
7. J. Roy Stockton, "Extra Innings," *St. Louis Post-Dispatch*, June 8, 1943: 4B.
8. "Cooper Hurls One-Hitter, But Brecheen Loses, 1-0," *St. Louis Post-Dispatch*, June 1, 1943: 8A.
9. McGoogan.
10. Stockton.
11. Ibid.
12. Cuddy.
13. The next pitchers to toss consecutive one-hitters after Cooper were Whitey Ford of the New York Yankees (1955), Sam McDowell (1966), Dave Stieb (1988), and R.A. Dickey (2012).

MARIUS RUSSO'S ONE-MAN SHOW LEADS TO YANKEES WIN OVER CARDINALS

October 10, 1943: New York Yankees 2, St. Louis Cardinals 1, at Sportsman's Park

Game Four of World Series

BY MIKE HUBER

THE 1943 WORLD SERIES WAS A rematch of 1942's fall classic, with the St. Louis Cardinals and the New York Yankees topping their respective leagues. However, in 1942, the first two games were played in St. Louis and the next three were played in New York. In 1943 the first three games were played in New York due to World War II travel restrictions, so the Cardinals did not get a chance to capitalize on their home-field advantage until Game Four, when the Series moved to Sportsman's Park.[1]

In 1943 the Cardinals had lost "three of their most important starters—Enos Slaughter, Terry Moore, and Johnny Beazley" to military service.[2] Even so, the Cards won 105 games in the regular season. For New York, Joe DiMaggio, Tommy Henrich, Red Ruffing, and Phil Rizzuto were off at war but they still won 98 games and captured the pennant by 13½ games.

The Yankees entered the game up two games to one. The three games in New York were characterized by sloppy Cardinals defense (eight errors leading to five unearned runs), a lack of St. Louis hitting (no more than seven hits in a game), and late Yankees rallies (two—almost three—come-from-behind victories). For Game Four, the visiting Yankees made a surprise move and put Marius Russo on the hill. He had been a 1941 All-Star, but his 1943 record was 5-10 and he spent much of the season nursing a bad arm and contemplating retirement.[3] Yet in this game he brought forth "his talented left-handed pitching and even more astonishing right-handed batting."[4]

Russo had been used both as a starter (14 games) and reliever (10 games) during the season. St. Louis turned to Max Lanier, its star southpaw, to try to even the series. He sported a record of 15-7 with a league-leading 1.90 ERA. Lanier had lost Game One, 4-2, "the victim of a harrowing wild pitch that ruined his opening game effort."[5] A crowd of 36,196 jammed into Sportsman's Park for the show.[6]

The pitchers controlled the game in the first few innings. Ray Sanders got the first Cardinals hit in the bottom of the second but was forced at second by Danny Litwhiler for the inning's final out. In the top of the third, Russo became the Yankees' first baserunner by drawing a two-out walk. Tuck Stainback reached on an error by second baseman Lou Klein, and New York had a rally going. Frankie Crosetti stroked a shot to right field for a single. Russo rounded third and headed home, but the relay from right to first to home cut down the sliding pitcher for the third out.

In the New York half of the fourth, Joe Gordon doubled with two outs. Bill Dickey, appearing in his 37th World Series game with the same club, a new record (he broke Babe Ruth's record of 36 games),[7] came to the plate and singled for an RBI, "before anybody could think of walking him."[8] New York led, 1-0. An inning later Russo doubled with one out, but his teammates could not capitalize with a runner in scoring position, as Lanier kept the Yankees in check.

Russo defended his one-run advantage until the seventh inning. With two outs Sanders reached on an error, as shortstop Crosetti dropped an easy pop fly, losing the ball in the glaring sun. Litwhiler then drove a ball that struck the first-base bag and bounced into right field for a double. Yankees manager Joe McCarthy played percentage baseball, loading the bases by intentionally walking Marty Marion. Now with the bases loaded and Lanier due up, Cardinals skipper Billy Southworth had to make a decision. He "elected to shoot straight for victory and, without any further hesitation, called upon the veteran outfielder, Frank Demaree, to pinch hit for Lanier."[9]

Demaree grounded to third baseman Billy Johnson, who fumbled the ball, and everyone was safe as Sanders scored the tying run and pandemonium broke out at Sportsman's Park. The Cardinals fans in the left- and center-field bleachers showed their exuberance by giving "the outfield grass a shower of bottles,"[10] which caused a delay in the game and perhaps caused the St. Louis momentum to fade while the grounds crew came out to clean up. With the bases loaded, Klein smashed a hard shot to the right of second base. Gordon scooped it up and flipped to shortstop Crosetti, covering the bag at second, for out number three. But the Cardinals had tied the score.

Another lefty, Harry Brecheen, now came on in the top of the eighth inning. Russo greeted him with a double into the left-field corner, his second two-bagger of the game. Stainback laid down a perfect sacrifice bunt, allowing Russo to move to third. He scored when Crosetti lifted a long sacrifice fly to center. The Yankees had manufactured the go-ahead (and winning) run.

The St. Louis fans urged their team on in the bottom of the eighth. With one out, National League MVP Stan Musial got his second infield hit of the game. Walker Cooper, who had driven with his brother Mort (a Cardinals pitcher) through the night from Independence, Missouri, where they attended the funeral of their father a day earlier,[11] hit a ball over second base that shortstop Crosetti knocked down, but Cooper reached with a single as Musial stopped at second. Suddenly the Cards had a rally. Whitey Kurowski[12] flied out to left. Sanders then hit a hard, skimming grounder toward second base.

Gordon bobbled it and threw late to Crosetti for the force on Cooper. Cooper was initially called safe, but he overran the bag, and Crosetti tagged him out. According to the *St. Louis Post-Dispatch*, Cooper's "determination was fine, but the momentum played old ned with the situation and when he couldn't apply the brakes he just fell away from second base,"[13] allowing Crosetti to slap a tag on Cooper and bringing a loud groan from the fans.

New York loaded the bases with two outs in the ninth, thanks in part to a pair of intentional walks, one of which brought Russo to the plate again. McCarthy stuck with his pitcher instead of bringing in a pinch-hitter and Russo struck out to bring up the Cardinals in their final at-bat. After Litwhiler grounded out to short, Marion doubled to left field. But Russo buckled down and retired pinch-hitter Sam Narron and then Klein to end the game.

Game Four of the fall classic featured a tight pitching duel. Lanier pitched well enough to win, scattering four hits and striking out five, but his opponent was better. Russo was the hero for the Yankees. Until the seventh inning, he allowed only three singles and no runners had reached second base. Had his defense held up, he might have pitched a complete-game shutout. At bat he was 2-for-3 with two doubles and a walk. Although the middle of the Cardinals batting order got hits, there weren't many opportunities to drive in runners. With the 2-1 victory, the Yankees took a commanding three-games-to-one lead in the Series and moved to the threshold of another championship.

SOURCES

In addition to the sources mentioned in the Notes, the author consulted baseball-almanac.com, baseball-reference.com, and retrosheet.org. The author also recommends a video recap of the 1943 World Series produced by the American League of Professional Baseball Clubs (the 22-minute video can be found online at *youtube.com/watch?v=hdMLEaC1haQ*).

NOTES

1   In 1943, the World Series moved to a new 3-4 format in order to reduce travel for teams during the war.

HOME OF THE BROWNS AND CARDINALS AT GRAND AND DODIER

2. Gregory H. Wolf, "The St. Louis Cardinals in Wartime," in *Who's on First: Replacement Players in World War II* (Phoenix, Arizona: Society for American Baseball Research, 2015), 175.

3. Cort Vitty, "Marius Russo," sabr.org/bioproj/person/f12997d8.

4. John Drebinger, "Yanks, With Russo, Beat Cards by 2-1; Lead, 3-1, in Series," *New York Times*, October 11, 1943: 1.

5. Ibid.

6. The size of the crowd at Sportsman's Park was a few thousand over capacity (34,023), yet this number was dwarfed by the approximately 69,000 who watched each of the first three games in Yankee Stadium.

7. Dickey played in Game Five as well, extending his record to 38 games. Another Hall of Fame Yankees catcher, Yogi Berra, played in 14 World Series with a total of 75 games with the same club. Both Dickey and Berra wore number 8 for New York.

8. J. Roy Stockton, "Yankees Victors in 4th Game," *St. Louis Post-Dispatch*, October 11, 1943: 10.

9. Drebinger.

10. Stockton.

11. Drebinger.

12. Kurowski was playing with a handicap, as he had suffered a gall-bladder attack the night before the game. He was given strong sedatives to relieve the pain and spent the morning sleeping under the influence of the medication.

13. Stockton.

THE YANKEES BRING THE CHAMPIONSHIP BACK TO NEW YORK

October 11, 1943: New York Yankees 2, St. Louis Cardinals 0, at Sportsman's Park

Game Five of the World Series

BY JAMES FORR

IF YOU WERE LISTENING CAREFULLY, you might have picked up on it—a subtle, perhaps unconscious acknowledgement that the curtain was falling.

As Sportsman's Park public-address announcer George Carson introduced the home team, he left something out. For the first time all season he didn't refer to them as the "World Champion Cardinals."[1]

The New York Yankees led St. Louis three games to one as they closed in on their 10th World Series title on this sunny Monday afternoon. It was a battle of 20-game winners as the Yankees' Spud Chandler (20-4, and the winner of Game One) took on Mort Cooper (21-8).

According to Cardinals left fielder Danny Litwhiler, the Yankees had the Cardinals' pitchers figured out to some extent. Apparently third-base coach Art Fletcher had deciphered St. Louis's signs by observing how catcher Walker Cooper moved his elbow as he put down his fingers.[2] However, that didn't help them against Mort Cooper in Game Two, when he threw a complete-game six-hitter. It wouldn't help them much on this day, either.

St. Louis manager Billy Southworth shook up his lineup for Game Five, benching Litwhiler for Debs Garms and center fielder Harry Walker for Johnny Hopp. Southworth's logic was unclear because he refused to speak to the press before the game—he had all but thrown the writers out of the clubhouse after the Cardinals' 2-1 loss in Game Four, snarling, "How did you fellows become sportswriters—some of the stupid questions you ask?"[3]—but the move reeked of desperation. Although Walker and Litwhiler struggled at the plate in the first four games, Garms and Hopp both had endured miserable regular seasons.

The Sportsman's Park crowd, somnolent throughout Game Four, finally came alive when Cooper struck out the side in order in the top of the first. The St. Louis right-hander then fanned the first two hitters in the second, coming within one of Hod Eller's 24-year-old Series record of six consecutive strikeouts, before walking Nick Etten. Walker Cooper's errant pickoff throw allowed Etten to scoot into scoring position, but Joe Gordon grounded sharply to third baseman Whitey Kurowski, who knocked the ball down and whipped it to first to end the inning. "Mort Cooper was looking great. ... [He] was throwing hard," recalled Chandler years later. "The only way we were going to beat him was to hold the Cardinals down and wait for something to happen."[4]

Chandler was far from dazzling but he did, indeed, hold the Cards down. The first man he faced, Lou Klein, smacked one back to the box and off his shin for an infield hit. Garms laid down a perfect sacrifice, nearly beating the throw from third baseman Billy Johnson. Stan Musial walked, but Chandler escaped the jam with groundballs off the bats of Walker Cooper and Kurowski.

More trouble awaited Chandler in the second. After Ray Sanders opened with a single, Hopp hit what appeared to be a routine double-play ball back to the mound. Chandler fired to second in plenty of time, but shortstop Frank Crosetti dropped the ball as he took it out of his glove to make the relay to first. American League umpire Joe Rue initially put up his right arm, but then changed his call and declared Sanders safe. New York manager Joe McCarthy stormed from the dugout, contending that Crosetti had the ball long enough for the force, but Rue stood his ground. *New York Times* columnist Arthur Daley cracked, "Officially, it was scored as an error for Crosetti. Unofficially, the press-box tenants scored it as an error for Rue."[5]

The Cardinals, however, let Chandler off the ropes. With men at first and second, eighth-place hitter Marty Marion, an All-Star who batted .280 for the season, curiously laid down a bunt. He was credited with a sacrifice that moved two Cardinals into scoring position, but all that did was pass the buck to Mort Cooper, a .170 hitter, who struck out. Klein flied to deep right, and that was the end of the threat.

St. Louis rallied again in the fourth as Kurowski legged out a bunt single down the third-base line and Sanders coaxed a walk. After Chandler missed with the first three pitches to Hopp, catcher Bill Dickey stomped out to the mound.

"What's the matter?" he asked.

"Nothing," muttered Chandler.

"Then get the ball over the plate," Dickey suggested helpfully.[6]

Chandler's next two pitches were called strikes, setting up a critical 3-and-2 pitch. "I'll never forget it as long as I live," said Chandler. "It was a fastball and it had to be at least eight to ten inches outside — and he swung at it and missed." Marion and Mort Cooper both grounded into force outs to end the inning and Chandler returned to dugout in a buoyant mood. "I said, 'Fellows, there's no way I can lose today.'"[7]

In the top of the fifth, with a man on third and two outs, Walker Cooper took a foul tip off his bare hand and suffered a grotesque compound dislocation of his right index finger. He kicked his mitt toward the dugout as he trudged off and Ken O'Dea took his spot behind the plate. Unfazed, Mort Cooper got Crosetti to loop a lazy fly ball to Garms in left to extinguish the threat.

New York finally broke through in the sixth. With two out Charlie Keller slapped a single past second baseman Klein and into right field. Klein had been shading the right-handed-hitting Keller up the middle, and was unable to move to his left quickly enough to make the play. Next came Dickey, who turned on Cooper's first pitch, powering it onto the roof of the right-field pavilion for his fifth career World Series home run and a 2-0 lead. "Boy, that certainly felt good," Dickey remarked after the game. "It was a high fastball and I gave it a ride."[8]

Over the final innings, the desperate Cardinals continued to jab at Chandler but he kept bobbing out of the way. O'Dea led off the sixth with an infield single but was immediately erased on a double play. Harry Walker, pinch-hitting for Mort Cooper, delivered a single with two away in the seventh but Chandler stranded him when he struck out Klein. With two gone in the eighth, O'Dea and Kurowski strung together consecutive singles but Sanders grounded to second. It was that kind of series for St. Louis; they batted .152 (5-for-33) with runners in scoring position and stranded 37 men in the five-game series.

In the top of the ninth Cardinals right-hander Murry Dickson became just the second active member of the military to see action in a World Series. Dickson, on furlough at the request of Commissioner Kenesaw Mountain Landis after being inducted into the Army in September, retired the final two Yankees hitters to keep his team within range.

St. Louis put something together again in the bottom of the ninth. With one out, Marion singled to left and Litwhiler followed with a pinch-hit single to center. However, Chandler buckled down once more. Klein went down on strikes on three pitches, nearly corkscrewing himself into the ground on his final swing, and then Garms hit a harmless roller to Gordon for the game's final out.

Chandler scatted 10 hits and walked two, but got the outs when he needed them in going the distance. Mort Cooper, pitching just a few days after the death of his father, was brilliant other than that one pitch to Dickey, allowing just five hits and striking out six through seven innings.

The Yankees were champions for the sixth time in the last eight seasons. Joe Gordon, the goat of the

1942 fall classic against St. Louis, redeemed himself by setting a Series record, handling 43 errorless chances at second base over the five games, and leading his club with an OPS of .821. Chandler gave up just one earned run in 18 innings.

Southworth lamented the lack of timely hitting and his club's ragged defense; they made at least one error in every game and 11 overall. "If anyone had told me that I would get as good pitching as we had in the Series, I would have thought the Series was in the bag," he said.[9] His club left 11 men on base in Game Five and set ignominious Series records for the most hits in a game without scoring and the most hits in a game without an extra-base hit.

Meanwhile the Yankees sang at the top of their lungs in the clubhouse, and even got Landis to join in the chorus. "That wound up 1943," Chandler mused. "That beautiful year."[10]

NOTES

1. W.J. McGoogan, "Series Sidelights," *St. Louis Post Dispatch*, October 11, 1943: 2,1.
2. Danny Litwhiler, *Danny Litwhiler: Living the Baseball Dream* (Philadelphia: Temple University Press, 2006), 86.
3. "Feudin' Goes on Between Southworth and Writers," *St. Louis Star-Times*, October 11, 1943: 18.
4. Donald Honig, *Baseball When the Grass Was Real* (New York: Coward, McCann, and Geoghegan, 1975), 220.
5. Arthur Daley, "Sports of the Times: Champions of the World," *New York Times*, October 12, 1943: 32.
6. *Baseball When the Grass Was Real*, 220.
7. Ibid.
8. "Sonic Boom Across Yankee Clubhouse in Boisterous Victory Demonstration," *New York Times*, October 12, 1943: 31.
9. "Series Reel Cutbacks," *The Sporting News*, October 21, 1943: 8.
10. *Baseball When the Grass Was Real*, 220.

LANIER PITCHES MARATHON GEM AS HOPP DELIVERS WINNER

July 2, 1944: St. Louis Cardinals 2, Brooklyn Dodgers 1 (14 Innings, Game One of Doubleheader), at Sportsman's Park

BY GORDON GATTIE

THE ST. LOUIS CARDINALS ENTERED July 1944 with an eight-game lead over the second-place Pittsburgh Pirates. The reigning NL champions compiled a 42-19 record through June 30, the best record in the majors. Manager Billy Southworth guided the Cardinals to successive World Series appearances in 1942-43 and a 17-5 record during June 1944. Their success during early 1944 was attributable to a balanced offensive and defensive attack, supported by roster consistency.

The Cardinals had lost several players to World War II service, including pitchers Johnny Beazley, Howie Pollet, Ernie White, and Howie Krist;[1] second baseman Lou Klein; and outfielder Harry Walker. However, position players including catcher Walker Cooper, first baseman Ray Sanders, shortstop Marty Marion, third baseman Whitey Kurowski, and outfielders Stan Musial and Danny Litwhiler remained in St. Louis. In addition to that stability, the Cardinals featured the youngest team in baseball for the third consecutive season.[2]

The Brooklyn Dodgers struggled to a 33-33 record through June. After five consecutive winning seasons, Leo Durocher was enduring the worst season in his young managerial career. Brooklyn was particularly hurt by the war; by the start of the 1944 season, the Dodgers had lost Hugh Casey, Billy Herman, Kirby Higbe, Pee Wee Reese, Pete Reiser, and Johnny Rizzo to the war effort.[3] Brooklyn subsequently filled its roster with youngsters like 16-year-old shortstop Tommy Brown and 21-year-old Eddie "The Fiddler" Basinski, and timeworn veterans like 41-year-old Paul Waner. Entering July, the Dodgers were in fifth place, 11½ games behind the Cardinals.

Starting July 1, the Cardinals hosted Brooklyn for three games. In an 8-3 victory in the opener, St. Louis pounded Brooklyn pitcher Curt Davis for 18 hits and seven earned runs in 7⅓ innings, while Cardinals starter Al Jurisich allowed just one run on one hit, with seven walks, through five innings for his fifth win.[4] The series featured top NL hitters; just before the series began, Musial recaptured the batting lead with a .3786 average to Brooklyn's Dixie Walker's .3780.[5] In the series opener, Musial tied Walker for the NL lead in doubles by hitting his 22nd two-bagger.

Max Lanier was the Cardinals' game-one starter in the July 2 doubleheader. Lanier earned his first NL All-Star Game appearance in 1943, leading the league with a 1.90 ERA. Through 14 starts so far in 1944, Lanier was 7-5 with a 2.50 ERA in 104⅓ innings. Lanier had begun the season strong, pitching complete-game victories in six of his first seven starts.[6] However, he had lost four of his previous six starts, including his last one, on June 28 against Philadelphia. Lanier's repertoire included an overhead curve, fastball, changeup, and knuckleball, which he had developed just two years earlier. His approach was pitching mostly overhand to right-handed batters and side-arm to left-handed batters, with a high leg kick in his full windup.[7]

Rube Melton started for Brooklyn. His career began with Philadelphia, where he was 10-25 over two seasons. Scouts raved about Melton's potential, but he never overcame his wildness. On December 12, 1942, Philadelphia traded Melton to Brooklyn for Johnny Allen and $30,000; this was Brooklyn's second attempt to acquire Melton. Commissioner Kenesaw Landis nullified a 1939 deal sending him to Brooklyn because of suspected collusion.[8] Melton entered this game with a 5-5 record and 3.20 ERA. He had last appeared four days earlier in the final inning of the second game of a doubleheader; before that scoreless appearance, he won three of his last five starts, including a 10-inning complete-game victory against Philadelphia on June 25.

Both teams had scoring opportunities during the early innings, but neither crossed the plate. The Cardinals had runners reach second base during each of the first three frames, but couldn't push across a run. Brooklyn placed runners on first base in the second and third innings, but neither advanced beyond first base. Spanning the fourth to sixth innings, Lanier and Melton each faced only one batter over the minimum.

The Dodgers threatened in the seventh inning; Augie Galan singled and Dixie Walker followed with a fielder's choice, forcing Galan at second. Frenchy Bordagaray walked, advancing Walker to second with one away. However, Mickey Owen ended the threat by hitting into a 5-4-3 double play. The Cardinals' Emil Verban singled in the bottom of the seventh, and the Dodgers' Eddie Stanky doubled in the top of the eighth, but neither runner advanced. In the bottom of the eighth with two outs, Musial walked and Ken O'Dea singled, but Kurowski popped out to third base, ending the threat. Both teams went down 1-2-3 in the ninth to send the scoreless game into extra innings. This was Melton's third time pitching into the 10th inning in 1944, while Lanier ventured into extra innings for the first time that season.

Both pitchers faced the minimum in the 10th inning; Lanier induced three groundouts and Melton benefitted from an 8-3 line-drive double play. In the 11th, Brooklyn moved a runner into scoring position when Stanky singled and advanced to second on a Melton sacrifice bunt. After an Eddie Miksis strikeout and Luis Olmo intentional walk, Galan grounded out to second for the third out.

In the top of the 12th, the Dodgers nearly broke the impasse. After one out Bordagaray and Owen delivered successive singles to place runners at first and second. Howie Schultz grounded out, and both baserunners advanced, resulting in runners on third and second. Stanky was intentionally walked so Lanier would face Melton. The strategy worked as Melton struck out, ending the inning. The Cardinals mustered a lone Verban single in the 12th as each starting pitcher remained in the game. Both Lanier and Melton set down the side in order during the 13th inning.

Brooklyn's Walker tripled to lead off the 14th inning, the first time a runner stood at third base with no outs. Bordagaray lifted a fly ball to left field, scoring Walker with the game's first run. After two Brooklyn groundouts, St Louis batted. Melton walked catcher O'Dea to start the Cardinals half. Kurowski hit into a fielder's choice, forcing pinch-runner Pepper Martin at second. Litwhiler singled, moving Kurowski to second, and then Marion singled, scoring Kurowski with the tying run and advancing Litwhiler to third base. Durocher replaced Melton with reliever Les Webber, who intentionally walked pinch-hitter Debs Garms. Southworth then pinch-hit for Lanier with Augie Bergamo, who lined out for the second out. With the game now exceeding three hours, Hopp stepped to the plate for the seventh time and delivered a single far over Olmo's head in center field that plated Litwhiler with the winning run.[9]

Lanier pitched 14 innings, allowing one run on seven hits while striking out nine and walking five. Melton nearly matched Lanier, pitching 13⅓ innings, allowing two runs on nine hits while striking out seven and walking five. Each pitcher allowed multiple hits in only one inning: Brooklyn off Lanier in the 11th and the Cardinals off Melton during the fateful 14th inning.

Coincidentally, National League All-Star Game rosters were announced later that day. Six Cardinals earned a trip to Pittsburgh: Marion, Kurowski, Cooper, Musial, George Munger, and Lanier.[10] Due to elbow soreness, Lanier didn't pitch in the game;[11] he finished the season with a 17-12 record and 2.65 ERA. Marty Marion won the 1944 National League MVP Award, the first NL shortstop to receive the honor. The Cardinals faced their Sportsman's Park landlords, the St. Louis Browns in the 1944 World

Series, the Browns' lone World Series appearance. The Cardinals defeated the Browns four games to two for their fifth title.

SOURCES

Besides the sources cited in the Notes, the author consulted Baseball-Almanac.com, Baseball-Reference.com, Retrosheet-org, and the following:

Bedingfield, Gary. Baseball in World War II, baseballinwartime.com/baseball_in_wwii/baseball_in_wwii.htm. Accessed November 11, 2016.

Thorn, John, and Pete Palmer, et al. *Total Baseball: The Official Encyclopedia of Major League Baseball* (New York: Viking Press, 2004).

NOTES

1 Frederick G. Lieb, "Cards' Service Staff Best," *The Sporting News*, June 29, 1944: 2.

2 Gregory H. Wolf, "The Cardinals in Wartime," in Marc Z. Aaron and Bill Nowlin, eds., *Who's on First: Replacement Players in World War II* (Phoenix: Society for American Baseball Research, 2015), 177.

3 Peter Golenbock, *Bums: An Oral History of the Brooklyn Dodgers* (Lincolnwood, Illinois: Contemporary Books, 2000), 71.

4 J. Roy Stockton, "Three-Ply Killing Halts Dodger Threat in Third; Birds Collect 18 Hits," *St. Louis Post-Dispatch*, July 2, 1944: 35.

5 Associated Press, "Musial Regains N.L. Batting Lead," *St. Louis Post-Dispatch*, July 1, 1944: 6.

6 Gregory H. Wolf, "Max Lanier," SABR Biography Project, sabr.org/bioproj/person/587c5c76.

7 Bill James and Rob Neyer, *The Neyer/James Guide to Pitchers: An Historical Compendium of Pitching, Pitchers, and Pitches* (New York: Fireside Books, 2004), 274.

8 Jack Morris "Rube Melton," SABR Biography Project, sabr.org/bioproj/person/2e93db95.

9 Herman Wecke, "Munger and Brechen to Pitch in Twin Bill With Giants Tomorrow," *St. Louis Post-Dispatch*, July 3, 1944: 6.

10 "Six Cardinals, Three Brownies Are Named on All-Star Squads," *St. Louis Post-Dispatch*, July 3, 1944: 6.

11 "Cardinals Likely to Bat Against Konstanty or Southpaw Clyde Shoun," *St. Louis Post-Dispatch*, July 13, 1944: 18.

FINALLY, THE BROWNS!

October 1, 1944: St. Louis Browns 5, New York Yankees 2, at Sportsman's Park

BY MIKE WHITEMAN

BY OCTOBER 1, 1944, THE UNITED States was fully engaged in World War II. War had raged for almost three years on opposite ends of the world, far from home. In a conflict that saw over 16 million Americans serve, almost 400,000 of them were killed in action.[1] The American public was becoming wearily accustomed to daily news of the deaths of young men in the defense of their country.

With this as the backdrop, the national pastime continued. In fact, the president of the United States insisted on it. In his famous Green Light Letter of 1942, Franklin D. Roosevelt shared his thoughts with Commissioner Kenesaw Mountain Landis, saying, "I honestly feel that it would be best for the country to keep baseball going. There will be fewer people unemployed and everyone will work longer hours and harder than ever before. And that means that they ought to have a chance for recreation and for taking their minds off their work even more than before."[2]

While Roosevelt expressed his enthusiasm about the good the game could do for the morale of the country, winning the war was the first priority. Those ballplayers who could reasonably serve in the armed forces did, leaving behind decimated major-league rosters by 1944. In fact, by Opening Day 1944 only 40 percent of those in the Opening Day lineups in 1941 were still in the majors, and several more were awaiting the call to duty. Seventeen of those who participated in the 1942 All-Star Game and 13 from the 1943 contest were now serving in the military.[3]

By any means of measurement, the quality of the game on the field was suffering. Those suiting up for the 1944 season were largely considered physically unable to serve in the military (4-F), were too old, too young in a few cases, or had families to support. Teams scoured the landscape looking for capable players.

Despite the turnover, there were some predictable results. On September 21, 1944, the St. Louis Cardinals clinched the National League title, their third in a row. This was not unexpected, as it was also their third consecutive season with 100 or more wins. They won the flag in dominant form, residing in first place all but three days of the season.

The American League pennant was also going through St. Louis, but this was *not* expected. The Browns had a long history of mediocre baseball, having never won an AL title, and rarely even contended for one. In fact, the team had not finished within 15 games of first place in 22 years.

This Browns team, though, looked different from the start, as they shot out of the gate with nine victories in a row. A long-suffering fan base needed to be convinced at first; on April 27 the hometown team ran its record to 8-0 in front of a mere 1,106 spectators at Sportsman's Park.

The Browns did come back to earth but throughout the summer, which included a suspension of play during the D-Day invasion, they battled Detroit, New York, and Boston for the pennant. On September 3 all four squads were all within 1½ games of one another. *The Sporting News* adorned the front page of its September 14 issue with the headline "AL Pennant Race Most Dramatic in History."[4]

Eventually the race came down to the Detroit and St. Louis. On Sunday, October 1, the last day of the regular season, the Tigers and Browns woke up tied for the American League lead. The Tigers were sending out ace Dizzy Trout, who had already won 27 games, in their season finale against last-place Washington.

The "Sewellmen," led by manager Luke Sewell, had a bit of a longer hill to climb. They would face off against the defending champion New York Yankees, still a formidable foe (83 wins) despite having fallen out of the race. The Yankees would send out rookie Mel Queen with the intent of spoiling the Browns' pennant chances.

Taking the mound for the Browns was 34-year-old Sig Jakucki. One year earlier, the right-hander was working at shipyards in Houston. Prior to this season, he had last pitched in the major leagues in 1936. "He was a mean son of a bitch, a big strong bastard that would turn over a juke joint every night if he could," teammate Ellis Clary said of Jakucki. "But you could not help but like him if he was on your side."[5] Jakucki had a reputation as a carouser, but was an effective pitcher, with a 12-9, 3.67 record up to this day.

Jakucki took the mound in front of a sellout crowd, the first in 20 years, of 35,518, with some accounts of an additional 15,000 turned away.[6] The Yankees were poor guests and started the scoring immediately with an RBI single by Johnny Lindell in the first inning. They added another when Hersh Martin doubled in Bud Metheny in the third. In the bottom of the fourth the Browns pulled even when Chet Laabs, whom Sewell almost benched before reinstating him after watching him in batting practice, followed a single by Mike Kreevich with a two-run homer to make it 2-2.

Shortly after Laabs' blast, the scoreboard informed the players and faithful that Detroit had lost to Washington, 4-1, and the pathway to the AL pennant was now clear. Just win, and take the elusive pennant for the first time ever. The Browns didn't waste any time; Laabs went deep again, this time a 400-foot shot, to give St. Louis a 4-2 lead. Vern Stephens ripped a solo homer of his own leading off the eighth.

This would be all they would need as Jakucki held the Yanks scoreless the rest of the way. After 1 hour and 38 minutes of play, New York's Oscar Grimes fouled out to first baseman George McQuinn to end the game.

As reported in *The Sporting News*, "After McQuinn clutched Oscar Grimes' foul for the last out, the crowd was dazed for the moment. Then it let out a terrific shout. However, as it was Sunday and the third year of our entry in World War II, there was no aftermath like the wild celebration in St. Louis after Hornsby's Cardinals clinched their first National League pennant in 1926. … With thousands of young fans of the harum-scarum age in the armed services, and gasoline rationed, there were not many youthful spirits on hand to repeat the Hellraising of 18 years ago."[7]

Thus set into motion "The Streetcar Series" against their city mates. The week of the World Series was proclaimed as St. Louis Baseball Week by Mayor Aloys Kaufman. The series created great civic interest; tickets went quickly, and were sometimes scalped at significantly inflated prices.[8]

The first order of business prior to the first pitch was to deal with accommodations. With wartime housing not always plentiful, Sewell and Cardinals manager Billy Southworth had shared an apartment during the season. Since the teams never playing in town at the same time during the season, there was never a conflict. Now there was. Southworth found another apartment for the Series.[9]

The Series looked to be a mismatch from the start, with the 105-win Cardinals, who led the majors in most team batting and pitching categories, matching up against perhaps the worst pennant winner in history. The Browns' 89-65 mark was tied with that of the 1926 World Series champion Cardinals for the worst record of a pennant-winning team. The Browns were playing to win, though, and Sewell was confident. "Billy (Southworth) has a mighty good team; they must be good to win over 100 games for the third straight season," he said. "But I think we can show them some pitching that might bother them."[10]

Would the "Team of Destiny," as labeled by Fred Leib, be able to generate four more wins and shock the baseball world? The Browns were sure of it. "Now, bring on those Cardinals."[11]

SOURCES

In addition to the sources cited in the Notes, the author also consulted Baseball-Reference.com, Retrosheet.org, and Skelton, David E., Chet Laabs, SABR BioProject, SABR.org.

NOTES

1. H.P. Willmont, Charles Messenger, and Robin Cross, *World War II* (New York: DK Publishing, 2009), 305.
2. Rob Felder and Steven Hoffman, *The Baseball Book* (New York: Sports Illustrated, 2006), 105.
3. Clifford Kachline, "60 Per Cent Turnover in Majors Since '41," *The Sporting News*, April 13, 1944.
4. Daniel M. Daniel, "A.L. Pennant Race Most Dramatic in History: Four-Club Fight Sets Precedent," *The Sporting News*, September 14, 1944.
5. Peter Golenbock, *The Spirit of St. Louis: A History of the St. Louis Cardinals and Browns* (New York: HarperCollins, 2001), 294.
6. Golenbock, 303.
7. Carl Felker, "Big Sig Gets Beer Shampoo in Brownies' Victory Party," *The Sporting News*, October 5, 1944.
8. William Mead, *Even the Browns: Baseball During World War II* (New York: Dover, 1982), 180.
9. Mead, 181.
10. Frederick G. Leib, "Hitless Wonders Win the Hard Way," *The Sporting News*, October 5, 1944.
11. Leib. The Browns came into the World Series confident, and took two of the first three games, with the loss coming in extra innings. The Cardinals took over though, and allowed only two Browns runs over the last three games to take the Series in six games.

BROWNS SURPRISE CARDS IN OPENING SALVO OF THE TROLLEY WORLD SERIES

October 4, 1944: St. Louis Browns 2,
St. Louis Cardinals 1, at Sportsman's Park

Game One of the World Series

BY RICHARD RIIS

OHIO GOVERNOR AND Republican candidate for vice president John W. Bricker posed for photographers before the game with two fellow Buckeyes, Cardinals manager Billy Southworth and Browns skipper Luke Sewell. Pressed by a reporter for a series prediction, Bricker simply grinned and said, "I hope St. Louis wins."[1]

The first intracity World Series outside of New York since Chicago's Cubs and White Sox squared off against one another back in 1906, and the first single-park series since the Yankees and Giants shared the Polo Grounds in 1922, came as a something of a shock to most baseball observers. The Cardinals had been expected to take their third straight NL flag in 1944 and did, in handy fashion, finishing 14½ games ahead of the Pittsburgh Pirates and winning 105 games. The Browns, though, had surprised nearly everyone by winning 89 games and taking the American League pennant by a single game over the Detroit Tigers on the final day of the season after blowing a seven-game lead in August. The Browns' sizzling finish, which included 11 wins in their last 12 games, had some predicting the upstart AL squad to win the World Series, but Sewell's announcement the day before the opening game had many rethinking the odds.

Sewell bypassed his ace, Nelson Potter, winner of 19 games, in favor of journeyman hurler Denny Galehouse for Game One. The right-handed Galehouse had put together an 81-88 won-lost record in his 10 years in the major leagues and had gone just 9-10 in 1944, pitching most of the season only on Sundays, when he would travel by overnight train to St. Louis from his defense job in a Goodyear Aircraft plant in Akron, Ohio.

When asked by reporters why he'd selected Galehouse to start, Sewell declined to explain, commenting only that "Galehouse is my man."[2]

Galehouse likely made an impression on Sewell by winning two of three starts down the stretch. After a six-hit, 3-1 victory over the Philadelphia Athletics, Galehouse yielded only one run in five innings in losing at Boston. His last outing, a five-hit, 2-0 whitewash of the Yankees on September 30, kept the Browns even with Detroit and set the stage for their pennant-clinching win over New York on October 1.

"It's the biggest thrill of my life," Galehouse said. "I've yearned for this through the 15 years I've been playing ball but never came close."[3]

The opposing moundsman came as a surprise to no one. The Cardinals' Mort Cooper was a 20-game winner for the third straight season, compiling a 22-7 record with a stingy 2.46 ERA and seven shutouts, which tied him with Detroit's Dizzy Trout for the most in the majors.

The weather was cool and damp that morning, but by game time, 2:00 P.M., the sun was out and the skies clear.

Series-opening festivities were subdued in keeping with wartime sensibilities, and outside of Governor Bricker, visiting dignitaries were few. Baseball Commissioner Kenesaw M. Landis, who was ill, remained in Chicago, missing his first World Series since he assumed the office in 1920.[4] With 33,242 fans filling the stands, and tens, if not hundreds, of thousands of GIs listening on shortwave radio sets as they attempted to breach Germany's Siegfried Line at Aachen or sweltered in the South Pacific, the Cardinals took the field.

The Cardinals were the first to threaten when Marty Marion doubled down the third-base line with two outs in the bottom of the second inning and Emil Verban singled sharply to center, sending Marion to third. Mort Cooper took a called third strike, though, to end the threat.

Cardinals center fielder Johnny Hopp may have deprived the Browns of a scoring opportunity in the third when, after a walk to Galehouse, Don Gutteridge lifted a fly ball to center. Hopp stumbled but recovered in time to make the catch.

The Cardinals threatened again in the bottom of the third when Hopp drove a one-out single just out of reach of George McQuinn's glove at first, and Sanders' drive to right field clanked off the glove of a sprinting Gene Moore. Hopp moved to second on what was scored a base hit.

Southworth called on Stan Musial, the NL leader with 51 doubles and a .990 OPS, to bunt. It was a perfect sacrifice. Galehouse, who scooped it up, could only toss the ball to McQuinn at first, with Hopp and Sanders advancing to second and third.

Walker Cooper, Mort's brother and batterymate, was intentionally passed to load the bases, and as Bob Muncrief began to warm up in the Browns bullpen, Whitey Kurowski fouled off Galehouse's first two pitches, and then went down swinging on the third. Danny Litwhiler then grounded to third, and the Browns' Mark Christman made the force play unassisted for the third out.

In the top of the fourth inning, Chet Laabs took Mort Cooper deep to right field, but Musial made the catch at the wall. Vern Stephens popped out to second for the second out, but Moore followed by poking a single between first and second for the Browns' first hit of the game.

George McQuinn stepped up to the plate. Cooper's first pitch was high and inside for a ball. The next pitch was over the plate, and McQuinn connected, driving the ball onto the roof of the right-field pavilion for a two-run homer. The crowd, clearly leaning to the long-hapless Browns, erupted, and Moore and McQuinn were mobbed by their teammates as they crossed home plate. In the tumult, home-plate umpire John "Ziggy" Sears was forced to temporarily halt play until the crowd settled down enough to allow Christman to step in and ground out to shortstop Marion to end the inning.

Neither team managed a hit through the next three innings. With Ray Sanders on first and one out in the fifth inning, Browns second baseman Don Gutteridge executed what was called the "smartest play of the game."[5] Jogging back for Musial's soft fly,

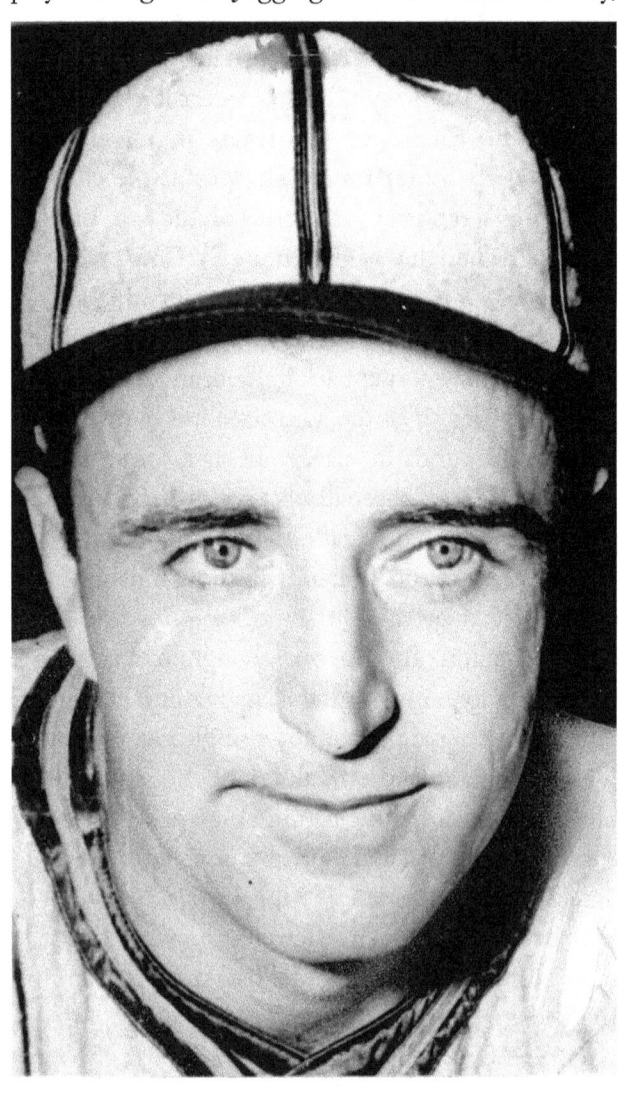

Denny Galehouse went 9-10 for the pennant-winning Browns in 1944. In parts of 15 big-league campaigns, he compiled a 109-118 record. (National Baseball Hall of Fame, Cooperstown, New York)

he chose to let the ball bounce. He tossed the ball to shortstop Vern Stephens, covering second, who relayed to McQuinn at first for the inning-ending double play.

With the score still 2-0 in the bottom of the seventh and Augie Bergamo, who had drawn a walk batting for Emil Verban, on first, Mort Cooper, who had pitched seven innings of two-hit ball, was lifted for a pinch-hitter. Debs Garms grounded out to first, advancing Bergamo, but Galehouse retired Hopp and Sanders, leaving Bergamo stranded at second.

Right-hander Blix Donnelly took the mound for the Cardinals in the eighth. Donnelly, a 30-year-old rookie who had contributed a 2-1 record with a 2.12 ERA in 27 games as a spot starter and reliever, retired the Browns in order in the eighth and ninth innings.

Marion led off the bottom of the ninth for the Cards by lining to center. Kreevich made a diving stab at the ball, snaring it in his glove for a moment before it popped out and Marion pulled into second with a double. Bergamo, who had remained in the game in left field, grounded out to Gutteridge for the first out, with Marion moving to third. Southworth sent left-handed Ken O'Dea to hit for Donnelly. O'Dea flied to Kreevich in center, while Marion tagged up and scored to pull the Cardinals within a run. Kreevich, though, pulled in Hopp's fly ball to put the game away for the Browns.

The improbable Browns had won the first game in their first World Series. In the process, they had come out on top despite only two hits, the first team to win a World Series game with such a meek attack.

Denny Galehouse pitched all nine innings, yielding only seven hits and one run. Although he looked somewhat shaky in the early innings, Galehouse subsequently bore down, allowing only two hits over the final six innings.

"Did Southworth blunder when he called on Stan Musial to bunt?" asked sports editor Sid Keener in the next day's *St. Louis Star-Times*.

"After it was all over," Keener wrote, "and the fans walked slowly from the park, and the press box gathered to review the stunning defeat of the National League champions, one managerial flaw was noted in Southworth's strategy.

"Two on, none down, and the Cardinals' leading batter at the plate. Would you play the old army game of bunting for a sacrifice, or call out some inside stuff like the hit-and-run or let Stan Musial swing with full power and no strings attached? Southworth played it safety-first for the bunt and the sacrifice, and with Musial the batter, it is repeated.

"And this is the story of how two hits won over seven hits—how the Browns, baseball's Cinderella ball club, captured the first game from their National League rivals."[6]

SOURCES

In addition to the sources listed in the Notes, the author also consulted the *New York Times*, *St. Louis Post-Dispatch*, and *The Sporting News*.

NOTES

1   F.W. Crawford, "Series Sidelights," *Indianapolis Star*, October 5, 1944: 16.

2   Orlo Robertson, "N.L. Champs 2-1 in Opener, 20-9 for Title," *Des Moines Register*, October 4, 1944: 6.

3   "Galehouse to Face Cooper," *Daily Chronicle* (DeKalb, Illinois), October 4, 1944: 11.

4   Landis eventually checked in to St. Luke's Hospital in Chicago, where he died on November 25 after suffering a heart attack.

5   "Bricker, at Series, Praises Gutteridge," *Los Angeles Times*, October 5, 1944: 1.

6   Sid Keener, "Browns First Team in World Series History to Win Game on Two Hits; Galehouse Brilliant in the Clutch," *St. Louis Star-Times*, October 5, 1944: 20.

UNKNOWNS LEAD CARDS TO VICTORY

October 5, 1944: St. Louis Cardinals 3, St. Louis Browns 2, at Sportsman Park

Game Two of the World Series

BY KELLEN NIELSON

"They looked more like a softball team than a baseball team, but that was okay. They were different. They were allowed to look different. They were always in last place," opined sportswriter Joe Falls about the St. Louis Browns.[1] But this year was different. The Browns, a ragtag bunch of 4Fs and misfits, were in the World Series and had taken the first game of the Series, 2-1, against the heavily favored in-town rival St. Louis Cardinals, despite only two hits.[2]

The "Streetcar Series" or "Trolley Series," as it was known in St. Louis, was the first intracity World Series that didn't include a team from New York since 1906, when the Chicago Cubs and White Sox squared off. It was also only the third time World Series opponents had shared the same home field.[3]

Browns manager Luke Sewell, in a surprise move, had started Denny Galehouse in Game One, but for Game Two Sewell went to his ace, Nelson Potter. Potter was enjoying what was probably the finest year of his career. He had won 19 games for the Browns that year, and might have won 20 if not for being ejected from a game for using the spitball. Potter had a good September and had not allowed a run in his last 20 innings.

Cardinals manager Billy Southworth countered with Max Lanier, who also enjoyed a fine 1944 season. Lanier had gone 17-12 with a 2.65 ERA. Lanier, a natural righty, had become a left-hander after breaking his right arm several times in his youth. Unlike Potter, Lanier had struggled down the stretch. He hadn't won a game since a complete-game victory against the Boston Braves on August 22. He had lost his last seven starts with an ERA of 6.29.

The first inning went smoothly for both pitchers; both retired the side in order. Lanier had an easy second, but Potter gave up a leadoff double to Walker Cooper. Potter struck out Ray Sanders and retired the next two batters on groundouts. The Browns went down easily in the third, but Potter once again ran into trouble. Emil Verban led off with a single. Lanier squared to bunt and popped it up. Potter missed the easy catch, fumbled the ball, and compounded his mistake when he threw wild to first. Verban ended up at third and Lanier at first. Potter was charged with two errors on the play. (Ironically, the last World Series pitcher to make two errors in an inning was Lanier, who did it in Game One of the 1942 Series. Next up was Augie Bergamo, who hit an RBI grounder to second as Verban came home to make it 1-0. Potter erased Johnny Hopp and Stan Musial to end the inning.

Potter got into trouble again in the bottom of the fourth, when he walked Ray Sanders with one out and Whitey Kurowski singled sharply to left. League MVP Marty Marion grounded to third for what looked like an easy double play, but the ball was booted by Mark Christman and skipped into left field. With the bases loaded, Verban lofted a fly ball to left field and Sanders scored to give the Cardinals a 2-0 lead, with both runs being unearned.

The Browns mounted their first offensive threat in the top of the fifth when Gene Moore bunted for the Browns' first hit of the game. (Moore, a left-handed batter, got a surprise start against the left-handed Lanier.) The threat evaporated as the Browns offense continued to fizzle with a couple of groundouts and a fly out.

In the bottom of the sixth, Kurowski doubled to deep center with two outs. Marion was then intentionally walked, bringing up Verban, who popped up to first.

The Browns' first serious threat tied the score, 2-2. With two outs in the seventh, Moore got his second hit, a single to center. Red Hayworth doubled to left, scoring Moore, then Frank Mancuso pinch-hit for Potter and singled to center, scoring Hayworth.

The top of the eighth began with Mike Kreevich's double to left off Lanier. Manager Southworth went to his bullpen, bringing in 30-year-old rookie reliever Sylvester "Blix" Donnelly. In the bullpen Bud Byerly and Fred Schmidt had both been warming up, but Southworth decided to play a hunch. "I sent word down there for Donnelly to get ready," he said. "Yes, I know he worked the day before, but I had a hunch he was the right man for the relief job."[4] Donnelly had pitched admirably for the Cardinals in 1944 with a 2.12 ERA in 76⅓ innings, and had pitched two hitless and scoreless innings in Game One. Chet Laabs, who became a hero for the Browns on the last day of the season by hitting two homers and helping the Browns clinch their first pennant, struck out when he fouled off a bunt attempt with two strikes. Donnelly recorded another strikeout when he got Vern Stephens swinging. After intentionally walking George McQuinn, Donnelly struck out Christman, who flung his bat in disgust, to end the Browns threat.

Neither team scored in the ninth and the game moved to extra innings. It was the first extra-inning game in the World Series since 1939, when the Yankees closed out the Reds in Game Four, 7-4. In the 11th the Browns threatened to take the lead. McQuinn doubled off the screen in right field to lead off the inning. Christman bunted down the third-base line, but Donnelly grabbed the ball quickly and fired to third to nab McQuinn for the first out. Southworth said of the play, "He's like a cat out there on the mound, a swell fielding pitcher."[5] Arthur Daley of the *New York Times* said of the play, "Donnelly's astounding executed play made all the difference between victory and defeat."[6] Donnelly retired the next two batters with a fly ball and a strikeout.

The Cardinals wasted no time in their half of the 11th. Sanders singled to center. Kurowski bunted him to second and Marion was intentionally walked for the second time. Southworth sent Ken O'Dea to pinch-hit for Verban. O'Dea was no stranger to the pressures of pinch-hitting in the World Series. A backup catcher, he had appeared in four previous World Series going 5-for-10 with one home run and four RBIs. He had also knocked in the only run for the Cardinals in Game One with a pinch-hit sacrifice fly. It was even noted in the World Series program, "Though not a consistent hitter, [O'Dea] has swatted many timely wallops to turn defeats into victories."[7] O'Dea did not disappoint Cardinals fans when he sent a Bob Muncrief pitch into right field to bring home the winning run and even the Series at one game apiece. O'Dea modestly said of the hit, "I caught one of Muncrief's curve balls just right and that was that."[8]

Muncrief made no excuses for the loss, saying, "You'll never see me with my chin in my hands over a ball game. I do the best I know how and if I lose I try harder the next time."[9] Browns manager Sewell took the loss in stride, saying, "I don't like it a bit when we lose a ball game, but we didn't fold up in the pennant race and we won't fold in the Series."[10] When asked if the Browns would take Game Three Sewell replied confidently, "You're damn right we will."[11]

Donnelly went four innings for the win, giving up two hits and walking one while striking out seven.[12] Southworth said of Donnelly's performance, "His last few games were great and today he came through when the chips were down."[13]

SOURCES

Besides the sources mentioned in the Notes, the author consulted Baseball-Reference.com, SABR.org, and Retrosheet.org.

NOTES

1   John Heidenry and Brett Topel, *The Boys Who Were Left Behind* (Lincoln: University of Nebraska Press, 2006), 4.

2   The format for home field for the World Series during World War II was 3-4 to reduce traveling. Since both teams shared

Sportsman's Park, a 2-3-2 format was used and the Browns were the "road" team for Games One and Two.

3   The 1921 and 1922 World Series between the New York Giants and New York Yankees were played at the Polo Grounds, the Giants' home field. The Yankees played at the Polo Grounds from 1913 through 1922. Yankee Stadium opened in 1923.

4   J. Roy Stockton, "Tie Broken on O'Dea's Pinch Hit," *St. Louis Post-Dispatch*, October 6, 1944.

5   Charles Dunkley, "Donnelly's Firearm Act May Mean Starting Role," *Detroit Free Press*, October 6, 1944.

6   Heidenry and Topel, 96.

7   Ibid.

8   "Donnelly, Relief Pitcher, Is Also Magician," *Cincinnati Enquirer*, October 6, 1944.

9   Lou Smith, "Big Hand Played by Donnelly," *Cincinnati Enquirer*, October 6, 1944.

10 Dunkley.

11 "Donnelly, Relief Pitcher, Is Also Magician."

12 Stan Musial said of Donnelly's performance, "Without Donnelly's pitching and field, we would have been down three games because the Browns won the third contest, 6-2, as Jack Kramer beat Ted Wilks." Stan Musial, as told to Bob Broeg, *Stan Musial: The Man's Own Story* (New York: Doubleday, 1964), 81.

13 "Donnelly, Relief Pitcher, Is Also Magician."

THE BROWNS' JACK KRAMER SUBDUES THE REDBIRDS

October 6, 1944: St. Louis Browns 6, St. Louis Cardinals 2, at Sportsman's Park

Game Three of the World Series

BY MICHAEL HUBER

WHILE THE NATION WAS STILL heavily engaged in World War II, two teams from the Gateway City battled for the 1944 world championship in baseball. The postseason was affectionately known as the "St. Louis Showdown"[1] and the "St. Louis Streetcar World Series."[2] Historian Roger Launius wrote, "The championship series certainly dripped with symmetry and irony. Both the Browns and the Cards shared Sportsman's Park in St. Louis. Moreover, with the wartime shortage of housing the two teams' managers, the Browns' Luke Sewell and the Cardinals' Billy Southworth, shared an apartment in the city during the year."[3] Further, "the Cardinals had long been considered the best of the National League. Its roster was filled with stars whose fingers were weighed down with championship rings. The Browns had long been the doormats of the American League."[4] The Browns had clinched the American League pennant on the very last day of the 1944 season, winning only their 89th game. Before 1944, only the Chicago White/Black Sox of 1919 made it to the World Series with fewer victories.[5] The Cardinals cruised to a 105-49 record, securing the National League pennant. Had they been in the National League, the Browns would have finished 16 games behind the Cardinals.

Because both teams called Sportsman's Park home, there was no day off between games, since they did not have to travel. However, the Cardinals were actually tenants; Donald Lee Barnes, majority owner of the Browns, owned the ballpark. The first two games were close, each decided by a single run, with the Cardinals as the home team. The Browns had taken Game One with only two hits, 2-1, and the Cardinals had rallied for an 11-inning walk-off victory, 3-2, in Game Two. In Game Three, two 17-game winners faced off, Jack Kramer (17-13) for the Browns and rookie Ted Wilks (17-4) for the Cardinals, before a packed crowd of 34,737. The Browns wore their white home uniforms for the first time, and "a blazing sun had the thermometer on the playing field soaring in the nineties."[6]

The "visiting" Cardinals scored first. In the top of the first inning, Johnny Hopp reached on an error by Browns shortstop Vern Stephens. Two batters later, Walker Cooper singled to left, giving the Cardinals an unearned run. The Browns threatened in the bottom of the second, when Wilks walked the bases loaded, but he struck out his counterpart Kramer to end the inning.

An inning later, the Browns' offense offered ample support to Kramer by mounting a two-out rally. Five players (Gene Moore, Stephens, George McQuinn, Al Zarilla, and Mark Christman) hit consecutive singles. Three runs had scored, and Southworth strode to the mound, trying to buy some time. Until Christman's hit, no one was warming in the Cardinals bullpen.[7] Wilks appeared to have good stuff, but the Browns were hitting it, so Southworth replaced Wilks with another rookie, Freddy Schmidt. Schmidt intentionally walked Red Hayworth, in order to pitch to Kramer. But he then uncorked a wild pitch, and Zarilla scored the fourth tally of the inning. Kramer grounded out, but his Browns now had a 4-1 lead. In 37 games pitched in the 1944 season, "Fred [Schmidt] never had cut loose with a wild pitch, but he chose this unhappy moment to do so."[8]

Kramer was dominant. After the first inning he was perfect for five innings, except for Stan Musial's single in the third. In the top of the seventh, Ray Sanders led off with a single to right-center. Whitey Kurowski grounded to short. Stephens threw to Don Gutteridge at second for the force out, but Gutteridge overthrew first trying for the double play, and Kurowski was awarded second base. Marty Marion singled past second, plating Kurowski, and the Cardinals had their second unearned run of the game.

The Browns answered in their half of the seventh on a pair of doubles and a walk. Al Jurisich started the inning in relief of Schmidt. Gutteridge doubled off the right-field pavilion wall and moved to third on Moore's groundout. Jurisich walked Stephens, and his fourth ball got away from Cardinals catcher Cooper, who was known as "the premier catcher of the National League."[9] Cooper was charged with a passed ball as Gutteridge scored and Stephens moved to second. McQuinn then doubled to right field, driving in Stephens. The 6-2 score would hold as the final.

However, there was a little more drama to be had. In the Cardinals' eighth inning, Hopp led off with a hard single to center, Musial smacked a line drive to right that Moore caught at the wall, but Cooper doubled to left, with Hopp taking third. After this "third straight drive of authority,"[10] manager Sewell walked to the mound. Kramer told his skipper he wasn't tired and his catcher Hayworth echoed that Kramer's control was good. Sewell told reporters, "After that, there was nothing for me to do on the mound, so I went back to the bench."[11] Sanders struck out looking and Kramer escaped the threat as Kurowski ended the inning with a fly ball to right. After the game, Musial praised Kramer, commenting that "he made us hit at the bad ones."[12] After a leadoff single, Kramer closed out the game in the ninth by striking out George Fallon, getting pinch-hitter Ken O'Dea to ground out and then fanning top-of-the-order batter Danny Litwhiler. He had silenced the Cardinals by striking

Jack Kramer went 17-13 with a staff-low 2.49 ERA for the pennant-winning Browns in 1944. He produced a 95-103 record in parts of 12 big-league campaigns. (National Baseball Hall of Fame, Cooperstown, New York)

out 10 and not allowing an earned run in a complete-game victory.

For the Browns, McQuinn was a perfect 3-for-3 plus a walk, scoring a run and driving in two. Stephens, who batted in front of McQuinn, was a table-setter, going 1-for-2 with two walks and two runs scored. McQuinn had also been the hero of Game One, stroking a two-run home run to clinch the game. Through the first three games of the World Series, McQuinn was as hot as the weather, going 5-for-8 (.625), with four walks and four runs batted in. For the Cardinals, Cooper and Marion had an RBI and two hits each in Game Three. After the game, it was reported that Wilks had been in the hospital the day before the game, being treated for stomach ulcers, and the Browns' third-inning barrage "doubtless sent Ted back to his sick bed."[13]

The Browns' third-inning offensive was their only outburst of the Series. Over the final three games of the World Series, they mustered only two more runs (one in Game Four and one in Game Six). The Cardinals would be tasting the champagne. The 1944 season was the only time the Browns won the pennant (out of 52 seasons in St. Louis), and this game proved to be the last game they would win in World Series play. According to the *New York Times*, "Despite their defeat in the third game today, the Cards remained favorites to take the world series. They were quoted at 4 to 5 in the series and 11 to 20 in tomorrow's game."[14]

The 1944 fall classic remains the most recent World Series played outside New York City that featured two teams from the same city (as of 2016). The only other such Series to be played prior to 1944 was the 1906 World Series between Chicago's White Sox and Cubs. It was also the first time in 22 years that all the games were played in the same ballpark. (In 1922, the five World Series games between the New York Yankees and New York Giants were all played in the Polo Grounds, including Game Two, which ended in a 3-3 tie).[15]

Years later, Musial said, "The funny thing about that World Series (in 1944), the fans were rooting for the Browns, and it kind of surprised me because we drew more fans than the Browns during the season. The fans were rooting for the underdog, and I was surprised about that, but after you analyze the situation in St. Louis, the Browns in the old days had good clubs. They had great players like George Sisler and Kenny Williams, and the fans who were there were older fans, older men, old-time Brownie fans. But it was a tough series."[16]

Fans can view a description with original footage from the six games, narrated in 1944 by Lieutenant Bob Elson, United States Naval Reserve, at youtube.com/watch?v=M6WrnmkxNJE.

NOTES

1. "1944 World Series," baseball-almanac.com/ws/yr1944ws.shtml.
2. "The Great St. Louis Streetcar World Series of 1944," launiusr.wordpress.com/2010/12/06/the-great-st-louis-streetcar-world-series-of-1944/.
3. Ibid.
4. Ibid.
5. In 1919, the Chicago White Sox won 88 games in an abbreviated season. The 1926 St. Louis Cardinals and the 1938 Chicago Cubs each won 89 games. In 1945, the Detroit Tigers won the World Series after claiming the AL pennant with a record of 88-65. These do not include the 1918 World Series, played between the Boston Red Sox (75-51) and the Chicago Cubs (84-45); that wartime season no major-league team played more than 129 games with the season ending after Labor Day.
6. John Drebinger, "Browns Win, 6 to 2, for 2-1 Series Lead," *New York Times*, October 7, 1944: 1.
7. J. Roy Stockton, "Kramer Is Hero of Third Game," *St. Louis Post-Dispatch*, October 7, 1944: 7.
8. Drebinger.
9. Ibid.
10. Stockton.
11. "Sewell Heaps Praise on Kramer; Jakucki to Face Brecheen Today," *New York Times*, October 7, 1944: 17.
12. Ibid.
13. Drebinger.
14. "Cards Still Favored," *New York Times*, October 7, 1944: 17.
15. In 1922, the Browns had their best season ever (measured by winning percentage), ending the season with a 93-61 record. However, they finished one game behind the New York Yankees in the American League race.
16. baseball-almanac.com.

MUSIAL'S BLAST HELPS CARDINALS LEVEL THE TROLLEY CAR SERIES AT TWO GAMES EACH

October 7, 1944: St. Louis Cardinals 5, St. Louis Browns 1, at Sportsman's Park

Game Four of the World Series

BY KEN CARRANO

THE 1944 BASEBALL SEASON IN ST. Louis was the same as it had been the last few years, and remarkably different at the same time. The Cardinals won 105 games for second straight year and captured the flag by a comfortable 14½ games. That the Browns were able to win the 1944 pennant—regardless of the circumstances—shocked the baseball world.[1] The Browns won the AL crown on the season's last day, beating the New York Yankees while the Detroit Tigers lost.

Manager Billy Southworth's Cardinals were favorites to win the Series. "Those who dabble with figures set up the Cardinals as favorites. But there are in this World's Series situation elements which cannot possibly be articulated in cold arithmetic" stated columnist Dan Daniel.[2] The Redbirds, 91-30 after 121 games, at that point a record better than even the 1906 Chicago Cubs, slumped in September and lost 19 of their last 33 games entering the Series, but were 2-to-5 favorites to win back the Series title after falling to the Yankees the previous October.[3]

Browns skipper Luke Sewell was elated with his team, saying, "No veteran club could have held up better. I am proud of all my players. The boys were wonderful. And how they played when the checks were down."[4] Even though the teams shared a town and ballpark, they were unfamiliar with each other. "We didn't know them much, and they didn't know us, because when we were at home, they were on the road," said Cardinals shortstop Marty Marion.[5]

Only the most loyal Browns supporter could have favored them over the juggernaut with which they shared Sportsman's Park. The Cardinals won the "team triple crown" by leading the NL in batting average, home runs, and RBIs, as well as hits, doubles, and on-base and slugging percentage. The Cards also led the league in ERA, fewest runs allowed, and double plays. The Browns were led by their pitching, coming in second in the AL in ERA, but had struggled at the plate, finishing the season seventh in team batting average. The comparisons to the 1906 all-Chicago World Series were apt, with the Cardinals playing the role of the Chicago Cubs, winners of 116 games that season, against the "Hitless Wonder" White Sox.[6] Browns fans were hoping for a similar result in the Series.

The momentum that carried the Browns to the pennant carried over into the first three games of the Series. Denny Galehouse scattered seven hits over nine innings as the Browns scraped by with a 2-1 victory in Game One. The Browns notched their runs and only hits in the fourth when George McQuinn homered after Gene Moore recorded their first hit with two outs. The Cardinals tied the Series the next day when Ken O'Dea's walk-off single plated Ray Sanders for a 3-2 win in 11 innings. Game Three saw the Browns prevail, 6-2, thanks in part to a four-run third. Jack Kramer made the runs hold up, scattering seven hits and striking out 10.

The Browns were two games from glory, and if the Cardinals didn't get themselves out of the funk that started in September, they would be on the wrong side of one of baseball's biggest upsets. Cincinnati Reds general manager Warren Giles told NL President Ford Frick, "[I]f they played this kind of ball all season they wouldn't have been in the Series."[7]

No team since 1937 had lost Game Four of the World Series and gone on to win it. To turn around the Series, the Cardinals turned to left-hander Harry Brecheen, who was 16-5 during the season with a 2.85 ERA in 30 appearances (22 starts). Brecheen had the makeup to right the Cardinals' floundering ship. "Deadpanned and apparently nerveless," wrote the United Press's Stan Mockler, "Brecheen has a reputation for having ice water in his veins."[8] The Browns would counter with Sigmund "Sig" Jakucki, 13-9 with a 3.55 ERA in his return to the majors after an eight-year absence. Jakucki was out of Organized Baseball from 1938 through 1943. He worked as a painter and paper hanger, as well as in the shipyards, and played semipro baseball.[9] In March 1944 the 34-year-old Jakucki was surprised to receive a letter from Browns general manager Bill DeWitt inviting him to spring training. Praised for his "fast one," Jakucki made the team.[10] Prior to Game One, Jakucki complained of an abscessed tooth, but by the time he took the mound for Game Four he said there was no pain.[11]

The Browns were the home team for Game Four, and the largest crowd of the Series, 35,455, enjoyed a cool October day. Jakucki struck out leadoff hitter Danny Litwhiler, but then the real 1944 Cardinals showed up. Johnny Hopp singled, bringing up Stan Musial. Musial had hits in all three games of the Series so far and didn't wait long to get his fourth, driving Jakucki's first offering to the far edge of the right-field pavilion for what would be the only World Series home run of his career, giving the Cards a 2-0 advantage. After going down in order in the second, the Cards doubled their advantage in the third. Brecheen struck out to start the inning, and then Litwhiler singled to left for his first hit in the Series. After Hopp struck out, Musial reached on a slow grounder past the box that was scored a single. Walker Cooper then looped a single to left, scoring Litwhiler. Second baseman Don Gutteridge could not handle Ray Sanders' hot smash, and Musial scored from second to give the Cardinals an unearned run and a 4-0 lead.

While the Cardinals appeared to have awakened, the Browns were frustrated at every turn. With one on and one out in the first, Gene Moore hit a long drive to right-center that Hopp turned into a spectacular grab. "Had that ball been a foot more to Hopp's left, he never could have reached it, we'd have a run in, a man on second or third and one out, but he caught it and it certainly was a great catch, the Browns remarked" to W.J. McGoogan.[12] The Associated Press's W.F. Crawford described the catch as "first degree robbery."[13] The Browns had another chance in the second, but with runners on first and third a broken-bat grounder from Red Hayworth turned into an around-the-horn double play, ending the threat.

The Browns had runners in each of the next three innings, but Brecheen's resolve and the Cardinals' glove work kept their lead at four runs. Brecheen's excellent defense was on display in the fourth when he retired Vern Stephens, who tapped a slow roller up the middle, especially important since the next hitter, Chet Laabs, lined a single to center. Hayworth led off the fifth with a high pop foul outside first base that Sanders turned into a great catch—he appeared to overrun the ball but was able to reach back and make the play. After a groundout and a single, Brecheen made another fine play, grabbing a low line drive off the bat of Mike Kreevich.

The Cards scored their final run of the contest off Al Hollingsworth, who relieved Jakucki in the fourth. Sanders led off the inning with a single, and one out later NL Most Valuable Player Marion doubled to left-center to score Sanders and make it 5-0.

The Browns had another excellent chance in the sixth when Laabs doubled to left with two down and McQuinn followed with a walk, but Mark Christman hit into a fielder's choice to end the inning. The Browns recorded their only run in the bottom of the eighth. Brecheen's third walk of the game—to Moore—started the frame, and Vern Stephens' single moved Moore to third. With the count one ball and two strikes on Laabs, Southworth went to the mound to talk to Brecheen after two foul balls. His advice paid off; Laabs hit a sharp grounder that Marion grabbed and turned into a 6-4-3 double play as Moore scored. Another grounder to Marion ended the inning. The Browns had one more chance in the ninth, but with two on and two out Kreevich grounded into a fielder's choice to end the game.

Brecheen leveled his World Series record at 1-1 with the victory. His line was not impressive with nine hits and four walks, but timely pitching and the Cardinals defense was enough to square the Series. The Cardinals would go on to break the Browns' hearts by winning the next two games to claim their second crown in three years, and would dominate the NL for the rest of the decade. The Browns finished third in the AL in 1945, but would never rise higher than sixth place until the team moved to Baltimore in 1954.

SOURCES

In addition to the sources noted in this game account, the author accessed Retrosheet.org, Baseball-Reference.com, SABR's BioProject via SABR.org, *The Sporting News* archive via Paper of Record, the *Cincinnati Enquirer*, *Detroit Free Press*, and *St. Louis Post Dispatch* via newspapers.com, and the *Chicago Tribune* archive.

NOTES

1. Peter Golenbock, *The Spirit of St. Louis—A History of the St. Louis Cardinals and Browns*, (New York: Harper Collins e-books, 2000), 305.
2. *The Sporting News*, October 5, 1944: 1.
3. *St. Louis Post Dispatch*, October 3, 1944: 15.
4. *The Sporting News*, October 5, 1944: 2.
5. Golenbock, 261.
6. *The Sporting News*, October 5, 1944: 2.
7. *Cincinnati Enquirer*, October 8, 1944: 34
8. Gregory H. Wolf, "Harry Brecheen," in Bill Nowlin, ed., *Van Lingle Mungo—The Man, The Song, The Players* (Phoenix: Society for American Baseball Research, 2014), 204.
9. Wolf, 94.
10. Wolf, 95.
11. David Allen Heller, *As Good as It Got: The 1944 St. Louis Browns (Images of Baseball)*, (Charleston South Carolina: Arcadia Publishing, 2003).
12. *St. Louis Post Dispatch*, October 8, 1944: 20.
13. Ibid.

BIG MORT AND BIG BLASTS

October 8, 1944: St. Louis Cardinals 2, St. Louis Browns 0, at Sportsman's Park

Game Five of the World Series

BY JOHN BAUER

THE STREETCAR SERIES WAS EVEN. BY winning 5-1 the previous day, the Cardinals tied the Browns at two wins apiece in the 1944 World Series. Game Five would provide a rematch between Game One starters, the Browns' Denny Galehouse and the Cardinals' Mort Cooper. Galehouse outdueled Cooper in the opener and the Browns "entered this crucial contest confident that their cool-headed Galehouse ... would repeat that performance against the Cards' strapping right-hander. ..."[1] St. Louis baseball fans responded to the high stakes of the occasion, buying up every unreserved bleacher and pavilion seat two hours before first pitch. On a sunny, 64-degree day, more fans—36,568 of them—would squeeze into Sportsman's Park than in any of the previous Series games.

Now established as the betting favorite, the Cardinals sought to maintain their momentum. Danny Litwhiler immediately set the tone when he belted Galehouse's first pitch of the game into left-center field for a double. Galehouse struck out Johnny Hopp, but pitched cautiously to Stan Musial and walked the Cardinals slugger. With two men on base, Galehouse struck out Walker Cooper and Ray Sanders, showing that "it would take concentrated power to beat him."[2]

In the Browns' half of the inning, Don Gutteridge fouled off Mort Cooper's first five pitches before claiming first base via a walk. Mike Kreevich stared at a third strike for the first out, then Musial caught Gene Moore's fly ball in right field. Vern Stephens, whose 109 RBIs led the AL in 1944, singled to left field and advanced Gutteridge to second, but George McQuinn's groundball to Marty Marion at short ended the inning.

Whitey Kurowski provided the Cardinals with another leadoff hit in the second, this time an infield single after beating shortstop Stephens' throw to first. Marion attempted to advance Kurowski, but his bunt popped up and was nabbed by catcher Red Hayworth on the first-base line. Emil Verban successfully advanced Kurowski with a single that created another two-on, one-out situation, but Mort Cooper's hard grounder to Stephens resulted in a double play that ended the threat. Taking the mound in the bottom half of the inning, Cooper allowed nothing. He struck out Al Zarilla, then got a pop fly by Mark Christman and a fly ball by Hayworth.

The third inning concluded with the game remaining scoreless, but not before two-out doubles by each team. Moore, whose defense in right field had received notice, tried to play it safe with Musial's ball, but watched it bounce over his head to the outfield wall. Galehouse snuffed out the threat by striking out Walker Cooper for the second time. In the Browns' half, Kreevich claimed a double when his hit to left took an unusual bounce away from Litwhiler. Mort Cooper struck out Moore for the final out, however.

At the time, the fourth inning appeared uneventful with neither side reaching base. After the game, however, it was revealed that Mort Cooper had wrenched his ankle jumping to grab a bounder from Zarilla.[3] Cooper recovered to make the throw to first and end the inning, but it was learned later "that the big fellow had hurled the last five innings with a painfully sprained right ankle."[4]

Verban opened the fifth by reaching first base when Stephens bobbled his grounder for an error. Mort Cooper's sacrifice bunt to Galehouse moved up Verban, who gained another 90 feet on Litwhiler's long fly ball to Kreevich next to the center-field flagpole. With a runner on third, Hopp struck out to end the inning. Christman opened the Browns' fifth by popping up to Verban at second. With one out, Hayworth whacked a single into right field. The Browns catcher "thundered" to second base when the "usually flawless" Musial fumbled the ball for the Cardinals' first error of the Series.[5] The Browns stranded their backstop when Galehouse popped up to Verban and Gutteridge grounded back to Cooper. After five innings, Game Five was still scoreless.

Musial, the NL's slugging and on-base-percentage leader, led off the sixth inning with a bunt; however, Galehouse fielded the ball cleanly and made the throw to McQuinn at first. Walker Cooper flied out to Moore, which brought Sanders to the plate with two outs. Sanders worked the count to 3-and-1 before hitting a "towering smash that cleared the right-field pavilion."[6] Not only did Sanders' drive clear the stands, but the ball "would have fallen into the street beyond except for the high screening which projects above the roof."[7] After the game, Sanders commented, "It's about time I connected with one. I've been up there swingin' and missin' long enough."[8] With his home run, Sanders became the second Cardinal to hit two home runs in the World Series, matching George Watkins' four-baggers in the 1930 and 1931 World Series.[9] Kurowski popped up in foul territory near the Browns dugout for the third out, but the Cardinals had the game's first lead, 1-0.

The Browns threatened to tie the game in their half of the sixth. Kreevich led off with a single to right field. Moore laid down a bunt, but Mort Cooper "went after that bunt with a speed that belied his poundage, and his snap throw"[10] to Marion forced Kreevich at second. With Moore on first and one out, Stephens singled to center field and Moore raced around to third. Cooper walked McQuinn "trying to cut the corners,"[11] and Cardinals manager Billy Southworth paid his pitcher a visit. There was no question of Southworth making a change. Rather, the manager wanted to give his pitcher a short break. With bases loaded and one out, he told Cooper, "You can get those next two men — now go ahead and do it."[12] Do it Cooper did. Zarilla watched as Cooper "blazed"[13] a third strike over the plate, and Christman looked at a big curveball for his third strike and the third out of the sixth inning. With that clutch performance, even the Browns fans "had to give the rosy-cheeked Mort a tremendous round of applause."[14] Despite loading the bases, the Browns finished their sixth inning as they started it, down 1-0.

In the seventh, Galehouse put down the Cardinals in order. After Hayworth's slow grounder to Marion resulted in the first out in the bottom of the inning, the Browns pitcher came to the plate. Galehouse singled to right field, becoming the first pitcher to get a hit in the Series. While Browns manager Luke Sewell had resisted the temptation to lift his pitcher for a pinch-hitter, he had no concerns about doing so for his leadoff hitter. Sewell brought in Floyd Baker for Gutteridge, but Cooper struck out the weak-hitting utilityman on three pitches. Kreevich's foul pop to third baseman Kurowski ended the inning.

Litwhiler, leading off the Cardinals' eighth, drove Galehouse's first-pitch slider into the Sportsman's Park pavilion. Litwhiler's blast "soared deep into the pavilion in right-center beyond the protective screening, with a carry of more than 400 feet."[15] The Cardinals had doubled their advantage, 2-0. Hopp followed with another strikeout, his third of the game, and Musial and Walker Cooper both flied out to Kreevich to end the Cardinals' half of the inning. After Moore's leadoff strikeout, cleanup hitter Stephens doubled into center field. The Browns shortstop stood witness, however, as center fielder Hopp "hauled down two towering flies"[16] by McQuinn and Zarilla to end the inning.

The Cardinals went down in order in the top of the ninth, leaving the Browns with three outs to make up a two-run deficit. Sewell opted to pinch-hit for each of his scheduled batters. Cooper, however, was unfazed. Milt Byrnes and Chet Laabs stared at called third strikes for the first two outs. Mike Chartak, to his credit, went down swinging, but struck out nonetheless. With Cooper's 12th strikeout, the Cardinals took the Series lead, 3 games to 2. Although Cooper fell one short of Howard Ehmke's single-game Series strikeout record established in 1929, he became the first pitcher to strike out three pinch-hitters in succession in a World Series game.

As the winning pitcher, Mort Cooper received most of the postgame plaudits. *Post-Dispatch* columnist Ed Wray observed, "[T]his must be eminently satisfactory to him because there have been many times when critics have not thought Mort was good in a pinch."[17] Cooper and Galehouse combined to establish a World Series record for total strikeouts in a game, 22, and umpire Ziggy Sears offered compliments to both pitchers afterward. Despite the loss, Galehouse was sanguine in defeat: "They just tagged a couple."[18] Those home runs, though, left the Cardinals one win away from a World Series triumph.

SOURCES

In addition to the sources listed in the notes, the author also consulted

baseball-reference.com and SABR.org.

NOTES

[1] John Drebinger, "Cards, With Cooper, Beat Browns on Homers, 2-0, to Lead in Series," *New York Times*, October 9, 1944: 1.

[2] "Mort Cooper Fans 12 In Winning by 2-0," *St. Louis Post-Dispatch*, October 9, 1944: 5B.

[3] Drebinger: 18.

[4] Ibid.

[5] Ibid.

[6] Ibid.

[7] Ibid.

[8] "Cards En Masse Hail Mort Cooper," *New York Times*, October 9, 1944: 18.

[9] Herman Wecke, "Cooper, Galehouse in Strikeout Masterpiece; Denny More Accurate," *St. Louis Post-Dispatch*, October 9, 1944: 5B.

[10] "Mort Cooper Fans 12."

[11] Ibid.

[12] "Cards En Masse Hail Mort Cooper."

[13] Drebinger: 18.

[14] "Mort Cooper Fans 12."

[15] Drebinger: 18.

[16] Ibid.

[17] Ed Wray, "Wray's Column," *St. Louis Post-Dispatch*, October 9, 1944: 5B.

[18] "Cards En Masse Hail Mort Cooper"

ST. LOUIS WINS! CARDINALS DEFEAT BROWNS IN TROLLEY CAR FALL CLASSIC

October 9, 1944: St. Louis Cardinals 3, St. Louis Browns 1, at Sportsman's Park

Game Six of the World Series

BY GREGORY H. WOLF

"Most of the crowd at the series seemed to be eager for the underdog Browns to upset the Cardinals," wrote the *St. Louis Post-Dispatch* about Game Six of the Trolley Car World Series in the Gateway City.[1] Described by sportswriter Sid C. Keener as the "people's choice," the Brownies hoped to even the Series and extend the fairy-tale season in which they captured their only pennant by sweeping the New York Yankees in four games on the last weekend of the season.[2] The Redbirds, playing in their eighth fall classic since 1926, were on the precipice of their NL-leading fifth championship.

The Series had been more competitive than many had expected. The Cardinals had looked invincible for most the season, owning an 89-29 record before slipping into a prolonged funk and losing 20 of their last 36 games. Nonetheless, their 105 victories marked the first time in NL history that a club had reached the century mark in wins for three consecutive seasons. Skipper Billy Southworth's squad still looked vulnerable as the Series opened, the first and only one featuring two St. Louis teams. The Browns took two of the first three games, leading many to wonder if David could slay Goliath, but the sleeping giants eventually woke up. The Cardinals, in the words of J. Roy Stockton in the *Post-Dispatch*, "shook the lethargy and faltering gait of the late season slump" to win Games Four and Five behind distance-going gems by Harry Brecheen and Mort Cooper.[3]

For Game Six, Sportsman's Park was crowded with 31,630 spectators, many of whom "dressed in fur coats, overcoats, and wrapped in blankets, [and] tried to ignore the chilly weather," noted sportswriter John R. Bell.[4] Temperatures hovering in the mid-50s at the 2:00 P.M. game time and overcast skies led to the smallest crowd of the Series with unoccupied swaths of seats in the bleachers and pavilion.

The Cardinals, in their home white uniforms, sent Max Lanier to the mound. Among baseball's best southpaws, Lanier had a 66-45 record in seven seasons, including a 17-12 slate in 1944 while earning his second straight All-Star berth. He looked sharp early, setting down the side in order and fanning two in the first. Manager Luke Sewell counted on Nels Potter, a journeyman right-hander who had emerged as a staff ace, winning 19 games to even his career record at 51-51. He, too, set down the first three batters he faced.

The Browns struck first when Chet Laabs smashed a one-out triple off the center-field wall. Donald H. Drees of the *St. Louis Star and Times* described it as "one of the longest hits seen here in years" and compared it to Babe Ruth's moon shot in the 1926 World Series.[5] With the infield playing in, George McQuinn sent a bounder over Lanier's head and just out of reach of second baseman Emil Verban to drive in Laabs. Swingman Ted Wilks began warming up to replace Lanier, who had struggled down the stretch, losing his last seven starts with a 6.29 ERA while plagued by chronic shoulder pain.

"Lanier mixed his fastball with slower stuff effectively," wrote Stockton; however, the southpaw looked shaky most of the game.[6] He escaped a scare in the third when center fielder Johnny Hopp couldn't reach Mike Kreevich's rapidly sinking liner, resulting in a two-out double, followed by a walk before Lanier got out of the jam. Laabs led off the fourth with a walk and made it to third with two outs, but was stranded after Lanier intentionally walked Red Hayworth to face Potter, who grounded out.

Meanwhile, Potter's "dypsy-dew assortment of twisters" kept the Cardinals off balance, wrote Keener.[7] Shortstop Vern Stephens saved a likely extra-base hit when he made what sportswriter W.J. McGoogan called "one of the most sensational plays of the series," snaring Walker Cooper's screeching liner in the webbing of his glove for the first out of the second.[8] Potter also got into the highlight reel by picking off Whitey Kurowski to end the frame. In the third, Potter escaped trouble after consecutive one-out singles by Verban and Lanier.

Potter came unraveled in the fourth thanks to porous defense, the Browns' glaring Achilles' heel throughout the Series. Cooper walked on four pitches with one out and moved to third on Ray Sanders' single. Kurowski hit a tailor-made double-play grounder to Stephens, but his high throw pulled second baseman Don Gutteridge off the bag.[9] As Cooper crossed the plate, Gutteridge's throw to McQuinn was late. Instead of an inning-ending twin killing, the Redbirds had tied the game and still threatened. After Marty Marion flied out, Verban and Lanier connected for RBI singles for a 3-1 lead.

Though the rest of the game was scoreless, it was not without its tense moments. Lanier was "hanging on the ropes" by the sixth inning, according Keener.[10] After one out, he yielded consecutive walks to Laabs and McQuinn, drawing manager Southworth to the mound. Both runners moved up on Lanier's next pitch, a wild one in the dirt, prompting Southworth to summon the right-handed rookie Wilks, coming off an impressive campaign (17-4; 2.64 ERA). Sewell drew heavy criticism after the game for his decision to remain with right-handed Mark Christman, mired in a 2-for-21 slump, instead of opting for a left-handed pinch-hitter. Kurowski scoped up Christman's grounder to third and fired a strike to catcher Cooper, who easily tagged Laabs, who came to the plate standing up. Wilks retired Hayworth on a fly out to end the frame.

Browns relievers Bob Muncrief and Jack Kramer held the Redbirds scoreless over the final 4⅓ innings, though they did yield four hits and walked three. One of those hits was by Hopp, who rounded first and then headed for the dugout apparently under the impression that Laabs had caught his fly in left. He hadn't, and Hopp was subsequently out at second.

Wilks "swept the Browns down like they were tenpins," gushed sportswriter John Drebinger in the *New York Times*.[11] Given the start in Game Three, Wilks had yielded four runs and eight baserunners in just 2⅔ innings and was saddled with the loss. It was a completely different script in this contest; he retired all 11 batters he faced, including four by strikeout. Pinch-hitter Mike Chartak went down swinging for the final out, ending the game in 2 hours and 6 minutes.

"The celebration of the Cardinal victory must merge with deep regret that the gallant Browns [lost]," mused Stockton in the *Post-Dispatch*.[12] The Cardinals' depth proved to be too much for the underdog Browns. Lanier and Wilks combined on a soul-crushing three-hitter with nine strikeouts; Cardinal batters banged out 10 hits, all singles, and for the fifth time in the Series, the Redbirds played flawlessly in the field.

One of the stories of the game was the Cardinals' pitching, which had led the majors in ERA the last three seasons. Cardinals hurlers limited the Browns to a paltry .183 batting average (36-for-197) and .254 slugging percentage. McQuinn, the offensive star of the Series, had seven of those hits (in 16 at-bats) and drove in a Series-high five runs. The Redbirds yielded only 12 runs and struck out a record 49 batters, one of at least 26 records that were tied or broken in the Series.

Far from lighting up the scoreboard, the Redbirds hit just enough to win, batting .240 and slugging .338, numbers that normally would not portend a World Series championship. Cooper, Musial, and Verban paced the club with seven hits each; Sanders scored a Series-high five runs, and no Cardinal knocked in more than two while the club tallied just 16 runs.

As much as the moundsmen, Cardinals fielders were the difference maker in the Series. The best-fielding team in the majors (.982 fielding percentage) committed only one error all Series, an innocuous one by right fielder Stan Musial in Game Five. Their .996 fielding percentage tied the 1918 Boston Red Sox for best in World Series history. The Browns, on the other hand, committed 10 miscues, leading to seven unearned runs (including two in Game Six).

With America at war in the European and Pacific theaters, people had more than baseball on their minds as the 1944 season officially ended. The day after the conclusion of the World Series, baseball was pushed from the front pages of the *Post-Dispatch*, *Star and Times*, and *St. Louis Globe-Democrat*, each of which ran stories about the Allies' siege of Aachen in Germany, while the fall classic was relegated to the sports sections. There was no victory parade for the Cardinals, or a last goodbye to the Browns in the Mound City, either. Gas rationing made sure of that.

SOURCES

In addition to the sources cited in the Notes, the author also accessed Retrosheet.org, Baseball-Reference.com, SABR.org, and *The Sporting News* archive via Paper of Record.

NOTES

1. "Crowd Was for the Underdog, But Had Little to Cheer About," *St. Louis Post-Dispatch*, October 10, 1944: 1B.
2. Sid C. Keener, "American Leaguers Get Only 3 Hits as Birds Take Finale, 3-1," *St. Louis Star and Times*, October 10, 1944: 17.
3. J. Roy Stockton, "Cards Champions of Baseball World for Fifth Time," *St. Louis Post-Dispatch*, October 10, 1944: 1B.
4. John R. Bell, "Shivering Fans Cheer Sun as Well as the Teams," *St. Louis Post-Dispatch*, October 10, 1944: 4B.
5. Donald H. Drees, "Browns' 45th Strikeout Breaks 33-Year-Old Mark," *St. Louis Star and Times*, October 10, 1944: 17.
6. J. Roy Stockton, "Potter Batted Out in Fourth; Wilks Replaces Lanier in Sixth," *St. Louis Post-Dispatch*, October 9, 1944: 4B.
7. Keener.
8. W.J. McGoogan, "Shave Brings Potter Bad Luck, Whiskers Bring a Calamity," *St. Louis Post-Dispatch*, October 9, 1944: 1B.
9. Though the error was charged to Stephens, the *Post-Dispatch* noted that there was some initial confusion on the play. According to Stockton, official scorers attempted to consult with players and umpires about the play to determine if Stephens' throw was too high, or if Gutteridge was late to the bag with poor footwork. Players and umpires dismissed the official scorer who charged Stephens with the error. See "Crowd Was for the Underdog, But Had Little to Cheer About."
10. Keener.
11. John Drebinger, "Cards Take Series by Beating Browns," *New York Times*, October 10, 1944: 1.
12. Stockton, "Cards Champions of Baseball World for Fifth Time."

PETE GRAY'S MAJOR LEAGUE DEBUT

April 17, 1945: St. Louis Browns 7, Detroit Tigers 1, at Sportsman's Park

BY CHIP GREENE

ON APRIL 17, 1945, JUST TWO weeks before Adolf Hitler committed suicide in a Berlin bunker, the St. Louis Browns prepared for Opening Day of the major-league baseball season. Their starting lineup was expected to contain some unfamiliar faces. For several years, as the Allies fought to defeat both Hitler and Japan, hundreds of major-league veteran players had left the game in service to their country. As a result, teams searched far and wide for men with some degree of baseball skill to fill the void among depleted major-league rosters.

Of all those replacement players, perhaps none was a more unlikely professional than Pete Gray. When he was 6 years old, Gray, a coal-miner's son from Nanticoke, Pennsylvania, fell off a farmer's wagon, caught his right arm in the wagon wheel's spokes, and subsequently lost the arm to an above-the-elbow amputation. In spite of his disability, though, Gray, who was born Peter Wyshner, nonetheless pursued a love of baseball.[1] Naturally right-handed, Gray became a left-handed hitter. To defend, he removed almost all the padding from his glove; this allowed a greater feel during catches and also aided Gray in getting the ball out of the glove when he placed the glove under the stump of his right arm. Asked once how he had developed the ability to transition the ball from his glove to his hand, Gray denied any special rehabilitation, explaining instead simply that when playing with the neighborhood kids, "I couldn't figure how to get the ball out, how to get rid of the ball. And then that just came. It just came, and that was it."[2] So adept did Gray become with his technique that in 1944, when playing in the Southern Association for the Memphis Chicks, he led all league outfielders in fielding percentage.

Gray's improbable road to the major leagues began very close to home. "I was playing up in Scranton [Pennsylvania]," Gray recalled decades later, "Sunday baseball, and the pitcher, Skelton, he went to Canada, and he knew what I could do. They were playing six days a week. They didn't play Sunday ball at that time. So, he called me up and he said would I come up there [Canada]. … it's everyday baseball except Sunday, and we practiced on Sundays.

"So, I went up there, and I done all right. It was a better class of ball than when I [later] went up there to play in the Canadian-American League; older fellas; minor-league fellas; they were paying good money. Then about three, four years later, they got into Organized Baseball, and they sent me a contract. That's how I got into professional baseball."

Gray's first minor-league season, with the Class-C Three Rivers Renards, occurred in 1942. Although Gray was initially slowed by an injury, he still was a tremendous success. "On Opening Day," Gray said, "I broke my collarbone. I was out for two months and I came back and hit .381."

That performance caught the eye of the Southern Association's Memphis Chicks, for whom Gray started the next two seasons. If there were any doubts about his ability, he dispelled them with his performance in 1944. That season, in addition to his league-best fielding, Gray also excelled offensively: in 501 at-bats, he batted .333, smashed five home runs, and also stole 68 bases. For his all-around play, Gray was named the league's Most Valuable Player.

As Gray produced his signature season in 1944, the Browns that year, for what would be the only time in their history, won the American League pennant. Despite that accomplishment, however, the team drew only 508,644 fans to Sportsman's Park.

Whether through genuine belief in Gray's abilities or, as some would later contend, a sense of exhibitionism, Browns general manager Bill DeWitt purchased Gray's contract for $20,000 in the fall of 1944.[3] The next spring, Gray would have the chance to make the Browns roster.

As St. Louis's Browns and Cardinals met the following spring in their annual city exhibition series, the hometown press got their first look at Gray. According to one report, the 30-year-old rookie fared well. He handled 14 defensive chances without a miscue and registered an assist while playing in each of the six games, and also batted .240. In the first inning of the series' final game, after a single by the leadoff hitter, Gray, batting second, singled to right field and advanced the runner to third, from where the runner subsequently scored on a fly ball. Given that, as well as his full body of work throughout the six games, one baseball scribe assessed that Gray "showed enough to warrant the belief that he will be a useful member of the club."[4] When the Browns broke camp, Gray had made the team.

On April 17, 1945, Opening Day, the Detroit Tigers came to Sportsman's Park for the first of a three-game series. "The weather was chilly and the crowd disappointingly small, estimated at no more than 4,000," reported the press, as Browns righthander Sig Jakucki took the mound.[5] Behind him defensively, in left field, was Gray. In an interview he gave in 1989, Gray was not asked, nor did he volunteer, what his thoughts were that afternoon. If he was at all nervous in the field, however, it took just two batters for those nerves to be tested, as the Tigers' Eddie Mayo doubled to left field. By all accounts, Gray seems to have fielded the ball cleanly and returned it to the infield. Regardless, Mayo's hit gives us our only glimpse at Gray's defensive performance that afternoon. It must have been quite a relief to him to get that first one out of the way.

The Tigers failed to advance Mayo beyond second base. As things turned out, however, it didn't matter, for this game belonged to the Browns. In the bottom of the first inning, left-hander Hal Newhouser took the mound for Detroit. Following a leadoff out, Gray grounded out to shortstop for the second out, but two Browns hits, a walk, and a Tigers error gave the Browns a 2-0 lead, one they would never relinquish. After Paul Richards of the Tigers homered in the top of the third, Gray struck out leading off the bottom of the inning, as Newhouser retired the side in order. Through three innings, the Browns led, 2-1.

Over the next two innings, neither side realized many opportunities. In the Browns' fifth, however, against Newhouser, Gray momentarily brought the crowd to its feet when he drove a ball to center field for what appeared to be a sure double. But as the ball headed toward the gap, Tigers center fielder Doc Cramer made a tremendous catch, somersaulting as he caught the ball near the ground for the final out. In the seventh inning, in his final at-bat, Gray singled against pitcher Les Mueller, who'd relieved Newhouser, and eventually scored the sixth of seven Browns runs in what became a 7-1 St. Louis victory.

So how good was Pete Gray? In his single season, Gray batted just .218 in 234 at-bats. While he proved adept at hitting fastballs (he struck out just 11 times), the momentum needed to swing his 35-ounce bat—and the force needed to stop it—made it difficult for Gray to adjust to changeups. Also, infielders played in against him, which neutralized Gray's "skillful bunting."[6] In the field, the fraction of a second it took Gray to transfer the ball from his glove to his hand gave runners that same split-second advantage.

In the opinion of manager Luke Sewell, Gray "didn't belong in the major leagues and he knew he was being exploited. Just a quiet fellow, and he had an inferiority complex. They were trying to get a gate attraction in St. Louis."[7] Teammate Don Gutteridge opined, "Some of the guys thought Pete was being used to draw fans late in the season when the club was still in the pennant race and he wasn't hitting well. But I certainly marveled at him. He could do things in the outfield that some of our other outfielders could not."[8]

In the end, though, it was left for Gray to judge himself. When asked once how good he might have been if he had had both arms, Gray responded, "Who knows? Maybe I wouldn't have done as well. I probably wouldn't have been as determined."9

SOURCES

In addition to the sources cited in the Notes, the author also consulted Baseball-Reference.com, Retrosheet.org, and SABR.org.

NOTES

1. Gray changed his name once he began to play professional baseball. His brother, Joe, had been a pro boxer who fought several fights under the pseudonym Whitey Gray, so Pete appropriated the same last name.
2. Pete Gray interview contained in SABR Oral History collection; conducted April 1989, by Steve Svetovich. Unless otherwise noted, all Gray quotations are from this interview.
3. Ibid.
4. *St. Louis Post-Dispatch*, April 16, 1945: 14.
5. *St. Louis Post-Dispatch*, April 17, 1945: 14.
6. Goldstein.
7. Ibid.
8. Ibid.
9. Ibid.

SLUGFEST AT THE BOTTOM OF THE AMERICAN LEAGUE

August 10, 1945: St. Louis Browns 14, Philadelphia Athletics 13 (11 Innings, Game Two of Doubleheader), at Sportsman's Park

BY JOHN BAUER

There remained the matter of a ballgame on August 10, 1945. Two, in fact. Newspaper headlines revealed a nation with its collective mind elsewhere, and St. Louisans likely also thought of events far away from Sportsman's Park. The previous day, the United States dropped an atomic bomb on the Japanese city of Nagasaki, three days after a similar event at Hiroshima. With newspapers reporting on the Japanese offer to surrender, provided Emperor Hirohito could remain on his throne, World War II appeared to be reaching its coda. That Friday's doubleheader between the St. Louis Browns and Philadelphia Athletics paled in significance to world events —even if it was ladies' night at the ballpark.

The seventh-place Browns began the day 46-50, nine games behind first-place Detroit. Defending their wartime pennant from 1944, the Browns had spent most of the past two months mired in the second division. Connie Mack's Athletics opened the season with a 6-2 record, before a six-game losing streak started a downward spiral in which Philadelphia had last place to itself from May 23 through the end of the season. The Athletics stood at 33-63, trailing even the Browns by 13 games. The day's doubleheader was the third in a week for the Browns, prompting an annoyed St. Louis general manager Bill DeWitt to point out, "There wasn't a single twilight game on our original schedule. They were made necessary by weather and travel conditions."[1]

Before the action on the field, there occurred action in the Browns' boardroom. During that morning's Board of Directors meeting at the Ambassador Theater, Browns president Donald Barnes sold his stock to club vice president Richard Muckerman. With this transaction, Muckerman now owned 56 percent of the Browns and assumed the presidency from Barnes.[2] Muckerman announced his intention to retain DeWitt as well as manager Luke Sewell. With Barnes credited for building the Browns "into a strong organization . . . well fortified in players and in money for the post war years,"[3] there seemed little reason for a dramatic shake-up.

The Browns won the first game of the twin bill, as George McQuinn's sixth-inning home run provided the margin of victory in St. Louis's 2-1 win. In the nightcap, Steve Gerkin started for Philadelphia. Despite an 0-12 record, Gerkin had posted a respectable 3.24 ERA throughout the Athletics' struggles. The 1945 season proved to be the only major-league season for the 32-year-old, and this game would be his last. Swingman Bob Muncrief took the mound for St. Louis with a 5-1 record and a 2.62 ERA. Overall, the Browns were in a weakened state through a combination of trades and injuries. In the past week, St. Louis had sold two veterans to pennant contenders, with outfielder Mike Kreevich going to Washington and pitcher George Caster to Detroit. Regular third baseman Mark Christman, meanwhile, remained in St. John's Hospital after being knocked unconscious by an Allie Reynolds pitch in the August 6 game against Cleveland. A recurring groin injury kept pitcher Jack Kramer on the sidelines and, although they played, Chet Laabs and Lou Finney were less than 100 percent.

The Athletics jumped on Muncrief right away. Irv Hall singled to open the game and Hal Peck followed with his fourth home run of the season. Two batters into the game, the Athletics led 2-0. Mayo Smith and Dick Siebert also reached base, but Muncrief escaped without further damage. Muncrief's role in the contest proved short, however. Greek George opened the second inning with a single before being forced out on Gerkin's bunt. Hall and Peck continued their hit parade with back-to-back singles — Peck's hit scoring Gerkin — and Muncrief's day was over. Sewell called upon "stocky southpaw pitcher" Earl Jones, who had became a father again that week, to cool Philadelphia's bats.[4] Hall scored on Bill McGhee's fly ball to Laabs in left field, a run charged to Muncrief, but Jones managed to keep the score to 4-0, Philadelphia.

Gerkin retired McQuinn and Vern Stephens to open the bottom of the second, yet the Browns managed to tie the game. Laabs and Len Schulte hit consecutive two-out doubles, with Laabs crossing the plate on Schulte's hit. Gerkin walked Frank Mancuso to set up Jones for a classic case of a pitcher helping his own cause. With two on and two out, Jones hit the first and only home run of his short wartime career to make the score 4-4. After Jones got through the third allowing only an Ed Busch single, the Browns went back to work on Gerkin in the bottom half. When Milt Byrnes singled to open the inning, Mack had seen enough from his starter. Charlie Gassaway, making his only August appearance for Philadelphia, would face the heart of the Browns' order. Lou Finney's bunt single made it two on with none out. After Gassaway struck out McQuinn, Stephens doubled to right to score Byrnes and give the Browns a 5-4 lead.

Jones permitted the Athletics only one baserunner in each of the fourth and fifth innings, and then his teammates broke it open in the bottom of the fifth. Gassaway surrendered a leadoff walk to Byrnes, who then beat the throw to second on Finney's sacrifice bunt. With two on, the heart of the order would really get to work. McQuinn's double into left field brought home Byrnes, and Stephens's infield single loaded the bases for Laabs, who singled to score Finney and McQuinn. Schulte followed with his own single to score Stephens. The Browns now possessed a 9-4 advantage with none out against the helpless Gassaway. Although the Athletics pitcher would create another bases-loaded jam for himself with a walk, he got Byrnes on a called third strike to end the fifth. In the sixth the Browns added two more runs when Stephens hit his 16th home run of the season with McQuinn on base. With the score 11-4 after six innings, the Browns "seemed to have the game salted away."[5]

Philadelphia scratched out a series of singles and walks against Jones in the seventh, with the result being two runs and an end to Jones's day. In the bottom half of the inning, St. Louis got back one of those runs. After Don Gutteridge and Byrnes singled with one out against Joe Berry, Finney's single scored Gutteridge. Lefty West, who had replaced Jones, held a 12-6 lead and retired Peck to start the eighth. West walked Smith before successive singles by McGhee and Siebert loaded the bases. Bobby Wilkins, who had replaced George Kell in the sixth inning, struck out, and light-hitting Busch came to the plate. Busch popped up for what appeared to the third out; however, second baseman Gutteridge "permitted an ordinary pop fly . . . to bounce out of his hands . . . ."[6] Smith and McGhee scored on the error, but the Browns led 12-8 and needed just one more out to end the threat.

That out proved difficult to find. George singled to right field, scoring Siebert and Busch and knocking out West. With Sam Zoldak allowing run-scoring doubles to his opposite number Berry as well as Hall, the game was now tied, 12-12. Sewell called upon Sig Jakucki to close out the inning, which Jakucki did by striking out Smith, but only after Peck singled home Hall to grab a 13-12 lead. Philadelphia scored seven runs in the inning, all unearned. Mancuso and Jakucki hit consecutive two-out singles in the eighth, but Gutteridge could not atone for his error and made the third out.

After Jakucki pitched a three-up, three-down ninth, the Browns rallied in the bottom half of the frame. Byrnes led off by hitting a single to center field, and Finney moved him to second on a sacrifice bunt. McQuinn's grounder to second baseman Hall accounted for the second out but also moved Byrnes to third. With the tying run 90 feet from scoring,

Stephens singled into right field, his fourth hit of the day, plating Byrnes and tying the game, 13-13. Gene Moore, who replaced the sore Laabs in the seventh, made the third out, and the game headed to extra frames.

With Berry and Jakucki remaining on the mound, the 10th inning proved scoreless. In the top of the 11th, Jakucki allowed a leadoff walk to Hall, but afterward retired the Athletics in order. Milt Byrnes, who was already 3-for-5, led off the bottom of inning for St. Louis. Byrnes drove a pitch from Berry onto the roof of the right-field pavilion, ending the game, 14-13, with his fifth home run of the season.[7] Jakucki notched his 11th win of the season with 3⅓ innings of scoreless relief, "and if ever a pitcher deserved that kind of triumph it is the big blond."[8] The Browns failed ultimately to defend their pennant, but they rebounded over the remainder of the season to finish in a respectable third place.

SOURCES

In addition to the sources in the Notes, the author also consulted baseball-reference.com, retrosheet.org, and the *New York Times* of August 11, 1945.

NOTES

1　*The Sporting News*, August 16, 1945: 10.
2　*St. Louis Post-Dispatch*, August 11, 1945: 8A.
3　*St. Louis Post-Dispatch*, August 10, 1945: 2B.
4　*The Sporting News*, August 16, 1945: 18.
5　*St. Louis Post-Dispatch*, August 11, 1945: 8A.
6　Ibid.
7　Ibid.
8　Ibid.

THEY NEEDED EXTRA GAMES

October 1, 1946: St. Louis Cardinals 4, Brooklyn Dodgers 2, at Sportsman's Park

BY ALAN COHEN

GOING INTO THE LAST DAY OF the 1946 baseball season, Brooklyn and St. Louis were tied for the National League lead with identical 96-57 records. When each team lost on that day, the Dodgers to the Braves and the Cardinals to the Cubs, it became necessary for the teams to engage in the first-ever playoff to determine the pennant winner. The powers-that-be elected to have a best-of-three series with the first game scheduled at Sportsman's Park in St. Louis on October 1, 1946.

As noted in the *New York Herald Tribune*, "A dozen or more photographers and about fifty writers lent a semblance of World Series importance. Four umpires officiated (three was the norm during the regular season)."[1]

The Cardinals had won 14 of 22 regular-season meetings with Brooklyn and were hoping to maintain that edge in the playoff. First-year Cardinals manager Eddie Dyer, a Btanch Rickey disciple who had taken over at the beginning of the season for Billy Southworth, chose Howie Pollet to take the mound for the Cardinals against Brooklyn's young Ralph Branca. The 20-year-old Branca was in his third season with Brooklyn and had started nine games during the 1946 season. He was 3-0 coming into the game and had pitched two shutouts, including one over the Cardinals, during the September stretch drive.

Pollet, the Cardinals ace, was pitching in pain after pulling a muscle in the left side of his back in a prior start. He had not been particularly effective down the stretch, notching his 20th win on September 17 and failing to add to that number in his two remaining September starts, in which he was knocked out of the box on each occasion.

The Tuesday-afternoon encounter drew a paid crowd of 26,012, about 8,000 short of capacity, but a strong showing considering that there was virtually no advance sale of tickets. Most of the empty seats were in the bleachers.

The Cardinals broke out on top in the first inning. Team captain and center fielder Terry Moore singled over shortstop with one out and advanced to third base on a single by Enos "Country" Slaughter that just eluded the grasp of Dodgers second baseman Eddie Stanky. With two outs, young catcher Joe Garagiola stepped to the plate. Garagiola hit a grounder between third baseman Cookie Lavagetto and shortstop Pee Wee Reese. By the time Reese grabbed the ball and threw to first, Garagiola had arrived safely, just beating the throw. Moore scored on the play. Dodgers manager Leo Durocher argued the call with arbiter Babe Pinelli to no avail. There was no scoring in the second inning, and the Dodgers knotted the score on a leadoff home run to the left-field bleachers by Howie Schultz leading off the top of the third. But the tie did not last long.

In the bottom of the third inning, Stan Musial walked, was singled to third by Slaughter and scored when Whitey Kurowski's grounder forced Slaughter at second base. Garagiola's second single in as many at-bats advanced Kurowski to second base, before Whitey scored on a single by Harry "The Hat" Walker, brother of Brooklyn right fielder Dixie Walker. Walker's single made it 3-1 and spelled the end for Branca. Durocher brought in Kirby Higbe, who escaped the inning without further damage, thanks to a defensive gem by Stanky on a hard-hit ball to second by Cardinals shortstop Marty Marion.

Pollet was in command and through six innings and kept the lead intact. The Dodgers mounted a threat in the fifth, loading the bases on singles by Reese and Bruce Edwards and a walk to Stan Rojek, but the threat came to a halt when Stanky grounded into an inning-ending double play, started by Red Schoendienst. Rojek did everything in his power to thwart Marion's throw to first base, but the great Cardinals shortstop was able to complete the double play. It was the second of three double plays that the Cardinals would use to snuff out potential Dodger rallies during the game's first six innings. John Drebinger of the *New York Times* provided the following analogy concerning hitting a ball toward the Cardinals' middle infielders: "[N]ext to ramming your head against a concrete wall, there is no surer way to bring an immediate halt to whatever it is you are trying to do."[2]

The Dodgers completed their scoring for the day in the top of the seventh inning. With one out Reese and Edwards hit back-to-back singles, and then Reese scored on Schultz's single to center field, which cut the lead to 3-2. However, the Cardinals defense once again frustrated Brooklyn when Slaughter cut down Edwards trying to advance from first to third on Schultz's single.

The Dodgers used pinch-hitters for their pitchers in the fifth and seventh innings, and by the bottom of the seventh the Dodgers' fourth pitcher, Vic Lombardi, was in the game. Stan Musial greeted Lombardi with a triple off the right-field screen and held at third base when Slaughter's fly ball to short left field was caught by Ducky Medwick, who had played with St. Louis during the years of the Gas House Gang, winning the Triple Crown and being selected the National League MVP in 1937. The ever-impatient Durocher removed Lombardi from the game at that point and brought in Rube Melton. Melton recorded the second out of the inning before Garagiola, on an 0-and-2 pitch, looped a ball over the infield and out of the reach of Lavagetto and Reese. It went into left field for his third single of the game, driving in Musial with the Cardinals' last run.

Pollet stranded two Dodgers in scoring position in a scoreless eighth inning when Marion at shortstop ranged to his right to intercept a dart hit by Brooklyn's Carl Furillo for the final out of the inning. Pollet retired Reese and Edwards for the first two outs of the ninth inning before Howie Schultz stepped in. Schultz had already propelled the Dodgers offense with a homer, sacrifice bunt, and an RBI single. What was left in his bat? Not enough. This time around Pollet struck out Schultz. The Dodgers went in order in the ninth inning and Pollet had his 21st win of the season. The loss in the game, which was completed in 2:48, went to Branca. (Statistics from these playoff games became part of the 1946 season record.)

The ever-resilient Dodgers fans had listened to the game on radio at any number of places in the borough. Brooklyn Borough President John Cashmore urged all firms in Brooklyn to allow their employees to listen in, saying, "Collective rooting of the borough will bring us victory and prepare us for the tremendous parade and celebration when the Dodgers win the pennant."[3] At game's end, one fan at a local watering hole was heard echoing a familiar refrain, "Wait till we get them Cards at Ebbets Field!"[4]

Pollet's 21st win made him the league leader in that category, and his 2.10 ERA also led the league. He was the NL ironman, too, pitching 266 innings.

Branca, whose loss was his only one of the season, would once again take the mound in playoff competition in 1951, starting and losing the first game and facing only one man—Bobby Thomson—in the fateful third game.

Registering the most hits for St. Louis on October 1 were Terry Moore and Joe Garagiola. Although Moore would play two more years with the Cardinals, he wasn't the same player as he was before missing three seasons during World War II. Although greatness eluded Garagiola on the playing field, his self-deprecating sense of humor and engaging personality took him to a very successful career as a writer, broadcaster, and television personality.

Schultz, the Dodgers' hitting hero of the game, had started his last game at first base for the Dodgers. Relegated to the bench and having appeared as a late-inning substitute in only two of his team's first 16 games, he was sold to the Philadelphia Phillies on May 10, 1947.

The second and final playoff game was held in Brooklyn two days later and the Cardinals won to advance to the World Series against the Boston Red Sox, who were appearing in their first World Series since 1918. The Cardinals won the Series in seven games. It marked their last appearance in the Series until 1964. The Dodgers would come back to win the 1947 pennant.

The Cardinals and the Dodgers were the two most dominant teams that played in the National League from 1926 through 1968. The teams were particularly dominant from 1941 through 1949, winning seven of nine pennants between them. During these years, the Cardinals finished first or second in every season, winning four pennants and three World Series. They passed the torch of league domination to the Dodgers. It was no coincidence that Branch Rickey played a significant role in molding each of the teams whose paths crossed in 1946 with the Cardinals (Rickey's first dynasty) about to win their ninth pennant in 21 years, and the Dodgers (Rickey's second dynasty) one year away from a series of 20 seasons that would see them win 10 pennants and four world championships.

SOURCES

In addition to the sources cited in the Notes, the author used Baseball-Reference.com and the following:

Fraley, Oscar (United Press). "Today's Sports Parade," *Traverse City* (Michigan) *Record-Eagle*, October 2, 1946: 10.

Hand, Jack (Associated Press). "Cardinals Loose and Confident," *Sedalia* (Missouri) *Democrat*, October 2, 1946: 6.

Leib, Fred. "Cards Hold Mastery Over Dodgers to End," *The Sporting News*, October 9, 1946: 8.

Mileur, Jerome M. *The Stars Are Back: The St. Louis Cardinals, the Boston Red Sox, and Player Unrest in 1946* (Carbondale, Illinois: Southern Illinois University Press, 2014), 219-220.

Mockler, Stan (United Press). "Pollet Pitches Cardinals to Playoff Lead," *Nevada State Journal* (Reno), October 2, 1946: 10.

Talbot, Gayle (Associated Press). "Red Birds Roar Out of Batting Slump to Smash Out Dozen Hits Off Five Pitchers," *Kokomo* (Indiana) *Tribune*, October 2, 1946: 9.

NOTES

1   Rud Rennie, "Cardinals Defeat Dodgers 4-2, in Opener of Pennant Playoff," *New York Herald Tribune*, October 2, 1946: 1B.

2   John Drebinger, "Cardinals Defeat Dodgers in Opening Game of Play-Off Series for Pennant," *New York Times*, October 2, 1946: 35.

3   Roscoe McGowen, "Gloom Surrounds Flatbush Rooters," *New York Times*, October 2, 1946: 35.

4   Bob Cooke, "Morose Dodger Fans Moan, 'Wait 'Til We Play 'Em Here!" *New York Herald Tribune*, October 2, 1946: 32A.

THE RED SOX TAKE THE OPENER

October 6, 1946: Boston 3, St. Louis 2 (10 Innings), at Sportsman's Park

Game One of the World Series

BY CECILIA TAN AND BILL NOWLIN

The Red Sox had not won a World Series since 1918, almost 30 years. As all the teams reassembled their full rosters in the wake of World War II, the Red Sox found themselves with a superb team and jumped out to a very strong start. They were 21-3 by May 10. They clinched on September 13, one of the earliest clinches a team has ever enjoyed, but it left the Sox marking time as they awaited the outcome of the National League race to learn which team would be their opponent. As they played the schedule, to keep in shape, they inevitably lacked some of the fire that characterized the St. Louis Cardinals, who fought the Brooklyn Dodgers right to the final day — and then some. The Cards and Dodgers tied and had to fight it out in a three-game playoff for the pennant. St. Louis won the first two games, and the pennant.

Irving Vaughan of the *Chicago Tribune* declared that the Sox "had such a formidable lead that they merely had to stumble into a pennant" but that they should therefore be in a "delightfully relaxed state." Rather than being worn ragged by the pennant race and playoffs, though, the Cardinals may have been "put in the mood that convinces them they are tough."[1]

The day of the first playoff game, the Sox scheduled an exhibition game against a collection of American League all-stars, recruited to help them keep in form. Williams was hit in the elbow by a Mickey Haefner pitch. X-rays were negative, but the elbow was badly bruised. On October 3, team physician Dr. Ralph McCarthy told the press, "Ted will be able to start the series, but he won't have the proper use of his elbow for at least another week."[2]

Cardinals manager Eddie Dyer was taking no chances. Having noted that the Yankees had held Williams to an average of under .200 on the season, Dyer figured he'd better learn how.[3]

Odds were cited at 11 to 5 in favor of the Red Sox. The first two games were played in St. Louis. Dyer decided to start back-to-back southpaws, with Howie Pollet (21-6, league-leading 2.10 ERA) pitching the first game against Joe Cronin's ace, Tex Hughson (20-11, 2.75). Dyer tapped Harry Brecheen to pitch the second game, and Cronin was expected to start Mickey Harris.

The game got underway in unseasonably warm weather at 82 degrees. It turned out to be, for Cardinals fans, "a game to sire nightmares."[4]

The Sox scored first with a run in the top of the second, taking advantage of a Pollet pitch that hit Rudy York and a walk to Bobby Doerr on a 3-2 count that moved York into scoring position. Third baseman Pinky Higgins singled to center to drive in York.

Enos Slaughter tripled with two outs in the fourth, and even rounded third heading for home, when Johnny Pesky fumbled the relay, but Pesky got ahold of the ball and Slaughter retreated to third.

The Cardinals did not score until the bottom of the sixth when Red Schoendienst singled, took second on a bit of a bumble scored a fielder's choice, and then cruised home on Stan Musial's double off the right-field wall at Sportsman's Park to the delight of the largest crowd in park history. Musial took third on Tom McBride's wild throw in. Slaughter was walked intentionally, and Hughson hit Kurowski, loading the bases, but rookie catcher Joe Garagiola struck out.

St. Louis had something going in the seventh, when Harry Walker walked and Marty Marion sacrificed him to second. Pollet whiffed, but Schoendienst beat out an infield hit and Walker took third. Schoendienst then stole second, with Sox catcher Hal Wagner electing to throw to third rather than second, hoping to catch Walker off the bag. Moore flied out deep to Ted Williams in left.

The Redbirds broke the 1-1 tie in the bottom of the eighth. With two outs, Whitey Kurowski singled down the third-base line. Garagiola drove a high fly ball deep to DiMaggio in center field and Dominic lost sight of the ball. It has nothing to do with the sun; there was a heavy haze hanging over the field.[5] Dom was just a fraction of a second too late and the ball ticked off his outstretched glove. He fired the ball to Pesky, who expertly relayed to Higgins, and Garagiola was cut down at third—before Kurowski crossed the plate. Kurowski was awarded home plate, though, with obstruction called against Higgins for blocking him as he'd come around third. Higgins admitted he'd been in the way, so Cronin's squawk was cut short.[6] St. Louis had a one-run lead to defend heading into the ninth inning. Pollet had given up just four hits and the one run.

Doerr struck out, leading off the ninth. Higgins hit a ball right to Marion at short, but it scooted through his legs. "It just stuck to the ground," said Cardinals pitcher Red Barrett.[7] It was ruled a single, but it was a big break for Boston. Both teams agreed after the game that it was the play that turned things around. Don Gutteridge pinch-ran for Higgins. Cronin put in Rip Russell (.208 on the season) to pinch-hit for Boston's catcher Hal Wagner, and Russell ripped a solid single to center. Gutteridge took third. His third substitution of the inning, Roy Partee, came in to hit for Hughson, but Partee struck out. Tom McBride was 0-for-4 on the day; he hadn't gotten the ball out of the infield. And Pollet had two strikes on him. This time, though, McBride hammered a one-hopper between short and third, and drove in Gutteridge to tie the score. Johnny Pesky flied to Enos Slaughter in right, and the Sox were retired. "The Earl of Emergency" - Earl Johnson—took over for Hughson and set the Cardinals down 1-2-3, and the game went into extra innings. Pollet was tiring, though; he'd given up four hits in the last two innings.

In the top of the 10th, Pollet showed he still had some stuff. He got DiMaggio on a grounder to short. Ted Williams was 1-for-2 on the day, a single, and Pollet had walked him twice. In the 10th, Ted hit a "towering foul fly" to Musial.[8] Two outs, but the Cardinals feared York as much as Williams. Earlier in the season, on July 27, York had hit two grand slams in the same day against the St. Louis Browns, in this very same ballpark.

Pollet's first two pitches to the veteran York were both out of the strike zone. He had to get one over and fired a curve which York pounded "almost to the concession stand high up in the [left-field] bleachers" to give the Red Sox a 3-2 lead.[9] Doerr singled, but Earl Johnson's ground ball forced Doerr at second base.

Johnson didn't have an easy time of it. Pesky erred on Schoendienst's ground ball, and Terry Moore sacrificed Schoendienst to second. With the Cardinals' best two hitters - Stan Musial and Enos Slaughter - coming to the plate, Cronin took McBride out of right field, replacing him with the more experienced Wally Moses. Musial grounded to Doerr, but Schoendienst took third on the play. With two outs, Slaughter hit a ball to right-center field but Moses ran it down for the third out.

Boston won the first game of the World Series, 3-2, in 10 innings. In the clubhouse after the game, Hal Wagner jumped on a trunk wearing just his shorts, and shouted, "Let's give a little hand to ol' Rudolph!"[10] York took a deep bow to sustained applause. He was one of only three Red Sox with previous Series experience. Gutteridge and Higgins were the other two Sox who'd seen Series play. The Cardinals had 15 players with Fall Classic resumes.

"It was a fast ball, inside," York explained. "At least that's what I thought it was the last time I saw it. Then I closed my eyes and swung."[11] Cronin thought the pitch was a slow curve. The *Herald*'s Burt Whitman thought it a change of pace. Pollet himself said it was a "fast curve"—the same pitch he'd gotten

York on twice before. Whatever pitch it was, York converted it into an arcing shot traveling 410-450 feet, and snared one-handed by a "steel-fisted fan."[12] In the dressing room after Game One, York said, "I stopped at second to watch it."

An earlier version of this article first appeared in Cecilia Tan and Bill Nowlin, *The 50 Greatest Red Sox Games* (New York: John Wiley, 2006).

NOTES

1 Irving Vaughan, "Red Sox and Cardinals Launch World Series Tonight," *Chicago Tribune*, October 1, 1946: A1.

2 Hy Hurwitz, "Injured Elbow Will Handicap Williams in Opener; Sox Head West," *Boston Globe*, October 4, 1946: 1.

3 Dyer pulled an extreme "Cleveland shift" on Ted Williams—moving the third baseman all the way to the other side of the second base bag, and leaving the shortstop in place. It worked in the second inning, but in the sixth Ted singled past the unorthodox defense. He wrote in his column, "I got a single into right field over the third baseman's head. Brother, that's one for the books." In the third inning, Ted had hit a deep drive that had home run distance but landed foul, then was walked by a wary Pollet.

In the daily *Boston Globe* newspaper column written by Williams on October 1, he admitted betting on a World Series game—back in 1931 at age 13, when he'd been rooting for the St. Louis Cardinals. The junior high school student wagered 25 cents on the Cardinals to win, and presumably collected since they defeated the Philadelphia Athletics, four games to three. Ted Williams, "Ted's Column," *Boston Globe*, October 1, 1946: 9.

4 J. Roy Stockton, "York's Homer Deciding Blow in 3-2 Victory in First Game," *St. Louis Post-Dispatch*, October 7, 1946: 2B.

5 Ted Williams wrote in his column: "It's wonder the outfielders didn't lose more. I never saw a worse haze in the outfield than the one that hung over Sportsman's Park." Ted Williams, "Ted Williams Says: 'Whee! I Singled to Right Field Over the Third Baseman's Head,'" *Boston Globe*, October 7, 1946: 7.

6 The play was described in detail in W. J. McGoogan, "Ump Explains Play on Which Kurowski Scored," *St. Louis Post-Dispatch*, October 7, 1946: 2B.

7 Associated Press, "Cards Grumble Over Beating By Red Sox," *Los Angeles Times*, October 7, 1946: 9.

8 Associated Press, "Red Sox's Late Surge Overcomes Cards in Frist Game of Series," *New York Times*, October 7, 1946: 24.

9 J. Roy Stockton, who added, "It was the only run of the afternoon that wasn't tainted." York thought it was a fastball, but Pollet said it was "a curve exactly like the one he had thrown two innings before, when York, a big broad-shouldered giant of an athlete, had popped helplessly in foul territory to Joe Garagiola."

10 Associated Press, "York Takes A Bow As Mates Applaud in Dressing Room," *Chicago Tribune*, October 7, 1946: 27.

11 Will Cloney, "Rudy Says: Closed Eyes and Swung," *Boston Herald*, October 7, 1946: 1.

12 Burt Whitman, "York Homer Wins in 19th, 3-2," *Boston Herald*, October 7, 1946: 1.

THE CAT PURRS AND THE KID CRACKS

October 7, 1946: St. Louis Cardinals 3, Boston Red Sox 0, at Sportsman's Park

Game Two of the World Series

BY JOHN BAUER

DESPITE THE LOSS TO THE BOSTON Red Sox in the 1946 World Series opener, Cardinals fans approached Game Two with enthusiasm. Thousands of unreserved seats were sold the morning of the game. Pregame entertainment—comprised Frank Miller's 25-piece jazz band and a 77-year-old bricklayer from Ohio dancing behind home plate in a white linen suit with a red parasol[1] — helped set the festive mood. Unseasonably warm temperatures in the 80s caused many fans in the outfield pavilion to strip to their undershirts.

For Game Two, Cardinals manager Eddie Dyer handed the ball to Harry "The Cat" Brecheen. The Cardinals starter went 15-15 for the NL champions, but "[his] work during the 1946 campaign, including assignments in most of the tough ones, is not truly pictured by his season's record."[2] In the season's final days and with the pennant on the line, Brecheen shut out the Cubs at Wrigley Field on September 23 and then held Chicago to a single run in a September 28 victory.

Brecheen would face Red Sox left-hander Mickey Harris, who played in his only All-Star Game that season and completed the season with a 17-9 record and a 3.64 ERA. The heat pleased Harris, who believed the weather suited his game.[3] Facing a southpaw, Dyer adjusted his lineup from Game One. Enos Slaughter dropped in the order so Whitey Kurowski could assume the cleanup spot; Erv Dusak took Harry Walker's place in left field; and Del Rice was the catcher in place of Joe Garagiola. Rice caught Brecheen regularly during the season and usually started against lefties.[4]

Brecheen's day commenced inauspiciously when Tom McBride sent his first pitch past second baseman Red Schoendienst and into right field for a single. After two failed attempts to bunt, Johnny Pesky stared at Brecheen's fastball for strike three. Dom DiMaggio sent a grounder past Brecheen only for Marty Marion to nab the ball, step on second to force McBride, and complete the double play with a toss to first baseman Stan Musial. Harris put down the Cardinals in order, with possible assistance from gusts blowing in from center field. Leading off, Schoendienst sent a long fly to DiMaggio but the wind may have spared the Red Sox an early deficit.

Ted Williams led off the second for the Red Sox, greeted by what would be known variously as the Boudreau shift, the Williams shift, or the Dyer shift, moving the fielders drastically to the right. Cardinals fans also gave Williams a "greeting"; they "booed lustily" on this and every occasion Williams came to the plate. With a 1-and-2 count, Williams grounded sharply to Musial for the out. Rudy York's 10th-inning home run to deep left field had provided Boston's winning margin in Game One, so Brecheen pitched him cautiously on this day. York worked the count full, and Brecheen's payoff pitch missed. On Bobby Doerr's bounding grounder to Schoendienst the only play was to first base, and York advanced to second. After Brecheen intentionally walked Pinky Higgins, Roy Partee's grounder to Schoendienst ended the Red Sox second. In the bottom of the inning, Whitey Kurowski singled, but Harris set down the next three batters to keep the game scoreless.

After Brecheen's three-up, three-down third inning against the Red Sox, the Cardinals grabbed

Harry "The Cat" Brecheen won three games in the 1946 World Series, the first southpaw to achieve that feat in the Fall Classic. (National Baseball Hall of Fame, Cooperstown, New York)

the lead in the bottom of the inning. Rice drove Harris's pitch against the wall in left field for a double. Brecheen showed bunt before lashing a 1-and-2 pitch into right field, scoring Rice. Seeking to advance Brecheen, Schoendienst laid down a bunt. First baseman York fell down fielding the ball, but recovered to throw out Schoendienst as Doerr covered first. With Brecheen on second, Terry Moore's groundout moved the Cardinals pitcher to third base but Brecheen was stranded there when Musial flied out to DiMaggio.

DiMaggio led off the fourth by flying out to Moore, his center-field counterpart. Williams again faced the shift and the boos. After taking two pitches for strikes, Williams swung and missed at an inside fastball for the second out. The Red Sox rallied as Doerr followed York's second walk with a single. Higgins's groundball to Marion ended the threat, however. Harris allowed a two-out walk in the bottom half of the inning, but otherwise scattered three fly outs to keep the score 1-0.

Harris's single in the top of the fifth was the only base hit for the Red Sox in that half-inning. In the home half, Rice reached first on another leadoff hit, a low line drive into left-center. Brecheen bunted down the third-base line and Higgins went for the lead runner with unfortunate consequences for the Red Sox. His throw sailed wide and deflected off Pesky's glove into center field. While Pesky scrambled to retrieve the ball, Rice made it to third and Brecheen raced safely to an unguarded second base. Doerr held the runners on Schoendienst's groundout, but Moore's subsequent grounder took a bad hop off Doerr's glove and rolled into right-center field. Rice crossed the plate for a 2-0 Cardinals lead. When the Red Sox proved unable to turn the double play on Musial's groundball to Doerr, Brecheen scored from third. Kurowski's grounder to Pesky ended the inning, but the Cardinals had expanded their lead to 3-0.

DiMaggio's grounder to Marion produced the first out of the sixth, bringing Williams to the plate. After a first-pitch strike, Williams swung hard and missed at Brecheen's next offering. The force of the swing caused the bat to fly out of Williams's hands and crash into the Red Sox dugout. Cardinals partisans stopped their jeering long enough to gasp at the sight of the flying bat before resuming the boos. Williams eventually lined out to Schoendienst on a ball that might have been a single but for the shift.[5] Kurowski's stop of York's sharp grounder to third was the final out.

Slaughter led off the Cardinals sixth with a groundball to York, whose throw to the pitcher was just in time as Harris dawdled a bit getting to the bag. After working a full count by staring at five straight pitches, Dusak sent Harris's next pitch into the screen in right-center field for a double. Facing Marion, Harris delivered a pitch that catcher Partee scrambled to dig out of the dirt. For his effort, Partee suffered a badly bruised right thumb that required Boston manager Joe Cronin to replace him with Hal Wagner. After Marion flied out to McBride in right, Harris intentionally walked Rice in order to face Brecheen. The Cardinals pitcher struck out to end the inning but not for lack of effort: He swung so hard he fell down twice during the plate appearance.[6]

Neither team struck a blow in the seventh inning. Harris's day ended when Cronin sent up pinch-hitter Leon Culberson to start the eighth, but the utilityman flied out to Slaughter in right field. Brecheen then induced a fly out and groundout from McBride and Pesky, respectively, to put out the side. Joe Dobson replaced Harris on the hill for the Red Sox. Slaughter flied out to McBride in short right field for the first out. Dyer gave Dick Sisler his Series debut as a pinch-hitter for Dusak.[7] He grounded to Doerr for the second out, before Marion did the same for the final out.

Brecheen took the mound for the ninth, seeking his sixth shutout of the year. DiMaggio reached base by beating the throw to first after dropping a slow-rolling bunt along the third-base line. Facing the shift once more, Williams made an effort to overcome the Cardinals defense but managed only a pop fly that Marion caught in foul territory near the Cardinals dugout on the third-base side. York and Doerr launched "towering flies"[8] toward the outfield, but their balls landed in Cardinal gloves for the final outs of the game.

The postgame comments centered on Brecheen's stellar performance and Williams's struggles against the shift. Dyer praised his starter. "He won for us today. You can't say anything else."[9] Brecheen boasted, "I threw plenty of screwballs at them, and they couldn't do a thing with them."[10] Dyer laughed about Williams: "We had Ted crazy before it was over."[11] For his part, Williams declared, "I know that those wide-open spaces in left loom invitingly, but with that short right-field fence, the percentages are still in my favor for hitting to right."[12] The percentages went against Williams in Game Two, and the teams headed to Boston for Game Three with the Series knotted at one game apiece.

SOURCES

In addition to the sources listed in the notes, the author also consulted

baseball-reference.com and SABR.org.

NOTES

1   Selwyn Pepper, "35,815 Roaring Fans See Cards Win and Even Up World Series," *St. Louis Post-Dispatch*, October 7, 1946: 3A.

2   "Brecheen Stops Red Sox With Hill Magic, Big Bat," *The Sporting News*, October 16, 1946: 6.

3. "Cards Found a Way to Still York Bat," *New York Times*, October 8, 1946: 27.
4. Bob Broeg, "Series Sidelights," *St. Louis Post-Dispatch*, October 7, 1946: 1B.
5. J. Roy Stockton, "Cardinals Win, 3-0, and Square Series," *St. Louis Post-Dispatch*, October 7, 1946: 1B.
6. Ibid.
7. Dick Sisler, a St. Louis native and a son of Browns legend George Sisler, thus achieved a feat that eluded his father: appearing in a World Series game.
8. John Drebinger, "Cards Even Series With Red Sox, 3-0, as Brecheen Stars," *New York Times*, October 8, 1946: 27.
9. "Brecheen Says He Used Screwball to Check Red Sox in Masterful Exhibition," *New York Times*, October 8, 1946: 28.
10. Ibid.
11. "Brecheen Stops Red Sox With Hill Magic, Big Bat."
12. Arthur Daley, "Sports of the Times," *New York Times*, October 8, 1946: 28.

JOYOUS CARDS HAIL GAMENESS OF BRECHEEN AND SLAUGHTER

October 13, 1946: St. Louis Cardinals 4, Boston Red Sox 1, at Sportsman's Park

Game Six of the World Series

BY PHILLIP BOLDA

ON SUNDAY, OCTOBER 13, 1946, the St. Louis Cardinals faced the sixth game of the World Series against the Boston Red Sox with their backs, once again, against the wall. They had played that way for the entire bruising 1946 season, and now they needed another win to tie the Series and force a seventh and deciding game in Sportsman's Park.

The 1946 National League season ended with the Cardinals, who were seven games back on the Fourth of July, tied with the Brooklyn Dodgers, forcing the first tiebreaker playoff in major-league history. The Cardinals won the best-of-three series in two straight games despite being underdogs.

The Boston Red Sox were restless as the World Series was delayed. They had won 104 regular-season games and captured the American League pennant by 12 games over the Detroit Tigers. They finally clinched on September 13 after uncharacteristically dropping six games in a row. To keep his club fine-tuned for the coming series, Boston general manager Eddie Collins scheduled three exhibition games against a team of AL players. In one of the games, Ted Williams was struck on the elbow by a pitch from knuckleballer Mickey Haefner, a mishap that some blamed for his poor hitting in the Series.

The Cardinals won National League championships in 1942, '43, and '44, and had been in nine World Series since 1926. Red Sox fans pointed out that their team had never lost a World Series, sometimes failed to note that this was their first Series appearance in 28 years, since 1918, a year before the club traded Babe Ruth to the Yankees.

The Red Sox were heavily favored against the Cardinals—as the Dodgers had been in the playoff. Boston's Dom DiMaggio thought he knew the reason for the Red Sox' success in 1946—"Red Sox players were lucky enough to be able to resume playing at our prewar level of performance."[1] This was remarkably true for Williams, who returned in 1946 after three full years of military service and picked up right where he left off, batting .342 with 38 home runs and earning the AL Most Valuable Player Award.

The 1946 Series featured the MVPs of both leagues in Williams and Stan Musial of the Cardinals. But the key to the Series quickly became the Cardinals' pitching staff, which had compiled a league-best ERA of 3.01 during the regular season. First-year manager Eddie Dyer's "money man"[2] turned out to be left-hander Harry "The Cat" Brecheen, who had won 15 games for the second straight season. Game Six featured Brecheen against Red Sox left-hander Mickey Harris in a rematch of Game Two, which Brecheen and the Cardinals won, 3-0. Brecheen also saved the clinching game in the playoff against the Dodgers, getting the last two outs in relief of Murry Dickson. Boston manager Joe Cronin held back his ace, Dave "Boo" Ferriss, who had won Game Three on a six-hit shutout, for a possible seventh game.

In the second game of the Series, Brecheen gave up four hits and shut out a powerful Red Sox lineup that included Williams (.342 batting average, .497 on-base percentage, .667 slugging average), Dom DiMaggio (.316/.393/.427), Johnny Pesky (.335/.401/.427), Rudy York (119 RBIs), and Bobby Doerr (116 RBIs).

Game Six did not start well for Brecheen as he struggled to control his screwball; Dyer had George Munger warming up in the first and second innings. The Red Sox loaded the bases in the first with singles by Pesky and DiMaggio and a walk to Williams. But with one out Rudy York grounded to third baseman Whitey Kurowski, who started an around-the-horn double play to extinguish the threat.

The Red Sox opened the second inning with singles by Doerr and Pinky Higgins. But Erv Dusak threw Doerr out from left field as he attempted to advance to third and the Red Sox were unable to score against Brecheen.

Harris gave up five hits and three runs in the third. Del Rice singled to left field but was forced out at second on Brecheen's bunt. Red Schoendienst doubled to right, advancing Brecheen to third. Brecheen scored on Terry Moore's fly ball to right. What followed convinced the fans in Sportsman's Park there would be a Game Seven—consecutive singles by Musial, Kurowski, and Enos Slaughter produced two more runs before Cronin summoned 20-game winner Tex Hughson from the bullpen. Dyer countered with pinch-hitter Harry Walker, Hughson, who pitched four strong innings of relief, retired Walker on a fly ball to center to end the inning.

Brecheen held Boston at bay until the seventh, when he gave up a triple to York that Moore almost caught near the left-center-field wall. Doerr then knocked in Boston's only run of the day with a fly ball to left.

The Cards scored an insurance run in the eighth on a walk to Slaughter followed by a double by Marty Marion. As the eighth inning ended, the Cardinals were startled by a public-address system announcement to the 35,768 fans in attendance that tickets for Game Seven were now on sale. "That guy on the PA system scared me to death." Enos Slaughter said. "Announcing tickets on sale for the seventh game in the ninth inning. We still had three men to get out."[3]

Brecheen gave up a single to Williams in the ninth, one of only five hits, all singles, that Williams would get in the Series. The game ended when York's smash deflected off Brecheen to second baseman Schoendienst, who turned it into a double play.

York grounded into two of the three double plays the Cardinals turned in the game (DiMaggio was the victim of the third) and the Red Sox left only four men on base. Slaughter reached base three times for the Cardinals, drove in a run and made a running catch of Leon Culberson's line drive in fifth inning despite having spent the previous night having his injured elbow X-rayed. No fracture had been discovered, but the elbow was puffy and inflamed. A physician declined to give an opinion whether Slaughter could play in Game Six but Cards owner Sam Breadon said, "Enos will be in there, all right."[4]

In 1 hour and 56 minutes of work, Brecheen assured that there would be a Game Seven. "Yahoo, one run off me in 18 innings," the pitcher said with a smile. "Ain't that something?"[5]

The rescheduling of World Series games to accommodate the three-game NL playoff meant Game Seven could not be played until Tuesday afternoon. Many in the jubilant crowd stayed for hours until an orderly process was established to sell tickets.

Although box-seat holders were assured of their regular seats, 25,000 tickets were sold at the box office in a single day. The Cardinals, on behalf of the St. Louis fire marshal, also announced that people buying standing-room tickets could not enter the park with stools, chairs, or ladders, and that only one person could sit in the aisle in each row.

The postwar housing shortage meant that out-of-town fans turned out by their hotels spent the offday trying to secure another place to stay. Their problems were made worse as a convention of state medical examiners and a parent-teacher conference were also in town. Baseball visitors were forced to sleep on cots in hotel dining rooms or on park benches.[6]

The *New York Times* observed that in the clubhouse, "Dyer was more than happy. He was overjoyed." Talking about the deciding game, he said "I'll toss Brecheen back in there again, if need be."[7]

Dyer was pressed to explain his team's success against Ted Williams, "the most publicized hitter in baseball." Brecheen was a screwball pitcher, but had teased Williams with a well-controlled curveball and jammed him with a fastball close to the wrists. "They certainly know how to pitch to me," said the Boston slugger before Game Six, "'cause I'm getting what I'm not expecting."[8]

Dyer had also used a shift against Williams during the Series, switching one infielder from the left side of the infield to the right, a strategy slightly more conservative than the shift introduced during the season by Lou Boudreau of the Cleveland Indians, which positioned three infielders to the right of second base. Dyer thought his shift got into Williams's head. "We had Ted crazy before it was over," he said.[9]

In the Boston clubhouse, the postgame atmosphere was tense. York reminded his teammates that Game Seven was their turn—as the Cardinals had won Games Two, Four, and Six of the Series and the Red Sox had won Games One, Three, and Five. As Cronin explained his pitching strategy to sportswriters, he was interrupted by the noise of Mickey Harris tossing furniture and tearing apart the contents of his locker in frustration over failing to win either of his two starts in the Series.[10]

"One thing I you can quote me on," said St. Louis catcher Joe Garigiola as waves of sportswriters pressed for more quotes, "the next game is definitely the last one."[11]

NOTES

[1] Dom DiMaggio with Bill Gilbert, *Real Grass, Real Heroes; Baseball's Historic 1941 Season* (New York: Kensington Publishing Corporation, 1990), 233.

[2] "Brecheen Stops Red Sox With Hill Magic, Big Bat," *The Sporting News,* October 16, 1946.

[3] Jimmy Cannon, *St. Louis Star and Times*, October 14, 1946.

[4] "X Ray Shows No Fracture. Slaughter Says He'll Play," *St. Louis Post-Dispatch*, October 13, 1946.

[5] John Schlegel, First Cards-Red Sox Series in '46 had its own twists, MLB.com, October 29, 2013. m.mlb.com/news/article/63480966//.

[6] Selwyn Pepper, "Most Seats Sold Quickly for Deciding Series Game," *St. Louis Post-Dispatch,* October 14, 1946.

[7] James P. Dawson, "Joyous Cards Hail Gameness of Brecheen and Slaughter; Cronin Downcast," *New York Times*, October 14, 1946.

[8] Bob Broeg, "Musial's Leg Work on a Leg Hit Called Turning Point of the Game," *St. Louis Post-Dispatch*, October 14, 1946.

[9] "Brecheen Stops Red Sox."

[10] Dawson.

[11] Cannon.

COUNTRY'S MAD DASH AND THE CAT'S THIRD VICTORY

October 16, 1946: St. Louis Cardinals 4, Boston Red Sox 3, at Sportsman's Park

Game Seven of the World Series

BY GREGORY H. WOLF

"SLAUGHTER'S GREAT GALLOP FROM first to score will rate with Paul Revere's ride in the history of our country," gushed sportswriter Whitney Martin about one of the most enduring plays in World Series lore.[1] Enos "Country" Slaughter's mad dash from first on Harry Walker's eighth-inning smash to center field coupled with shortstop Johnny Pesky's hesitation on the relay throw gave the St. Louis Cardinals a 4-3 lead in the bottom of the eighth in Game Seven of the World Series against the Boston Red Sox—a lead they would not relinquish. "[I]t was anybody's contest," suggested Redbird beat reporter J. Roy Stockton, "with thrill following thrill."[2]

On a warm, sunny Tuesday afternoon, Sportsman's Park was packed with a "wildly-delirious" standing-room-only crowd of 36,143, wrote Selwyn Pepper in the *St. Louis Post-Dispatch* about the atmosphere for just the seventh deciding game in the history of the fall classic.[3] That mood quickly changed when Cardinals starting pitcher Murry Dickson yielded a leadoff single to Wally Moses. Pesky followed with what appeared to be a routine grounder, but the ball took a "weird hop," according to Stockton, and bounced over shortstop Marty Marion's glove.[4] Dom DiMaggio's fly to deep right-center drove in Moses for the first run. In a play that foreshadowed the Cardinals' fielding highlights the entire game, center fielder Terry Moore made a running stab to rob Ted Williams of a possible extra-base hit. Missed scoring opportunities proved costly for the Red Sox. Bobby Doerr led off the second with a single, moved to second on third baseman Whitey Kurowski's throwing error, and reached third with one out, but failed to score.

Boston starter Dave Ferriss, who had won 25 games in the regular season and tossed a shutout in Game Three against Dickson, looked shaky from the get-go despite five days' rest. Red Schoendienst tried to stretch his leadoff single when Williams fumbled the ball in left field, but Williams recovered quickly and threw him out. Two batters later, Stan Musial doubled down the left-field line, but was stranded. The Redbirds tied the contest in the second when Kurowski led off with a double and later scored on Harry Walker's fly ball.

Notwithstanding his early-game jitters, Dickson, a 15-game winner as a swingman in the regular season, found his groove and, with help from his fielders, held the Red Sox hitless from the third inning through the seventh (issuing only a sixth-inning walk to DiMaggio). Described by Pepper as the "favorite whipping boy of the bleacherites,"[5] Williams led off the fourth with another deep fly, but left fielder Harry Walker made what Sid Keener of the *St. Louis Star and Times* called a "phenomenal" catch near the flagpole to again rob the "The Kid" of an extra-base hit.[6] The slumping Williams, hounded by sportswriter Hy Hurwitz of the *Boston Globe* as a "pathetic figure," finished the series with just five hits (all singles) in 25 at-bats and one RBI.[7] It was déjà vu in the fifth when Pinky Higgins led off with a shot to deep center. Moore raced at least 50 yards to make what Keener called the "greatest catch of his notorious career," a running backhanded stab near the wall.[8] Moore, once regarded as the premier center fielder in the

Ten-Time All-Star Country Slaughter batted .300 with 2,383 hits in his 19-year big-league career. (National Baseball Hall of Fame, Cooperstown, New York)

NL, discovered the fountain of youth despite having missed the three previous years to World War II. The 34-year-old suffered from swelling in his left knee and requiring what sportswriter W. Vernon Tietjen called "special 'dope' ointment" from team trainer H.J. "Doc" Weaver before each game.[9] After Moore's gem, Kurowski atoned for his earlier miscue by racing deep into foul territory to snag Hal Wagner's popup.

The Redbirds pounded Ferriss savagely in the fifth. Walker led off with a single and moved to second on Marion's sacrifice bunt. Dickson, no slouch at the plate, lined a double to score Walker and give the Cardinals a 2-1 lead.[10] After Schoendienst's single drove in Dickson, Moore's single sent Ferriss to the showers while "bedlam reigned" in Sportsman's Park.[11] Right-hander Joe Dobson put out the fire by retiring Musial on a grounder and, after an intentional walk to Slaughter to fill the bags, getting Kurowski to ground into a force play to end the threat.

Tension mounted as neither the Red Sox nor Cardinals managed a hit in the sixth or seventh inning. Down 3-1 to start the eighth, Boston's Rip Russell, pinch-hitting for Wagner (who was hitless in 13 Series at-bats), lined a single. Cardinals first-year skipper Eddie Dyer motioned to Harry Brecheen and Red Munger to hastily warm up in the bullpen, while Red Sox manager Joe Cronin sent George Metkovich to pinch-hit for Dobson. Metkovich's double pushed Russell to third and spelled Dickson's demise. To the mound came Brecheen, the slightly built, 5-foot-10, 160-pound southpaw whose quick movements earned him the nickname "The Cat." A 15-game winner with a league-best five shutouts during the regular season, Brecheen had tossed a complete-game seven-hitter two days earlier to force Game Seven and had blanked the Red Sox on four hits in Game Two.

Brecheen retired Moses and Pesky, but then surrendered his first hard-hit ball of the Series, DiMaggio's double off the wall in right field, out of reach of the leaping Slaughter, to drive two runs and tie the game. DiMaggio's dramatic hit proved costly, however, as he pulled a muscle in his leg and was replaced by Leon Culberson. After Williams's foul tip split the finger of catcher Joe Garagiola, necessitating his replacement by Del Rice, the Red Sox slugger popped up harmlessly to Schoendienst to end the inning.

The eighth inning is one of the most torturous and second-guessed frames in Red Sox history. Right-handed reliever Bob Klinger took the mound and yielded a leadoff single to Slaughter, then retired Kurowski and Rice. Next was Walker, described by Bob Broeg as a "regular season flop" after batting just .237,[12] Slaughter darted from first in a hit-and run as Klinger made his delivery home. Walker belted a line drive to center field, where Culberson was playing deep. Slaughter had almost reached third as Culberson made a relay throw to Pesky in shallow center. J. Roy Stockton was sure Slaughter would meet "certain death" as third-base coach Miguel "Mike" Gonzalez waved him home.[13] Pesky, momentarily caught off guard by Slaughter's aggression, dropped his arms and "pivoted slowly" before firing home, according to Jerry Nason of the *Boston Globe*.[14] Slaughter slid across home plate well ahead of Pesky's weak throw as Walker advanced to second.[15] "I hesitated," admitted Pesky after the game. "I thought he'd hold up at third so late in the game."[16] After Klinger intentionally walked Marion, new reliever Earl Johnson retired Brecheen to end the threat.

The ninth inning proved to be equally gut-wrenching. Rudy York and Doerr led off with singles; Higgins's grounder forced Doerr at second. Needing just a long fly to tie the game, Roy Partee popped one of Brecheen's slow screwballs to first for the second out. Tom McBride, pinch-hitting for Johnson, hit what Keener called, a "tough bounder, a hippety-do-hopper" to Schoendienst.[17] "[I]t was a screwy, curving ball," said Schoendienst. "It hit me ... on the right wrist ... and rolled up my forearm. Then I clamped my arm over it ... under the shoulder in time to grab the ball."[18] His shovel toss to Marion at second forced Higgins, ending the game in 2 hours and 17 minutes and giving the Cardinals their sixth championship since 1926.

Sportswriters heaped praise on the Cardinals for their unlikely victory over the Red Sox, who had won 104 regular-season games. Nason described the Cardinals as a "fighting, snarling ball team";[19] while George C. Carens of the *Boston Traveler* thought the club "showed indomitable courage, opportunism, and clutch pitching."[20] Syndicated columnist Grantland Rice observed that "smart, keen Cardinal pitching shackled Red Sox power," as the majors' highest-scoring team tallied just 20 runs in seven games.[21] Brecheen became the first left-hander and ninth pitcher to win three games in a World Series.[22] "The Cardinals outhit, outslugged, outscored, outran, outfielded, and," opined Broeg, "... outhustled the 7-to-20 favored American League champions."[23] The difference in the game, according to Stockton, was that the Cardinals took chances while the Red Sox "played it extremely safe" late in the game.[24]

The notoriously harsh Boston media was direct in its criticism of the Red Sox. Harold Kaese of the *Globe* summed up the team's stunning loss as a result of "World Series inexperience, winning the pennant too soon, and Williams' slump."[25] Cronin's decisions were openly questioned, especially why he did not lift the left-handed Moses for a pinch-hitter against Brecheen in the eighth with the game on the line and right-handed hitters on the bench; or why Klinger pitched instead of staff co-ace Tex Hughson, who had won 20 games and was in the bullpen.[26] Though some fans might have perceived Pesky as a goat, Nason rejected any overtures assigning blame to him for the Red Sox loss; instead he suggested the Cardinals won because of their defense, especially Moore's heroics.[27]

The game, gushed Whitney Martin, was "sheer undiluted, spine-tingling drama."[28]

SOURCES

In addition to the sources cited in the Notes, the author also accessed Retrosheet.org, Baseball-Reference.com, SABR.org, and *The Sporting News* archive via Paper of Record.

NOTES

1. Whitney Martin (Associated Press), "Slaughter Run Like Paul Revere's Ride," *Boston Globe*, October 16, 1946: 19.
2. J. Roy Stockton, "Slaughter's Run to Certain Death Is Winning Gamble; Brecheen and Walker Also Heroes of Epic Finish," *St. Louis Post-Dispatch*, October 16, 1946: 2B.
3. Selwyn Pepper, "Fans Wildly Delirious as Home Team Takes Final Series Contest," *St. Louis Post-Dispatch*, October 15, 1946: 1B.
4. J. Roy Stockton, "Walker Drives In Slaughter in 8th to Beat Red Six, 4-3," *St. Louis Post-Dispatch*, October 15, 1946: 1B.
5. Pepper.
6. Sid Keener, "Brecheen Is Team's Hero in Dramatic 4-3 Victory; Decisive Run by Slaughter," *St. Louis Star and Times*, October 16, 1945: 20.
7. Hy Hurwitz, "Ted Just Sits and Stares for Half-Hour After Game," *Boston Globe*, October 16, 1946: 1.
8. Sid Keener, "Moore and Walker Race to Distant Sectors to Haul Down Drives by Red Sox," *St. Louis Star and Times*, October 15, 1946: 2.
9. W. Vernon Tietjen, "Step Right Up, Folks, and Pick Your Series Hero—Cardinals Have Them by the Dozens," *St. Louis Star and Times*, October 16, 1946: 20.
10. Dickson batted .277 (18-for-65) with six extra-base hits in the regular season.
11. Pepper.

12 Walker had been an All-Star in 1943, batting .294 in his last full season before missing the next two seasons during the war. Bob Broeg, "Eight Records Set, 10 Tied in Series," *St. Louis Post-Dispatch*, October 16, 1946: 4N.

13 Stockton, "Slaughter's Run to Certain Death Is Winning Gamble; Brecheen and Walker Also Heroes of Epic Finish."

14 Jerry Nason, "Slaughter, Brecheen Give Cards Series Finale," *Boston Globe*, October 16, 1946: 1.

15 A video of this exciting play can be seen on You Tube. youtube.com/watch?v=t7IgTE5930A.

16 Harold Kaese, "Why Did Sox Lose? Series Inexperience, Soft Pennant Race, Williams' Slump," *Boston Globe*, October 16, 1946: 20.

17 Keener, "Brecheen Is Team's Hero in Dramatic 4-3 Victory; Decisive Run by Slaughter."

18 Tietjen, "Right Up, Folks, and Pick Your Series Hero — Cardinals Have Them by the Dozens."

19 Nason.

20 George C. Carens, "DiMaggio Injury Big Game Break," *Boston Traveler*, October 16, 1946: 32.

21 Grantland Rice, "Not Best I've Seen, but Gamest, Says Dyer of Cards," *Boston Globe*, October 16, 1946: 22.

22 The other pitchers to win three games in a single World Series were Deacon Phillippe (Pittsburgh Pirates) and Bill Dineen (Boston Americans) in 1903; Christy Mathewson with the New York Giants in 1905; the Pirates' Babe Adams in 1909; Jack Coombs (Philadelphia Athletics) in 1910; Smoky Joe Wood of the Red Sox in 1912; Red Faber (Chicago White Sox) in 1917; and finally Stan Coveleski (Cleveland Indians) in 1920.

23 Broeg's pronouncement was hardly the stuff of homerism; the Cardinals bettered the Red Sox in almost every meaningful offensive and defensive category. The final batting slash for the Cardinals was .259/.320/.371 compared with .240/.309/.330 for the Red Sox. The Cardinals team ERA was 2.32; Red Sox 2.95; and finally the Cardinals committed four errors to the Red Sox' 10.

24 Stockton, "Slaughter's Run to Certain Death Is Winning Gamble; Brecheen and Walker Also Heroes of Epic Finish,"

25 Kaese.

26 Hughson started games One and Four, though lasted just two innings in the latter. In game Six he hurled 4⅓ innings of scoreless relief.

27 Nason.

28 Martin.

A DARK CHAPTER: JACKIE ROBINSON DEBUTS IN THE GATEWAY CITY

May 21, 1947: Brooklyn Dodgers 4, St. Louis Cardinals 3 (10 Innings), at Sportsman's Park

BY CHIP GREENE

JACKIE ROBINSON NEVER THOUGHT the abuse would happen in New York City. He was accustomed to receiving this kind of racial vilification — the vitriol and vulgarity heaped on him simply because of the color of his skin — in the Jim Crow South, where blacks, if not inured to the humiliation, at least knew it was coming, and how to tolerate it. Not here, however. Robinson never expected it in the north, in one of the world's most cosmopolitan cities.

Yet, there it was: every conceivable racial slur leveled at this proud man; every despicable, deplorable invective one could imagine, pouring forth from the Philadelphia Phillies dugout, each time Robinson took the field at Brooklyn's Ebbets Field. Yes, he had agreed to keep his anger in check, to turn the other cheek. Robinson had given Branch Rickey his word that he would not fight back. How much was one man expected to take, though, when every fiber of his being cried out for him to stride to the Phillies' bench and, as Robinson recalled years later, "grab one of those white sons of bitches and smash his teeth in with my despised black fist."?[1]

That day, April 22, 1947 (as well as the remaining two games of the three-game series), as the Phillies' manager, Ben Chapman, a Southerner, led the torment of Robinson from the Phillies dugout, has been endlessly chronicled in the years since Robinson broke baseball's color barrier. With each telling of the narrative, it is perhaps the most infamous and notorious example of the vicious treatment Robinson endured that season, as he integrated modern baseball. Indeed, Robinson himself later conveyed his sense of desperation at the time, relating in his autobiography that although "I tried just to play ball and ignore the insults," the Phillies' racist taunts left him "tortured" and "brought me nearer to cracking up than I ever had been."[2] It was a shameful and disgusting display of man's inhumanity toward man.

If that Phillies series, however, marked the nadir of Robinson's degradation, it also formed cohesion among the man and his teammates; even, to a degree, those who shared the same views as did the Phillies' racist manager. As Branch Rickey opined years later, "Chapman did more than anybody to unite the Dodgers."[3] For as the other Dodgers witnessed the abuse Robinson was taking, a solitary figure unable to fight back, many began to sympathize with his plight and to stand up for him — to see him, simply, as a man. Perhaps they weren't all to become instant friends, and perhaps Rickey would have to defend Robinson against those Dodgers who refused to fully accept a black man, but as the season went on, Robinson became one of theirs, and they gradually learned to live with each other. That Robinson was possessed of undeniable talents assuredly made his presence that much easier to take.

As important as it was for Robinson to gain acceptance within the clubhouse, it was equally important that he be accepted outside as well. In that, he had a most effective advocate: The sporting press was critical in humanizing Robinson and generating empathy in the eyes of the mostly white public. And no single reportage was more important than an exclusive that was published by the *New York Herald Tribune's* legendary sports editor, Stanley Woodward.

In his autobiography, Robinson incorrectly remembered that Brooklyn was scheduled to make its first visit to St. Louis, baseball's southernmost city, where he was certain to receive his most vehement abuse, on May 9, 1947. In actuality, though, it wasn't until May 21 that the Dodgers and Cardinals met for the first time in St. Louis. Just before that date, however, Woodward discovered that the Cardinals players were plotting to execute a last-minute strike in protest of Robinson's inclusion on the Brooklyn squad. Woodward printed the story. The ramifications of the exposed plot were immediate.

"If you do this," warned National League President Ford Frick, "you will be suspended from the league. You will find that the friends you think you have in the press box will not support you, that you will be outcasts. I do not care if half the league strikes. Those who do it will encounter quick retribution. They will be suspended and I don't care if it wrecks the National League for five years. This is the United States of America, and one citizen has as much right to play as another.

"The National League will go down the line with Robinson whatever the consequences. You will find if you go through with your intention that you have been guilty of complete madness."[4]

The Cardinals' planned strike was never carried out.

Against that backdrop, on Wednesday afternoon, May 21, the Dodgers and Cardinals took the field at Sportsman's Park. The struggling Cardinals had the worst record in the majors (9-18), while the Dodgers (14-13) were in fifth place, 1½ games behind the Chicago Cubs. Despite the game's racial overtones, the Cardinals front office likely breathed a sigh of relief that the strike hadn't taken place, because the 16,249 fans in attendance that day were the Cardinals' largest weekday crowd thus far in the season. That number included, reported the press the next day, an estimated "6,000 Negroes."[5] Starting for the Cardinals was left-hander Harry Brecheen, who came in with a 4-1 record, picking up where he left off as the pitching star of the previous fall's World Series. Batting second for Brooklyn and playing first base, was Robinson. Fittingly, he was to be instrumental in the game's final outcome.

In their first at-bats, Brooklyn struck quickly. That a Cardinals defensive blunder helped must certainly have exacerbated the chastened Cardinals' undoubtedly already surly dispositions. After leadoff batter Eddie Stanky flied out, Robinson drew a walk and quickly advanced to third on a single by Pete Reiser. The next batter was Carl Furillo. Playing first base for St. Louis was Stan Musial. As Brecheen delivered, Furillo hit a hard grounder to Musial, so hard, that Robinson could not advance. That quickly changed, however. Fielding the ball cleanly, Musial stepped on first, but then made an ill-advised decision. As Reiser bolted for second, Musial ignored Robinson and fired a throw to second, where shortstop Marty Marion awaited. Because Musial had stepped on first, Marion had to tag Reiser, but Musial's throw was low and wide, and Marion failed to hold on to the ball. On the throw, Robinson trotted home, giving the Dodgers a 1-0 lead as the inning ended. It was to be a critical run.

For posterity, history records that the Dodgers went on to win this game 4-3, in 10 innings, when Cookie Lavagetto singled home Reiser in the top of the 10th. The victory ran their record to 15-13, a modest start on their way to the National League pennant, with a 94-60 record. They couldn't have done it without Jackie Robinson, though. After finishing the season with a .297 batting average and a league-leading 29 stolen bases, the 28-year-old Robinson was named the league's Rookie of the Year. Two years later he was named the league's Most Valuable Player, and by the time he retired after the 1956 season, he had cemented his legend as a baseball immortal, and perhaps the most transformative athlete in the history of sports.

That the Dodgers won this, their 28th game in a long 154-game season, and that Robinson, despite going 0-for-4, contributed to the victory, was certainly important. Of far greater importance, however, was the fact that here, in the South, this black man "was cheered each time he went to bat and the Dodgers as a team received more vocal encouragement than they usually [got] at Sportsman's Park."[6]

In the end, no one could have synopsized that season better than Robinson himself. In his autobiography, Robinson wrote eloquently: "I had started the season as a lonely man, often feeling like a black Don Quixote tilting at a lot of white windmills. I ended it feeling like a member of a solid team. The Dodgers were a championship team because all of us had learned something. I had learned how to exercise self-control—to answer insults, violence, and injustice with silence—and I had learned how to earn the respect of my teammates. They had learned that it's not skin color but talent and ability that counts. Maybe even the bigots had learned that, too."[7]

SOURCES

In addition to the sources listed in the Notes, the author also consulted Retrosheet.org and Baseball-Reference.com.

NOTES

[1] Jackie Robinson, as told to Alfred Duckett, *I Never Had It Made: An Autobiography of Jackie Robinson* (New York: Harper Collins, 1972), 69.

[2] Ibid.

[3] Robinson, 72.

[4] Robinson, 73.

[5] J. Roy Stockton, "Cardinals 'Health Resort' Makes Rivals Feel Better, Fans Worse," *St. Louis Post-Dispatch*, May 22, 1947: 10C

[6] Ibid.

[7] Robinson, 75.

HARRY BRECHEEN'S ALMOST-PERFECT GAME

May 8, 1948: St. Louis Cardinals 5, Philadelphia Phillies 0, at Sportsman's Park

BY RICHARD A. CUICCHI

HARRY "THE CAT" BRECHEEN HAD previously entered major-league baseball's record books in 1946 by becoming the first left-handed pitcher to win three games in a World Series. He figuratively came within a cat's whisker of making history again on May 8, 1948, when he missed hurling a perfect game because of a close call on an infield grounder.

Brecheen had already established himself as one of the best St. Louis Cardinals pitchers of the 1940s. And the 1948 season turned out to be his best year, as he won 20 games for the Cardinals, the only season in which he reached that mark. It was his fifth consecutive season with 15 or more wins. Cardinals manager Eddie Dyer said of his gritty and tenacious pitcher, "What a man to have around when you really have to win a ballgame. The Cat's got a head, heart, and guts."[1]

Brecheen earned his feline nickname by virtue of his superior fielding ability. He reminded people of a cat when he sprang off the mound to pounce on groundballs hit near him.[2] His smallish physical stature, 5-feet-10 and 160 pounds, also contributed to the analogy.

After beginning the 1948 season with two shutout wins, the 38-year-old Brecheen got his third start on May 8 against the Philadelphia Phillies at Sportsman's Park. Blix Donnelly drew the starting assignment for the Phillies.

In front of 15,471 spectators, Brecheen blitzed through the Phillies' starting nine the first time by recording outs via three strikeouts, three fly balls, two popups and one groundout. The Phillies' lineup that day featured rookie Richie Ashburn, who had gotten off to a solid start and had an average near .300 at the time.

The Cardinals got their first run against Donnelly in the bottom of the fourth inning on a two-out walk by Enos Slaughter and a run-scoring double by Whitey Kurowski.

Brecheen retired the entire Phillies lineup the second time through in a similarly routine fashion as in the first three innings, including three more strikeouts.

The Cardinals scored their second and third runs in the bottom of the sixth inning by loading the bases on a double, walk, and single before Nippy Jones's single scored Stan Musial and Terry Moore.

In the top of the seventh inning, Brecheen retired Putsy Caballero and Richie Ashburn for his 19th and 20th consecutive batters without allowing a runner. The next batter, rookie Johnny Blatnik, was playing in place of the regular left fielder, Harry Walker, who was working himself into condition after an early-season bout with the flu.[3] Blatnik drew two strikes before hitting a slow groundball along the third-base line.

Cardinals third baseman Whitey Kurowski aggressively fielded the ball in front of the bag. His throw to the stretching Nippy Jones at first base appeared to arrive simultaneously with Blatnik, and veteran umpire Babe Pinelli called Blatnik safe, spoiling Brecheen's perfect-game bid.[4]

Brecheen retired the next seven batters to record his first one-hitter. The Cardinals had added two more runs in the eighth inning on Jones's two-run homer for a final score of 5-0.

As one might expect, there were different points of view on Pinelli's fateful call.

Sportswriters in the press box were divided in their opinions on the outcome of the play, although they acknowledged that their vantage point was unreliable.[5]

Eddie Dyer commented after the game, "I don't want to dispute Umpire Pinelli's decision, but everybody on the ball club thought Blatnik was out. From the dugout, I'd have sworn he was out, but naturally we see the play at an odd angle from our bench and we could have been wrong." However, Dyer added, "I'm glad I talked to Pinelli after the game, as we walked toward our dressing room. He told me that while he knew the Cat was pitching a perfect game, he only did his duty and called the play as he saw it. I wouldn't have wanted him to call it any other way." Nippy Jones, however, firmly insisted that Kurowski's throw beat Blatnik by "a good half-step."[6]

Pinelli firmly backed up his call. He said he was aware of Brecheen's bid for a perfect game, but that "[T]here was no doubt on the play."[7] In his 1952 autobiography, *Mr. Ump*, Pinelli recollected the close call in Brecheen's game as an example of the tensions an umpire faces in performing the job. He wrote, "Had I called (Blatnik) out, Brecheen would have had a perfect no-hit game. Later I felt sorry for Brecheen; for a moment I regretted I had had to make that call. But not for long. The hitter had been safe, and I knew I would have had to call him safe if he had been the last batter in the ninth against a perfect game. I did what the ball commanded me to do."[8]

Brecheen said after the game, "I thought (Blatnik) was out," then quickly added, "but of course I'm prejudiced.[9] The one-hit gem was Brecheen's third consecutive shutout of the young season, although he didn't think it was his best performance of the three.[10]

Had Brecheen successfully recorded the perfect game, it would have been only the sixth in the major leagues at that time. In 2010 Detroit's Armando Galarraga found himself in a similar situation when his unsuccessful perfect-game bid also came down to an umpire's call.[11]

Brecheen finished the season with a 20-7 record, winning 11 of his last 14 decisions. He led the league in ERA (2.24), shutouts (7), and strikeouts (149), even though he wasn't generally known as a strikeout pitcher. From a statistical standpoint, he was arguably the league's best pitcher, although the Braves' Johnny Sain also turned in a spectacular season with 24 wins, a 2.60 ERA, and a second-place finish in the league's MVP voting.

The combination of Brecheen's pitching and Stan Musial's hitting essentially kept the Cardinals in contention during the 1948 season. However, the Boston Braves took the National League lead on June 13 and never relinquished it. The Cardinals wound up topping Brooklyn and Pittsburgh for second place. Only two games separated the three teams in the final standings.

If there had been instant replay technology in 1948, Pinelli's self-assured call at first base would have been reviewed and possibly overturned, and Brecheen would have secured another rare place in baseball history with a perfect game. But on that day in May, the umpire's call was the final word.

SOURCES

In addition to the sources mentioned in the Notes, the author also consulted:

Baseball-Reference.com.

"Brecheen Continued Southpaw's Reign in N.L.," *The Sporting News*, December 29, 1948: 15.

Nowlin, Bill, ed., *Van Lingle Mungo: The Man, the Song, the Players* (Phoenix: Society for American Baseball Research: 2014), 202.

Pietrusza, David, Matthew Silverman, and Michael Gershman, eds. *Baseball: The Biographical Encyclopedia* (New York: Total Sports Illustrated, 2000), 120.

NOTES

1 Mike Eisenbath, *The Cardinals Encyclopedia* (Philadelphia: Temple University Press, 1999), 140.

2 Gene Karst and Martin J. Jones Jr., *Who's Who in Professional Baseball* (New Rochelle, New York: Arlington House, 1973), 100.

3 Bob Broeg, "Shutout No. 3 for Southpaw as Cards Clip Phillies, 5-0: Jones Wields the Big Stick," *St. Louis Post-Dispatch*, May 9, 1948:1D.

4 John Wickline, "Johnny Blatnik," SABR BioProject, sabr.org/bioproj/person/cdfd30f7.

5 Broeg.

6 Ray Gillespie, "The Cat Misses Perfect Game by a Whisker," *The Sporting News*, May 19, 1948: 7.

7 Broeg.

8 Babe Pinelli, *Mr. Ump* (Philadelphia: Westminster Press, 1952), 128.

9 Broeg.

10 Gillespie.

11 Jerry Crasnick. "Perfect Moment Stolen in Time," June 3, 2010, espn.go.com/mlb/columns/story?id=5245331&columnist=crasnick_jerry.

STAN THE MAN HOMERS AT HOME IN ALL-STAR GAME

July 13, 1948: American League 5, National League 2, at Sportsman's Park

1948 All-Star Game

BY C. PAUL ROGERS, III

BASEBALL'S 15TH ALL-STAR GAME took place in Sportsman's Park on July 13, 1948, before a capacity crowd of 34,009. It was the second time St. Louis had hosted the summer classic. The first time, in 1940, the host team was the St. Louis Browns. That game took place in 1940 and resulted in a 4-0 National League win behind a three-run first-inning home run by Max West of the Boston Bees. It was the first shutout in All-Star Game history. This time the American League prevailed, 5-2, in 2 hours 27 minutes behind stellar pitching by Vic Raschi of the New York Yankees and Joe Coleman of the Philadelphia A's, each of whom threw three shutout innings at the Nationals.

The National League had lost five of the last six All-Star Games and 10 of 14 overall, but it appeared to have the advantage coming into this one. The pitching staff selected by manager Leo Durocher of the Brooklyn Dodgers was well rested and the 25-man team was mostly healthy. In contrast, four of the top stars of the American League were limited because of injury and six of their pitchers had worked just two days earlier. One was Hal Newhouser, who came into the All-Star break with a 13-6 record on his way to a 21-win season. He had thrown 7⅔ innings on Sunday and asked not to be used. In addition, Joe DiMaggio was afflicted with sore heels and a swollen knee, Ted Williams was battling torn rib cartilage, and George Kell had a bum ankle. As a result, all three would-be starters were limited to pinch-hitting duties.[1]

The American Leaguers were also without Bob Feller, who had withdrawn from the game.[2] Feller was only 9-10 at the break, but his withdrawal drew a firestorm of criticism, particularly from American League manager Bucky Harris, who said that if he had his way, Feller would never be asked to another All-Star Game.[3] St. Louis Cardinals shortstop Marty Marion also drew criticism for his last-minute withdrawal from the game, all of which prompted a letter from the Cincinnati Reds, signed by veteran pitcher Bucky Walters, urging a fine equal to three days' pay for any player selected who skipped the game. That prompted Commissioner Happy Chandler to issue a statement expressing his concern "over the failure of club owners and players to take seriously the All-Star Game" and promising to take whatever steps were necessary in the future to assure participation by those selected.[4]

Although major-league baseball was integrated the previous year, no African-American players were selected for the All-Star Game until 1949. In 1948 Jackie Robinson was passed over at second base even though he was hitting a hard .295 at the break. Larry Doby was similarly bypassed in the American League despite hitting .288 for a team in the thick of the pennant race.

With his choices limited, Harris named Washington Senators right-hander Walt Masterson to start the game, even though he had only a 6-6 record and had also pitched on Sunday.[5] Durocher, who had broken convention by picking only six pitchers instead of the usual eight, started Ralph

Branca, his ace from the Dodgers, who was 10-6 at the break and well rested.[6]

The game began under a blistering sun in hot, muggy conditions. Center fielder Richie Ashburn, the only rookie on either squad, led off for the National League. Ashburn had taken the National League by storm, hitting .351 to earn the starting spot.[7] He swung at the first pitch of the game and legged out a groundball to Joe Gordon at second for an infield single.[8] Ashburn stole second and advanced to third on a groundout before hometown hero Stan Musial thrilled the St. Louis fans by homering to the top of the right-field pavilion to put the National League into the lead, 2-0.[9] Although the NL threatened in the third and sixth innings with men in scoring position, they were unable to score again.

Branca sailed through the bottom of the first against the American Leaguers, striking out the first two batters. But in the second, Detroit's Hoot Evers, DiMaggio's replacement in center field, belted a one-out home run into the left-field bleachers to bring the score to 2-1. Evers thus became the second player in history to homer in his first All-Star at-bat.[10]

The National League put together singles by Musial and Slaughter in the top of the third but were unable to score as Andy Pafko hit into a force out at second to end the inning. In the American League third, Branca lost command and walked the first two batters, Mickey Vernon and Pat Mullin. He recovered to strike out Tommy Henrich looking, but Vernon and Mullin surprised by executing a double steal, aided by the fact that third baseman Pafko was playing deep and had to take Walker Cooper's throw on the run.[11] Lou Boudreau followed with a fly ball to deep right to bring in Vernon easily with the tying run.

After Johnny Schmitz relieved Branca to start the fourth inning, the American League quickly took control of the game. With one out Ken Keltner singled to left, George McQuinn singled to center, and Birdie Tebbetts walked to load the bases. Vic Raschi, a .243 hitter who had relieved Masterson on the mound in the top of the inning, got behind in the count on a couple of wild swings before lining a single to left to drive in two runs and knock Schmitz from the game.[12] Durocher brought in Johnny Sain to face Joe DiMaggio, pinch-hitting for Mullin. On the first pitch DiMaggio lined out to Musial in left, deep enough to bring in Tebbetts from third and put the American League ahead 5-2. Despite its best efforts, the National League would not be able to recover from that big inning.[13]

After five hot, muggy innings, dark thunderclouds moved in during the sixth inning accompanied by lightning bolts around the ballpark.[14] With spitting rain falling, the National League mounted a serious rally in the top of the sixth on one-out singles by Bob Elliott and Phil Masi off Raschi, who was pitching his third and final inning. Buddy Kerr then grounded out to Keltner at third, advancing both runners. With two outs, pinch-hitter Eddie Waitkus followed by working a walk to load the bases. Raschi next faced Ashburn, who already had two hits. With the count at 2-and-2 Ashburn backed away from an inside fastball that caught the corner for a called third strike.[15] It ended the uprising and was the last serious National League challenge.

In the bottom of the sixth the American League threatened against Ewell Blackwell of the Reds, who relieved Sain to start the inning. With one out McQuinn singled to left and then stole second as Tebbetts was called out on strikes. Bucky Harris surprised everyone by sending up Ted Williams, who was not expected to play, to pinch-hit for Raschi. Williams drew a walk and Newhouser, who was also not expected to participate, pinch-ran. Blackwell quickly quelled the threat by getting Al Zarilla to ground to Red Schoendienst at second for a force out.

Light rain fell intermittently through the seventh and eighth innings but it didn't bother Joe Coleman of the A's, who relieved Raschi and set the National Leaguers down in both frames, giving up only a walk to Musial in the seventh. For the Nationals, Sain pitched 1⅔ innings of scoreless baseball, while Blackwell finished with three scoreless innings, although he walked three.

The drama in the ninth was largely whether the thunderstorms would hold off long enough for the game to finish. The National League cooperated, however, and, with rain falling, could muster only a two-out walk by Bill Rigney off Coleman before Musial grounded out to second baseman Bobby Doerr to end the game on the short end of a 5-2 score.

If an All-Star MVP award had existed, it surely would have gone to Raschi, the winning pitcher, whose fourth-inning single drove in the winning run. As for the National League, its frustration would continue in 1949 with an 11-7 loss in Ebbets Field in Brooklyn before it finally broke through with a 5-4 win in 1950 in a 14-inning thriller in Chicago's Comiskey Park.

NOTES

1 David Vincent, Lyle Spatz, and David W. Smith, *The Midsummer Classic—The Complete History of Baseball's All-Star Game* (Lincoln: University of Nebraska Press, 2001), 90.

2 Feller had controversially skipped the 1947 All-Star Game due to a back injury suffered in his last start before the game. He recovered well enough, however, to pitch two days after the game. In 1948 Indians owner Bill Veeck allegedly told Feller to fake an injury because, in the midst of a pennant race, he did not want to send both Bob Lemon and Feller to the game and risk injury. John Sickels, *Bob Feller—Ace of the Greatest Generation* (Washington: Brassey's, 2004), 193-94; Bob Feller with Bill Gilbert, *Now Pitching—A Baseball Memoir* (New York: Birch Lane Press, 1990), 152-53.

3 Frank Graham, *Baseball Extra* (New York: A.S. Barnes, 1954), 143-44. Harris selected Boston's Joe Dobson to replace Feller. Vincent, et al., 90.

4 Vincent et al., 90-91.

5 Masterson was on his way to an 8-15 record for the seventh-place Senators, who won only 56 games.

6 Durocher picked two sluggers instead, Sid Gordon of the Giants and Bob Elliot of the Braves. Vincent et al., 91.

7 Ibid.

8 John Debringer, "American League Beats National 11th Time in 15 Games With Three Runs in 4th," *New York Times*, July 14, 1948: 28; Gordon's throw was wide but the official scorer ruled it an infield hit, Vincent et al., 91.

9 Debringer.

10 Max West's three-run homer off Red Ruffing in the first inning of the 1940 game, also in Sportsman's Park, was in his first All-Star at-bat.

11 Cooper was starting his sixth consecutive All-Star Game for the National League.

12 "American Leaguers Humble Nationals, 5-2," *Los Angeles Times*, July 14, 1948: 9.

13 Donald Honig, *The All-Star Game—A Pictorial History, 1933 to Present* (St. Louis: The Sporting News, 1987), 70.

14 *Los Angeles Times*, July 14, 1948: 9.

15 *Los Angeles Times*, July 14, 1948: 11.

MUNGER'S $50 NIGHT

September 13, 1949: St. Louis Cardinals 1, New York Giants 0, at Sportsman's Park

BY JOHN BAUER

IN 1949, THE *ST. LOUIS POST-DISPATCH* DIStributed $50 savings bonds to Cardinals players for on-field heroics. Sluggers were rewarded for hitting home runs, and pitchers for shutouts. Preparing to face the New York Giants on the evening of Tuesday, September 13, 1949, starting pitcher George "Red" Munger noticed a *Post-Dispatch* reporter slipping savings bonds into the lockers of those players who had recently achieved the required feats. With the clubhouse otherwise quiet, the Cardinals starter called out to the reporter, "Get one of those ready for me. I'm going to pitch a shutout tonight."[1] The 30-year-old Munger, an affable veteran considered "as friendly as a St. Bernard,"[2] would take the mound with his club opening a 12-game homestand. With a 1½-game lead over Brooklyn in the season's homestretch, the Cardinals had little margin for error. That seemed not to faze Munger, who called out again as the reporter left the clubhouse, "Don't forget, get that bond ready."[3]

The game conditions suited Munger. With recent heavy rains and a sharp dip in temperature, the setting for the 8:30 P.M. first pitch was "topcoat weather."[4] Munger commented, "I like cool weather because if you've got a good fastball this kind of night, you sting the hitters' hands, and they don't have as much fun up there."[5]

Sportsman's Park proved happy hunting grounds for the Cardinals, who had played .662 baseball at home in padding their league-leading 87-50 record. Pennant hopes were beyond the 67-70 Giants, who sat 20 games behind the Cardinals in a fourth-place tie with Boston. Because fourth-place finishers earned a sliver of World Series money, though, the Giants had financial incentive to remain engaged for the season's final weeks.[6] To counter Munger, who already owned three wins over the Giants, New York manager Leo Durocher sent Dave Koslo to the mound. Based on his 9-11 record, it might have appeared that Koslo was having a season as mediocre as the Giants', but despite his team's lackluster year and his own lackluster won-lost mark, Koslo would complete the season as the NL's ERA leader.

Munger faced Bill Rigney to begin the game. Rigney hit the ball sharply toward left-center, but Cardinals center fielder Chuck Diering prevented an extra-base hit when his "swift sprint"[7] allowed him to make the catch for the game's first out. Whitey Lockman flied out to right and Hank Thompson grounded to shortstop Marty Marion, which allowed Munger to open the game unscathed. In the home half of the inning, Diering grounded out and second baseman Red Schoendienst popped out to his opposite number, Thompson.

With two out, Schoendienst's roommate, Stan Musial, batted for the Cardinals. Trailing only Brooklyn's Jackie Robinson and teammate Enos Slaughter in the NL batting race, Musial needed 21 hits in his final 17 games to reach the 200-hit mark for the fourth time in his career.[8] Musial attempted to pull away from Koslo's offering but hit a checked-swing roller past third baseman Sid Gordon that died just beyond the lip of the outfield grass. He alertly raced to second with his 33rd double of the season. When Nippy Jones lined a single into right field, Musial scored to give the Cardinals a 1-0 lead.

Munger's second inning started the same way his first inning ended, with a groundout to his shortstop. After Bobby Thomson flied out to Diering, Sid Gordon came to the plate. With the count 3-and-1, Munger "got the ball where I wanted it—a low fast ball."[9] Gordon proved equal to the pitch, lining a single into center field in front of Diering. *The Sporting News* suggested later that Diering "might have made a desperate, diving catch of the ball, had he chosen to try."[10] The commentary seems harsh, and even *The Sporting News* acknowledged that Diering probably made the smart play to keep the ball in front of him with two outs.[11] How would Diering (or anyone) have known Gordon's hit would be New York's only one? The Giants could not convert the opportunity as Joe Lafata's pop fly to Marion ended the inning.

Marion and Del Rice began the Cardinals' second with fly outs to Thomson. Thomson "roamed far and wide in center," making seven putouts and robbing at least two Cardinals of extra-base hits.[12] When Koslo struck out Munger after a single by Tommy Glaviano, the game moved to the third inning. Munger retired the Giants in order in the top half of the third. In the bottom half, Schoendienst, who entered the game hitting .299 as he chased his first .300 season,[13] singled to left field with one out; however, Musial's double-play ball back to Koslo ended the inning. Perhaps lost in Munger's evening was Koslo's performance for the Giants. After surrendering a run in the first inning, Koslo "hurled airtight ball."[14] He scattered nine hits while allowing no walks to St. Louis, and "was as rugged as a pitcher must be to hold a pennant-contending team to one run on nine hits."[15]

The game settled into a pattern: Munger would retire the Giants in order, while Koslo gave up the occasional hit. The fourth inning exemplified the game. The heart of the Giants order caused no trouble for Munger. Against Koslo, Slaughter looped a one-out double just inside the left-field foul line but would not score. Slaughter was returning to the lineup after leaving the second game of a doubleheader in Cincinnati two days earlier with cramps in both calves.[16] The Cardinals captain was enjoying a fine season after a rough start. Manager Eddie Dyer benched the 33-year-old on May 11 with Slaughter hitting .254. After sitting out two games, Slaughter recovered his All-Star form and his current .339 average was well above his previous single-season high.

The Giants caught a break in the eighth inning when Munger made one of his few mistakes. Behind 3-and-1 in the count, Munger missed with his fastball and Thomson claimed first base. With Gordon batting, Giants manager Durocher called for a hit-and-run. To Thomson there must have been no doubt that the line drive off Gordon's bat would find the grass. He streaked around second base, which only made it easier for Marion to tag Thomson and complete an unassisted double play after he had snared Gordon's ball. Lafata lined out to Schoendienst for the third out. Koslo then continued his effective evening, for which he would receive no reward, by getting successive outs from Musial, Jones, and Slaughter.

Munger, on the other hand, stood three outs from his reward: a win and a savings bond. Monte Irvin pinch-hit for Ray Mueller and grounded to Schoendienst for the first out. Durocher finally lifted Koslo from the game, not for performance on the mound, but for another pinch-hitter, Bert Haas. On a night in which Munger's "assortment of hooks and slants [had] the Giants completely baffled,"[17] Haas struck out. With the Giants down to the final out, Rigney came to bat. Marion slipped as he charged Rigney's slow groundball but "got away a hard and accurate throw as he plunged head-first to the infield grass."[18] When the ball hit Jones's glove at first, Munger had completed his second shutout of the season and the first one-hitter of his career.

Considering the wintry conditions, the 16,418 fans in attendance likely appreciated the efficiency of the two pitchers. At one hour, 31 minutes, the game clocked in as the fastest of the season at Sportsman's Park. Cardinals players lingered in the clubhouse to catch the result of the Dodgers game in Cincinnati. After learning that the Dodgers tied the game in the ninth, the players slowly filed out and did not stick around for word of Brooklyn's extra-inning win. St. Louis maintained a slim lead over Brooklyn until the final week of season. In the end, Brooklyn claimed the NL pennant by one game over the Cardinals, but for one night in September, Red Munger was king.

SOURCES

In addition to the sources cited in the Notes, the author also consulted baseball-reference.com and retrosheet.org.

NOTES

1 Bob Broeg, "Munger Calls Shot on Shutout — Word as Good as Bond; Big Red's One-Hitter Keeps Cards Game and a Half Ahead," *St. Louis Post-Dispatch*, September 14, 1949: 2B.

2 "George Did It, Just Like That — And With Great Performance," *St. Louis Post-Dispatch*, September 14, 1949: 2B.

3 Ibid.

4 Broeg, "Munger Calls Shot."

5 Ibid.

6 Bob Broeg, "Cards Ready for Sportsman's Park Showdown With Heads Up," *St. Louis Post-Dispatch*, September 13, 1949: 2B.

7 "George Did It."

8 Broeg, "Cards Ready."

9 Ray Gillespie, "Year of One-Hitters in Majors — Three Hurled in 6-Day Period," *The Sporting News*, September 21, 1949: 10.

10 Ibid.

11 Ibid.

12 James P. Dawson, "Munger Hurls 1-Hit, 1-0 Victory for St. Louis, Facing 28 Batsmen," *New York Times*, September 14, 1949: 42.

13 Broeg, "Cards Ready."

14 Dawson.

15 "George Did It."

16 Broeg, "Cards Ready."

17 Dawson.

18 "George Did It."

BRECHEEN, SCHMITZ BOTH GO THE DISTANCE IN EXTRA-INNING DUEL

April 30, 1950: St. Louis Cardinals 1, Chicago Cubs 0 (13 Innings), at Sportsman's Park

BY KEN CARRANO

WHEN FANS OF THE ST. LOUIS Cardinals woke up on the morning of April 30, 1950, they probably didn't have much to look forward to that day. The Cardinals had been rained out the day before, and today didn't look very promising. The team was not off to a great start, either, having gone 4-5 after a loss in Pittsburgh on the 28th, and was already three games behind the first-place Brooklyn Dodgers after only nine games played.

Cardinals management had other concerns than the weather. The St. Louis Browns, who owned Sportsman's Park, were suing the Cardinals, the Browns' tenants, for violating the terms of their lease. In 1948, after Sam Breadon sold the team to Fred Saigh and Robert Hannegan, the club's lease on Sportsman's Park was assigned within the Cardinals ownership and the Browns contended that they should have been informed. "While the primary objective of the suit ostensibly was to eject the Cardinals from the park, actually the Browns appeared more interested in getting what they termed more reasonable rental," *The Sporting News* opined. "The Cardinals pay $35,000 annual rental and the clubs share alike on maintenance, which amounted to about $130,000 (in 1949). The Browns, pointing to the larger crowds of the Cardinals, have argued that maintenance costs should be on a per capita basis."[1] The Cardinals who missed the pennant by just one game in 1949, drew 1,430,676 spectators to Sportsman's Park that year, while the seventh-place Browns drew only 270,936. A judgment in the case was close at hand.

Cardinals manager Eddie Dyer's squad entered the game shorthanded. Stan Musial, although in uniform, was not available to play, having twisted his knee rounding first a few days earlier in Pittsburgh. The Cardinals were also without ailing veteran shortstop Marty Marion, who made his 1950 debut the next day. For Cubs manager Frankie Frisch, injuries were not the main concern—the weatherman was. The Cubs had had more postponements (five—four due to rain, one due to cold) than games played, and with three scheduled offdays for travel in the early-season schedule, Frisch's men had played only one game since April 22. "It's a treat to hear Frisch moan about the way in which his boys are losing the benefits of their spring training toil," wrote Irving Vaughan in the April 28 *Chicago Tribune*. "Having his lads eat themselves out of shape for the lack of exercise is only part of the manager's concern about the series of delays. Spring postponements make for summer double headers and the bargain bills burn up pitching in a hurry. Frisch isn't sure that he has a staff able to absorb, without distress, even a normal diet of one game per diem. But he's hoping."[2]

Somehow the baseball gods relented, and 9,645 people headed to Sportsman's Park to see Harry "The Cat" Brecheen, two years removed from leading the league in ERA, make his second start of the season against Johnny Schmitz for the 3-1 Cubs. Brecheen's first start of the season, on April 21, was a 2-0 complete-game loss to the Cubs, although he gave up just three hits (two of them triples) and two walks while striking out seven. Cubs hurler Schmitz wasn't as sharp as Brecheen in his 1950 debut, getting the decision but allowing five runs and a dozen hits over eight innings in a 9-6 win in their season opener at Cincinnati. Schmitz was trying to bounce back after a subpar 1949 season, which saw his win total drop from 18 to 11 (he lost 13 games both seasons) and his

ERA rise from 2.64 in 1948 to 4.35 in 1949. It wasn't Schmitz's turn in the rotation, but Frisch decided to go with him over Bob Rush, who was scheduled to start on the 29th before the rains came.[3]

Once the game started, Brecheen didn't need the help from the Cardinals' missing stars. After an uneventful first inning, the Cubs had a chance to scratch out a run in the second. Andy Pafko led off with a single but was thrown out by Enos Slaughter trying to make third on Bill Serena's hit. Hal Jeffcoat then grounded out to short to end the uprising.

The Cubs threatened again in the third, this time with a two-out rally. Leadoff man Wayne Terwilliger singled off Brecheen and stole second. Bob Borkowski was beaned by Brecheen on an errant throw after he laid down a bunt, and the Cubs had men at first and third. But Brecheen escaped trouble by getting Preston Ward to ground to short. The Cubs had no more baserunners until the 10th inning. Brecheen was perfect from the fourth through the ninth, striking out four during that span.

Schmitz was every bit Brecheen's equal on this cold April day. He walked one in each of the first two innings without harm, and didn't give up a hit until Johnny Blatnik reached with a two-out single in the fourth. The Cardinals saw their first runner in scoring position in the fifth on a leadoff double by Del Rice. The catcher made it to third after a long fly to center by Eddie Miller, but was left stranded as Schmitz got Brecheen to ground out to the mound, and Tommy Glaviano to ground to shortstop. The Cardinals got a two-out single from Steve Bilko in the sixth, but Schmitz retired every batter from then until the fateful 13th. Slaughter nearly had extra bases in the ninth, but a diving catch by Jeffcoat saved Schmitz's streak.

That was not the last of the excitement, though, as the Cubs had great opportunities in the 10th and 12th to take the game's first lead. In the 10th Chicago got its first hit since the third on Pafko's leadoff double, but his attempt to advance to third on Roy Smalley's fly ball was denied by center fielder Chuck Diering's throw to Glaviano, then Serena struck out. In the 12th the Cubs put a runner on third on a leadoff hit by Wayne Terwilliger, a sacrifice, and a groundout. After giving Pafko an intentional walk, Brecheen fanned Smalley, the pitcher's eighth and final strikeout of the game.

The proceedings ended shortly thereafter. Brecheen breezed through the 13th with a 1-2-3 inning, bringing up the bottom of the order for the Cardinals. Schmitz retired Red Schoendienst for his 20th consecutive out. Del Rice ended the streak—and the game. After fouling off the first pitch, he put a charge into Schmitz's next offering, smashing a low line drive into the pavilion near the 405-foot mark.[4] It was Rice's first homer of the campaign and the only walk-off home run of his career, and it put an end to one of the better pitching duels witnessed at Sportsman's Park. "That was a big game for us fellas," Dyer said after the game. "Beating Schmitz without a Musial, Marion or (Ted) Wilks is good any time."[5] On a day tailor-made for pitching, the pitchers did not disappoint. Hard-luck loser Schmitz scattered four hits and two walks, and lowered his ERA by nearly 3 runs. Brecheen showed his mettle in getting out of several jams, and also retired 19 consecutive Cubs.

The next day, Judge Robert L. Aronson ruled in favor of the Cardinals in the suit by the Browns. "In sustaining the Cardinals' contention," Judge Aronson said, "We have concluded that the merger agreement was not a violation of the non-assignment clause of the lease of 1937. Therefore, the plaintiff had no valid basis for a declaration of forfeiture thus no valid basis for institution of this suit in ejectment."[6] This may have been the final push that sent the Browns to Baltimore four years later.

SOURCES

Wolf, Gregory H. "Harry Brecheen," in Bill Nowlin, ed., *Van Lingle Mungo—The Man, The Song, the Players* (Phoenix: Society for American Baseball Research, 2014).

Also, in addition to the sources listed in the notes, the author accessed Retorsheet.org, Baseball-Reference.com, SABR's BioProject via SABR.org, *The Sporting News* archive via Paper of Record, the *St. Louis Post Dispatch* via newspapers.com, and the *Chicago Tribune* archive.

NOTES

1. *The Sporting News*, May 10, 1950: 11.
2. *Chicago Tribune*, April 28, 1950: Part 3, page 1.
3. *Chicago Tribune*, April 30, 1950: Part 2, page 2.
4. *St. Louis Post Dispatch*, May 1, 1950: 16.
5. Ibid.
6. *St. Louis Post Dispatch*, May 1, 1950: 1.

BROWNIES SET SCORING RECORD AT HOME

August 18, 1951: St. Louis Browns 20, Detroit Tigers 9, at Sportsman's Park

BY J.G. PRESTON

THE 1951 ST. LOUIS BROWNS WERE ONE of the sorriest teams in the Browns' often sorry history. They won barely one-third of their games, finishing with a record of 52-102, and they were the only team in the American League that averaged fewer than four runs a game.

That would make the Browns an unlikely candidate to set the record for the most runs in a game at Sportsman's Park by any St. Louis team, Browns or Cardinals. But that's exactly what happened on August 18, 1951—helped by the worst pitching performance in major-league history.

It started out as a typically dismal day for the Browns that Saturday afternoon in front of 4,699 spectators, more than half of whom were women admitted free of charge on Ladies' Day.[1] The second batter of the game for the visiting Detroit Tigers, Dick Kryhoski, homered onto Grand Avenue off the Browns' Fred Sanford, and later in the first inning Bud Souchock singled home Vic Wertz.[2] Then in the third inning, after Sanford retired the first two Tigers, Wertz walked and Pat Mullin hit a home run to put Detroit ahead, 4-0.

The Browns got on the board in the bottom of the third thanks to a pair of Tiger errors. A wild throw by third baseman George Kell on a groundball by Matt Batts allowed two Browns to score, and Batts later scored when Hank Arft's groundball went through the legs of Detroit second baseman Jerry Priddy.[3] But the Tigers added to their lead in the top of the fourth when Priddy and Kryhoski hit consecutive doubles and Wertz greeted rookie relief pitcher Bob Mahoney with a two-run homer to make it 7-3, Detroit.

More Tigers miscues allowed the Browns to take the lead in the bottom of the fourth. After Batts singled in a run, Detroit catcher Joe Ginsberg made a wild throw to first base in an attempt to pick off Batts, allowing Jim Delsing to score from third, which cut the lead to 7-5. Cliff Mapes followed with a walk, and then Arft singled to score Batts and send Mapes to third. Hal White entered the game to relieve Tigers starter Marlin Stuart and tried to pick off Mapes, but his wild throw allowed Mapes to come home with the tying run, and Ken Wood then doubled to score Arft and put the Browns in front, 8-7.[4]

The Tigers tied the game on Priddy's home run in the top of the sixth. The Browns recaptured the lead on Fred Marsh's fly ball in the bottom of the inning, but the Tigers tied it again in the seventh on a home run by Mullin—his second of the game and the Tigers' fifth. That made it 9-9 as the home team came to bat after the seventh-inning stretch.

Sixteen Browns would come to the plate before they would have to take the field again.

Mahoney struck out to start the inning, but after leadoff man Bobby Young singled and Delsing walked to put the go-ahead run in scoring position, Tigers manager Red Rolfe called veteran Hank Borowy to the mound to relieve White. The 35-year-old Borowy had been one of the major leagues' top pitchers during World War II. From 1942 through 1945, his first four seasons in the big leagues, Borowy had a record of 67-32 and ranked fifth in the majors in wins during that period.[5] He also won three World Series games, one in 1943 for the New York Yankees and two in 1945 after he was sold to the Chicago Cubs. (Prior to 2016 he was the last pitcher to win a World Series game for the Cubs.) But Borowy did not have as much success after the war, and by 1951 he was hanging on as a seldom-used member of the Detroit bullpen.

Batts was the first batter to face Borowy. He singled to score Young and put the Browns on top, 10-9. Mapes then singled to score Delsing, and Arft followed with a three-run homer, which made it 14-9. Wood singled, Marsh singled, and Bill Jennings walked to load the bases.

With the pitcher, Mahoney, due to bat again, Browns manager Zack Taylor summoned rookie Frank Saucier to hit for him. Saucier's professional career got off to a blazing start after he graduated from Missouri's Westminster College in 1948. He led all of professional baseball in 1949 with a .446 batting average for Wichita Falls of the Class-B Big State League, and in 1950 he was named Minor League Player of the Year by *The Sporting News* after winning the Texas League batting title with a .343 mark for San Antonio.[6] But after not receiving a contract offer to his liking in 1951, Saucier held out and worked for an oil company in Oklahoma. He didn't sign with the Browns until Bill Veeck paid him a visit after taking over control of the team in July.[7]

Borowy walked Saucier to force in a run, the first—and, as it turned out, the last—RBI of Saucier's brief major-league career. He wasn't able to play much in 1951 because of a shoulder injury, and then spent the 1952 and 1953 seasons in the military. (He had also served in World War II.) After he returned to civilian life he turned down offers to play baseball in order to stay in the oil business.[8] But Saucier remains well known to trivia buffs, because on August 19, 1951, the day after his pinch-hit RBI, he was the man replaced so that 3-foot-7 Eddie Gaedel could be used as a pinch-hitter.[9]

The Browns still had the bases loaded after Saucier's walk. Borowy then issued two more walks, to Young and Delsing, making the score 17-9. At that point, manager Rolfe had finally seen enough. "Rolfe indicated his disgust at Borowy's work by allowing him to take a cruel beating in a game in which the Tigers still had a chance," Tommy Devine wrote in the next day's *Detroit Free Press*.[10] "Rolfe never made a gesture to warm up a replacement until the contest was hopelessly lost and it was obvious that Borowy's chances of ever retiring the side were slight."[11]

Borowy faced nine Browns, allowing five hits and four walks. No other pitcher in major-league history has ever faced as many batters in a game without retiring any of them. And all nine of the batters he faced scored. Fred Hutchinson, who came on in relief of Borowy, gave up a two-run single to Batts—his fourth hit of the day—and an RBI single to Arft before finally retiring the side.[12] The Browns' 11 runs in the inning tied a team record set in the sixth inning of the first game of a doubleheader on July 21, 1949, at Sportsman's against the Philadelphia Athletics.

Forty-five-year-old Satchel Paige shut out the Tigers over the final two innings to wrap up a 20-9 win for the Browns. The 20 runs exceeded the previous team record of 19, set on May 11, 1925, at Sportsman's Park against the Yankees. The most runs the Cardinals ever scored in a game at Sportsman's Park was also 19, against the Philadelphia Phillies on May 15, 1922. The record for most runs in a game at Sportsman's Park by any team was set by Cleveland on August 12, 1948, in the second game of a doubleheader, a 26-3 rout of the Browns. Fred Sanford was the Browns' starting pitcher in that game—as he was the day the Browns scored 20.

The Browns had only two extra-base hits in scoring their 20 runs, an RBI double by Ken Wood and a three-run homer by Hank Arft. But the Browns took full advantage of 11 walks (three with the bases loaded) and five Tigers errors.

The next day it was back to normal for the Browns' offense, as they scored a total of four runs in losing both games of a doubleheader. But of course no one paid much attention to that—not after the Browns sent a 3-foot-7 batter to the plate.

Notes

Thanks to Retrosheet's David Smith for sharing the *St. Louis Globe-Democrat* game story. Other game stories were accessed via Newspapers.com.

HOME OF THE BROWNS AND CARDINALS AT GRAND AND DODIER

NOTES

1 "Cards Lose To Reds, 1-0; Browns Maul Tigers, 20-9," *St. Louis Post-Dispatch*, August 19, 1951: 2D. The paid attendance is given by retrosheet.org and baseball-reference.com as 1,871.

2 Harry Mitauer, "Browns Pet Tigers With Mallet, 20-9," *St. Louis Globe-Democrat*, August 19, 1951.

3 Associated Press, "Tribe Blanks Chisox, 7 to 0; Browns Blast Tigers, 20 to 9," *State Journal* (Lansing, Michigan): fourth section, 1.

4 Harry Mitauer, "Browns Pet Tigers."

5 Borowy avoided active military duty during the war, as he worked in defense industries during the winter months and was classified 2-B for the draft. After he was sold to the Cubs he was reclassified as 2-A ("contributing to the war effort, but not actually on the assembly line") but was not called to serve. Lyle Spatz, "Hank Borowy," Society for American Baseball Research Baseball Biography Project, sabr.org/bioproj/person/ea042adc.

6 Dick Peebles, "Browns' Saucier Hits the Top as 'Minor Leaguer of Year,'" *The Sporting News*, January 3, 1951: 2.

7 Ray Gillespie, "Negro Stars, Plus Jap Ace, Slated as New Brownies," *The Sporting News*, July 11, 1951: 16; Bob Burnes, "Sport Shirt Veeck Collars Browns' Fans," *The Sporting News*, July 18, 1951: 4.

8 Details of Saucier's military service are in Gary Bedingfield's "Baseball in Wartime" newsletter, Issue 41, January 2016, 14-15, baseballinwartime.com/BIWNewsletterVol8No41Jan2016.pdf.

9 Saucier looked back on that day in Ira Berkow, "The Man for Whom Gaedel Hit," *New York Times*, July 21, 1991, and Darren Rovell, "Short on Size, Long on History," ESPN.com, August 16, 2001, static.espn.go.com/mlb/s/2001/0816/1240553.html.

10 Tommy Devine, "Borowy at End of Tiger Trail," *Detroit Free Press*, August 19, 1951: Section C, 1.

11 Tommy Devine, "St. Louis Browns Tattered Tigers to a Crisp, 20-9," *Detroit Free Press*, August 19, 1951: Section C, 1.

12 The most complete account of the Browns' seventh inning is in Associated Press, "Tribe Blanks Chisox, 7 to 0; Browns Blast Tigers, 20 to 9," *State Journal* (Lansing, Michigan): fourth section, 1.

THE SMALLEST PINCH-HITTER IN THE GAME

August 19, 1951: Detroit Tigers 6, St. Louis Browns 2 (Game Two of Doubleheader), at Sportsman's Park

BY CHIP GREENE

SEARCH ONLINE FOR A DEFINITION OF the word *incongruous* and among several provided on the Merriam-Webster website is "inconsistent within itself." Well, that's perfectly clear. In other words, something that just seems out of place.

Now, consider this: In one of baseball's most iconic photographs, a batter, a catcher, and the home-plate umpire, each frozen in time in their customary positions, fill the frame: the umpire, at the left of the photo, standing with knees bent behind the catcher, peers over the kneeling catcher's head; in the catcher's upraised mitt, held slightly higher than the batter's head, the ball is clearly visible, indicating that a pitch has just been delivered; and, crouching in the right-hand batter's box, the batter, apparently having let the pitch go by, remains stationary in his stance, in anticipation of the pitcher's next offering. It's the classic triumvirate of contestants in America's national pastime.

There is, however, one thing dramatically out of place in the photo. It is the "inconsistency," the *incongruity*. The batter is very small; so small, in fact, the catcher, despite kneeling, nevertheless appears to tower over him. Though clearly short of stature, the batter is made even smaller as he leans slightly back over his flexed right leg. Although the faces and expressions of the fans in the background are blurred and difficult to make out, they undoubtedly share with the viewer the same shocked realization: The batter is, in the parlance of the day, a midget.

The idea for such an audacious stunt had been percolating in the mind of one man practically his whole life. St. Louis Browns owner, Bill Veeck Jr., for whose team the lilliputian had gone to the plate, was 4 years old when his father became president of the Chicago Cubs. As a teenager, the younger Veeck learned about team management during various stints as a vendor, ticket salesman and junior groundskeeper. He also got to know many of baseball's most famous personalities, including New York Giants manager John McGraw, whom Veeck later credited with inspiring what would come to be his masterpiece as a baseball showman.

"McGraw," Veeck recalled, "had been a great friend of my father's. … Once or twice a season McGraw would come to the house, and one of my greatest thrills would be to sit quietly at the table after dinner and listen to them tell their lies.

"McGraw had a little hunchback he kept around the club as sort of a good-luck charm," Veeck said. "He wasn't a midget but was sort of a gnome. By the time McGraw got to the stub of his last cigar, he would swear to my father that one day before he retired he was going to send his gnome up to bat."[1] While McGraw never did, Veeck eventually sent his own diminutive batter to the plate.

It happened August 19, 1951. By then, Veeck had already firmly established a reputation for grandiose promotion that would, 40 years later, earn him enshrinement in the baseball Hall of Fame. In 1946, after five years as owner of the Double-A Milwaukee Brewers, during which time Veeck scheduled morning games for night-shift workers and staged weddings at home plate, he purchased a minority stake in the Cleveland Indians, which he held for three years, until a divorce in 1949 forced him to sell his share of the team. There, in addition to a World Series championship in 1948, Veeck expanded on his creativity by hiring a clown as coach, and also burying the Indians' pennant when they couldn't repeat as champions.

Veeck arrived in St. Louis in 1951 when he purchased the Browns. who shared Sportsman's Park with the Cardinals. The Browns were an abysmal team. Despite recording their 36th win of the season during an impressive 20-9 thumping of the visiting Detroit Tigers the previous afternoon, the Browns had nonetheless lost an astounding 77 games, and Veeck was desperate to boost attendance."What can I do," he pondered, "that is so spectacular that no one will be able to say he had seen it before? The answer was completely obvious: I would send a midget up to bat."[2] And so, he did.

Twenty-six-year-old Eddie Gaedel stood 3-feet-7-inches tall and weighed 65 pounds. Veeck had found him through a talent booking agent and had signed him, importantly, to a standard, valid major-league contract worth $15,400, which would amount to $100 for a single game. On this day, the Browns and Tigers were scheduled to play a doubleheader, the final two games of their four-game series. To maximize attendance, Veeck had decided to celebrate two birthdays—the 50th anniversaries of both the American League and the Browns' sponsor, Falstaff Brewing Company. Veeck's plan was to unveil Gaedel between the first and second games of the doubleheader. After the first game, won by the Tigers, 5-2, the intermission's entertainment took the field, a motley crew of performers accompanied by an eight-piece band that featured, on drums, 45-year-old Browns' pitcher Satchel Paige. Finally, after a parade of old cars and motorcycles circled the field and clown Max Patkin danced crazily on the mound, a seven-foot-tall birthday cake was wheeled to home plate. When Gaedel popped out, little could the fans have guessed the role he was about to play.

After Browns starting pitcher Duane Pillette got out of the first inning by stranding two Tigers runners, Detroit's starter, right-hander Bob Cain, took the mound. Scheduled to lead off for the Browns was Frank Saucier. He never made it to the plate, however. As the public-address announcer notified the crowd of a Browns pinch-hitter, Gaedel emerged from the dugout wearing a uniform with the number ⅛ on the back and swinging three tiny bats, and strode toward home plate.

"Hey, what's going on here," bellowed home plate umpire Ed Hurley, advancing toward Browns' manager Zach Taylor in the St. Louis dugout.[3] Immediately Taylor, who had fully anticipated Hurley's protest and was fully prepared to defend the move, was on the field. Taylor showed Hurley Gaedel's contract; a telegram announcing Gaedel's signing, which had been sent to American League headquarters and was noted with a requisite time stamp; and a copy of the Browns' active roster, proof that St. Louis had room to add another player. In light of this evidence, Hurley allowed Gaedel to enter the game.

In his autobiography, Veeck later described what happened next. "The place went wild wild*[sic]*. Bob Cain, the Detroit pitcher, and Bob Swift, the catcher, had been standing peaceably for about 15 minutes. … I will never forget the look of utter disbelief that came over Cain's face when he finally realized that this was for real."[4] Cain could not know that Veeck had given Gaedel instructions not to swing. Regardless, Cain missed the strike zone with his first two pitches, then, continued Veeck, Swift "did just what I hoped he would do. He went to the mound to discuss the intricacies of pitching to a midget with Cain. And when he came back, he did something I had never dreamed of. To complete the sheer incongruity of the scene and make the picture of the event more memorable he got down on his knees to offer his pitcher a target."[5] With Swift on his knees, Cain threw two more fastballs, each missed, and Gaedel trotted to first base with a walk. As Gaedel stepped on first, Jim Delsing came in to run for him, and Gaedel's major-league career was ended.

For those interested readers, the Tigers won the game, 6-2, behind Cain's artful pitching. In the bottom of the first, Delsing advanced to third after replacing Gaedel, but Cain stranded two runners to end the inning. With the score tied 2-2, in the top of the seventh inning, the Tigers plated three runs on four hits to break the game open, 5-2. The following inning they scored their sixth run and an inning later handed the Browns their 79th loss of the season. Undoubtedly, though, on their way out of the park, the 18,369 fans in attendance, the largest American League crowd at Sportsman's Park of the season, could talk about only one thing: the day a midget came to bat.

SOURCES

espn.com/classic/veeckbill000816.html

Gillespie, Ray. "Short Career for Midget in Brownie Uniform," *The Sporting News*, August 29, 1951: 6.

NOTES

1. Jerome Holtzman, "Veeck's Midget Plan Was Picture Perfect," *Chicago Tribune*, July 23, 1991.
2. baseballhall.org/hof/veeck-bill.
3. Holtzman.
4. Ibid.
5. Ibid.

BROWNS FANS MANAGE TO GET IT RIGHT

August 24, 1951: St. Louis Browns 5, Philadelphia Athletics 3, at Sportsman's Park

BY NORM KING

IT WAS A "VEECK" OF A BALLGAME FOR the St. Louis Browns and their 1,115 managers in the stands at Sportsman's Park on August 24, 1951, in yet another amazing stunt pulled by the Browns' legendary owner Bill Veeck Jr.

Since winning the American League pennant in 1944 and finishing third in 1945, the only two things the Browns could guarantee were lousy baseball and terrible attendance. From 1946 to 1950 the Browns averaged 59 wins and 95 losses, and were last in league attendance each season.[1] Despite the team's abysmal record and popularity, Veeck decided to buy the Browns in 1951 after being out of baseball since he sold the Cleveland Indians in 1949. He took over ownership in July 1951, intending to make the Browns the dominant team in the St. Louis market over the National League Cardinals.

That was a tall order, as the Cardinals had a history of World Series success and drew over a million fans each season from 1946 to 1950, while the Browns drew 1,700,540 for the entire five-year period. The Cardinals almost equaled that total in 1949 alone, when they attracted 1,430,676 people to Sportsman's Park (which, incidentally, Veeck owned).

Veeck knew these were desperate times, and we all know what kinds of measures are needed in these instances. He decided to go for the outrageous, starting on August 19, when, in the second game of a doubleheader he brought in 3-foot-7 Eddie Gaedel to pinch-hit for Frank Saucier in the bottom of the first inning. Gaedel walked on four pitches, then sauntered down to first base and into baseball lore.

"The austere American League, celebrating its fiftieth anniversary this year, will reach the ripe old age of 100 before anyone other than Phineas T. Veeck, the Barnum of baseball, tops the colorful substitute for winning ball the sport-shirted showman offered yesterday at Sportsman's Park," wrote Bob Broeg.[2]

What Broeg didn't know was that ol' "Phineas T." would top that stunt five nights later, when the lucky fans (including Veeck, his wife, and A's owner Connie Mack) sitting in a special section behind the Browns' dugout got to play Manager for a Day and guided the Browns to a 5-3 win over the Philadelphia A's.

The groundwork for the stunt started even before the Gaedel game, when the *St. Louis Globe-Democrat* printed the following notice on August 15:

How to Become the Manager

If you would like to be a Grandstand Manager of the Browns on the night of Aug. 24 in their game against the Athletics, fill in your name, address, zone number and city or town below … If you would like to be one of the coaches, append a brief letter, stating your reasons. The shorter the better. Your membership card, entitling you to admission to park upon payment of tax, will be mailed to you.[3]

Veeck received 4,000 letters from across America, even as far away as Anchorage, Alaska. He chose two gentlemen, Clark Mitze and Charles E. Hughes, to be the coaches, although they weren't allowed onto the field because the American League office did not receive their contracts by game time. Mitze, it seemed, was qualified because, according to his letter, he went to a batting cage, missed the first nine pitches, and then fouled off the 10th, bopping himself in the nose.

This idea of having the fans manage wasn't surprising coming from Veeck, as he usually watched games from the bleacher seats. "I have discovered in 20 years of moving around a ballpark that the knowledge of the game is usually in inverse proportion to the price of the seats," Veeck said.[4]

Here's how the stunt worked: Each fan in the section received a placard with "yes" printed on one side and "no" printed on the other. When either Mitze or Hughes determined that a decision was in order, they contacted Veeck's right-hand man, Bob Fishel, via walkie-talkie; Fishel then would raise a sign asking the fans a question, such as whether a runner should steal, if the infield should move back for a batter, even "Shall we jerk the bum," and the fans would display their placards according to what they thought the team should do. A circuit judge, one James E. McLaughlin, estimated the votes to ensure fairness, and relayed the results to player-coach John Berardino.

The ballots from the notice had also asked the fans to select the starting eight for that night's game, although Veeck did stop short of having 1,000-plus people bring the lineup card to home plate — probably because he didn't think of it. Six of the starting eight from the Browns' previous game — a 9-3 loss to the Red Sox — started for St. Louis. Sherm Lollar replaced Matt Batts at catcher and Hank Arft resumed playing first base after missing three games. Ned Garver, who got the mound assignment, had lost his previous start in the first game of the doubleheader at which Gaedel made his appearance. Nonetheless he had a fine 14-8 record with a 3.89 ERA, and would go onto win 20 games for a team that won only 52 the entire season. (He ended up second in American League MVP voting behind the Yankees' Yogi Berra.) Journeyman Alex Kellner started for Philadelphia. Kellner had lost his last four decisions and was 7-12 with a 5.19 ERA at game time.

The game was almost a disaster for the Browns from the get-go, as Garver gave up three runs in the first inning. With one out, Ferris Fain and Elmer Valo both singled and Gus Zernial, who smacked 12 of the 33 home runs he hit that season off Browns pitching, belted a three-run shot to put the A's ahead. Hank Majeski then reached on an error and Dave Philley singled Majeski to third.

At this point the "managers" were called upon to make their first decision, whether to move the infield in to cut the run off at the plate or move back for a possible double play. They voted, McLaughlin tabulated, and the decision was to move the infield back. That proved to be the right call, as Pete Suder grounded into an inning-ending double play.

Fans didn't high-five each other in those days, or else there would have been 1,115 sore palms just from getting the first decision right. Besides, they had to contend with a three-run deficit. The Browns tied it in the bottom of the first. With one out, Jim Delsing doubled to center. Lollar showed his appreciation for the fans choosing him by hitting a single to drive Delsing home with the first St. Louis run. With the count 3-and-2 on Cliff Mapes, the fans were polled as to whether Lollar should be off with the pitch. They voted no, which proved smart as Mapes struck out. Ken Wood then hit the first of his two doubles in the game, sending Lollar to third. The fans looked like out-and-out geniuses when Arft singled to drive home two runs and tie the score, 3-3.

Ah, but then the realities of life at the helm hit home. The fans were asked if Arft should steal second, which, when you think about it, was the equivalent of having the PA announcer tell the other team that Arft was on his way. The fans voted for the theft, but Arft was out by two feet.

Lollar proved to be the hero of the evening. He hit a solo shot in the third to give St. Louis a 4-3 lead, and then scored the insurance run in the eighth when Mapes singled him home after he hit a two-out double. The final score was 5-3, with Garver going all the way for the win.

Zack Taylor, the Browns' regular manager, spent the game sitting in a rocking chair wearing civilian clothes. He took over the team again the next night, but he must have longed for the rocker as St. Louis lost, 9-1. Veeck fired him after the season. Taylor piloted the Browns for four years (plus a 30-game stint in 1946) and never managed in the majors again.

The game was also memorable for Mitze, as Veeck gave him a trophy after the game inscribed: "One of the Best Coaches Ever Banned from the Coaching Lines." He also didn't have to jerk any bums.

SOURCES

In addition to the sources listed in the Notes, the author also used Baseballhall.org, Baseballhotcorner.com, and the *New York Times*.

NOTES

1 The numbers exceed 154—the number of games in a season in those years—due to rounding.

2 Bob Broeg, "Lots of Frosting on Brownies' A.L. Birthday Cake, But Filling Turns Bitter With Two Defeats," *St. Louis Post-Dispatch* August 20, 1951: 1C.

3 Steve Wulf, "Vote, Vote Vote for the Home Team," *espn.com*, September 16, 2014.

4 Wayne Stewart and Roger Kahn, *The Gigantic Book of Baseball Quotations* (New York: Skyhorse Publishing, 2007), 32.

WARREN SPAHN EARNS 20TH WIN WITH ONE-HITTER IN RARE DAY-NIGHT, THREE-TEAM DOUBLEHEADER

September 13, 1951: Boston Braves 2, St. Louis Cardinals 0, at Sportsman's Park

BY MICHAEL HUBER

ON SEPTEMBER 13, 1951, Sportsman's Park hosted an extremely rare event: a three-team doubleheader. In the first game, the third-place Cardinals defeated the second-place New York Giants, 6-4. In the second game, the Boston Braves' Warren Spahn pitched a masterful one-hitter as the Braves blanked the Cardinals, 2-0.

This was the first time since June 25, 1899, that a team had played two different rivals on the same day.[1] The Cardinals-Giants game scheduled for September 12—the Giants' last scheduled game at Sportsman's Park in 1951—had been rained out. The 13th had originally been an open date for the Cardinals, but the club had filled it by rescheduling a rained-out game against the Braves. Horace Stoneham, owner of the Giants, objected to the unusual doubleheader, but Ford Frick, the National League president, "gave his blessing to the arrangement because no other date was available"[2] to fit the New York-St. Louis game into the two teams' schedules. So "novel scheduling"[3] meant that the Cardinals hosted the Giants in the afternoon before 4,160 fans. The Cardinals-Braves game, played under the lights, brought a mere 4,706 spectators to Sportsman's Park.

In the afternoon opener, Monte Irvin led the Giants' cause with a 3-for-3 day at the plate, scoring two runs and driving in three, but it wasn't enough as St. Louis prevailed, 6-4. The Cardinals had a balanced attack with six different batters driving in runs, all in the second inning. The St. Louis lineup featured seven left-handed batters in a row.[4] New York's Sal Maglie had won his previous five starts, but "six hits and two walks figured in the Cardinals' splurge" against Maglie and reliever Monty Kennedy.[5] Harry Walker, batting seventh in the St. Louis lineup, went 3-for-4 with a run scored and a run batted in to lead his team.

At night, St. Louis sent Al Brazle to the mound to battle Boston's Spahn. Brazle had a rough start, yielding singles to Sibby Sisti and Sam Jethroe to start the game. Then, in what should have been the start of a strike-'em-out, throw-'em-out double play, Earl Torgeson struck out. Jethroe was caught off first base but catcher Del Rice's throw went past first baseman Stan Musial into right field. Sisti scored an unearned run on Rice's throwing error and Jethroe ended up on third base. Cleanup batter Bob Elliott then hit a sharp grounder to second, and Red Schoendienst threw to Rice at home, nailing Jethroe at the plate. Sid Gordon flied out to center field, and the wild first frame had the Braves on top, 1-0.

With the one-run cushion, Spahn set down the first six batters he faced. Chuck Diering walked to lead off the third inning for the Redbirds. He advanced to second on a wild pitch by Spahn. Rice sent a hard line drive up the middle that caromed off Spahn's pitching hand, but the pitcher snared the ball and threw to first baseman Torgeson for the out; Diering remained at second base. Spahn's ring finger got the worst of it, but he shrugged it off. "Oddly enough, it didn't bother me," he said after the game.[6] "I hold it against my ball for my fast one—and it was numb from the third inning on." Spahn threw mostly fastballs in the game, mixing in an occasional curve, and he said the numbness was the reason why

Cardinals batters popped out so much in the game.[7] Spahn retired the next two hitters and stranded Diering at second. That was the farthest a St. Louis batter would get, as the left-hander pitched with precision and efficiency.

After the improbable first inning, Brazle also settled into a routine. He retired 12 Braves in a row before Willard Marshall singled in an unusual fifth inning that featured four straight hits by the Braves but no runs. On Roy Hartsfield's single, Marshall tried for third but was gunned down by Cardinals center fielder Diering. With two outs, Spahn singled, putting runners at first and second. Sisti followed with the fourth consecutive single of the inning. However, Hartsfield fell rounding third base and Spahn, who had rounded second base too far, was tagged out at second before diving back to the base. Four straight hits but no runs for the Braves.

After Diering's walk in the third inning, Spahn retired 10 batters in a row. But with one out in the sixth his no-hitter was broken up by, of all people, his mound opponent. Jack Barry of the *Boston Globe* wrote that "a soft hump-backed liner off the bat of Alpha Brazle … kept the Braves' Warren Spahn from baseball glory tonight."[8] Brazle was stranded when the next two batters were retired, and Spahn finished the game by retiring 11 straight Cardinals.

Brazle kept the Braves in check until the top of the ninth. With one out, former Cardinals catcher Walker Cooper doubled and moved to third on a groundout by Marshall. Hartsfield was intentionally walked, bringing Spahn to the plate. The Braves' hero singled to center, bringing home Cooper with the Braves' second run. Spahn took the mound and retired the Cardinals in order in the bottom of the ninth, completing the one-hitter as Boston prevailed 2-0.

Facing only 29 batters, Spahn took just one hour and 48 minutes to defeat the Cards and earn his 20th victory of the season. He helped his own cause with a 2-for-3 performance plus a sacrifice and that RBI single for the insurance run in the ninth. Hartsfield and Sisti also recorded two hits each for Boston.

Both pitchers notched complete games.[9] Spahn, using only 95 pitches, allowed just one hit, and he walked one while striking out two. Brazle scattered nine hits and three walks. The 37-year-old St. Louis left-hander struck out eight Boston batters, including Torgeson four times.

Spahn reached the 20-win plateau for the third straight season and fourth time in his career.[10] He joined Maglie as the only National League pitchers at this point of the season with 20 wins.[11] Spahn's accomplishment was the 13th one-hitter of the season. After the game he told reporters about the experience. "This is the one I wanted. I wasn't thinking in terms of a no-hitter. I just wanted the 20th. Even when I was warming up, I felt as though I had it."[12]

For the season, 1951 featured four no-hitters: the Pittsburgh Pirates' Cliff Chambers (versus the Braves, May 6), the Cleveland Indians' Bob Feller (versus the Detroit Tigers, July 1—his third career no-hitter), and two by the New York Yankees' Allie Reynolds (versus the Cleveland Indians, July 12, and the Boston Red Sox, September 28).

With the conclusion of the unique three-team doubleheader, the Cardinals had a record of 73-66. The Giants fell to 84-57 and the loss dropped them to six games behind the league-leading Brooklyn Dodgers. However, the Giants went 14-2 to close the season, clinching the 1951 National League crown on Bobby Thomson's legendary walk-off home run off the Dodgers' Ralph Branca.[13] Brazle and St. Louis finished the season in third place and Spahn and the Braves ended in fourth.

The author thanks Lisa Tuite from the *Boston Globe* for her valued assistance with sources.

NOTES

1. According to Baseball-Reference.com, the National League's St. Louis Perfectos played the New York Giants in Game One and the Cleveland Spiders in Game Two on June 25, 1899. The Perfectos lost both games.
2. Joseph M. Sheehan, "Cards Halt Polo Grounders, 6-4, Routing Maglie in 6-Run Second," *New York Times*, September 14, 1951.
3. "Games of Thursday, September 13," *The Sporting News*, September 26, 1951.

4   Jack Barry, "Spahn Allows One Hit, Scores 20th Victory, 2-0," *Boston Globe*, September 14, 1951.

5   Sheehan.

6   Barry.

7   Spahn got 17 outs on balls hit in the air. Six of them were pop fouls (three to the catcher and three to the first baseman).

8   Barry.

9   Spahn led the major leagues in 1951 with 26 complete games and seven shutouts. Brazle finished the 1951 season with five complete games.

10 Spahn finished the 1951 season with a 22-14 record, and he ended his career with 13 20-win seasons.

11 In 1951 Maglie tied his New York Giants teammate Larry Jansen for the major-league lead in wins with 23. Spahn's 22 victories tied Brooklyn Dodgers pitcher Preacher Roe and Cleveland Indians ace Bob Feller. Three other pitchers amassed 21 wins, and five more notched 20.

12 Barry.

13 The Giants lost the 1951 World Series to the New York Yankees in six games.

NED GARVER WINS 20TH FOR THE 102-LOSS BROWNIES

September 30, 1951: St. Louis Browns 9, Chicago White Sox 5, at Sportsman's Park

BY GREGORY H. WOLF

THE NL DOMINATED THE HEADLINES on the last day of the 1951 regular season. With identical 95-58 records, the Brooklyn Dodgers and the New York Giants squared off against their respective opponents, Philadelphia and Boston, on the road with the chance to claim the pennant or end the season in a tie, thus necessitating a best-of three tie-breaker series beginning the next day. In the AL, where the New York Yankees had already captured the flag, there was a refreshing diversion from the Gotham-focused attention of the baseball world. Tension mounted in St. Louis, where hurler Ned Garver of the 102-loss, last-place Browns took aim at an improbable accomplishment—a 20-win season — against the fourth-place Chicago White Sox (81-72).

The Browns had floundered since capturing their first and only AL pennant, in 1944, followed by a second straight winning season for just the second time in the franchise's 51-year history. They averaged a dismal 56-98 record under skipper Zack Taylor (1948-1951), yet there was some glimmer of hope in July 1951 when former Cleveland Indians owner Bill Veeck Jr. purchased the moribund team. "Our club will be fifth—at the worst—in 1952," he said confidently as the season wrapped up.[1]

A major reason for Veeck's optimism was Garver, one of the best, most underrated and most forgotten pitchers of the era.[2] Since debuting with the Browns in 1948, Garver had posted a misleading 51-58 record, including 19-12 thus far in '51, despite playing for baseball's worst team. Not known as a hard thrower, Garver took a cerebral approach to pitching. "I was a sinker-slider ball pitcher," he told the author.[3] "I accidentally developed the slider playing catch in St. Louis. I had good control and could throw from different spots—side-arm or overhand. I already had a curveball and a sinker. All of a sudden I threw a slider. I could feel it when it left my hand. I threw the ball again with the same pressure from my finger and that son-of-a-biscuit moved. Ted Williams always said that he could not pick up the spin from my slider. That pitch made the difference in my major-league career." Garver had two different sliders with different breaks. "One I threw like a football pass to left-hand hitters, but I tried to throw it only belt-high," he said. "It would break back in and hit you on the fist of the bat. I had another slider I'd throw three-quarters. I could make the ball drop out and down and I threw it a lot to right-hand hitters." Blessed with superior command of his breaking balls, Garver threw few pitches in the strike zone and rarely gave batters a "good" pitch to hit.

Determined to give fans something to remember during the long offseason, the showman Veeck organized a day of festivities for this warm Sunday afternoon, September 30, with all of the proceeds going to the Community Chest of Greater St. Louis.[4] Shrouded in a carnival-like atmosphere, Sportsman's Park was filled with 14,771 spectators, the third largest crowd of the season and almost four times the season average. At 1:30 the Harlem Globetrotters basketball team faced a ragtag squad of former college stars and Browns players, including Sherm Lollar, Al Widmar, and Jim Delsing, on a court set up in the infield between second and third base. (The Globetrotters won, 29-17.) Afterward, one of the basketball players, Tony Lavelli, also a renowned accordion player, engaged the crowd with a virtuoso performance before the Browns took the field. For his last gag of a season filled with them, including the appearance of 3-foot-7 pinch-hitter Eddie Gaedel and Grandstand Managers Day, Veeck delighted fans by rearranging the outfield flags depicting the position of all eight AL teams, so that the Browns sat on top, in first place. He also promised to keep the crowd regularly informed about the Giants and Dodgers games.

The Browns tallied the game's first run, in the second inning, when Hank Arft sprinted home from second on Fred Marsh's one-out single off Chicago starter Joe Dobson. (Marsh was thrown out trying for two.) Two batters later, Garver lined a single that center fielder Ray Coleman misplayed, enabling Bill Jennings, who had also singled, to score.

Coleman atoned for his miscue an inning later when he belted a two-out bases-loaded single, driving in Nellie Fox and Al Zarilla, both of whom had also singled, to tie the game. Garver had beaten the Pale Hose in their three previous meetings, allowing only three runs in 27 innings, but he was making his third consecutive start on three days' rest and looked fatigued.

Dobson, an 11-year veteran with a 118-88 career record, including 7-6 as a part-time starter thus far in '51, appeared equally ineffective. He squandered the lead by yielding three consecutive hits to start the third, including Earl Rapp's two-run single plating Cliff Mapes and Bob Nieman for a 4-2 Browns lead.

"[Garver] looks, acts, and pitches like the college hero on the cover of a boy's novel," opined the *St. Louis Post-Dispatch*, and it was the good-looking pitcher's game to win or lose even after a two-run homer by light-hitting rookie shortstop Joe DeMaestri, the first of his career, tied the game in the fourth.[5] Not a stir was seen in the Browns' bullpen. After yielding almost as many hits (6) and walks (2) as he had registered outs (9), Garver repaid Taylor's trust by retiring the next three hitters and tossing solid ball the rest of the game. Manager Taylor's biggest concern was whether the AL's lowest-scoring team could provide Garver enough support to eke out a win.

Garver didn't wait for his teammates' help. With one out in the fourth, he picked an opportune occasion for his first homer of the season and third in his career, a solo shot off right-handed reliever Randy Gumpert. Adept at the plate, Garver batted .305 (29-for-95) with nine RBIs in '51.

Garver was far from assured of his 20th victory with five innings to go. The Browns had little margin for error; they had a deplorable relief corps, boasted the highest team ERA in the majors (5.18), and also led the league in errors (172). In the bottom of the fifth Marsh gave St. Louis some breathing room by belting a two-out, two-run homer for a 7-4 lead. The Browns tacked on more insurance in the seventh on an RBI double by Arft, who subsequently scored on Lollar's groundout.

Garver had a hiccup in the eighth when Bud Stewart led off with a single, moved to second on the hurler's fielding error on Red Wilson's chopper back to the mound, and then scored on DeMaestri's grounder. But Taylor had no intention of pulling the AL's most durable pitcher in the ninth. Garver had

Ned Garver completed 24 of 30 starts and won 20 games in 1951, finishing second in MVP voting despite playing for a last-place team. (National Baseball Hall of Fame, Cooperstown, New York)

led the circuit by going the distance 22 times (in 31 starts) in 1950 and was shooting for his league-best 24th complete game in 1951. As he had all game, Garver fed the White Sox a steady diet of breaking balls which they pounded into the dirt. He gave up a one-out single to Jim Busby, but recorded all three outs on infield grounders, finishing a 9-5 victory in 1 hour and 45 minutes.

Overcoming a rocky start, Garver yielded 11 hits and five runs (four earned) to became the first Browns hurler to win 20 games since Bobo Newsom in 1938. The loss went to Gumpert (9-8). Baseball has always had a peculiar fascination with successful pitchers on terrible teams. Garver (20-12, 246 innings, 3.73 ERA) became the first hurler to reach the 20-win plateau for a last-place team since Hollis "Sloppy" Thurston of the Chicago White Sox in 1924. Howard Ehmke, who won 20 for the Boston Red Sox in 1923, was the only other hurler in the live-ball era to hold that dubious distinction. Two Hall of Famers joined the club in the 1970s: Steve Carlton picked up the Cy Young Award in 1972 for winning 27 games for the Philadelphia Phillies; two years later Nolan Ryan recorded 22 victories for the California Angels. Garver remains the only live-ball hurler to win 20 games on a club that lost 100 or more. He also finished a close second in the MVP voting in '51, behind the Yankees' Yogi Berra.

Garver's success made him one of the most coveted pitchers in baseball. The New York Yankees had been attempting to acquire him since at least 1950. One day after Garver's milestone victory, Veeck added fuel to the speculation by boldly claiming, "[I] will trade anyone, I mean anyone."[6] The *St. Louis Post-Dispatch* reported that the White Sox GM, Frank "Trader" Lane, had offered a package worth at least $250,000 for Garver.[7]

Ignoring trade rumors the best he could, Garver went on a barnstorming tour in October with Browns venerable reliever Satchel Paige, whom Veeck signed soon after acquiring the club. Garver was ultimately traded, but not until August 14, 1952, in an eight-player deal with the Detroit Tigers.

SOURCES

In addition to the sources cited in the Notes, the author also accessed Retrosheet.org, Baseball-Reference.com, the SABR Minor Leagues Database, accessed online at Baseball-Reference.com, SABR.org, and *The Sporting News* archive via Paper of Record.

NOTES

1. Neal Russo, " 'Will Trade Anyone,' Says Veeck, About to Tie Into Rebuilding Job; Garver Shaky, but Lands No. 20," *St. Louis Post-Dispatch*, October 1, 1951: 2E.

2. By one advanced metric, Garver was the most valuable pitcher in the AL in both 1950 and 1951 when he led all pitchers in WAR (Wins Above Replacement), which attempts to measure a player's contribution. WAR calculates the number of wins a player provides his team compared with a replacement-level player. Garver's 8.2 WAR in 1950 led all major leaguers, regardless of position. His 6.8 WAR in 1951 was the highest among pitchers in the AL, and second only to Ted Williams in the league.

3. Author's interview with Ned Garver on April 27, 2012. All quotations from Garver are from this interview. See also, Gregory H. Wolf, "Ned Garver," *SABR Biography Project*, SABR.org. sabr.org/bioproj/person/78230a19.

4. "Garver Could Expand Chest Today Along With the Community Chest," *St. Louis Post-Dispatch*, September 30, 1951: 1E.

5. "Excitement in the Cellar," *St. Louis Post-Dispatch*, September 27, 1951: 2B.

6. Russo.

7. International News Service, "White Sox Want 'In' if There Is Open Bidding for Ned Garver," *St. Louis Post-Dispatch*, October 3, 1951: 1B.

SATCH TURNS BACK TIME TO SPIN 12-INNING SHUTOUT AGAINST TIGERS

August 6, 1952: St. Louis Browns 1, Detroit Tigers 0, at Sportsman's Park

BY GREGORY H. WOLF

"Never was Paige more tantalizing," mused the *St. Louis Post-Dispatch* about 45-year-old "Old Satch's" remarkable 12-inning shutout of the Detroit Tigers. "[He] wins games [and] entertains in the process. He whirled his arm twice in a full windup; sometimes just once. His slow ball … seemed to hang in the air, as though manipulated by wire."[1] "[Paige] unwound his ancient right arm," gushed the *Detroit Free Press*, and "proved himself the master," momentarily putting the St. Louis Browns on the front pages of sports pages across the country.[2]

Since capturing an unlikely pennant in 1944, the Browns had been among the worst teams in baseball, and struggled to draw fans in a city long dominated by the Cardinals. In 1951 Bill Veeck bought a controlling interest in the club and vowed to make changes as he did when he purchased the Cleveland Indians in 1946. The visionary owner had integrated the AL with the signing of Negro Leagues star Larry Doby in 1947. In July 1948 he signed Satchel Paige, who by some estimates had probably already pitched in excess of 2,000 games in the Negro Leagues, most notably with the Pittsburgh Crawfords and Kansas City Monarchs, and on barnstorming tours.[3] The 41-year-old "rookie" became the first African-American pitcher in the major leagues, going 6-1 as the Indians went on to win the World Series. When Veeck was forced to sell the Indians after the 1949 season as part of a divorce settlement, Paige was subsequently released, his big-league career seemingly finished. A year and a half later, Satch got another chance when Veeck signed the ageless hurler to a Browns contract in July 1951. In his debut on July 18, he hurled eight innings in an eventual loss to the Washington Senators at Sportsman's Park.[4]

The seventh-place Browns (44-63) were in accustomed territory as they prepared to play the Tigers in the second game of a three-game set as part of a season-long 22-game homestand. Paige was one of the few bright spots for the Browns and skipper Marty Marion, the former Cardinals All-Star shortstop who had replaced Rogers Hornsby in the dugout about two months earlier. Paige had strung together 27⅓ scoreless innings over 12 appearances as a reliever (May 8 to June 11). On June 20, the 6-foot-3, 180-pound Alabaman hurled 10 scoreless innings of relief in a 5-5 tie against Washington; 11 days later he tossed 10⅔ innings of relief against Cleveland only to suffer a heartbreaking loss by surrendering two runs in the 19th inning. Paige's unlikely performance thus far in '52 was vindicated when New York's Casey Stengel named him to the AL All-Star team, though he didn't pitch in the game.

Paige (7-6, 3.00 ERA), making his 35th appearance and second start of the season, faced off against 35-year-old right-hander Virgil Trucks, long considered one of the hardest throwers in baseball. "Fire" Trucks entered the season with a stellar 103-72 career record in parts of 10 seasons, yet was in the midst of a confounding campaign. Despite his unsightly record (4-13), Trucks had already authored a no-hitter and one-hitter against Washington for the last-place Tigers (36-68). [Trucks would go on to toss his second no-hitter of the season, against New York, on August 25 en route to a 5-19 record].

Paige and Trucks weren't strangers. Trucks told the author that while growing up in Birmingham he'd sneak into games at Rickwood Field to see Paige pitch for the Birmingham Black Barons in the late 1920s.[5] Coincidentally, when Trucks was traded to the Browns for the 1953 season, Paige became his first black teammate, and they struck up a close friendship that included a barnstorming event featuring the two hurlers in 1959.

A Wednesday match-up of the league's two worst teams drew a sparse crowd of 6,162 to Sportsman's Park. The Browns threatened first when they filled the bases with no outs in the second on singles by Jim Delsing and Bobby Young and a walk to Joe DeMaestri. Paige hit a sharp grounder to first baseman Walt Dropo, who initiated a 3-2-3 double play by firing a strike to catcher Joe Ginsberg. Trucks whiffed Gordon Goldsberry to end the frame. The Browns had another good scoring opportunity in the fifth when Goldsberry led off with a double, only to have Trucks retire the next three batters in succession.

Described as a "venerable Negro," in the insensitive parlance of the time, Paige rolled through the first five innings, yielding only three hits.[6] The Tigers had their "first real chance," opined the *Detroit Free Press*, when Neil Berry and Fred Hatfield lined consecutive two-out singles in the sixth.[7] Paige dispatched cleanup hitter Dropo on a routine fly to left fielder Ray Coleman.

After Paige set down the Tigers in order in the seventh and eighth, Clint Courtney collected the Browns' sixth hit, a one-out double. But once again, Trucks defused the threat, retiring Jim Dyck and then corralling Delsing's "high bounder" and throwing to first to end the frame.[8]

The Tigers seemed to have Paige on the ropes in the 10th. But the oldest player in the league, whom the United Press tabbed as "Old Mr. Unbelievable," had a few more tricks up his sleeve.[9] After Cliff Mapes led off with a double, Paige intentionally walked Ginsberg, setting up a potential double play. Light-hitting rookie Al Federoff's bunt was perfectly placed to the third-base side, filling the bases with no outs. Skipper Fred Hutchinson sent Johnny Pesky to pinch-hit for Trucks, who had been on a roll, yielding only two of his six hits since the third inning. The move backfired as Pesky grounded sharply to first baseman Goldsberry, whose strike to Courtney nailed Mapes at the plate. Johnny Groth followed with a hard bouncer to rookie third baseman Dyck, whose missile to Courtney erased Ginsberg. Facing Berry with runners on second and third, Paige lofted "three very fast, sharp breaking curves," wrote the *Post-Dispatch*. "Each one started for Neil Berry's chest, then broke right over the heart of the plate."[10] Berry was called out on strikes to end the frame. The Browns' defense and Paige's performance were "hailed as actual victory," gushed the *Post-Dispatch*. "[Paige] broke the Tigers' spirit."[11]

Armed with what the *Free Press* described as "unusual baffling control," Paige retired all six batters he faced in the 11th and 12th innings.[12] One of those outs was by Dropo, who meekly grounded back to Paige to finish the game hitless in five at-bats. Frustrated by Paige the entire game and once falling after whiffing at a pitch, Dropo "exchanged heated words" with the pitcher at one point, according to the *Post-Dispatch*.[13]

St. Louis got a break when Young led off the 12th with a sharp blow that caromed off second baseman Federoff's glove for the Browns' first hit against Hal White. (The right-hander had relieved Trucks to begin the 10th.) After Marsh advanced Young to second on a sacrifice, Al Zarilla, pinch-hitting for Paige, was intentionally passed to set up a double play. Both Marsh and Zarilla moved up a station when Goldsberry's grounder was too slow to turn a twin killing. White loaded the bases by intentionally walking Coleman to set up a do-or-die scenario with rookie Bob Nieman. The Cincinnati native, who ended the season leading the Browns in homers (18), RBIs (74), and batting average (.289), stroked a single over shortstop Berry's head to drive in Young for the dramatic winning run, ending the game in 3 hours and 1 minute.

Nieman's clutch single made a winner out of Paige, who yielded only seven hits and struck out a career-high nine batters in the longest outing of his big-league career. "[He] outpitched one of the standouts of the decade," praised the *Free Press*.[14] Reporters gathered around the affable hurler in the clubhouse after the game. "I told Marty that I had 100 outs in my arm last night and I sure used them all up," said Paige in his Alabama drawl. "I made up my mind that there wasn't gonna be no morning workout," he continued, making reference to manager's Marion's practice of holding early-morning practices after losses.[15]

The most excited person after the game might have been Bill Veeck, who kept an office and a small apartment in Sportsman's Park, which he also owned. "This is the greatest baseball thrill I have had in many years," said the cash-strapped owner, whose controversial stunts, such as 3-foot-7 pinch-hitter Eddie Gaedel and grandstand manager day (both of which occurred within a week the previous August), had infuriated other baseball owners.[16] But "Ole Satch," who never forgot the trust the master showman had in him, knew Veeck must have been an anxious, miserable wreck during the game. "I was thinking of 'Old Burrhead' (Paige's pet name for Veeck) when I was going through those extra innings."[17] Paige finished his most productive campaign in the majors with a 12-10 record and a 3.07 ERA in 138 innings.

SOURCES

In addition to the sources cited in the Notes, the author also accessed Retrosheet.org, Baseball-Reference.com, the SABR Minor Leagues Database, accessed online at Baseball-Reference.com, SABR.org, and *The Sporting News* archive via Paper of Record.

NOTES

1. Dent McSkimming, "Paige Puts On His Greatest Show, Beating Tigers in 12 Innings, 1-0," *St. Louis Post-Dispatch*, August 7, 1952: 30.

2. "Old Satch Beats Tigers, 1-0, in 12 Innings," *Detroit Free Press*, August 7, 1952: 21.

3. According to Larry Tye's biography of Paige on SABR's BioProject site, it is impossible to determine how many games Paige pitched. The author notes that Paige kept his own pitching records, and supposedly pitched in more than 2,500 games in a professional career that spanned five decades. sabr.org/bioproj/person/c33afddd.

4. Outfielder Hank Thompson integrated the Browns on July 17, 1947.

5. Author's interview with Virgil Trucks on September 19, 2011. See author's biography of Trucks on the SABR BioProject site, sabr.org/bioproj/person/63151815.

6. *Detroit Free Pres.*

7. Ibid.

8. Ibid.

9. Carl Lundquist, United Press, "Double Header to Tax Pitchers of Both Teams," *Franklin* (Pennsylvania) *News-Herald*, August 7, 1952: 14.

10. *St. Louis Post-Dispatch*.

11. Ibid.

12. *Detroit Free Press*.

13. *St. Louis Post-Dispatch*.

14. *Detroit Free Press*.

15. United Press, *Franklin* (Pennsylvania) *News-Herald*.

16. *St. Louis Post-Dispatch*.

17. Ibid.

BOBO HOLLOMAN THROWS A NO-HITTER IN HIS FIRST MAJOR-LEAGUE START

May 6, 1953: St. Louis Browns 6, Philadelphia Athletics 0, at Busch Stadium

BY JOE SCHUSTER

BEFORE THE 1953 SEASON, PITCHER Alva "Bobo" Holloman predicted great things for himself. Acquired by the St. Louis Browns from the Triple-A Syracuse Chiefs the previous October, he immediately started a campaign to assure himself a spot as a starter, telling team owner Bill Veeck that he would be his number-one pitcher and asking, "Am I going to be a regular starter?"[1]

Holloman continued pursuing a shot at starting throughout the early spring. "The guy's a real character" Veeck said. "Every night since the season's opened, he's come pounding on [manager] Marty Marion's door. 'When you gonna start me?' he'd ask."[2]

Holloman gave little evidence early on that he deserved to start. In his first four relief outings, covering 5⅓ innings, he allowed five earned runs on 10 hits.[3] He justified his poor performance by claiming he was naturally a starter and insisting that if Marion did not accede to his wishes, he wanted a trade. Finally, largely to put an end to his wheedling, Marion gave in, a move many thought was a prelude to the Browns shedding the pitcher when the May 14 cutdown deadline required teams to reduce their rosters to 25: Holloman would prove no better a starter than reliever and the team would release him.[4]

Marion initially scheduled Holloman to start an April 28 home game against the New York Yankees, but with rain falling as Holloman finished his warm-up and Yankees leadoff hitter Phil Rizzuto stepping into the batter's box, home-plate umpire Bill Summers called the game, deferring Holloman's start.[5]

As it turned out, the delay likely kept him in the majors beyond the cutdown day, since in his eventual start, against the Philadelphia Athletics on May 6, Holloman threw an improbable no-hit, no-run game, the only one in the majors that season.

Opening the day, the Browns were 9-9, on their way to finishing last with their third 100-loss season in five years. The Athletics came in 10-8, bound for a seventh-place finish in the eight-team league. Opposing Holloman was southpaw Morrie Martin, in the fourth season of a 10-season major-league career, making his second start after missing a year of baseball when a line drive broke the index finger of his pitching hand the previous May.[6] In Martin's first appearance, on May 1, he pitched a complete-game 4-1 victory over Detroit.

As with Holloman's earlier attempt to start, it was raining and chilly at game time. The weather kept the crowd down to 2,473, such a poor showing that in the fifth inning, Veeck told his public-relations director, Bob Fishel, to announce that, due to the "bad night," the team would honor the rain checks for the game, even though by then it was official.[7]

As the game started, Holloman went through his usual ritual, scratching the initials of his wife and son into the foul line, "N" for Nancy and "G" for Garry.[8] The superstition seemed to pay immediate dividends. Relying primarily on his sinker and curve, with an occasional slider because his fastball lacked zip, he was perfect through the first two innings, although he needed a spectacular play by Browns left fielder Jim Dyck for the last out in the second, when A's slugger Gus Zernial hit a deep line drive. Dyck made what one writer described as a "circus performance" catch, leaping against the wall to make a one-handed grab.[9]

In the bottom of that inning, Browns catcher Les Moss hit a one-out double down the right-field line. After first baseman Roy Sievers struck out, Moss went to third when second baseman Bobby Young reached on an error, bringing up Holloman for his first major-league plate appearance. He singled, scoring Moss and giving the Browns a 1-0 lead. They added single runs in the third, fifth, and sixth innings before closing out the scoring with two in the seventh on Holloman's second and last major-league hit, also a single.

While game accounts describe most of the plays behind Holloman as routine, there were moments that challenged the eventual gem, including a few plays one writer characterized as "perils of Pauline fielding."[10] In the fifth, with one down, A's right fielder Allie Clark hit a fly to deep left that cleared the wall, but foul by a few feet. After Clark grounded to short, Zernial again threatened to end the no-hitter, sending a high bouncer back up the middle, which Holloman leaped to snag but it got caught in his glove. When he shook it out, it hit the ground and Zernial was safe, but the official scorer ruled it an error.[11]

Leading off in the sixth, A's catcher Joe Astroth trickled a groundball down the third-base line. Knowing he would be unable to throw Astroth out, Browns third baseman Bob Elliott hovered over it, hoping it would go foul, which it did; Astroth walked on the next pitch.[12] Astroth threatened the no-hitter again in the eighth, when he hit a hard grounder far to the left of shortstop Billy Hunter, who made what one reporter hyperbolically called "a 1000-yard dash," dropped to a knee to stop the ball and threw to first, nabbing Astroth.[13]

As Holloman went to the mound for the ninth, he was nervous and, for luck, touched his wife's and son's initials again in the foul line.[14] This time, it seemed to fail him, as he hit a streak of wildness, walking the first two, pinch-hitter Elmer Valo and shortstop Eddie Joost. When center fielder Dave Philley hit into a 4-6-3 double play, sending pinch-runner Joe DeMaestri to third, Holloman was one out away from his no-hitter, but extended things by walking third baseman Loren Babe, bringing up first baseman Eddie Robinson, who watched a strike go by and then fouled the next pitch before smashing a Holloman curve down the first-base line, only inches foul.[15]

Holloman and Moss figured that Robinson would be looking for a fastball and decided to come back with the curve instead. It was wise: Robinson flied out to right fielder Vic Wertz.[16] Holloman was in the record books as the first pitcher in the century to throw a no-hitter in his first start; the 6-0 victory was the first win of his major-league career.

After the game, Marion seemed to revise his opinion of Holloman, saying, "Some people would call him a screwball. ... But I'm mighty happy that he pestered me into giving him his chance to start. ... He proved to me that he's just about as good as he thinks he is."[17]

As it turned out, he wasn't. In Holloman's next start, on May 12, against the Athletics in Philadelphia, he lasted 1⅓ innings, walking the first three batters and giving up two runs and three hits before departing with a blister on his pitching hand.[18] Over his next four starts, he managed a total of 14⅓ innings, allowing 14 runs on 18 hits and 15 walks. From early June until late July, Holloman bounced between starting and relieving, finding one more moment of small glory, when he went eight innings against the Boston Red Sox on June 21, surrendering just two hits and no runs, earning what was his last major-league victory, 2-0, when Satchel Paige came on to save it.

On July 23, with his record at 3-7 with a 5.23 ERA, Holloman was sold to Toronto of the International League. Characteristically, he at first refused to report, saying he would devote himself to a Nashville trucking company he co-owned, However, he relented and reported to Toronto.[19] A bit more than a year later, after playing for five minor-league teams in the 1954 season, Holloman was out of baseball. By then the Browns were gone, too — moved to Baltimore, where they became the Orioles.

HOME OF THE BROWNS AND CARDINALS AT GRAND AND DODIER

NOTES

1. "Veeck Limits Holloman Pitching in Puerto Rico," *The Sporting News*, January 14, 1953: 23.
2. Lowell Reidenbaugh, "Holloman, Facing Axe, Hurls No-Hitter," *The Sporting News*, May 13, 1953: 13.
3. Unless otherwise noted, all stats and game accounts come from Retrosheet or Baseball Reference.
4. Reidenbaugh.
5. Louis Effrat, "Rain Washes Out 'Bout' at St. Louis," *New York Times*, April 29, 1953: 45.
6. Stan Opdyke, "Morrie Martin," sabr.org/bioproj/person/08084fff, accessed December 23, 2015.
7. Reidenbaugh.
8. "Bobo Does Some Boasting But It's About His Hitting," *St. Louis Post-Dispatch*, May 7, 1953: 4B.
9. Dent McSkimming, "Holloman Hurls No Hitter in His First Start," *St. Louis Post-Dispatch*, May 7, 1953: 4B.
10. Jack Rice, "Holloman Throws No-Hitter," *St. Louis Globe-Democrat*, May 7, 1953: 2B.
11. Reidenbaugh.
12. Ibid.
13. Rice.
14. "Bobo Does Some Boasting."
15. Ibid.
16. McSkimming.
17. Ibid.
18. "Browns Trounce Athletics, 7-3," *New York Times*, May 13, 1953: 35.
19. "Great Bobo Gives In, Goes to Toronto—and is Routed." *The Sporting News,* August 5, 1953: 32.

EXTRA-INNING FINALE ENDS WITH 100TH LOSS: THE ST. LOUIS BROWNS DEPART ST. LOUIS

September 27, 1953: Chicago White Sox 2, St. Louis Browns 1 (11 Innings), at Busch Stadium

BY JEFF FINDLEY

WHEN DUANE PILLETTE TOOK the mound for the woeful St. Louis Browns against the Chicago White Sox for the final game of the 1953 season there was little to cheer about for the home team's fans. The Browns already had 99 losses and were reported to be leaving St. Louis for a new home in Baltimore. Only 3,174 attended what *The Sporting News* described as a "wake."[1]

Pillette was opposed by All-Star southpaw Billy Pierce, who was concluding a solid season, with 17 wins and an ERA of 2.80 at game time, although he had failed to post a win in his previous five starts.

With the White Sox sitting solidly in third place in the American League, the game had little impact on the season's outcome, and other than nostalgia for longtime Browns fans—some of whom had hanged majority owner Bill Veeck in effigy a few nights earlier[2]—the contest was insignificant. Veeck, in fact, wasn't there.[3]

The game started slowly. Each team posted a hit in the first two innings, but neither pushed a runner past second base. After the White Sox were retired in order in the top of the third, the Browns' Johnny Groth doubled to left field with one out in the bottom of the inning, and Ed Mickelson singled to give the Browns and Pillette a 1-0 lead.

Pillette, who labored hard for some terrible teams and would win only 38 games in his eight-year career, is associated with several historical baseball moments. The son of former major-league pitcher Herman Pillette, he not only started the Browns' final game, but he was the winning pitcher in the first victory by the Baltimore Orioles in 1954, as well as the starter in the Orioles' initial home win. He was also the starting pitcher for the Browns the day 3-foot-7 Eddie Gaedel appeared as a pinch-hitter against the Detroit Tigers in 1951.

Pitching with a lead, Pillette charged on. He gave up a single to Minnie Miñoso, a former American League Rookie of the Year and future All-Star, in the fourth, but left him stranded at third when he struck out Tom Wright to end the inning.

Over the next three innings the White Sox mustered just a harmless single off Pillette. Pierce was just as efficient, allowing just two sixth-inning hits, and the score remained 1-0 into the eighth inning.

With one out in the White Sox' eighth, Pillette served up the tying run when Jim Rivera homered. Pierce also singled in the inning, his second hit of the game, but he was stranded at first when Pillette struck out Fred Marsh to end the inning. The Browns failed to answer in the bottom of the inning, and the score was tied, 1-1.

Minnie Miñoso singled with one out in the top of the ninth. Miñoso, who had stolen 25 bases so far in the season, tried for number 26, but was cut down by Browns catcher Les Moss. Wright followed with an infield single to second, but Bob Boyd flied out to center to end the inning.

The Browns were equally ineffective in the bottom of the inning, and the game moved to extra innings.

Pillette and Pierce remained in the game, having allowed one run and seven hits apiece. Both sides were retired in order in the 10th. But the 11th was a different story. After Pierce struck out to lead off,

Marsh singled, his first hit of the day. Nellie Fox's fly to center was the second out. Then Miñoso doubled to right field and drove in Marsh with the go-ahead run. Wright stranded Miñoso at second when he popped to third, but the White Sox led, 2-1.

Pierce struck out Groth and Mickelson and got Jim Dyck to fly to center to end the game, and the season, with his 18th win. It was the Browns' 100th loss of the season and, as it turned out, their final game in Sportsman's Park.

The *St. Louis Post-Dispatch* ran a page of photos the next day showing departing players, umpires, and grounds-crew members shaking hands, along with a photo of four fans who saw the first Browns game in St. Louis in 1902.[4] No one seemed to believe the Browns would be in St. Louis the next season.

Manager Marty Marion had his own analysis. "It's sad—sure," he said of the prospect of St. Louis losing the American League franchise it had held for 52 years. "When the attendance is down, the money is down, and it takes money to build a ball club."[5]

The St. Louis Browns' attendance for the 1953 season was a dismal 306,728.[6] But despite the miserable season, the 1953 Browns had some notable players on their roster.

Bob Elliott was named the National League Most Valuable Player by the Baseball Writers' Association of America as a member of the Boston Braves in 1947. Marion was the National League MVP in 1944. The 1953 season was his first as manager of the Browns, and despite being under contract, he did not manage the team in 1954, the franchise's first as the Baltimore Orioles.

Rookie Bob Turley went on to win the Cy Young Award and World Series MVP honors in 1958 as a member of the New York Yankees. He pitched in 15 games during five World Series with the Yankees, posting a 4-3 record.

Don Larsen, in his rookie season, started 22 games for the Browns in 1953, registering a 7-12 record in 192⅔ innings. As an Oriole the next season he went 3-21, but better days also awaited him in New York. After being traded to the Yankees in November 1954, he pitched a perfect game against the Brooklyn Dodgers in Game Five of the 1956 World Series, and was named the World Series MVP.

Satchel Paige, the ageless former Negro League star, pitched in 57 games for the 1953 Browns with 11 saves and an earned-run average of 3.53. Paige had posted his final big-league win just five days earlier, starting against the Detroit Tigers and allowing three runs in seven innings in a 7-3 victory, the final win ever for the Browns franchise. (Larsen worked two innings in relief and earned a retroactive save.)

Neither Elliott, Turley, Larsen, nor Paige played in the final Browns game.

An item in *The Sporting News* after the season summarized the Browns' plight: "With their working capital reduced to practically nothing, the Browns came close to being unable to finish their last game of the American League season. Unknown to the fans in the stands, September 27, the baseballs supplied by the home club ran completely out after the game with the White Sox passed the ninth inning and went into overtime.

"When Plate Umpire Art Passarella called for a new supply of baseballs, Bernie Ebert, who handled the baseballs for the Browns, informed him that the supply was exhausted and that the team had no more left. With that, the umpire looked over the scuffed up balls that had been tossed out of the game earlier and put several of them back into play—enough to finish up the game."[7]

The ball that White Sox center fielder Bill Wilson caught to end the game, and the season, was turned over to Browns publicist Bob Fishel. It had a large cut down the middle.

SOURCES

In addition to the sources cited in the Notes, the author also accessed Retrosheet.org and Baseball-Reference.com.

NOTES

1 Ray Gillespie, "3,174 at 'Wake' as Browns Bow Out at St. Louis," *The Sporting News*, October 7, 1953. Club owner Bill Veeck's attempt to move the Browns to Baltimore himself was thwarted by hostile American League owners. The desperate Veeck then sold the club to a Baltimore-based syndicate which transformed the team into the Baltimore Orioles.

2   "Necktie Party for Sport Shirt," *The Sporting News*, October 7, 1953.

3   Gillespie.

4   Was It "Goodby Browns" or Just "So Long 'Til '54?" *St. Louis Post-Dispatch*, September 28, 1953.

5   "Marion Predicts Big Rebuilding Job; Browns Wind Up With 100 Losses," *St. Louis Post-Dispatch*, September 28, 1953.

6   Ibid.

7   "Brownies Ran Out of Balls When Finale Went Overtime," *The Sporting News*, October 7, 1953: 5.

MUSIAL HITS FIVE HOME RUNS, SETS ML RECORD IN DOUBLEHEADER

May 2, 1954: St. Louis Cardinals 10,
New York Giants 6 (Game One);

New York Giants 9, St. Louis Cardinals 7
(Game Two), at Busch Stadium

BY RUSS LAKE

EARLY ON SUNDAY MORNING, MAY 2, 1954, a group of 37 people from Chillicothe, Missouri, boarded a chartered bus for the first leg of a round trip to Busch Stadium[1] in St. Louis to see a doubleheader between the Cardinals and New York Giants. The Midwestern town's depot agent, J.E. Brotherton, had arranged the excursion, which would be trailed by several carloads of locals.[2] The 235-mile route to the big riverfront city would proceed east via US 36 to Hannibal, and then southeast on US 61 before intersecting with US 40 eastward until a north turn onto Grand Boulevard.

Jack Buck arrived at the ballpark long before the 1:30 P.M. start of the first game to go over the between-innings copy he would read for D'Arcy Advertising Agency during the radio broadcast of the twin bill. A couple of months before, the 29-year-old Buck had packed his family and belongings into a 1950 Plymouth and driven from Rochester, New York, to join the Cardinals' announcing team of Harry Caray and Milo Hamilton.[3]

Horace Stoneham, president of the Giants; his son, Pete; and other representatives from the New York ballclub were attending the doubleheader. They were much impressed with the recent improvements to Busch Stadium.[4] A persistent morning rain fell long enough to cancel batting practice. Thirty minutes before game time, St. Louis skipper Eddie Stanky was on the steps of the third-base dugout when he was approached by a reporter. Arch Murray, an enterprising scribe for the *New York Post*, was working on a magazine story when he posed a carefully phrased question. "Who," Murray inquired, "is the best player in baseball? Stan Musial?" Stanky wasted little time with his reply, "You," said manager to writer, "have just asked and answered your own question." Murray nodded and explained that all other managers had agreed.[5]

Game One — The 33-year-old left-handed Musial, limping slightly with a charley horse, was batting .346, and starting in right field for St. Louis.[6] The Giants, managed by former Gas House Gang shortstop Leo "The Lip" Durocher, were in fifth place at 8-7, while the Redbirds, at 8-6, found themselves in a virtual tie for second with the Philadelphia Phillies and Brooklyn Dodgers in the early-season bottleneck of the National League standings. Johnny Antonelli (2-1, 1.12), a 6-foot-1 southpaw, would make his fourth start of the season for New York. The Cardinals' starter, 6-foot right-handed veteran Gerry Staley (2-1, 5.59), had struggled a bit during five appearances, which included three starts.

This would be the season's only scheduled Sunday doubleheader in St. Louis.[7] Staley benefited from a groundball double play to end a scoreless top half of the first. Antonelli, who had been obtained from the Milwaukee Braves in February, had not allowed a home run this season, but that changed quickly when the Cardinals' leadoff hitter Wally Moon, hammered his third homer of the year. After that blast Antonelli immediately found himself in an early jam after allowing consecutive walks to Red Schoendienst and

Musial. A force play and a strikeout followed, but with two outs rookie first baseman Tom Alston, who a few weeks earlier had become the Cardinals' first African American player, singled home Schoendienst to put the Cardinals up 2-0.

Antonelli had retired five consecutive batters when he faced Musial with one out in the third. Musial parked a slow curveball onto the right-field pavilion roof for his fourth round-tripper of the season and a 3-0 St. Louis lead. Staley set down seven straight Giants until second baseman Davey Williams, who entered the day batting .137, singled to open the fourth. With one away, back-to-back doubles by Hank Thompson and Monte Irvin, followed by Don Mueller's single, produced three quick runs to tie the score. Staley escaped further trouble when Willie Mays bounced into an around-the-horn double play.

Mays, who would turn 23 in four days, had not regained his admirable major-league skill set since returning to the Giants in March from nearly two years in the US Army. In the bottom of the fourth, the left-handed-swinging, 6-foot-5 Alston launched a high "wind-blown" drive to the deep center that the "Say Hey Kid" lunged for and missed. It then bounced away toward left field while Alston circled the bases for an inside-the-park home run to give the lead back to St. Louis.[8] But the tide turned quickly when Whitey Lockman and Wes Westrum popped back-to-back home runs to begin the top of the fifth and put New York up, 5-4.

The Cardinals once again struck back quickly in the bottom half as Schoendienst reached first on shortstop Al Dark's error. Musial stepped to the dish and crouched in his trademark stance. Antonelli fired a low, inside fastball out of the strike zone, but Musial uncoiled to send another shot up and away to the right-field roof as St. Louis moved in front, 6-5.[9] Ray Jablonski singled to end Antonelli's appearance, with Durocher bringing in right-hander Jim Hearn, an ex-Cardinal who had not pitched in nine days and was rumored to be in Durocher's doghouse.[10] Burdened with an early-season ERA of 8.31, Hearn seemed to bring a gasoline can with him to put out the fire after Rip Repulski doubled Jablonski to third and Alston walked to load the bases with no outs. The veteran Hearn, though, reached back to notch a groundball force at home and followed with successive strikeouts to keep it a one-run game.

With Staley out of the game, lefty Al Brazle took the mound in the sixth for St. Louis and looked good when he fanned Thompson. That "look" certainly proved deceiving when Irvin pounded his fourth homer of the season to tie the back-and-forth affair at 6-6. Hearn, who certainly displayed some moxie a couple of innings earlier, was still toeing the rubber for the Giants in the bottom of the eighth. Moon singled, Schoendienst walked, and up strode Musial who was 3-for-3 with a pair of runs scored and three RBIs. The fans, who had been watching dark clouds move in, turned their attention back to the playing field, and the stands echoed with the rhythmic staccato clapping that traditionally accompanied Redbird rallies. Hearn pondered before he went into his stretch and fed Musial a slider. Musial ripped into it and pulled a shot down the line to right toward the 37-foot-high screen attached to the roof in front of the pavilion seating area. This drive looked too low to clear the screen, but it just made it onto the roof for Musial's third home run of the contest.[11] Hearn hung his head, and the home crowd went wild as the Cardinals took a 9-6 lead. St. Louis added another run on a pair of singles followed by a Giants fielding miscue to increase its margin to 10-6.

With threatening clouds moving closer, the stadium lights were now on as the 40-year-old Brazle had some room to work with in the top of the ninth. After the first two Giants went down easily, St. Louis native son Bobby Hofman was tabbed as a pinch-hitter. The side-armer Brazle, who was the NL's oldest player in 1954, struck out Hofman to end the lid-lifter at 2 hours and 48 minutes.

Both teams retreated quickly via the Cardinals' dugout to their respective clubhouses to rest and relax a bit before the second contest got underway. The line score for the opener showed St. Louis with 10 runs, 14 hits, and no errors. New York plated six runs on nine hits and two errors. The winning pitcher was Brazle (1-0) while the loser was Hearn (0-2). Brazle, pleased to be credited with a win, offered Musial a bonus for the upcoming game: "Hit three more, kid, and I'll buy you a beer."[12]

Musial removed his spikes and uniform number 6, draped a towel over his shoulders, and sat stoically in front of his locker while munching on a ham sandwich and drinking a glass of milk. His wife, Lil, could not attend today's action because their daughter, Jan, was sick. Lil called Stan to teasingly remind him that this was the second time she had missed seeing her husband hit three home runs in a game during his professional baseball career. At age 20, playing for Springfield (Missouri) of the Class C Western Association in 1941, Musial had swatted three round-trippers against Topeka. Lil was at this game, but not sitting in the stands during any of her husband's homers because of a trio of "under-the-stands diaper-duty trips" for their infant son, Dickie.[13]

Game Two—Before returning to the diamond, a teammate kiddingly asked Musial, "Going to change uniforms, Stosh?" Musial grinned and replied, "Heck, no."[14] Stanky also appeared superstitious when he posted the same starting lineup and batting order from the first game with the exception of the batteries. Each starting pitcher in the nightcap was making his initial start of the season. Durocher selected 5-foot-10 lefty Don Liddle (0-1 with a 9.00 ERA), while Stanky went with 5-foot-9 right-hander Joe Presko, who sported a pair of relief wins.

Presko performed admirably for the first three innings while holding the Giants scoreless on one hit. After Schoendienst's one-out double, Liddle tried to pitch around trouble in the first and walked Musial to a chorus of boos from the faithful. That strategy failed after he issued another free pass to Repulski, and Alston doubled to clear the bases for a 3-0 St. Louis lead. Leading off the third, Musial faced the southpaw again. The crack of the bat and the trajectory of the ball brought the fans to their feet once more as it appeared to be another home run. However, Mays was able to get under this 410-foot blast on the gravel warning track in dead center for an out.[15] The Cardinals threatened to score again in the frame, but left two runners on base.

During three of their previous six losses, the St. Louis pitching staff had displayed the inability to stave off a "crooked number" inning. That achilles heel flared up in the top of the fourth when New York tallied eight runs on as many hits while facing a trio of Cardinals hurlers. Three of the Giants' safeties went for extra bases with the big blow being Hofman's three-run pinch-hit home run against left-handed reliever Royce Lint. Right-hander Mel Wright entered to suppress the uprising, but he allowed both inherited runners to score on a single by Mays. Musial spared the manual scoreboard operator some grief when he nailed catcher Ebba St. Claire trying to stretch his hit into a double for the third out.

Rain had started to fall and it was enough to cause an 18-minute delay before knuckleball specialist Hoyt Wilhelm came in and retired the Cardinals in order. St. Louis was looking at an 8-3 deficit, and some in the crowd were considering departure. Wright got three quick outs from New York in the fifth, and suddenly the Redbirds' bats fired up in their half. Schoendienst tripled and Musial followed by knocking a slow curve from Wilhelm over the right-field roof onto Grand Avenue.[16] Jablonski immediately trailed "The Man's" act with a blast of his own into the left-field bleachers, and it was now 8-6.

Anticipation grew in the bottom of the sixth with a runner on second, but Wilhelm struck out Moon and got Schoendienst on a groundball to second to end the inning with Musial on deck. Right-hander Tom Poholsky dispatched the Giants in order in the seventh, and the fans eagerly waited for Musial to come to the plate. Wilhelm disdained his curveball and floated in a knuckler, but it never made it to his catcher's mitt. Musial's timing this day was impeccable as he unleashed a swing that tattooed another baseball. The crowd knew it was gone, and roared with delight as the sphere grew tinier, cleared the roof in right-center, and struck a taxi beyond the ballpark on Grand Avenue. The driver, who had been listening intently to the game on KXOK, pulled over and exited his vehicle to retrieve the baseball.[17]

Musial had just become the first major leaguer ever to hit five home runs in a doubleheader. The

All-Star from Donora, Pennsylvania, smiled broadly as he started yet another trot around the Busch Stadium bases. The usually reserved Musial could not contain himself, and actually laughed for joy as he rounded third with the large crowd and his teammates cheering loudly for him.[18] Folks in the stands had to set aside their applause to realize that New York was still in front, 8-7, but that fact did not seem to matter. Jablonski stroked a single, and that was all for Wilhelm as Durocher called for veteran right-hander Larry Jansen to quell the uprising.

The 33-year-old Jansen certainly performed yeoman service for his team. He coaxed Repulski to hit into a 5-4-3 double play, then issued a pair of walks before retiring Solly Hemus on a comebacker to end the seventh. In the eighth Jansen allowed a one-out single before stabbing Schoendienst's hard grounder and starting a 1-6-3 twin killing. This defensive play occurred with the all-too-familiar uniform number 6 kneeling in the circle. Later, Jansen, batting for himself with two outs in the ninth, singled home an important insurance run to increase the Giants' slim spread to two runs. Jansen's clutch hit was struck off right-hander Cot Deal, who was Stanky's fifth hurler of the nightcap.

Nearing 8:00 P.M., Jansen strode to the mound for the last of the ninth. As Musial trekked to the plate, the crowd of 26,662 was buzzing while preparing themselves to erupt one more time for another long one. Jansen got the sign, wound up, and fired. Musial swung heartily and watched the flight of another baseball take shape. However, this one traveled a mere 90 feet and fell harmlessly into the glove of first baseman Whitey Lockman. The St. Louis fans then stood and gave Musial a thunderous ovation, and then, as if an evacuation alarm had just sounded, whisked themselves toward the nearest exit of the ballpark. Many folks had their backs to the action when Jablonski grounded out and Repulski fanned.[19] The 2-hour and 58-minute contest officially ended when Westrum picked up the dropped third strike and pegged it to first to preserve New York's 9-7 triumph.

The line score in the second game for New York read 9 runs, 13 hits, and 1 error, with the Cardinals notching 7 runs on 10 hits and no errors. The winning pitcher, with three innings of one-hit relief, was Jansen (1-0), and the loser was Lint (1-1). With the doubleheader split, the Cardinals (tied for second) and Giants (in fifth place) remained where they had started the day in the NL standings. For the two games the teams combined for 12 home runs, eight by St. Louis.

Despite Musial's setting the record for home runs hit by a player in a doubleheader, there was little celebration in the clubhouse as Stan forced a grin posing for numerous photographs. He lamented, "You can't smile too much when you lose a ballgame."[20] Musial also had his name next to a new mark for total bases (21) in a twin bill. His offensive numbers for the two games were six hits in eight official at-bats, nine RBIs, and six runs scored. His batting average jumped 54 points to .400, and his slugging percentage soared from .654 to .917. For his fast start to the season, Musial credited Stanky for playing him more during spring training, but offered, "I've never had a day like this one."[21]

The weary outfielder dutifully answered questions about the pitches he hit and the last at-bat. "Jansen got me out on a bad pitch—a high fastball, inside." He admitted, "Yeah, I was going for one that time."[22] Cab driver Joe Capraro, who had recovered the record-setting ball, returned it to the Cardinals' dressing room, and Peanuts Lowrey gave him another one to replace it.[23] Baseball Hall of Fame director Sid Keener phoned Musial from Cooperstown to request the history-making bat after he was through with it. "I'll send it right away," Stan said without delay. "I got a lot of bats."[24] The more he thought about it, the more amazed Musial was by his feat. "I still can't believe it. You mean real sluggers like Babe Ruth, Lou Gehrig, Ralph Kiner—men like them—never hit five homers in a doubleheader?"[25]

Lost in all the record-setting clamor were three other players with big days. For New York, it was Bobby Hofman[26] and Don Mueller, both natives of St. Louis. Hofman, who had starred at nearby

Beaumont High School,[27] hit the big round-tripper in the nightcap to highlight the eight-run fourth inning, while Mueller went 6-for-9. The Cardinals' Tom Alston enjoyed a 5-for-6, 5-RBI total, and joked with reporters in comparing himself to Musial, "Man, every time I watch Stan hit, I'm ashamed to take a bat up to the plate."[28]

Musial was last player to get dressed and leave the clubhouse. He was beaming when he finally arrived home to his family. However, the feeling of accomplishment was tempered after he was greeted by his 13-year-old son, Dick, who inquired, "They must have been giving you fat pitches, eh, Dad?"[29]

Jack Buck just had fun being at Busch Stadium for the historic day. He was not concerned that Harry Caray was at the microphone for all five of Musial's home runs. It was just as well, since Buck already knew that it bothered Caray if something really big happened when he was not calling the game.[30]

The chartered bus finally returned to Chillicothe, Missouri, past midnight. The tired passengers smiled as they thought about the baseball history they had witnessed, courtesy of Stan "The Man" Musial.[31]

SOURCES

In addition to the sources noted in these two game accounts, the author also accessed Retrosheet.org, Baseball-Reference.com, SABR.org/bioproj, and *The Sporting News* archive via Paper of Record. Additional websites accessed were newspapers.com, mapquest.com, and modot.org.

NOTES

1 Ray Gillespie, "Busch Buys Sportsman's Park From Browns, $400,000 Improvement Program Started," *The Sporting News*, April 15, 1953: 8.

2 "Chartered Bus Takes 37 to St. Louis Ballgame," *Chillicothe Constitution-Tribune*, May 3, 1954: 1.

3 Jack Buck with Rob Rains and Bob Broeg, *Jack Buck, That's a Winner!* (Champaign, Illinois: Sagamore Publishing, 1997), 81, 83-84.

4 Bob Broeg, "Raschi to Pitch Tonight," *St. Louis Post-Dispatch*, May 3, 1954: 4C.

5 Broeg, "Musial's Five Homers in Doubleheader a New Major League Mark," *St. Louis Post-Dispatch*, May 3, 1954: 4C.

6 Jerry Lansche, *The Man Musial, Born to Be a Ballplayer* (Dallas: Taylor Publishing, 1994), 130.

7 *St. Louis Post-Dispatch*, February 5, 1954, 22. Three additional Sunday doubleheaders were played at Busch Stadium to make up weather postponements.

8 Robert L. Tiemann, *Cardinal Classics, Outstanding Games From Each of the St. Louis Baseball Club's 100 Seasons, 1882-1981* (St. Louis: Baseball Histories, Inc., 1982), 194.

9 Broeg, "Musial's Five Homers."

10 Stan Baumgartner, "Ragged Start Gives Phillies 'Job Jitters,'" *The Sporting News*, May 5, 1954: 8.

11 Tiemann.

12 Associated Press, "Loss of Game More Important to Musial Than Batting Feat," *Kansas City Times*, May 3, 1954: 22.

13 Stan Musial as told to Bob Broeg, *The Man Stan: Musial, Then and Now* (St. Louis: Bethany Press, 1977), 24, 61.

14 *Kansas City Times*, May 3, 1954: 22.

15 Broeg, "Musial's Five Homers."

16 Ibid.

17 *Kansas City Times*, May 3, 1954: 22.

18 Broeg, "Musial's Five Homers."

19 Ibid.

20 *Kansas City Times*, May 3, 1954: 22.

21 Ibid.

22 Broeg, "Musial's Five Homers."

23 *Kansas City Times*, May 3, 1954: 22.

24 Broeg, "Stan Sends Five-Homer Bat to Museum at Cooperstown," *The Sporting News*, May 12, 1954: 6.

25 Broeg, "Musial's Five Homers."

26 Hofman was the nephew of Arthur Frederick "Circus Solly" Hofman, who played in all three major leagues from 1903 to 1916.

27 Beaumont High School (opened in 1926 and closed in 2014), located at 3836 Natural Bridge Avenue, St. Louis, was built on the same grounds that housed League Park/Cardinal Field/Robison Field (home of National League baseball in St. Louis from 1893 to 1920). Joan M. Thomas, SABR BioProject, sabr.org/bioproj/park/88929e79.

28 Broeg, "Alston Knows How Gehrig Felt Hitting Behind Ruth," *The Sporting News*, May 12, 1954: 6.

29 Broeg, "'Fat Pitches?' Asks Dickie After Dad Stan's Big Day," *The Sporting News*, May 12, 1954: 6.

30 Buck, 85.

31 "Chartered Bus."

CARDINALS OUTSLUGGED BY CUBS BUT FINALLY WIN IN 14

April 16, 1955: St. Louis Cardinals 12, Chicago Cubs 11 (14 Innings), at Busch Stadium

BY RUSS LAKE

ON SATURDAY, APRIL 16, 1955, PRE-game activity at Busch Stadium was lively hours before the 1:30 p.m. tilt between the Cubs and the Cardinals. While Chicago manager Stan Hack amused reporters talking about his badly swollen hand, St. Louis skipper Eddie Stanky and his coaching staff were busy hosting a morning baseball clinic for more than 1,000 high-school-age baseball players and their mentors. After the two-hour training session concluded, the athletes, plus their tutors, were admitted to the game as guests of the ballclub.[1] With a ladies day promotion drawing more than 5,500 walk-ups, the 9,075 paid admissions swelled attendance to 15,678 on an early-spring day under partly cloudy skies that reached an above-normal high temperature in the mid-80s.[2]

Hack, known as Smiling Stan from his playing days as an All-Star third baseman, was questioning his laughable injury. Three days earlier in Cincinnati, Hack reached for a chaw from the chewing tobacco pouch he stuffed in his rear pants pocket. He quickly removed his grip on the contents after feeling a stinging sensation, and saw a bee quickly fly away from the scene. "I thought I knew about bees," Hack joked. "I've been stung before. But what do you suppose that bee was going to do with my chewin' terbaccy?"[3] Despite the discomfort, Hack was grinning broadly because his Northsiders had won their season's first three games for the first time since 1950.

Stanky, assessing his squad's roster a few days before, had remarked, "This is the best club I have ever managed. But it's young; be patient with it."[4] Stanky, who was *The Sporting News* Major League Manager of the Year in his first season in 1952, had guided the Cardinals to a pair of third-place finishes before he experienced a bumpy ride piloting a sixth-place team in 1954. Always a fiery competitor, and nicknamed "The Brat," Stanky had been ejected 15 times as the Cardinals manager. As it happened, all four of the seasoned arbiters working today's contest had banished Stanky at least once. The Cardinals were 1-1 with a lopsided loss sustained in Chicago, followed by a comeback extra-inning home-opening win over the Milwaukee Braves.

St. Louis starting pitcher Tom Poholsky had to first appear in morning traffic court and plead guilty to a speeding charge, costing him an $8 fine.[5] Chicago countered with a rookie hurler, "Toothpick Sam" Jones. In the first inning, the 6-foot-3 right-handed Poholsky pitched around a two-out single. Jones, a 6-foot-4 righty with a herky-jerky motion, had a rough bottom half as he allowed two runs on three hits and a walk.

Just as fans flipped their scorecards, the game took an eventful turn and the Cardinals' lead became a memory. Randy Jackson drove an offering from Poholsky into the left-field bleachers. Before Jackson was done receiving kudos, shortstop Ernie Banks blistered a one-strike pitch for another drive into the left-field seats. Not to be outdone, left-handed-hitting Dee Fondy powdered a full-count pitch that hit a flag perched on the right-center-field pavilion roof and Chicago had a 3-2 lead. These back-to-back-to-back home runs tied a major-league record held by several teams; the last time it had occurred for the Cubs was August 11, 1941. Back then, the successive blasts were also socked in St. Louis when Phil Cavaretta, Hack, and Bill Nicholson connected off Lon Warneke.[6]

Jones settled down in the next two frames, even striking out the side in the third. Poholsky, too, was doing better until two outs in the third, when Jackson cracked a 400-foot shot into the right-center-pavilion seats for his second solo home run of the game and a 4-2 lead.[7] Poholsky, who had given up four runs on seven hits in three innings, was replaced by Brooks Lawrence. The barrage the Cubs put on Poholsky was not an aberration as Chicago had entered this contest with a .375 team batting mark while scoring 27 runs on 42 hits during their first three games.

A penchant for wildness hurt Jones in the fourth: He walked the first two batters, and they came around as the Cardinals plated three on just one base hit to go back up, 5-4. St. Louis added another run in the sixth. Del Rice singled with two outs. Alex Grammas received the fifth free pass allowed by Jones, then Lawrence singled home Rice for his second RBI of the day. With the Cubs trailing 6-4, Hack removed Jones for southpaw Jim Davis, who retired Wally Moon on an unassisted grounder to Fondy at first base.[8]

Chicago's Bob Speake made his major-league debut memorable as the 24-year-old left-handed batter delivered a pinch single leading off the seventh. Speake went to second on a walk and scampered home on a knock by Frank Baumholtz to cut Chicago's deficit to one. Hank Sauer smacked the next pitch for another run-scoring single, tying the score, 6-6. Veteran right-handed submariner Frank Smith, who was obtained from Cincinnati during the offseason, took over for St. Louis and brushed back the heavy-hitting Jackson. Notwithstanding, Jackson drove a double off the left-field wall to score Baumholtz with the go-ahead run and send Sauer to third. Smith departed, and right-hander Bobby Tiefenauer was beckoned to stifle the Cubs' parade around the bases. Banks fouled out to left fielder Moon, but it was deep enough for Sauer to tag and score. Fondy's single plated Jackson to increase the Cubs' edge to 9-6.[9]

In the bottom of the seventh, 32-year-old right-hander John Andre made a forgettable major-league debut, defaulting to wildness by walking fellow rookie Bill Virdon, uncorking a wild pitch, and then issuing another walk to Stan Musial. Hack summoned right-hander Hal Jeffcoat, who had been a Cubs outfielder from 1948 through 1953 before successfully converting to pitching in 1954. Rip Repulski greeted Jeffcoat with a double to center to score Virdon and send Musial to third. Red Schoendienst grounded out, plating Musial. Rookie Ken Boyer singled to score Repulski and tie the game, 9-9. The highly touted Boyer, who earlier made a heads-up dash home to slide around catcher Harry Chiti in the fourth, stole second, but was held at third by Stanky on Rice's third single. After lefty-swinging pinch-batter Solly Hemus was announced, Hack motioned for ex-Cardinals' lefty Howie Pollet, and Hemus was lifted for right-handed batter Harry Elliott. Pollet had allowed a two-run double to Elliott the last time they faced each other two seasons ago, but this time the veteran southpaw fanned his adversary. Another pinch-hitter, Bill Sarni, was retired to strand two Redbird runners.

Right-handed knuckleballer Barney Schultz entered for St. Louis in the eighth. The 28-year-old Schultz, who had already represented 11 different minor-league cities from 1944 to 1954, surprisingly stabilized the Cardinals' mound efforts for four innings. Schultz worked out of a bases-loaded 10th frame when Gene Baker fouled out. St. Louis threatened to win the contest in the 11th, but Boyer flied deep to left with two runners on to end the threat.[10]

Chicago finally solved Schultz's flutter pitch for twin tallies in the 12th when Banks and Fondy again swatted consecutive homers to provide Chicago with an 11-9 margin. In the bottom half, Cubs right-hander Bubba Church began his third inning of relief by walking pinch-hitter Joe Frazier. Dick Schofield ran for Frazier, but he remained stationary as Church retired pinch-hitter Tom Alston on a fly ball and fanned Sarni. With a two-run cushion, another out and the Cubs would start a season with four straight victories for the first time since 1934. Moon had other thoughts, however, as he parked a two-run homer onto the right-field rooftop to knot the game, 11-11.[11] Virdon singled and Church was replaced by right-hander Vicente Amor. The Cuban-born Amor, also making his major-league debut, got Musial to pop out to the catcher.

The ballpark lights were on, and the available bench for both teams was dwindling. Despite an ineffective start in the Cardinals' home opener two days before, left-hander Harvey Haddix opened the 13th and hurled two scoreless frames. Amor pitched out of trouble in his portion of the 13th after Repulski doubled and Schoendienst was intentionally passed to start the inning. Sarni opened the Cardinals' 14th with an easy pop fly to short left. Banks moved back to make the catch, but then inexplicably gave way to left fielder Sauer, who was in no position to glove it, and the ball fell safely for a fluke double. Moon, who had extended the game, singled to right on the next pitch.[12] Stanky waved Sarni home and the Cardinals walked off with an unforgettable 12-11 triumph.

Haddix was the winner with Amor charged with the loss. Forty players, including 13 pitchers, appeared in the contest, which took 4:39 to play.[13] Chicago accumulated 37 total bases to 24 for St. Louis as the clubs combined for 33 hits. Lack of control from Cubs pitching was the difference as their nine walks permitted five extra St. Louis runners to eventually score. Four of the seven home runs were hit to right field, but none of the circuit clouts this day were due to the pavilion screen being removed prior to the start the season.[14]

SOURCES

In addition to the sources noted in this game account, the author also accessed Retrosheet.org, Baseball-Reference.com, and *The Sporting News* archive via Paper of Record.

NOTES

1. *St. Louis Post-Dispatch*, April 15, 1955: 6C.
2. Bob Broeg, "Cards Win In 14th, 12-11, Despite Six Cub Homers," *St. Louis Post-Dispatch*, April 17, 1955: 1.
3. *The Sporting News*, April 27, 1955, 3.
4. Herb Heft, "Youthful Cards Hailed by 1,000 at Dinner as Team of Future," *The Sporting News*, April 20, 1955: 26.
5. *The Sporting News*, April 27, 1955: 6.
6. Edward Prell, "Card Pop Fly Wins, 12-11, In 14th; 6 Cub Homers," *Chicago Tribune*, April 17, 1955: 1F.
7. Ibid.
8. Ibid.
9. Ibid.
10. Ibid.
11. Broeg.
12. Prell.
13. According to Baseball-Reference.com, this marathon was the third longest major-league game of the 1955 season. The Washington Senators and Cleveland Indians took the '55 top spot for "Time of Game" at 4:46 in 17 innings on April 27, followed by the Pittsburgh Pirates and Milwaukee Braves lasting 4:44 in 19 innings on July 19.
14. *St. Louis Post-Dispatch*, May 7, 1955: 1C; The "Redbird Notes" column reported that Cardinals public-relations man Jim Toomey affirmed that Bill Virdon's sixth-inning home run off Milwaukee's Chet Nichols on May 6 was the first to land into the right-field pavilion seats instead of remaining in play after striking the screen that was removed before the 1955 season started. When the opposing batters ended up hitting more homers than the Cardinals into the available area, the screen was re-installed prior to the 1956 campaign. The 25-foot 8-inch covering went from the 310-foot right-field foul line and ended at the 354-foot right-center power alley and stayed in place through the final game on May 8, 1966.

"ALL MY REPLACEMENTS DID WELL." — CASEY STENGEL[1]

July 9, 1957: American League 6, National League 5, at Busch Stadium

1957 All-Star Game

BY ALAN COHEN

IN 1957, THE FANS, WITH SOME HELP from Commissioner Ford Frick, selected the starters for the All-Star Game. The folks of Cincinnati exercised their franchise by stuffing the ballot box and selecting Reds players at all but one position. Five Reds started the game, as Frick named outfielders Willie Mays and Henry Aaron to start in place of Gus Bell and Wally Post.

American League manager Casey Stengel was disappointed with the fans' selections of Harvey Kuenn, Vic Wertz, and George Kell to the starting lineup, and early on vowed to remove the trio after three innings. His reasoning was that these players were not having particularly good years.

It was the 24th All-Star Game and the first in St. Louis since the Browns departed Sportsman's Park, now called Busch Stadium, for Baltimore after the 1953 season. The park had also hosted the game in 1940 and 1948.

Under sunlit skies on what evolved into a glorious afternoon weatherwise, the players took the field and managers Stengel and Walter Alston met each other for the second consecutive year. Each manager selected seven pitchers for the contest and the American League squad, batting first, faced Curt Simmons of the Philadelphia Phillies. The left-hander from Egypt, Pennsylvania, put down the American Leaguers in order in the first inning. The AL starter, Detroit's Jim Bunning, matched him by setting down the first three batters he saw in the bottom half of the inning.

The American League, which had lost five of the six games Stengel had managed, broke on top in the second inning. Mickey Mantle, batting right-handed, led off the inning with an infield single before Simmons walked Ted Williams to put runners at first and second base. The left-handed-hitting Wertz singled to the opposite field, scoring Mantle with the game's first run. Yogi Berra walked on Simmons's last pitch of the game and Alston called in Lew Burdette to snuff out the rally. Burdette retired Kell and Bunning but walked Kuenn to force in Williams with the second run of the inning. Nellie Fox was retired on a fly ball to conclude the half-inning.

After the American League had batted in the top of the fourth inning, Stengel, as promised, removed Kuenn, Kell, and Wertz, and replaced them with Gil McDougald, Frank Malzone, and Bill Skowron. He explained, "I'm in favor of leaving the balloting in the hands of the fans, but the system should be changed to prevent a repetition of the 'Cincinnati and Kuenn, Kell, and Wertz incidents.' Kuenn, Kell and Wertz should not have been picked because they're not having good years."[2]

Bunning left the game after three perfect innings and was replaced by Billy Loes. Bunning, playing in his first full season and making his first appearance on center stage in the midseason classic, would have preferred to stay in the game. "I know that the rule prohibits a pitcher from working more than three innings, except if he is a reliever during an inning or if he is an extra-inning pitcher, but I would have liked to continue today," he said. "Maybe it would have been pressing my luck, but I still would have liked to keep pitching."[3]

Loes allowed three hits in his three innings of work but kept the opposition from scoring. Burdette, meanwhile, after the second inning kept the American League in check. In all, he pitched four scoreless innings and yielded just two hits, though he pitched in luck, especially in the fifth inning. Frank Robinson led off the fifth with a single, and Eddie Mathews stepped to the plate. Mathews pulled a line drive to short right field as Al Kaline gave chase. Robinson, thinking the ball might be caught, stopped halfway to second base as Kaline attempted a shoestring catch. Kaline trapped the ball but was able to force Robinson at second base for the first out of the inning. Ernie Banks than hit into a double play and the score remained 2-0 as the game entered the sixth inning.

Philadelphia's rookie ace Jack Sanford came in to pitch for the National League and was done in by a pair of Yankees. Moose Skowron doubled with one out and, after advancing to third base on a wild pitch, scored easily on a single by Berra. It was Yogi's first RBI in 31 All-Star plate appearances over nine games. That was the only run allowed by Sanford, who gave way to Larry Jackson in the seventh inning.

Loes came out of the game after three scoreless innings and was replaced by Cleveland's Early Wynn as the game advanced to the bottom of the seventh. Wynn had pitched seven innings on the Sunday before the All-Star Game, a decision that infuriated Stengel, and he was ineffective on Tuesday. With one out, Mays singled and moved to third on a single by Cincinnati's Ed Bailey. In a move that could only happen in an All-Star Game, Alston removed Frank Robinson and inserted left-handed pinch-hitter Gus Bell. Bell doubled down the left-field line, scoring both Mays and Bailey, and the National League trailed by only one run. That was it for Wynn. Billy Pierce came on in relief and the White Sox lefty retired Mathews and Banks.

Going into the ninth inning, the AL still led 3-2 as Jackson and Pierce each pitched a scoreless eighth. In the top of the eighth, after Mantle led off with a walk, Williams sent a fly ball to deep center field that Mays had been able to track down for the first out. Although the catch paled against some of the circus catches for which Mays was famous, it nonetheless showcased the fielding capabilities of the New York star, who over the years shined in All-Star Games. He appeared in a record 24 games, and holds or shares the career records for runs scored (20), hits (23), extra-base hits (8), triples (3), stolen bases (6), and total bases (40). In 1963, he stole two bases in an inning, and in 1965 led off the game with a homer. He was selected as the All-Star Game MVP in 1963 and 1968.

Alston brought in Dodgers ace reliever Clem Labine to pitch the ninth inning, but Labine faltered. Stengel elected to have Pierce, who had retired the five batters he faced, three by strikeout, bat for himself, and Billy hit a leadoff infield single that eluded Labine and rolled slowly up the middle. Red Schoendienst was able to get a glove on the ball, but could not make a play. The normally reliable Schoendienst then misplayed a potential double-play groundball hit by McDougald, dropping the ball as he pivoted to throw to the shortstop, for the game's only error—and a critical one at that.

After Fox's sacrifice bunt put runners at second and third with one out, Kaline singled both runners home to give the AL a three-run cushion. Labine struck out Mantle, but Minnie Miñoso, who had replaced Williams in left field in the eighth inning, stroked a double to right-center that was out of the reach of Mays and brought home Kaline with the sixth American League run. The American League took a 6-2 lead and the National League was down to its final three outs.

Pierce retired not a batter in the ninth inning. A walk to hometown favorite Stan Musial, playing in his 14th All-Star Game, was followed by a triple off the bat of Mays. Mays came home with the fourth of his team's runs on a wild pitch, and Pittsburgh's Hank Foiles singled to center field to continue the rally. Pierce's last pitch was ball four to Bell, and the tying runs were on base. Stengel brought in the Indians' Don Mossi, who struck out Mathews. Banks followed with a single that plated Foiles, but Miñoso cut down Bell trying to advance from first to third. "Minnie made a whale of a throw to Malzone to get

Bell," Alston said. "It had to be a perfect throw and that's what he made. That was the biggest out of the game, maybe."[4]

Banks took second on the throw to third and was in scoring position with the tying run. Stengel brought in one of his eight Yankees All-Stars, Bob Grim, to pitch to Gil Hodges, batting for his Dodgers teammate, Labine. Hodges made a bid for extra bases, lining a ball into the left-field corner, but Miñoso ran down the liner to make his second superb play of the inning and secure the 6-5 win for the American League. The decisions in the contest, which took 2:43 to play, went to the starters, with Bunning getting the win and Simmons absorbing the loss.

SOURCES

In additional to the sources cited in the Notes, the author used Baseball-Reference.com and the following:

Daniel, Dan. "Who Were the All-Star Heroes, Goats? No Horns After Game," *The Sporting News*, July 17, 1957: 8.

NOTES

1   Louis Effrat, "Berra's Handling of Bunning is Key Factor in Triumph at All-Star Contest," *New York Times*, July 10, 1957: 31.

2   "Stengel Quickly Benches Trio Fans Picked; Expects Change," *The Sporting News*, July 17, 1957: 9.

3   "Berra's Handling."

4   Roscoe McGowen, "Alston Defends Running of Bell," *New York Times*, July 10, 1957: 31.

STAN MUSIAL KNOCKS IN SEVEN RUNS

June 23, 1961: St. Louis Cardinals 10, San Francisco Giants 5, at Busch Stadium

BY TOM HAWTHORN

THE TURNSTILES AT BUSCH STADIUM, the renamed Sportsman's Park in St. Louis, counted 15,444 customers for a game played on June 23, 1961, a Friday evening in early summer. The San Francisco Giants were in town, trying to halt a three-game losing streak against a hometown club not yet playing .500 ball.

The Giants starter was Billy "Digger" O'Dell (3-3), a left-hander who, as a member of the Baltimore Orioles, had been named the Most Valuable Player of the 1958 All-Star Game after retiring the nine National League batters he faced. Behind him on this night was a lineup that included future Hall of Famers Orlando Cepeda and Willie Mays. Willie McCovey, another future inductee, would pinch-hit later in the game.

Veteran lefty Curt Simmons (2-6), the one-time schoolboy phenom from Egypt, Pennsylvania, who made his major-league debut at age 18 in 1947, took to the mound for the hometown side. The Cardinals had some offensive stars of their own, including Ken Boyer at third base and Bill White at first base. Tim McCarver, a chatty rookie, was behind the plate, though he would spend most of the season in the minors. The lineup included Stan Musial, Stan the Man, the Donora Greyhound (after his Pennsylvania birthplace), the surefire future Hall of Famer whose name had been on the roster for nearly two decades. The left fielder had marked his 40th birthday seven months earlier and his numbers, while solid, were no longer spectacular. He went into the game hitting .305 with 7 home runs and 27 runs batted in.

Musial was nursing the lingering effects of a head cold, as well as the nuisance of a sore heel. He was also approaching the 20th anniversary of his major-league debut, on September 17, 1941. The newspapers were already speculating whether this season would be his last. In the end, he would not retire until the end of the 1963 campaign, missing out on the Cardinals' pennant and World Series championship the season after that.

The third-place Giants (36-27) were starting to slip in pursuit of the Cincinnati Reds, whom they now trailed by four games. The Cardinals were already a disappointing 11 games back with a 28-33 record in sixth place, ahead of only the Chicago Cubs and Philadelphia Phillies.

Both teams went out in order in the first. Mays got things going for the Giants in the second with a single and a stolen base, only to be picked off by Simmons. The putout went 1-4-5, Simmons to second baseman Bob Lillis to Boyer at third. The Cardinals sandwiched two singles around a Musial fly out to right to open their half of the second inning, but the rally ended without damage when Simmons struck out with the bases loaded.

The game remained scoreless until the bottom of the third, when Musial stepped to the plate with two outs, White on third and Boyer on second, both getting on base via walks and advancing on a groundout to first. Musial promptly sent an O'Dell pitch over the screen and onto the roof of the pavilion in right field to give his club a 3-0 lead.

The Giants got on the board in the fourth when Mays reached on a single and scored on Cepeda's two-out double to left. The Cardinals responded in the fifth by pushing across a run on four singles in an inning in which Musial popped out to shortstop.

The Giants chased Cardinals starter Simmons in the sixth by bunching two singles, a Harvey Kuenn double, and a Cepeda triple, which tied the game, 4-4. Ernie Broglio coaxed a flyout, with Cepeda tagging up and scoring the go-ahead run, before he issued a walk to Ed Bailey. Manager Solly Hemus pulled Broglio for Craig Anderson, a 6-foot-2 reliever called up from Portland of the Pacific Coast League the previous day. The 22-year-old right-hander was making his major-league debut. With one out, Bailey was caught stealing second before Anderson ended the inning by striking out O'Dell. But the Giants led 5-4.

The Cardinals tied the game in the bottom of the inning, with Boyer scoring on a double by Charlie James. Stu Miller came in to walk Musial intentionally. He then walked Curt Flood before ending the inning by inducing McCarver to pop out to Cepeda at first.

In the seventh, the Cardinals retook the lead on back-to-back doubles by Anderson, in his first major-league at-bat, and Julio Gotay. A single by White chased Miller, who was replaced by righty Bobby Bolin. The new reliever intentionally walked Boyer before fanning James.

Next, Musial came to the plate with the bases loaded and two outs. A *St. Louis Post-Dispatch* photographer captured the veteran completing his swing, an image that appeared in the paper the next day. It showed Musial erect, the result of a fluid swing whose grace belied the power behind it, his left foot pivoting on the toes, his right foot bent slightly to the outside from the torque, his upper hand leaving the bat in the follow-through, his mouth open as his 40-year-old eyes followed the trajectory of the ball over the head of right fielder Kuenn toward the fence and, beyond that, the stands. "I didn't hit the second one real good, and I thought it would just hit the screen," Musial said after the game.[1]

The ball landed in nearly the same spot as the first homer.[2] The grand slam was the ninth of Musial's career, giving him seven RBIs for the game. The blast also gave him 2,340 extra bases on long hits, as he surpassed Lou Gehrig on the all-time list (2,339), trailing only Babe Ruth (2,926). (Musial had once recorded seven RBIs in a spring-training game against the Philadelphia Phillies on March 23, 1954, on a homer, triple, and a single. He also recorded seven RBIs in a doubleheader sweep of the Chicago Cubs on May 27, 1956.) Carl Warwick replaced Musial in the field for the next inning, as the Cardinals won, 10-5. Anderson earned the win in his debut, while Miller suffered his first loss of the season against six wins.

After the game Musial insisted he was not considering an imminent retirement. "I don't feel any older than, say, seven years ago when I hit five homers in a doubleheader off the Giants," he told a reporter.[3] Musial recorded nine RBIs in those games on May 2, 1954.

St. Louis manager Hemus was hopeful the victory would spark the Cards. "A big win can make a turning point," he said. "It's not just that Musial hit the grand slammer. He doesn't surprise you when he does anything. People get to expect it, because he's so great. The new momentum goes to everything we did right, especially getting a relief pitcher to come in and stop them."[4]

In the Giants clubhouse, manager Alvin Dark was asked his opinion of Musial's work after the two-homer, seven-RBI performance. "He sure can hit 'em, can't he?" Dark said, echoing what managers had been saying about Stan the Man for 20 years.[5]

The outfielder got the next day off, standard practice for the veteran when a day game followed a night game. Musial posed on the infield for teenage photographers before the game as part of a Camera Day promotion.

Hemus's optimism turned out to be misplaced. The Cardinals won just three of their next 11 games and Hemus was fired on July 6, replaced by his lieutenant, Johnny Keane, a St. Louis-born career minor leaguer who days later would make an example of pitcher Mickey McDermott by releasing him after he missed a bedcheck before a doubleheader in San Francisco. (At the same time as the change in manager was announced, second baseman Red Schoendienst was made a playing coach. He'd replace Keane as manager after the Cards won the 1964 World Series.) The Cardinals improved their play considerably over the rest of the season, finishing 80-74, but managed to overtake only the Pittsburgh Pirates in the standings, finishing fifth, 13 games behind the Reds.

SOURCES

In addition to the sources listed in the Notes, the author also consulted the *St. Louis Post-Dispatch*, the *Oakland Tribune*, the *Daily Capital* (Jefferson City, Missouri), the *Hayward* (California) *News*, *The Sporting News*, and Retrosheet.org.

NOTES

1. "Ailing Musial Rocks Giants With Grand Slam and 3-Run Homer," *St. Louis Post-Dispatch*, June 24, 1961: 6.
2. "Giants Losing String Hits 4," *Oakland Tribune*, June 24, 1961: 11.
3. "Cards Gain Steam," *Oakland Tribune*, June 24, 1961: 11.
4. Ibid.
5. Ibid.

KEN BOYER'S 11 TOTAL BASES AND 11TH-INNING HOME RUN DRIVE CARDS TO DEFEAT CUBS IN WALK-OFF FASHION

September 14, 1961: St. Louis Cardinals 6, Chicago Cubs 5 (Game Two of Doubleheader), at Busch Stadium

BY MICHAEL HUBER

KEN BOYER COLLECTED HIS FIRST career five-hit game in propelling the St. Louis Cardinals to victory over the Chicago Cubs in the second game of a doubleheader at Busch Stadium before a crowd of 5,835. Four of those five hits enabled him to hit for the cycle. He had two hits in the opener as well, contributing to another Cardinals win and giving him a 7-for-11 day at the plate.

In game one of the doubleheader, Boyer singled in the fourth inning and stroked a two-run triple in the fifth. Sammy Taylor and George Altman homered for the Cubs, while hometown favorite Stan Musial went 3-for-4 with a home run for St. Louis. The Cardinals won on a bizarre walk-off play. In a tie game, with two outs and the bases loaded in the bottom of the ninth inning, Jimmie Schaffer came to bat for the Cardinals. According to the *Chicago Tribune*, "Barney Schultz's puzzling knuckler slithered away as a passed ball in the ninth inning while Bob Lillis scored," suddenly giving St. Louis an 8-7 victory.[1]

Game two featured Curtis versus Curtis. The Cardinals started Curt Simmons and the Cubs sent Jack Curtis to the mound. In four previous starts against the Cubs in 1961, Simmons had allowed 14 earned runs in 23⅔ innings.[2] He fared slightly better in this game, allowing five runs (two earned) in 4⅔ innings. Simmons finished the season with a 3.13 earned-run average, third best in the National League. He seemed to like pitching in his home park. In 16 starts that season at Busch Stadium, Simmons had six complete games and two shutouts. (By contrast, he did not have any complete games while pitching on the road.)

Jack Curtis was a 24-year-old Cubs rookie in 1961. He started 27 games and allowed 220 hits in 180⅓ innings. His earned-run average hovered between 4.00 and 5.00 all season. Curtis liked pitching in Wrigley Field, with four complete games, but at Busch Stadium he struggled, with a 5.25 ERA.[3]

The Cardinals struck first, in the bottom of the opening inning. Julian Javier walked with one out and scored when Bill White tripled to right field. Boyer's single to left scored White. In the third Boyer singled again, this time with two outs, but the Cardinals did not score.

Chicago plated two runs in the top of the fourth. Billy Williams doubled to center field and scored when Ernie Banks doubled to right. Ron Santo singled, advancing Banks to third base, and Altman brought Banks home with a sacrifice fly. The score was tied. St. Louis responded by manufacturing a run in its half of the fourth. Don Taussig walked, stole second, and scored on a single by Curt Flood.

The seesaw scoring continued in the fifth inning. Williams reached on a two-out error by first baseman White. Banks reached on an infield single, and then Santo deposited a Simmons pitch beyond the fence in deep left field to give Chicago a 5-3 lead. Altman singled and Simmons, "victim of three unearned runs, soon was on his way to the showers."[4] Bob Miller came on in relief and shut the door on the Cubs, allowing just one hit and two walks as he pitched through the eighth inning.

Meanwhile, Curtis allowed a solo home run to Charlie James in the bottom of the fifth (after Boyer had grounded out and Gene Oliver had flied out), and St. Louis was within one run. Curtis scattered 10 hits and gave up three walks in 6⅓ innings, but he left in the seventh with the lead. With one out in the bottom of the seventh, Boyer sent a shot to left field and legged out a triple, but Bob Anderson came on in relief for Chicago and retired the next two batters. Anderson continued to keep the Cards batters in check until the bottom of the ninth. With St. Louis trailing by one run, White coaxed a one-out walk. Boyer delivered an opposite-field double into the right-field corner, driving in White with the tying run and sending the game into extra innings.

Cubs manager El Tappe inserted Don Elston to pitch the bottom of the 11th inning. Boyer, leading off, smashed a home run, driving an Elston slider onto the right-field roof and giving the Cardinals their second walk-off victory of the day.[5] Boyer became the first major-league player to complete the cycle with a walk-off home run.[6]

The Cubs had rallied from behind four times in the doubleheader, but had managed to lose both games in walk-off fashion. The doubleheader featured 15 runs and 20 hits in the first game and 11 runs and 23 hits in the second. The Cubs left 23 runners on base in the two contests. (The Cardinals stranded 20.) The first game started at 5:30 P.M., and Boyer's solo blast closed the doubleheader almost seven hours later, at 12:21 A.M.

Boyer, team captain and a perennial All-Star[7] and Gold Glove Award winner for the Cardinals, posted his highest batting average in 1961, finishing the season at .329, the third best in the National League (behind Roberto Clemente and Vada Pinson). After the game, Boyer told reporters, "I've always had one bad month a season until this year,"[8] adding that he was worried more about his team getting into the first division than with his chances of increasing his batting average to .340. He added, "Maybe we can waltz into third place, and a $1,200 slice wouldn't be a bad Christmas present. And then we'd know we'd go into next season with a good club."[9]

A seven-time All-Star, Ken Boyer was named NL MVP in 1964 for the world champion Redbirds. (National Baseball Hall of Fame, Cooperstown, New York)

Boyer's rare feat was the only cycle of the 1961 season. It came 13 months after his teammate White hit for the cycle against the Pittsburgh Pirates. On June 16, 1964, Boyer again defied the odds and hit for the cycle again, this time against the Houston Colt .45s. This second accomplishment was a natural cycle.[10] Boyer is the only Cardinals player to ever hit for the cycle twice.

NOTES

1 Richard Dozer, "Cubs Add Two Verses to the St. Louis Blues," *Chicago Tribune*, September 15, 1961.

2 Simmons had been a three-time All-Star with the Philadelphia Phillies in the 1950s. For his career, Simmons had a 193-183 record, coupled with a 3.54 earned-run average. He pitched 163 complete games.

3 Curtis pitched only three seasons in the major leagues, compiling a 14-19 record and a 4.84 ERA. He had six complete games and finished third in the 1961 Rookie of the Year voting in the National League.

4 Neal Russo, "Boyer's Seven Hits Help Cards Beat Cubs Twice, 8-7, 6-5," *St. Louis Post-Dispatch*, September 15, 1961: 22.

5   Ibid.

6   retrosimba.com/2015/04/20/ken-boyer-added-special-twists-to-rare-pair-of-cycles/. Accessed April 14, 2016. Since Boyer's walk-off cycle in 1961, four other ballplayers have completed their cycles with a walk-off home run: César Tovar (Minnesota Twins, September 19, 1972), George Brett (Kansas City Royals, May 28, 1979), Dwight Evans (Boston Red Sox, June 28, 1984), and Carlos González (Colorado Rockies, July 31, 2010).

7   There were two All-Star Games played in 1961: on July 11 at Candlestick Park in San Francisco, and on July 31 at Fenway Park in Boston. The Cardinals were represented in both games by White (who started at first base), Musial, and Boyer. White was a combined 3-for-7 with two runs batted in, while Musial and Boyer were hitless. Ernie Banks, George Altman, and Don Zimmer were the Cubs players in the two midseason classics. The 1961 NL Rookie of the Year, Billy Williams, was not selected to the National League's squad.

8   Russo.

9   Ibid.

10 A "natural cycle" is accomplished when the batter hits a single, double, triple, and home run in that exact order.

ONE MORE RUNG ON THE RECORD BOOK LADDER FOR MUSIAL

September 2, 1962: New York Mets 4, St. Louis Cardinals 3, at Busch Stadium

BY ALAN COHEN

THERE WAS NOT MUCH TENSION IN the air as the New York Mets concluded a series against the St. Louis Cardinals at Busch Stadium on September 2, 1962. The Mets had long since secured their place in baseball lore as a truly horrific enterprise. Coming into the game, their record stood at 34-103 and they were 55½ games and seven years removed from first place. Their current losing streak was at five games. The Cardinals were in fifth place, 15½ games out of first place. They were two key players away from being a contender.

On this day, the Cardinals were pinning their hopes for a win on right-hander Ernie Broglio. Broglio had labored in the minor leagues for six seasons before a trade at the end of the 1958 season brought him and Marv Grissom to the Cardinals from the Giants organization. In his first three seasons with the Cardinals, he had gone 37-33, including a breakout season in 1960, when he went 21-9 and finished third in the Cy Young Award balloting. He came into the September 2 contest with a record of 10-7 in 1962.

The Mets pitcher was Alvin Jackson, called "Little Al" by Mets announcer Bob Murphy. Jackson had been chosen off the roster of the Pittsburgh Pirates by the Mets in the expansion draft and was one of the team's better pitchers despite a 7-17 record.

The size of the crowd, 9,169, was consistent with the perceived importance of the game, but by day's end, although the Mets announcers would be doing their 35th "happy recap" of the season, Cardinals fans had witnessed a moment of greatness.

After a scoreless first inning, the Mets broke into the scoring column when Frank Thomas led off the second inning with his 30th home run of the season. Jackson kept the Cardinals from scoring in the first two innings, stranding two runners. He was aided in the second inning when center fielder Jim Hickman gunned down Charlie James, who was trying to advance from first to third on a single by Jimmie Schaffer. The Cardinals tied the score in the third inning. After Jackson hit Curt Flood with a pitch, Julio Gotay slammed a double that plated Flood.

Next, second baseman Rod Kanehl grabbed Bobby Gene Smith's grounder and threw late to first baseman Marv Throneberry. Smith's single advanced Gotay to third base. Throneberry felt that the throw had beaten the runner and began to discuss his feelings with umpire Shag Crawford. As the two argued, Gotay took the opportunity to run home from third. However, home-plate umpire Ed Vargo ruled that time had been called and sent Gotay back to third base. Cardinals manager Johnny Keane lodged a protest. With runners at the corners, Jackson retired Bill White and Ken Boyer to prevent further scoring.

Jackson and Broglio dueled for the next three innings and the score was still 1-1 as the Mets came to bat in their half of the seventh inning. Clarence "Choo Choo" Coleman, one of four Mets catchers who saw action in the game, led off with a single and advanced to second base when Charlie Neal successfully executed a sacrifice bunt to the right side of the infield. Hickman's single brought home Coleman with the lead run but there was no further scoring as Kanehl and Jackson grounded out. The lead was short-lived. Schaffer led off the Cardinals' half of the inning with a single and left for a pinch-runner, Bob Gibson. Gibson advanced to second on a sacrifice by Dal Maxvill, who was pinch-hitting for Broglio;

went to third on Coleman's passed ball; and scored on a single by Flood.

Bobby Shantz came on to pitch in the eighth inning for St. Louis and the Mets mounted a rally against him in the ninth to regain the lead. With one out, Hickman singled and Kanehl reached on a bobble by Cardinals second baseman Gotay. The runners advanced to second and third when Jackson executed a sacrifice bunt. Richie Ashburn then walked to load the bases for Joe Pignatano, who had replaced Coleman behind the plate.

Pignatano, who had put on his first professional uniform in 1949, was batting .235 and Mets manager Casey Stengel was looking for more firepower. He called on Joe Christopher who, like Jackson, had been plucked off the roster of the Pirates. Although he was batting only .201 at the time, 13 of his 38 hits had been for extra bases. Christopher hit the third pitch from Shantz into left field, driving home two runs, before Shantz struck out Throneberry for the final out of the inning.

The Cardinals were down two runs as they came to bat in the final inning. But not for long. Gene Oliver led off with a homer off Jackson and the Cardinals were within one run of tying things up again. It was Oliver's eighth homer of the season, but his first of the year at home. Jackson retired Fred Whitfield and Shantz was due up. Shantz was not a bad hitter. Coming into the 1962 season, he had a .202 batting average with 104 career hits. In 1961, he had batted .438 (7-for-16) with the Pirates. But Johnny Keane had a fellow on the bench with 3,515 hits.

Stan Musial was called upon to keep the hopes of the Cardinals alive. Musial singled and was accorded a hero's ovation when he was removed for pinch-runner Julian Javier. The single was Musial's 3,516th career hit and moved him past Tris Speaker into second place on the all-time hit list. The day before, when he went 1-for-3 against New York, he had tied Speaker. Regardless of how he was performing against the rest of the league, Musial had always loved his trips to New York. It was in Brooklyn that he had first been called "The Man." When New York rejoined the National League in 1962, Musial went 21-for-46 against the Mets. He had slugged four homers against the Mets in 1962. The four homers, all at the Polo Grounds, came in as many at-bats as he homered in his last at-bat on July 7, and had three homers and a walk in his first four plate appearances on July 8.

Stengel, displaying the sort of genius that won him 10 pennants in 12 years with the Yankees, switched catchers. He summoned strong-armed Chris Cannizzaro (a.k.a. "Canzineri" in Stengelese) to take over for Sammy Taylor, who had taken over for Pignatano, who had taken over for Coleman. With Flood at the plate representing the winning run, Javier took off for second base, hoping to get into scoring position. Shortstop Felix Mantilla covered the base and took the throw from Cannizzaro. Mantilla applied the tag and the Mets were one out away from the win. Could Jackson retire the red-hot Flood? Curt already had two hits in the game and was in the midst of a hitting streak, having gone 7-for-12 in the three games with the Mets, but he grounded harmlessly to Kanehl at second and the game was over.

National League President Warren Giles disallowed the protest filed by the Cardinals, although it is conceivable that Throneberry had not called time out before engaging in his discourse with Crawford.

The Mets win was their fifth in 18 games against the Cardinals in 1962.

Jackson's victory was his eighth win of the year and his 11th complete game. It was his last win of a season in which he finished at 8-20. He continued to pitch through 1969 and became a pitching coach after his playing days.

Shantz was charged with the loss. The 36-year-old, who had won the American League MVP award in 1952 with a 24-7 record, pitched two more years before calling it a career after the 1964 season.

Broglio had a 12-9 record in 1962 and followed it up with a stellar 18-8 in 1963. In 1964, he was 3-5 with the Cardinals in June when he was dealt to the Cubs in the trade that sent Lou Brock to St. Louis.

Flood, who made the game's last out, would go on to extend his hitting streak to 10 games. The following year he won the first of seven consecutive Gold Glove awards. At the end of the 1969 season, he was traded to the Philadelphia Phillies and refused to report, setting off a challenge to baseball's reserve clause. Although he was unsuccessful in his challenge, he paved the way to a stronger baseball union and the reserve clause was ultimately overthrown.

Musial retired at the end of the 1963 season with 3,630 hits and more than a half-century later was still in the top five on the all-time hit list, trailing only Pete Rose, Ty Cobb, and Hank Aaron.

SOURCES

The author used Baseball-Reference.com, the *St. Louis Post-Dispatch*, and

Tuckner, Howard M. "Bases-Filled Hit Tops St. Louis, 4-3," *New York Times*, September 3, 1962: 18.

SAY HEY TIMES THREE

June 2, 1963: San Francisco Giants 6, St. Louis Cardinals 4, at Busch Stadium

BY ALAN COHEN

"Those homers all felt good. They all do. That second one was one of the hardest I've ever hit, and it came off a curve ball!" —Willie Mays.[1]

ON THE FIRST SUNDAY OF JUNE in 1963, 22,857 fans arrived at Busch Stadium to see their second-place Cardinals try to tie the visiting Giants for the league lead. The Cardinals had won five games in a row, including the first two of the three-game series against the Giants. The defending National League champions had their ace, Juan Marichal, on the mound and the Cardinals countered with Ernie Broglio and his 5-1 record. The game-time temperature of 88 degrees was an indicator that summer had arrived in the Gateway City.

The Giants wasted little time scoring. Harvey Kuenn led off the game with a single to left. After Chuck Hiller flied out, Willie Mays slammed his eighth homer of the season to give the Giants a 2-0 lead. It was the 376th career blast for Mays, who earlier in the season had moved past Gil Hodges into the all-time lead for homers by a right-handed batter in the National League. Mays, a notorious streak hitter, had not homered since May 17, and prior to the series with the Cardinals had been in an 0-for-16 slump that brought his season's batting average down to .236. His bat got healthy in St. Louis. The first-inning homer was his fourth hit in his first seven at-bats during the three games.

Marichal kept the Cardinals in check and the Giants added to their lead in the third inning. Kuenn, in his second at-bat, once again led off an inning with a hit, this time an infield hit that Cardinals third baseman Ken Boyer was unable to convert into an out. Hiller bunted Kuenn to second base and Orlando Cepeda singled him home to make the score 3-0. Two innings later, the Cardinals thwarted an attempt by the Giants to extend their lead when Hiller was gunned down at home trying to score on a double by Cepeda.

The Cardinals finally broke through against Marichal in the fifth. Julian Javier led off with a double to left, his second double of the game. Against conventional wisdom, he advanced to third base when Tim McCarver grounded out to shortstop Jose Pagan. The daring baserunning put him in position to score on a groundout by pinch-hitter Carl Sawatski (batting for Broglio) and give the Cardinals their first run.

Bob Humphreys took over for Broglio and stifled the Giants for two innings with his "tick-tock" pendulum windup delivery.[2] The eighth inning was Humphreys' undoing. After retiring Hiller on a fly ball, Humphreys surrendered back-to-back homers to Mays and Cepeda. The shot by Mays was a monster blow off the scoreboard in deep left-center field. Cepeda's blast, which landed on the right-field roof, was his 10th homer of the season and temporarily put him one up on Mays. After Humphreys walked Ed Bailey, he was removed and Ed Bauta was able to get the Cardinals out of the inning. However, they trailed by four runs as the game went to the bottom of the eighth.

Marichal needed some eighth-inning defensive help after giving up singles to McCarver and Charlie James. With runners on first and second, second baseman Hiller, who had recently returned from the DL after breaking his left wrist on May 1, fielded Curt Flood's grounder, tagged James, and threw to first base for the Giants' first double play in 71 innings. McCarver advanced to third but was left stranded when Marichal got Bill White to ground out to end the inning.

The Giants led 5-1 as the Cardinals brought in Bobby Shantz to pitch the ninth inning. With two out and none on, Mays came to the plate for the fourth time in the game and slammed his third homer. It was the third time in his career that he had hit as many as three home runs in a game. With Marichal pitching, the Giants seemed to have the game secured with a five-run lead.

However, the Cardinals were able to mount a rally. Dick Groat, in his first year with the Cardinals after nine seasons with the Pirates, led off with a triple. Stan Musial, playing left field for the Cardinals, singled in Groat. Musial, who had been playing with a pulled muscle, ruptured a blood vessel in the back of his right knee running out his single, and had to come out of the game. Ray Sadecki went in as a pinch-runner. After Boyer fouled out, George Altman doubled to right field and the Cardinals, trailing 6-2, had two runners in scoring position. Julian Javier delivered both runs with his third double of the game, a shot past Mays in center. The tying run came to the plate in the person of McCarver, batting at a torrid pace that had produced six hits in 12 at-bats over the prior three games. Giants manager Alvin Dark decided that Marichal, who had yielded four ninth-inning hits (three for extra bases), had had enough. He brought in hard-throwing Bobby Bolin. Bolin retired McCarver on a fly ball and struck out pinch-hitter Leo Burke to end the contest and gain the save, his sixth of the season. Marichal, with the win, saw his record go to 8-3, tying him for the team lead in wins with Billy O'Dell. Broglio's record, with the loss, went to 5-2.

The Cardinals and Giants remained in contention for most of the season, but fell short of the pennant as the Dodgers, with their great pitching, outdistanced the second-place Cardinals by six games. The Cards were within one game of first place in mid-September but lost eight of their last 10 games, including three in a row to Los Angeles. The Giants were within three games of first place in mid-August before fading to third place, 11 games behind the Dodgers.

Mays left St. Louis with a .254 batting average, having raised it 18 points during the three games against the Cardinals. He also left town with his first multi-extra-base-hit game of 1963. By season's end, the average was at .314 with 38 homers. Marichal would compile a record of 25-8, leading the National League in wins and innings pitched (321⅓).

After the game, Dark, happy that his team could salvage the finale and leave town with a two-game lead, was highly respectful of the Cardinals. He thought that the acquisition of Groat was a major factor in the team's success. "Groat adds tremendously to the ballclub. He already has made a much better player out of Julian Javier. Groat has helped Javier in the field and I'm sure that has also made Javier a better hitter."[3]

The Cardinals, one year later, would make another key trade and that trade involved Broglio. He compiled an 18-8 record in 1963 and tied Bob Gibson for the staff lead in wins. His 2.99 ERA was second best on the team to Curt Simmons (2.48). But in June 1964, the Cubs were in need of a starter. Broglio by then was 3-5, and was expendable. Furthermore, the Cardinals needed an outfielder. At the end of the 1963 season, Musial retired and Altman was traded to the Mets. They needed an outfielder to complement Flood and Mike Shannon. The Cubs had a surplus of power in their lineup, making outfielder Lou Brock expendable. Brock joined the Cardinals on June 15, and showed a new dimension. With the Cubs, he had stolen 50 bases in 327 games. With the Cardinals, he stole 888 bases over the course of 16 seasons, leading the league on eight occasions and stealing more than 50 bases in 12 consecutive seasons. Broglio, on the other hand, would not be the answer for the Cubs. In parts of three injury-ravaged seasons in the Windy City, he struggled to a 7-19 record and pitched his last game in 1966.

At the time of the game, Cepeda, who delivered an RBI single and a double before homering behind Mays in the eighth inning, was embroiled in a lawsuit against *Look* magazine.[4] An article in the magazine had taken issue with his ability to hit in the clutch, and implied that his selfishness caused him to put his own interests ahead of those of the team. It would take a trade, not a lawsuit, to silence his detractors. Despite a rookie-of-the year award in 1958 and a 1961 season in which he led the league in homers (46) and RBIs (142), it wasn't until he was traded to the Cardinals early in the 1966 season that the Baby Bull showed the leadership qualities that took the Cardinals to the National League pennant and world championship in 1967 and earned him the only MVP award of his Hall of Fame career.

SOURCES

In addition to the sources included in the Notes, the author used Baseball-Reference.com.

NOTES

1 "Willie: Sure Home Slump's Over," *San Francisco Chronicle*, June 3, 1963: 51.

2 Bob Stevens, "Willie Shakes Slump — And 'Tick-Tock'; Giants Win 6-4," *San Francisco Chronicle*, June 3, 1963: 51.

3 Neal Russo, "Giants Don't Quite Lay Egg, So Dark Drops Hard-Boiled Act," *St. Louis Post Dispatch*, June 3, 1963: 34.

4 Charles McCabe, "Who's Cepeda REALLY Suing?" *San Francisco Chronicle*, June 3, 1963: 51.

STAN MUSIAL'S FINAL GAME

September 29, 1963: St. Louis Cardinals 3, Cincinnati Reds 2, at Busch Stadium

BY JOE SCHUSTER

THERE WAS SYMMETRY TO THE FIRST weeks of Stan Musial's career in September 1941 and the last weeks 22 autumns later: Both saw the St. Louis Cardinals chasing the Dodgers for the pennant. Both saw them fall short but in each case, despite having the nucleus in place that would help them win the World Series the following season.

Even Musial's first and last games echoed one another: In both, Musial had two hits and drove in crucial runs in contests that ended in identical 3-2 Cardinal walk-off wins.

In between lay one of the finest baseball careers ever. By the time he played the last of his 3,026 games, Musial had been an All-Star in all but his first full season, 1942. He had collected a then-league-record 3,630 hits. Although his 475 home runs seem modest today, when he retired they ranked second in the National League, behind only Mel Ott's 511. All in all, when he retired as a player Musial held 17 major-league and 29 National League records.[1]

By the time Musial made the formal announcement that he was retiring, he had been considering it for quite a while. He had publicly floated the idea in 1958, when he signed the National League's first $100,000 contract, saying that he saw himself playing "one or two more years."[2] In the offseason after 1962—when Musial had something of a career second wind, hitting .330 after three consecutive uncharacteristic seasons of sub-.300 averages—he actually found himself in the middle of a controversy about the subject. That fall, Cardinals owner August A. Busch Jr. hired legendary baseball executive Branch Rickey as a senior consultant to general manager Bing Devine.[3] Almost immediately, Rickey—someone used to pulling the strings and not merely suggesting which strings someone else should pull—ended up in a power struggle with Devine that created "[a] schism … so deep that both seriously considered quitting."[4] One of Rickey's most drastic declarations was that Musial should retire to make way for younger players but Busch was quick to quash the notion: "Since when do you ask a .330 hitter to retire…?"[5]

Early in 1963 it became evident that Rickey may have been correct: By mid-May, Musial was hitting .215. By the All-Star break, his average was up to .279 but despite the mild offensive surge, he began to recognize this would be his final season. Selected for the National League squad as a reserve, he later said, "I knew, in my heart, that this would be my last All-Star appearance."[6]

Musial made his official announcement at the team's annual picnic at Busch's estate, Grant's Farm, on August 12, saying, "I figured on quitting, no matter what kind of year I had. … After all, I'll be 43 next season and I feel I've had more than my share from baseball."[7]

For a while it seemed to energize the team: Six games behind the Dodgers the day of the picnic, they went 27-8 over the next five weeks, pulling within one. However, a late September 1-8 stretch pushed the team seven back by the time of Musial's finale on September 29.

His departure was marked with tribute after tribute: Nationally, ABC aired a special that evening celebrating his career.[8] In St. Louis, the *Post-Dispatch* ran a five-page photographic feature in its Sunday magazine supplement; radio station KMOX, which broadcast Cardinals games, did an hour-long program about Musial before the game, while two St. Louis television channels also ran features about him.[9]

HOME OF THE BROWNS AND CARDINALS AT GRAND AND DODIER

In the ballpark, before a standing-room-only crowd, a pregame ceremony included a jazz band and speeches by team officials, media figures, the presidents of the National and American Leagues, and Commissioner Ford Frick, who famously declared of Musial, "Here stands baseball's happy warrior, here stands baseball's perfect knight."[10] After the speeches, Musial toured the ballpark in a convertible while fans tossed confetti.[11]

The game itself carried little weight. Win or lose, the Cardinals were assured of second place, as they stood five games in front of third-place San Francisco; their opponents, the Cincinnati Reds, came in 13 games behind the Dodgers, tied with Philadelphia for fourth place. On the mound were future Hall of Famer Bob Gibson, 18-9 as the day began, and Jim Maloney, 23-7, whose 254 strikeouts stood second to eventual Cy Young Award winner Sandy Koufax's 306.

Both pitchers were sharp early and the game remained scoreless through five. To that point Gibson had six strikeouts and no walks, while the only hit he had surrendered was a leadoff single by rookie Pete Rose. Maloney struck out eight Cardinals through five innings, giving up two walks and a single by Musial in the fourth that just eluded Rose at second base.[12]

The Cards finally broke through in what turned out to be an emotional sixth inning. Curt Flood led off with a double. After Dick Groat struck out, Musial came to the plate for what would be his final at-bat. He fouled off the first pitch, took two balls, and then lined a curveball past first baseman Gordy Coleman, who dove for the ball but couldn't snag it. Musial's single drove in Flood, giving St. Louis a 1-0 lead.[13]

The crowd's cheers shifted to boos as manager Johnny Keane sent Gary Kolb to pinch-run for Musial. Before the game Keane had promised Musial would play most of it so he would "go out on a good note, not a popup," and an RBI single was that note.[14] To a resounding ovation, Musial jogged off the field for the last time as a player and went to the clubhouse to wait for the final out. There, he slipped off his iconic number-6 jersey for the last time as a player and hung it up, pausing for a moment to touch his name above the number, and said, "If I do say so myself, pal, you're all right."[15]

In a way, it was as if no one else wanted it to end. The Cards added a second run in the sixth on singles by Ken Boyer and Bill White.

The lead held in the seventh and eighth innings, though the Reds put two runners on in both innings, and the Cardinals mustered an eighth-inning single by Boyer against Jim O'Toole, who was on the mound after Bob Skinner pinch-hit for Maloney in the top of that inning. In the top of the ninth, however, Gibson finally broke. After retiring the first two hitters, he gave up consecutive singles to Coleman and Don Pavletich, threw a wild pitch, and then gave up a game-tying single to Leo Cardenas.

The Cardinals tried to win it in regulation against Al Worthington, loading the bases on two walks and a single with one out, but Flood grounded to Rose, who forced the runner at home, and then Dal Maxvill, who had replaced Groat at short, flied out to send the game into extra innings.

The Reds threatened in the top of the 10th. Rose doubled leading off and went to third on a sacrifice. After an intentional walk, Ron Taylor, who relieved Gibson after nine, struck out Frank Robinson for a huge second out. Coleman drew a walk but Taylor retired Pavletich to leave the bases full. While the Cardinals were going down quietly from the 10th through the 13th, the Reds threatened again in the 14th, when Cardenas singled and Ernie Broglio, who relieved Taylor in the 12th, threw two wild pitches, putting a runner on third with one out. Cincinnati could not push him across, though, as Joey Jay (the fifth Reds pitcher of the day) struck out and, after Rose walked, Tommy Harper popped out to first.

The game ended in the bottom of the inning. Jerry Buchek singled. Broglio tried but failed to advance him on a bunt, and Buchek was out at second. Flood singled, moving Broglio to second, and then the notoriously light-hitting Maxvill doubled, bringing Broglio in for the victory.

Not surprisingly, Musial was the "Star of the Game" on broadcaster Harry Caray's postgame show on KMOX radio.[16] There, the conversation centered on Musial's reflection on his career; among other things, he pointed to Warren Spahn as the best pitcher he had faced and Willie Mays as the best all-around player he had seen before giving way to an emotional admission: "This has been a terrific way to end my career, on a victorious note. Several times I came close to tears before the game, but I thought I had some reason.["17]

A half-hour later, Musial drove away from the ballpark. A *St. Louis Post-Dispatch* reporter wrote that kids with programs chased after him, yelling, "One more! One more!"[18]

But there weren't any more. Musial was finished.

SOURCES

In addition to the sources cited in the Notes, the author also consulted the *New York Times*, Baseball-Reference.com, and Retrosheet.org.

NOTES

1 "Musial's Record," *St. Louis Post-Dispatch*, September 30, 1963: 6B.

2 Bob Broeg, "Stan at $100,000 on First Hike in 6 Years," *The Sporting News*, February 5, 1958: 3.

3 Bob Broeg, "Rickey, 80, Hired by Redbirds as Player Personnel Consultant," *St. Louis Post-Dispatch*, October 29, 1962: 5C.

4 Bob Burnes, "B.R.'s Return Ruffles Redbird Feathers," *The Sporting News*, November 17, 1962: 7.

5 Bob Broeg, "Rickey's Proposal to Retire Musial Stirs Discord," *St. Louis Post-Dispatch*, November 6, 1962: 4C.

6 Stan Musial and Bob Broeg, *Stan Musial: The "Man's" Own Story as Told to Bob Broeg* (Garden City, New York: Doubleday & Company, 1964), 236.

7 Neal Russo, "Even in Auld Lang Syne, The Man Hits Grand Slam," *The Sporting News*, August 24, 1963: 7.

8 Don Page, "Dodger Banjo Parade vs. the Yankee Ballet," *Los Angeles Times*, September 28, 1963: 33.

9 Neal Russo, "The Last Stan Like the First: A Hero in a Cardinal Victory," *St. Louis Post-Dispatch*, September 30, 1963: 4B.

10 Ibid.

11 Ibid.

12 Ed Wilks, "Day Was Long for Stan, Not Long Enough for Fans," *St. Louis Post-Dispatch*, September 30, 1963: 4B.

13 Ibid.

14 Russo, "The Last Stan."

15 Lowell Reidenbaugh, "'A Day I Will Always Remember,'" *The Sporting News*, October 12, 1963: 19.

16 Ibid.

17 Ibid.

18 Wilks.

CARDS ALMOST METS THEIR MATCH, BUT WIN PENNANT

October 4, 1964: St. Louis Cardinals 11, New York Mets 5, at Busch Stadium

BY NORM KING

THE ST. LOUIS CARDINALS MUST HAVE been pinching themselves. On September 22 they were in third place in the National League, five games behind the first-place Philadelphia Phillies. Nine days later, after the Phillies' epic collapse and their own eight-game winning streak, the Cardinals were in first place, one-half game up on the Cincinnati Reds, while the Phillies had fallen to third. Even better, the Cardinals were home to the New York Mets, the lowly, awful, 51-108 Mets, the team that needed a telescope just to see ninth place. Not only that, but the Reds and Phillies could beat each other up in a two-game series at Crosley Field.

You would think the Cards were salivating when Casey Stengel and his New York Mets came a'callin' for a three-game series to end the 1964 season, especially when they had future Hall of Famer Bob Gibson on the mound. So what happens? He loses a 1-0 decision to Al Jackson.

In 2008, Jackson recalled for *Newsday* the Cardinals' reception for him as he walked through their clubhouse on that last Friday night to appear on Harry Caray's postgame show. "Oh, did they call me a bunch of names. They said, 'You guys are 59 games out of first place and you've got to pitch a game like this?' Man, did they rip me."[1]

The next day the teams played in an alternate universe; the Cardinals committed two first-inning errors and 20-game winner Ray Sadecki gave up five runs, four of them earned, in one-plus innings as Casey's Amazins battered St. Louis, 15-5.

"Somebody's been putting Yankees into the Mets' uniforms," said Lou Brock. "Tomorrow they'll play like the Mets again."[2]

Well, so much for the easy time with the Mets. St. Louis was still in first place as dawn arose on October 4, but they were tied with Cincinnati (both with 92-69 records) and Philadelphia was one game back (91-70). St. Louis had to defeat the Mets and have Philadelphia beat the Reds to win the pennant.

St. Louis starter Curt Simmons was having the best season of his career at age 35. He had a career-best 18 wins with a respectable 3.38 ERA going into the game. His Mets counterpart, Galen Cisco, was 6-18 at game time, but also with a respectable ERA, at 3.45.[3]

After a scoreless first, the Cardinals got on the board in the second when Tim McCarver doubled and trotted home on Mike Shannon's single. The score stayed 1-0 until the two teams began a back-and-forth tussle in the middle innings. The Mets tied it up in the top of the fourth on a Charley Smith home run, but the Cardinals regained the lead thanks to a 150-pound stringbean of a second baseman named Dal Maxvill—playing in place of the injured Julian Javier—who very nearly wasn't around to perform the feat.

When the Cardinals wanted to send down him on loan to the Chicago White Sox' Triple-A affiliate in Indianapolis in May, Maxvill thought very seriously about quitting baseball to work as an electrical engineer with the Bussmann Fuse Company. Maxvill's wife encouraged him to accept the demotion, and after returning to the big club, he found himself playing in the team's most important game of the year. Maxvill came up with two out and singled home Dick Groat, who was on second after hitting a double, to give St. Louis a 2-1 lead.

But the Mets were more like Gnats in the top of the fifth because they were so pesty. With one out, George Altman singled to center, and moved to second on Cisco's sacrifice. Bobby Klaus hit a popup just behind first base, but when Maxvill went to make the catch, the wind caught the ball, played some tricks with it, and allowed it to land beyond his reach. Altman was only able to reach third on the play. However, both Altman and Klaus scored when Roy McMillan doubled, which gave New York a 3-2 lead and Cardinals manager Johnny Keane a major headache. Keane decided he had had enough of this nonsense and brought Gibson in to relieve Simmons, even though Gibson had pitched eight innings two nights before. In his fourth relief appearance of the season, Gibson induced Joe Christopher to fly to right and got Jim Hickman to ground out.

The Cardinals decided in the bottom of the fifth that enough was enough. Cisco made the big mistake of walking Brock, the leadoff hitter. Bill White followed with a single that moved Brock to second. Ken Boyer doubled to score Brock and tie the game, with White going to third, after which Stengel brought Bill Wakefield in to relieve Cisco. Wakefield got Groat to ground out to second, but that scored White with the second run of the inning. With Boyer still on second, Wakefield walked McCarver intentionally, hoping to set up the double play. He struck out Shannon, but then faced Maxvill, that very lean run-producing machine. Maxvill singled Boyer home from second, making it 5-3 Cardinals. That was it for Wakefield as Jack Fisher came on and struck out Gibson to end the inning.

While the Cardinals fans were watching this, they were also tuning in to the Reds-Phillies matchup. Even when their game was quiet, the fans had a lot to cheer about as the Phillies were pounding the Reds 10-0. A Reds loss guaranteed the Cards at least a tie for the NL crown.

"Nothing was happening on the field [in the third inning], yet the cheers rolled in waves through Busch Stadium, where every other customer had a transistor radio," wrote Red Smith. "They were following a doubleheader — the game they saw and the game they heard — and over the air had come word that the Phillies had flattened [Reds pitcher] John Tsitouris with a two-run attack in Cincinnati."[4]

The Mets moved close again in the top of the sixth as Gibson's control got away from him. After Hawk Taylor hit a one-out single, Gibson walked Ed Kranepool and retired Altman on a groundout to first. He then walked pinch-hitter Jesse Gonder intentionally to load the bases. A most unintentional walk to Klaus followed, forcing Taylor home and bringing the Mets to within one run at 5-4.

The Ol' Perfesser may have overmanaged this one by pinch-hitting for Fisher.[5] Willard Hunter came in to pitch the bottom of the sixth, and the Cardinals went to town on him. Brock doubled with one out, and then trotted home on White's two-run blast. The next batter, Boyer, walked, and after Groat struck out, McCarver stroked another double to score Boyer. It was now 8-4 Cardinals and the champagne was on its way to their dressing room. And just to put an exclamation point on the affair, St. Louis scored three more runs in the eighth on a Curt Flood home run and a two-run single by McCarver. The Mets scored a meaningless run in the ninth. It was only fitting that McCarver, who went 3-for-4 with two doubles and three RBIs, caught a foul popup for the final out to clinch the pennant and a World Series date with the New York Yankees.

While the Cardinals celebrated their first flag since 1946 in the clubhouse, Groat explained that his team had such a tough time against the Mets because they had just gone through a rough series in sweeping the Phillies. "When we got through that big roadblock– now we had to play the Mets," he said. "There had to be a letdown."[6]

As for the St. Louis-born Keane, the win meant that he would see a World Series game live for the first time since he was 14 and woke up at 5:00 A.M. to buy bleacher tickets for the 1926 fall classic, also between the Cardinals and Yankees. But this time he was guaranteed a better seat.

SOURCES

In addition to the sources listed below, the author also used:

New York Times.

SABR biography of Dal Maxvill by Loretta Donovan.

NOTES

1. Greg W. Prince, " Al Jackson," sabr.org/bioproj/person/9bc53b1d.
2. William Leggett, "Miracle in St. Louis," *Sports Illustrated*, October 12, 1964: 26.
3. Cisco proved the old adage: "If you can't do, teach." After accumulating a 25-56 lifetime record, he went on to serve as a pitching coach for 30 years with the Kansas City Royals, Montreal Expos, San Diego Padres, Philadelphia Phillies, and Toronto Blue Jays. He won World Series rings with the Jays in 1992 and 1993.
4. Red Smith, "Airwaves Bubbling at Busch," *St. Louis Post-Dispatch*, October 5, 1964: 6B.
5. The Ol' Perfesser was Stengel's nickname.
6. Ed Wilks, "Dick Groat Says Cards Are Like 1960 Bucs," *St. Louis Post-Dispatch*, October 5, 1964: 6B.

SCHULTZ, CARDINALS IGNORE THE ODDS TO DEFEAT YANKEES

October 7, 1964: St. Louis Cardinals 9, New York Yankees 5, at Busch Stadium

Game One of the World Series

BY FREDERICK C. BUSH

THE CITY OF ST. LOUIS WAS ECSTATIC that it would get to host at least two games of the 61st World Series during its bicentennial year. In addition to thrusting the Midwestern metropolis itself into the spotlight, "two sons of St. Louis," Johnny Keane and Yogi Berra, were managing the Cardinals and New York Yankees respectively.[1] The only negative aspect of the matchup was that the Yankees, playing in their fifth consecutive World Series and ninth in the past 10 years, were favored by the Las Vegas odds makers to win their 21st championship.[2]

The Yankees and Cardinals had met four times previously in the World Series, with St. Louis prevailing in 1926 and 1942 and New York taking the title in 1928 and 1943. The Cardinals were set to move into new Busch Memorial Stadium early in the 1966 season; thus, barring another Cardinals World Series appearance in 1965, there was a strong chance that the 1964 fall classic would be the last hurrah for venerable old Sportsman's Park. The facility had the character of "a pleasant stadium, in the Norman Rockwell genre" and, for fans, "the feeling in the park [was] one of inclusion, of being in a whole of which the diamond is only a focal part."[3] After the venue passed into the hands of August "Gussie" Busch Jr., who had purchased the Cardinals franchise in 1953, it had been renamed Busch Stadium, but the new name had never caught on with the hometown fans.[4]

Whatever the preferred name of the ballpark, 30,805 fans filled it for Game One on October 7, 1964. The Yankees sent left-hander Whitey Ford to the mound for the opener. Ford was making his 22nd start in 11 World Series and already had six titles and a record 10 postseason victories to his name. St. Louis countered with Ray Sadecki, who had posted a 20-11 record during the season, in lieu of ace Bob Gibson, who was unavailable after pitching 12 innings in the Cardinals' final series against the New York Mets.

Sadecki held the Yankees in check in the top of the first and was staked to a 1-0 lead in the bottom of the frame. Lou Brock lined a one-out single to right field, used his speed to advance to third on Dick Groat's single to center, and scored on Ken Boyer's sacrifice fly. Third baseman Boyer no doubt was happy to draw first blood against the Yankees and his brother, Clete, who manned the hot corner for the New Yorkers.

The Yankees wasted no time in erasing their deficit. Elston Howard opened the top of the second with a single, and then Tom Tresh smashed a homer to deep left-center field for a 2-1 Yankees advantage. Clete Boyer, looking to do Ken one better, lashed a one-out single, stole second base, and scored on Ford's single to extend the lead to 3-1. Sadecki walked Phil Linz, who was playing shortstop in place of the injured Tony Kubek, then was fortunate to catch a break when Ford tried to score from second on Bobby Richardson's single to left field. Brock fired a perfect throw to catcher Tim McCarver to cut down Ford at home plate, and Sadecki struck out Roger Maris to end the inning.

After surrendering three runs, Sadecki sought to help his cause with his bat. Mike Shannon led off with a single and advanced to second on Dal Maxvill's one-out comebacker to Ford. Sadecki drove in Shannon with a base hit to right field to narrow the score to 3-2 and advanced to third base on Mickey Mantle's errant throw to home; however, he was stranded there when Curt Flood's grounder to Linz resulted in the third out.

After the early excitement, the third inning was uneventful as each pitcher worked around a walk. Sadecki also issued a two-out walk in the fourth but escaped without further adventure. In the bottom of the fourth, Ford, in what would be his final World Series appearance, gave a demonstration of his postseason acumen. After McCarver blasted a one-out triple to the right-center-field gap between Mantle and Maris, Ford struck out Maxvill and Sadecki to strand McCarver at third base.

Not only had the Cardinals missed the opportunity to tie the score, but they then saw the Yankees extend their advantage in the top of the fifth. Mantle lashed a two-out single and advanced to third on Howard's second base hit of the game, after which Tresh garnered his third RBI with a double that drove in Mantle for a 4-2 lead.

Ford cruised through the bottom of the fifth. However, after Sadecki held the Yanks scoreless in the top of the sixth, Ford encountered trouble. Ken Boyer led off with a single and advanced to second on a passed ball. After Bill White struck out, Shannon mashed one of the longest home runs in the history of Sportsman's Park to tie the score, 4-4; aided by a 16-mph southeast wind, the ball was estimated to have traveled between 475 and 500 feet before it hit the scoreboard past the left-field bleachers.[5] McCarver followed Shannon's blast with a double that ended Ford's day.

Al Downing took the mound and induced a pop fly from pinch-hitter Charlie James. Carl Warwick, batting in place of Sadecki, singled to score McCarver with the go-ahead run and advanced to second on Tresh's throw to home. After Julian Javier entered the game to pinch-run for Warwick, Flood hit the second wind-assisted drive to the left-field-bleacher area, only his ball bounced off the fence for a triple rather than clearing it altogether; Javier scored on the play to give the Cardinals a 6-4 lead. Downing retired Brock to stop the bleeding, but the game had turned in the Redbirds' favor.

Keane now sent 38-year-old Barney Schultz to the hill to face the heart of the Yankees' order in the top of the seventh inning. Schultz was an unlikely hero, since he had pitched for 18 different franchises in 13 different leagues—counting major- and minor-league stints—over the past 20 seasons. After developing arm trouble early in his career, he had come to depend upon the knuckleball, but he had found success at the major-league level to be elusive.

What Schultz had found was the support of manager Johnny Keane. Schultz first came under Keane's leadership while he was with the Columbus Red Birds in 1954, and they were reunited on the Omaha Cardinals in 1956-58. Schultz appreciated Keane's role in his career, saying, "He's the one who made me a relief pitcher. He's the one who had faith in me. He's done more for me than any other man in baseball."[6]

In 1963, with a shot at the NL pennant, Keane persuaded general manager Bing Devine to trade for Schultz. Though Schultz was released after the season, he worked out at the Cardinals' spring-training camp in 1964 and was assigned to the Triple-A Jacksonville Suns. The Cardinals called him up at the end of July, and he contributed a 1-3 record with 14 saves and a 1.64 ERA over 30 appearances down the stretch.

Schultz rewarded Keane's confidence in him by allowing the Yankees only one run over the final three innings. In the top of the eighth, pinch-hitter Johnny Blanchard hit a one-out double, and pinch-runner Mike Hegan scored on a two-out single by Richardson to draw the Yankees to within one run of the Cardinals.

St. Louis responded in the bottom of the inning by putting the game away with three unearned runs off relievers Rollie Sheldon and Pete Mikkelsen. Shannon, the leadoff batter, reached base on a Clete Boyer error. Sheldon walked McCarver but got Schultz to line into a double play; after he intentionally walked pinch-hitter Bob Skinner, he gave way to Mikkelsen. Flood greeted the new Yankees pitcher with a single that plated Shannon, and Brock followed with a double that drove in pinch-runner Jerry Buchek and Flood for a 9-5 lead.

After the scoring outburst, Schultz earned a save as he set the Yankees down in order to preserve the Cardinals' Game One victory.

SOURCES

In addition to the sources listed in the Notes, the author also consulted Baseball-Reference.com and *The Sporting News*.

NOTES

1 Joseph Durso, "Yanks, with Kubek Out, 7-5 to Top Cards in Opener Today," *New York Times*, October 7, 1964: 59.

2 Ibid.

3 "Fans Hail Cards with Propriety," *New York Times*, October 8, 1964: 55.

4 Gussie Busch had a penchant for attaching his family's name to various arenas. In addition to renaming Sportsman's Park, he also changed the name of Houston's Buffalo Stadium—home of the Cardinals' longtime minor-league affiliate, the Buffaloes—to Busch Stadium in 1958. In both cities, most fans continued to refer to the structures by their old names. Busch finally obtained ego gratification via stadium name with the opening of Busch Memorial Stadium (a.k.a. Busch Stadium II) in 1966.

5 Joseph Durso, "Cards Rally to Beat Yanks in Series Opener, 9 to 5," *New York Times*, October 8, 1964: 1.

6 "Schultz Is Cardinal Hero With Three Innings of Effective Relief Pitching," *New York Times*, October 8, 1964: 54.

ROOKIE HURLER MEL STOTTLEMYRE GOES THE DISTANCE AS YANKEES TIE WORLD SERIES

October 8, 1964: New York Yankees 8, St. Louis Cardinals 3, at Busch Stadium

Game Two of the World Series

BY FREDERICK C. BUSH

THE NEW YORK YANKEES HAD ENtered the 1964 World Series as favorites to extend their record number of championships to 21, but they had blown a Game One lead and found themselves in an early hole. Though it was true that this Yankees squad carried no "superman aura, either by their manner or in the thinking of the opposition, they remain[ed] a symbol of glamour."[1] The Bronx Bombers had dominated the major leagues for so long that it seemed to be their birthright to be champions. Still, the difference between the current Yankees and the juggernauts of the 1930s and 1950s came to the fore as this 1964 squad resorted to sending a rookie, Mel Stottlemyre, to the mound to try to even the Series at one game apiece on a cloudy, blustery afternoon.

Stottlemyre was 13 years younger than the venerable Whitey Ford, who had started Game One for New York. He was also the antithesis of St. Louis's Game One pitching hero, Barney Schultz, who had embarked upon his professional career in 1944, when Stottlemyre was 2 years old, and had struggled to make it to the major leagues. Stottlemyre, on the other hand, was a hotshot rookie who had compiled a 13-3 record, including 10 consecutive victories at one point, with the Triple-A Richmond Virginians of the International League before being called up by the Yankees on August 11.[2] After arriving in New York, he went 9-3 with a 2.06 ERA to help the Yankees capture the American League pennant. Now, in his first postseason start, Stottlemyre found himself pitted against Bob Gibson, the Cardinals' fiery ace.

Gibson opened the game by walking shortstop Phil Linz, but then showed Stottlemyre and the Yanks what they would be up against as he struck out Bobby Richardson, Roger Maris, and Mickey Mantle in succession. Stottlemyre was not intimidated, however, and was determined not to be outdone. He set the Cardinals down in order and registered two strikeouts of his own, catching both Curt Flood and Bill White looking at called third strikes.

In the top of the second, Gibson set New York down in order while adding Elston Howard and Tom Tresh to his list of early strikeout victims. Stottlemyre kept pace by retiring the side on three groundball outs in the bottom of the frame.

Linz registered the first hit for either side when he hit a two-out single in the top of the third. He advanced to third base on Richardson's double but was stranded there when Maris grounded out to shortstop Dick Groat.

Just as Stottlemyre had followed Gibson's lead in setting batters down over the first two innings, he now followed suit by allowing the Cardinals' first hits of the game. Mike Shannon and Dal Maxvill led off with back-to-back singles, and both advanced one base on Gibson's sacrifice bunt. Shannon scored on Flood's grounder to shortstop to give St. Louis a 1-0 lead. It was all the Cardinals would get for the moment as Stottlemyre induced a Lou Brock comeback grounder to end any further threat.

The Yankees struck back in the top of the fourth. After Howard lined a one-out double, Joe Pepitone hit a short fly ball to shallow left field. Brock missed a shoestring catch, and the ball rolled away for a double, but Howard was unsure whether the ball would be caught and had to hold up at third base. Gibson walked Tresh intentionally to load the bases, and Clete Boyer drove in Howard with a sacrifice fly that tied the score at 1-1 before Gibson struck out Stottlemyre for the third out.

In the top of sixth, a controversial call cost Gibson the second Yankees' run of the contest. After Mantle drew a leadoff walk, Howard smashed a liner toward right-center field but was robbed by second baseman Maxvill, who made a diving catch for the first out. The controversy ensued as the next batter, Pepitone, was at the plate. Gibson threw an inside curveball on a 1-and-2 count, and home-plate umpire Bill McKinley ruled that the close pitch hit Pepitone on the right thigh. As boos rained down on McKinley, Cardinals manager Johnny Keane argued that the ball had hit Pepitone's bat. Several Cardinals players "pointed out that Pepitone made no move to go to first, a normal reaction, until McKinley waved him there."[3]

Groat had run in from shortstop to pull an irate Gibson out of the fray; though he may have prevented Gibson from being ejected, he did not settle him down. Once play resumed, Tresh lined Gibson's first pitch into center field, and Mantle scored to give the Yankees a 2-1 lead. Gibson retired Clete Boyer and Stottlemyre to end the inning, but the Yankees were not about to relinquish the advantage they had gained.

Stottlemyre quickly set the Cardinals down in order in the bottom of the sixth, and Gibson ran into further troubles in the top of the seventh. Linz led off with a single and advanced all the way to third base when Gibson uncorked a wild pitch with Richardson at the plate. Richardson drove in Linz with a broken-bat single, advanced to third on Maris's base hit, and scored on Mantle's grounder to second base. New York now held a 4-1 lead.

The Cardinals were unable to mount much of a threat against the Yanks' rookie hurler throughout the game, but it was not for lack of trying. In the bottom of the eighth, Carl Warwick pinch-hit for Maxvill and led off the inning with a single. Bob Skinner, pinch-hitting for Gibson, smashed a ground-rule double to left field to put runners at second and third with no outs, but Stottlemyre buckled down. Warwick scored on Brock's one-out grounder to make it a 4-2 game, but it was the only run the Cardinals could muster after a promising start to their half of the inning.

Although four runs would have sufficed for the Yankees on this day, they added four more as the Cardinals' relief pitching corps came undone in the top of the ninth. Schultz took the mound for the Redbirds, but his Game One magic abandoned him. He surrendered a leadoff home run to Linz, who had hit only five homers in 368 at-bats during the regular season, and then was replaced by Gordie Richardson after giving up a one-out single to Maris.

Mantle greeted Richardson with a double that drove in Maris and extended the Yankees' lead to 6-2. Richardson intentionally walked Howard but then allowed a Pepitone single that plated Mantle. Tresh followed with a sacrifice fly that scored Howard for New York's eighth run. After an intentional walk of Boyer, Roger Craig replaced Richardson and struck out Stottlemyre to end the Cardinals' misery.

In the bottom of the ninth, a tiring Stottlemyre gave up a leadoff triple to Groat, who scored when Tim McCarver followed with a single to center field. The Yankees had a large enough lead, 8-3, that manager Yogi Berra allowed his rookie pitcher to finish what he had started. After Shannon hit into a double play, Stottlemyre punctuated his first—and what turned out to be his only—World Series victory with a strikeout of pinch-hitter Charlie James.

The Cardinals, though still unhappy about the Pepitone hit-by-pitch call, were impressed by Stottlemyre's composure. Third baseman Ken Boyer said, "He never wavered. The few times he was in a jam, he just worked a little harder and kept hitting the corners. He was great."[4] Keane, alluding to Stottlemyre's repertoire, added, "We knew his sinker ball was excellent, but we may have underestimated his fastball, which was live."[5]

As for Stottlemyre himself, he conceded that he was most successful on days when he could keep the ball low and induce a lot of groundouts. This had been one of those days as "only nine of the 35 batters he faced had managed to hit the ball into the air."[6] Thanks to Stottlemyre's pitching prowess, the Yankees had tied the 1964 World Series, 1-1. The fact that the next three games would take place in New York shifted the Series back in the Yankees' favor, which was exactly the way things had been — with the exception of the early 1940s war years — for almost four decades.

SOURCES

In addition to the sources listed below, the author also consulted Baseball-Reference.com.

NOTES

1   Leonard Koppett, "Talk of the Series," *New York Times*, October 9, 1964.

2   "Stottlemyre Reaches High Point of Short Career by Keeping Pitches Low," *New York Times*, October 9, 1964.

3   "Stottlemyre Stifles Cards, Gives Bombers a Big Lift," *The Sporting News*, October 24, 1964: 24.

4   "Second Game" *The Sporting News*, October 24, 1964: 25.

5   Ibid.

6   "Stottlemyre Reaches High Point of Short Career by Keeping Pitches Low."

BOUTON EARNS SECOND VICTORY TO EXTEND WORLD SERIES TO SEVENTH GAME

October 14, 1964: New York Yankees 8, St. Louis Cardinals 3, at Busch Stadium

Game Six of the World Series

BY FREDERICK C. BUSH

AFTER THE CARDINALS TOOK TWO out of three games from the Yankees in New York, the World Series returned to St. Louis with the home team on the verge of capturing its seventh championship. Each of the games in New York had been tightly contested, and each game's outcome had been determined by a home run. Mickey Mantle had clouted the game-winner off Barney Schultz in the bottom of the ninth inning of Game Three; Ken Boyer's sixth-inning grand slam had provided the winning margin for St. Louis in Game Four; and Tim McCarver's three-run blast in the 10th inning of Game Five had given the Cardinals their 3-2 advantage in games. Whitey Ford, the Yankees' postseason ace, was still suffering from a heel injury incurred in Game One, so manager Yogi Berra sent Game Three winner Jim Bouton to the mound on October 14 in the hopes of extending the series to seven games.

The partisan St. Louis crowd of 30,805 was every bit as confident as Cardinals manager Johnny Keane, who had asserted, "We're the favorites at last."[1] Indeed, Keane's squad looked ready to claim the crown in the early going of Game Six. The Cardinals started left-hander Curt Simmons, who had pitched eight strong innings of one-run ball in Game Three, though he had received a no-decision for his effort in what turned out to be a losing cause. In the top of the first, Simmons allowed a one-out single to Bobby Richardson, who then stole second base, but the veteran lefty quickly put down any thoughts of a Yankees rally with strikeouts of Roger Maris and Mantle.

In the bottom of the frame, Curt Flood registered a leadoff single, advanced to third on Lou Brock's base hit, and scored on Bill White's double-play grounder to give the Cardinals a quick 1-0 lead against Bouton. After this early tally, Simmons and Bouton made quick work of both sides' batters from the second inning through the fourth.

True action resumed when Tom Tresh led off the top of the fifth for the Yankees with a ground-rule double to left field. Joe Pepitone struck out, but Tresh advanced to third on Clete Boyer's ground-out to second base. With two outs, Bouton aided his own cause with a single to left-center field that drove in Tresh to tie the game, 1-1. Bouton then kept the Cardinals off the scoreboard in the bottom of the frame, which set the stage for two iconic Yankees heroes of the early 1960s to turn the tide of the game.

Richardson led off the sixth inning with a pop fly to shortstop, but Maris and Mantle clobbered back-to-back home runs on consecutive pitches—both to deep right field—to give the Yankees a 3-1 lead that they would not relinquish. The dual blows were more hard luck for Simmons in this Series. He had matched Bouton by allowing only one run through eight innings in Game Three, only to see Schultz give up a game-winning homer to Mantle in the ninth. He had again pitched well for five innings on this day until he surrendered the two round-trippers in the sixth. Simmons said afterward, "Outside of those

360

two bombs, my stuff was all right. You know, when you throw a hanging pitch to a good hitter, he jumps on it. That's what Maris did. And Mantle just simply creamed that fastball outside."[2]

Bouton, having been given the lead, set the Cardinals down in order in the sixth and seventh innings. At one point in the bottom of seventh, however, Berra came to the mound to confer with his starter. Bouton had developed stiffness in his arm in the sixth inning, and Berra thought he was beginning to labor a bit. Bouton assured his manager that he was fine and asserted, "I've got all winter to rest,"[3] so he remained in the game.

His mound opponent, Simmons, had been removed in favor of Ron Taylor with one out in the top of the seventh. Now Schultz took the hill for the Cardinals in the eighth; his relief effort had been the story of Game One, but he had not fared successfully in Game Two and had lost Game Three. Though Schultz would not suffer the ignominy of adding another loss to his World Series record, he and fellow reliever Gordie Richardson allowed the Yankees to put Game Six further out of the Cardinals' reach.

Phil Linz led off the top of the eighth inning with a single, advanced to second on Bobby Richardson's sacrifice bunt, and moved on to third base on Maris's grounder to second. Even though there were now two outs, Keane decided to have Schultz issue an intentional walk to Mantle, whose sixth-inning homer had landed on the grandstand roof of Sportsman's Park.[4] The strategy didn't work. Elston Howard drove in Linz with a base hit, and then Schultz unintentionally walked Tresh to load the bases. At that point, Keane had seen enough, and he pulled Schultz in favor of Gordie Richardson.

Unfortunately for Keane and all of St. Louis, *R-i-c-h-a-r-d-s-o-n* did not spell *relief* for the Cardinals. Pepitone worked a 2-and-2 count against Richardson before clearing the bases with a grand slam over the right-center-field wall that gave the New Yorkers a commanding 8-1 lead. Pepitone's blast was the second grand slam of this Series—Boyer's four-bagger in Game Four had been the other—which tied the World Series record; the record had initially been set in 1956 when Berra and Bill Skowron had both hit grand slams for the Yankees against the Brooklyn Dodgers.[5]

Though the Yankees' lead appeared to be insurmountable, the Cardinals refused to give up. Flood drew a walk to lead off the bottom of the eighth, and Brock followed with a double. White's grounder to first allowed Flood to score to make it an 8-2 ballgame, but that was the only run the Cardinals could manage against Bouton after the promising start to the frame.

Reliever Bob Humphreys set the Yankees down in order in the top of the ninth, and the Cardinals continued to show their fighting spirit in the bottom half. Bouton quickly retired McCarver on a pop fly to second baseman Richardson, but he then allowed consecutive singles to Mike Shannon and Jerry Buchek that ended his day. Berra knew that Bouton was tiring and had Steve Hamilton ready in the bullpen. Berra had drawn a laugh earlier when he had "raised his hands high over his head, indicating he wanted 'the tall one'" to warm up;[6] the 6-foot-7 Hamilton was a former professional basketball player with the NBA's Minneapolis Lakers. Upon entering the game, Hamilton allowed pinch-hitter Bob Skinner's single that drove in Shannon to make the score 8-3, but he then induced Flood to hit into a double-play grounder to end the game.

Though Bouton had tired at the end, he had earned his second victory in the 1964 World Series and had given the Yankees the opportunity to steal back the championship from the Cardinals. As reporters crowded around Mantle, Maris, and Pepitone, Bouton joked, "How about that? You take one swing with the bat, hit the ball out of the park, and everybody congratulates you. But nobody pays any attention to the pitcher. All I did was work like a Trojan, getting in and out of jams all day."[7]

Bouton had not actually been in that many jams over the course of Game Six, but he claimed that he had not felt comfortable until the fourth inning. When a reporter mentioned that Bouton's cap had begun falling off his head as he delivered pitches in the fourth inning, Bouton responded, "Yeah, that proves it."[8] Bouton's issue with his headgear may not have been quite the indicator of success that he thought it was, though. He lost his cap only 12 times over the course of Game Six compared with 38 times in Game Three.[9]

What Bouton and his home-run-hitting teammates had done was to send the World Series to a deciding seventh game for the 19th time. Every player on both sides would have his cap and his game face on when the Cardinals started Bob Gibson against the Yankees' Mel Stottlemyre to determine the 1964 World Series champion on October 15.

SOURCES

In addition to the sources listed below, the author also consulted Baseball-Reference.com.

NOTES

1. Joseph Durso, "Keane Confident of Title Victory," *New York Times*, October 14, 1964.
2. "Two Bad Pitches Cost Simmons Chance to Fill Hero's Role in Sixth Game," *New York Times*, October 15, 1964.
3. "Kink Can't Stop Bouton," *The Sporting News*, October 24, 1964: 32.
4. Joseph Durso, "The Home Run Is the Decisive Weapon as Yankees Beat the Cardinals," *New York Times*, October 15, 1964.
5. "Pepitone Makes '64 Series Second with Pair of Slams," *The Sporting News*, October 24, 1964: 32.
6. "Kink Can't Stop Bouton."
7. "Bouton Says Arm Tightened in Sixth, But It Wasn't Cause for His Removal," *New York Times*, October 15, 1964.
8. Ibid.
9. "Kink Can't Stop Bouton."

GIBSON PITCHES CARDINALS TO CROWN, EARNS MVP HONORS

October 15, 1964: St. Louis Cardinals 7, New York Yankees 5, at Busch Stadium

Game Seven of the World Series

BY FREDERICK C. BUSH

PRIOR TO THE START OF GAME SEVEN of the 1964 World Series, Cardinals starter Bob Gibson grudgingly obliged the press by posing for pictures with his mound opponent, the Yankees' Mel Stottlemyre. By this time in the Series, Gibson was running on fumes; after his 10-inning, complete-game victory in Game Five, he had commented, "I feel as though I'd just come out of a 10-round bout."[1] In light of Gibson's fatigue, and taking his bulldog competitive nature into account, it should have come as no surprise that—after the photo-taking was at an end—he shook hands with Stottlemyre and said to him, "Hope all of your luck is bad today."[2] As it turned out, Gibson's gutsy pitching on two days' rest and some bad plays by the Yankees, rather than bad luck, gave the Cardinals the edge they needed to prevail against the Yankees.

Gibson came out gunning and set the Yanks down in order in the first inning, striking out Bobby Richardson in the process. Stottlemyre, who had defeated Gibson in a complete-game effort in Game Two, allowed a two-out double to Bill White in the Cardinals' half of the first, but he escaped trouble with a strikeout of his own against Ken Boyer.

In the top of the second, Gibson set a World Series record when he fanned leadoff batter Mickey Mantle for his 24th strikeout of this Series; the old record had been set by Los Angeles Dodgers lefty Sandy Koufax against the Yankees just one year earlier.[3] In spite of his strikeout skein, Gibson soon ran into his first jam of the day. Elston Howard singled and, following Joe Pepitone's out, Tom Tresh singled and Clete Boyer reached first safely on shortstop Dick Groat's error to load the bases. Gibson responded by striking out Stottlemyre on three pitches to end the scoring threat.

Stottlemyre matched Gibson pitch-for-pitch as both men put up zeroes for the first three innings. In the bottom of the fourth, however, Gibson's hoped-for misfortune befell New York; though the Yankees committed only one official error in the inning, they actually made four costly mistakes. Ken Boyer stroked a leadoff single and advanced to second when Stottlemyre, perhaps suffering under Gibson's bad mojo, pitched too cautiously to Groat and walked him on four pitches. Tim McCarver then hit what should have been a certain double-play grounder to Pepitone at first base, but shortstop Phil Linz threw the ball away on the relay back to first and was charged with an error; Boyer scored on the errant throw to give St. Louis a 1-0 lead.

The Cardinals were not finished scoring just yet. McCarver advanced to third base on Mike Shannon's single to set up the next Yankees misplay which, ironically, occurred due to a Cardinals mistake. As Dal Maxvill swung and missed on a hit-and-run play, Shannon broke for second base. Howard failed to throw him out at second, and second baseman Richardson's throw back to home plate was not good enough to nail McCarver, who scored the Cardinals' second run. Maxvill then singled, and Mantle committed the final Yankees mistake of the inning when his throw home was wide of the plate and allowed Shannon to score for a 3-0 St. Louis lead. Stottlemyre

Celebration time! Bob Gibson was lights-out in World Series competition, attested by his 7-2 record, eight complete games in nine starts, and a 1.89 ERA in 81 innings.

retired Gibson and Curt Flood to end the inning; after that, his day was at an end.

Cardinals manager Johnny Keane later affirmed, "There's no doubt that those three runs gave Gibson something to work with. ... I've never had a gutsier ballplayer, but it was getting the lead that enabled him to last."[4] Indeed, courage did not equal energy, and Gibson was laboring through this game. He walked Tresh to lead off the Yankees' fifth, and issued another walk—with one out—to pinch-hitter Mike Hegan, but he escaped unscathed courtesy of a double-play grounder from Linz.

Al Downing took the mound for New York in the bottom of the fifth, but he did not last long. After a sequence in which he surrendered a leadoff homer to Lou Brock, a single to White, and a double to Boyer without registering a single out, manager Yogi Berra pulled him out of the game and replaced him with Rollie Sheldon. Groat's grounder to second base enabled White to score, and McCarver's sacrifice fly drove in Boyer for a 6-0 edge in favor of the home team. Shannon struck out to end the onslaught, but the Yankees looked to be finished.

Still, the proud New Yorkers did not go down without a fight, and they scored their first runs of the game against an increasingly tired Gibson in the top of the sixth inning. Richardson and Roger Maris opened the frame with back-to-back singles, and then Mantle hit his 18th home run in World Series play to narrow the margin to 6-3.[5] Gibson dug deep once more and, though he issued another walk to

Tresh, he struck out Howard and Clete Boyer to hold the Yankees at bay.

Sheldon retired the Cardinals in order in the sixth inning, and Gibson allowed only a harmless Richardson single in the top of the seventh before the Cardinals added to their lead. Steve Hamilton, the Yankees' fourth pitcher of the day, struck out the first two batters he faced—Brock and White—before allowing a solo home run by Ken Boyer that gave St. Louis a 7-3 advantage.

A momentarily-reinvigorated Gibson then set down the Yankees one-two-three in the top of the eighth inning. In the Cardinals' half of the eighth, Hamilton found himself in a quick jam after a leadoff single by McCarver and an error by Clete Boyer on Shannon's grounder put men at first and second with no outs. After Maxvill advanced both runners with a sacrifice bunt, Pete Mikkelsen relieved Hamilton. Gibson came to bat and hit a grounder to Clete Boyer, who threw home to retire McCarver after a rundown. Mikkelsen kept the Cards from adding to their lead by retiring Flood on a liner to Boyer.

Now it was do-or-die time for the Yankees, and they alternated between the two outcomes in the top of the ninth inning. Tresh, the leadoff batter, fell into the *die* category by striking out, but Clete Boyer followed with a *do* in the form of a home run. The pattern repeated itself when pinch-hitter Johnny Blanchard, batting for Mikkelsen, struck out and Linz followed with an unlikely homer of his own to draw New York to within two runs, 7-5. With Maris and Mantle waiting in the wings, Gibson got Richardson to pop out to Maxvill at second base to give the Cardinals their seventh World Series championship. It was the first time the Yankees had lost consecutive World Series since 1921-22.

Gibson had amassed a 2-1 record and a 3.00 ERA; his two ninth-inning strikeouts had extended his record for a single World Series to 31. When he was informed of his strikeout record, he commented, "It's nice to know … but I'd rather have the money."[6] In addition to getting a winner's share of the World Series money, Gibson also received a 1965 Corvette convertible when he was named the Series' MVP; the car was a gift from *Sport* magazine, which sponsored the award.[7]

All was well for the Cardinals after they won the championship on October 15, but the next day brought a surprising development when Keane resigned as the team's manager. Keane's letter of resignation was dated September 28, which was when he had decided that he would quit St. Louis no matter what the Cardinals' postseason fate turned out to be.[8] Though Keane refused to disclose why he was leaving, it was well-known that he had been unhappy about two issues: 1) the ouster of his friend Bing Devine as the general manager on August 13, and 2) the persistent rumors that Keane would be replaced by Leo Durocher.[9]

That same day—October 16—the Yankees fired Yogi Berra from his managerial post; in a strange twist of fate, they then hired Keane to be their new manager on October 20.[10] Thus, while the 1964 World Series marked only the beginning of Gibson's postseason exploits, it denoted the end of Keane's tenure with the Cardinals, the end of the Yankees' long dynasty, and the end of playoff baseball at old Sportsman's Park in St. Louis, Missouri.

SOURCES

In addition to the sources listed below, the author also consulted Baseball-Reference.com.

NOTES

1. Joseph Durso, "Keane Confident of Title Victory," *New York Times*, October 14, 1964.

2. "Bad Luck for Mel: Gibson's Hopes Come True," *The Sporting News*, October 24, 1964: 34.

3. Koufax's record of 23 strikeouts was for a World Series of seven games or fewer. Bill Dinneen of the Boston Americans had struck out 28 batters in an eight-game World Series against the Pittsburgh Pirates in 1903. As it turned out, Gibson bested both marks with his 31 strikeouts in the 1964 World Series.

4. Leonard Koppett, "Talk of the Series," *New York Times*, October 16, 1964.

5. With his World Series-record-extending 18th home run, Mantle garnered additional records with 40 RBIs and 42 runs scored, surpassing Yogi Berra by one in both categories.

6. "Yankees Walloped 'Good Fast Balls,' Gibson Notes at Victory Celebration," *New York Times*, October 16, 1964.

7   "Gibson Voted Outstanding Player of Series, Wins Car," *The Sporting News*, October 24, 1964: 33.

8   Joseph Durso, "St. Louis Manager Turns in Notice Dated Sept. 28," *New York Times*, October 17, 1964.

9   Ibid.

10 There was one additional ironic result from the 1964 World Series: Little more than two months after being fired by St. Louis, Bing Devine was named Executive of the Year after winning *The Sporting News'* poll of baseball's general managers. Ed Wilks, "Devine Acclaimed as Executive of the Year: Rival Bosses Cite Former Redbird GM," *The Sporting News*, October 24, 1964: 1.

CARDINALS' LAST GAME IN SPORTSMAN'S PARK

May 8, 1966: San Francisco Giants 10, St. Louis Cardinals 5, at Busch Stadium

BY GREG ERION

ON MAY 8, 1966, SPORTSMAN'S Park hosted its last major-league baseball game. The venerable facility stood on grounds that had been in use for baseball since 1866. St. Louis's first professional team played there in 1875. Over the years the Cardinals and their late intracity rival Browns shared the ballpark. It was the site of 10 World Series, home turf for the likes of Hornsby, Sisler, Dean, Musial, and Gibson as well as a field where players like Ruth, Gehrig, and Williams walked. Where Enos Slaughter made his "mad dash" to win the 1946 World Series. And where 3-foot-7 Eddie Gaedel famously worked a walk in his only major-league appearance. And no ballpark in the country had hosted more big-league games.

With all this and much more in the way of historical lore, the last game would end with a celebration. Pregame ceremonies honored the Browns' greatest player, George Sisler, and the Cardinals' beloved Stan Musial just three years after his retirement. Fans were interviewed before the game and shared memories of Browns and Cardinal contests which hearkened back to the 1920s. Nostalgia was in full force.[1]

Playing the Cardinals were the league-leading San Francisco Giants, led by Willie Mays, who just days before had smashed his 512th major-league home run to take over the all-time National League record from Mel Ott. Alongside Mays played two future Hall of Famers, Orlando Cepeda and Willie McCovey. Thirty-two year-old Bob Shaw (1-3) started for the Giants. Eighth-place St. Louis countered with 22-year-old rookie Larry Jaster, who had a 2-2 record. Despite their slow start, the Cardinals were just two years removed from winning the World Series and still boasted a formidable lineup with Lou Brock, Curt Flood, and Tim McCarver among others. They were slumping, however, having lost their last three games, including a 15-2 shellacking the day before, thanks in part to Cepeda's grand slam.

Before 17,503 spectators, the game opened with what looked to be a repeat of the previous day's performance as the Giants plated three runs, the big blow Cepeda's two run-double. In the third, San Francisco struck again, this time when Jim Ray Hart launched his fifth home run of the young season. The two-run shot gave the Giants a 5-0 lead.

With the makings of another blowout at hand, St. Louis got back in the game in the bottom of the fourth on the strength of a walk and three hits, including two-run homers by McCarver and pinch-hitter Bob Skinner. An inning later Mike Shannon came to bat with the Cardinals now down by one run. Shannon, a St. Louis area native who played ball for the Catholic Youth Council as a 14-year-old, homered to tie the game, 5-5. It would prove to be the last home run hit by a Cardinal in the old ballpark.

Visions of a stirring comeback were dashed the next inning when McCovey hit a three-run homer off Jaster's replacement, Tracy Stallard. After Jesus Alou hit an RBI single in the eighth, Mays ended the Giants' scoring in the ninth with his eighth home run of the season to set the final margin at 10-5. Trivia reigned in the bottom of the ninth when Jerry Buchek became the last Cardinal baserunner, via a walk. (Charlie Smith made the last St. Louis hit—a single in the fifth.) Buchek was erased on a double-play ball hit by Alex Johnson, the last man to bat at Sportsman's Park. Ironically, the winning pitcher for the Giants was longtime Cardinal Lindy McDaniel, whose five innings of scoreless relief earned him his first win of the season.

While the game might have ended, the various festivities hadn't. Longtime groundskeeper Bill Stocksick, who had originally "placed" home plate in the field in 1909, dug it up and carried it to a helicopter that took it to Busch Stadium, where Stan Musial and Joan Nolan, "Miss Redbird of 1966," replanted it later that evening.

The remaining crowd sang "Auld Lang Syne" and with that, the ceremonies ended. Youngsters were allowed to run around on the playing field. One of Red Schoendienst's daughters went out to second and scooped up some earth where her All-Star father had played for years. A fan who had occupied the same seat in the ballpark for years dismantled it and took part of it home.

Scarcely had the ceremonies ended when the Cardinals announced a major trade. Not only were they getting a new ballpark but a new first baseman was on the way as well. The Giants' Orlando Cepeda was coming to the Redbirds in exchange for pitcher Ray Sadecki. San Francisco, which would rattle off four straight second-place finishes in the 1960s, needed a left-handed starting pitcher. Sadecki, a 20-game winner in 1964, had the potential to fill that need, but that potential went largely unrealized during his four-year, 32-39 stay with San Francisco. His 3-7 record with the Giants in 1966 proved a significant contribution to their razor-thin 1½-game loss of the pennant to the Los Angeles Dodgers.

The power-hitting Cepeda, whose chronic knee injuries limited him to just 33 games in 1965, became a cornerstone for St. Louis as the Cardinals built teams that captured consecutive pennants in 1967 and '68. Cepeda hit .325 and had a league-leading 111 RBIs for the 1967 world champions, on the way to being selected as the National League's Most Valuable Player.

Stands for the old ballpark would soon be torn down, the field remaining in place to be used for recreation by the Herbert Hoover Boys Club.[2]

Four days after the final game was played at Sportsman's Park, the Cardinals—with Cepeda in the lineup—hosted their first league game in the new, more spacious, more modern Busch Stadium, beating the Atlanta Braves in 12 innings, 4-3, before 46,048 fans, a then all-time attendance record for St. Louis.[3] Not only did the new facility represent a success for the Cardinals, but it also provided a major boost to revitalizing the Gateway City.

Closing the old ballpark was part of St. Louis's bicentennial efforts to refurbish the downtown area, a 31-block district that had not kept up with the times and was an increasing blight on the city's image. The city used eminent domain to tear up parking lots and raze timeworn hotels and warehouses, and dilapidated buildings.[4] Just a few blocks from the new ballpark the iconic Gateway Arch had been completed in late 1965; months later Busch Stadium was ready for its debut. Sportswriters trying to describe the new ballpark were taken by its vastness. A facility that could accommodate both professional baseball and football was encircled by wide concourses and ramps, upper and lower decks completely surrounding the playing field and a prominent state-of-the-art scoreboard. The seating capacity was at 49,275, well above Sportsman's Park's 30,500.[5]

Modern stadiums were replacing the old ballparks. Within the decade beginning in 1961, Griffith Stadium, the Polo Grounds, Sportsman's Park, Crosley Field, Connie Mack Stadium, and Forbes Field saw their last major-league games. They had become antiquated, less relevant in changing times. Many structures were in need of major restoration or repair. As was the case with Sportsman's Park, most of these edifices were located in run-down parts of the city that were inconvenient to get to. Demographics reflected a shift of populations from inner city to suburban living. In the years after World War II fans found that rather than using intra-urban bus or subway systems, they had to drive to ballgames. Therefore, parking, designed for a minimal number of drivers prior to the war, was woefully inadequate.

The new stadiums were certainly more fan-friendly with greater parking capacity, easier access and egress, modern restroom facilities and concession stands, as well as pyrotechnically enticing scoreboards, fan appreciation days, and numerous other marketing initiatives.

But with this something was lost. Ballparks lost their uniqueness. Various idiosyncrasies such as the Polo Grounds' oddly configured playing field or Crosley Field's left-field terrace were replaced by "cookie cutter" venues. As ballplayer Richie Hebner stated, "When I'm at bat, I can't tell whether I'm in Cincinnati, Philly, or St. Louis."[6]

Perhaps Cardinals pitcher Nelson Briles captured the change from old to new best when he observed. "[T]he transition from the ballpark — small, close to fans, electric atmosphere — to a big stadium, which was a compromise for everybody because you are removed from the field and you lose that intimacy and the closeness to the action, and you lost a good angle of view. And as a result fans suffered a bit."[7]

In 2006 the "new" Busch Stadium was replaced another "new" Busch Stadium.

SOURCES

In addition to the sources cited in the Notes, the author also accessed Retrosheet.org and Baseball-Reference.com.

NOTES

1. youtube.com/watch?v=ZArYa5lEIcQ.
2. Neal Russo, "Million Memories — They're All That's Left in Cards' Old Park," *The Sporting News*, May 21, 1966: 25.
3. Neal Russo, "Something New in St. Louis — Spacious Stadium," *The Sporting News*, May 28, 1966: 15.
4. Tim O'Neill, "A Look Back: In 1966 New Busch Stadium Was a Tub-Thumping Civic Cause," *St. Louis Post-Dispatch*, May 11, 2013: 13.
5. Philip J. Lowry, *Green Cathedrals: The Ultimate Celebration of Major League and Negro League Ballparks*, (New York: Walker & Company, 2006), 202, 204; Russo, "Something New in St. Louis."
6. Curt Smith, *Storied Stadiums: Baseball's History Through Its Ballparks* (New York: Carroll & Graf Publishers, 2001), 301.
7. Peter Golenbock, *The Spirit of St. Louis: A History of the St. Louis Cardinals and Browns* (New York: Avon Books, Inc. 2000), 477.

SPORTSMAN'S PARK III/ BUSCH STADIUM I BY THE NUMBERS

BY DAN FIELDS

Sportsman's Park III: 1909-1952

Busch Stadium I: 1953-1966

0

Runs scored in a 15-inning tie on April 20, 1912, between the St. Louis Browns and Chicago White Sox. George Baumgardner of the Browns allowed nine hits and eight walks in a complete-game effort. Jim Scott of the White Sox also went the distance, allowing six hits and two walks.

0

Fielding chances by first baseman Bud Clancy of the White Sox, who played the full nine innings of an April 27, 1930, game against the Browns.

0

Strikeouts in a 12-inning game between the Browns and White Sox on July 7, 1931.

0

Hits allowed by Bobo Newsom of the Browns through 9⅔ innings against the Boston Red Sox before Roy Johnson singled, on September 18, 1934. The Red Sox won 2-1 in 10 innings.

1ST

Career grand slam by Babe Ruth of the Red Sox on May 20, 1919, off Dave Davenport of the Browns. Ruth pitched a complete game as the Red Sox won 6-4.

1ST

AL player to hit three home runs in a game: Ken Williams of the Browns on April 22, 1922, against the White Sox. George Sisler was on base each time. In an August 7 game against the Washington Senators, he became the first ALer to hit two home runs in one inning (sixth inning).

1ST

Player to hit three home runs in a World Series game: Babe Ruth of the New York Yankees on October 6, 1926, against the St. Louis Cardinals. He repeated the feat in St. Louis during the 1928 World Series against the Cardinals (October 9).

1ST

Major-league pitch faced by Eddie Morgan of the Cardinals in which he hit a home run off Lon Warneke of the Chicago Cubs on April 14, 1936. It was also the only home run in his 39-game career.

1ST

Black player to hit a home run in AL history: Willard Brown of the Browns on August 13, 1947 (second game of doubleheader), off Hal Newhouser of the Detroit Tigers. It was the only home run of Brown's 21-game major-league career. Brown was renowned as a power hitter in the Negro Leagues and was elected to the National Baseball Hall of Fame in 2006.

1ST

Season-opening night game in major-league history, on April 18, 1950. The Cardinals beat the Pittsburgh Pirates 4-2.

1ST

Career home run by Hank Aaron of the Milwaukee Braves on April 23, 1954, off Vic Raschi of the Cardinals.

HOME OF THE BROWNS AND CARDINALS AT GRAND AND DODIER

1ST

Brothers to hit a home run in the same World Series game: Clete Boyer on the Yankees and Ken Boyer of the Cardinals, on October 15, 1964.

1

Hit allowed each by Bob Cain of the Browns and Bob Feller of the Cleveland Indians in complete-game outings on April 23, 1952. The Browns won, 1-0.

2

Consecutive one-hit shutouts thrown by Mort Cooper of the Cardinals on May 31, 1943, in the first game of a doubleheader against the Brooklyn Dodgers and on June 4 against the Philadelphia Phillies.

2

Shutouts in his first two major-league starts, by Fred Sanford of the Browns on September 15, 1946, in the first game of doubleheader against the Yankees and on September 22 in the first game of a doubleheader against the White Sox. In his other 96 career starts, Sanford had one shutout.

2:07

Combined time of the first game (1:12) and second game (0:55) of an 18-inning doubleheader between the Browns and the Yankees on September 26, 1926.

3

All-Star Games played at Sportsman's Park III/Busch Stadium I. On July 9, 1940, the NL won 4-0 in the first shutout in All-Star Game history. On July 13, 1948, the AL won 5-2 for its third consecutive victory and sixth in seven games. On July 9, 1957, the AL won 6-5; ballot stuffing by Cincinnati fans led to the election of Redlegs to seven of the eight starting field positions, but Commissioner Ford Frick appointed Hank Aaron and Willie Mays to start instead of Cincinnati's Gus Bell and Wally Post.

4

Hits by one-armed center fielder Pete Gray of the Browns in the first game of an August 19, 1945, doubleheader against the Red Sox. He also scored three runs in the 13-inning game. Gray lost his right arm at the age of 6, after a truck accident. In his only season in the majors, he batted .218 in 77 games, including 61 games as an outfielder (.959 fielding percentage).

4

Home runs allowed by Charlie Bicknell of the Phillies in the sixth inning of the first game of a June 6, 1948, doubleheader against the Cardinals.

4

Consecutive strikeouts recorded by Jim Davis of the Cubs during the sixth inning in the first game of a May 27, 1956, doubleheader against the Cardinals. When St. Louis pitcher Lindy McDaniel fanned for the third strikeout, the ball got away from Chicago catcher Hobie Landrith, and McDaniel reached first base safely. Don Blasingame then struck out looking.

4

Consecutive home shutouts thrown by Curt Simmons of the Cardinals between August 16 and September 13, 1963.

5

Nine-inning complete-game no-hitters thrown at Sportsman's Park III/Busch Stadium I: by Eddie Cicotte of the White Sox on April 4, 1917, against the Browns; Ernie Koob of the Browns on May 5, 1917, against the White Sox; Bob Groom of the Browns on the very next day, May 6, 1917, in the second game of a doubleheader against the White Sox; Jessie Haines of the Cardinals on July 17, 1924, against the Boston Braves; and Bobo Holloman of the Browns on May 6, 1953, against the Philadelphia Athletics (first major-league start and only complete game of his 10 career starts).

5

Home runs by Stan Musial of the Cardinals in a doubleheader on May 2, 1954, against the New York Giants.

6

Would-be base stealers thrown out by catcher Wally Schang of the Philadelphia Athletics on May 12, 1915, against the Browns.

6
Consecutive games in which Ken Williams of the Browns hit a home run, from July 28 through August 2, 1922.

6
RBIs by Gil McDougald of the Yankees in the ninth inning on May 3, 1951, against the Browns. He hit a two-run triple off Irv Medlinger and a grand slam off Bobby Herrera.

6.42
ERA of the Browns at home in 1936. Their ERA on the road that year was 6.07.

7
Doubles hit by the Boston Bees in the first inning of the first game of an August 25, 1936, doubleheader against the Cardinals. Boston scored 11 runs in the inning and won, 20-3.

7
Home runs by the Cardinals on May 7, 1940, against the Brooklyn Dodgers. Eddie Lake and Johnny Mize each homered in the third and eighth innings. The Cardinals won, 18-2.

8
Hits by Nap Lajoie of the Cleveland Naps in a season-ending doubleheader on October 9, 1910, against the Browns. In an apparent effort to help Lajoie catch Ty Cobb for the AL batting title, St. Louis manager Jack O'Connor ordered third baseman Red Corriden to play deep, which allowed Lajoie seven bunt hits. Lajoie finished the day with a .384 average and appeared to edge Cobb for the title, but AL President Ban Johnson said a recalculation showed that Cobb had won with a .385 average.

9
Runs scored by Mel Almada of the Washington Senators in a July 25, 1937, doubleheader against the Browns. He scored four runs as the Senators won 16-10 in the first game and five runs as the Senators won 15-5 in the second game.

9
Pitchers used by the Browns in the first game of an October 2, 1949, doubleheader against the White Sox. Each pitched for one inning. The White Sox won 4-3.

10
Consecutive games with an extra-base hit by Rogers Hornsby of the Cardinals from August 20 (first game of doubleheader) through August 26, 1924.

10
World Series played at Sportsman's Park III (1926, 1928, 1930, 1931, 1934, 1942, 1943, 1944, and 1946) and Busch Stadium I (1964). The Cardinals played in all 10 and won seven championships (including in 1944 against the Browns, in their only appearance in the World Series).

11
Players who hit for the cycle at Sportsman's Park III/Busch Stadium I: Tris Speaker of the Red Sox on June 9, 1912; George Sisler of the Browns on August 8, 1920 (second game of doubleheader); Chick Hafey of the Cardinals on August 21, 1930; Chuck Klein of the Phillies on May 26, 1933 (14 innings); Babe Herman of the Cubs on September 30, 1933; Sam Chapman of the Philadelphia Athletics on May 5, 1939; Johnny Mize of the Cardinals on July 13, 1940 (first game of doubleheader); George McQuinn of the Browns on July 19, 1941 (first game of doubleheader); Jackie Robinson of the Brooklyn Dodgers on August 29, 1948 (first game of doubleheader); Ken Boyer of the Cardinals on September 14, 1961 (11 innings; second game of doubleheader); and Willie Stargell of the Pirates on July 22, 1964.

12
Runs allowed by the Browns in the eighth inning on April 14, 1925, against the Indians. St. Louis committed five errors during the inning. Cleveland won 21-14.

12
Assists by Brooklyn Dodgers second baseman Jim Gilliam during a nine-inning game on July 21,

1956, against the Cardinals. He was the third second baseman (after Fred Dunlap in 1882 and John Montgomery Ward in 1892) to accomplish the feat.

14

Hits by Bill White of Cardinals on July 17 and 18, 1961, against the Cubs. On the 17th, he went 4-for-5 in each game of a doubleheader. On the 18th, he went 3-for-4 in each game of a doubleheader. During the two-day span, he raised his batting average from .289 to .317.

16

Total bases by Ty Cobb of the Tigers on May 5, 1925, against the Browns. He hit two singles, a double, and three home runs in six at-bats. In a rematch the next day, he had nine total bases (with a single and two home runs).

17-20-3

Record of the St. Louis Cardinals football team at Busch Stadium I from 1960 through 1965.

18

Consecutive home wins by the Cardinals from May 29 through July 18, 1935.

18

Innings in a game on June 20, 1952, in which the Browns and Washington Senators tied 5-5. There were no runs scored after the top half of the eighth inning.

18-59-1

Home record of the Browns in 1939 (.234 winning percentage). The Browns went 0-11 against the Yankees at home.

19-0

Score by which the Pirates beat the Cardinals on August 3, 1961. The Pirates scored all of their runs in the first six innings.

20

Age in years of Bob Feller of the Indians when he became the youngest player to win 20 games in a season, on September 8, 1939, against the Browns.

20

Consecutive home losses by the Browns from June 3 through July 7, 1953.

23

Doubles in the second game of a doubleheader on July 12, 1931, between the Cardinals (13 doubles) and Cubs (10 doubles). A crowd of more than 45,700 overflowed onto the field, and balls hit into the outfield area occupied by spectators were declared ground-rule doubles. The Cardinals won 17-13.

26-3

Score by which the Browns lost to the Indians in the second game of a doubleheader on August 12, 1948. Six players on the Indians had at least three hits; pitcher Gene Bearden had three singles and hit a three-run home run.

32

Consecutive home games with a base hit by Mel Almada of the Browns, from June 21 through August 11 (second game of doubleheader), 1938. During the streak, he batted .396 (55 for 139).

32 AND 7

Home runs hit at home and on the road, respectively, by Ken Williams of the Browns in 1922.

34

Years that both the Browns and the Cardinals played at Sportsman's Park III/Busch Stadium I (1920 through 1953).

39

Players who appeared in a nine-inning game on May 5, 1940, between the Brooklyn Dodgers (22 players) and Cardinals (17 players). Brooklyn won 9-6.

41ST

Consecutive games (all ballparks) in which George Sisler of the Browns had a base hit. He reached this mark on September 17, 1922, against the Yankees, breaking the AL record set by Ty Cobb in 1911.

43

Inches in height of Eddie Gaedel, who made a single plate appearance for the Browns on August 19,

1951, in the second game of a doubleheader against the Tigers. With surely the smallest strike zone in major-league history, he was walked by a laughing Bob Cain on four consecutive pitches before being lifted for a pinch-runner.

46

Age in years of Jimmy Austin of the Browns when he stole home in the second game of a September 26, 1926, doubleheader against the Yankees. It was also the age of Satchel Paige of the Browns when he threw a 12-inning shutout against the Tigers on August 6, 1952.

54-23

Home record of the Browns in 1922 and 1944 (.701 winning percentage).

57

Extra-base hits at home by Joe Medwick of the Cardinals in 1937, with 34 doubles, 5 triples, and 18 home runs. On the road, he had 40 extra-base hits.

58

Home runs in regular-season games by Babe Ruth at Sportsman's Park III, the most at the stadium by any player who was never on the Browns or Cardinals. He hit seven with the Red Sox and 51 with the Yankees.

60-17-1

Home record of the Cardinals in 1942 (.779 winning percentage).

97TH

Stolen base of the season by Maury Wills of the Los Angeles Dodgers on September 23, 1962, against the Cardinals. He broke Ty Cobb's modern-day single-season record of 96 steals set in 1915.

217-233-1

Record in regular-season games of Philadelphia Athletics manager Connie Mack at Sportsman's Park III from 1909 through 1950 (.482 winning percentage). He had a 3-4 record in Word Series games there (1930 and 1931).

241

Total bases at home by George Sisler of the Browns in 1920. He had 158 total bases on the road.

258

Losses in regular-season games as manager by Rogers Hornsby at Sportsman's Park III/Busch Stadium I, the most by any manager at the stadium. He had a record of 93-51-2 with the Cardinals (1925 and 1926), 4-3 with New York Giants (1927), 2-5 with Boston Braves (1928), 7-12 with the Cubs (1931 and 1932), 138-175-7 with the Browns (1933 through 1937 and 1952), and 4-12 with the Reds (1952 and 1953). In addition, he had a record of 1-2 with the Cardinals at Sportsman's Park III in the 1926 World Series.

.329

Batting average of the Browns at home in 1920, their highest single-season average at Sportsman's Park III/Busch Stadium I. The Browns hit .287 on the road that year.

.332

Batting average of the Cardinals at home in 1930, their highest single-season average at Sportsman's Park III/Busch Stadium I. The Cardinals hit .298 on the road that year.

346

Wins in regular-season games as manager by Billy Southworth at Sportsman's Park III, the most by any manager at the stadium. He had a record of 324-148-9 with the Cardinals (1929 and 1940 through 1945) and 22-33 with Boston Braves (1946 through 1951). In addition, he had a record of 5-5 in World Series games there (1942, 1943, and 1944 Cardinals).

400TH

Career home run by Stan Musial of the Cardinals, on May 7, 1959, off Don Elston of the Cubs. Musial became the first major-leaguer with 400 homers and 3,000 hits.

600TH

Career home run by Babe Ruth of the Yankees, on August 21, 1931, off George Blaeholder of the Browns.

HOME OF THE BROWNS AND CARDINALS AT GRAND AND DODIER

736

Extra-base hits by Stan Musial at Sportsman's Park III/Busch Stadium I, the most by any player at any one stadium.

.800

Career batting average of Ray Jansen, who played third base for the Browns on September 30, 1910, and went 4-for-5 in his only major-league game.

1,357TH

Career extra-base hit by Stan Musial of the Cardinals on May 8, 1963, against the Los Angeles Dodgers. He broke Babe Ruth's record, which had stood since 1935.

1,614-1,797-40

Regular-season record of the Browns at Sportsman's Park III/Busch Stadium I from 1909 through 1953 (.473 winning percentage). In their only World Series appearance (1944), the Browns won two games and lost four against the Cardinals (all games at Sportsman's Park III).

1,815 AND 1,815

Career hits at Sportsman's Park III/Busch Stadium I and hits on the road by Stan Musial.

1944

Year in which Sportsman's Park III allowed black fans to purchase tickets in the grandstand. Previously, blacks had been restricted to the bleachers and pavilion. It was the last major-league stadium to desegregate seating.

2,122-1,421-28

Regular-season record of the Cardinals at Sportsman's Park III/Busch Stadium I from July 1, 1920, through May 8, 1966 (.599 winning percentage). They had a record of 16-17 in World Series games there.

3,145

Total bases by Stan Musial at Sportsman's Park III/Busch Stadium I, the most by any player at any one ballpark.

3,174

Attendance at the last Browns game at Sportsman's Park III/Busch Stadium I, on September 27, 1953. The Browns fell to the White Sox 2-1 as they lost their 100th game of the season.

5,810

Days between home runs at Sportsman's Park III by White Sox shortstop Luke Appling from June 4, 1933 (second game of doubleheader), to May 1, 1949 (first game of doubleheader).

17,503

Attendance at the last major-league game at Sportsman's Park III/Busch Stadium I, on May 8, 1966, between the Cardinals and San Francisco Giants. Willie Mays hit the last home run at the ballpark. The Giants won 10-5.

80,922

Home attendance of the Browns for the entire 1935 season, an average of 1,065 per game.

712,918

Home attendance of the Browns in 1922 (an average of 9,259 per game), highest in a single season for the team at Sportsman's Park III/Busch Stadium I.

1,430,676

Home attendance of the Cardinals in 1949 (an average of 18,110 per game), highest in a single season for the team at Sportsman's Park III/Busch Stadium I.

CAREER LEADERS AT SPORTSMAN'S PARK III/BUSCH STADIUM I

Batting

Games

1524	Stan Musial
949	Red Schoendienst
917	Enos Slaughter
844	George Sisler
836	Ken Boyer

Plate appearances

6332	Stan Musial
3885	Red Schoendienst
3835	Enos Slaughter
3673	George Sisler
3507	Ken Boyer

At-bats

5402	Stan Musial
3545	Red Schoendienst
3366	George Sisler
3343	Enos Slaughter
3148	Ken Boyer

Runs

999	Stan Musial
618	George Sisler
568	Red Schoendienst
559	Enos Slaughter
538	Harlond Clift

Hits

1815	Stan Musial
1229	George Sisler
1056	Enos Slaughter
1033	Red Schoendienst
968	Jim Bottomley

Doubles

394	Stan Musial
244	Joe Medwick
221	Jim Bottomley
217	Red Schoendienst
197	Frankie Frisch

Triples

90	Stan Musial
90	George Sisler
67	Enos Slaughter
54	Jim Bottomley
39	Baby Doll Jacobson

Home runs

252	Stan Musial
138	Ken Williams
130	Ken Boyer
104	Jim Bottomley
102	Rogers Hornsby

RBIs

1056	Stan Musial
630	Enos Slaughter
602	Jim Bottomley
564	Ken Boyer
516	George Sisler

Walks

857	Stan Musial
525	Harlond Clift
441	Enos Slaughter
310	Jim Bottomley
308	Ken Boyer

Intentional walks

159	Stan Musial
45	Ken Boyer
43	Enos Slaughter
25	Del Rice
23	Joe Cunningham

HOME OF THE BROWNS AND CARDINALS AT GRAND AND DODIER

Strikeouts

398	Ken Boyer
338	Stan Musial
306	Bill White
290	Harlond Clift
265	Marty Marion

Hit by pitch

27	Solly Hemus
25	Ray Blades
25	Stan Musial
23	Enos Slaughter
21	Curt Flood

Batting average (min. 1,400 at-bats)

.392	Rogers Hornsby
.365	George Sisler
.351	Joe Medwick
.345	Johnny Mize
.342	Chick Hafey

On-base percentage (min. 1,400 at-bats)

.468	Rogers Hornsby
.427	Stan Musial
.427	Johnny Mize
.422	Ken Williams
.404	George Sisler

Slugging percentage (min. 1,400 at-bats)

.660	Rogers Hornsby
.628	Ken Williams
.616	Johnny Mize
.605	Chick Hafey
.582	Stan Musial

OPS (min. 1,400 at-bats)

1.127	Rogers Hornsby
1.050	Ken Williams
1.043	Johnny Mize
1.009	Stan Musial
1.004	Chick Hafey

Stolen bases

175	George Sisler
103	Frankie Frisch
96	Burt Shotton
79	Del Pratt
77	Ken Williams

Pitching

ERA (min. 500 innings)

2.27	Earl Hamilton
2.52	Carl Weilman
2.61	Mort Cooper
2.75	Max Lanier
2.97	Harry Brecheen

Wins

105	Jesse Haines
72	Bill Sherdel
71	Harry Brecheen
71	Dizzy Dean
69	Urban Shocker

Losses

67	Jesse Haines
58	Bill Sherdel
54	George Blaeholder
43	Jack Kramer
43	Urban Shocker

Winning percentage (min. 40 wins)

.747	Mort Cooper
.702	Ernie Broglio
.682	Al Brazle
.667	Bill Hallahan
.655	Gerry Staley

SPORTSMAN'S PARK IN ST. LOUIS

Games pitched

269	Jesse Haines
225	Al Brazle
198	Bill Sherdel
183	Lindy McDaniel
180	Larry Jackson

Games started

186	Jesse Haines
119	Harry Brecheen
116	Larry Jackson
114	Bill Sherdel
113	Curt Simmons

Complete games

99	Jesse Haines
70	Dizzy Dean
69	Bill Sherdel
68	Urban Shocker
61	Harry Brecheen

Shutouts

15	Urban Shocker
13	Harry Brecheen
13	Harvey Haddix
12	Mort Cooper
12	Max Lanier

Saves

43	Lindy McDaniel
23	Al Brazle
19	George Caster
14	Ted Wilks
13	Satchel Paige

Innings pitched

1555⅓	Jesse Haines
1100⅓	Bill Sherdel
956⅓	Harry Brecheen
948	Urban Shocker
924	Dizzy Dean

Walks

407	Jesse Haines
342	Dixie Davis
342	Bobo Newsom
303	Bill Hallahan
302	Bump Hadley
302	Elam Vangilder

Intentional walks

36	Al Brazle
28	Murry Dickson
28	Howie Pollet
23	Larry Jackson
22	Curt Simmons

Strikeouts

638	Bob Gibson
595	Dizzy Dean
538	Larry Jackson
516	Jesse Haines
482	Harry Brecheen

Home runs allowed

91	George Blaeholder
88	Jesse Haines
82	Larry Jackson
75	Bob Gibson
72	Lon Warneke

Hit by pitch

28	Gerry Staley
25	Allen Sothoron
24	Larry Jackson
23	Bob Gibson
22	Jesse Haines

Wild pitches

37	Bill Hallahan
26	Lindy McDaniel
26	Ray Sadecki
25	Jesse Haines
22	Bob Gibson

SINGLE-SEASON LEADERS AT SPORTSMAN'S PARK III/ BUSCH STADIUM I

Batting

Games: 81 by Del Pratt, Browns, 1914; Johnny Mize, Cardinals, 1938; Stan Musial, Cardinals, 1943; Bill White, Cardinals, 1963; Ken Boyer, Cardinals, 1963 and 1964; Curt Flood, Cardinals, 1964

Plate appearances: 374 by Jimmy Brown, Cardinals, 1939

At-bats: 345 by Jimmy Brown, Cardinals, 1939

Runs: 90 by George Sisler, Browns, 1920

Hits: 150 by George Sisler, Browns, 1920

Doubles: 34 by Jack Burns, Browns, 1933; Joe Medwick, Cardinals, 1936 and 1937

Triples: 13 by George Sisler, Browns, 1922; Heinie Manush, Browns, 1928

Home runs: 32 by Ken Williams, Browns, 1922

RBIs: 102 by Ken Williams, Browns, 1922

Walks: 67 by Harlond Clift, Browns, 1938

Strikeouts: 57 by Bruce Campbell, Browns, 1932

Hit by pitch: 10 by Solly Hemus, Cardinals, 1952

Batting average: .478 by Rogers Hornsby, Cardinals, 1925

On-base percentage: .565 by Rogers Hornsby, Cardinals, 1925

Slugging percentage: .902 by Rogers Hornsby, Cardinals, 1925

OPS: 1.467 by Rogers Hornsby, Cardinals, 1925

Stolen bases: 32 by Lou Brock, Cardinals, 1965

Pitching

ERA: 1.04 by Max Lanier, Cardinals, 1943

Wins: 15 by Dizzy Dean, Cardinals, 1934

Losses: 11 by Allen Sothoron, Browns, 1917; Milt Gaston, Browns, 1926; George Blaeholder, Browns, 1928 and 1933; Sam Gray, Browns, 1931; Fred Sanford, Browns, 1948

Games pitched: 36 by Lindy McDaniel, Cardinals, 1960

Games started: 23 by Bobo Newsom, Browns, 1938

Complete games: 17 by Bobo Newsom, Browns, 1938

Shutouts: 5 by Harvey Haddix, Cardinals, 1953

Saves: 17 by Lindy McDaniel, Cardinals, 1960

Innings pitched: 185⅓ by Bobo Newsom, Browns, 1938

Walks: 109 by Bobo Newsom, Browns, 1938

Strikeouts: 135 by Bobo Newsom, Browns, 1938; Bob Gibson, Cardinals, 1964 and 1965

Home runs allowed: 24 by Bob Gibson, Cardinals, 1965

Hit by pitch: 12 by Gerry Staley, Cardinals, 1953

Wild pitches: 9 by Bill Hallahan, Cardinals, 1935

SINGLE-GAME LEADERS AT SPORTSMAN'S PARK III/ BUSCH STADIUM I

* denotes extra-inning game

Batting

Runs: 5 by Bill Wambsganss, Indians, 9/10/1921 (second game of doubleheader); George Watkins, Cardinals, 5/7/1930; Rabbit Maranville, Boston Braves, 6/10/1931; Ski Melillo, Browns, 6/22/1931; Bob Johnson, Philadelphia Athletics, 8/25/1933; Ripper Collins, Cardinals, 7/6/1934; John Stone, Washington Senators, 6/16/1935 (first game of doubleheader); Roy Hughes, Indians, 7/2/1936 (first game of doubleheader); Fabian Gaffke, Red Sox, 7/14/1937; Mel Almada, Washington Senators, 7/25/1937 (second game of doubleheader); Jimmie Foxx, Red Sox, 6/9/1939 (second game of doubleheader); Barney McCosky, Philadelphia Athletics, 7/17/1947; Pee Wee Reese,

SPORTSMAN'S PARK IN ST. LOUIS

Brooklyn Dodgers, 5/21/1949; Hank Edwards, Cubs, 6/30/1949; Solly Hemus, Cardinals, 5/20/1953; Al Dark, New York Giants, 6/3/1954

Hits: 6 by Ty Cobb, Tigers, 5/5/1925; Sam West, Browns, 4/13/1933*; Terry Moore, Cardinals, 9/5/1935; Bruce Campbell, Indians, 7/2/1936 (first game of doubleheader); Stan Spence, Washington Senators, 6/1/1944; Jim Piersall, Red Sox, 6/10/1953 (first game of doubleheader)

Doubles: 4 by Paul Waner, Pirates, 5/20/1932; Joe Medwick, Cardinals, 8/4/1937

Triples: 3 by Charlie Hollocher, Cubs, 8/13/1922; Baby Doll Jacobson, Browns, 9/9/1922

Home runs: 3 by Ken Williams, Browns, 4/22/1922; Ty Cobb, Tigers, 5/5/1925; Mickey Cochrane, Philadelphia Athletics, 5/21/1925; Jack Fournier, Brooklyn Robins, 7/13/1926; Babe Ruth, Yankees, 10/6/1926 (World Series); Babe Ruth, Yankees, 10/9/1928 (World Series); Goose Goslin, Browns, 6/23/1932; Joe DiMaggio, Yankees, 6/13/1937 (second game of doubleheader)*; Hal Trosky, Indians, 7/5/1937 (first game of doubleheader); Johnny Mize, Cardinals, 7/13/1938; Johnny Mize, Cardinals, 7/20/1938 (second game of doubleheader); Johnny Mize, Cardinals, 9/8/1940 (first game of doubleheader); Stan Musial, Cardinals, 5/2/1954 (first game of doubleheader); Hank Thompson, New York Giants, 6/3/1954; Ted Kluszewski, Reds, 7/1/1956 (first game of doubleheader)*; Willie Mays, San Francisco Giants, 6/2/1963; Jim Hickman, New York Mets, 9/3/1965

RBIs: 10 by Rudy York, Red Sox, 7/27/1946

Walks: 6 by Jimmie Foxx, Red Sox, 6/16/1938

Intentional walks: 3 by Ted Williams, Red Sox, 5/18/1946; Dixie Walker, Brooklyn Dodgers, 7/14/1946 (second game of doubleheader)*; Alex Grammas, Cardinals, 4/17/1955 (first game of doubleheader)

Strikeouts: 5 by Dick Allen, Phillies, 6/28/1964 (first game of doubleheader)

Stolen bases: 4 by Home Run Baker, Yankees, 5/17/1917; Wally Moon, Cardinals, 5/25/1954; Willie Mays, New York Giants, 5/6/1956 (second game of doubleheader)

Pitching

Innings pitched: 17 by Roy Parmelee, Cardinals, 4/29/1936*

Runs allowed: 16 by Johnny Stuart, Cardinals, 6/22/1925

Hits allowed: 20 by Jesse Haines, Cardinals, 6/21/1930

Walks: 16 by Tommy Byrne, Browns, 8/22/1951*

Intentional walks: 5 by Robin Roberts, Phillies, 9/10/1957*

Strikeouts: 17 by Dizzy Dean, Cardinals, 7/30/1933 (first game of doubleheader)

Home runs allowed: 6 by Tommy Thomas, Browns, 6/27/1936

Hit by pitch: 3 by Dwight Stone, Browns, 5/22/1913; Rube Foster, Red Sox, 9/24/1914; Grover Lowdermilk, Browns, 4/19/1915; Howard Ehmke, Tigers, 4/25/1922; Hub Pruett, Boston Braves, 8/22/1932 (second game of doubleheader); Hugh Casey, Brooklyn Dodgers, 5/7/1940; Brooks Lawrence, Cardinals, 8/11/1954; Harvey Haddix, Cardinals, 5/13/1955*; Bob Purkey, Cardinals, 4/15/1965

Wild pitches: 3 by Ray Keating, Yankees, 7/15/1913; Elmer Myers, Philadelphia Athletics, 9/22/1916; Joe Engel, Washington Senators, 8/6/1920; George Boehler, Brooklyn Robins, 7/15/1926; Bill Hallahan, Cardinals, 5/11/1932*; Johnny Welch, Red Sox, 6/19/1935 (second game of doubleheader); Bill Hallahan, Cardinals, 8/7/1935; Lefty Mills, Browns, 9/29/1937; Paul Calvert, Washington Senators, 7/17/1949 (second game of doubleheader); Cloyd Boyer, Cardinals, 8/27/1950; Karl Drews, Phillies, 9/16/1951; Lindy McDaniel, Cardinals, 9/14/1961 (first game of doubleheader); Ernie Broglio, Cardinals, 5/19/1964; Al Jackson, New York Mets, 5/21/1965; Gerry Arrigo, Reds, 6/8/1965; Jim Maloney, Reds, 8/13/1965; Ray Sadecki, Cardinals, 8/14/1965

Balks: 3 by Adrian Zabala, New York Giants, 8/6/1949; Bob Hall, Boston Braves, 6/9/1950

SOURCES

Nemec, David, ed. *The Baseball Chronicle: Year-by-Year History of Major League Baseball* (Lincolnwood, Illinois: Publications International, 2003).

Society for American Baseball Research. *The SABR Baseball List and Record Book* (New York: Scribner, 2007).

Solomon, Burt. *The Baseball Timeline* (New York: DK Publishing, 2001).

Sugar, Bert Randolph, ed. *The Baseball Maniac's Almanac* (fourth edition) (New York: Skyhorse Publishing, 2016).

baseball-almanac.com

baseball-reference.com

nationalpastime.com

retrosheet.org/boxesetc/S/PK_STL07.htm

thisgreatgame.com

SPORTSMAN'S PARK: THE SABR TEAM OF PLAYERS

MARK ARMOUR writes about a variety of baseball subjects from his home in Oregon.

JOHN BAUER resides with his wife and two children in Parkville, Missouri, just outside of Kansas City. By day, he is an attorney specializing in insurance regulatory law and corporate law. By night, he spends many spring and summer evenings cheering for the San Francisco Giants and many fall and winter evenings reading history. He is a past and ongoing contributor to other SABR projects.

PHILLIP BOLDA was born in Milwaukee and grew up within walking distance of Milwaukee County Stadium. A graduate of Ripon College, he spent his career on campuses as a university fundraiser and now lives in Tempe, Arizona. He became a member of SABR in 1979 and has contributed to several book projects. He currently serves as the chair of the Fund Raising and Development Committee.

FREDERICK C. (RICK) BUSH is a college English instructor in the Houston area, where he resides with his wife, Michelle, and their three sons, Michael, Andrew, and Daniel. A diehard Houston Astros fan, he had high hopes for their 2017 squad, though history instilled in him the fear that the franchise's World Series drought would continue. Rick co-edited the SABR volume titled *Bittersweet Goodbye: The Black Barons, the Grays, and the 1948 Negro League World Series*. He is currently working on a biography of former Negro League baseball player and Texas high-school football coaching legend Andrew "Pat" Patterson.

Surrounded by Cubs fans in the northern suburbs of Chicago, lifelong White Sox fan **KEN CARRANO** works as a chief financial officer for a large landscaping firm and as a soccer referee. Ken and his Brewers fan wife, Ann, share two children, two golden retrievers, and mutual disdain for the blue side of Chicago.

ALAN COHEN has been in SABR since 2011, and serves as vice president/treasurer of the Connecticut Smoky Joe Wood Chapter. He has written more than 30 biographies for SABR's BioProject, and has contributed to over 20 SABR publications. He is expanding his research into the Hearst Classic (1946-1965), an annual youth All-Star game that launched the careers of 88 major leaguers. He lives in Connecticut with his wife, Frances, a cat (Morty), and two dogs (Sam and Sheba).

RICHARD CUICCHI joined SABR in 1983 and is an active member of the Schott-Pelican Chapter. Since his retirement as an information technology executive, Richard authored *Family Ties: A Comprehensive Collection of Facts and Trivia about Baseball's Relatives*. He has contributed to numerous SABR BioProject and Games publications. He does freelance writing and blogging about a variety of baseball topics on his website TheTenthInning.com. Richard lives in New Orleans with his wife, Mary.

GREG ERION is retired from the railroad industry and currently teaches history part-time at Skyline Community College in San Bruno, California. He has written several biographies and game articles for SABR. Greg is one of the leaders of SABR's Baseball Games Project. He and his wife, Barbara, live in South San Francisco, California.

DOUG FELDMANN is a professor in the College of Education at Northern Kentucky University and a former part-time scout for the San Diego Padres, Seattle Mariners, and Cincinnati Reds. He is the author of 12 books, six of which are on the St. Louis

Cardinals. More information on his books is available at dougfeldmannbooks.com.

Fresh off his first book, *Motor City Champs: Mickey Cochrane and the 1934-35 Detroit Tigers*, **SCOTT FERKOVICH** is scrambling for what to write about next. He has been a card-carrying SABR member for longer than he cares to admit. Scott lives a life of quiet rectitude in his home near Detroit. He could use a few more followers on Twitter @Scott_Ferkovich

DAN FIELDS is a senior manuscript editor at the *New England Journal of Medicine*. He loves baseball trivia, and he enjoys attending Boston Red Sox and Pawtucket Red Sox games with his teenage son. Dan lives in Framingham, Massachusetts, and can be reached at dfields820@gmail.com.

JEFF FINDLEY is a native of Eastern Iowa, where he did the logical thing growing up in the heart of the Cubs/Cardinals rivalry—he embraced the 1969 Orioles and became a lifelong fan. An informational security professional for a large insurance company in central Illinois, he compiles a daily sports "Pages Past" column for his local newspaper

JAMES FORR is past winner of the McFarland-SABR Baseball Research Award and the co-author (along with David Proctor) of *Pie Traynor: A Baseball Biography*, which was a finalist for the 2010 CASEY Award. He lives in Columbia, Missouri.

GORDON J. GATTIE serves as a human-systems integration engineer for the US Navy. His baseball research interests involve ballparks, historical records, and statistical analysis. A SABR member since 1998, Gordon earned his Ph.D. from SUNY Buffalo, where he used baseball to investigate judgment/decision-making performance in complex dynamic environments. Ever the optimist, he supports the Cleveland Indians and nearby Washington Nationals. Lisa, his lovely bride, who also enjoys baseball, challenges him by supporting the Yankees. Gordon has contributed to multiple SABR publications.

CHIP GREENE, the grandson of former Brooklyn Dodgers pitcher Nelson Greene, joined SABR in 2006. A frequent contributor to SABR's BioProject, Chip edited the SABR book *Mustaches and Mayhem: Charlie O's Three-Time Champions: The 1972-74 Oakland A's*. Chip and his wife, Elaine, live in Waynesboro, Pennsylvania.

TOM HAWTHORN is a journalist, author, and bookseller who lives in Victoria, British Columbia. His latest book is *The Year Canadians Lost Their Minds and Found Their Country: The Centennial of 1967* (Douglas and McIntyre). He has also contributed to more than a dozen SABR titles. He is a member of the selection committee for two sports halls of fame in his native Canada.

MIKE HUBER is a professor of mathematics and former dean of academic life at Muhlenberg College in Allentown, Pennsylvania. A SABR member for more than 20 years, he enjoys researching rare events in baseball, to include games where a player has hit for the cycle or pitched a no-hitter. He began rooting for the Baltimore Orioles a decade after their move from St. Louis.

DWAYNE ISRIG lives in Missouri and enjoys researching the hidden history of the Negro Leagues.

NORM KING is a retired civil servant from Ottawa, Ontario. Since joining SABR in 2010, he has written numerous biographies and game summaries, focusing primarily on the Montreal Expos. He was the lead writer and senior editor of *Au jeu/Play Ball: The 50 Greatest Games in the History of the Montreal Expos*, which was SABR's top-selling book of 2016.

RUSS LAKE lives in Champaign, Illinois, and is a retired college professor. The 1964 St. Louis Cardinals remain his favorite team, and he was distressed to see Sportsman's Park (aka Busch Stadium I) being demolished not long after he attended the last game there, on May 8, 1966. His wife, Carol, deserves an MVP award for watching all of a 13-inning ballgame in Cincinnati with Russ in 1971—during their honeymoon. In 1994, he was an editor for David Halberstam's baseball book *October 1964*.

LEN LEVIN, a lifelong Red Sox fan, wishes he had seen some of the games whose stories he edited here. A longtime newspaper editor in New England and adjunct professor of journalism, he now edits the decisions of the Rhode Island Supreme Court.

KELLEN NIELSON was born in Price, Utah, and was raised in Blanding, Utah, where he now resides with his wife, Lydia, and three children, Madison, Austin, and Charlotte. He graduated from Utah State University with a BA in history. He is a lifelong fan of the Atlanta Braves and the game of baseball.

BILL NOWLIN has been on the SABR board of directors since 2004 (a good year for Red Sox fans) and has helped shepherd many a SABR book to completion. He wrote this brief bio from the country of Moldova, sitting in the airport, "watching" the Sox take a 3-0 lead over the Yankees.

DENNIS PAJOT was born in Milwaukee, raised and schooled in Milwaukee, worked for and retired from the City of Milwaukee, still lives in Milwaukee. Happily or sadly, that says it all about Dennis.

RYAN PARKER is a lifelong Cardinals fan. At age 4 he started listening to radio broadcasts of their games sitting next to his grandpa on his back porch in South St. Louis. From there they could see the lights of the stadium and hear the roar of the crowd. He now sits next to his own five-year-old son as they watch Cardinals games on a computer tablet. He learned of SABR only a few years ago but quickly became a member as he knew it was the perfect marriage of his love of both history and baseball. He still resides in the St. Louis area where he works as a teacher.

J.G. PRESTON is a writer and communications consultant in Santa Fe, New Mexico. He has contributed to several SABR publications and writes about baseball at prestonjg.wordpress.com/.

RICHARD RIIS hails from South Setauket, New York, where he is a professional writer, researcher, and genealogist, and an avid baseball historian. He has contributed to SABR books on the Yankees, Tigers, Pirates, Astros, Brewers, Braves, and 19th century Red Stockings, and is currently collaborating on the memoirs of a well-known television and film actress.

PAUL ROGERS is a law professor at Southern Methodist University, where he served as dean for nine years. When not writing about antitrust law or legal history, he has co-authored four baseball books, including two with his boyhood hero Robin Roberts, *The Whiz Kids and the 1950 Pennant* and *Throwing Hard Easy — Reflections on a Life in Baseball*. He has also collaborated on baseball memoirs with Eddie Robinson and Bill Werber and co-edited the SABR book *The Team That Time Won't Forget: The 1951 New York Giants*. He is president of the Ernie Banks—Bobby Bragan DFW SABR Chapter, has authored about 30 biographies for the SABR BioProject, and previously served as a judge for the Casey Award.

JOE SCHUSTER is the author of the novel *The Might Have Been*, a finalist for the CASEY Award as the Best Baseball Book of 2012, as well as *One Season in the Sun*, a short book about ballplayers whose major-league careers lasted a few weeks or less, which he wrote for Gemma Open Door's adult literacy project. A professor at Webster University in St. Louis, he is a frequent contributor to the St. Louis Cardinals' *Gameday* magazine, the team's official publication. He is married and the father of five rabid Redbird fans.

LYLE SPATZ has written and edited several books on baseball history and has edited two record books. He has been a member of SABR since 1973.

STEVE STEINBERG is a historian of early twentieth-century baseball, with a focus on St. Louis and New York baseball. He has co-authored two award-winning books with Lyle Spatz: *1921: The Yankees, the Giants, and the Battle for Baseball Supremacy in New York* and *The Colonel and Hug: The Partnership that Transformed the New York Yankees*. His latest book, *Urban Shocker: Silent Hero of Baseball's Golden Age*, was published by University of Nebraska Press in 2017.

MARK S. STERNMAN works in Boston and, though a diehard fan of the New York Yankees, holds a partial season-ticket plan for the Boston Red Sox. He enjoys writing game recaps for World Series games involving the Yanks and has done so for several SABR books. He has visited St. Louis just once, but has many fond memories of the trip involving the Arch, baseball, custard, pizza, and the zoo.

CECILIA TAN became Publications Director for SABR in 2011 and has written for *Baseball Prospectus*, *Yankee Magazine*, *Gotham Baseball*, and many other publications.

DOUG WALDEN is a physician and medical educator in St. Louis, a contributor to the SABR BioProject, and a longtime fan of the Cardinals and White Sox. He attended Northwestern University, and on nice spring evenings was known to defer his studies to head to old Comiskey Park to watch the White Sox. He counts the 1964, 1967, and 1982 Cardinals and 1977 White Sox seasons among his favorite baseball memories.

JOSEPH WANCHO lives in Westlake, Ohio. He has been a SABR member since 2005. He serves as chair for the Minor League Research Committee. His major pursuits in life are Nicaraguan cigars and Kentucky bourbon.

JOHN J. WATKINS, a retired law professor, is the author of three books and more than 40 scholarly articles. A lifelong St. Louis Cardinals fan, he lives with his wife, Joan, in Fort Worth, Texas. His great-uncle, George "Watty" Watkins, played right field for the Cardinals from 1930 through 1933, hitting .309 over that span.

Upon realizing he couldn't hit a curveball, **MIKE WHITEMAN** took to reading and researching about the national pastime. This is the third SABR project he has contributed to. He enjoys sitting on his porch in Lancaster, Pennsylvania, in the summertime listening to ballgames on the radio. His home team includes his wife, Nichole, and two daughters.

JIM WOHLENHAUS has been a baseball fan since the Golden Days. Having grown up in Denver, he found his following confined to the Game of the Week, *The Sporting News,* and the local paper. However, in his career as a faceless, humorless government bureaucrat, he was assigned to locales that had teams and he became a fan of those teams, while remaining an overall generalist baseball fan. Jim's biggest baseball claim to fame is being batboy for the Denver Bears Triple-A team in 1961.

A lifelong Pirates fan, **GREGORY H. WOLF** was born in Pittsburgh, but now resides in the Chicagoland area with his wife, Margaret, and daughter, Gabriela. A professor of German studies and holder of the Dennis and Jean Bauman Endowed Chair in the Humanities at North Central College in Naperville, Illinois, he has edited seven books for SABR. He is currently working on projects about Crosley Field in Cincinnati, Wrigley Field and Comiskey Park in Chicago, and the 1982 Milwaukee Brewers. As of January 2017, he serves as co-director of SABR's BioProject, which you can follow on Facebook and Twitter.

BRIAN P. WOOD (Woodie) is a longtime San Francisco Giants fan and resides in Pacific Grove, California, with his wife, Terrise. They have three sons, Daniel, Jack, and Nathan, and a dog, Bochy. A retired US Navy commander and F-14 Tomcat flight officer, Woodie is a research associate on the faculty at the Naval Postgraduate School in Monterey, California, specializing in field experimentation of new technologies before they are sent to military forces.

SABR BioProject Team Books

In 2002, the Society for American Baseball Research launched an effort to write and publish biographies of every player, manager, and individual who has made a contribution to baseball. Over the past decade, the BioProject Committee has produced over 6,000 biographical articles. Many have been part of efforts to create theme- or team-oriented books, spearheaded by chapters or other committees of SABR.

THE 1986 BOSTON RED SOX:
THERE WAS MORE THAN GAME SIX
One of a two-book series on the rivals that met in the 1986 World Series, the Boston Red Sox and the New York Mets, including biographies of every player, coach, broadcaster, and other important figures in the top organizations in baseball that year. .
Edited by Leslie Heaphy and Bill Nowlin
$19.95 paperback (ISBN 978-1-943816-19-4)
$9.99 ebook (ISBN 978-1-943816-18-7)
8.5"X11", 420 pages, over 200 photos

THE 1986 NEW YORK METS:
THERE WAS MORE THAN GAME SIX
The other book in the "rivalry" set from the 1986 World Series. This book re-tells the story of that year's classic World Series and this is the story of each of the players, coaches, managers, and broadcasters, their lives in baseball and the way the 1986 season fit into their lives.
Edited by Leslie Heaphy and Bill Nowlin
$19.95 paperback (ISBN 978-1-943816-13-2)
$9.99 ebook (ISBN 978-1-943816-12-5)
8.5"X11", 392 pages, over 100 photos

SCANDAL ON THE SOUTH SIDE:
THE 1919 CHICAGO WHITE SOX
The Black Sox Scandal isn't the only story worth telling about the 1919 Chicago White Sox. The team roster included three future Hall of Famers, a 20-year-old spitballer who would win 300 games in the minors, and even a batboy who later became a celebrity with the "Murderers' Row" New York Yankees. All of their stories are included in Scandal on the South Side with a timeline of the 1919 season.
Edited by Jacob Pomrenke
$19.95 paperback (ISBN 978-1-933599-95-3)
$9.99 ebook (ISBN 978-1-933599-94-6)
8.5"x11", 324 pages, 55 historic photos

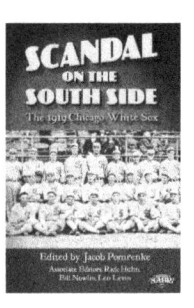

WINNING ON THE NORTH SIDE
THE 1929 CHICAGO CUBS
Celebrate the 1929 Chicago Cubs, one of the most exciting teams in baseball history. Future Hall of Famers Hack Wilson, '29 NL MVP Rogers Hornsby, and Kiki Cuyler, along with Riggs Stephenson formed one of the most potent quartets in baseball history. The magical season came to an ignominious end in the World Series and helped craft the future "lovable loser" image of the team.
Edited by Gregory H. Wolf
$19.95 paperback (ISBN 978-1-933599-89-2)
$9.99 ebook (ISBN 978-1-933599-88-5)
8.5"x11", 314 pages, 59 photos

DETROIT THE UNCONQUERABLE:
THE 1935 WORLD CHAMPION TIGERS
Biographies of every player, coach, and broadcaster involved with the 1935 World Champion Detroit Tigers baseball team, written by members of the Society for American Baseball Research. Also includes a season in review and other articles about the 1935 team. Hank Greenberg, Mickey Cochrane, Charlie Gehringer, Schoolboy Rowe, and more.
Edited by Scott Ferkovich
$19.95 paperback (ISBN 9978-1-933599-78-6)
$9.99 ebook (ISBN 978-1-933599-79-3)
8.5"X11", 230 pages, 52 photos

THE TEAM THAT TIME WON'T FORGET:
THE 1951 NEW YORK GIANTS
Because of Bobby Thomson's dramatic "Shot Heard 'Round the World" in the bottom of the ninth of the decisive playoff game against the Brooklyn Dodgers, the team will forever be in baseball public's consciousness. Includes a foreword by Giants outfielder Monte Irvin.
Edited by Bill Nowlin and C. Paul Rogers III
$19.95 paperback (ISBN 978-1-933599-99-1)
$9.99 ebook (ISBN 978-1-933599-98-4)
8.5"X11", 282 pages, 47 photos

A PENNANT FOR THE TWIN CITIES:
THE 1965 MINNESOTA TWINS
This volume celebrates the 1965 Minnesota Twins, who captured the American League pennant in just their fifth season in the Twin Cities. Led by an All-Star cast, from Harmon Killebrew, Tony Oliva, Zoilo Versalles, and Mudcat Grant to Bob Allison, Jim Kaat, Earl Battey, and Jim Perry, the Twins won 102 games, but bowed to the Los Angeles Dodgers and Sandy Koufax in Game Seven
Edited by Gregory H. Wolf
$19.95 paperback (ISBN 978-1-943816-09-5)
$9.99 ebook (ISBN 978-1-943816-08-8)
8.5"X11", 405 pages, over 80 photos

MUSTACHES AND MAYHEM: CHARLIE O'S THREE TIME CHAMPIONS:
THE OAKLAND ATHLETICS: 1972-74
The Oakland Athletics captured major league baseball's crown each year from 1972 through 1974. Led by future Hall of Famers Reggie Jackson, Catfish Hunter and Rollie Fingers, the Athletics were a largely homegrown group who came of age together. Biographies of every player, coach, manager, and broadcaster (and mascot) from 1972 through 1974 are included, along with season recaps.
Edited by Chip Greene
$29.95 paperback (ISBN 978-1-943816-07-1)
$9.99 ebook (ISBN 978-1-943816-06-4)
8.5"X11", 600 pages, almost 100 photos

SABR Members can purchase each book at a significant discount (often 50% off) and receive the ebook edtions free as a member benefit. Each book is available in a trade paperback edition as well as ebooks suitable for reading on a home computer or Nook, Kindle, or iPad/tablet.
To learn more about becoming a member of SABR, visit the website: sabr.org/join

The SABR Digital Library

The Society for American Baseball Research, the top baseball research organization in the world, disseminates some of the best in baseball history, analysis, and biography through our publishing programs. The SABR Digital Library contains a mix of books old and new, and focuses on a tandem program of paperback and ebook publication, making these materials widely available for both on digital devices and as traditional printed books.

Greatest Games Books

TIGERS BY THE TALE:
GREAT GAMES AT MICHIGAN AND TRUMBULL
For over 100 years, Michigan and Trumbull was the scene of some of the most exciting baseball ever. This book portrays 50 classic games at the corner, spanning the earliest days of Bennett Park until Tiger Stadium's final closing act. From Ty Cobb to Mickey Cochrane, Hank Greenberg to Al Kaline, and Willie Horton to Alan Trammell.
Edited by Scott Ferkovich
$12.95 paperback (ISBN 978-1-943816-21-7)
$6.99 ebook (ISBN 978-1-943816-20-0)
8.5"x11", 160 pages, 22 photos

FROM THE BRAVES TO THE BREWERS: GREAT GAMES AND HISTORY AT MILWAUKEE'S COUNTY STADIUM
The National Pastime provides in-depth articles focused on the geographic region where the national SABR convention is taking place annually. The SABR 45 convention took place in Chicago, and here are 45 articles on baseball in and around the bat-and-ball crazed Windy City: 25 that appeared in the souvenir book of the convention plus another 20 articles available in ebook only.
Edited by Gregory H. Wolf
$19.95 paperback (ISBN 978-1-943816-23-1)
$9.99 ebook (ISBN 978-1-943816-22-4)
8.5"X11", 290 pages, 58 photos

BRAVES FIELD:
MEMORABLE MOMENTS AT BOSTON'S LOST DIAMOND
From its opening on August 18, 1915, to the sudden departure of the Boston Braves to Milwaukee before the 1953 baseball season, Braves Field was home to Boston's National League baseball club and also hosted many other events: from NFL football to championship boxing. The most memorable moments to occur in Braves Field history are portrayed here.
Edited by Bill Nowlin and Bob Brady
$19.95 paperback (ISBN 978-1-933599-93-9)
$9.99 ebook (ISBN 978-1-933599-92-2)
8.5"X11", 282 pages, 182 photos

AU JEU/PLAY BALL: THE 50 GREATEST GAMES IN THE HISTORY OF THE MONTREAL EXPOS
The 50 greatest games in Montreal Expos history. The games described here recount the exploits of the many great players who wore Expos uniforms over the years—Bill Stoneman, Gary Carter, Andre Dawson, Steve Rogers, Pedro Martinez, from the earliest days of the franchise, to the glory years of 1979-1981, the what-might-have-been years of the early 1990s, and the sad, final days.and others.
Edited by Norm King
$12.95 paperback (ISBN 978-1-943816-15-6)
$5.99 ebook (ISBN978-1-943816-14-9)
8.5"x11", 162 pages, 50 photos

Original SABR Research

CALLING THE GAME:
BASEBALL BROADCASTING FROM 1920 TO THE PRESENT
An exhaustive, meticulously researched history of bringing the national pastime out of the ballparks and into living rooms via the airwaves. Every play-by-play announcer, color commentator, and ex-ballplayer, every broadcast deal, radio station, and TV network. Plus a foreword by "Voice of the Chicago Cubs" Pat Hughes, and an afterword by Jacques Doucet, the "Voice of the Montreal Expos" 1972-2004.
by Stuart Shea
$24.95 paperback (ISBN 978-1-933599-40-3)
$9.99 ebook (ISBN 978-1-933599-41-0)
7"X10", 712 pages, 40 photos

BioProject Books

WHO'S ON FIRST:
REPLACEMENT PLAYERS IN WORLD WAR II
During World War II, 533 players made the major league debuts. More than 60% of the players in the 1941 Opening Day lineups departed for the service and were replaced by first-times and oldsters. Hod Lisenbee was 46. POW Bert Shepard had an artificial leg, and Pete Gray had only one arm. The 1944 St. Louis Browns had 13 players classified 4-F. These are their stories.
Edited by Marc Z Aaron and Bill Nowlin
$19.95 paperback (ISBN 978-1-933599-91-5)
$9.99 ebook (ISBN 978-1-933599-90-8)
8.5"X11", 422 pages, 67 photos

VAN LINGLE MUNGO:
THE MAN, THE SONG, THE PLAYERS
40 baseball players with intriguing names have been named in renditions of Dave Frishberg's classic 1969 song, Van Lingle Mungo. This book presents biographies about all 40 players and additional information about one of the greatest baseball novelty songs of all time.
Edited by Bill Nowlin
$19.95 paperback (ISBN 978-1-933599-76-2)
$9.99 ebook (ISBN 978-1-933599-77-9)
8.5"X11", 278 pages, 46 photos

NUCLEAR POWERED BASEBALL
Nuclear Powered Baseball tells the stories of each player—past and present—featured in the classic Simpsons episode "Homer at the Bat." Wade Boggs, Ken Griffey Jr., Ozzie Smith, Nap Lajoie, Don Mattingly, and many more. We've also included a few very entertaining takes on the now-famous episode from prominent baseball writers Jonah Keri, Joe Posnanski, Erik Malinowski, and Bradley Woodrum.
Edited by Emily Hawks and Bill Nowlin
$19.95 paperback (ISBN 978-1-943816-11-8)
$9.99 ebook (ISBN 978-1-943816-10-1)
8.5"X11", 250 pages

SABR Members can purchase each book at a significant discount (often 50% off) and receive the ebook edtions free as a member benefit. Each book is available in a trade paperback edition as well as ebooks suitable for reading on a home computer or Nook, Kindle, or iPad/tablet.
To learn more about becoming a member of SABR, visit the website: sabr.org/join

SABR BioProject Books

In 2002, the Society for American Baseball Research launched an effort to write and publish biographies of every player, manager, and individual who has made a contribution to baseball. Over the past decade, the BioProject Committee has produced over 2,200 biographical articles. Many have been part of efforts to create theme- or team-oriented books, spearheaded by chapters or other committees of SABR.

THE YEAR OF THE BLUE SNOW:
THE 1964 PHILADELPHIA PHILLIES
Catcher Gus Triandos dubbed the Philadelphia Phillies' 1964 season "the year of the blue snow," a rare thing that happens once in a great while. This book sheds light on lingering questions about the 1964 season—but any book about a team is really about the players. This work offers life stories of all the players and others (managers, coaches, owners, and broadcasters) associated with this star-crossed team, as well as essays of analysis and history.
Edited by Mel Marmer and Bill Nowlin
$19.95 paperback (ISBN 978-1-933599-51-9)
$9.99 ebook (ISBN 978-1-933599-52-6)
8.5"X11", 356 PAGES, over 70 photos

THE MIRACLE BRAVES OF 1914
BOSTON'S ORIGINAL WORST-TO-FIRST CHAMPIONS
Long before the Red Sox "Impossible Dream" season, Boston's now nearly forgotten "other" team, the 1914 Boston Braves, performed a baseball "miracle" that resounds to this very day. The "Miracle Braves" were Boston's first "worst-to-first" winners of the World Series. Refusing to throw in the towel at the midseason mark, George Stallings engineered a remarkable second-half climb in the standings all the way to first place.
Edited by Bill Nowlin
$19.95 paperback (ISBN 978-1-933599-69-4)
$9.99 ebook (ISBN 978-1-933599-70-0)
8.5"X11", 392 PAGES, over 100 photos

DETROIT TIGERS 1984:
WHAT A START! WHAT A FINISH!
The 1984 Detroit tigers roared out of the gate, winning their first nine games of the season and compiling an eye-popping 35-5 record after the campaign's first 40 games—still the best start ever for any team in major league history. This book brings together biographical profiles of every Tiger from that magical season, plus those of field management, top executives, the broadcasters—even venerable Tiger Stadium and the city itself.
Edited by Mark Pattison and David Raglin
$19.95 paperback (ISBN 978-1-933599-44-1)
$9.99 ebook (ISBN 978-1-933599-45-8)
8.5"x11", 250 pages (Over 230,000 words!)

THAR'S JOY IN BRAVELAND!
THE 1957 MILWAUKEE BRAVES
Few teams in baseball history have captured the hearts of their fans like the Milwaukee Braves of the 1950s. During the Braves' 13-year tenure in Milwaukee (1953-1965), they had a winning record every season, won two consecutive NL pennants (1957 and 1958), lost two more in the final week of the season (1956 and 1959), and set big-league attendance records along the way.
Edited by Gregory H. Wolf
$19.95 paperback (ISBN 978-1-933599-71-7)
$9.99 ebook (ISBN 978-1-933599-72-4)
8.5"x11", 330 pages, over 60 photos

SWEET '60: THE 1960 PITTSBURGH PIRATES
A portrait of the 1960 team which pulled off one of the biggest upsets of the last 60 years. When Bill Mazeroski's home run left the park to win in Game Seven of the World Series, beating the New York Yankees, David had toppled Goliath. It was a blow that awakened a generation, one that millions of people saw on television, one of TV's first iconic World Series moments.
Edited by Clifton Blue Parker and Bill Nowlin
$19.95 paperback (ISBN 978-1-933599-48-9)
$9.99 ebook (ISBN 978-1-933599-49-6)
8.5"X11", 340 pages, 75 photos

NEW CENTURY, NEW TEAM:
THE 1901 BOSTON AMERICANS
The team now known as the Boston Red Sox played its first season in 1901. Boston had a well-established National League team, but the American League went head-to-head with the N.L. in Chicago, Philadelphia, and Boston. Chicago won the American League pennant and Boston finished second, only four games behind.
Edited by Bill Nowlin
$19.95 paperback (ISBN 978-1-933599-58-8)
$9.99 ebook (ISBN 978-1-933599-59-5)
8.5"X11", 268 pages, over 125 photos

RED SOX BASEBALL IN THE DAYS OF IKE AND ELVIS: THE RED SOX OF THE 1950S
Although the Red Sox spent most of the 1950s far out of contention, the team was filled with fascinating players who captured the heart of their fans. In *Red Sox Baseball*, members of SABR present 46 biographies on players such as Ted Williams and Pumpsie Green as well as season-by-season recaps.
Edited by Mark Armour and Bill Nowlin
$19.95 paperback (ISBN 978-1-933599-24-3)
$9.99 ebook (ISBN 978-1-933599-34-2)
8.5"X11", 372 PAGES, over 100 photos

CAN HE PLAY?
A LOOK AT BASEBALL SCOUTS AND THEIR PROFESSION
They dig through tons of coal to find a single diamond. Here in the world of scouts, we meet the "King of Weeds," a Ph.D. we call "Baseball's Renaissance Man," a husband-and-wife team, pioneering Latin scouts, and a Japanese-American interned during World War II who became a successful scout—and many, many more.
Edited by Jim Sandoval and Bill Nowlin
$19.95 paperback (ISBN 978-1-933599-23-6)
$9.99 ebook (ISBN 978-1-933599-25-0)
8.5"X11", 200 PAGES, over 100 photos

SABR Members can purchase each book at a significant discount (often 50% off) and receive the ebook editions free as a member benefit. Each book is available in a trade paperback edition as well as ebooks suitable for reading on a home computer or Nook, Kindle, or iPad/tablet.
To learn more about becoming a member of SABR, visit the website: sabr.org/join

The SABR Digital Library

The Society for American Baseball Research, the top baseball research organization in the world, disseminates some of the best in baseball history, analysis, and biography through our publishing programs. The SABR Digital Library contains a mix of books old and new, and focuses on a tandem program of paperback and ebook publication, making these materials widely available for both on digital devices and as traditional printed books.

Classic Reprints

BASE-BALL: HOW TO BECOME A PLAYER
by John Montgomery Ward
John Montgomery Ward (1860-1925) tossed the second perfect game in major league history and later became the game's best shortstop and a great, inventive manager. His classic handbook on baseball skills and strategy was published in 1888. Illustrated with woodcuts, the book is divided into chapters for each position on the field as well as chapters on the origin of the game, theory and strategy, training, base-running, and batting.
$4.99 ebook (ISBN 978-1-933599-47-2)
$9.95 paperback (ISBN 978-0910137539)
156 PAGES, 4.5"X7" replica edition

BATTING by F. C. Lane
First published in 1925, *Batting* collects the wisdom and insights of over 250 hitters and baseball figures. Lane interviewed extensively and compiled tips and advice on everything from batting stances to beanballs. Legendary baseball figures such as Ty Cobb, Casey Stengel, Cy Young, Walter Johnson, Rogers Hornsby, and Babe Ruth reveal the secrets of such integral and interesting parts of the game as how to choose a bat, the ways to beat a slump, and how to outguess the pitcher.
$14.95 paperback (ISBN 978-0-910137-86-7)
$7.99 ebook (ISBN 978-1-933599-46-5)
240 PAGES, 5"X7"

RUN, RABBIT, RUN
by Walter "Rabbit" Maranville
"Rabbit" Maranville was the Joe Garagiola of Grandpa's day, the baseball comedian of the times. In a twenty-four-year career that began in 1912, Rabbit found a lot of funny situations to laugh at, and no wonder: he caused most of them! The book also includes an introduction by the late Harold Seymour and a historical account of Maranville's life and Hall-of-Fame career by Bob Carroll.
$9.95 paperback (ISBN 978-1-933599-26-7)
$5.99 ebook (ISBN 978-1-933599-27-4)
100 PAGES, 5.5"X8.5", 15 rare photos

MEMORIES OF A BALLPLAYER
by Bill Werber and C. Paul Rogers III
Bill Werber's claim to fame is unique: he was the last living person to have a direct connection to the 1927 Yankees, "Murderers' Row," a team hailed by many as the best of all time. Rich in anecdotes and humor, Memories of a Ballplayer is a clear-eyed memoir of the world of big-league baseball in the 1930s. Werber played with or against some of the most productive hitters of all time, including Babe Ruth, Ted Williams, Lou Gehrig, and Joe DiMaggio.
$14.95 paperback (ISNB 978-0-910137-84-3)
$6.99 ebook (ISBN 978-1-933599-47-2)
250 PAGES, 6"X9"

Original SABR Research

INVENTING BASEBALL: THE 100 GREATEST GAMES OF THE NINETEENTH CENTURY
SABR's Nineteenth Century Committee brings to life the greatest games from the game's early years. From the "prisoner of war" game that took place among captive Union soldiers during the Civil War (immortalized in a famous lithograph), to the first intercollegiate game (Amherst versus Williams), to the first professional no-hitter, the games in this volume span 1833–1900 and detail the athletic exploits of such players as Cap Anson, Moses "Fleetwood" Walker, Charlie Comiskey, and Mike "King" Kelly.
Edited by Bill Felber
$19.95 paperback (ISBN 978-1-933599-42-7)
$9.99 ebook (ISBN 978-1-933599-43-4)
302 PAGES, 8"x10", 200 photos

NINETEENTH CENTURY STARS: 2012 EDITION
First published in 1989, *Nineteenth Century Stars* was SABR's initial attempt to capture the stories of baseball players from before 1900. With a collection of 136 fascinating biographies, SABR has re-released *Nineteenth Century Stars* for 2012 with revised statistics and new form. The 2012 version also includes a preface by **John Thorn**.
Edited by Robert L. Tiemann and Mark Rucker
$19.95 paperback (ISBN 978-1-933599-28-1)
$9.99 ebook (ISBN 978-1-933599-29-8)
300 PAGES, 6"X9"

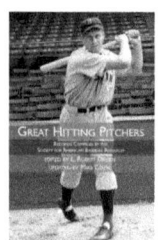

GREAT HITTING PITCHERS
Published in 1979, *Great Hitting Pitchers* was one of SABR's early publications. Edited by SABR founder Bob Davids, the book compiles stories and records about pitchers excelling in the batter's box. Newly updated in 2012 by Mike Cook, *Great Hitting Pitchers* contain tables including data from 1979-2011, corrections to reflect recent records, and a new chapter on recent new members in the club of "great hitting pitchers" like Tom Glavine and Mike Hampton.
Edited by L. Robert Davids
$9.95 paperback (ISBN 978-1-933599-30-4)
$5.99 ebook (ISBN 978-1-933599-31-1)
102 PAGES, 5.5"x8.5"

THE FENWAY PROJECT
Sixty-four SABR members—avid fans, historians, statisticians, and game enthusiasts—recorded their experiences of a single game. Some wrote from inside the Green Monster's manual scoreboard, the Braves clubhouse, or the broadcast booth, while others took in the essence of Fenway from the grandstand or bleachers. The result is a fascinating look at the charms and challenges of Fenway Park, and the allure of being a baseball fan.
Edited by Bill Nowlin and Cecilia Tan
$9.99 ebook (ISBN 978-1-933599-50-2)
175 pages, 100 photos

SABR Members can purchase each book at a significant discount (often 50% off) and receive the ebook editions free as a member benefit. Each book is available in a trade paperback edition as well as ebooks suitable for reading on a home computer or Nook, Kindle, or iPad/tablet.
To learn more about becoming a member of SABR, visit the website: sabr.org/join

Society for American Baseball Research

Cronkite School at ASU
555 N. Central Ave. #416, Phoenix, AZ 85004
602.496.1460 (phone)
SABR.org

Become a SABR member today!

If you're interested in baseball — writing about it, reading about it, talking about it — there's a place for you in the Society for American Baseball Research. Our members include everyone from academics to professional sportswriters to amateur historians and statisticians to students and casual fans who enjoy reading about baseball and occasionally gathering with other members to talk baseball. What unites all SABR members is an interest in the game and joy in learning more about it.

SABR membership is open to any baseball fan; we offer 1-year and 3-year memberships. Here's a list of some of the key benefits you'll receive as a SABR member:

- Receive two editions (spring and fall) of the *Baseball Research Journal*, our flagship publication
- Receive expanded e-book edition of *The National Pastime*, our annual convention journal
- 8-10 new e-books published by the SABR Digital Library, all FREE to members
- "This Week in SABR" e-newsletter, sent to members every Friday
- Join dozens of research committees, from Statistical Analysis to Women in Baseball.
- Join one of 70 regional chapters in the U.S., Canada, Latin America, and abroad
- Participate in online discussion groups
- Ask and answer baseball research questions on the SABR-L e-mail listserv
- Complete archives of *The Sporting News* dating back to 1886 and other research resources
- Promote your research in "This Week in SABR"
- Diamond Dollars Case Competition
- Yoseloff Scholarships

- Discounts on SABR national conferences, including the SABR National Convention, the SABR Analytics Conference, Jerry Malloy Negro League Conference, Frederick Ivor-Campbell 19th Century Conference, and the Arizona Fall League Experience
- Publish your research in peer-reviewed SABR journals
- Collaborate with SABR researchers and experts
- Contribute to Baseball Biography Project or the SABR Games Project
- List your new book in the SABR Bookshelf
- Lead a SABR research committee or chapter
- Networking opportunities at SABR Analytics Conference
- Meet baseball authors and historians at SABR events and chapter meetings
- 50% discounts on paperback versions of SABR e-books
- Discounts with other partners in the baseball community
- SABR research awards

We hope you'll join the most passionate international community of baseball fans at SABR! Check us out online at SABR.org/join.

SABR MEMBERSHIP FORM

	Annual	3-year	Senior	3-yr Sr.	Under 30
Standard:	☐ $65	☐ $175	☐ $45	☐ $129	☐ $45

(International members wishing to be mailed the Baseball Research Journal should add $10/yr for Canada/Mexico or $19/yr for overseas locations.)

Canada/Mexico:	☐ $75	☐ $205	☐ $55	☐ $159	☐ $55
Overseas:	☐ $84	☐ $232	☐ $64	☐ $186	☐ $55

Senior = 65 or older before Dec. 31 of the current year

Participate in Our Donor Program!

Support the preservation of baseball research. Designate your gift toward:
☐ General Fund   ☐ Endowment Fund   ☐ Research Resources   ☐ _____
☐ I want to maximize the impact of my gift; do not send any donor premiums
☐ I would like this gift to remain anonymous.

Note: Any donation not designated will be placed in the General Fund.
SABR is a 501 (c) (3) not-for-profit organization & donations are tax-deductible to the extent allowed by law.

Name _____

E-mail* _____

Address _____

City _____ ST _____ ZIP _____

Phone _____ Birthday _____

* Your e-mail address on file ensures you will receive the most recent SABR news.

Dues $_____
Donation $_____
Amount Enclosed $_____

Do you work for a matching grant corporation? Call (602) 496-1460 for details.

If you wish to pay by credit card, please contact the SABR office at (602) 496-1460 or visit the SABR Store online at SABR.org/join. We accept Visa, Mastercard & Discover.

Do you wish to receive the *Baseball Research Journal* electronically? ☐ Yes   ☐ No
Our e-books are available in PDF, Kindle, or EPUB (iBooks, iPad, Nook) formats.

Mail to: SABR, Cronkite School at ASU, 555 N. Central Ave. #416, Phoenix, AZ 85004